Roller-Coaster

IAN KERSHAW

Roller-Coaster

Europe, 1950–2017

ALLEN LANE
an imprint of
PENGUIN BOOKS

ALLEN LANE

UK | USA | Canada | Ireland | Australia
India | New Zealand | South Africa

Allen Lane is part of the Penguin Random House group of companies
whose addresses can be found at global.penguinrandomhouse.com

First published 2018
001

Copyright © Ian Kershaw, 2018

The moral right of the author has been asserted

Set in 10.5/14 pt Sabon LT Std
Typeset by Jouve (UK), Milton Keynes
Printed and bound in Great Britain by Clays Ltd, Elcograf S.p.A.

A CIP catalogue record for this book is available from the British Library

ISBN: 978–0–241–18716–6

Contents

List of Illustrations

List of Maps

N

300 miles

500 km

IRELAND

UNITED
KINGDOM
(Due to leave in 2019)

North Sea

DENMARK
(Inc. Greenland
which left in
1985)

NETHERLANDS

BELGIUM

GERMANY

LUXEMBOURG

W. GERMANY

ATLANTIC

OCEAN

English Channel

Thames

Loire

Marne

Rhine

Danube

FRANCE

Po

AU

PORTUGAL

SPAIN

I T

Mediterranean Sea

•Gibraltar

The European Union 2018

Expansion of the EEC

- Countries forming the EEC in 1957
- Countries joining in 1973
- Countries joining in 1981
- Countries joining in 1986
- Countries joining in 1995
- Countries joining in 2004
- Countries joining in 2007
- Countries joining in 2013

SWEDEN

FINLAND

ESTONIA

Baltic
Sea

LATVIA

LITHUANIA

Niemen

Don

GDR
joined on
unification with
W. Germany
(1990)

POLAND

Donets

Dnieper

Vistula

CZECH REP.

SLOVAKIA

STRIA

HUNGARY

ROMANIA

SLOVENIA

CROATIA

Black Sea

Adriatic Sea

BULGARIA

ITALY

Aegean
Sea

GREECE

CYPRUS

MALTA

Preface

To Hell and Back, I wrote in the Preface, was the hardest book I had ever attempted. That was until this book. This second volume on the history of Europe from 1914 to our own times posed still greater problems in both interpretation and composition. This is in no small measure because Europe's history between 1950 and the present day has no single overriding theme comparable to the obvious centrality of world war which dominates the predecessor volume that covers the period 1914 to 1949. *To Hell and Back* followed a linear progression in and out of war, then again, in and out of war. No straightforward linear development adequately describes the complexity of European history since 1950. This is rather a story of twists and turns, of ups and downs, of volatile shifts, of a great and accelerating speed of transformation. Europe since 1950 has been a roller-coaster ride, complete with thrills and scares. This book aims to show how and why it lurched during those decades from one era of great insecurity to another.

The metaphor of the roller-coaster is not perfect. After all, a roller-coaster, for all its thrills and excitement, runs along fixed lines in a circuit and ends at a known point. Perhaps, too, its fairground imagery sounds too trivial and light-hearted for the seriousness, weightiness and, indeed, often tragedy of Europe's history since the war. But it does capture the unevenness, the breathtaking moments, and the experience of being swept along by uncontrollable forces that affected – though in different ways – practically all Europeans during these decades.

The complexity of Europe's history in this era poses significant problems for the 'architecture' of the book. These are compounded by the division of Europe for over forty years by the Iron Curtain. Other than as an *idea* of shared cultural identity (though one fragmented through religious, national, ethnic and class differences), Europe in these decades did not exist. Its two halves – western and eastern Europe – were themselves purely political constructs. The internal development of each half of the continent over that period is so different that it is impossible to integrate them in any coherent fashion until the fall of communism between 1989 and 1991. Although Eastern and Western Europe also thereafter remain profoundly different, the impact of rapidly accelerating globalization – a key theme of the volume – then makes it feasible to deal with them together, rather than separately.

The nature of such a wide-ranging work means, as in *To Hell and Back*, that I had to rely heavily upon the research and writing of others – even more so, in fact, since I have never undertaken specialized research on any aspect of this period. Having lived through it is no substitute. Someone suggested to me as I was starting the writing that this book should be easy, since the period coincided with much of my lifetime. But living through history produces memories that can be distorting or inaccurate, as well as possibly helpful. In a tiny number of places I have added a personal recollection in a footnote. But I have kept them out of the text. Personal anecdote and historical evaluation are in my view best kept apart. Leaving aside the frailties of memory, most of what passes by on a daily basis has only ephemeral resonance. Assessment of the significance of major occurrences nearly always requires not just detailed knowledge but the passage of time in which to digest it.

So the scholarly work of others is indispensable. Many works are specialist monographs or essays in learned journals. I mentioned in the Preface to *To Hell and Back* a number of excellent general histories of Europe in the twentieth century, to which I could now add Konrad Jarausch's *Out of Ashes*. Specifically on the second half of the twentieth century the most compelling general study has been Tony Judt's *Postwar*. Timothy Garton Ash's books, brilliantly combining high-quality journalism and contemporary historical insight, have proved invaluable, especially on Central Europe. And a number of books by German historians – Heinrich August Winkler, Andreas Wirsching, Harmut Kaelble, Andreas Rödder and Philipp Ther – have helped me greatly. They are listed, along with other works that I have found particularly useful, in the select bibliography. They are only the tip of a very large iceberg. As in the predecessor volume, and in accordance with the format of the Penguin History of Europe series, there are no endnote references. As before, I have marked with an asterisk works in the bibliography from which I have drawn direct quotations.

My approach follows that of *To Hell and Back*. As in that volume, I have been anxious to portray the drama, often the uncertainty, of the unfolding of history, occasionally by blending in contemporary views of events. So I have organized the book chronologically, in chapters covering relatively brief periods, with thematic subdivisions. The short Foreword outlines the nature of the interpretation. The first three chapters begin with Europe's first post-war era of insecurity, moving from the tensions of the Cold War to the building of the two opposed blocs of Western and Eastern Europe down to the mid-1960s. Chapters 4 and 5 deal with the astonishing and long-lasting post-war economic boom and its social implications, then with the bifurcation of culture – the doleful legacy of the recent past on the one hand, and conscious invocation of a new, modern and exciting atmosphere on the other. How this burst into youthful protest in the late 1960s, and the changing social and cultural values that were left from the period of student revolt, is explored in Chapter 6. Chapter 7 focuses upon a key decade: the fundamental change that occurred during the 1970s and early 1980s. Although the problems east of the Iron Curtain were by the 1980s mounting alarmingly for the leaders of communist states, Chapter 8 emphasizes the personal part played by Mikhail Gorbachev in unintentionally but fatally undermining Soviet rule, while Chapter 9 turns the spotlight on the part played in Europe's 'velvet revolution' of 1989–91 by pressure for change from below. How difficult and often disillusioning the transition to pluralist democracies and capitalist economies was for the countries of Eastern Europe, and the disastrous collapse into ethnic war in Yugoslavia, form the main topics of Chapter 10. Chapter 11 examines the changes within Europe in the wake of the 2001 terrorist attacks in the United States and the subsequent wars in Afghanistan and Iraq. Finally, in Chapter 12, I explore the concatenation of crises that have afflicted Europe since 2008 and cumulatively amount to a serious general crisis for the European continent. The Afterword turns from the past to Europe's future, both the short-term prospects and the longer-term problems that will face the continent in a new era of insecurity.

To Hell and Back ended on a positive note. As Europe emerged between 1945 and 1949 from the double catastrophe of two world wars, the signposts to a brighter future were plainly visible – if under the cloud of the atomic bomb in possession of both superpowers. This book's finale is more ambivalent – certainly as regards the longer-term future of Europe.

Things can change rapidly. So can historiography. Eric Hobsbawm, writing in the early 1990s, looked gloomily at the long-term crises likely to beset Europe and emphasized the destructive force of capitalism in his pessimistic conclusion. Most analysts, though, were far more positive about Europe's recent history. A number of prominent studies of Europe's twentieth century, written just before or after the millennium, struck a distinctly upbeat tone. Mark Mazower thought the 'international outlook' appeared 'more peaceful than at any time previously'. Richard Vinen spoke of an 'era of sound money'. Harold James wrote of the 'almost complete ascendance of democracy and capitalism' (though he did qualify this by pointing to increased disenchantment with that ascendancy) and saw globalization in almost entirely positive terms as the 'recreation of an international society, culture and economy'. Developments in the still young twenty-first century might call such positive verdicts into question.

Tony Judt's magisterial work, completed five years after the millennium, also ended on a broadly optimistic note. 'Nationalism had come and gone' in Europe, he adjudged. 'The twenty-first century might yet belong to Europe' were his concluding words. In the light of Europe's disarray since 2008, the rise of nationalist and xenophobic parties in many countries, the long-term challenges that the continent faces, and the apparently irresistible rise of China's position of world power and influence, these look like highly dubious presumptions.

Of course, short-term change is largely unpredictable. Europe's future – still riding the roller-coaster – can climb up and swoop down in quick succession. At present (autumn 2017) the auguries are better from what they had been only a few months ago, though the crystal ball remains clouded. Long-term change is another matter. And here, the problems facing Europe (and the rest of the world) are daunting. Climate change, demography, provision of energy, mass migration, tensions of multiculturalism, automation, the widening income gap, international security and dangers of global conflict: all pose major challenges for the decades ahead. Just how well equipped Europe is to deal with these problems is hard to say. How to meet the challenges, to shape the future of the continent, lies not solely, but nevertheless in good measure, in the hands of Europeans themselves. In dangerous waters the convoy is best staying close together, not drifting apart. That means building upon and strengthening the levels of unity, cooperation and consensus, imperfect as they are, that have been gradually constructed since the war. With good navigation, everyone may traverse the perilous straits ahead to reach safer shores.

Writing the history of my own time has been enormously challenging. But I found it a rewarding task. I have learnt immeasurably more than I knew before about the events and changes that have shaped my life. At the end, I have a better sense than I did earlier about how my own continent has arrived at the present. For me, that in itself makes the enterprise worthwhile. As for the future: on that a historian's predictions are no better than anyone else's.

Ian Kershaw, Manchester, November 2017

Acknowledgements

For stimulating discussions, advice on specialist literature, supply of off-prints or books, interest in my venture and help in various other ways I am grateful to Patrick Argent, Joe Bergin, John Breuilly, Archie Brown, Franz Brüggemeier, Detlef Felken, Christian Göschel, Mike Hannah, Geoffrey Hosking, Thomas Karlauf, Thomas Kielinger, Frances Lynch, Frank O'Gorman, Paul Preston, Colin Steele, Alan Steinweis, Frank Trentmann, Heinrich August Winkler, Charlotte Woodford and Benjamin Ziemann. I would also like to record my thanks, without knowing those involved personally, to leading journalists of major British, German and American newspapers on whose excellent reportage and analysis of political, economic and foreign affairs I was able to draw extensively, especially for the last chapter of the volume. And I am greatly obliged (again without personal acquaintance) to the distinguished *Guardian* columnist Martin Kettle, who was kind enough to read the text and save me from a number of gratuitous factual errors.

My warmest thanks go to Traude Spät who, together with her husband, Ulrich, made me as welcome as ever when I stayed in Munich, ensuring, too, through frequent supplies of German press cuttings, that I was kept aware of different perspectives on European affairs from those I would regularly see in British media. Not least, I'm grateful to Traude for coming up with the title 'Achterbahn' (Roller-Coaster), as we struggled to find a suitable image for the vagaries of Europe's history during the last seven decades. Other friends were also helpful beyond any call of duty. Laurence Rees, Nicholas Stargardt and David Cannadine generously gave up their time to read and comment on the typescript, providing many insights, corrections and suggestions. My periodic discussions with Laurence, a wonderful friend since the time when we worked together on television productions, were an invariable stimulus. My wife, Betty, and elder son, David, also read the typescript and posed numerous detailed queries that helped to improve the text.

Simon Winder has been, as ever, a superb editor – never pestering me, but always there with cheerful encouragement when called for, and offering invaluable suggestions. He was also a great help in selecting the photos. As with previous books, my thanks also go to all the members of the splendid team at Penguin who have contributed in different ways to the production, especially to Ellen Davies for her editorial assistance and to Richard Duguid for his work on the maps. I'm also most grateful to Richard Mason, who again showed skill, knowledge and precision in his excellent copy-editing of the text. Dave Cradduck has produced a magnificent index. Once more I have been able to depend on the continued support, which I value greatly, of Andrew Wylie in New York and James Pullen at the Wylie Agency in London.

My loving thanks go, as always, first and foremost to my family – to Betty (and Hannah), David, Stephen and Becky, and to our grandchildren, Sophie (and Paul), Joe, Ella, Olivia and Henry. For our grandchildren and their generation, my greatest hope is that Europe's future will still rest on the peace, freedom and prosperity that the post-war generation strived, however imperfectly, to construct.

Ian Kershaw, Manchester, January 2018

Foreword:
Europe's Two Eras of Insecurity

It is the same with history as with nature, as with all profound problems, whether past, present or future: the more deeply and seriously one enters into problems, the more difficult are those that arise.

Johann Wolfgang von Goethe

In 1950 Europe was reawakening from the dark years of the worst war in history. The physical scars were to be seen throughout the continent in the ruins of bombed-out buildings. The mental and moral scars would take far longer to heal than the time to rebuild towns and cities. The inhumanity of the recent past would, in fact, cast a deep shadow over Europe throughout subsequent decades. Important steps towards shaping a new Europe had been taken since the war's end in 1945. But the most striking legacy of the war for the immediate post-war world was twofold: Europe was now a continent divided down the middle by the Iron Curtain; and the new age was a nuclear era, with both of the super-powers in possession of super-weapons of mass destruction.

Europe was no longer at war. But a nuclear war, which seemed far from a distant prospect, threatened the entire basis of the continent's capacity to survive as a civilization. And the threat of nuclear war, hanging over Europe like the sword of Damocles, did not depend solely upon events in Europe itself. For Europe was now fully exposed to the global confrontation between the nuclear superpowers. Events far from European shores, the outbreak of the Korean War in 1950 and the Cuban Missile Crisis of 1962, mark the beginning and end of the most dangerous phase of the

Cold War for Europe (though a second, briefer period of heightened threat occurred in the early 1980s).

The children, products of the post-war 'baby boom', born into this new era would live to see changes that their parents could not have imagined. They would also experience an acceleration of change – political, economic, social and cultural – that exceeded anything known in earlier peacetime conditions. They were born into a time of searing austerity, much of it the direct consequence of war. Living accommodation was often makeshift as housing programmes tried to find homes for the millions of displaced and bombed-out families in much of the continent, especially in Central and Eastern Europe. Even houses left standing after the war were often in a poor state of repair. Sanitary conditions for much of the population were primitive. There were widespread shortages of food and clothing. Only wealthy families would have such crucial pieces of household equipment, which freed women from regular household drudgery, as a washing machine, or a telephone, a fridge, a car. Even then, few probably possessed a television.

The post-war baby-boom generation benefited in their lifetimes from astounding medical advances. They were immeasurably helped by the establishment and extension of the welfare state, made possible by high levels of economic growth. Although living standards in countries behind the Iron Curtain soon lagged well behind those in Western Europe, far-reaching systems of social welfare and support were intrinsic to communist systems (if usually corrupt in their practice). This was the first crucial breakthrough, offering a level of social security that earlier generations had not known in both halves of Europe. In some respects, at least in Western Europe, the lengthy post-war economic boom, the social advances that it facilitated, and the early flourishing of consumerism that also encouraged optimism about the future, distracted from the underlying insecurity of a continent endangered by the potential for nuclear war.

The material progress since those times has been astonishing. The plethora of food available in the average supermarket in any European country today would have been met with sheer disbelief in 1950 or indeed in any previous time. Today's families would look with horror at a home without a bathroom and with a toilet (often shared with other families) outside in the yard. Commodities that would have been extreme luxuries available only to a tiny minority are now commonplace. Most families have a car. Two cars for a single household is nothing unusual. A fridge to keep food cool is taken for granted. Foreign travel – the preserve of the wealthy in 1950 – is now available to millions. Nearly every home has a television. Satellites in space allow people to see television news, or watch a sporting event, live from the other side of the globe. Unimaginable until relatively recently, television can now even be viewed on mobile phones. And where once a trip abroad invariably necessitated phone calls home from a telephone box or a post office, mobiles now serve not just for making such calls effortlessly, or for sending instant messages around the world, but as mini-computers that offer an array of services. These include constant access to news and the possibility of not just speaking to but actually seeing on screen friends and relatives who live thousands of miles away. The availability of ever smaller and more readily available computers has transformed life in ways unthinkable only a short time ago, let alone in 1950.

Not just material possessions, but attitudes and mentalities have changed drastically as well. Most people in Europe in 1950 held views that seventy years later would be regarded as anathema. The Universal Declaration of Human Rights (arising from their catastrophic breach during the Second World War) had been adopted by the United Nations as recently as December 1948, but there was little popular understanding of what it meant in practice. Racist views and blatant racial discrimination were widely accepted and scarcely seen as remarkable. Few people of skin colours other than white lived in European countries. Capital punishment was still in existence, and executions were routinely carried out for people found guilty of the worst crimes. Homosexuality remained a criminal offence. Abortion was illegal. The influence of the Christian churches was profound, and attendance at church services still relatively high. By the time post-war children approached old age, human rights were taken for granted (however imperfect the practice), holding racist views was among the worst of social stigmas (though less so in Eastern and Southern than in Western Europe), multicultural societies were the norm, capital punishment had disappeared from Europe, gay marriage and legal abortion were widely accepted, and the role of the Christian churches had diminished greatly (though the spread of mosques, a feature of modern European cities almost wholly unknown in 1950, testified to the importance of religion among Muslim minorities).

Such patterns of transformation – and many others – can be seen as part of the process of what has come to be termed 'globalization'. This describes not just economic integration arising from the free movement of capital, technology and information, but the interweaving of social and cultural patterns of progress across national boundaries and throughout developing areas of the world. Globalization was far from simply a positive trajectory to ever better material provision. It had obvious dark sides. It has caused, for example, massive damage to the environment, a widening gulf between rich and poor, intensified (largely uncontrollable) mass migration, and loss of employment through automation made possible by technological change – and it continues to do so. The transformation brought through globalization runs like a thread through the following chapters. It is far from an unequivocal story of success. Europe's new era of insecurity is inextricably enmeshed with the deepening of globalization.

* * *

This book explores the twists and turns, ups and downs, that have led from one era of insecurity to another – from the threat of nuclear war to the multilayered and pervasive sense of present-day insecurity. It attempts to explain the complex, multifaceted patterns of change in Europe between 1950 and the present day. Epochal turning points – 1973, 1989, 2001, 2008 – mark the way. Advances, progress and improvements lie alongside setbacks, disappointments and at times disillusionment.

A continuing thread of Europe's transformation over the seven decades since 1950 has been the central importance of Germany. Change here, in the country that did more than any other to destroy the continent during the first half of the twentieth century, has been especially profound. Despite its destruction as a nation state at the end of the Second World War, Germany has remained at the heart of Europe's development – central to post-war economic recovery, central to the Cold War, central to the ending of the Cold War, central to widening European integration, central to the creation of the Euro, central to the crisis of the Eurozone, central to the migration crisis, and central to the still-embryonic steps to reform the European Union after its recent serious travails. In the meantime Germany has become a vital pillar of stable liberal democracy, it presides over Europe's strongest economy, has overcome forty years of division to attain national unity, and has reluctantly acquired the mantle of European leadership. Germany's own transformation has played a key role in Europe's post-war story – and is far from the least successful part.

No simple explanations of Europe's transformation will suffice. Political, economic and cultural dynamics were too closely interwoven to permit a neat parcelization of the agents of change. Much of the transformation reflects deep-rooted social and economic change, not confined to Europe, which the term 'globalization' encapsulates. The rebuilding of Europe after the Second World War took shape under the impact of unprecedented global, not just European, economic growth that lasted over two decades. The collapse of that growth in the 1970s marked a decisive turn in development that influenced the remainder of the twentieth century.

Europe's astonishing recovery in the immediate post-war decades had been conditioned by what might be called a 'matrix of rebirth', already outlined in the concluding part of *To Hell and Back*, the first volume on the history of Europe from 1914 to today. The elements of this matrix were the end of German great-power ambitions, the geopolitical reordering of central and eastern Europe, the subordination of national interests to those of the two superpowers, the upsurge of unprecedented economic growth, and the deterrent threat of nuclear weapons. By about 1970 all the points in this matrix had much less salience than they did in the early years after the Second World War. But the most crucial change was that economic growth was manifestly slowing. The long boom was over. The post-war economic order was about to alter fundamentally. The paradigm shift signified the beginning of what, in retrospect, can be viewed as an embryonic new matrix, which only gradually took shape over the subsequent two decades. What turned eventually into a 'matrix of new insecurity' comprised liberalized, deregulated economies, unstoppable globalization, a dramatic revolution in information technology, and, after 1990, the growth of multipolar bases of international power. Over time, the amalgamation of these components transformed Europe in many positive ways – but also led to kinds of insecurity that were quite different in character from the existential insecurity caused by the threat of nuclear war during the 1950s and early 1960s.

After the fall of the Iron Curtain the pace of globalization intensified markedly, the result in no small measure of the explosion of technological change and the rapid spread of the internet, especially after the World Wide Web (invented in 1989) became widely available from 1991 onwards. Already before then major cultural change was well under way. Central to this were the fight for social liberties, an emphasis on individualism and the onset of identity politics. From the mid-1960s onwards, value systems and lifestyles were altering in ways that would make Europe in many ways more tolerant, more liberal and more internationalist in outlook than had earlier been the case. But many earlier certainties and norms were dissolving.

Into these wide-ranging impersonal dynamics, the role of individuals and short-term political decision-making has to be added. The actions of a small number of key individuals – Mikhail Gorbachev and Helmut Kohl prominent among them – cannot be reduced simply to reflections of structural determinants of change. At crucial junctures such individuals *personally* played a decisive part in Europe's transformation.

The balance sheet of Europe's transformation over the seven decades since 1950 will present itself in the chapters that follow. It is by no means an unqualified success story. Europe's recent history has been far from purely benign. There have been some extraordinarily positive developments. But the picture is chequered.

And grave problems lie ahead.

I

The Tense Divide

... it is likelier to put an end to large-scale wars at the cost of prolonging indefinitely a 'peace that is no peace'.

George Orwell, on the atomic bomb, 1945

By 1950, as the immediate aftermath of the Second World War subsided, a new Europe, riven in two – ideologically, politically and socio-economically – had emerged. It was the beginning of a completely changed era in the continent's history, one of unprecedented insecurity. It was an era intrinsically shaped by the division that the war had left as its over-riding legacy – and by the appalling threat of nuclear annihilation.

For more than four decades the Cold War was to drive the two halves of Europe apart. The largely separate development took place, however, with one vital feature in common: the primacy of military power. This military power, the dominant feature of post-war Europe on both sides of the Iron Curtain, was now controlled by only two countries: the United States of America and the Soviet Union. Both were preoccupied with security. Both were determined to prevent the enemy dominating Europe. The novelty in their tense relationship was that it rested ultim-ately on weaponry of such fearful destructiveness that neither side dared use it. Within the space of only a few years it became the power of com-plete destruction. Both the United States and the Soviet Union – one already a superpower, the other on the verge of becoming one – had built atomic bombs by 1949. Four years later both the USA and the USSR had acquired the immensely more powerful hydrogen bombs and were soon in possession of nuclear arsenals capable of destroying civilized life on the planet several times over.

During the years 1950 to 1962 the Cold War was at its most intense, and most dangerous. For much of this period Europe was the centre of the Cold War – though in a nuclear age superpower confrontation anywhere on the globe could have had the direst repercussions for the European continent.

THE HEAT OF THE COLD WAR

The emerging conflict between the United States and the Soviet Union in the immediate post-war years had been threatening at times but had avoided disaster. No sooner had the new decade begun, however, than a dangerous crisis threatened to have grave consequences. That the crisis erupted over distant Korea was the most obvious indicator that Europe could not avoid being part of a global conflict between the superpowers. Whereas before 1945 the United States had been reluctantly drawn into European affairs to fight in two world wars, Western Europe now became in essence an appendage – if an important one – of American foreign policy. Meanwhile the eastern bloc (apart from Yugoslavia, which had in the aftermath of the war successfully asserted its independence from Moscow) was even more directly committed to support of the USSR in its worldwide confrontation with the USA.

Korea had been annexed by the Japanese in 1910 and ruled by them until the end of the Second World War. The Korean peninsula was then divided more or less in half at a demarcation line on the 38th parallel by an agreement between the Americans and Soviets to split the administration of the country temporarily. By 1948 expectations of a reunited Korea had disappeared. The division congealed into a communist republic in the north, effectively a Soviet satellite and seen by Moscow as part of the Soviet sphere of influence, and a vehemently anti-communist republic in the south, dominated by American interests. But the victory of communism in China in September 1949, after more than two decades of bitter civil war with Chiang Kai-shek's Nationalists (which had run alongside the immensely bloody war against the Japanese invaders between 1937 and 1945), had left the Korean peninsula exposed. The south remained a non-communist enclave in a vast region of communist dominance. When, on 25 June 1950, the North Koreans crossed the demarcation line and attacked the south of the partitioned country, superpower confrontation escalated dangerously. The United States, committed to the containment of Soviet power and highly allergic to the prospects of further expansion of communism, in Southeast Asia as well as in Europe, could not contemplate the loss of South Korea and the evident threat that Japan would then face.

The Americans correctly presumed that the North Koreans would not have attacked without Stalin's authorization. The Soviet dictator had, in fact, given a green light some weeks earlier, though he was unwilling to send combat forces, looking to the Chinese to provide military assistance, if necessary. The American leadership took the view that communist expansion had to be halted there and then if a domino effect were to be prevented. If the fall of Korea were not arrested, argued President Harry Truman, then the Soviets would 'swallow up one piece of Asia after another'. And 'if we were to let Asia go, the Near East would collapse and [there was] no telling what would happen in Europe'. Not for the last time in post-war Europe, the failed appeasement policy of the 1930s was cited as a motive for military action. The appeasers had failed to stop Hitler. If the communist advance were not now stopped in its tracks, it would lead to a third world war.

The United States gained the backing of the United Nations, established in October 1945, to use force to defend a member nation under attack. This was the first time that this had happened, and it arose from a Soviet mistake. Both Stalin and the United States leadership were satisfied, when it was agreed at the Yalta Conference in February 1945 to create the United Nations Organization, that they would have the right of veto in any vote in the envisaged Security Council, whose five permanent members would also include Britain, France and China. Through a Security Council controlled by the great powers, it was imagined that the United Nations would prove far more effective than the League of Nations had been. The fallacy of such a presumption was to be repeatedly demonstrated during the Cold War when the use of the veto by one or the other superpower almost invariably produced stalemate on the Security Council. The exception was in 1950 when a temporary Soviet boycott of the Security Council in protest at the refusal to give a seat to Communist China enabled approval for the aid necessary to repel the invasion of South Korea and to re-establish peace and security. Stalin quickly realized his error and the Soviets again took their seat on the Security Council. But it was too late to stop a United Nations Command force, dominated by the USA, being sent to support the South Korean military. By the time the war ended the United Nations Command, which had incorporated the South Koreans, totalled almost 933,000 troops. The overwhelming majority of them were South Koreans (591,000) and Americans (302,000). A number of European countries – Britain and, with far smaller contingents, France, Belgium, Greece and the Netherlands, along with a tiny contribution from Luxembourg – sent combat troops.

The Americans took the initiative throughout, expelling the North Koreans from the south, then pushing on beyond the demarcation line and into the north. Fearful of outright hostilities with the United States, Stalin rejected North Korean requests for Soviet intervention. The Chinese leader, Mao Zedong, however, was not prepared to see Korea fall wholly under American control, perhaps offering a gateway to an attack on a future date on China itself (whose relations with the Soviet Union were already less than harmonious). In autumn 1950 Mao had dispatched a sizeable force, eventually numbering about 300,000 troops, and forced the US Eighth Army into panicky retreat. It was a first indication that the West would have to reckon with China as a major military power. Within two months, the whole of North Korea was again under communist control and the South Korean capital, Seoul, had fallen. An alarmed Washington considered dropping an atomic bomb.

The United States still possessed a huge supremacy – 74 to 1, according to some estimates – in operational atomic bombs, compared with the Soviet Union. But what, exactly, would be the targets? In a war fought overwhelmingly in the Korean countryside, this was not obvious. And the prospects of a massive retaliatory escalation of what was a regional war, possibly extending to a Soviet invasion of Western Europe, or even atomic bombs dropped on European cities, had to be contemplated. Towards the end of 1950 the prospect of the widening of the conflict leading to a third world war was a very real one. The American military leadership had drawn up a list of Russian and Chinese cities as targets and considered delivering an ultimatum to China to retreat beyond the Yalu river. If necessary there would be a resort to 'prompt use of the atomic bomb'.

Wiser counsels prevailed. And by spring 1951, by which time the Chinese offensive had been blocked with much bloodshed, the Americans had regained the initiative, and the UN Command troops had eventually forced back the communist army. For the next two years both sides remained mired in a horrible war of attrition. In the armistice concluded in July 1953 the Korean War ended much as it had started, with each side behind the demarcation line at the 38th parallel. The three-year bitter war had cost the lives of nearly three million dead and wounded – the vast majority of them Koreans from both sides of the divide. American casualties numbered almost 170,000, over 50,000 dead, and those of the European contingents over 8,000, the majority of them British.

Although far away and not primarily involving Europeans, the Korean War had significant consequences for Europe, resulting from the dramatic rise in American defence expenditure. The first test explosion of a Soviet atomic bomb in August 1949, before the Korean War, at the Semipalatinsk test site in modern-day Kazakhstan, had already concentrated American minds on the need to advance the development of nuclear technology to keep ahead of the Soviets. President Truman had commissioned not just the accelerated production of atomic bombs but also, on 31 January 1950, the building of a 'super-bomb'. Military spending was already set to escalate by the time the outbreak of the Korean War sent it soaring. Within a year the US defence budget more than quadrupled. By 1952 military expenditure was consuming little short of one-fifth of American gross domestic product, up from less than a twentieth only three years earlier. On 1 November that year the Americans carried out the first test of their 'super-bomb' – a hydrogen bomb that 'blotted out the whole horizon' and obliterated the Pacific island (Eniwetok Atoll) where the explosion had taken place. Only nine months later, on 12 August 1953, the Soviets followed suit with their own test in a Central Asian desert. Winston Churchill later aptly spoke of a 'new terror' that brought 'equality in annihilation'.

Unsurprisingly, the Americans felt obliged to review not just their expenditure but also their overseas commitments in the light of a policy of global containment of a Soviet threat that was perceived to be a rapidly growing menace. This obviously affected Europe. The Americans thought increasingly of aid to Europe in military terms. The Marshall

Plan, established in 1947 to stimulate European economic recovery after the war through the provision of around $13 million over four years, was wound down. But by the end of 1951 American military aid to Europe had amounted to almost $5 billion. By 1952, as the build-up of arms increased in the wake of the Korean War, up to 80 per cent of American aid to Western Europe was directed at military purposes rather than civilian reconstruction.

In April 1949 the North Atlantic Treaty Organization (NATO) had been established as a pact that bound, initially, twelve countries – the United States, Canada, Britain, France, Italy, Denmark, Norway, the Netherlands, Belgium, Luxembourg, Portugal and Iceland (extended in 1952 to include Greece and Turkey) – to the defence of Western Europe. But it was plain to American leaders from the start that NATO's armed strength was inadequate. And they felt European countries needed to contribute more to their own defence costs; that the United States, starting to see itself as the world's policeman, could not continue to carry a hugely disproportionate burden of European defence. Each of NATO's European partners accordingly increased defence expenditure. West Germany, prohibited from the manufacture of arms but producing military machinery, tools and vehicles in ever greater numbers, benefited greatly from the demand for steel, increasing output by over 60 per cent between 1949 and 1953 – a boost to its burgeoning 'economic miracle'. Expenditure had to be turned into military strength. So at a NATO meeting in Lisbon in 1952, members determined to raise at least ninety-six new divisions within two years.

However, the elephant in the room could not be ignored for much longer. Strengthening NATO could make little progress without the rearming of West Germany. Such a short time after it had taken a mighty alliance to crush Germany's military power, once and for all it was thought, the prospect of a resurgent German militarism not surprisingly held scant appeal for her European neighbours (as well, understandably, as terrifying the Soviets). The Americans had raised the question of West German rearmament already in 1950, not long after the outbreak of the Korean War. They continued to press, and Western European NATO partners had to acknowledge that there was logic in their case. Why should the Americans continue to foot the lion's share of the bill for the defence of Europe if the Europeans were prepared to do so little? From the European point of view, there was always the lingering fear that the United States might even retreat from Europe, as it had done after 1918 and had initially been envisaged following the end of the Second World War. And there was also the need to ensure that West Germany remained bound to the Western alliance, something that Stalin was prepared to test with an overture in 1952 – rejected outright by Western leaders – that dangled before German eyes the inducement of a unified, neutral Germany. Stalin's initiative was interpreted in the West as an attempt to press the Americans to leave Europe. It also plainly aimed to head off the closer incorporation of the Federal Republic in the Western alliance (which the West German government, under its Chancellor, Konrad Adenauer, was keen to attain). This was by now closely bound up with the question of a West German armed force.

Already in 1950 a proposal that appeared to offer a potential break-through in the conundrum of how to make West Germany a military power while not alienating European countries vehemently opposed to such a step had, surprisingly perhaps, come from the French. The French proposal, advanced in October 1950 by the Prime Minister René Pleven, was intended to avoid the accession of West Germany to NATO, the step sought by the Americans, by the formation of a European defence organ-ization that would incorporate but control German involvement. It envisaged a European army that would include a West German compon-ent under European, not German, command (ensuring, in effect, French supervision). This proposal was the basis of what became by May 1952 a treaty to establish a European Defence Community (EDC).

The title was misleading. The envisaged EDC did not even extend to all the countries in Western Europe. From the outset it encountered the fundamental problem that would bedevil all steps towards European integration over subsequent decades: how to create supranational organ-izations while upholding the national sovereignty of individual members. The Schuman Plan of 1950 (named after the French Foreign Minister, Robert Schuman) had formed the basis of the European Coal and Steel Community, established the following year, which would emerge as the embryo of the Common Market and subsequently the European Eco-nomic Community. Its members were France, West Germany, Italy, the Netherlands, Belgium and Luxembourg. But Great Britain chose to remain aloof. The EDC built on a similar model, with the same membership. But Great Britain, possessing alongside France the largest armed forces in Europe, while welcoming the EDC and pledging its closest cooperation through its membership of NATO, was not part of it. Britain was not prepared to commit troops indefinitely to the defence of Europe or to participate in a project whose aim, according to the British Foreign Secretary, Anthony Eden, in 1952, was 'to pave the way for a European federation'. The diminution of national sovereignty that membership of a supranational EDC would have entailed could not be contemplated. Scandinavian members of NATO took a similar view. So the EDC was confined, as indeed was initially intended, to the countries that were starting to converge on economic policy. But the treaty had to be ratified. And here it came to grief in the country that had proposed it in the first place, France. The issue of national sovereignty was, here too, the decisive issue. When EDC ratification came before the French National Assembly on 30 August 1954, it was resoundingly rejected. With that the EDC was dead.

German rearmament, however, was not. Adenauer had deeply regretted the demise of the EDC, which he had viewed as an important step towards the integration of Western Europe. He had initially seen the vote in the French National Assembly as destroying his hopes of regaining German sovereignty. In fact, however, with its failure the prospect opened up of what Adenauer (the British and Americans, too) had wanted all along: the militarization of West Germany as a fully fledged member of NATO and recognition of his country as a sovereign state. The time was now propitious for such a step. Stalin had died in March 1953. The Korean War was over; West Germany was firmly committed to the Western alliance; and lingering notions of West German neutrality and reunification (which the opposition Social Democratic leadership, supported by a sizeable proportion of German opinion, had continued to entertain) were as good as buried. At conferences in London and then Paris, in September and October 1954, NATO members agreed to end the occupation of Germany (though Allied troops would remain by German agreement), to accept West Germany as a sovereign state, and to incorporate the Federal Republic into NATO. On 5 May 1955 West Germany attained its state sovereignty. Four days later it formally joined NATO. The Federal Republic was now allowed an army (not to be larger than half a million men), air force and navy, though prohibited totally from the possession of nuclear weapons.

From the Soviet perspective the developments in the West were deeply worrying. America was the only country actually to have used atomic bombs in war. It had been the first to develop the hydrogen bomb. It had intervened militarily in Korea. It had a lead in the unfolding arms race. And it had now consolidated an anti-Soviet alliance in Western Europe, including a rearmed West Germany. The Soviet Union had done all it could do to prevent this happening. Alarmed at the prospect of restored 'German militarism', the USSR had in 1954 even suggested to the Western powers, in a vain attempt to weaken or split the alliance's resolve, its own readiness to join NATO – a suggestion that was briskly rejected by the West.

Since the Soviet overtures predictably fell on stony ground, and given the perception that NATO was an aggressive alliance directed at the USSR and dominated by hawks in the American leadership, it was little wonder that a quick riposte to the inclusion of West Germany in NATO followed only ten days later, on 14 May 1955, with the formation of the Warsaw Pact. This bound Poland, Czechoslovakia, Hungary, Romania, Bulgaria, Albania and the German Democratic Republic (GDR) to the Soviet Union in a military alliance. At the same time the USSR took steps to improve relations with strategically important 'floating' European countries, especially Yugoslavia and Austria, to ensure that they were not drawn into the Western alliance. The schism with Yugoslavia, unmitigated since Tito's split with Stalin in 1948, was ended, at least officially, with a declaration in Belgrade on 2 June 1955 of mutual respect for independence and territorial integrity and commitment not to interfere in internal affairs. Already on 15 May, the day after the Warsaw Pact had come into existence, the signing by the four wartime powers – the USA, the USSR, Great Britain and France – of an Austrian State Treaty (to come into effect on 27 July) brought the occupation of Austria to an end and established the country as an independent sovereign state. The Soviet Union had been ready to make this step possible once Austria undertook to disallow the presence of any military bases on its territory and not to join any alliances. Austria's neutrality was formally announced on 26 October 1955, the day after the occupying powers had left the country. And in the previous month the closing of a Soviet naval base near

Helsinki signalled a readiness to allow Finland more firmly to establish its neutrality, genuinely independent of its giant Soviet neighbour but not aligned with NATO.

The formalization of opposed military alliances facing each other across Europe's Iron Curtain, each alliance presided over by a super-power in possession of weaponry of unimaginable destructive force, introduced a brief moment when the ice forming over the Cold War, if not starting to thaw, at least did not thicken. Both the Soviet and the American leadership seemed ready to defuse the tension. On 18 July 1955, the heads of government of the USA, the USSR, Great Britain and France met in Geneva. It was the first time in ten years they had come together; the last time had been during the Potsdam Conference, imme-diately following the end of the Second World War in Europe. The summit meeting (as such gatherings started to be called) ranged widely, especially over issues affecting security. It appeared to offer a glimmer of hope of attaining something like a basis for peaceful coexistence. At least the leaders of the superpowers were prepared to sit down and talk to each other. That was a straw to be grasped from the conference. But nothing worthwhile materialized. President Eisenhower proposed an 'open-skies' policy, aimed at allowing the United States and the Soviet Union to con-duct aerial reconnaissance over each other's territory. The Soviets, cautious of allowing the Americans any insight into their nuclear instal-lations and the potential of recognizing how limited their long-range bombing capability was, were quick to reject the proposal. (To the USA this mattered little. They were soon flying new U-2 spy planes over the Soviet Union, until one was shot down in May 1960 and the pilot, Gary Powers, was captured, causing an international incident.) The 'spirit of Geneva' was quick to evaporate. Within a year the Cold War reasserted itself. The savage repression of the Hungarian uprising against Soviet rule, coinciding in early November with the culmination of the Suez Cri-sis (which included a threat from the Soviet leader, Nikita Khrushchev, to use 'rocket weapons' against Britain and France), brought a renewed and terrible tension to international relations.

By this time the nuclear arms race had reached truly overwhelming proportions – not that most ordinary people on either side of the Iron Curtain had any genuine inkling of the scale of the stockpiling of weap-onry. Britain had decided already in 1947 that it had to build its own atomic bomb (seen as guaranteeing a place at the 'top table' of inter-national diplomacy). The Labour Prime Minister, Clement Attlee, had strongly advocated this step as early as August 1945, immediately after the Americans had dropped atomic bombs on Hiroshima and Nagasaki. His Foreign Secretary, Ernest Bevin, a dominant member of the post-war Labour government, had then decisively argued the following year in favour of a British bomb when others, including Attlee himself, wavered: 'We've *got* to have this,' declared Bevin, whatever the cost. 'We've got to have the bloody Union Jack on top of it.' Britain duly became the third nuclear power in October 1952 when it carried out its first test, in the Monte Bello Islands off Western Australia. Within two years of the test the British government had decided on the manufacture of a hydrogen bomb. By 1957 a British bomb was added to the growing thermonuclear arsenal. Winston Churchill, Attlee's successor as Prime Minister, had contended that it was 'the price we pay to sit at the top table' of world leaders. France, like Britain, regarded possession of an independent atomic (then hydrogen) bomb as the indispensable sign of great-power status. It would join 'the nuclear club' as its next member, testing its first atomic bomb in February 1960 near Reggane in the Algerian Sahara des-ert, then producing a thermonuclear weapon in 1968. These steps amounted to a worrying proliferation of nuclear weapons, if still con-fined to the victorious powers of the Second World War. But the crucial development was the competition between the two superpowers for ever greater destructive capacity.

In March 1954, on Bikini Atoll in the Marshall Islands, the Americans had exploded a hydrogen bomb 750 times more powerful than the atomic bomb that had devastated Hiroshima. The fallout from the explosion led to deaths from exposure to radiation over eighty miles away. Not to be outdone, the Soviets exploded a still larger bomb that September, near the village of Totskoye in Orenburg Oblast in the southern Urals, and the following year their first airborne hydrogen bomb a hundred times more powerful than their first bomb. The United States was by this time work-ing on the manufacture of small 'tactical' nuclear weapons that could be fitted into the nose cone of a missile. From autumn 1953 the Americans began creating what would become a sizeable stockpile of tactical nuclear weapons in Europe. Trainee officers in America were soon being pre-sented with scenarios of Europe as a nuclear-torn battleground. The hawkish American Secretary of State, John Foster Dulles (who conceived of policy in new terms, no longer of the 'containment' of Soviet communism but of its 'roll-back'), told NATO leaders the following year that atomic weapons had now to be regarded as a conventional part of the Western alliance's defence capability. A limited nuclear war, with Europe as the battleground, seemed a real possibility. The United States contemplated a rapid knock-out attack on the Soviet Union. At a briefing of representatives of the US military services in March 1954, General Curtis LeMay, head of Strategic Air Command (and who had directed the bombing campaign against Japanese cities towards the end of the Second World War), outlined plans for a massive air attack, envisaging 'that virtually all of Russia would be nothing but a smoking, radiating ruin at the end of two hours'. LeMay was 'firmly convinced that 30 days is long enough to conclude World War III'.

The escalation in nuclear firepower was breathtaking. In 1950 the US military was in possession of 298 atomic bombs. By 1962 it had no fewer than 27,100 nuclear weapons and over 2,500 bombers capable of carrying out long-range attacks. The Soviets had some long-range bombers that could reach American targets, but lagged behind the United States in their numbers and capabilities. But in 1957 the Soviet Union caused renewed anxiety with a double-coup in the arms race. In August it launched an intercontinental ballistic missile, the first the world had experienced. Even more spectacularly, in the early morning of 5 October (Moscow time), using the missile, it launched the first space satellite, which it called *Sputnik*, meaning 'fellow traveller'. Although most Europeans rejoiced at what they saw as an extraordinary achievement, the first step towards space exploration, American scientists and politicians were not slow to realize what *Sputnik* meant. The Soviet Union might soon be in a position to launch a nuclear attack from space on the United States. An American report pointed to an alarming inferiority to Soviet technology and called for a big build-up of a US missile force – necessitating, of course, a major increase in funding. By 1959 military spending accounted for half of the US federal budget. Already the previous year the Americans had followed the Soviets into space with the launch of their Explorer and (after an earlier embarrassing failure) Vanguard rockets to put their own satellites into orbit. The National Aeronautics and Space Administration (NASA) was founded the same year, in July 1958, to undertake the scientific exploration of outer space, but – emphasizing the military significance of the rapidly expanding programme – with part of its funding derived from the Pentagon (US military headquarters) and directed at missile research. In fact, though American political and military leaders continued to be almost paranoid about the 'missile gap' with the Soviet Union, believing they were lagging behind, by the time John F. Kennedy was elected President of the United States in November 1960 the Americans had perhaps seventeen times as many usable nuclear weapons as the Soviets.

Which of the superpowers possessed the larger nuclear arsenal had by now, however, become largely meaningless. For by the early 1960s the nuclear arms race had long reached the point of Mutually Assured Destruction (MAD), as it was aptly labelled. Interballistic missiles could deliver their devastating load within minutes. Fleets of bombers and submarines were armed with nuclear weapons, ready to unleash them should the command be given. The world had to live with the possibility that a crisis could escalate to the point where the button would be pressed; or that a nuclear bomb could wreak devastation by accident (such as came close to wiping out East Anglia when in 1957 an American bomber crashed into a repository holding three nuclear bombs). A reminder of the scarcely imaginable devastation that a nuclear war would bring was provided when, on 30 October 1961, the Soviets detonated what would prove to be the largest and most powerful bomb of the Cold War, north of the Arctic Circle over the Novaya Zemlya archipelago in the Arctic Ocean. The mushroom cloud stretched forty miles into the stratosphere. The flash from the explosion could be seen 600 miles away. The 50-megaton monster's scarcely conceivable destructive capability was said to have been 1,400 times more powerful than the combined force of the atomic bombs dropped on Hiroshima and Nagasaki and far greater than all the explosives used by all the belligerents during the Second World War.

For three years up to that point superpower tension had once more revolved around the issue of Berlin. There had already been one major Berlin crisis, in 1948 when Stalin had attempted to force the Western Allies out of the city. Berlin, though under four-power occupation, was located around 100 miles within the Soviet-controlled zone. The Soviet dictator had eventually backed down in spring 1949 after the Western

Allies had carried out the 'Berlin airlift' that lasted almost a year to beat the blockade he had imposed. In 1958 Stalin's successor, Khrushchev, judged the time right to impose new pressure on the Western Allies over Berlin. This was in response to American plans, encouraged by the West German government, to station intermediate-range nuclear weapons in West Germany – itself a reaction to the Soviet launching of space satellites and Khrushchev's boasting of Soviet nuclear capability.

Nikita Khrushchev had boxed his way through a power struggle in the Kremlin that had lasted for more than two years after Stalin's death in 1953 to emerge as the Soviet leader. As both Chairman of the Council of Ministers and First Secretary of the Communist Party – effectively combining the position of state premier with the all-important leadership of the party – he had outright supremacy in the Soviet system. A former protégé of Stalin (and collaborator in his purges), from a poor, uneducated background, Khrushchev was crude but quick-witted. His superficial amiability could rapidly give way to temper tantrums and outright menace. In the mid-1950s the West had briefly hoped that under his leadership better, less tense relations with the Soviet Union could be established. But Khrushchev was a volatile character, less predictable in foreign affairs than Stalin had been. That enhanced the danger that superpower conflict could quickly spin out of control.

The status of Berlin had remained a thorn in the side both of the East German leadership and of their masters in the Soviet Union. West Berlin was a small Western-run island in a Soviet-controlled ocean. But members of the Western occupying forces had the right to go in and out of East Berlin (just as Soviet military patrols occasionally still entered West Berlin, since the entire city technically remained under the control of all the four occupying powers). And East Berliners could without difficulty cross into West Berlin, which functioned as a showcase for the more prosperous West. They did not just come and go. Many of them stayed to find work, settling and enjoying the higher living standards in western Germany. Between 1953 and the end of 1956 more than 1.5 million East Germans had voted with their feet and left. Almost half a million more followed in 1957–8. The levels of departure were not compatible with either the economic or the political plans of the East German leadership, or of maintaining East Germany as a bulwark against the capitalist West. Beyond the economic considerations lay the recent developments that had seen West Germany remilitarized, part of NATO and with American nuclear weaponry on its soil. Furthermore, West Berlin was a hotbed of Western espionage and propaganda (to which increasing numbers of East Berliners were exposed on a daily basis through television transmitted from West Berlin). Khrushchev reckoned it was time to challenge the status quo. And to reopen the question of Berlin's status meant reopening the German question itself.

On 27 October 1958 Walter Ulbricht, the East German leader, announced in a major speech that 'the whole of Berlin stands on the territory of the German Democratic Republic' and fell within its sphere of sovereignty. This was an outright contradiction of Berlin's status as a city under the control of the four occupying powers. Ulbricht had obviously cleared the speech with Khrushchev, for only two weeks later, in Moscow on 10 November, the Soviet chief stated that the time had come for the occupation of Berlin to end. He followed this up on 27 November with an ultimatum to the Western powers – the USA, Great Britain and France – to accept the demilitarization of West Berlin within six months and thereby the end of their 'occupation regime' or face unilateral action to achieve this goal by the Soviet Union and the German Democratic Republic. The wartime agreement, on which the occupation rested, would in that case be deemed to be invalid.

Plainly, to accept the ultimatum would have meant a serious weakening of the Western powers, and not just in Berlin. A potential showdown was, however, averted by semi-conciliatory diplomacy (without actually yielding anything) on the part of the Western powers, and by an invitation from President Eisenhower to Khrushchev to visit the United States in 1959. The initial ultimatum deadline came and went without incident. And on 15 September 1959 Khrushchev began a twelve-day visit to America which, although it produced nothing of substance, provided an opportunity for the leaders of the superpowers to meet face to face and brought a temporary warming of the previously frosty atmosphere.

The crisis that had been brewing subsided temporarily. Deteriorating relations with China (epitomized by Mao Zedong's scant regard for Khrushchev) were among the reasons that the Soviet Union was willing to reduce the tension in Central Europe. This tension was bound to recur, however, since the problem that underlay it – the haemorrhaging of the East German population across the border into West Berlin – continued unabated. The constant drain of population to the west had prompted the East German regime, already in 1952, to seal off the demarcation line to the Federal Republic. But the border in Berlin was not closed, and it remained a way out of East Germany for those wanting to enter the west.

Hundreds of East Germans were by now crossing the border every day. At the high point of the refugee flood as many as 2,305 people headed from East to West Berlin on a single day, 6 April 1961. Most of those leaving were young. Many were farmers, choosing this way out of the collectivization of agricultural production that had been introduced in June 1958. Skilled workers, newly qualified students and young professionals – none of which the East German state could afford to lose – were also prominent among the droves seeking a better life in western Germany. In 1960 some 200,000 East Germans left. The numbers threatened to grow even larger in 1961. In April that year alone 30,000 crossed the border for good. Between the foundation of the GDR in October 1949 and August 1961 no fewer than 2.7 million East Germans (15 per cent of the population) had cast their own verdict on the socialist system of the east and moved to western Germany.

When Khrushchev and Kennedy met for the first time in Vienna on 3–4 June 1961, the question of Berlin was at the centre of their uneasy deliberations. Khrushchev was little more than contemptuous of the new and inexperienced American leader. Kennedy had been badly bruised by the 'Bay of Pigs' debacle in April – an ill-fated invasion sponsored by the Central Intelligence Agency (CIA) aimed at toppling Cuba's communist government. Seizing the initiative at their meeting, Khrushchev posed a new ultimatum. If the Western powers would not agree to making Berlin a 'free state' and renounce their rights of access, he would transfer all Soviet rights over the air corridor between West Berlin and the Federal Republic of Germany to the German Democratic Republic, forcing Western planes to land on East German territory. Kennedy, undaunted by the Soviet leader's bluster, raised the prospect of war if Khrushchev persisted in his demands.

A few weeks later reports that the council of NATO had agreed to take military measures to prevent the blockage of access routes to West Berlin caused Khrushchev to revise his initial view that there was no serious threat of war. Only at this point did he agree to a request that Ulbricht had made already in March at a meeting of Warsaw Pact representatives in Moscow to seal off the border between West Berlin and the territory of the German Democratic Republic. (Plans to wall off West Berlin to block access to and from the east dated, in fact, to as far back as 1952.) On 24 July 1961 the Politburo – the ruling body – of the Socialist Unity Party (SED, the GDR's Communist Party) decided to make the appropriate preparations. The Warsaw Pact states backed the step in early August, and on 12 August Ulbricht gave the orders for the border to be closed from midnight. The next day, 13 August – first with swiftly erected barbed wire but soon with a twelve-foot-high concrete wall nearly a hundred miles long backed by guard towers, minefields, police dogs and orders to shoot anyone crossing the 'death strip' on either side of the wall – the border between East and West Berlin was sealed. It would remain so for the next twenty-eight years.

The West's response was muted. It suited all of the Western powers, in fact, to calm the crisis. Britain, an overstretched imperial power, wanted to cut its occupation costs in Germany. The French, equally over-stretched, were even less willing 'to die for Berlin' (as their Defence Minister commented), preoccupied as they were by a severe crisis in their colony of Algeria. And the Americans, obviously the dominant Western power, had no interest in war over Berlin. So there were predictable ver-bal protests from the West but little more, beyond a symbolic show of solidarity through a visit to West Berlin a few days after the closing of the border by the American Vice-President, Lyndon B. Johnson, and the for-mer hero of the airlift, General Lucius D. Clay. Equally symbolic was the dispatching of 1,500 American combat troops to the city – who were given a rapturous reception from West Berliners as they marched down the main boulevard, the Kurfürstendamm.

Signals from Washington had, in fact, already hinted that the United States would not stand in the way of blocking off *East* Berlin, as long as there were no Soviet moves to alter the status of *West* Berlin. In late July, President Kennedy, addressing the American people on television on essential stipulations over Berlin – the right of the Western Allies to a presence in the city, right of free access, and right of self-determination for West Berliners – had not mentioned East Berlin or its population. He had acknowledged legitimate Soviet security concerns in Central and Eastern Europe (though, to Khrushchev's fury, he also stated that he would be seeking the approval of Congress for a further $3.25 billion of military spending, mainly for conventional forces). The President had told one of his closest aides that he could hold the Western alliance together to defend West Berlin, 'but I cannot act to keep East Berlin open'. And on 30 July the chairman of the American Senate's foreign policy committee, William Fulbright, had almost seemed to invite the East Germans to seal their border, indicating in a television interview his belief that they had the right to do so. Khrushchev, who wanted war just as little as did the Western powers, had his way out of the crisis that he had initiated.

The closing of the border on 13 August 1961 was well timed. It was a Sunday morning when Berliners awoke to find that East German workers under armed guard had overnight erected barbed-wire fencing throughout the city. Kennedy was only informed in mid-morning – late afternoon in Berlin. He and his leading advisers decided that, despicable as the barrier was, it was preferable to war. 'It's not a very nice solution,' Kennedy stated, 'but a wall is a hell of a lot better than a war.' Privately the US Secretary of State, Dean Rusk, admitted that the closure of the border 'would make a Berlin settlement easier'.

It was not to be expected that the other Western powers would adopt a more aggressive stance. The British ambassador in Berlin, Sir Christopher Steel, expressed his surprise that it had taken the East Germans so long to seal their boundary. The French commander in Berlin had to await instructions from Paris. Those could not be expected instantaneously: most of the Foreign Ministry staff were on holiday. Charles de Gaulle, President of France, remained unperturbed at his country residence in Colombey-les-Deux-Églises, returning to Paris only on 17 August. In England, the day before the Berlin border was sealed was the 'glorious twelfth' – the start, each year on 12 August, of the season when the British upper class indulge in their sport of grouse-shooting; the Prime Minister, Harold Macmillan, was not to be diverted from his enjoyment on the Yorkshire estates of his nephew, the Duke of Devonshire.

Two months later, in October 1961, there was a further flashpoint over Berlin, caused by the dangerous and unnecessary escalation of a minor incident. This arose when an American diplomat and his wife refused to show East German border guards their passports and were consequently denied passage to cross into the east to visit the theatre. The Americans responded by sending a squad of soldiers to escort the diplomat into East Berlin, and over the next days soldiers in jeeps with rifles at the ready accompanied civilians across the border in what was little more than a provocation. The hawkish General Clay then had ten American tanks brought up to the crossing at Checkpoint Charlie. The Soviets responded by bringing in their own tanks and lining ten of them up a hundred metres away across the border. Any minor provocation in the standoff could have imperilled world peace. But no one wanted nuclear catastrophe over a triviality – 'this childish nonsense' in the words of Harold Macmillan. It was obvious to the leadership on both sides that the issue had to be defused. President Kennedy had already decided that enough was enough. He sent a message to Khrushchev (who had equally little interest in further escalation) ensuring him that the Americans would match any withdrawal. After a sixteen-hour standoff, both sides pulled back – slowly at first, but the crisis was over.

With that, not only Berlin but Germany and Europe ceased to be the epicentre of the Cold War. The people who had to pay the price for the attainment of superpower stasis in Europe for almost three decades to come were the peoples of Eastern Europe, and not least the East Germans. Although the Wall encircled West Berlin, the population of the German Democratic Republic were the ones actually walled in – deprived of their freedom to travel across the continent, their means of communication curtailed, often separated from relatives and friends, condemned to a regime of high restriction and constant surveillance, and unable to benefit from the rapid improvements in the standard of living of their compatriots in the west (which they could witness on Western television).

There was no longer any population flow to the west. East Germans seeking to leave now ran a high risk of being killed as they tried to cross the border. One of the first killings took place shortly after marking the first anniversary of the building of the Wall had brought serious disturbances in West Berlin. An eighteen-year-old boy, Peter Fechter, who tried to escape near Checkpoint Charlie on 18 August 1962, fell in a hail of bullets a yard from freedom as he attempted to scramble over the last barbed-wire fence before reaching West Berlin. A West German television crew filming a documentary on the Wall happened to be on the spot and filmed the death agony of the boy as he screamed in pain while the East German border guards remained at their posts and did nothing. Officially – though other estimates are far higher – the number of deaths at the Wall in the twenty-eight years that it stood totalled 139 persons (the first a week after it went up, the last six months before it came down).

These were the most awful human costs of the Wall. Politically, the Wall had a calming effect. Continued crisis over Berlin, with its potential to spiral into nuclear disaster, was intolerable for all the major parties. No one wanted war. The Wall was an appalling indictment of Soviet-style socialism. But without it, the drain on the East German economy would have been intolerable, undermining the political system of the GDR. And without East Germany the entire eastern bloc of Soviet satellite states would have been endangered. The Soviet leadership is unlikely to have remained passive. The Wall, cynical and inhumane as it was, brought calm not only to Germany but to the whole of Central Europe.

There was still, however, one moment of utmost tension – actually the only time in over four decades of Cold War that the world stood on the brink of nuclear war. That it happened thousands of miles away, on the sea approaches to Cuba, but could have enveloped Europe in a nuclear holocaust, shows the extent to which the superpower conflict had by now become a worldwide confrontation.

The crisis arose when Khrushchev decided in October 1962 to station intermediate- and medium-range nuclear missiles on Cuba. The American leadership continued during the crisis to think that Cuba was also related to the Berlin question – a way of putting pressure on America to give way on West Berlin. This indeed appears to have been an indirect reason for Khrushchev's dangerous initiative; he remained obsessed with the German question, aware that the Berlin Wall had actually constituted a defeat for the socialist East and a humiliation in the eyes of the world for Marxism-Leninism. But he also had other motives. The impulsive Kremlin chief was acutely aware that the Soviet Union lagged far behind the United States in long-range missile capability. And he was more than sensitive to the fact that American intermediate-range missiles were aimed at the Soviet Union from bases in Britain, Italy and Turkey. Part of his thinking was to pay back the Americans in kind and give them 'a little of their own medicine' by exposing them to the fear of missiles pointing at them and based just off their own coast. Khrushchev seems also, however, to have been motivated by the need he felt to uphold Soviet prestige in Cuba (where a second American attempt to overthrow the communist leader, Fidel Castro, was expected) and to stimulate wider revolution in Latin America.

When Kennedy's administration responded on 21 October to the shock news that forty-two intermediate-range nuclear missiles were on their way to Cuba, by threatening to intercept the Soviet ships and at the same time placing American forces on the highest state of nuclear alert short of war, the world stood on the verge of Armageddon. The high-stakes brinkmanship between Kennedy and Khrushchev lasted a week. After days of unbearable tension Khrushchev finally backed down on 28 October and ordered the return of the missiles to the Soviet Union. The whole world could breathe with relief. The Americans could claim a victory (even if some hotheads in the Pentagon regretted that it had not come to military action). But the Soviets did not emerge completely empty-handed. Kennedy pledged publicly to make no further attempt to invade Cuba. He also agreed to remove the missile bases in Turkey, a part of the deal kept secret at the time since these were technically NATO bases that the United States was unilaterally preparing to dismantle. The missiles were removed from Turkey the following year – without any admission that this was connected to the Cuban crisis.

Never before during the Cold War had nuclear war been so close. No one could know that it would never come so close again. This realization, in Washington and in Moscow, persuaded American and Soviet leaders to end – or at least pose limits to – the lunatic arms race. The installation in 1963 of a 'hot line' between the White House and the Kremlin was a sign of a willingness to defuse tension rather than run the risk of escalation to the point of nuclear conflict. And in Moscow on 5 August 1963 the United States, the Soviet Union and Great Britain agreed to a limited Nuclear Test Ban Treaty, prohibiting other than underground testing. (France did not sign.) It was a modest step, but it amounted at least to a start.

Little over a year later, in October 1964, Khrushchev was removed from power in a 'palace coup' in the Kremlin. His action in provoking the Cuban missile crisis, seen to have damaged the Soviet Union's international standing, was among the reasons for his deposition. So was his authorization of the building of the Berlin Wall. With Khrushchev's departure, the Cold War lost an erratic, blustering, unpredictable component. Two new Soviet leaders replaced him: Leonid Brezhnev as General Secretary of the Communist Party and Alexei Kosygin as Prime Minister. The shift of power in the Kremlin began a new phase of the Cold War. There would be future points of tension, certainly, but the erection of the Berlin Wall, the defusing of the Cuban crisis and the toppling of Khrushchev saw the worst of the heat evaporate from the Cold War. For a time, in international affairs, Europe remained quiet.

LIVING WITH THE BOMB: FEAR OR FATALISM?

'We were all living in a kind of nervous hysteria,' recalled Eric Hobsbawm, one of Europe's greatest historians, nearly fifty years later when reflecting on the 'black shadow of the mushroom clouds'. That was an intellectual's understanding. But how far did the generalization apply to the mass of ordinary Europeans? Did most people experience perpetual fear and live in 'nervous hysteria'? It is not an easy question to answer.

After a generation dominated by war, bloodshed, suffering and devastation, most people in Europe, east and west, longed more than anything for peace and 'normality'. Although there had been little 'normality' to speak of in previous decades, this in essence meant a return to lives revolving around family and work, spent in decent material circumstances, protected from the worst inroads of poverty and insecurity. As the horrors of the Second World War gradually receded and the contours of a new Europe began to emerge from the wreckage, what mattered to the great majority of people were security, stability and prosperity. They began to dream of better times. But the prospect of nuclear war between the new powers which now controlled Europe, and glowered at each other over the Iron Curtain that divided the continent, cast a long shadow. The capacity of nuclear weapons to inflict total destruction rendered Europe's citizens powerless. People throughout Europe (and beyond) had to learn to live with the bomb. Fear and fatalism existed side by side. There was good reason for both.

How people adjusted to the new reality of the threat to their very existence varied, of course, with personal circumstances, beliefs and convictions, social class, nationality, geography, and a myriad of other factors. It was not least greatly influenced by the information they received from political parties and their leaders, the mass media and social commentators and influential individuals at various levels. However difficult it is to arrive at generalizations, it appears to have been the case, paradoxically, that when Cold War confrontation was at its most dangerous, between 1950 and 1962, opposition to nuclear weapons was relatively muted.

Anti-nuclear movements were in their infancy during the hottest part of the Cold War and unable to win wide popular resonance. Western European governments were successful for the most part in instilling in the citizens of their countries profound anti-Soviet views and its counterpoint – a belief in the security provided by the United States of America, widely seen as Western Europe's saviour and the guarantee of its future wellbeing. In the other emerging nuclear powers, Britain and France, there was also widespread readiness to accept the deterrent effect of independently possessed nuclear weapons. Therefore, in Western Europe the fear of nuclear weapons was, it could be said – with pardonable exaggeration – largely one-sided. Soviet weapons were a source of fear; NATO, meaning in effect, American (and British and French) weapons, were a source of security. The anti-Americanism, which would feed into a widening anti-nuclear protest movement from the late 1960s onwards, greatly influenced by reactions to the Vietnam War, played a far smaller role in the 1950s.

One set of impressions of reactions in Britain to the prospect of nuclear war in the early 1950s can be gleaned from the diary entries of Nella Last, a lower-middle-class married woman, in her sixties, a supporter of the Conservative Party living quietly in the suburbs of Barrow-in-Furness in the north of England. On New Year's Day in 1950 she felt depressed at what the future might hold. She had been reading an article in an American magazine, passed on to her by some friends, which had spoken of war as inevitable after 1951 and suggested that atomic bombs were a trivial matter 'when compared to the germ bombs Russia was concentrating on'. Her reading of newspapers and magazines, listening to the radio and conversations with friends, had shaped and confirmed her clear views on the developing Cold War. In May, concerned about the threat of atomic weapons and hearing about '70-foot atom-proof shelters' being built in Stockholm, Nella worried about the likelihood of a new war and pondered about mankind eking out some kind of life deep underground. When the Korean War began in late June she had 'a sick feeling' that events there might 'destroy civilisation as we know it' and wondered what Russia held behind the Iron Curtain. She favoured Western action to 'put a stop to the Communist drive and urge'. Later in the month, attending instruction on civil defence and watching gas masks being fitted, she was depressed to hear of the devastating effect that the explosion of an atomic bomb would have on Barrow and the pessimism of the man sitting next to her, who had remarked: 'sooner it's over, sooner to sleep'. 'Ordinary people can do so little,' Nella concluded, 'only pray.'

Towards the end of July she expressed her foreboding at the testing of 'this dreadful H-bomb' and wondered whether America would drop an atomic bomb in Korea (thereby giving Stalin just cause, she added, to claim that the West stood for 'death and mutilation'). A weak Britain, she thought, could not influence such a decision. 'And if such a dreadful thing *did* happen (she went on) – and Russia *has* them [atomic bombs] – all hell could easily be let loose. A terrifying outlook.' Mrs Last continued to harbour a 'deep fear that another atom bomb will be dropped' and saw the chances of this growing, with 'no other weapon against such odds'. Towards the end of the year she 'felt that never before in the world's history was so difficult a situation facing men, or countries' in the light of 'the certainty of Stalin's deep-laid plans to engulf Europe, and, if Europe, the whole of the world'. Her fear of, and anxiety about, the Soviet Union knew no bounds. 'Beside Stalin,' she wrote, 'Hitler seems a boy scout. *He* is the Anti-Christ and not Hitler.'

Nella Last's worries about the atomic bomb, so frequently expressed in 1950, appear, however, to have dissipated once the most acute phase of the Korean War passed. She may have been more politically aware than many of her British contemporaries, though her views were perhaps fairly typical for her generation and social class as the outbreak of the Korean War stirred new anxieties. Whether her palpable fears were representative of the views of wider sections of the population is, however, doubtful. Certainly on the left there were strong feelings about rearmament. Fifty-seven members of the Labour parliamentary opposition rebelled in March 1952 against the party leadership in condemning the British rearmament programme. In autumn that year Britain tested its first atomic bomb and vehement denunciation on the Labour left of

Britain's possession of nuclear weapons started to mount sharply. By 1957, when Britain tested the far more devastating hydrogen bomb, the Labour Party seemed to be approaching a split on the issue. At the annual conference in 1957 as many as 127 motions called for disarmament and there were vehement attacks, led by the left-wing firebrand Aneurin Bevan, on the leader of the party, Hugh Gaitskell, and the support for an independent nuclear deterrent. The party's leadership, however, backed by the great majority of party members, remained resolutely against Britain's unilateral nuclear disarmament.

Some members of the Anglican clergy also voiced their opposition to Britain's nuclear capability. But when a petition signed by fifty-one members of the clergy urged the British people to reject Britain's acquisition of the bomb, the people took no notice. Opposition to Britain becoming a nuclear power was confined to a small minority. One former Labour minister acknowledged the general disinterest of most people. Social and economic matters were what concerned them. Towards the bomb there was a 'collective shrug of the shoulders'.

People no doubt felt the bomb was terrible; but it was better to have it than not, and there was little that ordinary people could do about it anyway. By the later 1950s, however, fear of the bomb and demands that Britain end its possession of nuclear weapons were growing. The sense of anxiety was expressed directly or obliquely in a variety of works of literature and in film – though the bleakest depiction of the impact of a nuclear attack on Britain, *The War Game* (1965), was deemed by the BBC to be too horrifying for a mass audience and was banned.

Fear of nuclear weapons had given rise by the late 1950s to the first organized forms of popular opposition. The Campaign for Nuclear Disarmament (CND), founded in February 1958, was backed by a number of prominent left-wing intellectuals and public figures. Among them were Bertrand Russell, the eminent philosopher and longstanding anti-war activist, and John Collins, a well-known Church of England clergyman, a canon of St Paul's Cathedral in London, an ardent pacifist. Its inaugural meeting in London the following year, demanding Britain's unilateral nuclear disarmament, was attended by 5,000 people, in the main Labour supporters. By 1959 it had over 270 branches throughout Britain. Increasingly impressive numbers – an estimated 150,000 by 1962 – joined the march at Easter each year from 1958, the first from

London to the nuclear research base fifty miles away at Aldermaston, subsequent marches taking the reverse route. The marchers were predominantly middle class and well educated, the majority of them supporters of Labour. They came from all age groups. Two-thirds of them were male, almost a half of them had a Christian belief, and a similar proportion were uncompromising pacifists.

Some were unworldly idealists. Dora Russell (Bertrand's second wife), a strong feminist and prominent campaigner on social issues, on whom the Russian Revolution had left an indelible mark, supplied tea to the marchers from the back of her battered campaign coach. The Aldermaston March in 1958 gave her the idea of linking with women from Eastern Europe and the Soviet Union on a joint peace initiative. The Women's Caravan for Peace that she organized at the age of sixty-four (actually comprising her old coach and a Ford lorry), comprising nineteen women, took their crusade on an extraordinary journey lasting fourteen weeks through much of Central and Eastern Europe, ending up in Moscow, where they met the Soviet Peace Committee and were treated to an approved tour of agricultural cooperatives. They returned to England by train. Few in London, however, were interested in the epic tale they tried to tell.

Fear of imminent nuclear war was never as acute as during the Cuban missile crisis in October 1962.* It marked for nearly twenty years the high point of the CND's protest. The Test Ban Treaty the following year saw its support slump. The CND had always been a minority movement – significant certainly, but never gaining the backing of the majority, even in the Labour Party. Most people recognized the fallacy of the notion that possession of the bomb gave Britain any genuine autonomy from the United States should it come to nuclear war. It was plain during the anxiety at the time of the Cuban missile crisis that, should it come to nuclear war, Britain would most likely be attacked whether it had the bomb or not. Opponents of the country's nuclear capability argued that it was pointless, therefore, to have the bomb. That was not, however, the

---

* This was the only time during the entire Cold War that I personally felt this fear. I had just gone to university but was sufficiently worried by the prospect of Britain being subjected to nuclear attack that I thought of returning home to be with my family. Within a few days the danger had passed and my fear with it.

reaction of most people. The majority of the population did not favour giving up Britain's independent nuclear weapons. The bomb was seen as a safeguard, a deterrent against attack – almost universally considered as most likely to come from the Soviet Union. When, if ever, it might be used, and whether a decision on its deployment could be taken independently of America, were seldom questioned. The belief that Britain could rely upon its victorious wartime ally, the United States, indeed perhaps fostered a degree of confidence, even complacency.

It did not follow that there was enthusiastic backing for Britain's nuclear weapons. People instead largely combined fatalistic acceptance of what they could not change with cautious optimism about the future. Of those asked in an opinion survey conducted in 1959 to gaze into the crystal ball and imagine what might happen by 1980, only 6 per cent thought an atomic war was likely, and 41 per cent thought the Soviet Union and the West would probably by then 'be living peacefully together'. And five years later, in the general election campaign of 1964, a mere 7 per cent highlighted defence as their most important concern. Daily bread-and-butter issues, not worries about nuclear Armageddon, were what shaped the lives of most people.

Britain and West Germany were in the 1950s and early 1960s in many ways at opposite ends of the spectrum of reactions to the threat posed by the Cold War. Britain saw itself as largely detached from the European continent, a victor in the Second World War, still a great power in possession of a world empire and, since 1952, of its own nuclear weapons. West Germany bore all the psychological as well as material scars of total defeat in the Second World War. Beyond this, divided and (until 1955) still occupied and demilitarized, West Germany stood in the absolute front line of Cold War confrontation, the obvious battleground if hostilities between the superpowers should become a reality, the most likely site of nuclear devastation should confrontation become uncontrolled. While there were some similarities in the way people in the two countries responded to the danger of nuclear war, there were also substantial differences.

So often in the eye of the storm in the post-war years, West Germans were especially sensitive to the threat to world peace posed by an international crisis. In October 1956, for instance, the double crisis over the popular insurrection in Hungary and the ill-fated Suez adventure of

Britain and France prompted fears of war in West Germany that were not widely felt in Britain. The extensive sympathies in Britain with the Hungarians who had suffered bloodshed and repression at the hands of the Soviets had not generally been coupled with anxieties that the uprising might lead to war. And the invasion of Egypt by Anglo-French and Israeli forces, though sharply dividing opinion, was as it was taking place backed by a majority of the population (when the invasion failed so dismally, it was another matter). In West Germany, by contrast, in November 1956 well over half of the population feared another war. Almost as large a proportion of public opinion thought that the Soviets would have carried out their threat to launch rocket attacks on Britain and France had there been no ceasefire in Suez. A majority of West Germans thought in the early 1950s that the Western democracies and the communist East would not in the long run be able to live together in peace. Nearly half of those asked between 1951 and 1963 were apprehensive about the imminent outbreak of another war, and felt that they had to reckon with another world war. And a third of the population thought that a future war would entail the use of atomic weapons.

These were certainly the fears of an elderly lower-middle-class citizen of West Berlin, Franz Göll, who lived alone and confided his reflective analysis solely to his diary. Göll thought in 1958 that 'we are already so close to a Third World War as to be prepared for its outbreak "by the hour"'. He completely opposed the stationing of nuclear weapons on German soil since it made Germany a target in any future war but also restricted the country's options in any superpower confrontation. He was not assured by the integration of West Germany into NATO, and feared that some unpredictable incident could trigger an American nuclear response. The larger the stockpile of weapons, the more likely it was in his view that an imminent threat 'will bait the button-pushers'. Rearmament and nuclear weapons, he concluded therefore, threatened rather than guaranteed Germany's security.

Despite such evident anxieties, anti-nuclear protest made relatively little ground in West Germany during the most dangerous phase of the Cold War. When eighteen internationally famous West German atomic physicists – including Carl Friedrich von Weizsäcker, Otto Hahn and Werner Heisenberg – signed an appeal in 1957 against the use of tactical nuclear arms by the recently established federal army or Bundeswehr (a stance that the federal government was considering), their manifesto evoked a response worldwide but only a muted one within West Germany itself. Nevertheless, spurred by this protest and by the example of the CND in Britain, an organization to lead West German opposition to nuclear weapons, backed by sections of the Social Democratic Party (SPD), some well-known intellectuals, a number of public figures and some Protestant theologians, was founded in early 1958. It called itself the 'Fight against Atomic Death' (*Kampf dem Atomtod*). Among its leading representatives were the Protestant theologian Martin Niemöller and the Catholic intellectual Eugen Kogon (both of whom had been incarcerated in Nazi concentration camps), one of West Germany's most eminent writers, Heinrich Böll, and Gustav Heinemann, a significant voice in the Protestant Church and a political figure of importance (a one-time CDU minister in Adenauer's first government, but in the meantime an SPD member and later to become the President of West Germany).

While the Protestant Church, though deeply divided on the issue, was heavily engaged in the debate over nuclear weapons, West Germany's Catholic Church officially kept its distance. It had taken the stance, voiced in 1950 by Cardinal Josef Frings, Archbishop of Cologne, that it was a moral duty to bear arms against totalitarianism. Acceptance of the possibility of a 'just war', even using nuclear weapons, remained the Catholic Church's position – one derived from the experience of Nazism, but now transferred to the perceived evil of Soviet communism. One extreme (if not outrightly zany) view expressed by a Jesuit theologian, Gustav Grundlach, in 1959 (and denounced by other Catholic writers), was that destruction of the world in a nuclear war was preferable to the evil of totalitarian rule.

'Fight against Atomic Death' sought to mobilize public feeling against the possibility of the newly established Bundeswehr acquiring nuclear weapons, and to force the removal from West Germany of Allied nuclear weapons. Building on the Aldermaston example, Easter marches of anti-nuclear demonstrators began in 1960 after press reports the previous winter that German troops had tested atomic weapons. The marches gained in popularity over the following years. By 1964 they were taking place in nearly all big German cities and towns; an estimated 100,000 citizens in total took part. Intellectuals, clergy, writers and artists, lawyers and trade unionists were prominent among them, as were young people. But the main political parties (the Christian Democrats, Free Democrats and Social Democrats) and most of the press remained hostile towards the anti-nuclear movement.

Unsurprisingly, given such strong influence on public opinion, the protests held little appeal for the majority of the German population. The proximity of the perceived communist threat obviously posed a major problem to the prospects of winning support for disarmament proposals. And the beginning of the protest movement had coincided with the start of the Berlin crisis instigated by Khrushchev. For most people, the worries about the escalating conflict did not translate into opposition to nuclear weapons. The time did not seem right to take the risk of disarmament. And the takeover in West Berlin of the leadership of 'Fight against Atomic Death' by Communists (though the official West German Communist Party had been banned in 1956) hardly helped. The 'Fight against Atomic Death' campaign had very limited success and was of short duration. It would be more than two decades before the anti-nuclear movement in West Germany would gain new strength.

In France, the second country in Western Europe to acquire its own atomic bomb, the anti-nuclear protest movement also faced great difficulties. Public opinion was evenly split in 1959 on France building its own bomb. The conservative press was in favour, the left-wing press against. Over the next few years increasing proportions of those questioned in opinion polls favoured multilateral nuclear disarmament. But a *French* bomb was seen as a prestige symbol, an indication that France was a great power. Important voices opposed a French bomb. But they were not backed by most of the population, who were more concerned by the bitter Algerian war than by the prospect of France becoming a nuclear power. Hundreds of writers and public figures (including Jean-Paul Sartre and Simone de Beauvoir), academics, scientists and religious leaders appealed in 1959 to Charles de Gaulle, who the previous year had become President of the new French Fifth Republic, to abandon nuclear testing. But the first French nuclear test went ahead on 13 February 1960, to widespread popular approval according to an opinion poll the following month. Some 67 per cent of respondents took the view that possession of the atomic bomb gave France higher standing in international affairs. By 1964, however, a year after the partial Test Ban Treaty (which France had not signed), more people opposed than supported a French nuclear defence force. The division mirrored the sharp political division within France on this and other issues. The non-Gaullist parties were by the mid-1960s opposed to France's nuclear bomb, the conservatives in favour of it.

In most of Western Europe a fairly common pattern emerged. The anti-nuclear movement gained support, especially among the well-educated middle classes and the far left, but ran up against the opposition of the political establishment, the military and most of the press. Frequently, as in the Netherlands, none of the major parties supported the anti-nuclear campaign. Here, the Dutch Labour Party joined conservatives in backing the installation of NATO's nuclear weapons. In Catholic countries anti-nuclear protest had to contend with the opposition of the Church. This was the case in Italy, where the Catholic Church backed the pro-nuclear policy of the dominant Christian Democrats (though this started to change following the publication of Pope John XXIII's encyclical letter *Pacem in Terris*, Peace on Earth, in 1963, which exerted a powerful influence internationally on Catholic thinking on war and peace).

Accordingly, anti-nuclear campaigns everywhere failed to win over the majority of the population. Opinion surveys demonstrated widespread and increasing support for complete nuclear disarmament of *all* countries and, as a step on the way, approval of a ban on the testing of nuclear weapons. But one-sided disarmament was another matter altogether.

Some of the strongest support for the anti-nuclear campaign outside Britain and West Germany arose in Greece (somewhat curiously, since there had been no strong pacifist tradition) but there, too, it ran into strong headwinds from the political and military establishment. The CND Aldermaston marches once more provided the main inspiration. And the fear provoked by the Cuban missile crisis swelled the ranks of its activists, especially among students. Some of its support also came from communists whose party had been banned since the civil war of the late 1940s. The conservative government saw revolutionary tendencies in the anti-nuclear protest movement and resorted to heavy-handed repression. It not only banned a march (a copy of Aldermaston) from Marathon to Athens in 1963, but arrested 2,000 protesters and injured several hundred

31

others. The tactic backfired. Support increased rather than fell away. When a Greek independent MP, Grigoris Lambrakis, the only person (because of his parliamentary immunity) to complete the banned Marathon march in 1963, was subsequently murdered by right-wing paramilitaries, no fewer than half a million people joined his funeral procession. The following year, the Marathon march was permitted, with an estimated 250,000 people participating in its final stages. But the anti-nuclear movement remained somewhat disorganized, unclear in its political aims, dependent on communist support, which alienated many Greeks, and relentlessly opposed by the political establishment and the armed forces. Despite the impressive levels of mobilization for the Marathon marches, it would be as well not to exaggerate the support for the anti-nuclear campaign in Greece. This was, as in all countries in Western Europe, divided over the frightening new weapons but mostly favoured their retention if getting rid of them meant exposure to domination by Soviet communism.

Even in neutral Switzerland fear of the bomb did not readily convert into support for anti-nuclear protest. Public opinion was again heavily shaped by a press that reflected the pro-nuclear position of the political establishment and the military. When a grassroots movement to block arming Swiss armed forces with tactical nuclear weapons forced a referendum on the issue, the proposal was opposed by two-thirds of voters. Despite the referendum victory, however, the government, anxious not to incite opposition and divide the country on such a contentious issue, took no steps to arm the military with nuclear weapons.

Only in Denmark and Norway did opposition to nuclear weapons accord with, rather than contest, government policy. Demonstrations against nuclear weapons were aimed at preventing their governments from acquiring them or allowing them to be stationed in their countries. But Danish protesters were largely pushing at an open door, since none of the main political parties favoured the deployment of nuclear weapons in Denmark. Much the same was true of Norway, where parliament had rejected the stationing of nuclear weapons. This move was widely popular, but otherwise Norwegian anti-nuclear agitation gained only limited support owing to its lack of obvious practical objectives. Growing opposition to nuclear armament in the wake of the escalating arms race between the superpowers did score a success in Sweden. Support for the building of a

Swedish bomb dropped sharply after the nuclear debate began in 1957. At first backed by 40 per cent of the population, it was a decade or so later opposed by 69 per cent. By the mid-1960s the Swedish government was committed to non-nuclear defence.

Every country in Western Europe, often initially inspired by the CND in Britain, developed its own movement against nuclear armament. Sometimes, as in Britain, the emphasis was on unilateral nuclear disarmament, but in most cases the aim was a worldwide end to nuclear weapons and an immediate ban on their testing. Such feeling mingled with pacifism, though extending far beyond it, and reached a peak between 1957 and 1963 before subsiding as tensions eased following the Test Ban Treaty of 1963. The widespread influence of the CND demonstrates the international character of the peace movements. Even so, national considerations predominated. Whether a country's background and cultural tradition had been as a 'great power' or generally rooted in neutrality and non-alignment strongly affected attitudes. So did the relative weighting of influence from the Christian Churches, the extent of popular support for parties of the left, levels of education, and the role of the mass media in promoting fear of communism and undermining protest through their backing for the policies of governing parties.

Difficult though it is to gauge levels of fear, fatalism and opposition to nuclear weapons in Western Europe during this period, it is absolutely impossible to reach any clear notion of genuine opinion among the peoples of Eastern Europe. Opposition to the Soviet slant on nuclear weaponry, the Cold War and the West could not be publicly expressed. Public opinion was determined by the leadership of the Soviet Union and its satellites, orchestrated to produce maximum uniformity in support of the regime's policy. Dissident voices could not be publicly heard and were, in any case, few. Relentless and ferocious propaganda was levelled at Western 'imperialists', 'warmongers' and 'fascists' who threatened the peace, democracy and socialism of the Soviet Union and other socialist countries. Lurid prose was used to denounce the Americans who were 'brandishing the atomic bomb' while the Soviet Union 'stood vigilantly in defence of peace'.

This stance in the Soviet bloc had hardened as the Cold War had deepened in the late 1940s. By 1950 the self-portrayal of the Soviet Union as the leader of a vast international movement of ordinary people seeking peace and freedom from the tyranny of nuclear weapons in the hands of

'Western imperialists' had taken shape. In March that year, driven more than anything by fear of war with the United States, a Permanent Committee of the Partisans of Peace, an international organization of pro-Soviet campaigners, met in Stockholm to devise its programme. Out of this emerged the Stockholm Peace Appeal, demanding 'the unconditional prohibition of the atomic weapon'. A vast, meticulously organized campaign was then launched with intense mobilization of the population through mass meetings, rallies and propaganda in factories, workshops and homes to gather signatures throughout the Soviet bloc and beyond for a petition in support of the Appeal.

The petition gained, so it was claimed, the signatures of over 500 million citizens from 79 countries, 400 million of them from communist countries, the rest largely from Soviet sympathizers elsewhere. By the end of 1950 it had been signed by more than 115 million Soviet citizens, more or less the entire adult population of the USSR. In Hungary an unlikely total of 7.5 million signatures from a total population (including children) of 9.2 million was announced. In Poland it was signed by 18 million people. The 190,000 who had failed to sign it (sometimes, individuals claimed, because they had been ill or incapacitated) were denigrated as 'kulaks, urban speculators . . . the reactionary section of the clergy and members of Jehovah's Witnesses'. Only Yugoslavia, constantly assailed by the Soviet Union since the schism of 1948, trod a different path. Its own peace movement attacked 'Soviet imperialism' as a threat to world peace as well as the aggression of Western powers.

Even though the worst of the repression of deviant views was ended with Stalin's death in 1953, outright opposition to the regime's policy on nuclear weapons could still not be openly expressed. A number of leading scientists, sometimes emboldened by contacts with their counterparts involved in anti-nuclear protest in the West, argued behind the scenes for nuclear arms control and disarmament. But even at a high level this was not without risks. The nuclear physicist Andrei Sakharov had played an important part in developing the Soviet hydrogen bomb, but by the 1970s he was persecuted for his outspoken views on human rights and suppression of liberties in the Soviet Union. When he opposed plans for a resumption of nuclear tests at a meeting of government leaders and scientists in Moscow in 1961, he was denounced by Khrushchev before the entire General Assembly in a tirade lasting half an hour.

Opposition expressed in a closed meeting did not, of course, seep out to the general public. A hint that the official stance of the regime did not wholly match popular views on nuclear weapons might be gleaned from the warm reception given by hundreds of passers-by in many towns and villages to a remarkable trek in 1961 by thirty-one peace marchers. They walked from San Francisco to Moscow and were permitted to travel through the Soviet Union on the last stages of the 5,000-mile journey. What people privately thought of the escalation of the nuclear arms race and how extensive their fears were can, however, only be surmised.

A reasonable assumption is that the views of most people amounted to practically a mirror image of Western fears of the Soviet Union. The scaremongering about Western 'imperialists', the emphasis on the nuclear danger posed by the United States and NATO (far from always unjustified), and the civil-defence propaganda that drew attention to the threat of nuclear attack, probably contributed to enhancing the anxieties of ordinary citizens. At the same time, there is no reason to doubt that most people believed much of what they were told about the Cold War (from exactly the opposite viewpoint of those in Western Europe) and were convinced that Soviet strength offered them the best safeguard against NATO-led aggression. Probably, therefore, people in the Soviet bloc welcomed the displays of Soviet military hardware and nuclear prowess (seen in the West as threatening) as their own guarantee against the danger from the West, specifically from the United States.

The great divide across the Iron Curtain thus separated attitudes towards the nuclear threat as it did so much else. The threat of nuclear devastation was common, however, to both halves of the continent – a continuing backcloth to people's lives even if the population (or their representatives) reacted to it in different ways. And at certain critical junctures, most especially during the Cuban missile crisis of 1962, it intruded sharply, though usually briefly. The evidence, difficult though it is to assemble and interpret, does not, however, tend to support Eric Hobsbawm's notion (mentioned earlier) that people lived in 'a kind of nervous hysteria' about The Bomb.

Unquestionably, there was near universal support for limiting the arms race, and preferably stopping it altogether. Most people, too, favoured nuclear disarmament by all powers – though unilateral nuclear disarmament was a different proposition altogether. The anti-nuclear movement gained momentum, starting in Britain, in practically all Western European countries in the late 1950s, as the horrific destructive potential of the hydrogen bomb became widely evident and Europe faced the dangerous crisis over Berlin. But nowhere did it win the support of the majority of the population. Anti-Soviet propaganda and the perceived threat from the USSR were sufficient to ensure that the bulk of the population in Western European countries backed the Cold War stance of their governments. In the Soviet bloc regime control of opinion was even more successful in blotting out any possibility of a challenge to nuclear policy, at the same time ensuring near total official commitment to peace, reinforced through the image, incessantly hammered home, of the dangerous, warlike ambitions of the United States and NATO.

In the east, too, in so far as it is possible to detect, the population ideally wanted worldwide nuclear disarmament and in any case limitations on nuclear arms. In both Eastern and Western Europe there was a good deal of realism behind the differently structured peace movements. A world completely free of nuclear arms was the ideal of most people. But there was also recognition that nuclear weapons, once invented, could not be wished away. They were a fact of life – a terrifying one if allowed to preoccupy the mind. So there was little tendency to dwell upon the prospect of nuclear Armageddon. People shut it out of their minds. They simply got on with their lives, aware of the threat of the mushroom cloud but not allowing it to dominate their existence, let alone reduce them to a state of hysteria. People acclimatized to fear. The dread of nuclear conflict was a latent presence rather than (apart from passing episodes) an acute anxiety. This allowed people to live with fear. It made them, for the most part, fatalistic about their survival in a world that might continue to exist without nuclear war. Some – how many is impossible to calculate – even no doubt welcomed the presence of nuclear weapons on both sides of the Cold War divide, seeing it as the best hope of avoiding a third world war. And in Western Europe at least people generally had other things on their mind – most obviously how to make the most of the remarkable upturn in economic prospects that was bringing about a dramatic improvement to their living standards.

2

The Making of Western Europe

Instead of unity among the great powers – both political and economic – after the war, there is complete disunity between the Soviet Union and the satellites on one side and the rest of the world on the other. There are, in short, two worlds instead of one.

Charles E. Bohlen, diplomat, expert on the Soviet Union,
and adviser to President Truman, August 1947

From the beginning of the 1950s, exacerbated by the international superpower confrontation over Korea and the terrifying escalation of nuclear destructive capability, the political arteries in Europe hardened. The divide between the political systems of Eastern and Western Europe, inexorably growing since 1945, widened to become an unbridgeable chasm.

Travellers in pre-modern times had seen a division running from north to south through Europe, usually at the line where allegiance to the Orthodox Church began. And well before the Second World War a clear fault line had divided the more prosperous, more industrialized northern and western parts of Europe from the much poorer, overwhelming agrarian south and east. But the division that emerged after 1945 was of a different nature altogether. The Iron Curtain that had descended soon after the end of the war ensured that East and West were now separated by irreconcilably opposed political systems, driven by mutually hostile ideologies, which meant in turn that economies, societies and the mentalities of citizens developed along utterly different lines.

As the era recedes into a more distant past the division seems increasingly surreal. For generations familiar only with Europe since the end of the Cold War it is difficult to 'feel' (even if it can be abstractly understood) what it was like for Western Europeans to be cut off from great capitals like Warsaw, Prague or Budapest, or for citizens from Eastern and Central Europe to be unable to travel to Paris, Rome or London. Not only were the two halves of Europe physically separated from each other; to cross the Iron Curtain in either direction was to experience a wholly different world, a sense of alienation mixed with apprehension and isolation in an intimidating as well as strange environment.

The Cold War determined the new geography. Neutral countries, even if formally 'non-aligned' to either of the superpower-dominated defensive organizations (NATO and the Warsaw Pact), could not in practice avoid being seen (like Austria or Finland) as part of 'the West' or (like Yugoslavia) 'the eastern bloc'. Greece and Turkey, despite their geographical position, were regarded as part of 'the West' whereas their Balkan neighbours belonged to 'the East'. Spain and Portugal, although dictatorships stuck in a time warp, were also incorporated into 'the West' because of their vehement anti-communism and strategic significance as the bridge between the Atlantic and the Mediterranean.

The two blocs separated by the Iron Curtain were by no means monolithic. Within the blocs Europe, east as well as west, remained a continent of nation states. The nation state was the accepted basis of political organization and identity. In this sense, the Second World War, for all its unparalleled destructiveness, had at the outset of the new era changed nothing. But there was a significant difference. Most of the nation states in the east had been newly created at the end of the First World War. They had often looked west for their political inspiration. Most in the west had a longer – sometimes extremely long – history of development behind them. National identities, histories, traditions, cultures and political developments that had shaped a continent of nation states ran too deep to be easily or quickly diluted by supra-national attachments. Soviet communism had proved incapable of forcing Yugoslavia, a nation state itself only a generation old, into line. And other countries in the eastern bloc, as Poland and Hungary in particular were also soon to show, were prepared to struggle to uphold national interests and resist pressure to comply with Moscow's demands – even if they had to realize that power ultimately came out of the turret of a Soviet tank. This military power ensured that the challenge to Soviet domination could not prevail. After seeming to loosen between 1953 and 1956, the grip of the Soviet Union over Eastern Europe tightened remorselessly again and was not to be broken for over three decades.

The varied character of nation states in Western Europe, their recent history and their dominant features of political culture, all determined that there would be far less uniformity in political development than was the case east of the Iron Curtain. Nevertheless, certain features crossed national boundaries. The destabilizing pressures of the interwar era no longer existed. Fascism and National Socialism were now only favoured by discredited residual minorities. Communism, as the Cold War set in, lost popularity, its revolutionary alternative to liberal democracy unappealing, except for a minority – sizeable in Italy, France and Finland, but otherwise negligible.

If the political constraints were less overt than in the Soviet bloc, they nonetheless existed, largely determined by the Cold War. American influence, shaped above all by the need to harden Western Europe into a firm bulwark against communism, was a vital unifying factor. International bonds were forged and strengthened by the Western defensive alliance in NATO – in good measure the arm of American foreign policy in Europe. Whatever the variations in the Western European political systems, anti-communism provided a unifying ideological force.

A level of political convergence among the countries of Western Europe was also imposed by the demands of rapidly growing market economies (see Chapter 4). The specific interests of the individual nation states posed, it is true, a major barrier, more than in Eastern Europe, to supranational politics that threatened to compete with, let alone override, issues touching on national sovereignty. The two pre-war 'great powers' and victors in the war, Britain and France, were especially sensitive to any such perceived threat to national interests. Nevertheless, in Western Europe, too, governments of individual countries faced similar pressures and had in their aims and policies much in common. Some of these were starting to push in the direction of greater integration, initially at least of their economies, which would find formal recognition in the creation of the European Economic Community (EEC) comprising France, Italy, West Germany and the Benelux countries, established by the Treaty of Rome in 1957.

International and economic pressures combined in the first post-war decades to mould Western Europe, whatever the national differences, into a recognizable political entity, sharing established principles of liberal democracy, based on increasingly interwoven capitalist economies, and with far closer bonds with the United States than had existed before the war. Another, quite dramatic, change came over this half-continent in these years. Its nation states ceased (apart, for a little while yet, from Portugal) to be colonial powers. The war had left European imperialism on the defensive, but intact. The once great powers, Britain and France, had no intention of giving up their immense colonial possessions. Yet two decades after the end of the war they were gone, apart from a few minor remnants. The speed of the demolition of empires marked an astonishing shift, with far-reaching consequences not just for the newly independent countries but also for the political consciousness of the former colonial powers, and for their international status. It meant in the long run, too, that Western Europe looked predominantly to the consolidation of its own political, economic and cultural identity. Any expansionist notions, whether overseas or within Europe itself, now belonged to the past.

DEMOCRACY CONSOLIDATED

In the 1950s the western half of the European continent comprised seven constitutional monarchies (the United Kingdom, Belgium, the Netherlands, Denmark, Norway, Sweden, Greece), a grand duchy (Luxembourg), and ten republics (Austria, Finland, France, Ireland, Italy, Switzerland, Turkey, West Germany, Portugal and Spain – the last two of these being authoritarian states that would last until the mid-1970s). In addition there were some tiny independent states, principalities left over from feudal times: Andorra, Liechtenstein and Monaco, the ancient little republic of San Marino (where Communists participated in government between 1945 and 1957), and the Vatican City (whose independence had been established by the Lateran Treaty of 1929). Malta was to gain its independence from Britain only in 1964. Gibraltar remains to this day an anomalous British dependency.

Western Europe, even geographically no more than a loose conglomerate of nation states, did not exist as a political concept before the Cold

War. The making of Western Europe was a gradual and piecemeal process, but was taking shape by 1949 as a group of liberal democracies based on the rule of law and international cooperation that were institutionally bound together through common interests, particularly in defence. It was forged in the first instance by commitment to the US-led anti-Soviet alliance, formalized in the foundation of NATO in April 1949.

That same year ten countries (Belgium, Denmark, France, Ireland, Italy, Luxembourg, the Netherlands, Norway, Sweden and the United Kingdom, all apart from Sweden founder members of NATO) came together in the Council of Europe, established to promote democracy, human rights and the rule of law (building on the Universal Declaration of Human Rights, adopted by the United Nations in December 1948). Within little more than a year they had been joined by Greece, Turkey, Iceland and West Germany. By the mid-1960s membership had been extended to Austria (1956), Cyprus (1961), Switzerland (1963) and Malta (1965). The first major step taken by the Council of Europe was to establish in 1950 (ratified in 1953) the Convention for the Protection of Human Rights and Fundamental Freedoms, which set up that same year the European Court of Human Rights to offer recourse to individuals for alleged breaches of the Convention by member states. The Convention sought to establish a basis for preventing any recurrence of the grotesque assault on humanity that had taken place during the Second World War and to offer a different framework for social and political development than that unfolding in Soviet-dominated Eastern Europe.

The crucial development during the 1950s and first half of the 1960s was the firm establishment, directly or indirectly assisted by American military and financial support, of liberal democracy in most of Western Europe. Without this foundation the freedom that soon benefited from the extraordinary and sustained economic growth of the 1950s and 1960s would not have flourished. It was a clear case of the primacy of politics.

On much of the southern rim of Western Europe, however, democracy either did not exist, or struggled to establish itself. The overriding priority of defence against communism nevertheless necessitated American (and other Western) backing here too, although this went in support of repressive regimes or countries where democracy was upheld more in lip service than practice.

The weakness of democracy in Southern Europe had deep roots.

Turkey, Greece, Portugal and, to a lesser extent, the more heavily industrialized Spain had been among the poorest countries in Europe before
the Second World War. Wealth had been (and continued to be) concentrated in the hands of small, powerful elites while much of the population,
still heavily dependent upon agricultural production, lived in dire poverty. Where pluralist politics existed they had been clientelist. The role of
the military had frequently proved the dominant factor in political systems contested by irreconcilably hostile sectors of ideologically divided
societies. Political violence had been commonplace. Authoritarianism of
one kind or another had predominated, or had at least never been far
from the surface. In Portugal and Spain the Catholic Church had also
exerted its great influence in support of repressive right-wing authoritarianism. During the war, Greece had undergone huge destruction and
massive human suffering under German occupation, followed immediately by a ruinous and horrifically violent civil war between 1946 and
1949. Turkey, Portugal and Spain had avoided devastation by their neutrality during the Second World War. All three countries had, however,
long been under forms of authoritarian rule – Turkey in the one-party
regime that had existed since 1925, following the establishment of Turkey
as a nation state by Mustafa Kemal Pasha (Atatürk), Portugal after a
military takeover in 1926, and Spain since the nationalist victory in 1939
following a devastating civil war.

The accoutrements of General Francisco Franco's atavistic dictatorship did not prevent the United States from welcoming Spain as part of
the West's anti-communist defensive umbrella. The worst of Franco's
savage revenge against his socialist and communist opponents during the
Civil War had indeed subsided by the mid-1940s. But Spain remained
desperately poor. Returning to the country where he had lived before the
Civil War, Gerald Brenan was forcibly struck everywhere he went in 1949
by the extreme poverty afflicting the population. He found the country
'corrupt and rotten and conditions are so bad that everyone except for a
few black marketeers wants a change. But no revolution can take place.
The police and the army see and will continue to see to that: they are the
one solid and dependable thing in this ramshackle regime.' A veneer of
national unity was layered over a still deeply divided country, in which
the defeated left-wing elements, especially in the industrial regions of
Catalonia, Asturias and the Basque Country, were sullenly forced to

comply with the demands of a reactionary and repressive dictatorship backed by a narrow ruling caste, economic elites, the Catholic Church and the numerically bloated officer corps of the army. There was sufficient left-wing opposition in other European countries to prevent Spain's admission to NATO. But the United States entered an agreement in 1953 to place naval and air bases in Spain, which received American military aid in return. By the end of the 1950s Spain, by now accepted as a member of the World Bank, the IMF and the GATT trading arrangements, was starting to liberalize its economy and to recognize the potential of the tourist trade that was beginning to entice citizens from Northern Europe to spend some of their increased wealth on holidays in the Spanish sun.

For the time being the regime, increasingly anachronistic, could coexist alongside, and profit from, rapid economic modernization. But it was living on borrowed time. By the later 1960s as economic growth rates soared, the traditional rural heartlands of regime support declined with the drain of labour to the cities and more prosperous sectors of the economy. And as industrial workers recognized their increased bargaining power, even under repressive conditions, their new militancy started to challenge the rigid controls of the authoritarian state.

Portugal, one of the poorest and most backward countries of Western Europe, had been ruled since 1932 by António de Oliveira Salazar, a former professor of economics at Coimbra University. The ideological basis of the Salazar regime comprised little more than belief in the Portuguese nation, strong anti-communism, fervent commitment to traditional Catholic values, and maintenance of its overseas empire (the oldest of any imperial power). The commitment to its empire, which it controlled with an iron fist, was an obstacle to American support. But Cold War strategy outweighed objections. Portugal was a recipient of Marshall Aid and a founding member of NATO in 1949. The key to Portugal's admission to NATO had been the strategic significance of the Azores to the United States in the emerging Cold War. In the early 1960s the importance of the Azores bases meant that the USA, though in principle supportive of anti-colonial movements in Africa, was prepared to overlook Portuguese repression of Angolan rebels.

The American commitment to military and financial aid to Greece and Turkey, announced by President Harry Truman in 1947 in the 'doctrine' he promulgated to defend 'free nations' against communism, was a strong inducement to the Turkish elite to move towards democracy and liberalization of the economy. By 1950 Turkey had joined the Organization for European Economic Cooperation, benefiting from Marshall Aid, and was a member of the Council of Europe. A Turkish contingent of troops had been among the first to join the United Nations Expeditionary Force to Korea in 1950, and had helped pave the way for NATO membership – the cause of great national rejoicing as the guarantee of Western military support against any Soviet aggression, and also as a source of American financial aid – two years later.

The pluralist political system introduced in Turkey in 1946 was only superficially democratic. And as the country was beset by mounting economic difficulties in the later 1950s the government became increasingly illiberal and repressive until it was toppled by a military coup in 1961. Although a return to pluralist politics soon followed, the influence of the military lurked as a constant threat and a second, more right-wing, strongly anti-communist coup followed a decade later. Despite its doubtful democratic credentials, Turkey's strategic position ensured strong American backing.

Like Turkey, Greece – deeply polarized and poverty-stricken – had a pivotal position in NATO's Cold War defence strategy. Greece was heavily dependent upon extensive American aid, while the CIA gave support to the strongly anti-communist military and security services. The complex internal politics of the country were strongly influenced by the deep split between the socialist left (the Communist Party had meanwhile been banned) and the conservative right, the historic enmities with Turkey (though relations improved somewhat during the 1950s) and continued tension in the British colony of Cyprus, where the majority of the population favoured union with Greece while the Turkish minority wanted partition. The intense anti-communism of Greece's political leaders helped to ensure American backing for a parliamentary system that was often murky and corrupt, descending by the mid-1960s into great governmental instability and eventually a coup d'état in 1967 by military leaders fearful that elections planned for that year would bring a predicted lurch to the left and open the door to communist influence.

Beyond the politically and socio-economically backward southern rim of Western Europe, however, liberal democratic forms of government were able to establish themselves during the 1950s more firmly than ever before as the accepted framework of society. Inevitably, the characteristics of democracy varied from country to country. A number of democracies, notably in the British Isles, France, Scandinavia, the Low Countries and Switzerland, could extend long-existing firm roots, whatever the drastic interruptions some had suffered through German occupation. Vital for Europe's future, though, was that democracy became consolidated during the 1950s in the former Axis countries – Italy, Austria and, above all, West Germany – that had earlier destroyed the peace of Europe.

This was a major advance, not only on the troubled interwar period but also on the first years after the war, which had inevitably seen continued great political upheaval. How the reformation of political parties and restoration of pluralistic politics would work out was at that time uncertain. Initially, it looked as if the left might profit from the prestige of its wartime resistance. But conservative parties had generally gained ground as the Iron Curtain descended, and until the mid-1960s conservatism triumphed throughout most of Western Europe.

The main exception to the general pattern of conservative dominance was Scandinavia, where there was a deepening of the distinctive form of social and political development that had started before the war, which proved an interruption rather than a fundamental break. The key before the war had been the readiness, deriving from perceived common interest, to reach a basis of cooperation both between labour and capital and between the political representatives of labour and the agrarian parties. The relatively high degree of consensual politics continued in the postwar decades. Geographical distance from most of the European continent probably played its part in the cultural underpinning of Scandinavian exceptionalism. A relatively low population size (no more than a total of around 20 million citizens in the whole of Scandinavia in 1950) and a small number of major urban and industrial centres were conducive to promoting social cohesion. But above all, the model worked. Although the internal development of Sweden, Norway and Denmark varied, the compromises that underlay consensual politics helped to turn the Scandinavian countries from a relatively poor part of Europe into one of its most prosperous regions. A stepping stone along the way was the establishment in 1952 of the Nordic Council, allowing citizens free movement without passports and providing the framework for a common labour market (joined by Finland in 1955). As elsewhere, Scandinavian prosperity benefited from the extraordinary economic growth throughout Europe in the post-war era. A hallmark of the Scandinavian development (with national variations) was, however, the extensive network of social services and welfare provision, paid for by high taxation, carried through by stable governments dominated not by Conservatives, as was more common in post-war Europe, but by Social Democrats.

Finland was a partial exception, forced by its proximity to the Soviet Union to tread a careful path, cooperating with the other Scandinavian countries while upholding its neutrality (as did Sweden) and avoiding becoming part of the western bloc. (Finland did not join NATO and became a member of the Council of Europe only in 1989.) It remained during the first post-war decades the poorest part of Scandinavia, with an electorate divided in the main between four blocs (Social Democrats, Agrarians, Communists and Liberal-Conservatives), unstable governments (twenty-five between 1945 and 1966), and a high communist presence of around 20 per cent of the electorate. This was in stark contrast to Sweden, where the Communists were, with no more than 5 per cent of the vote, a negligible presence and Social Democrats, at around 45 per cent, remained the dominant political force throughout the post-war years. Soviet pressure helped to ensure that Finland's Social Democrats played little part in government before the mid-1960s. Gradually, even so, Finland moved inexorably into the Western orbit, with a social and economic system growing closer to that of the other Scandinavian countries and the beginnings of the transformation from a poor agrarian nation to a technologically advanced country with a high standard of living.

On Europe's western perimeter Ireland also stood in some ways outside the more typical political development. Class was not, as was usually the case, the determining factor in political allegiance. Particularly in the south, politics reflected the legacy of the civil war of 1922–3. Ideologically, there was little to distinguish Fianna Fáil, the dominant party of government, from the main opposition party, Fine Gael (whose short periods in government were only attainable through coalition with smaller parties). Local patronage and family connections, rather than a distinctive political vision, were often the key to political power. A Labour

Party existed, but, like Sinn Féin – the most uncompromising voice of the struggle to unite Ireland – it had only minority support. Most obvious of all in the Republic was the political and social dominance of the Catholic Church – welcomed by the overwhelming majority of the population (whose church attendance outstripped that of any other Western European country) – which left a big imprint on the social welfare, education and public morality of a still largely agrarian country. Even after the mid-1950s, when new initiatives started to be adopted to stimulate economic growth, the Republic remained a European backwater.

In Northern Ireland, too, the partition was a crucial determinant of political and social life. The six counties of the province of Ulster had a population rigidly divided on near-apartheid lines between the majority Protestants, whose loyalties towards the British Crown veered from firm to fanatical, and the minority Catholics, discriminated against in housing, education, the workplace and most other forms of life, who often looked towards the Irish Republic across the border for their identity and in the hope of a better future. The Ulster Unionist Party (UUP) was electorally unchallengeable, regularly winning more than two-thirds of the vote, thereby ensuring continued Protestant dominance in the province – a dominance that began to be eroded only in the rapidly changing, and increasingly turbulent, conditions from the mid-1960s onwards.

In most of Western Europe, however, the consolidation of democracy rested on the more conventional lines of a division between socialism and conservatism, which had already been established in the immediate post-war years. As communist parties lost ground in the late 1940s under the impact of the Cold War, socialism meant in practice Social Democratic parties rooted mainly in the industrial working class and supportive of pluralistic democracy. Conservatism most commonly expressed itself as Christian Democracy. This attached considerable importance to traditional religious values, though its concrete form varied. In West Germany it consciously set out to transcend the narrowly denominational politics that had been so damaging between the wars. In the Netherlands, on the other hand, the continuation of the pre-war 'pillarized' subcultures (Catholic, Protestant and socialist) meant that Christian Democracy, in the shape of the Catholic People's Party, did not reach out beyond its denominational support. Italian Christian Democracy differed again. In a country with no major denominational divide, it penetrated Catholic organizational networks and built its substantial basis of support in the countryside and among the urban middle class in good measure on its appeal to Catholic social and moral values, and by its outright opposition to communism (as well by its dispensation of political patronage). Unlike some of its ideological antecedents, Christian Democracy, whatever its form, was unequivocally committed to democratic principles and prepared to accommodate (and manipulate) rather than resist social change. Although in electoral terms there was often only a narrow gap between left- and right-wing levels of support, conservative parties of one kind or another tended to dominate between 1950 and the mid-1960s, building on the platform they had established during the early years of post-war recovery.

Reinforcing the resort to conservatism was the widespread desire for 'normality', for peace and quiet, for settled conditions after the immense upheaval, enormous dislocation and huge suffering during the war and its immediate aftermath. Stability was paramount for most people. As the ice formed on the Cold War, every country in Western Europe set a premium on internal stability. Governments saw this as their key objective, and were prepared to support the welfare reforms that they saw as a prerequisite to sustaining it. It was a virtuous circle. Stability gave people a sense of security that underpinned the likelihood of further stability (and continued conservative success). Where political systems had been newly established or wholly reconstructed after the war, following German occupation and the deep internal enmities it had engendered, this required a level of collective amnesia – a readiness to avoid dwelling on the painful past in order to favour the stability and prosperity of the present.

A strong desire for 'normality' would probably not have been enough in itself but for the fact that these were years of unparalleled economic growth (to be explored in Chapter 4) which produced unheard-of levels of prosperity. The rapid material improvement in the standard of living for most people encouraged a readiness to stick with what appeared to be working so well. Political parties proposing radical alternatives faced an uphill task. That would start to change by the mid-1960s, aided by a declining deference towards authority, especially among a new generation born since the war, and by the diminishing influence of the Churches, which had stood firmly behind Christian Democracy.

Underpinning the success of conservatism in the consolidation of liberal democracy in Western Europe was the Cold War. By the early 1950s the Cold War was itself contributing substantially to the stabilization of politics as support for communism dwindled more or less everywhere. Awareness of the ruthlessness of Stalinism in Eastern Europe and fear of communist expansion were easy to exploit by Western anti-communist propaganda, much of it sponsored by the United States. Although nowhere as paranoid as in the USA (where the 'reds under the bed' hysteria that accompanied the witch-hunts pursued by Senator Joe McCarthy in the US Senate was at its height during the 1950s), the vehemence of anti-Soviet feeling helped to solidify Western liberal democracy. The Korean War in the early 1950s intensified anti-communism and further boosted conservative parties (of different kinds) which were its chief beneficiaries, while Social Democratic parties on the more moderate left joined in the outright rejection of Soviet communism.

Britain fitted the common European pattern in the turn to conservatism – the country was run by Conservative governments between 1951 and 1964. It was nevertheless in many ways an exception among the states of Western Europe. Britain had been the only European belligerent power to escape enemy occupation. It had emerged from the war victorious, if exhausted and nearly bankrupted, with its political, economic and social institutions intact. The war had produced unprecedented levels of national solidarity, temporarily at least overriding deep class divisions, and there was national pride in the victory over Nazism. The monarchy enjoyed great popularity. The British parliamentary democracy had almost total backing from the population. The 'first past the post' electoral system, unlike the proportional representation systems of most countries in Western Europe, strongly militated against small parties and tended to produce stable governments with sizeable majorities.

Clear election winners emerged even though, in fact, the electorate was almost evenly split between Conservative and Labour. At five general elections between 1950 and 1964 the Conservative vote ranged between 43.4 and 49.7 per cent of votes cast, Labour's vote between 43.9 and 48.8 per cent. Most of the remainder voted for the Liberals, a once-mighty party but now reduced to only around 9 per cent of the vote (falling in 1951 in fact to as low as 2.6 per cent). Parties of the extremes were in electoral terms an irrelevance. Fascism, never in possession of a single parliamentary seat in Britain even during the 1930s, was a non-entity, completely discredited. The Communist Party was almost devoid of electoral support; the 100 Communist Party candidates in the 1950 election averaged no more than 2 per cent of the vote. All these factors went far towards ensuring a high level of continued stability and policy adjustments rather than seismic shifts.

For many in Britain the Conservative victory at the polls in 1951, returning to office as Prime Minister the war-hero Winston Churchill, by now almost seventy-seven years old, was reassuring. There was, in fact, no sharp break with the policies of the previous Labour government. The Conservatives, placing a high premium upon social peace, were conciliatory towards the powerful trade unions (backed by nearly ten million members). They did not try to reverse the nationalization of industries carried through by their Labour predecessors, apart from denationalizing iron, steel and road haulage in 1953. The welfare state was sustained. Expenditure on the National Health Service was increased. The programme of house-building was extended. There was even a new term 'Butskellism', coined by journalists in 1954, to indicate convergence of economic policy between the former Labour Chancellor, Hugh Gaitskell, and his successor, the Conservative R. A. Butler ('Rab'). Continuity was also marked in foreign and defence policy. The winding-up of the empire, begun under Labour, was extended as the move to a self-governing free Commonwealth advanced in Africa and Asia. There was no change in commitment to the Korean War, NATO, the building of an 'independent nuclear deterrent', or relations with the United States. The Conservatives also followed directly from Labour in keeping their distance from the early tentative steps towards integration in continental Europe. Britain still saw itself as a great power, playing an important role in world affairs. The bridge across the Atlantic was far more important than the bridge across the English Channel.

The Conservative government in Britain was, in fact, though unwilling to admit it, the beneficiary of the austerity that the post-war Labour administration had been forced to endure. By the early 1950s economic conditions were improving markedly. The terms of trade were running in Britain's favour. Fewer exports were needed to pay for imports. By 1955 national income was as much as 40 per cent higher than it had been in 1950. Rationing had finally been ended. Income tax at the standard rate was reduced to 42.5 per cent, where it would remain for a quarter of a century. The vital 'feel-good factor' was sustained, with a buoyant economy and expanding availability of consumer goods, throughout the remainder of the 1950s. It was the basis of further Conservative electoral victories in 1955 and 1959. The Prime Minister, Harold Macmillan, had aptly captured the positive popular mood three months before the 1959 election. He claimed that levels of prosperity surpassed anything in Britain's history. 'Let us be frank about it,' he declared in a speech in July 1959, 'most of our people have never had it so good.'

By the early 1960s, however, economic problems were starting to mount, unpopular wage controls were introduced, the government was beset by a scandal involving the sexual pecadillos of the War Minister, John Profumo, and the image of a tired and failing government was compounded by President de Gaulle's rebuff in January 1963 of Britain's belated attempt to join the EEC. In 1964 Labour, under the wily Harold Wilson, a leader with the popular touch who seemed to point the country towards the future, not the past, won a wafer-thin majority. Thirteen years of Conservative government were over. Britain entered a new and, as it proved, far less stable phase.

British conservatism, with its deep roots, differed from the more overtly religious ideals that underpinned the conservative parties on much of the continent, the more important of them explicitly committed to 'Christian Democracy'. The emerging success of Christian Democratic parties had, in fact, been the most significant development in the internal politics of Western Europe in the immediate post-war years. The more stable conditions of the 1950s were to provide the framework for the consolidation of this initial success.

Although the pattern varied, in Belgium, Luxembourg, the Netherlands, Switzerland, Austria, Italy and West Germany, Christian Democratic parties (in tone, if not always by name) played a significant, often the dominant, role in politics during the 1950s and early 1960s, their prominence generally waning only by the mid-1960s. Government in Switzerland was made more complex by strong cantonal loyalties and by frequent direct participation of the people in plebiscites (which makes for party-political compromise and cooperation, generally favouring conservatism in practice). Coalitions in each of these countries were the norm, driven by electoral systems based on proportional representation. As in the

Netherlands, where the traditional 'pillars' of Catholic, Social Democratic and liberal-conservative subcultures continued to exist side by side until their erosion in the mid-1960s, there was a readiness to work with rival parties to ensure stability and effective government.

The complexities of 'pillarized' subcultures in Belgium were compounded by the linguistic division of the country into the Flemish- and French-speaking regions. This made compromise between the major parties, the Socialists and the Christian Socialists, more difficult, and gave rise to continuing bitter conflict. The monarchy was, at least in the early post-war years, itself not a unifying element. King Leopold III's chequered wartime record – he was accused of being too friendly towards the German occupiers, and even of treason – was held against him by much of the population. In 1951, after his return from Swiss exile had provoked huge strikes in protest and he had gained the support of only a slight majority of the population in a referendum, he abdicated in favour of his son, Baudouin. Here, too, there was a regional split. Only 42 per cent of voters in Wallonia, where the Socialists were dominant, supported the monarch, whereas Flanders, where the Christian Socialist strongholds were located, provided him with 70 per cent support. Baudouin, who ruled Belgium until his death in 1993, did offer the symbol of unity that his father had not been able to supply. Somehow the country avoided falling apart. Ultimately, the two halves of Belgium had more to gain through staying together than through breaking up, especially once prosperity spread, though the country's linguistic antagonisms would continue to afflict politics for decades to come.

A willingness to look for compromise and cooperation was especially important in Austria in ensuring that there was no repeat of the crippling divisions that had paved the way for Hitler. Electoral support was almost evenly split during the 1950s and early 1960s between the Christian Democratic Austrian People's Party (the conservative descendant of the pre-war Christian Social Party) and the Socialist Party. Other parties, including the Communists (who had a tiny level of support), were of only minor significance. The Nazi Party had of course ceased to exist, although many former Nazis were able to conceal their own dubious pasts behind a wall of silence and amnesties for all but the very worst crimes of the Nazi era, not least since Austria was conveniently regarded internationally as Hitler's 'first victim', thereby overlooking the warmth of his welcome at the Anschluss in 1938 and the subsequent total absorption in his regime. Crucial in the Austrian politics of the post-war world was that the bitter hostility of the 1930s, which had led to a brief civil war in 1934 and the establishment of a quasi-fascist authoritarian state (ended with the German invasion of 1938), was now transcended.

Between 1947 and 1966 government in Austria was run by a 'grand coalition' of the two major parties. In this duopoly the Christian Democratic right and the Social Democratic left divided up government ministries and public administration by allocation of posts in accordance with their proportion of support in the country (which was almost equal). This inevitably produced a patronage system in which party allegiance provided the ticket to status and advancement, housing, jobs, trade licences and much more. But it worked. Economic growth and spreading prosperity brought with it a readiness to avoid labour disputes that could rock the boat. And Austria's close geographical proximity to the communist eastern bloc (and memories of the Soviet occupation until 1955 of part of the country) played its part in concentrating minds. From being a focal point of instability and upheaval in Central Europe in the 1930s, Austria was transformed into a pillar of democratic solidity.

Christian Democracy had emerged in the late 1940s as the largest political force in Italian politics, and retained around 40 per cent of electoral support during the 1950s and early 1960s. The combined socialist and communist left could usually garner some 35 per cent, though the better-organized and socially more radical Communists proved able to increase their support, especially in the northern industrial belt, at the expense of the divided Socialists. By the early 1960s the main opponents of Christian Democracy were the Communists, who were backed by about a quarter of the electorate and controlled bastions of support in the big industrial cities of the north. The rest of the votes went to a range of small parties – Liberals, Republicans, Monarchists and Neo-Fascists. The political split between the Christian Democrats (CDs) and the left-wing parties reflected the country's deep social and ideological divisions. What emerged were separate subcultures in which political allegiance – party membership was the largest of any country in Western Europe – was a necessary passport to jobs and personal advancement.

Italian governments came and went, each lasting in the period 1945–70 on average less than a year. And after Alcide de Gasperi, the towering figure of the formative years of Christian Democracy, was ousted in 1953 – he was to die the following year – his successor Guiseppe Pella was the first of twelve premiers to hold office by the end of the 1960s. De Gasperi had himself presided over eight administrations. Pella's government lasted for less than five months, the cabinet of his successor Amintore Fanfani a mere twenty-one days. But beneath the superficial change there was much continuity, both in personnel and policy. Cabinet ministers played musical chairs, much as they had done before the First World War. Fanfani was Prime Minister five times in all, Antonio Segni twice, Giovanni Leone twice. And the CDs remained the mainstay of every administration. In the intensely factionalized party, ideology was secondary to retaining the hold on power and, crucially, patronage – of the often corrupt kind that the Italians called *sottogoverno* (literally, 'sub-government'). In the impoverished south, the *mezzogiorno*, the success of the CDs owed much to the way they were able to take over deeply embedded clientelism through dispensation of the state's resources. And in the north, where the CDs had some of their greatest strongholds, they could exploit the extensive network of big Catholic associations to cement their support – and the important backing of the Catholic Church.

The ineffectiveness of the series of weak and short-lived centrist coalitions in the 1950s led to a brief attempt in 1960 to incorporate the neo-fascist right in government. But this provoked widespread protests in which the police killed a number of demonstrators. The CDs consequently did a volte-face and began overtures to the anti-communist centre-left. This eventually produced in 1963, under Aldo Moro, a coalition that even included the Socialists, though the Socialist Party split as a result when a significant faction on its left, including many trade unionists, found collaboration with Christian Democracy an intolerable prospect.

Moro's three administrations lasted for five years, but most of the promised social reforms came to nothing. The bloated civil service, which doubled in size between 1948 and 1969, remained unreformed and chronically inefficient. The judiciary, presiding over a legal system that operated with painful slowness and drawing disproportionately on the law schools of southern Italy for its membership, was a highly conservative caste with an anti-left bias, concerned above all to defend career prospects and independence from government interference. The large and well-financed armed forces had little to do, but maintained two admirals for every ship and a general for every 200 metres of the border with Yugoslavia. This was social and institutional stasis. But, for the Christian Democrats, holding on to power was an end in itself.

The obstacles to radical change in Italian politics and society were great and numerous. But Christian Democracy's efforts to bring about such change were modest indeed. At the same time it proved capable of blocking reformist forces on the left. Italy remained a deeply divided country, its divisions and internal problems simply managed rather than overcome throughout the long years of CD dominance. For the leaders of Christian Democracy that was enough. And though a hallmark of Italian politics, governmental instability was in fact quite compatible with stability of the system itself.

The pivotal country in the stabilization and democratization of Western European politics was unquestionably West Germany (meaning the Federal Republic of Germany and West Berlin – the latter still under the four-power occupation of the former capital city and not formally part of the FRG). At the foundation of the Federal Republic in 1949 stability had been far from guaranteed. The new state had been a product of defeat and division. Until 1952, when it was granted sovereignty in foreign affairs, it remained technically an occupied country and only gained full recognition as a sovereign state in 1955. It had no armed forces. It had no established political system. Its ideological divisions ran deep. Its very recent Nazi past left it intensely morally damaged, strongly distrusted by its European neighbours (as well as the United States and the Soviet Union), and facing the problem of integrating in a new democracy millions of refugees and expellees (whose pressure groups were able to exert significant influence on the government) – as well as the many citizens who had at one time avidly supported Hitler's dictatorship, including those directly implicated in its crimes against humanity.

More than anything else, West Germany was pivotal because its borders were not settled. And at the start of the 1950s the question of its borders divided the German public, much of which – according with the stance of the main opposition party, the Social Democrats – favoured early reunification and political neutrality rather than the country's indefinite division and its integration into the orbit of Cold War politics as practised in the West.

At the first federal elections in August 1949 the multiplicity of parties, though mostly now bearing new names, in many ways resembled that of the Weimar era. Konrad Adenauer's Christian Democratic Union (CDU) with the support of no more than 31 per cent of the electorate emerged only narrowly ahead of its main rival, the Social Democratic Party of Germany (SPD), which gained 29.2 per cent. Adenauer, who had been Mayor of Cologne during the Weimar Republic and was already aged seventy-three, managed through arm-twisting and hard bargaining to piece together a coalition dependent especially on the pro-business Free Democratic Party (FDP), though he also co-opted smaller parties. Bonn, a small town on the Rhine, rather than the more obvious Frankfurt am Main, was chosen as the capital of the Federal Republic. It was sarcastically dubbed the 'capital village'; for Adenauer it had the notable advantage that it was so close to his Rhineland home. Adenauer was elected Federal Chancellor by a majority of a single vote (his own). Yet by 1963, when he finally resigned office, most West Germans thought he had been a greater statesman than Bismarck.

Fourteen years of the Weimar Republic had ended with Hitler in power. Fourteen years of the Bonn Republic saw liberal democracy consolidated. Why did the second German democracy succeed so completely when the first failed so catastrophically?

Constitutional changes helped. They were not, however, the main reason. The framers of the Basic Law were certainly conscious of the flaws in the Weimar Constitution and successfully sought to overcome them. The Federal President was now given largely representative functions. It was made far more difficult to overthrow an existing government through a vote of no confidence. And, perhaps most significant in preventing small parties from exercising undue influence, only parties gaining more than 5 per cent of the vote (initially at regional, but from 1953 at federal, level) were allowed representation in the Bundestag.

Crucial above all in the successful consolidation of democracy in West Germany were two factors. The first was the extraordinarily rapid and strong economic growth, 'the economic miracle' as it was labelled, that enabled Germans to improve their standard of living beyond anything they might have imagined possible at the foundation of the Federal Republic. This gave ordinary citizens a big stake in the new political system. It showed them that democracy worked to their material advantage – something that the Weimar Republic had never achieved.

West Germany was fortunate, as were all Western European states, in profiting from the worldwide boom that followed the Second World War. It also had a number of uniquely favourable conditions for growth. It benefited from the flow of often well-qualified refugees, over ten million of them, who poured into the country, highly motivated, anxious to improve their lives, and willing to work for low wages. They were much needed, since the immense task of rebuilding the country itself, of course, offered vast opportunities for employment. Germany's formidable industrial capacity, though badly damaged, had not been completely destroyed by the war, had in fact partly been modernized, and was able to rebound swiftly. The Korean War brought an unexpected bonus to the economy. Since production of armaments was prohibited, West German industry turned to consumer goods that found ready markets abroad and fed a remarkable export boom as well as satisfying rapidly growing domestic demand. Economic growth was also spurred by the need to build new homes to cope with the acute housing shortage left by the war and the influx of refugees. Over five million homes were constructed during the 1950s, stimulating the myriad subsidiary industries that supplied the building trade.

The resurgence of world trade, liberalized and regulated under the arrangements agreed at Bretton Woods, New Hampshire, in 1944, and the General Agreement on Trade and Tariffs (GATT) three years later, provided the international framework within which West Germany's buoyant economy could flourish. The regulation of West Germany's commercial debt, agreed in London in 1953, to pay off at low and completely manageable rates of interest a total amount of around $15 billion over more than thirty years, down to 1988 (what was owed from before and during the war to external creditors, mainly American firms), was a further important step in the recovery in firmly establishing the country's debt-worthiness. In fact, the debt was, thanks to the scale of economic growth, already largely paid off by the end of the 1950s. The question of payment of reparations to Nazi victims, overwhelmingly located in the communist countries of Eastern Europe, was, however, postponed until a negotiated peace treaty. (A separate agreement was reached to pay a total of 3.45 billion marks in compensation (*Wiedergutmachung*) to Jews in Israel and elswhere.)

The second reason why democracy could firmly establish itself in West

Germany by the mid-1960s was the Cold War. The Korean War, which gave rise to renewed fears of a new world war, appeared to many West Germans, like others in Western Europe, to confirm the acute dangers of communism. And the existence of 'the other Germany' provided ideological cement. Even for opponents of Adenauer and the CDU, the existence of what almost all of them took to be a highly unattractive alternative model in Communist East Germany, so close to home – an image constantly reinforced by the mass media – built on and extended the anti-communism that been relentlessly hammered home by the Nazis.

The Cold War enhanced close dependence on the United States, and drove Adenauer's determination to seek forms of integration with other European countries, most especially – laying aside longstanding bitter enmities – with France. For Adenauer, a Rhinelander, this was a palatable as well as necessary move. The turn to the West was, however, highly controversial since it had a direct corollary: accepting that for the indefinite future there could be no expectation of East and West Germany uniting. This was a bitter pill to swallow. The leader of the SPD, Kurt Schumacher (whose personal standing drew on the ten years he had spent in a Nazi concentration camp), was unwilling to abandon the priority of reunification, though he shared the view that this could only come about under the absolute guarantee of freedom. For Schumacher and the third or so of the population that supported his party, a reunified and neutral Germany was a far more attractive proposition than binding the Federal Republic to the American-dominated capitalist (and militarized) West.

On 10 March 1952, alarmed by the prospect of West German integration in a Western military alliance directed against the Soviet Union, and just before the signing of a fundamental treaty between the Western powers and the Federal Republic aimed at restoring much of West German sovereignty (becoming fully effective in 1955), Stalin made an offer to the Western powers aimed at creating a united, neutral Germany. He envisaged a peace treaty and 'free activity of democratic parties and organisations'. The Americans, after consultation with the British and French, gave a cool though not altogether dismissive answer. A second 'Note' from Stalin on 9 April then specifically offered free elections in a united Germany, which would 'have its own national armed forces' for the country's defence.

Adenauer had immediately recognized the danger to his hopes of Western integration – for him the absolute priority – and, backed (after some initial hesitation) by his cabinet, rejected the initiative out of hand. For much of the West German population, however, there were distinct attractions to Stalin's offer. Putting Western integration before reunification was inevitably highly controversial. Adenauer had to tread carefully. He was, though, unbending in his stance. He argued that reunification could only come about through Western strength. The Western powers accepted his arguments and did not reply to the second 'Stalin Note'. On 26 May the 'Germany Treaty' between the Federal Republic and the Western powers cemented their relations for the foreseeable future. By then, the 'Stalin Note' was history.

At the time, and since, it has been asked whether this was a missed opportunity. It was not. The probability is that the establishment and consolidation of a stable liberal democracy would have proved far more difficult, if indeed at all possible, had the terms of the 'Stalin Note' been accepted. The risk that the whole country, even presuming that the terms offered had been genuinely upheld – a doubtful assumption – might gradually be sucked into the Soviet sphere of influence, was not worth taking. As it was, West Germany remained totally committed to integration into the West, above all to the defensive shield of the United States. It paid dividends. Although the proposal for a European Defence Community was eventually, in 1954, torpedoed by France, the very country that had advanced it in the first place, the upshot (as noted in Chapter 1) was the initially highly controversial creation of a West German army, the Bundeswehr, to form an integral part of NATO, and the fulfilment of Adenauer's aim of full sovereignty for the Federal Republic.

Reunification unsurprisingly held an emotional appeal for much of the population. Two-thirds of West Germans continued even in the mid-1960s, when asked in opinion polls, to state that unification of Germany was their key political objective. Most of them nonetheless accepted that this would remain for many years an unrealistic expectation. The Adenauer government itself held to national unity as the ultimate objective and refused to recognize the German Democratic Republic as a sovereign state. In practice, however, reunification was a dead letter long before the division of Germany became quite literally concrete with the erection of the Berlin Wall starting in August 1961.

By then Adenauer had twice, in 1953 and 1957, won convincing electoral victories. The narrow margins of 1949 had been replaced by a huge increase in support for his party. In the 1957 election to the Bundestag, the Federal Parliament, the CDU and its Bavarian sister-party the CSU (Christian Social Union) won an absolute majority (50.2 per cent of the vote), the only time that any party won such an outright victory in the history of the Federal Republic. Adenauer's slogan 'no experiments' had chimed perfectly with the popular mood, reflecting the satisfaction of the growing affluence resulting from the 'economic miracle'. The extraordinary record of growth allowed the Chancellor to offer an important extension of social benefits that proved a significant factor in his triumph: the guarantee of pensions index-linked to the cost of living. Affluence was now set to extend into old age.

In an age of growing affluence the old vocabulary of class warfare had lost much of its resonance. The SPD leadership drew its conclusions and in 1959, at a party conference in Bad Godesberg, on the Rhine adjacent to Bonn, dropped the Marxist rhetoric – it had in practice been no more than that – which by now appealed at best to a minority of its core vote in industrial regions. Aiming to court the middle classes and win the centre ground of politics, the SPD turned away from its hostility to capitalism and rejected the ultimate objective of state ownership of the means of production. The party had already abandoned its insistence on a foreign policy directed towards reunification. The following year, 1960, it confirmed its acceptance of Western integration, (West) German rearmament and membership of NATO. The fundamental changes in the SPD's programme were an indication that West Germany had turned into a modern democracy which, for all its own peculiarities arising from its history and the division of the Cold War, had a party-political system in essence similar to that elsewhere in Europe. Policy was now largely a matter of adjustments rather than any advocacy of an alternative system.

By the early 1960s the authority of the aged Chancellor, by now in his mid-eighties, was starting to weaken. In the 1961 elections the CDU/CSU's proportion of electoral support declined slightly for the first time. In October the following year Adenauer's standing was badly tarnished by the repercussions of a government raid, using methods reminiscent of those of the Nazis, on the offices of the news magazine *Der Spiegel*, after the publication of an article attacking the Minister of Defence, Franz-Josef

Strauss, and highlighting West Germany's inadequate conventional defence capability. Adenauer was seen by many, mobilized in mass protests, as ready to override legality in supporting a high-handed action that raised doubts about the firmness of democracy and fears of a return to arbitrary state power. The 'Spiegel-Affair' marked the beginning of the end for Adenauer's long Chancellorship. Even at eighty-seven years of age Adenauer did not leave office willingly. But he had stayed in government too long. He was effectively forced out by his own party in October 1963. This ushered in a more unsettled era in politics and society. The years of conservative dominance were over.

Many West Germans, especially left-liberal intellectuals, found much to criticize in what they saw, with some justification, as the stuffy, dull provincialism of the Adenauer era. They frequently bemoaned what they saw as a lack of artistic creativity, innovation and dynamism. The Weimar Republic had provided these in abundance. But its chronic political instability had ended in Hitler. The Bonn Republic was certainly a pale shadow in terms of cultural excitement. It did, however, create lasting stability and prosperity.

Some *literati* thought the critique among intellectuals had gone too far. The writer Johannes Gaitanides acknowledged in 1959 'the weaknesses, mistakes and failings of the Federal Republic', but claimed it was a mistake to dismiss its notable achievements. 'How would this critique of the Federal Republic look,' he asked, 'if it had not produced an economic miracle, full employment, improvement in the social status of workers, integration of expellees from the east and refugees from central Germany [by which he meant from the regions that had become the German Democratic Republic], further development of social security, shortened working hours, co-determination of workers in heavy industry and restitution to victims of Nazism?' He thought little of criticism that ignored the advances made, including reconciliation with France (for so long the 'arch-enemy'), the growing integration of West Germany into Europe, greater intellectual and artistic interchange with the West, and the breaking-down of barriers between Catholics and Protestants. Another writer, Kasimir Edschmid, raised similar points in January 1960: 'If in 1948 you had told one of the million poor mites who now drive round in their own cars that he would be seen as well-off, nicely set up, going on foreign trips with hard-currency deutschmarks in his pocket, overall a respectable person (so soon after collecting the cigarette ends of occupying soldiers on the streets), he would have rubbed his eyes and thought you were a madman.'

Adenauer's successes at home and abroad, most of all the securing of stable democracy in West Germany, had been remarkable. They had come, however, at a high price. This was not just the painful division of Germany (and the lasting, seemingly permanent, loss of its former eastern provinces beyond the Oder–Neisse line – West and East Prussia, most of Silesia, much of Pomerania and part of Brandenburg). There was also a moral price: the readiness to draw a veil over the crimes of the recent Nazi past and even accept former active Nazis into the federal government. The political activities of those still harbouring hopes of returning to a nationalist authoritarian government were strictly curtailed. The Socialist Reich Party (*Sozialistische Reichspartei*), numbering around 40,000 members, was banned in 1952. But most of the Allied denazification, limited as it had been, was reversed. Under amnesties between 1949 and 1954 all but the tiny minority of civil servants who had been convicted of the most serious offences in the Nazi era were rehabilitated, and allowed their pensions. Judges and lawyers, many with a dubious past, were able to continue in post. One of Adenauer's closest aides, Hans Globke, had served in the Reich Ministry of the Interior in Hitler's regime and had been the main author of the commentary on the racial laws introduced at Nuremberg in 1935. Another former Nazi, Theodor Oberländer, Minister for Displaced Persons, Refugees and Victims of War in Adenauer's governments between 1953 and 1960, had before the war been involved in racial planning for a future Eastern Europe under Nazi rule. Pensions paid to war widows included one for Lina Heydrich, whose husband, Reinhard, assassinated in June 1942 by a Czech resistance group trained by a British Special Operations Executive unit, had been chief of the Reich Security Head Office. Continuities with the Nazi past were also marked in the personnel of the Foreign Ministry. Many former Nazis, including some guilty of heinous actions before and especially during the war, managed to rebuild post-war careers and eventually die peacefully in their beds.

Morally, the rapid rehabilitation of former Nazis – even including some who had been involved as members of the security police in some of the worst crimes against humanity in Eastern Europe – was shameful.

Was it politically worthwhile, or even necessary? The Allied denazification had been widely unpopular. People were all too ready to push the blame for the catastrophe of which they saw themselves as victims on to Hitler and other leading Nazis. Unsurprisingly, most people, according to opinion polls, did not welcome the involvement of Nazi functionaries in the running of West Germany. But delving too closely into the actions of ordinary people during the dictatorship had implications for so many Germans that there was a widespread willingness to draw a line under what had happened and focus on the present and future. For the vast majority of the population, maximizing the benefits of the 'economic miracle' without rocking the boat by undue preoccupation with the recent past was what counted. Adenauer's amnesties and rehabilitation accorded, therefore, in good measure with popular mentalities in an age of amnesia. They involved him in some sharp controversies, over Globke for instance. But as election results showed, they did not dent his popularity. The reintegration of former Nazis perhaps also contributed to neutralizing undemocratic forces. More aggressively pursued denazification and prosecution of Nazi criminals might instead have continued to underscore the divisions and pain of the recent past, possibly making the swift stabilization of a functioning democracy more difficult. If the ends are seen to justify the means, then it could be argued that the high moral price for the political prize of a consolidated West German democracy was worth paying. The Federal Republic bore a stain, however, that would accompany it for decades to come.

Surprisingly, perhaps, the only country of Western Europe where the governmental system failed during the 1950s was France. Despite the bitter legacy of German occupation and the wartime Vichy regime, this would have been hard to foresee at the foundation of the Fourth Republic in October 1946. However, within twelve years, amid endemic governmental instability and a mounting crisis of the state, the Fourth Republic collapsed.

What is the explanation when, despite at least equally chronic governmental instability, the Italian Republic continued to stagger on? As a defeated country emerging from civil war in the final phase of the Second World War, it might have seemed improbable that Italy's political structures would survive those of liberated France, ranked among the victorious Western Allies. Yet they did.

Certainly, the constitution of the French Fourth Republic was a major handicap. Political instability was guaranteed by the ease with which governments could be brought down (though a well-functioning civil service ensured a significant level of economic stability). The powers given to the legislature over the executive more or less mirrored those of the weak Third Republic, encouraging factionalism and lack of party discipline among members of the National Assembly. If anything, in fact, such tendencies were even more pronounced in the Fourth Republic. Léon Blum, who had been Prime Minister in the Popular Front government of 1936, reflected in 1949 that the Fourth Republic was a repeat of the Third, 'as if French history had begun, in a senile way, to stutter its old thoughts, having refused to learn anything new'. However, Italy's constitution also promoted severe parliamentary factionalism and a similar readiness to topple governments (within a relatively stable state system). The main reasons for the divergent fates of the Italian and French political systems were not primarily constitutional.

They lay, first, in the relative cohesion – or lack of it – of the conservative right in the two countries. In France, a divided right was unable to exert anything remotely resembling the dominance of the conservative right attained by Christian Democracy in Italy. In the 1951 elections the nearest French equivalent to a Christian Democratic party, the *Mouvement Républicain Populaire* (MRP, Popular Republican Movement), seen to represent Catholic interests, was able to win only 13.4 per cent of the vote, slightly less than the total gained by various smaller conservative parties and significantly less than its main challenger, the Gaullists, who gained 21.7 per cent. The centre and left were also divided between the Radicals (the party of small business and the countryside) with 10 per cent, the Socialists with 15 per cent and the Moscow-aligned Communists – who stood outside all alliances – with 26 per cent. (As in Italy, the strength of early post-war communism owed much to the depth of pre-war social and ideological divisions that had been then sharply intensified in the fight for liberation in the last years of the war.) No party won even a fifth of the seats in the National Assembly, and all coalition arrangements were flimsy. The political landscape was as a consequence irredeemably fragmented.

Closely associated with the splintering of the right in France was the second reason: the unique figure of Charles de Gaulle. The war had turned de Gaulle into a national hero, the emblem of French resistance to

Nazi rule. It had also elevated de Gaulle's sense of his own indispensability to France's return to national greatness. Seeing himself as standing above the squabbling and bickering of parliamentary politics that filled him with disgust, his self-image was that of the national saviour in waiting. He had resigned in 1946 as head of the Provisional Government, created a new political movement, the *Rassemblement du Peuple Français* (Rally of the French People) in 1947, but six years later, as its fortunes waned and it suffered a bad electoral defeat, he abandoned it and in July 1955 once more withdrew from politics, ostensibly to write his memoirs. From then on, he was an aloof, brooding presence in retreat at his home in Colombey-les-Deux-Églises, disdainful of the Fourth Republic, certain that the time would come when France would need him again.

The crisis that indeed brought de Gaulle back to power was an expression of the most important of all the factors that undermined the Fourth Republic: the colonial question, and specifically the issue of Algeria (to which we will shortly return). Had Italy faced any external problem of such gravity, its political system might well have cracked under the strain. In France the issue of Algeria was a running sore in domestic politics. The intensifying gravity of the issue was sufficient to split the country, and ultimately to destroy the Fourth Republic.

France under the Fourth Republic was barely governable. The idealism that had followed the Liberation seemed light-years away. *Immobilisme* was the term used to describe the stagnation. As in Italy, governments came and went – twenty of them in all before de Gaulle – but to no noticeable effect. Constructing a government capable of surviving even for a short time was a difficult process. On occasion France was left for weeks in a state of near paralysis without a government. In early 1951, with the country beset by big strikes in the face of steeply rising prices, there was no government for nine days. In July and August there was a gap of thirty-two days between governments. In spring 1953 France went through what Janet Flanner, a well-informed American observer who had long lived in Paris, described as a 'record-breaking five-week political crisis' without a government. In autumn 1957 the country again went for over five weeks without a government and renewed waves of strikes by public employees, protesting at the inability of their pay to keep up with rapidly rising prices even though industry was prospering and the better off were sustaining a consumer boom.

The most impressive Prime Minister of the Fourth Republic, Pierre Mendès-France, a left-leaning member of the Radical Party, was able through bold decisions and great tactical skill to hold together his ministry for eight months in 1954–5 before his enemies on the right brought him down. By then France was embroiled in the deepening crisis over the civil war in Algeria that would beset the country for years to come. Yet French governments were ill-equipped to deal with the crisis. Elections to the National Assembly in January 1956 produced another hamstrung parliament. And now a new disruptive force on the right, the Poujadists (the creation, initially as a tax protest, of Pierre Poujade, a shopkeeper from southern France, which rapidly won support from small business) – a quasi-fascist movement that won 11.6 per cent of the vote and fifty-one seats in parliament – contributed to a bloc of relentless opposition, alongside their ideological enemies, the Communists and the Gaullists, to ensure parliamentary stalemate and continued political turmoil.

By May 1958 the four-year civil war in Algeria had exploded into an uprising of colonial white settlers led by army generals who threatened outright revolt by the French army unless General de Gaulle returned to power as head of a new national government. De Gaulle had long awaited the call. It now came. That month he made a triumphant return to politics. In circumstances of grave crisis the saviour-in-waiting agreed to fulfil what he saw as his sacred destiny. By the end of the year he had received wide plebiscitary backing for a new constitution, establishing the Fifth Republic as effectively a presidential regime. Foreign and defence affairs, in particular, were the prerogative of the President. Constitutional reforms introduced in 1962 gave de Gaulle even wider powers, now extended over many areas of domestic policy. The powers of parliament were in contrast greatly reduced. The National Assembly was in any case dominated by the Gaullists, tame adherents of the President, guaranteeing his complete control, while that of the left withered. It amounted to a conservative revolution from above.

The huge problem of Algeria remained. The surprising solution that de Gaulle came to was among his greatest achievements. The Algerian question that poisoned French politics in the 1950s was, however, part of the wider issue of decoupling from empire – an issue that also caused problems in varying ways for a number of European countries, especially Britain.

IMPERIAL RETREAT

The Second World War marked the beginning of the end for European imperialism. Germany's brutal imperialist ambitions in Eastern Europe had, at enormous cost, been halted once and for all. Italy had formally renounced its claims to colonies in the Treaty of Peace with the Allies of September 1947. But five Western European countries – Belgium, France, Great Britain, the Netherlands and Portugal – still held huge overseas possessions as hostilities ceased. And they had no intention of letting them go. Yet within twenty years of the end of the war these were nearly all gone, apart from Portugal's increasingly anachronistic colonies (which would be liquidated only in the mid-1970s) and a few remnants of the once mighty British and French empires.

Nationalist independence movements were emboldened by ideas of universal human rights embodied in the United Nations Charter. Doctrines of racial supremacy, the ideological basis on which imperialist rule rested, lost all legitimacy. And the weakening position of colonial powers was compounded by the increasingly unsustainable costs of empire. As it became both costly and ideologically indefensible to uphold colonialism as globalization gathered pace, and as anti-colonial forces gained strength (and encouragement from the success of parallel independence movements), imperialist powers gradually yielded to the pressures for independence.

The Dutch empire was the first to go. The Japanese conquest had revealed the sheer weakness of the Western colonial powers in East Asia and fostered the growth of nationalist movements that, once occupation ceased, took up the armed struggle for independence in the Dutch East Indies, what was to become Indonesia. The nationalist guerrilla movement sustained the anti-colonial struggle for four years. The Dutch tried to re-establish their colony – a rich supplier of rubber and other resources – but their forces were too weak to prevent the nationalist insurgents succeeding by 1949 in attaining independence, though the Dutch managed to hold on to two eastern provinces, which they called Netherlands New Guinea, until 1962.

Belgium's colony in the Congo had not been directly involved in conflict during the Second World War, which probably slowed the movement towards independence, compared with equivalent movements in East and South Asia or North Africa. With mounting difficulties, the Belgians – who in earlier decades had treated their possession with marked brutality and only belatedly introduced a more benign, paternalistic policy – were able to sustain their colony until armed conflict broke out in 1959. By then, the tide of anti-colonialism, backed by the United Nations, was surging strongly. Recognizing their own weakness and realizing the futility of trying to sustain colonial rule, the Belgians conceded independence to the Congo within a year, though they left behind a fragile state wracked by internal divisions that would soon descend into civil war.

The size and geographical spread of the British empire meant that decolonization was bound to be a more complex process than it was for the Netherlands or Belgium. As they had done when building their empire, British representatives usually tried to co-opt nationalist leaders and local power-brokers into the process of dissolving imperial rule. It was far from an invariable success, though it often helped to smooth the process of transition and avoid the descent into colonial war. Decisively, however, the growing independence movements encountered from the mid-1950s onwards a sharply diminished appetite for empire.

Surprising in some ways is how relatively painless – for the British people, though seldom those fighting for independence and inhabitants of the newly formed successor states – the unravelling was of such an immense overseas empire. This was probably at least in part because so few British citizens had any detailed knowledge, let alone any personal or direct experience, of the former colonies. Although many families had relatives in the white Dominions of Australia, Canada, South Africa and New Zealand, the empire had, in any tangible sense, mainly touched the lives of an elite educated in Britain's public schools with a view to later appointment to the colonial civil service, to an officer's commission in the army, or to a career in banking and commerce involving trade with overseas possessions. In any case, by the 1960s the Dominions were loosening their ties with Britain, and popular support for the empire was waning fast. There was no doubt much wider residual pride when people recalled schoolroom maps showing how much of the world Britain had once dominated, particularly among the population old enough to remember the empire at its height. But for many, perhaps most, among the younger generation growing up after the war, the empire was not much more than a historical relic, often little more than an array of exotic faraway places with strange-sounding names known only by the colourful contents of a stamp album.

That the dissolution of the empire caused so little trauma at home was a consequence, too, of its far from monolithic character and of the gradual process of change to the freer association of nations in a 'commonwealth'. The term 'British Commonwealth of Nations' dated from as early as 1917 – even then adapting still earlier expressions of a 'commonwealth of nations' reaching back to the 1880s. The formal equality of the Dominions was established in 1931. Indian independence in 1947 led to another change in nomenclature. In 1949 'British' was dropped from the title of what now became 'The Commonwealth of Nations'. That year the British monarch was accepted as the head of the Commonwealth, whose members were regarded as standing in free association, and could include independent nation states, which might themselves (as in the case of India) be republics. Although not all British overseas possessions chose to become members, most that went on to attain their independence did so. That a patchwork quilt of possessions lost dependent status piecemeal and adopted association with Britain through the Commonwealth meant that for most British people there was a relatively seamless transition – one certainly, in contrast especially with France, accepted fairly passively and with little political disturbance at home.

For the British government the liquidation of empire usually meant cutting losses. This had been the policy already in 1947 when Britain bowed to the inevitable and granted independence to India, Pakistan and Burma (and Ceylon the following year). India was no longer the 'jewel in the crown' of age-old cliché. British exports to India had already before the war been declining fast as Indian domestic industries, especially in textiles, expanded. Moreover, Britain, though once a major creditor, emerged from the war owing huge debts to India. Financially exhausted and unable to cover the costs of sustaining British rule, especially in the face of massive unrest and mounting internal violence between Hindus and Muslims, Britain yielded to the demands for independence that had already been so loudly voiced before the war as well as during the great conflict. Attempts to hand over a unified and peaceful country were hopeless. Uncontrollable religious violence and appalling atrocities prompted Britain's announcement in early 1947 that it would withdraw by the following summer come what may. Inability to calm the violence led to the decision to partition the South Asian subcontinent in order to create an independent Pakistan with an almost entirely Muslim population. India and Pakistan became independent nations on 15 August 1947 (eastern Pakistan would itself become a separate nation, Bangladesh, in March 1971).

Britain left India in a horrific mess. Far from leaving 'with honour and dignity', the historian Piers Brendon commented, 'the British left amid the clamour of homicide and the stench of death'. The religious violence, massive even before the British departure, far from subsiding escalated wildly thereafter. It spread through much of the country, but was especially bad in the densely populated provinces of Bengal in the east and Punjab in the north. Muslims, Hindus and Punjabi Sikhs had lived side by side there for generations but now discovered that new borders were to be driven straight through their provinces. Fear and violence went hand in hand as people fled, or were forced, across the frontier of the new countries. Those slaughtered are estimated to have numbered around a million, while about thirteen million refugees fled in an immense process of 'religious cleansing' in both directions across the new borders to safer havens. Tens of thousands of women were raped. Villages were set on fire. Relations between India and Pakistan would remain tense for decades. But the tragedy of the Indian and Pakistani people, and the loss of what for two centuries had been regarded as the cornerstone of Britain's overseas possessions, caused no great stir among a British public beset by post-war austerity and concerned chiefly with its own hardships and problems.

Cutting losses and withdrawal in the face of uncontrollable violence had also marked Britain's retreat from its involvement in the mandated territory of Palestine in 1947. 'Mandates', established by the League of Nations at the end of the First World War as the former Ottoman empire was carved up, were technically holding operations by colonial powers during a transition to self-government. Britain was given mandates in Palestine, Transjordan (later Jordan) and Iraq, and France mandates in Syria and Lebanon. Through the Balfour Declaration of 1917, Britain had supported the Zionist cause for the establishment of a 'national home for the Jewish people' in Palestine. The chief motive behind the Declaration was less humanitarian than to win the backing of Jews in the United States for American support for the Allies in the war and to encourage Russian Jews not to entertain notions of a separate peace with Germany. But the naive as well as somewhat cynical move laid down a minefield that, generations later, has still showed no signs of being cleared.

The Declaration did not specifically refer to a Jewish state, and Arthur Balfour, then the British Foreign Secretary, specifically pointed out that there was to be no prejudice to the rights of non-Jewish communities in Palestine. But that was wishful thinking. Arab hostility was magnified by the rapidly increasing numbers of Jewish settlers in the wake of persecution of Jews in Europe in the 1930s. The British rulers brutally suppressed what turned into a full-scale Arab revolt between 1936 and 1939. But their proposals first for partition, then for a unitary state with restricted Jewish immigration, satisfied neither Arabs nor Jews. When they persisted with their low immigration quotas even after the Second World War – while the Americans, backed by world opinion, pressed for large numbers of Holocaust survivors to be admitted to a safe haven in Palestine – the British had to contend with a wave of Zionist terrorist attacks. But they knew they were on the horns of a dilemma: to accept the American demand for higher levels of Jewish immigration would almost certainly trigger a new Arab revolt. Moreover, the costs of maintaining the mandate in Palestine – £40 million a year to keep 100,000 troops there – were far too high for post-war austerity Britain. 'The time has almost come,' the Chancellor of the Exchequer, Hugh Dalton, advised the Labour government in early 1947, 'when we must bring our troops out of Palestine altogether.'

With no way out of the impasse, and with the growing unpopularity of the mandate within Britain, the British government gave up, leaving the United Nations to do its best in 1947 to find a solution. But when the UN agreed to partition Palestine into Jewish and Arab states, Britain refused to implement the plan because of the considerable Arab hostility to it, and gave notice that it would end its mandate on 14 May 1948. At that point the Jewish leadership under David Ben-Gurion declared the establishment of a state of Israel. Many nations, including the United States and the Soviet Union, immediately recognized the new state. The suffering of European Jews in the genocide carried out by Nazi Germany had in the eyes of much of the world provided an urgent moral imperative to the creation of a Jewish homeland in Israel. But the Arab states utterly rejected what they saw as the outright annexation of Palestinian land. The scene was set for the first war between Israel and its Arab neighbours, the Arab-Israeli War of 1948–9.

Divisions among the Arab armies enabled Israel, by the time a series of armistice agreements were signed in February 1949, to extend its territorial hold beyond that envisaged in the initial United Nations proposal for partition. Israel had consolidated its existence by force of arms. But it had engendered deep, unquenchable hatreds among its neighbours as well as among the 750,000 Palestinians who became refugees in Jordan (formerly Transjordan), Syria, Lebanon and the Gaza Strip. The armistice of 1949 resolved nothing. It guaranteed, in fact, the eventual resumption of hostilities. The later ramifications of the Palestinian problem for Britain, and for the whole of Europe (as for most of the world), would be profound indeed. But at the time there was relief in the one-time colonial power that it had extricated itself from such an intractable issue. People in Britain got on with their lives, glad to be rid of a problem in the Middle East for which they had for the most part neither understanding nor concern.

Britain's withdrawal from India and Palestine did not signal a swift end to its other overseas possessions. British forces held back – for the time being – a nationalist movement in Malaya, a region with precious dollar-earning rubber resources, through the imposition of a state of emergency in June 1948 and the deployment of military power against insurgent communists. And they were engaged in Kenya between 1952 and 1956 in the brutal repression – in which thousands were killed – of the vicious Mau-Mau, whose anti-colonial struggle involved terrible atrocities. The dam walls of colonialism were yet to burst. However, they were soon to do so. And, curiously, what brought the surge that finally swept away Britain's former colonies took place in a country that was already independent and had never formally been part of the empire: Egypt.

In July 1952 a group of Egyptian army officers overthrew King Farouk – a playboy monarch whose squandrously lavish lifestyle compounded his utter uselessness as a ruler. One of the officers, Colonel Gamal Abdel Nasser, swiftly established himself as the dominant figure in the newly proclaimed republic. Within two years he had become its President and was regarded beyond Egypt's shores as the champion of Arab anti-colonialism. His anti-Western stance and overtures of friendship with the Soviet bloc (which provided arms denied him by the USA) stirred growing antagonism in the United States as well as in Britain and France. Nasser was viewed as a grave danger to the influence of the West in such a volatile region and threatened the rich oil resources so vital to Western economies. The British Prime Minister, Anthony Eden, who had succeeded an old and infirm Winston Churchill in April 1955, had in the 1930s witnessed at first hand the failure of appeasement to deal with the aggression of Hitler and Mussolini. This badly affected his judgement of Nasser, whom he portrayed, somewhat hysterically, as a dictator who this time had to be stopped in his tracks. The French Socialist Prime Minister, Guy Mollet, worried about the influence of Nasser's pan-Arabism on the Muslim inhabitants of French possessions in North Africa, wholeheartedly agreed; Nasser's intentions reminded him, he said, of Hitler's aims as laid down in *Mein Kampf*. The French, Janet Flanner reported, were united by 'the Munich complex', regarded Nasser as 'an Arab Hitler', and were prepared 'to risk a small war' to prevent a great war being ignited by 'pan-Arabism'.

Under an agreement dating back to 1936, British troops had been allowed to stay in Egypt to protect the Suez Canal zone, the crucial conduit of cheap oil supplies. But in 1954 Britain agreed to evacuate its forces, seen by Egyptians as no more than colonial occupiers, and British troops left the canal zone in June 1956. On 19 July the Americans, increasingly angered by Nasser's attempts to play them off against the Soviets, withdrew funding, which had always seemed highly likely to be forthcoming, for the building of the Aswan dam on the Nile, a major construction project important for national prestige and vital for Egyptian water supplies. The following week Nasser nationalized the Suez Canal.

When diplomatic efforts to change Nasser's mind failed, Britain and France decided to take the matter to the United Nations where, unsurprisingly, a Soviet veto put paid to hopes of a solution. Already behind the scenes, in any case, British and French leaders were preparing to ignore the UN and were plotting a military solution. Astonishingly, they thought they could act without even informing the American government of what they had in mind – a last show of the colonial powers' hubris in foreign-policy affairs. A top-secret conspiracy was hatched involving Israel. Its troops would occupy the Sinai peninsula before Britain and France, after demanding the withdrawal of both sides in the certainty that the proposal would be rejected, would launch air and sea attacks, 'restore order', and so regain control over the Suez Canal.

The Israeli invasion went ahead on 29 October 1956. Two days later Nasser closed the Suez Canal to shipping; it would not open again until early the following year. On 5 November British and French troops began an airborne landing in Egypt. Their early military successes – it was subsequently estimated that these would have led within a day or two to the retaking of the Canal – were, however, rapidly brought to a halt by intense international pressure. The Soviets raised the prospect of rocket attacks on the invaders and a crisis escalating into nuclear war. Serious or not, this encouraged the United States to bring the crisis to a speedy end. American leaders were furious at being kept in the dark about the invasion plot and their threat to undermine sterling if no ceasefire was forthcoming proved decisive. As the losses of its currency reserves – huge already during the first two days of the Suez operation – mounted to dangerous levels, the British bowed to necessity and agreed to a ceasefire without even consulting the French. A United Nations peacekeeping force was sent to Egypt. The British and French withdrawal duly took place by 22 December. The diplomatic debacle was complete.

The left in Britain was outraged at this return to gunboat colonial adventurism. The right was more appalled at the government's gross ineptitude in the Suez fiasco. Eden resigned as Prime Minister, officially on grounds of ill-health. He had waited in the wings for years as the heir apparent while Churchill clung to power. He had been an experienced and much respected Foreign Secretary, before and after the war. It was all the more ironic that he should make such a profound and damaging error in an issue of foreign policy. In domestic politics, though, Suez did remarkably little harm to the Conservative government that had so disastrously implemented it. Eden's successor, Harold Macmillan, went on to triumph in the 1959 election while Labour, which had vigorously attacked the government over Suez, remained in the doldrums. When it came down to what mattered most in the lives of ordinary people, Suez had a low ranking. Even so, Suez was a pivotal moment in Britain's post-war history, a lasting blow to national self-confidence and to the standing in the world of a country that had only recently been one of the 'Big Three'.

Relations with the United States were soon repaired. The much-vaunted 'special relationship' would be repeatedly emphasized and Anglo-American friendship advertised in the early 1960s by their contrasting leaders – Macmillan, the personification of patrician conservatism in Britain, and John F. Kennedy, the face of a youthful, dynamic American leadership. But it was a heavily imbalanced 'special relationship'. It was more obvious than ever after Suez that Britain could make no significant moves in international affairs without the backing of 'Uncle Sam'.

The British government realized that the game was up. Britain could no longer afford to sustain its military presence in so many parts of the globe. It had to accept that colonialism belonged to the past, that the most important consideration for the future was to establish friendly relations with the new independent states that would emerge from the end of the imperialist era. Once this fundamental reassessment was made, the end of empire came rapidly – and with remarkably little lamentation within Britain. Sudan's independence in January 1956 had in fact preceded Suez. Ghana (formerly the Gold Coast) gained its independence in March 1957. Malaya, the most economically valuable colony that remained, became independent in July 1957. In Cyprus independence (with British retention of military bases) was declared in August 1960, though in this case only after a violent and superficially resolved internal struggle between Greek and Turkish Cypriots. Between 1960 and 1966 a further nineteen former colonies (Nigeria, Sierra Leone, Tanganyika, Zanzibar, Uganda, Kenya, Nyasaland, Northern Rhodesia, Bechuanaland, Basutoland, Western Samoa, Jamaica, Barbados, Trinidad and Tobago, Malta, Singapore, Gambia, the Maldives and British Guiana) attained their independence.

Harold Macmillan captured the mood as well as stating the obvious in a speech in Cape Town in 1960 when he spoke of 'the wind of change' blowing through the African continent. The main resistance came not from Britain itself, but from white settlers in the Union of South Africa and in adjacent Southern Rhodesia. South Africa, refusing to yield on its system of racist apartheid, left the Commonwealth in 1961. The Rhodesian government declared independence in November 1965 in the teeth of

British opposition to such a move, aiming to retain the dominance of the white minority despite condemnation by the rest of the Commonwealth. This led Rhodesia into a brutal fifteen-year civil war but merely delayed the inevitable. Rhodesia eventually would be given independence as the new state of Zimbabwe in April 1980.

By then the British empire was – other than lingering, unimportant remnants – long gone, its obsequies effectively pronounced in the government's withdrawal in 1968 of British forces from bases 'East of Suez'. Britain could no longer afford expensive and unnecessary global commitments. And already by the early 1960s trade with the Commonwealth was shrinking fast. The Dominions were increasingly going their own way, loosening their once close bonds with the United Kingdom. Many political and business leaders were increasingly coming to recognize that Britain needed to reorientate its interests, to look for future prosperity less towards its former colonial possessions and more towards its European neighbours, whose economies were booming. Britain was on the way from a global imperialist to becoming little more than a European power. In 1962 the former US Secretary of State Dean Acheson remarked that 'Great Britain has lost an empire and has not yet found a role'. Decades later the remark was still apposite.

Suez had nothing like the same significance for the French as it did for the British. The bitter political debate and soul-searching about a global role that consumed the British political class were absent in France. There had been widespread support for the campaign in Egypt, and much of the blame for its failure was attributed not to the French government but to the United States and the United Nations which, it was claimed, had halted the attack when victory was imminent. Guy Mollet, unlike Eden, faced little serious clamour for his resignation and was given a big vote of confidence in the French parliament. Not Suez but Indochina and, beyond all else, Algeria symbolized the French retreat from empire. While the British surprisingly easily adjusted to the need to withdraw from their imperial commitments, the winding-up of the French empire was a traumatic business.

France's colonial empire – second only to that of Britain in size – had been put under great strain by the war. Political loyalties in the French colonies had at first mainly favoured the Vichy regime after France's calamitous defeat in 1940, but, often after bitter conflict, had by the middle of the war mostly been turned to Charles de Gaulle's Free French. At the same time France's military humiliation had strengthened anti-colonial feeling in its Middle Eastern and African possessions. The mandated territories in Lebanon and Syria emerged from the war as independent nations. Anti-colonial movements had gained ground notably in North Africa, where an armed uprising in Algeria was put down with force in 1945. The French possessions in Equatorial and West Africa remained quiet. But a revolt against French rule in the geographically isolated colony of Madagascar in 1947 was eventually suppressed with great cruelty. By some estimates as many as 100,000 Madagascans were killed before the rebellion was crushed the following year. An uneasy French colonial domination resumed and lasted until Madagascar finally gained its independence in June 1960.

The Provisional Government in France after the Liberation made a number of minor concessions of political and citizenship rights to its African colonies, granting limited extension of voting rights and representation in the French parliament. The new constitution in 1946 chose the name 'French Union' instead of 'empire', trying as with the British emphasis on 'commonwealth' to defuse the sense of subservience in the overseas territories. The worst instances of colonial abuse were greatly diminished. But outwardly the French colonial empire remained largely intact. And none of the insubstantial changes made much mark on opinion in France itself. While the French generally approved of them, few contemplated granting independence to the overseas possessions. There was certainly much liberal sentiment in favour of colonial reform, and opposition on the left to colonialism itself. But for most French people the empire remained a matter of national prestige.

This was about to be sorely tested in Indochina. The French Vichy authorities had continued to run Indochina (comprising the present-day countries of Vietnam, Cambodia and Laos) effectively as Japanese puppets until late in the war. In March 1945, fearing the transfer of allegiance to de Gaulle, the Japanese had moved to direct rule, encouraging national independence movements as a weapon against the imperialist powers. The problems that were to beset the French arose from their post-war attempts to restore their colonial supremacy. The main difficulties occurred in Vietnam, where Emperor Bao-Dai had abdicated and the Communist leader Ho Chi Minh, whose anti-colonialism had strongly emerged during his years in Paris immediately following the First World War, had declared a republic within days of the Japanese defeat in August 1945. (Remarkably, Ho had been significantly helped to establish his power base by American supplies of arms and military training for his guerrilla forces in the fight against Japan, provided by the OSS, the Office of Strategic Services, during the final months of the war.) The French, backed by public opinion in France, refused to accept the end of their rule and sent in over 30,000 troops to repel Ho's determined peasant army, the Viet Minh, setting up a puppet government in the south of the country (then known as Cochin-China). French obduracy brought the escalation of what would turn into a long and brutal, but unwinnable, war against Viet Minh guerrilla forces.

Increasing numbers of colonial troops were poured into the fight. By 1952 the total reached 560,000, though only about 70,000 of them were French volunteers while the remainder were drawn from the colonies, mostly from Vietnam itself. By that time the Indochina War was intolerably expensive for France, taking up 40 per cent of the entire defence budget, and could be sustained only through substantial and growing financial aid from the United States – where after Mao's triumph in China in 1949 and the outbreak of the Korean War there was intense worry about the 'domino effect' of the spread of communism in Southeast Asia.

The war in Vietnam was meanwhile highly unpopular within France. Losses were mounting. The numbers killed among the French colonial forces in Vietnam would eventually reach 92,000. While 52 per cent of the public questioned in an opinion poll in 1947 had been in favour of the war to keep Indochina as a colony, by February 1954 this had fallen to only 7 per cent. This was even before the greatest disaster in French colonial history: the defeat inflicted by the Viet Minh on 7 May 1954, following an eighty-day siege, on the French forces at Dien Bien Phu in north-west Vietnam. The French lost over 1,500 men in the siege, and a further 11,000 were captured. Dien Bien Phu was regarded as a national humiliation.

With that, the French had had enough. The government predictably fell. On taking office the new premier, Pierre Mendès-France, promised to resign if he did not accomplish a peace settlement in Vietnam within a month. Remarkably, he achieved his goal. A ceasefire was agreed at

Geneva on 21 July 1954 and approved by a huge majority in the National Assembly, which gave the premier 'a tremendous ovation'. Mendès-France became 'practically a national hero' in the eyes of the French public, weary of the costly and ruinous conflict in a distant part of the world known directly to only few French citizens. It was the signal for a rapid process of French disengagement from Indochina. There was no stomach for prolonging the presence of French troops in the region. By 1956 they were gone. The French government was more than happy to pass a poisoned chalice to the Americans and let them take over responsibility for the Vietnamese imbroglio.

In accordance with what was meant to be an interim arrangement reached at Geneva, Vietnam was divided along the 17th parallel. Elections were envisaged two years later to unify the country. The elections never took place. American opposition to a deal that they viewed as leading to conclusive victory for Ho Chi Minh saw to that. The Americans had given ten times as much aid to the French as Soviet and Chinese backers had given Ho. But such vast expenditure would have been in vain, Washington believed, if communism were to triumph after all in Vietnam. So the Americans continued to prop up a corrupt puppet government in the south of the country, which had as little interest as they had themselves in allowing the elections to take place – with the near certain outcome that the whole of Vietnam would become a communist state under the rule of Ho Chi Minh. French intransigence before rapidly vacating what they knew was a lost cause was replaced by American short-sightedness in failing to recognize a lost cause when they saw one. It meant that the worst of the torment for the people of Vietnam was yet to come. The tragedy would deepen much further, and last for another twenty years.

As one colonial war ended for the French another began. And while Indochina was far away, the new war that began in 1954 in Algeria was close to home. In a sense, in fact, it *was* home, for Algeria (colonized since 1830) had been administered as an integral part of France since 1848 and, unlike other parts of the French empire, had attracted settlement by hundreds of thousands of European (not just French) *colons* or *pieds-noirs* (as they came to be known, perhaps, it was thought, because of the black boots that early settlers had worn). The level of political and economic discrimination by the settlers against the Muslim majority had led to protests against colonial rule already in the 1930s and the suppression of a nascent nationalist movement. Demands for reform arose again in the middle of the war. Anger at the limited French concessions to reform led to an outburst of violent protest at the end of the war, which was ruthlessly suppressed by the army and police, who killed several thousand Muslims. In the aftermath the French set up an Algerian Assembly, though granting only a severely limited franchise to the majority Muslim population.

The tensions simmered just beneath the surface. An explosion was inevitable at some point. It came on 1 November 1954 when the *Front de Libération Nationale* (FLN, the Algerian National Liberation Front) attacked a number of targets of the colonial authorities, starting what became an eight-year war for an independent Algerian state based upon the principles of Islam. Mendès-France, fresh from his popular triumph in winding up the war in Indochina, was in this case prepared to make no concessions. He dismissed out of hand any notion that Algeria, a *département* of France, could break away. It was a popular stance.

Mendès-France had, in fact, set in train in 1954 the steps that would lead, by 1956, to independence for Tunisia and Morocco. Independence movements in those countries had faced colonial violence, and the anti-colonial struggle had involved bloodletting and atrocities, but the French government, also under international pressure, had eventually taken the sensible way out of a worsening situation. But Tunisia and Morocco were regarded as colonies; Algeria was seen as an integral part of France, administered from the Ministry of the Interior, not the Colonial Office. In French eyes (though not Algerian) the deepening conflict in Algeria was not a colonial but a *civil* war. This was the fundamental difference that determined French inflexibility over Algeria and produced long years of misery for so many of its inhabitants.

A pattern set in of escalating violence and extreme retaliatory counter-violence. In one flashpoint in August 1955 over a hundred civilian settlers were killed in a planned FLN action, prompting savage retaliation that left well over a thousand Muslims dead (by some estimates a far higher number). Terrorist attacks and localized atrocities met by a regime reliant upon gruesome reprisals was a recipe for a spiral of continued disaster. Guy Mollet, the Prime Minister, briefly tried a conciliatory policy in 1956 but in the face of the vehement opposition of the *colons* swiftly retreated to the objective of crushing the uprising. The number of troops was doubled. Torture was used extensively against FLN suspects. Great military force was deployed. But the FLN responded with further terrorist attacks. Public opinion turned against the savage war and, led by notable intellectuals on the left (prominent among them Pierre Vidal-Naquet and Jean-Paul Sartre), there were strong protests against the inhumanity of the French army in Algeria.

French opinion, however, while desperately wanting the war to end, did not favour independence for Algeria. In any case, the huge obstacle preventing any attempt to grant independence was the outright and violent refusal of the settlers to contemplate such an outcome. By early 1958 a crisis not just of the French government but of the state itself was brewing. When Pierre Pflimlin became Prime Minister on 14 May 1958 the crisis broke. Pflimlin favoured negotiations with the FLN. For the *pieds-noirs* this smelt of betrayal from Paris. They seized the government building in Algiers and chose the paratroop leader, General Jacques Massu, who had directed the ruthless counter-terrorist campaign the previous year, to head what amounted to a revolt against the French government. It was plain that the army backed the revolt. This was the background to the call for de Gaulle to take power. Pflimlin, newly installed as Prime Minister, was forced out of office towards the end of the month. It was the overture, described earlier, to the creation of the Fifth Republic.

The *colons* had thought de Gaulle was their man. They expected his prestige would succeed in ending the Algerian War to their satisfaction. But they were soon bitterly disappointed and incensed as de Gaulle, quickly realizing how intractable the problem was, gave indications that he was open to a negotiated settlement. This left the President uneasily balanced between the extremes of the FLN, unyielding in their demands for independence, and the *pieds-noirs*, ready to take up armed resistance against those demands. Disaffected generals, led by the one-time de Gaulle supporter General Raoul Salan, formed the *Organisation de l'Armée Secrète* (OAS). They planned more than one embyronic coup against the government, carried out a campaign of bombing in France, and tried to assassinate de Gaulle. Altogether the OAS was responsible for around 2,700 deaths, nearly all of them Algerian Muslims.

The Algerian War continued, amid huge violence, throughout 1960 and 1961. But de Gaulle prevailed. He was enough of a realist to know that eventual peace could only come through Algerian independence, and gradually moved to acceptance of that outcome. He used his immense standing and authority to gain the backing of 90 per cent of the French electorate for the ceasefire signed on 18 March 1962, which led to the declaration of Algerian independence on 5 July. Most of the embittered *pieds-noirs*, over 800,000 of them, recognized that they had no future in Algeria and moved to southern France, as did the Algerian Jewish community. Those Algerians, known as *harkis*, who had worked in some capacity for the colonial regime, often as lowly administrators, policemen or soldiers, faced terrible retribution by the FLN at the end of the war. A minority of them managed to flee to mainly southern France where they were treated abysmally by the French authorities, subjected to social discrimination, and shunned or despised by the majority population. The total numbers of victims of the vicious eight-year conflict are hotly disputed, though at a minimum they numbered not less than around 170,000. In all probability the number far exceeded this total. The great majority of those killed were Algerian Muslims. No Frenchmen were put on trial for murder in French courts. France's 'civilizing mission' – its ideological justification for rule over other peoples – had resulted in barbarity.

Remarkably, at the height of the dirty war in Algeria, de Gaulle was liquidating French colonialism throughout almost all of the rest of Africa. The constitution of the Fifth Republic in 1958 had replaced the 'French Union' with the 'French Community', which gave overseas territories extensive rights of self-government though it stopped short of granting them full independence. Only French Guinea initially rejected attachment to the Community. But this set an example, one rapidly to be followed by other former colonies. The wind of anti-colonialism was blowing strongly by the end of the 1950s, and Algeria was hardly a glowing advertisement for French rule. De Gaulle had offered overseas territories the right to choose. They chose. Between 1958 and the end of 1960 as many as fifteen former French colonies (Madagascar, French Sudan, Senegal, Chad, Middle Congo, Gabon, Mauritania, Ubangi-Shari, Cameroun, Togo, Mali, Dahomey, Niger, Upper Volta and Ivory Coast) followed Guinea into independence. By 1961 the French Community had dwindled into near obsolescence. The contrast is stark between the swift winding-up of empire elsewhere in recognition of the obviously unstoppable desire for independence and the tortured acceptance of the inevitable in Algeria only after the huge bloodshed of a lengthy war. The unique status of Algeria was the essential difference. It took de Gaulle's statesmanship and realism to end the largely nominal integration into France of what, despite the official denials, had in reality all along been a colony resting on discrimination against the nine million indigenous inhabitants by a million settlers.

By the mid-1960s only fragments of the once-mighty French and British empires were left. The age of empire was over.

*   *   *

The state funeral of Sir Winston Churchill – the last survivor of the 'big three' wartime leaders – on 30 January 1965 symbolized the passing of a generation wedded to the certainties of the nation state, imperialist domination and European great-power politics. The President of France, General de Gaulle, and the former President of the United States, General Dwight D. Eisenhower, who had stood alongside Churchill in the fight against Nazi Germany, were among the representatives from 112 countries who attended his funeral, an extraordinary display of pomp and ceremony. They saw a Europe that bore only scant resemblance to that which had emerged from the war twenty years earlier.

Most obviously, it was a Europe broken into two irreconcilable halves. The divide, already inexorably taking shape in the immediate post-war years, had widened to a point where, other than diplomatic formalities, there was little or no contact between the eastern and western parts of the continent. The two blocs, east and west, had meanwhile solidified. Western Europe, which had not existed even as a notion in 1945, was by now a definable entity. Two developments, examined above, had been of crucial significance to the making of Western Europe.

Most important of all was the consolidation of pluralist liberal democracy. This varied in its form from one country to the next, but was built everywhere on principles of law, human rights and personal freedom. It rested, too, on restructured capitalist economies that provided the platform for economic growth, prosperity and welfare systems which ensured a basis of social security for all citizens. The Cold War had provided an ideological impetus for the stabilization of Western European democracy. The American presence had provided a basis of security for its development. It was certainly far from perfect in any of its manifestations. When compared, however, with the chronic instability, divisive politics and social misery of the interwar years, the progress in the consolidation of democracy, the indispensable foundation of all that followed, was little short of astonishing.

The second major transformation had been the end of empire. This converted Western Europe into nation states of essentially similar status. Britain and France in particular, still clinging to notions of national grandeur, would not easily adjust to the fact that they were no longer great powers. They remained the most militarized states of Western Europe, possessors of nuclear weapons and seats on the United Nations Security Council. But in reality they were now little more than European powers. Dreams of empire increasingly became no more than the fading and often distorted nostalgia of a dwindling minority.

A third development remains to be explored. Economically, and in embryonic fashion also politically, Western Europe was moving in a direction difficult if not impossible to forecast in the early post-war years. It was starting to come together in institutions that coexisted with but to some extent transcended the nation state. This would prove a long, chequered and incomplete process, accompanied throughout by intrinsic tensions and conflicts but at the same time providing levels of cooperation and integration that would have seemed inconceivable in the years before the Second World War. It marked a major advance in building a foundation of lasting peace.

Eastern Europe stood wholly outside these patterns of fundamental transformation. There was change there, too, though it was much less far-reaching. Room for manoeuvre for Eastern European countries was closely confined. Its limits were tightly controlled by the clamp of Soviet domination.

3

The Clamp

We asked Marshal Konev, who was the commander of the War-saw Pact troops, 'How much time would it take if we instructed you to restore order in Hungary and to crush the counter-revolutionary forces?' He thought for a moment and replied, 'Three days, no longer.' 'Then start getting ready. You'll hear from us when it's time to begin.' So it was decided.

Memoirs of Nikita Khrushchev, 1971

While Western Europe was taking shape as a political entity under the aegis of the United States, the Soviet Union was consolidating its hold over the bloc of countries in its 'sphere of influence' on the other side of the Iron Curtain. The once independent Baltic countries – Estonia, Latvia and Lithuania – had been part of the Soviet Union since 1940. The other countries under Moscow's aegis were Albania, Bulgaria, Czechoslovakia, the German Democratic Republic, Hungary, Poland and Romania. Yugoslavia, however, continued to develop along the separate path it had followed since Marshal Tito's breach with Moscow in 1948.

A major caesura occurred in Eastern Europe – like 'Western Europe' a political construct rather than a precise geographical description – with the death of Joseph Stalin in March 1953. The end of the great tyrant ushered in a period commonly dubbed 'the thaw', a metaphor derived from the title of a novel published by Ilya Ehrenburg in 1954. The 'thaw' indicated de-Stalinization – a marked break with the system under Stalin. But the metaphor has its limitations. The Stalinist system had itself not been 'frozen', as a 'thaw' implies, but had been modified in several phases over time. Indeed, some change during the 'thaw' flowed from pressures that had built up in Stalin's last years or tapped into earlier ideas. Ehrenburg himself interpreted 'thaw' to imply impermanence, instability and mere uncertainty about what the weather would bring. A thaw could bring not just spring but new frosts as the ground froze over once again. But in its literal meaning a 'thaw' does eventually change the weather entirely. It reduces previous ice and snow to a formless slush that ultimately becomes water and drains away. Yet change under Nikita Khrushchev, though real and substantial, was *within* the Soviet system and did not dissolve it into a completely different form, let alone water it down to near disappearance. On the contrary: after Khrushchev's removal from office in October 1964 the system was stabilized and reinforced under his own successor, Leonid Brezhnev, lasting (even if stagnating) in much the same form and substance until the transformation of 1985–90. Finally, a thaw is a natural occurrence, not involving human agency. There was, however, little that was 'natural' about change in the Soviet Union after Stalin.

Perhaps a different metaphor, of a 'clamp' or 'vice', is therefore preferable to 'thaw'. A clamp can be loosened or tightened. But the object to which the clamp is applied remains the same. What happened under Khrushchev amounted to a loosening of the extremely tight clamp that Stalin had imposed on the Soviet Union. But the system remained in its essence intact. Moreover, there was a significant difference between Stalinism in the Soviet Union itself and in the nation states of Eastern Europe.

The possibilities of systemic change in the Soviet Union, given the firm establishment of communist rule over more than three decades since the 1917 Revolution and in a vast country lacking alternative forms and recent traditions of political organization, were as good as non-existent. In most of Eastern Europe, by contrast, only under Moscow's tutelage since the aftermath of the victory of the Red Army in 1944–5, Stalinism was an external and recent imposition. Here, the potential for fundamental change was real. Only the Soviet clamp of power prevented it. In each of the countries in the Soviet 'sphere of influence' there had been pre-war experience of pluralistic political systems, even if this had often amounted to no more than a façade of democracy. In some cases (most prominently East Germany and Czechoslovakia) there were longstanding democratic traditions, suppressed but still latently present. Most obvious of all, each of the satellites had a continuous sense of identity as an autonomous nation state. This was specially pronounced in Poland and Hungary.

It was, therefore, unsurprising that an initial loosening of the clamp after Stalin's death led, in some of the Soviet Eastern European satellites, to serious unrest that carried the potential to upturn, not just amend, the communist system itself in those countries. Nor was it surprising that the response of the Soviet Union was both nervous and heavy-handed, ultimately turning to the use of force as the clamp was sharply retightened.

LOOSENING THE CLAMP:
THE SOVIET UNION

The last years of Stalin were a miserable time for most Soviet citizens. The glories of the Red Army's victory over Nazism reverberated through the country. The human cost – over 25 million Soviet citizens had been killed – was barely imaginable. Whatever the embellishments of propaganda, there was great and genuine patriotic pride among the survivors at the feats of extraordinary courage and fortitude that the Soviet Union had shown in order to defeat and destroy the cruel invaders. But patriotic pride did not fill stomachs or provide decent homes. And patriotic pride was no guarantee against the insecurities of living in an intrusive police state without legal protection.

It is hard to exaggerate the extent of the physical destruction that the war had left behind in the western parts of the Soviet Union. Entire regions were desolate. The ravages of the fighting, or wilful destruction by the retreating Wehrmacht, had destroyed 1,710 towns and no fewer than 70,000 villages. Around 25 million people were homeless. Grain production had fallen by two-thirds, industrial production for civilian needs by well over a third. It took an extraordinary feat of reconstruction to recover from such devastation.

Recovery was indeed impressive. It was nevertheless accompanied by the rigidity, harshness and cruelty that had been an intrinsic part of the pre-war and wartime economy. Doubtless there were still many idealists and much readiness on the part of ordinary citizens, as in Western Europe, to work hard and endure hardships to help recovery and bring about improvements in their material circumstances. But what was demanded of them could only be achieved through heavy coercion. Wartime labour restrictions, with draconian penalties for lateness or any perceived misdemeanour, remained in place. The command economy retained its panoply of controls. Labour was mobilized where the state saw fit to deploy it. The results, in purely economic terms, were mixed. The human cost was, however, enormous, on top of the death and suffering during the war that had left scarcely a Soviet family untouched.

Production of iron, steel, coal, oil, electricity and cement was higher by 1950 than it had been before the war, and three times as many tractors were now being produced than ten years earlier (even if caveats have to be attached to all Soviet production statistics, leaving aside the age-old tactic of managers setting targets low in order to be able to show that they had been surpassed). But real wages only began to reach their 1928 level in 1952. Production of consumer goods and supplies of housing lagged far behind the improvements in heavy industry. The standard of living remained excruciatingly low. Housing was squalid and accommodation, often in communal apartments, grossly overcrowded. Much of the population continued to live in dire poverty. The priority accorded to capital goods (many still for armaments), whose output had increased by 83 per cent between 1945 and 1950, was retained. In 1952 a 45 per cent increase in output for the armed forces, compared with 1950, was included in the budget. As in the 1930s the countryside, quite especially, bore the brunt of the industrial recovery. Agricultural production was lower in the early 1950s than it had been before the war – productivity per acre even lower than before the First World War. Instances of cannibalism were reported from Ukraine, suffering in 1946 as it had grievously done in 1932–3 and once again from famine, despite the richness of its soil. This partly arose from natural causes, as drought badly affected the harvest. But far worse damage was done by the state removing food reserves from the peasants even though this condemned them to starvation.

Disaffection and unrest were kept under control by massive repression, which was ramped up again in the post-war years. The Gulag once more expanded as hundreds of thousands of new prisoners poured into the camps at the start of years of slave labour to help rebuild the ravaged country or to sustain armaments production (soon to include the making of nuclear weapons). Their numbers, reduced during the war, once more swelled to around five million prisoners. Disproportionate numbers came from deportees from the western borders of the Soviet Union or the former Baltic countries, the loyalties of whose populations were still regarded with high suspicion. Well over a million Red Army soldiers who had been captured by the Wehrmacht and spent years in horrendous conditions in Germany came back to their homeland to find themselves regarded as traitors and incarcerated anew in the Gulag.

Whatever minor relaxations in restrictions on expression and limits on interference by the party that had existed during the war were subsequently eliminated. The arts were throttled of anything that did not comply with the strict ideological guidelines laid down by the Communist Party's cultural head, Andrei Zhdanov. Science, too, was forced into line. The slightest sign of deviance invited the extreme disapproval of the regime, if not worse. The satirical tale of a monkey that had escaped from a zoo, observed Soviet life for a day, and preferred to return to captivity brought accusations against the author, Mikhail Zoshchenko, of 'rotten ideological nihilism' designed to poison attitudes towards the state.

The repression that was so close to the surface of Soviet life in Stalin's last years needed a huge apparatus of those ready to carry it out. Stalin ensured that the party, the army and the security police were well provided with privileges and power. Although much of the population had to scrape by with the bare minimum, the ruling elite still had their dachas, their holidays in the Crimea, special shops, good medical care and educational advantages for their children. And this kind of political bribery trickled down in some degree to lesser functionaries, bureaucrats in the service of the party or the state, members of the army and agents of the security service. The system of sticks and carrots – fear of retribution for any perceived failure, and material benefits, advancement, status and power over others – worked not just at the top but also as motivation to the millions of minions and 'little Stalins' who made the system work at the bottom.

Stalin's well-honed technique of 'divide and rule' among his paladins, deeply suspicious of each other and competing for the dictator's favour, continued down to his death. No one was secure in this system. But those in the ruling elite, most exposed to Stalin's whims, knew that they especially, for all their power, had only precarious tenure of their positions.

A word spoken out of turn or some well-meaning action that caused the dictator's displeasure could have incalculable consequences. There was no repeat, it is true, of the great purges of the 1930s. But selective purges of party cadres were carried out in Leningrad in 1949 and in part of Georgia in 1951. Stalin's decision to summon the Nineteenth Party Congress in October 1952, after a gap of thirteen years, was viewed by his subordinates as an ominous sign that he intended to purge the top leadership once again. Khrushchev thought another major purge was avoided only by Stalin's death.

Indeed, the dictator's paranoia was again running riot. 'I trust no one, not even myself,' Khrushchev claimed to recall him saying in 1951. A year later Stalin was absurdly suspecting Vyacheslav Molotov and Anastas Mikoyan, two of his most long-standing and loyal lieutenants, of being agents of foreign powers. Then, in January 1953, a group of Kremlin doctors, most of them with Jewish-sounding names, were suddenly arrested, accused of planning to wipe out the Soviet leadership. Stalin's own antisemitism was ingrained and obvious to his acolytes. And despite public condemnation of antisemitism, prejudice against Jews was widespread in Soviet society. Tens of thousands of Jews between 1948 and 1953 faced dismissal from their jobs and other forms of discrimination. Had Stalin lived, the 'doctors' plot', which triggered numerous arrests of Jews, would have spelled grave new danger for Soviet Jews. But the purge never took place. Immediately following Stalin's death the doctors were released and the 'plot' was acknowledged to be a fabrication.

On 1 March 1953 Stalin, in poor health for quite some time (though the fact was a close secret), collapsed after a stroke. No one rushed to provide medical care – not that it would probably have made any difference. Lavrenti Beria, the head of state security, seemed particularly keen that Stalin should not recover. Fear of the stricken dictator even as he lay dying combined with mutual suspicion and power ambitions to paralyse into inactivity his inner circle (reduced to Georgi Malenkov, Nikita Khrushchev, Nikolai Bulganin and Beria, with Molotov and Mikoyan largely sidelined). Stalin clung to life for four days before dying on 5 March, leaving his acolytes to fight over the spoils of power.

In the inevitable power struggle that immediately followed, Malenkov appeared to be the winner. He had used his various high positions, particularly his running of the party's secretariat, to become first among equals in the inner circle – in effect Stalin's heir apparent. His main ally – an alliance of convenience, no more – was Beria. No sooner was Stalin dead than Malenkov, proposed by Beria, was appointed by the inner circle both as Chairman of the Council of Ministers and as Secretary of the Party's Central Committee. Malenkov then proposed Beria as his first deputy. Beria was in addition given extended control over state security. The others in the leadership group felt obliged at first to accept this arrangement. But deep suspicions remained. One danger was the accretion of power in state and party in the hands of Malenkov. This was, in fact, quickly alleviated when Malenkov, already on 14 March, was forced to step down as Secretary of the Central Committee (in effect, head of the party). This opened the door to the most crucial position in the Soviet Union for Khrushchev, increasingly the coming man.

Bigger than the threat from Malenkov, as the inner group recognized, was that posed by Beria, whose ambitions had been barely disguised. They all feared Beria – and with good cause. He presided over an immense security and surveillance network and had a long history of ruthlessly dispatching any individuals who, on whatever trumped-up charge, could be portrayed as internal enemies. Nevertheless, the security chief had made his own powerful enemies, also among significant figures within the army – not least the former war hero, Marshal Zhukov. When the blow fell, Beria was on his own.

Khrushchev had lost little time in persuading the other leading figures in the Party Presidium (which in 1952 had replaced the Politburo) to join him in a plot to topple Beria. On 26 June 1953, a mere three months after Stalin's death, an unsuspecting Beria, attending a meeting of the Presidium, was denounced by his former comrades, arrested by Zhukov and a number of other generals, briefly held in military custody, then in December convicted in a secret trial on the ludicrous charge of being a British spy – the security chief hoisted on his own petard – and immediately shot. In March 1954 his security empire was split into two separate organizations, one to deal with ordinary criminality, the other with security matters.

Over the following months Khrushchev used his position as First Secretary of the party to consolidate his own power. He made numerous new appointments at regional and district level, creating an important base of support among those who were indebted to him. And his bold policy of opening up 'virgin lands' in Kazakhstan and Siberia to cultivation was trumpeted as a great success (though in reality contributing little to the bounty from the plentiful harvests of 1954 and 1955). Malenkov's star was by now on the wane, all the more so when Khrushchev set up a commission to investigate the crimes of the 1930s and 1940s, including Malenkov's role in the Leningrad purge of 1948–9. In February 1955 Malenkov lost his position as head of the Council of Ministers – effectively Prime Minister. His replacement, Bulganin, was, as soon became evident, the weaker component of the duopoly now running the Soviet Union.

The dramatic moment when Stalin's clamp was loosened came at the Twentieth Congress of the Communist Party of the Soviet Union on 25 February 1956. Khrushchev had suggested a fortnight earlier that a speech should be devoted to 'the Cult of the Individual and its Consequences'. Molotov, the arch-Stalinist, was opposed. So were Stalin's old stalwarts, Lazar Kaganovich and Kliment Voroshilov. But Khrushchev got his way. Those in the Presidium who supported him had all been involved, like Khrushchev himself, in implementing the horrific repression under Stalin. They were aware that the commission already at work would expose at least some of what had taken place. Anticipating that the many who would return from long periods in prisons and camps would ask questions, they had a vested interest in deflecting all blame to the dictator himself. So they backed what was a risky venture.

Khrushchev's four-hour speech to a closed session of the Congress was a bombshell. A key strategy was to separate Lenin's legacy from Stalin's abuses of power. Lenin was placed upon a pedestal to emphasize the gulf between him and his successor. Early in the speech Khrushchev cited Lenin's 1922 warning about Stalin – that he was not fit to be given the powerful position of the party's General Secretary. This was part of a sustained attempt to show that Stalin had completely abandoned Lenin's precepts and 'trampled on the Leninist principle of collective Party leadership' in building up his own absolute power, personality cult and reign of terror. Khrushchev's blistering attack on Stalin's crimes from the 1930s onwards (drawing a blanket over anything earlier) blamed him personally and solely – if aided by his willing minions, the heads of the security services (Nikolai Yezhov and Beria), acting under his express orders – for the terroristic repression and mass executions of loyal party members as 'enemies of the people' on completely falsified charges. 'Everything,' Khrushchev declared, 'was dependent upon the wilfulness of one man.'

By implication, subordinate party leaders were exonerated; they were, he added (with reference to the Leningrad purge), ignorant 'of the circumstances in these matters, and could not therefore intervene'. Not only did Stalin destroy the party cadres through his terroristic purges. His personalized power threatened the very existence of the country. Stalin, Khrushchev stated, was personally responsible for the calamitous mistakes made in 1941, when he had ignored warnings of imminent German invasion. Khrushchev continued his demolition of Stalin's reputation down to the abuses – including the supposed 'doctors' plot' – of the years immediately preceding his death. He ended his lengthy peroration with condemnation of 'the cult of the individual as alien to Marxism-Leninism' and urged his comrades 'to restore completely the Leninist principles of Soviet socialist democracy' and 'to fight wilfulness of individuals abusing their power'.

The denunciation of Stalin served, therefore, to underline both the ideological purity and the organizational principles of the Soviet system, as built by Lenin. In other words, the tyrant was gone and a line drawn under his crimes. But the system, now given new strength, would continue. When Khrushchev finished, 'the silence in the hall was profound', one delegate present later recalled. 'Whether from the unexpectedness of what had just occurred or from nervousness and fear', people, heads bowed, avoided looking each other in the eye as they came out.

The speech, leaked and swiftly published abroad, was a sensation. In Poland and Hungary its revelations contributed significantly to the mounting unrest that by the autumn would pose an outright challenge to Soviet rule. In the Soviet Union itself the press published no more than a brief summary of the speech. But the party's Central Committee itself ensured, probably directed by Khrushchev, that before long in the Soviet Union, too, copies of the speech were printed, circulated, and read out to party members.

Only three years earlier Stalin's death had produced a mass outpouring of grief, even near hysteria, among Soviet citizens. 'Everyone was in tears,' one woman recalled. 'We did not know what was going to happen next. We had never known anything different.' How genuine the grief was is impossible to ascertain. It was wise not to voice publicly the private reaction of a woman in Kazakhstan who simply said: 'Stalin's dead. And a good thing, too.' Even so, the personality cult of the great leader, cultivated over so many years, had not been without effect. Millions had come close to worshipping Stalin. Now they were asked utterly to disavow their recent idol. Unsurprisingly, therefore, many were shocked when they learnt the content of the speech; there was also great confusion.

Reactions were mixed. Portraits and busts of Stalin were destroyed, removed or defaced in places across the Soviet Union. There were demands to remove his body from its place of honour alongside Lenin's embalmed remains in the Kremlin mausoleum (though this was not, in fact, done until 1961). But many never forgave Khrushchev for toppling their idol from his pedestal. They defended Stalin, resisted attempts to remove his portraits, and praised his purges of those who had oppressed them. Nowhere was the Stalin cult upheld more fervently than in his native Georgia, where four days of protest at Khrushchev's denunciation of the former dictator marked the third anniversary of his death. Some 50,000 people gathered to pay homage to him on 5 March at his birthplace in Gori. A crowd of over 60,000 people attended a demonstration on 7 March to place flowers on Stalin's monument in Tblisi. During the following days, hundreds of others commandeered vehicles to carry portraits of 'the Great Stalin' around the city, shouting 'Down with Khrushchev' and 'Long Live Stalin'. Troops were sent in to quell the mounting disturbance. The events left twenty dead, sixty wounded and many others imprisoned.

Across the Soviet Union there was certainly far more open criticism than had been risked only a short time earlier. People, including those returning from the Gulag, felt emboldened to break their silence and to speak out. Party members queried the suggestion that other members of the Presidium had been ignorant of what Stalin was doing. They asked why it had taken so long to speak of Stalin's crimes. 'And where was Khrushchev himself?', asked one Stalin admirer, a retired colonel in the Red Army. 'Why did he keep quiet back then, but begin to pour all this muck on Stalin now he's dead?' Some asked why Khruschchev had made no mention of the many victims who had not been party members and questioned whether the system itself was not to blame? Such searching criticism was, however, exceptional. Critics more usually attacked abuses of Leninist ideals, not the Soviet system itself. Nearly forty years after the Revolution, it was as good as impossible to contemplate any alternative to a system that, whatever its faults, had proved victorious in the war. Most people were in any case still wary of voicing their opinions too loudly. Even so, the Central Committee was worried enough to send out a circular in June 1956 demanding tough action to curb the criticism.

It was like trying to nail down the lid of Pandora's box. Khrushchev's speech had awakened hopes and enthusiasm for reform, especially among students and other youth groups. There was a marked increase in political dissent in 1956 and 1957, most notably in and around universities in several parts of the Soviet Union. Thousands of anti-Soviet leaflets were distributed. Some, put through the letter boxes of houses in working-class districts of Moscow, called for reforms 'in the spirit of the Twentieth Congress', for the formation of genuine 'workers' soviets', for factory strikes, and for trials of those implicated in Stalin's crimes. The sending of anonymous anti-Soviet letters, possession of subversive literature and, most usual, individual verbal remarks attacking the regime, were the common forms of dissent detailed in a judicial review of almost 2,000 sentences for anti-Soviet activity in 1957. The World Youth Festival, a two-week-long carnival held in July that year in Moscow and briefly opening up the Soviet Union to an influx of over 30,000 people from 130 countries, contributed to the greater readiness of some young Soviet citizens to question their own political system – though, almost certainly, in order to improve it, not to embrace Western democracy.

Turning the spotlight back to the crimes and gross injustice of the Stalin era, as Khrushchev's speech had done, had a further unsettling effect as four million prisoners returned from prison camps and colonies under a series of decrees and amnesties between 1953 and 1958. Few met with a warm welcome. Most were marginalized and treated with suspicion. It was difficult to believe, many citizens felt, that there had been no grounds for their imprisonment. They were seen as a dangerous part of society, and often blamed for rising rates of crime. Those not directly affected by the mass arrests under Stalin had been indifferent towards the victims. They were unlikely now to show them much concern. For the victims themselves, though, there was a new readiness to speak of their ordeal, to confront their trauma. One woman, returning from exile to Leningrad in 1956, started after Khrushchev's speech to speak of her experiences for the first time, her daughter recalled. 'And the more we talked, the more our ideas changed – we became more sceptical.' But for victims and their families the new freedom was strictly qualified. They feared that repression could come back as quickly as it had receded. Most people remained cautious – and rightly so, for it was plain that the regime was prepared to tolerate criticism of Stalin's 'cult of personality' but not of the Soviet system itself.

It would be as well not to exaggerate the scale of the unrest within Soviet society. It was a minority taste. But it was sufficient to worry Soviet leaders of the old guard, and to heighten their criticism of Khrushchev. They disliked his domineering and impulsive style of leadership, though they had been used to far worse from Stalin. They had been antagonized by his outspoken attack on the leader they had served and often still revered, not least as the great Soviet wartime hero. At the very least they thought Khrushchev had made a grave error in opening up the past, of which they themselves were a part, to public scrutiny. Nor did they like his deviation from Stalin's foreign policy through re-establishing relations with the outcast, Tito, and through a professed readiness to seek 'peaceful coexistence' with the West. The strikes in Poland and the Hungarian uprising in autumn 1956 that had threatened to undermine Soviet rule were a further serious indicator to them that Khrushchev was completely mishandling Stalin's legacy.

The old-stagers Molotov, Malenkov and Kaganovich, all Stalinist stalwarts, plotted to overthrow him, proposing at a meeting of the Presidium on 18 June 1957 to abolish the post of First Secretary of the Communist Party, the base of his power. Khrushchev managed, however, to appeal to the decision of the Central Committee, placing his fate in the hands of its members. Most of these were his own placemen, who had benefited from advancement to positions of authority in the provinces. Rushed into a special meeting on 21 June, they backed Khrushchev. The plotters were defeated and dismissed from the Presidium. There was at least no reversion to the practices of Stalin's day. The disgraced leaders were not given a show trial, then executed. Instead they were dispatched to far-flung parts of the Soviet Union where they could cause no further mischief. Molotov was sent as ambassador to Mongolia. Malenkov became director of a power station in Kazakhstan. Kaganovich was made director of a cement works in Sverdlovsk in the Urals. Bulganin, too, had been implicated in the plot, and was dismissed as Chairman of the Council of Ministers. Khrushchev himself took over the post in 1958, following Stalin's example of 1941 by uniting it with his position as First Secretary of the Communist Party. The experiment with collective leadership was over. From now on, for the next six or so years, Khrushchev, heading both party and state, was the unchallenged leader of the Soviet Union.

The balance sheet of his period in office is chequered. During his time as Soviet leader gross national income rose by 58 per cent, industrial output by 84 per cent and consumer goods by 60 per cent. Despite the continued weighting towards capital goods, heavy industry and the military (including the development of nuclear weapons), the standard of living for most Soviet citizens improved as high rates of economic growth were sustained (if still poor by comparison with Western Europe). An indication was the increase in meat consumption by 55 per cent, and the fact that growing numbers (though still a tiny proportion of Soviet citizenry) could now afford a fridge, television and washing machine. Attempts were made to lessen some of the most dire poverty in the countryside. Higher prices were paid to collective farmers to procure their produce and they were allowed to make greater gains from private plots. Investment in agriculture was greatly increased. There was no longer the harsh punishment for minor misdemeanours at work that had prevailed under Stalin. Social security benefits were widened. A big housing programme went some way towards ameliorating the disastrous shortage of decent accommodation. Blocks of flats shot up in the big cities. Heating costs were minimal. Education and medical care were free. Substantial steps were taken to improve education, trebling the number of university students. And legal reforms removed the worst of the arbitrariness that had previously existed, even if the law remained ultimately subordinate to political imperatives. These were certainly notable improvements. But Khrushchev won few plaudits from Soviet citizens. Living conditions remained poor. The authoritarianism and arbitrariness of the system were somewhat reduced, but not removed.

Khrushchev also made huge mistakes. Some of the most costly were in his drive to improve agricultural productivity. His much-trumpeted 'virgin lands' policy was an initial success. Hundreds of thousands of young Soviet citizens were mobilized by the party's youth movement, the Komsomol, to travel to Kazakhstan or Siberia to help with the harvests.

Thousands of tractors ploughed huge new tracts of previously barren countryside which, by 1956, were producing three times as much as they had done in 1953. But the cost of maximizing production at the fastest possible pace was soon paid in soil erosion that seriously damaged millions of hectares of land, while the dreadful living conditions in the countryside caused many early idealists to return home. Despite the razzmatazz of the 'virgin lands' campaign, it had proved a failure. Agricultural production across the Soviet Union actually fell between 1958 and 1963.

Khrushchev made an equally damaging error when he returned from a visit to the United States in 1959 with enormous enthusiasm for turning hay meadows over to maize production in conditions quite unsuited for growing the crop. The experiment, carried out in the teeth of advice from leading agricultural experts, was a dire failure, as was the accompanying campaign to overtake the USA in dairy products. By 1962 food prices had to be raised (leading to riots in some cities), there were queues for bread even in Ukraine, long seen as the Soviet granary, the black market was thriving in major cities like Moscow and Leningrad, and hard-currency reserves had to be used to import grain from abroad. The price increases, shortages and other economic difficulties of 1961–2 had soured the popular mood. There were disturbances in some cities. In Novocherkassk, near Rostov in southern Russia, the army was called in to suppress serious riots in early June 1962 by striking workers, incensed at price increases and cuts in wages. Soldiers even turned a machine gun on unarmed workers, killing twenty-six and injuring a further eighty-seven.

It was little wonder that Khrushchev's enemies in the party were again sharpening their knives. The failures in planning, damaging economic problems and the expressions of popular resentment stood in glaring contrast to the boundless optimism and extraordinary promises – remarkable hostages to fortune – that Khrushchev had made only a year earlier, when presenting a revised party programme which he had personally devised to the Twenty-Second Party Congress on 18 October 1961. Khrushchev gave two speeches – gigantic even by Soviet standards – that lasted ten hours in total. He told the assembled 5,000 delegates that within ten years the whole population would be 'materially provided for', that the housing shortage would disappear by then, and that consumer goods would soon be plentiful, ensuring everyone 'a diet of high quality'. The crass gap between image and reality that was so blatantly revealed within less than a year could only undermine Khrushchev's authority, as well as his popularity.

The triumphalism of the Party Congress had a counterpoint: the final showdown with the cult of Stalin. Khrushchev's speech five years earlier, in 1956, had been to a closed meeting of party members. Although its contents swiftly became known there had been neither at that time, nor subsequently, an official, public denunciation of Stalin. On this occasion, however, it was open season on the former dictator; and now, also, on his former henchmen Molotov, Malenkov and Kaganovich, who had led the 'anti-party' plot of 1957 against Khrushchev – figures described in the official newspaper *Pravda* as 'swamp creatures grown used to slime and dirt'. Towards the end of the Congress an elderly woman who had joined the Bolsheviks in 1902 made her way to the podium and recounted her dream the previous night in which Lenin had appeared to her, saying: 'I do not like lying next to Stalin, who brought so much misfortune to our party.' This prompted a resolution, unanimously approved, to deem 'unsuitable the continued retention in the mausoleum of the sarcophagus with J. V. Stalin's coffin'. That same night Stalin's body was removed and thrown into a pit at the back of the Kremlin. Lorry-loads of concrete were reportedly poured into the pit and a granite slab was placed on top. It was as if the Soviet bosses were taking no chances – making absolutely sure that they were rid of the great monster once and for all.

Khrushchev had destroyed the cult of Stalin. But he had not replaced it with anything approaching the same level of commitment to his own personal rule. His own standing was soon on the wane as the extent of policy failure and popular discontent with his rule became apparent. Another poor harvest in 1963 aggravated the position. Khrushchev's agricultural policies had been costly mistakes. His reorganization of the apparatus of party and state had not led to marked improvement. There were worries that 'de-Stalinization' was going too far. Reductions in military spending and numbers of officers did not go down well in the leadership of the Soviet army. And Khrushchev's behaviour on the international stage – banging his shoe on the table to interrupt a speech that he did not like in the United Nations in 1960, and his mishandling of the Cuba Crisis in 1962 – were felt to have brought disrepute to the Soviet Union. He had succeeded in alienating important sectors of all the main power blocs – the party, the military, economic ministries and the security police.

In October 1964 Khrushchev was asked to return from holiday by the Black Sea to attend a meeting of the Party Presidium, ostensibly about agricultural matters. He was until the last minute blithely unaware that the meeting had been called to depose him. His successor was, in fact, nominated and ready to take over. It had already been agreed that Leonid Brezhnev, a one-time Khrushchev protégé, would become the next First Secretary of the Communist Party. He first had to preside over the meeting that would end Khrushchev's career. The meeting boldly attacked Khrushchev's failings of leadership, accusing him of trying to create his own personality cult, pointless administrative meddling, and disreputable conduct of foreign affairs. (An editorial in the party organ *Pravda* soon afterwards castigated 'harebrained scheming, half-baked conclusions and hasty decisions and actions divorced from reality, bragging and bluster, attraction to rule by fiat'.) The basis of support that had saved him in 1957 had meanwhile drained away. No one spoke in his favour. Khrushchev meekly accepted his fate: 'What can I say? I've got what I deserved,' he told his comrades. But there was no Stalinesque retribution. He departed, officially on grounds of ill-health, for comfortable retirement in obscurity, his name seldom to be heard again until his death in September 1971.

With Khrushchev's deposition dynamic dictatorship in the Soviet Union was over – replaced by dull dictatorship, now with a collective leadership. Already in October 1964 it had been decided that no single person could simultaneously be head of party and state. And Brezhnev made no attempt to gather all the reins of power into his own hands. So Aleksei Kosygin, if possible even less dynamic than Brezhnev, was made head of the Council of Ministers (Prime Minister), while Nikolai Podgorny, vying for dullness with the pair of them, was appointed chairman of the Presidium of the Supreme Soviet (head of state). In this collective leadership Brezhnev's position of first among equals metamorphosed only gradually over more than a decade into outright supremacy.

After decades of Stalin's autocratic rule followed by Khrushchev's upheavals, Brezhnev brought stabilization. His lacklustre personality contrasted sharply with Khrushchev's erratic ebullience. It was a complete antidote to anything resembling 'charismatic' rule. The system settled down to conservative repressive authoritarianism. The time for grand (but risky) experiments was over. The new head of the party reverted to being 'General Secretary', the title used from Stalin's time until Khrushchev had altered it to 'First Secretary'. The Politburo (which in 1952 had been restyled the Presidium) also regained its old name. Within the party the old insecurities disappeared. The new steadiness rested on armies of apparatchiks who were by and large left to enjoy their positions of power and comfortable corruption as long as they kept in line. Bureaucrats no longer needed to fear for their tenure, or even their lives. Draconian labour discipline was somewhat relaxed. Availability of consumer goods improved slightly, though there were still shortages of even basic commodities. People became used to queuing for foodstuffs. But the window to change that Khrushchev had opened a sliver was now firmly closed again.

The new regime under its collective leadership did not try to imitate the terroristic repression of bygone times. It made clear, however, that the communist system, whatever the changes in leadership, remained in all essentials intact and unchallengeable. The state security apparatus, now called the KGB (Komitet Gosudarstvennoy Bezopasnosti), was still in place, a crucial vehicle of regime control. Intellectuals who had thought that there was room in the system for a type of 'loyal opposition' – challenging abuses though not wishing to destroy a reformed communism – were disabused of their reformist hopes. The tentative steps taken under Khrushchev towards greater freedom and objectivity in the Soviet historical writing were halted or even reversed. Alexander Solzhenitsyn had gained international renown with the publication, personally approved by Khrushchev, in November 1962 of his book *One Day in the Life of Ivan Denisovich*, sensationally revealing the horror of the Gulag, but three years later he was not allowed to publish his novels, *The First Circle* and *Cancer Ward*, about life under Stalin. (He would later be expelled from the Soviet Union, his citizenship revoked.) The physicist Andrei Sakharov was prevented from expressing any criticism in public, then deprived of his privileges. He would subsequently be forced into internal exile. The satirists Andrei Sinyavski and Yuli Daniel were sent to the Gulag for spreading 'anti-Soviet propaganda'. The number of political prisoners or those who had vainly demanded freedom of religious expression grew to around 10,000 over the next few years. Surveillance, resting on huge networks of informers, was omnipresent.

It was nothing like a reversion to the days of Stalin. Arbitrary arrest, imprisonment and execution had gone. Keeping quiet brought relative security. But overt criticism or political deviation invited reprisals. Repression was immanent to the system. The clamp could be loosened somewhat, as it had been under Khrushchev. But it could not be removed.

YUGOSLAVIA'S 'HERESY'

One communist country stood out from those Eastern European states that belonged to the Soviet bloc. Yugoslavia, after Marshal Tito's rancorous split with Stalin in 1948, trod a separate path to that of the Soviet satellites where fears of contamination through the exquisitely labelled 'Titoist deviation' led to arrests, show trials and dire punishment for any – usually political opponents – accused of espousing it. Stalin had at first done all he could to put an end to Tito. Relentless vitriolic attacks in Soviet propaganda were accompanied by assassination attempts. Tito was, however, not one to be daunted by threats. A note found in Stalin's desk after his death read: 'If you don't stop sending killers, I'll send one to Moscow, and I won't have to send a second.' Khrushchev went some way towards mending fences with Tito in 1955. By then he was compelled to accept that Yugoslavia would remain a black sheep within the communist flock, continuing to reject subservience to the Soviet Union.

Stalin saw Tito's main crime in the refusal to bow to his supremacy. Ideologically, his 'heresy' was to pursue a form of 'socialism' that was diametrically opposed to the central tenets of Soviet rule. In Yugoslavian communism power was decentralized, not run by a highly bureaucratized party-state. Industrial production was steered through the 'self-management' of over 6,000 elected workers' councils, not by draconian managerial rule imposing the diktats of central planning. And Yugoslavia pursued 'non-alignment' – effectively neutrality in the Cold War through avoidance of formal commitment to either of the superpowers – rather than bow to Soviet imperatives in foreign policy.

The limited democratic form of communism in Yugoslavia, developed from the base upwards rather than from the top downwards, naturally raised vital questions about the role of the party. In the Soviet system the theory was clear: the party was the vanguard of the 'dictatorship of the

1. Protesters from the Campaign for Nuclear Disarmament, wanting to 'Ban the Bomb', march through London on their way to the nuclear research base at Aldermaston, about fifty miles away, on 7 April 1958. The march became an annual event and CND grew rapidly in popularity helping to inspire demonstrations against nuclear weapons in other parts of Western Europe.

2. A crowd of onlookers in West Berlin watch Soviet Army tanks at Checkpoint Charlie on 17 June 1953. That day, Soviet military might had been deployed to suppress the popular uprising against the East German regime, which threatened to undermine Communist rule.

3. The French Foreign Minister, Robert Schuman (*right*), and the West German Chancellor, Konrad Adenauer, two of the main architects of postwar Western Europe, meet in Paris on 21 November 1951. Franco-German friendship was the basis of what would take shape as the European Economic Community (and eventually the European Union).

4. Tears from women in Moscow at Stalin's funeral on 9 March 1953. Huge numbers of citizens turned out in bitterly cold weather to mourn their former leader. For countless Soviet citizens, Stalin was a great war hero, not a cruel dictator.

5. (*opposite*) Josip Broz Tito, the President of Yugoslavia, greets the Soviet leader Nikita Khrushchev as he arrives in Belgrade in 1963. The breach in relations between Yugoslavia and the Soviet Union, in existence since 1948, had been officially healed in 1955.

6. A Soviet tank and a building in Budapest destroyed by heavy fighting during the Hungarian uprising of 1956. The brutal Soviet crushing of the uprising shocked the West and gravely damaged the image of the Soviet Union among former admirers, many of whom now ended their membership of western Communist parties.

7. Algerian Harkis, whose former work for the French colonial regime forced them to flee independent Algeria, arrive at a refugee camp in Rivesaltes in southern France on 16 September 1962.

8. Then France's most prominent intellectual, the existentialist philosopher Jean-Paul Sartre, and his partner Simone de Beauvoir, who greatly influenced the early feminist movement, on 22 October 1963 during a visit to Rome.

proletariat' and as such controlled and directed the state. In Yugoslavia it was less clear. Tito set his face, however, against those who wanted to dilute the party's role to the point of near insignificance. Party organizations, Tito stipulated in 1954, would not interfere in the technical management of factories under the workers' councils. 'They must see,' he said, however, 'what general policies are pursued in the enterprises,' and 'they give the tone to the work of the workers' councils.' The vagueness of the demarcation lines did not disguise the ultimate control of the party.

The system functioned. Industrial production rose annually by over 13 per cent between 1953 and 1960, allowing an increase in income of nearly 6 per cent and, after the early years, a greater shift towards spending on consumption than in the Soviet bloc. The impressive economic growth, much of it flowing from investment channelled through the state-controlled banking system, was helped, though not caused, by financial aid from abroad – $553.8 million between 1950 and 1953 – as the United States, in particular, viewed Yugoslavia as a wedge to split communism still further. By the 1960s the beginnings of mass foreign tourism in Europe started to swell Yugoslavia's coffers still further and the extended liberalization of the system made it in Western eyes the most appealing form of communism. Already in the early 1960s, however, economic growth was slowing, and by the middle of the decade unemployment, inflation and a trade deficit were starting to rise – a harbinger of greater problems in the 1970s.

Popular support for Yugoslavian communism in the 1950s probably exceeded that for any of the Soviet satellites. Apart from a higher level of commitment that emanated from somewhat more democratic forms of government, two unique factors conditioned the relative success of Yugoslavian communism. One, certainly in the early years, was the unifying impact of the threat from Stalin. Fear of invasion fostered cohesion, producing 'negative integration' among the different peoples of Yugoslavia. More positively, a sense of identity was built around the figure of Josip Broz Tito himself. The creation of a Tito cult portrayed the leader as the personification of the new socialist Yugoslavia and the embodiment of the partisan heroism that had created the country. Tito's popular standing and prestige meant that he stood supreme over any internal factionalism within the party. The fact that he had a Croatian father and

Slovenian mother helped him, too, to transcend the ethnic divides that had earlier poisoned the country. Liberal disbursement of the usual positions of power, career advancement, privileges, material benefits and the fruits of corruption ensured that party activists and the security police remained loyal. Above all, Tito saw to it that the army – well funded, offering good pay, career opportunities and state housing – always stood behind him. Yugoslavian communism was fortunate that Tito – head of party, state and armed forces – lived so long, dying only in 1980. His personal qualities, political skill and 'charismatic' style of leadership were indispensable to the success and stability of the system. Without him, the divisions that would tear the country apart not long after his death might well have manifested themselves much earlier.

However appealing Tito's rule came to seem as a contrast to the Soviet bloc, it nevertheless had a dark side. Communists loyal to Moscow were heavily persecuted after 1948, around 16,000 of them interned in brutal 're-education' camps. Up to 3,000 of them died there, many of the effects of torture. Although purges within the party never remotely reached Stalinist dimensions, opponents were expelled and – most prominently Tito's arch-critic Milovan Djilas – imprisoned for lengthy terms, as were intellectuals and any others who overstepped the mark in their denigration of the regime. And, as within the Soviet bloc, when collectivization of agriculture – which underpinned the drive to industrialization – was vehemently resisted by the peasantry, prompting an outright rebellion (including former partisans and party members) in one region in 1950, the regime resorted to force. Hundreds of peasants were arrested, the leaders of the revolt sentenced to death. The regime learned the lesson. In 1953 the drive to collectivization was halted and land taken into unproductive cooperatives was given back to the peasants.

The greater flexibility and national roots of communism in Tito's Yugoslavia could cope far better than the Soviet satellites with adjustments to setbacks, and allowed moves to further liberalization of the economy as well as cultural activities in the 1960s. Cinemas showed some films from the West, including Hollywood productions (whose import was subsidised by the United States). Young people could enjoy the music of the Beatles, the Rolling Stones and Jimi Hendrix. Yugoslavia went further than any other Eastern European country in creating space for personal freedom. Yet the limits on behaviour were obvious.

There could be no challenge, not even fundamental written or verbal criticism, to the system. Ultimately, like the Soviet system, coercion – overt or implicit – lay behind it.

TIGHTENING THE CLAMP: THE SOVIET BLOC

The countries of the Soviet bloc were yoked together more tightly than were the liberal democracies of Western Europe. Nevertheless, they did not form a monolith. National traditions and cultures continued to shape their varied development beneath the blanket uniformity of Marxist-Leninist ideology. Their adjustment to the overlordship of the Soviet Union was also conditioned by the ways in which communist rule had been established and consolidated. They did not, therefore, react in uniform fashion to the changed climate following Stalin's death.

In the Balkan countries of Romania, Bulgaria and Albania there was, in fact, scarcely any loosening of the clamp at all. In Czechoslovakia, too, it remained tightly fastened. In the German Democratic Republic in 1953, then in Poland and, above all, Hungary in 1956, however, it was an altogether different story. There the scale of mass protest shook Soviet leaders, who responded with force to suppress the grave threat to their authority. What accounts for these differences within the Soviet bloc?

Of fundamental importance was whether the communist leadership in each country retained undisputed control of the apparatus of power and could direct policy without internal challenge or 'correction' from Moscow. The power of the regime's leadership itself rested heavily upon the support of the security services, whose loyalty was 'bought' by the extension of material benefits within the system. Extreme levels of repression then served to deter oppositional activity. Where repression was less extreme, and where the perception existed that the regime's leadership could be changed or policy substantially altered, the likelihood of significant expressions of political nonconformity was greatly enhanced. This was itself more probable where there was a well-established social and political infrastructure (such as through trade unions) that provided the capacity, even under a repressive regime, to organize forms of resistance. Where a particularly strong sense of nationality existed (which could tap long-standing aversions to Russia, only superficially varnished over by ideological 'fraternity' with the Soviet Union), as it did in Poland and Hungary, there was the potential for opposition to spread and gain extensive support. Organizational capacity was lower in the economically less advanced Balkan countries where traditional social and political infrastructures resting on large rural populations and a relatively small industrial working class persisted.

The Old Order Upheld

One of the most fanatical and ruthless communist leaders was the Romanian dictator, Gheorghe Gheorghiu-Dej. He had outmanoeuvred his rivals for power, Lucrețiu Pătrășcanu, Vasile Luca and Ana Pauker, and by the time of Stalin's death was in complete control as state premier and head of the party. He presided over a huge and utterly brutal security apparatus that ran a camp system reminiscent of the worst times of the Gulag in the Soviet Union under Stalin. Tens of thousands of Romanians from all sectors of society, but especially from the peasantry during the drive for collectivization of agriculture (which had begun in 1949–50), were incarcerated, many of them subjected to torture. Further tens of thousands became slave labourers on a massive construction project, the building of the Danube–Black Sea Canal. The slavery was pointless as well as grossly inhumane; reductions in Soviet economic support led to the suspension of work in 1953, leaving the canal unfinished. Work began again only two decades later.

Unchallenged in power and in control of a formidable police state, Dej was in a good position to resist the moves to reform introduced in the Soviet Union by Khrushchev. As a nod towards collective leadership he resigned as party leader in 1954 but took the post back again the following year, appointing his acolyte Chivu Stoica as Prime Minister. And he found scapegoats for earlier failings, denouncing his former rivals, Pătrășcanu, Luca and Pauker as 'Stalinists' – a classic case of the pot calling the kettle black. Control of the party and the security forces provided the basis of Dej's power. Internal unrest was contained. Peasant resistance, which had begun in the late 1940s in protest at collectivization, was, despite ruthless repression, far from fully extinguished, but the largely sporadic guerrilla activity in the hills and forests lacked the capacity to threaten the regime's existence. And when, in autumn 1956, encouraged by events in Poland and Hungary, student protest burst out in the universities, it was violently put down by the secret police, the notorious Securitate, among the largest and most brutal repressive organizations in Eastern Europe. Dej's strong support for the Soviet suppression of the Hungarian uprising in October gave him a bargaining counter with Khrushchev. Soviet economic impositions in Romania were pared back. And Dej's hold on power was left intact. Far from loosening the clamp of Stalinism, in Romania it was tightened.

By the later 1950s Romania not only had a largely unreconstructed Stalinist regime, but was in some ways developing a form of national communism, at odds with Soviet economic imperatives for the 'socialist division of labour' in its satellite states. In particular, the Romanian leadership's economic priority – to force the industrialization of the country – did not accord with Soviet expectations. These, pursued through the Comecon organization (set up in 1949 to coordinate the economies of Soviet bloc countries), were aimed at keeping Romania permanently as an agrarian state and mere supplier of agricultural products and raw materials. At stake especially, however, was the wider question of Soviet intervention in the internal affairs of other states. The Romanian leadership had to tread carefully, though it was helped by the Soviet Union's anxiety to avoid a showdown such as had taken place in Hungary. So the more semi-detached relationship of Romania with the USSR continued. The pursuit of quasi-independence within the Communist bloc was still in its early stages when Dej died in 1965, and was followed by his equally brutal successor Nicolae Ceauşescu.

In Bulgaria, too, the Stalinist clamp remained tightly applied. Unlike Romania, where long-ingrained anti-Russian feelings in the population had merely been glossed over by the imposition of communist rule (and, in fact, where the Soviet annexation of Bessarabia and northern Bukovina in 1940 still rankled), Bulgaria had a long tradition of pro-Russian and pan-Slavic sentiment and after the war became the most slavishly loyal of all the Eastern European satellites of the Soviet Union. The Bulgarian leader, Vâlko Chervenkov, was another Stalinist clone, by 1950 both Prime Minister and the party's General Secretary. Unlike Dej in Romania, however, he lost much of his power following Stalin's death.

This was not before he had done much to ruin the agricultural base of the country by destroying peasant smallholdings and forcing through inefficient collective farms that saw productivity fall sharply. Chervenkov followed Soviet demands in the immediate post-Stalin era in relaxing some of the most stringent controls and by improving housing and production of consumer goods. Bulgaria remained, however, an intensely poor and backward country with miserable living standards and a high economic dependency on the Soviet Union.

Chervenkov also complied with Soviet insistence on the separation of party and state positions of leadership, stepping down as party Secretary in 1954 in favour of Todor Zhivkov – born into a peasant family in 1911, and now, after working his way up the party's echelons, Europe's youngest communist leader. Two years later, following Khrushchev's denunciation of Stalin's cult of personality, Chervenkov was additionally forced to resign as Prime Minister. As was the case in Romania, however, Bulgaria did not publish Khrushchev's damaging speech. There was a very brief interlude of limited tolerance of literary expression before the clamp was put firmly in place again. Offending journalists were expelled and constraints imposed on publishing. The Soviet suppression of the Hungarian uprising was greatly welcomed as an opportunity to reimpose strict state controls. Stalinism had never gone away and was now again reinforced.

Factional infighting continued for some years at the top of the party, resulting in Chervenkov's removal from the Politiburo in 1961 after Khrushchev's second major attack on Stalinism at the 1961 party Congress. Zhikov was by this time Bulgaria's undisputed leader, now Prime Minister as well as party Secretary. His supporters were placed in all the key positions at the top of the party. Bulgaria, economically dependent upon the Soviet Union, remained a subservient Stalinist satellite – practically another Soviet republic. As Zhikov stated after Khrushchev had visited the country in 1962, Bulgaria's watch was set to Moscow time.

The poorest country in the Soviet bloc was the smallest, Albania. It had been under monarchical dictatorship for most of the interwar period and had then been occupied during the war by first Italy, then Germany. Unlike Romania and Bulgaria, Yugoslavian partisans and not the Red Army had been responsible for the establishment of a communist regime there. But when Tito broke with Stalin in 1948 the communist leadership,

which had become increasingly antagonistic towards Yugoslavian economic exploitation, abruptly switched allegiance to the Soviet Union,
gaining extensive economic assistance in return. Enver Hoxha, head of
party and state since 1946 and a fervent admirer of Stalin, crushed all
internal opposition in ruthless purges and, backed by a tight, nepotistic
ruling circle, gained absolute dominance over Albania that would last
until his death in 1985.

The greater the threats – real and perceived – from neighbouring
Yugoslavia, the more Hoxha could pose as a national leader defending
his country, one that he ruled with a rod of iron. Draconian repression,
including the execution of thousands of real or supposed adversaries,
was a hallmark of his regime. A quarter of party members had been
expelled or arrested in the purge that followed the break with Yugoslavia. The collectivization of agriculture from the mid-1950s, highly
unpopular as elsewhere among the peasantry, was accompanied by further heavy repression. Fully fledged Stalinism remained in place.
Following the death of the revered Stalin, however, problems with the
Soviet Union had started to mount. Hoxha had no truck with the post-
Stalin reforms, and was appalled by Khrushchev's denunciation of Stalin
in 1956. He fully approved of the suppression of the Hungarian uprising,
whose roots he saw in the revisionism of Tito. But he was alienated by
Khrushchev's rapprochement with the arch-enemy, Tito, as well as by
Soviet insistence on Albania's perceived future as a supplier of agricul-
tural produce, ignoring its industrialization programme.

The alienation led to Hoxha transferring his allegiance once more.
When China split with the Soviet Union in 1960–61, Hoxha switched to
backing Mao Zedong's China, which offered the economic support that
had been lacking from Moscow and a leadership model more amenable
to his own personality cult. Albania increasingly went its own way,
largely isolated from the rest of Europe, east and west, and declining still
further into an economic backwater that could provide only a miserable
standard of living for the Albanian people. This did not, however, undermine Hoxha's entrenched position as leader, which was upheld by further
repression and control of all the levers of power. Unlike the other communist countries of Eastern Europe, Albania remained staunchly
Stalinist. The clamp here had never been loosened at all.

On the face of it, Czechoslovakia had more in common with the

countries – East Germany, Poland and Hungary – where serious disturbances challenged Soviet domination than with the quiescent Balkan
regimes. Traditions of national independence, especially in the Czech
lands, had long roots. A democratic pluralist political culture had been
well established before Hitler destroyed it. A modernized industrial
economy, though less developed in Slovakia, had produced a strong
working class and a social infrastructure that bore little resemblance to
the clientelism of the heavily agrarian Balkan states. There was a large
intelligentsia and sizeable student population. Why, then, did the Soviet
Union encounter no significant trouble from Czechoslovakia in the years
after Stalin's death?

As elsewhere, the Soviet assault on the Hungarian rebels in 1956 had a
strong deterrent effect in Czechoslovakia. But why had the Soviet Union
faced no significant problem before then from the Czechs and Slovaks? In
fact, there *had* been a serious wave of strikes in Czechoslovakia in May
1953, triggered by the announcement of a swingeing currency devaluation to be introduced the next month (widely dubbed 'the Great Swindle')
and following months of sharply rising prices and falling living standards. Strikers from the Škoda factory in Plzeň had even thrown busts of
Lenin, Stalin and Klement Gottwald (the Czech communist leader, who
had died within days of Stalin's death) out of the window of the town
hall, which they had occupied. But the disturbances were savagely put
down by the police and never developed into the outright challenge to the
regime similar to that which was shortly to explode in the German
Democratic Republic.

The level of repression is itself a major part of the reason why unrest
in Czechoslovakia was contained relatively easily. Repression does not,
however, offer a complete explanation. Another strand lies in the appeal
of communism within Czechoslovakia. Unlike some parts of the Soviet
bloc, communism was not an alien ideology, imposed by an external
force. It enjoyed, in fact, a broad base of home-grown popular support.
The Communist Party had won more seats than any other party as far
back as 1925. Its support had swelled in the immediate aftermath of the
Second World War, bringing it nearly two-fifths of the votes in free elections in 1946. Early steps following the coup of 1948 to nationalize big
business and to eliminate the ownership of large landed estates were
widely popular. The party offered many a route to advancement. And it

could manipulate opinion. It was not only able to eliminate political rivals, but also to extend its own control and influence through the take-over of, for example, youth and sporting organizations, and through a monopoly of propaganda and orchestration of the mass media. Even so, repression was never far away – the unmistakable backcloth to the communist penetration of society.

The five years of communist rule had, in fact, been characterized by brutal repression under a leadership that repeatedly showed utter ruth-lessness in purging real or imagined opponents and in consolidating a firm hold on power that passed seamlessly on the death of Klement Gott-wald to Antonín Novotný, his successor as First Secretary of the party. Show trials of former political adversaries on trumped-up charges of treason and anti-state activity had begun in 1949, inevitably ending in death sentences or long terms of imprisonment. Stalin's suspicions of Czech and Slovak leaders' connections with foreign intelligence and their links with the Titoist anathema in Yugoslavia, together with his increas-ingly paranoid antisemitism, lay behind the purges.

These culminated in the arrest, show trial, forced false confession (reminiscent of the Stalinist purges of the 1930s) and execution as traitors and 'enemies of the people', in 1952, of the former General Secretary of the Czechoslovakian Communist Party, Rudolf Slánský, and eleven other communist leaders. Ominously, they were described as being 'of Jewish origin'. A sharp resurgence of antisemitism, prompted by the racist slurs of the party leadership, accompanied the purges in Czechoslovakia. Heda Margolius Kovály, herself Jewish, a former prisoner in Auschwitz, and married to a Jew, later recalled, 'When the arrests first started, it was generally assumed that the accused were guilty of something.' This was before her husband, Rudolf, was arrested, tried and executed as part of the imaginary Slánský conspiracy.

The spectacular show trials were only the tip of the iceberg of repres-sion in Czechoslovakia. Thousands of citizens were denounced and imprisoned, or worse, for alleged offences against the state. As elsewhere in Eastern Europe, however, the execution of the feared Lavrenti Beria in December 1953 sent a signal that a new wind was blowing in the Soviet Union. Czechoslovakia, too, had to adjust to the changed climate. The years between the death of Stalin and Khrushchev's assault on his mem-ory in February 1956 brought the release of many prisoners in

Czechoslovakia, though like released prisoners in the Soviet Union and elsewhere these faced an uncertain and often hostile welcome on their return from incarceration. There was a limited relaxation of controls on censorship, permitting some muted criticism of aspects of Soviet rule. And the atmosphere that brought the purges, fomented by the earlier antagonism between the Soviet Union and Yugoslavia, disappeared. But the repression had done its work. It had certainly not been without a basis of popular support. And the party leaders, bound together by their backing for the purges, made only minimal concessions to change.

Two years after his death, a colossal statue of Stalin, flanked by peasants, workers and intellectuals, was unveiled in 1955 in Prague. Standing high above the Vltava River the statue, 12 metres wide, 22 metres long, 15 metres high, could be seen all over the city. Ordinary citizens remarked – though not openly – that it looked like a queue for scarce meat. But it was a prominent sign of continuity at precisely the moment when Stalin's legacy was being called into question.

Khrushchev's denunciation of Stalin in 1956 posed difficulties for the Czech leadership. Their own purges and show trials had, after all, been carried out in accordance with Soviet imperatives. Novotný and the other Czech leaders found themselves obliged to pay lip service to the new course under Khrushchev while heading off major reforms. There was some cautious criticism of Stalinism in the lower ranks of the party. More strident demands for reform came from students in Prague and Bratislava, then at other universities and colleges across the country. Among the demands was the call for an investigation into the trials of Slánský and others together with punishment for those who carried out 'illegal procedures during interrogations'.

The student protest peaked in May 1956, then simmered, but did not escalate any further before events in Poland, then Hungary, posed a plain deterrent to action against the regime. Cultural dissent was vehemently attacked, and powerful voices in the Czech intelligentsia even backed the constraints on criticism. There was no liberalization as the party sustained its hold, introducing a new Five-Year Plan in 1956 that rested on the usual lines of maximizing production in heavy industry and the extended collectivization of agriculture.

The party leaders closed ranks. The changed climate in the autumn also gave them the opportunity to quash what would have been a damaging report on the purges and to reimpose their own stringent control. Novotný's position was strengthened in November 1957 when, on the death of Antonín Zápotocký (who had been responsible for handing Slánský over to the tender mercies of the security services), he became President of the Republic (head of state) as well as First Secretary of the party. A new constitution in 1960 substantially reduced Slovakian autonomy, and the control of the party's 'Fraternal Cooperation' with the USSR was expressly underlined. With that the threat to the party's power that had materialized in 1953, then again in 1956, had passed. Terroristic repression of the vintage of the early 1950s was no longer necessary, though the underlying intimidation continued. For the mass of the population the prospect of significant change seemed remote. So most Czech and Slovak citizens conformed. It was often without enthusiasm, sometimes resentfully. But more was not needed to sustain political stability. For now the regime remained firmly in place.

The Old Order Threatened

The German Democratic Republic (GDR, or East Germany as it was usually called in the West) came to be regarded as Moscow's most important ally. But in 1953 it was the first country east of the Iron Curtain in which an uprising had to be put down by Soviet armed force. Why, uniquely in the eastern bloc, did trouble flare up so strikingly in 1953? Why, in contrast, did the GDR remain quiet three years later when first Poland and then Hungary rebelled against Soviet domination? And how did the GDR change so categorically from being a trouble spot to the most dependable acolyte in the Soviet bloc?

East Germany in the early 1950s had an obvious Achilles heel. It was the only Soviet satellite that was an entirely new state, one created out of military occupation and the break-up of a former nation state. Only a narrow border separated it from the ideologically hostile political system and booming economy of West Germany. And that border was porous. Even after 1952, when it was sealed across its entire length, the special status of Berlin, under the control of four great powers, left a crucial opening. There it remained possible, if with difficulty, to cross to the West, and to a different (to many, more attractive) lifestyle. That very fact put the East German leadership under some pressure, since the growing exodus – over 360,000 in 1952 and early 1953 – could not be stemmed. The exodus itself reflected low living standards, a consequence of an economy directed, along Stalinist lines, towards the growth of heavy industry at the cost of production for consumer needs.

The East German regime also had to contend with another weakness. In Moscow's eyes East Germany was dispensable as the price for attaining a bigger goal – a reunified but neutral and demilitarized Germany. That goal had not been abandoned by the early 1950s. Stalin had tried to tempt the West into accepting it in 1952, but he met with a prompt rebuff. After his death the idea was resuscitated. Were it to succeed the East German leadership would see its power base vanish. But when, following Stalin's death, Soviet leaders – effectively the short-lived collective of Malenkov, Molotov and Beria – responded positively to Winston Churchill's suggestion of a Four-Power Conference to discuss a German peace treaty, involving free elections and the neutralization of a reunified country, a split opened up among East German leaders. The main faction, under the Stalinist diehard Walter Ulbricht, General Secretary of the Socialist Unity Party (SED, formed in 1946 from the forced merger of the Communist and Social Democratic parties, but wholly under communist domination), was utterly opposed. Another faction in the East German leadership, however, headed by Rudolf Herrnstadt (editor of the main SED newspaper, *Neues Deutschland*) and Wilhelm Zaisser (Minister of State Security), favoured economic reforms aimed at improving the living standards of the population (and reduced dependence on the Soviet model). They appeared at first to have backing in Moscow. Soviet leaders contemplated deposing Ulbricht. His leadership stood on shaky ground.

The factional disputes and divisions in leadership, in some respects mirroring the uncertainties in Moscow in the immediate aftermath of Stalin's death, were exposed even in the controlled press of the GDR and played a vital part in fostering the unrest that led to the uprising in June 1953. On 9 June the Politburo, bowing to the pressure to follow the Soviet Union's 'new course' (after Ulbricht and other top leaders had been summoned to Moscow and firmly told what was necessary), agreed to introduce limited economic reforms to improve living standards. The decision, made public two days later, prompted wild rumours about the reasons for the change. Some speculated that there had been a putsch against the party leadership, that Ulbricht had been arrested or shot, that the SED was on the point of breaking apart, and that the borders would be opened. Remarkably, the abrupt reversal of previous policy (hugely unsettling to those party workers who had faithfully upheld the need for unpopular measures) was accompanied by the damaging admission that mistakes had been made. Even more remarkably, while peasants, white-collar workers and the self-employed stood to gain in modest fashion, industrial workers – the very bedrock of the Marxist-Leninist ideology – faced a decline in their living standards. On 28 May the regime had already decreed a 10 per cent increase in production levels ('work norms'), which it saw as necessary to counter the country's severe economic problems. Workers would, therefore, have to work more for the same pay – in effect, a wage reduction. Amazingly, the communiqué of 9 June had made no mention at all of the raised work norms.

The divisions in the leadership soon became evident. On 14 June the increase in work norms was directly criticized in an article in *Neues Deutschland*. But two days later the diametrically opposite stance was presented in the official trade union newspaper, *Tribüne*, which supported the increases. It was unheard of for the leadership to air their fundamental disagreements in public. It served only to advertise weakness and confusion. It was later admitted that the *Tribüne* article triggered the conversion of the simmering discontent into open protest, first voiced by building workers in East Berlin.

In spontaneous meetings the workers demanded the cancellation of the increased productivity norms. The protests escalated and on 16 June a 10,000-strong angry crowd gathered outside the House of Ministers, the central government building. Once more the leadership sent mixed signals, suggesting with one voice that the raised work norms would be rescinded, but with another merely that they would be reconsidered. The crowd started to become more radical. Some demanded the resignation of the government. The demonstrations reflected the significant unrest that had been building for some days amid the speculation about the leadership and expectations that change was on the way. They were outbursts of spontaneous protest, without planning, orchestrated leadership or organization. But when one worker grabbed a loudspeaker and announced a general strike for the following day, there was immediate and widespread support. On 17 June the strikes spread to 373 towns and cities across East Germany. Half a million workers in 186 factories took part. Nor was the protest any longer confined to strikes. Other sectors of society joined in – over a million people in more than 700 places during the following five days. Around 250 party offices and other public buildings were attacked. Some 1,400 political prisoners were freed from jails (though most were soon rearrested). What had started as a protest about work norms had turned into a mass uprising against the regime.

SED leaders were in shock. The protests had quickly gained unexpected momentum. And there were concerns that the police might sympathize with the striking workers. The Soviet military commander in Berlin had on 16 June turned down a request for aid. A day later, however, presumably seeing that the protest was starting to run out of control and not trusting the GDR police to restore order, the Soviet authorities changed their mind. Warning shots were fired at midday. At 12.30 p.m. Soviet tanks started to rumble through the streets of East Berlin. Shortly afterwards the Soviet military administration imposed a state of emergency on the city, soon extending it to much of the GDR and retaining it until 11 July. At first the Soviet tanks advanced slowly, aiming to quieten the demonstrators through the show of intimidation. Tank crews even waved at the crowds, which in turn avoided any provocation, reserving their anger for the East German regime. But the uneasy stand-off could not last. It soon led to shots being fired. Demonstrators scattered, running for their lives. Some of those who remained threw stones at the tanks, shouting abuse at the Soviet occupiers.

By the evening of 17 June the show of Soviet might had done its work. There had been violent clashes of demonstrators with police and Soviet forces in a number of East German towns and cities – notably, outside Berlin, in Leipzig, Halle, Magdeburg and Bitterfeld – but the futility of combating Soviet military power was swiftly obvious to most protesters. One witness to events in Magdeburg, a schoolboy at the time, recalled that as the first Soviet tanks fired at the demonstrators, 'it was plain to everyone that the feeling of freedom had been a brief one'. Although signs of lingering unrest persisted for some weeks, the uprising was over.

What the disparate groups of protesters had wanted, apart from the remedying of immediate economic grievances, was not altogether clear. It is far from certain that the majority favoured Western capitalist liberal democracy, or had any specific alternative political model in mind. Many still believed in socialism. They had simply hoped – and in utopian fashion continued to hope – for a better way to a genuine socialist society. The demands – including cries of 'down with the SED', 'government resign', 'free elections', 'reunification', 'withdrawal of occupation forces from Germany' – nevertheless radically challenged the very existence of the GDR. Lacking the possibility of a clear oppositional stance, let alone a political programme, protest was bound to remain inchoate – an elemental outburst of anger and deep discontent rather than a preconceived and articulate expression of demands for a fundamental change of the system. The uprising nonetheless shook the SED regime at its roots.

Dozens of demonstrators – estimates vary between sixty and eighty – were killed in the clashes, along with ten to fifteen party functionaries and members of the security forces. The reprisals for the rebellion were ruthless. Over 6,000 people involved in the uprising were arrested by the end of June, another 7,000 later, and sentenced to lengthy periods of imprisonment. Several of those viewed as ringleaders were executed without any formal judicial procedure. Those in the party who had been seen to rock the boat were vigorously purged. Over the following months tens of thousands of functionaries and ordinary party members were denounced as 'provocateurs' and dismissed from their positions. And to ensure that the regime could never again lose control, the police and State Security Service (Stasi) were greatly strengthened, assisted by an elaborate network of informers constructed to spy on ordinary citizens.

The feeling of euphoria at challenging the regime had gripped the demonstrators only for a few hours. But the memory of Soviet tanks on East German streets firing on protesters, and the brutal way in which the uprising was suppressed, was long-lasting. Rebellion had brought bloodshed and repression. The hopes that some had placed in intervention by the Western powers had been illusory. (The GDR leadership had absurdly blamed 'American and West German sabotage organizations and fascists' for the uprising. In fact, the danger of sparking an international conflagration meant that the West refrained from any inkling of intervention.) The main and obvious lesson that contemporaries drew was that protest against overwhelming military power was pointless; the SED regime could not be overthrown as long as it had the backing of the Soviet Union. There was no willingness to repeat the failed experiment of 1953. That basic feeling sufficed to keep East Germany quiet when Poland and Hungary erupted in 1956.

Repression was only one side of the response to the uprising. It was accompanied by concessions. Within days the Central Committee of the SED retracted the unpopular increase in wage norms that had been the immediate cause of the trouble. Other modest but tangible improvements to living standards followed. Industrial production targets under the Five-Year Plan (to run over the years 1951 to 1955) were adjusted to reduce spending on heavy industry in favour of somewhat higher spending on consumer goods, while educational reforms stretching from primary school to university also sought to widen social advancement for children from working-class backgrounds. A new generation, socialized in the values of the regime from the cradle onwards, influenced too by incessant anti-Western propaganda, gradually formed the basis of more solid future political support than had existed in 1953.

Most people complied with the demands of the regime. But compliance is not consensus. Conformity was not just encouraged, but enforced. There was enormous resentment at the constraints of the system, the coerced uniformity, living standards inferior to those in West Germany, the presence of the security police, and the pervasive threat of denunciation. Informing, spying, denunciation ran through the society and provided an essential basis of social control for the regime. Those who did not conform encountered at the very least significant disadvantages – for example in housing, jobs, education – that affected living standards for themselves and their families. Some faced greater deterrents to non-conformist action. For the minority who still made their dissatisfaction openly felt, the big stick was never far away. The basic lack of freedom, except within the narrow parameters of the system, meant that, ultimately, it rested on the mechanisms of control and repression. Short of removing the system itself, this could not be altered.

Perversely, the uprising of June 1953 saved Walter Ulbricht. His leadership had been wobbling before the mass protest. Beria's arrest soon after the uprising had signalled that the die had been cast in Moscow against those who favoured a change of course in the GDR. Moscow's need to shore up the regime left Ulbricht in a far stronger position as the internal purges removed opponents and the SED tightened its control over state government. The removal of Ulbricht would have been seen as weakness, inviting further demands. The Soviet leadership had no wish to add to their troubles by trying to remove a loyalist hardliner in Berlin. The instability in the eastern bloc following Khrushchev's denunciation of Stalin in 1956, then, especially the uprising in Hungary in the autumn of that year, saved Ulbricht anew. It showed again what could happen if the clamp were loosened. Ulbricht was therefore able to silence his critics and bolster his own position of power once more.

He was helped, too, by Moscow's effective abandonment, as West Germany remilitarized then gained national sovereignty, of the quest for a unified, neutralized Germany and acceptance that the GDR was here to stay. A sign of this was Soviet relinquishment of further reparations from the GDR, which had inflicted great damage on its economy. Another was the extension of Soviet credit and restrictions on the cost of supporting Soviet troops in the GDR. Internationally, too, the GDR was more closely bound to the Soviet Union. Its fate, as the events of June 1953 had shown, depended entirely on Soviet backing. In May 1955 it became a member of the newly created Warsaw Pact, and remained over the following decades the Soviet Union's most staunch and loyal supporter in foreign affairs.

The building of the Berlin Wall starting in August 1961 was the culmination of the shift in the Soviet approach to the GDR and of the internal changes in the country that had followed the shock of the 1953 uprising. For the Soviet Union and for the East German regime, it brought lasting stabilization. For the people of East Germany it meant accepting what they could not change.

After the dramatic events in the GDR the Soviet Union faced no further great turbulence in its satellite countries of Eastern Europe until the aftermath of Khrushchev's sensational speech in February 1956. The intervening years had been unsettled across the eastern bloc as communist leaders had tried to adjust in different ways to the 'new course' in the Soviet Union. But Khrushchev, once his own pre-eminence as leader had been established, made attempts to weld the eastern bloc countries closer together. The formation of the Warsaw Pact in May 1955 – an immediate response to the remilitarization of West Germany – was an important step. So was the reconciliation with Tito in 1956 that restored relations between the Soviet and Yugoslav communist parties. This came at a time, however, when, in the months after Khrushchev's speech, the Soviet

Union faced an unprecedented challenge to its authority in Eastern Europe, one that even put the uprising in the GDR in the summer of 1953 in the shade.

The problems that arose in Poland and Hungary were separate but – certainly in Soviet eyes – interrelated. The unrest in Poland spilled over in the autumn of 1956 into the far greater threat from the mounting insurgency in Hungary. There were significant differences between the two countries, though also some common threads to the unrest. In both countries challenges to the party leadership made the respective regimes vulnerable, offering the chance for the disaffected to press for change – as had happened in the GDR. In both countries long-standing anti-Russian (and anti-Soviet) feelings, together with a notably strong sense of national identity, persisted beneath the blanket of communist rule. In both countries intellectuals and sizeable student populations felt choked by the constraints on free expression. And in both countries the priorities given to spending on heavy industry and capital products at the expense of consumer goods had led to significant discontent, notably among the working class. The pressures for reform, finally, in each country had been sharpened by the awareness of the post-Stalin atmosphere of change in the Soviet Union, especially after Khrushchev's speech in February 1956.

Poland had effectively been handed over to communist control through the triumph of the Red Army over Hitler's forces in 1944–5. Over the next decade the country became thoroughly 'Stalinized', creating an enormous bureaucratic machinery of control and massive state security system. By 1954 the Ministry of Public Security had a card index on 'criminal and suspicious elements' covering almost a third of the adult population – much of the information having been supplied through the denunciations of 85,000 informers scattered through all levels of society. The celebrated Polish writer Maria Dąbrowska lamented in her diary her country's 'great chalice of bitterness', its 'missed chance of socialism'.

Stalin had remarked, however, that 'introducing communism to Poland was like putting a saddle on a cow'. Under the Stalinist puppet leader, the President and General Secretary of the Party, Bolesław Bierut, and the Vice-Premier and Minister of Defence Marshal Konstanty Rokossowski (who was there to ensure Soviet control), the Poles were never happy to dance to Moscow's tune. After Stalin's death the reluctance became more evident. Some attempt was made to adjust to new times.

Moves to collectivize farming were slowed down on party orders. Censorship was relaxed. And in late 1954 the former communist leader, Władisław Gomułka, the chief rival to Bierut and long under house arrest following his advocacy of a more independent Polish route to communism, was released. In 1955 the Warsaw Youth Festival, attended by an estimated 30,000 young people drawn from 114 countries, then gave Poles a glimpse of a more open, less regimented outside world. After Bierut's death – he had died suddenly in Moscow after attending Khrushchev's speech, it seems from a heart attack or stroke presumably brought on by the shock at the denunciation of Stalin – his successor, Edward Ochab, continued the limited de-Stalinization, freeing and amnestying around 9,000 political prisoners in April. He spoke, too, the same month of possibilities of a 'new democratization of our political and economic life', though few specifics emerged to satisfy raised expectations.

There was little to be seen of reform and democracy when in June the complaints of factory workers in Poznań, incensed by a peremptory demand for a 25 per cent increase in productivity without a commensurate rise in wages (shades of East Germany three years earlier), fell on deaf ears. It sparked a strike by tens of thousands of workers in and around Poznań by the end of the month, and, as in East Germany, initial economic demands soon became political. Calls for 'bread and freedom' turned into 'Russians Go Home'. Prisoners were freed by workers from the local jail, weapons were seized from the guards, and the headquarters of party and police were attacked. The regime brought in 10,000 troops and 400 tanks from the Polish army to quell the trouble as unrest threatened to spread to other cities. The troops opened fire on the strikers leaving seventy-three dead and hundreds injured. They suppressed the rising within two days, though they could not eradicate the disaffection that lay behind it. Blame was largely directed at the Minister of Defence, Rokossowski (of Polish origin though a Soviet citizen), and a number of other Soviet citizens in the army leadership who had given the orders to fire on the striking workers. The result was increased pressure to end Soviet involvement in the army (specifically, the withdrawal of Rokossowski). There were also demands for a democratization of communist rule (including, for example, workers' self-management and a revival of parliament and local councils) in Poland and for the return of Gomułka, viewed as the face of the necessary reform.

There was powerful internal opposition to such a step from a conservative faction with influence in the Polish military and security services, which was anxious to prevent any weakening of ties with the Soviet Union and encouraged a tough stance from Moscow. Soviet worries that Gomułka would take Poland down a more independent route, enhanced by his demand for the release from office of Rokossowski, prompted a heavyweight delegation of Soviet leaders, including Khrushchev himself, and military top brass to Warsaw on 19 October. Tense deliberations headed by Khrushchev and Gomułka followed. The Soviet side pressed for a strengthening of the ties between the two countries. Gomułka repeated the demand for the removal of Rokossowski and fifty soviet military 'advisers' to the Polish army. While the negotiations proceeded, Gomułka was told that Soviet tank and military units were advancing on Warsaw. Polish combat units were ordered to take up defensive positions to protect the city. Armed conflict between Poland and the Soviet Union seemed close. Khrushchev blinked first, bowing to Gomułka's request to halt troop movements, and the immediate danger passed. On 21 October Gomułka was duly restored as First Party Secretary. Back in Moscow, Khrushchev was nonetheless heard to remark ominously that 'there's only one way out – by putting an end to what is in Poland'.

Within a few days he had backed away from immediate military intervention, saying it would be easy to find a reason for armed conflict, 'but finding a way to put an end to such a conflict later on would be very hard'. Soviet leaders believed that the Poles would put up strong armed resistance to intervention and would mobilize worker militias in the cause. There was agreement that the Soviet Union should 'refrain from military intervention' and 'display patience' for the time being. Khrushchev instead sought a political solution, reluctantly agreeing to the removal of Rokossowski, withdrawn as Minister of Defence on 29 October. Another indicator that Moscow was looking to calm the situation in Poland was the freeing on 28 October of Cardinal Stefan Wyszyński, the head of the Polish Catholic Church, from the detention in which he had been placed in 1953.

The massive displays of public support for Gomułka in huge rallies – over 100,000 in several major cities, half a million in Warsaw – probably encouraged Khrushchev to back down from all-out confrontation. Gomułka for his part assured Khrushchev that Poland would remain a loyal member of the Warsaw Pact and publicly condemned those who had expressed opposition to this. He exhorted citizens to return to work and to end the demonstrations. What undoubtedly most concentrated Soviet minds, however, and pushed Khrushchev to seek a rapprochement rather than order military intervention, was the deteriorating situation in Hungary, which by 26 October 1956 had already boiled up into a crisis far more dangerous than Poland's. And to deal with that, the Soviets wanted to ensure calm in Poland – indeed to have the support of the Polish leadership.

The tense conflict in Poland played a part in the immediate background to unleashing what soon became a full-scale revolution. Hungary had long been an uneasy component of the Soviet bloc. The country was kept under control by heavy repression, in which widespread disaffection with the Stalinist leadership was never far from the surface. Mátyás Rákosi had returned from wartime exile in Moscow to stamp his authority in Stalinist fashion on the path to dominance of the Hungarian Communist Party, destroying the far more popular Smallholders' Party in a prolonged, bitter struggle and cementing his complete control. Rákosi then demonstrated his credentials as Hungary's 'little Stalin' when in 1949, in toadying acquiescence with Moscow's line, he acceded to the show trial and execution (for supporting the 'Titoist deviation' and allegedly involvement with Western intelligence services) of László Rajk, the former Minister of the Interior. But with the introduction of the Soviet 'new course' after the death of Stalin, Rákosi's days were numbered.

With the economy in crisis, peasants resisting collectivization, workers striking on account of falling wages, and bulging jails, Rákosi and other party leaders were summoned to Moscow in June 1953 and told in no uncertain terms to put their house in order. Rákosi's 'high-handed and domineering style', Soviet leaders told him, had led to 'mistakes and crimes' and had taken Hungary 'to the brink of catastrophe'. Despite such an indictment, he was left in office as party leader though forced to surrender his position as head of government to Imre Nagy, the people's favourite and hope of disillusioned communists, who had been expelled from the Politburo in 1949 for opposing the speed of collectivization.

A crucial division in the communist leadership thereby opened up. This played no small role in boosting the growing unrest in the country, exposing Moscow's lack of confidence in Rákosi and indicating an alternative, more attractive form of leadership. Nagy lost no time in advocating economic changes to improve the supply of consumer goods. More radically, he proposed reinvigorating communism by democratization at the grass roots. He envisaged a mass base of support, organized in a new popular front, the Patriotic People's Party, which would blend national sentiment with democratic socialism. The Communist Party would play a leading role in Nagy's scheme, but would not simply rule from above. This was naturally anathema to Rákosi and the party hardliners. By early 1955 Rákosi's machinations against Nagy had proved successful. Nagy was condemned for ideological 'deviation', expelled from the party's Politburo and by the end of the year, from the party itself.

The situation in Hungary, therefore, was already brittle even before Khrushchev's speech in February 1956 created a new, hugely disturbed climate. Intellectuals and students, stirred by the prospect of a more democratic route to communism that Nagy had opened up and angry at repression and censorship, engaged in intense political debate about Hungary's future. Workers, incensed at their treatment in a supposedly 'workers' state', felt exploited by 'a bloodsucking government'. Groups of workers even met young intellectuals and joined in debates that were attended by growing numbers of people. Many of the debates were organized by the Petőfi Circle (named after a revolutionary fighter for Hungarian independence in 1848). It was from the Petőfi Circle, which had attracted as many as 6,000 people to an evening meeting in Budapest in June 1956, that the call came for Rákosi to be ousted and replaced by Nagy. Moscow responded. Rákosi duly resigned – officially on health grounds – in July. His replacement was, however, not Nagy but the hapless Ernő Gerő, cut from much the same ideological cloth as Rákosi himself.

Serious trouble was not long in coming. The start of the 'Budapest autumn' was 6 October 1956 when attacks on the regime were voiced by tens of thousands of demonstrators gathered for the solemn reburial (with Gerő's reluctant permission) of the rehabilitated László Rajk – the former security chief, now an unlikely symbol of the desired liberalization. By 23 October, inspired by events in Poland, student-led demonstrations in Budapest and other cities posed radical demands. These included the reinstatement of Nagy as Prime Minister (he had been readmitted to the party ten days earlier), the withdrawal of Soviet troops, punishment of those responsible for the terroristic repression, and free elections to end monopoly communist rule. A huge statue of Stalin in a Budapest park was hauled down and dragged by a lorry through the streets of the city. A placard was attached to the statue, admonishing the Soviets to go home. 'Don't forget to take me with you' was added. Members of the security forces inflamed the growing rebellion when they fired on unarmed demonstrators that evening. Gerő himself responded in a radio broadcast, condemning the chauvinism and nationalism of demonstrators that had been whipped up by hostile propaganda. The government was by this point close to panic.

Gerő had already a few hours earlier asked the Soviet Embassy for urgent military assistance, but Soviet officials in Budapest were unwilling to give their permission without authorization from Moscow. That evening the Soviet Party Presidium gave its permission. By the next day thousands of Soviet troops had already entered Budapest. By that afternoon at least twenty-five protesters lay dead and more than 200 had been wounded.

The show of military might had not proved effective, however, in quelling the unrest. A state of emergency was proclaimed. Party offices were attacked, Soviet symbols destroyed, and Budapest paralysed by a mass strike. Approaching tanks, manoeuvring only with difficulty through the barricades erected in Budapest's streets, found themselves the easy target of 'Molotov cocktails', hand grenades and even two anti-tank guns removed from army arsenals. An offer by Nagy (who had supported the request for Soviet military intervention and was reinstated as Prime Minister on 24 October) of an amnesty to rebels if they laid down their arms was whistling in the wind. The replacement of Gerő as head of the party by János Kádár, himself in earlier years a victim of Rákosi, also failed to calm the situation. The violent unrest continued on 25 October as demonstrators were shot by the police and party functionaries, and agents of the police in turn were killed by protesters. Workers' councils and revolutionary committees, without central organization, took over power in the localities. The party seemed to have become as good as superfluous.

Calm – after a fashion – only returned on 28 October when Nagy (who the previous day had appointed a cabinet of reformers) announced that he accepted the main demands of what he called the 'national democratic movement'. He spoke of Soviet troop withdrawal, dissolution of the political police, a general amnesty and reform of agriculture. The next day, 29 October, Soviet troops indeed began withdrawing from Budapest. The revolution had triumphed – or so it seemed.

In Moscow an uncertain Soviet leadership, dismayed by Nagy's stance, nonetheless decided on 30 October to pull back the troops from Budapest and avoid confrontation through large-scale military intervention. Reports from their emissaries in Budapest, Mikail Suslov and Anastas Mikoyan, however, were increasingly pessimistic. They described further violent attacks on party functionaries in Budapest and feared that the Hungarian army sided with the insurgents. In their view the situation could not be politically resolved in any way compatible with Soviet interests. 'Peacefully liquidating this hotbed is impossible,' they concluded. Calls from the Hungarian leadership on 30 October for a 'neutral Hungary', and Nagy's own approval, expressed that day to Mikoyan and Suslov, of the withdrawal of all Soviet troops and the country's departure from the Warsaw Pact, confirmed the gravity of the situation. Khrushchev pondered overnight whether the decision against renewed military intervention had been the correct one. In favour of intervention, beyond the worsening situation in Budapest, was the worry that any sign of weakness by the Soviet Union would be exploited by the imperialist Western powers (which on 29 October, amid the Suez crisis, had launched their attack on Moscow's Middle Eastern ally Egypt). A far more serious consideration was that Soviet weakness would encourage the spread of unrest – already being reported in neighbouring Romania and Czechoslovakia – to other parts of Eastern Europe. The risk of contagion was a grave one, as Soviet leaders were well aware. It was the critical factor. Accordingly, led by Khrushchev, Soviet leaders reversed their earlier stance and on 31 October unanimously agreed to deploy full-scale military force in Hungary to 'rebuff the counter-revolution'.

That day further units of Soviet troops entered Hungary. On 1 November Nagy announced that Hungary was leaving the Warsaw Pact and proclaimed the country's neutrality. In the evening a Soviet military plane flew Kádár to Moscow. When he returned to Budapest a few days later it was at the head of a new 'Provisional Revolutionary Workers' and Peasants' Government' installed by the Soviets to crush the 'fascist reaction' and defend socialism. Nagy took refuge on 4 November in the

Yugoslavian Embassy. Meanwhile, Khrushchev, along with Malenkov and Molotov, had lost no time in ascertaining that other communist states, including China and Yugoslavia, supported the intervention. It was a good moment to act. The Western powers were conveniently mired in the Suez crisis – though, whatever their sympathies for the Hungarian rebels, it was clear that they had no intention of risking a possible world war through intervening in the Soviet sphere of influence. Suez was, from the Soviet point of view, no more than a fortunate distraction. It had no determining role in the decision to crush the Hungarian uprising. It did, however, encourage the readiness to act while the Western powers were, as Khrushchev put it, 'in a real mess in Egypt'.

The end now came quickly. Soviet troops began their assault on Budapest in the early morning of 4 November 1956. The Soviet forces were this time better prepared for the intervention than they had been in October. 'The streets are swarming with Soviet tanks and arms,' a French journalist in the city registered. 'Guards have been posted at street-crossings. Shots are fired from all sides.' The Hungarian army took no part; the troops were confined to barracks and disarmed by Soviet forces. The fighting in Budapest and other cities was fierce for the next three days, but it was largely over by 8 November. Over the three days the casualties (dead and wounded) numbered around 22,000 Hungarians and nearly 2,300 Soviet soldiers – an indication of the scale of the revolution. The reprisals were swiftly under way. Over 100,000 people were arrested, 35,000 tried for 'counter-revolutionary acts', almost 26,000 given prison sentences and 600 executed. An estimated 200,000 Hungarians fled into lasting exile abroad. Nagy himself was lured out of the Yugoslavian Embassy by false promises of safety, taken captive by Soviet security forces, initially deported to Romania, then later put on trial and in June 1958 hanged.

There was a diplomatic price to pay. The prestige of the Soviet Union in non-aligned countries suffered, at least in the short term. And the scales fell from the eyes of many Western European communists, who until then had looked to the Soviet Union as their lodestar but now deserted communist parties in droves. None of this weighed heavily in the balance for Soviet leaders when preventing the eastern bloc of communist states from disintegrating was at stake. The cohesion of the Soviet bloc had been maintained – if only through the force of arms. That was the crucial factor. The demolition of the Hungarian uprising was the vital moment which showed potential dissidents that any attempt to overthrow Soviet power was futile. Any such action would be ruthlessly crushed.

There was recognition in Moscow that the policies which for years had held back living standards in the eastern bloc would have to change to prevent any recurrence of trouble. The crass imbalance between capital and consumer spending was as a result at least partially redressed. Living standards modestly increased across the Soviet bloc in the following years. The trajectory of the two countries at the centre of the storm in 1956, Poland and Hungary, was, however, not identical.

Władisław Gomułka turned out to be a sore disappointment for those who had dreamt that the 'Polish October' would usher in a more liberal socialism. At first the signs were promising. The circumstances of his compromise arrangement with Khrushchev gave him some leeway, which he initially exploited as far as he could without rocking the boat. His government was less rigid and less repressive than its predecessor and at first enjoyed much greater popularity. The security police were cut back in size and reduced in power – though not by any means to the point of insignificance. Polish intellectuals and students experienced a more liberal atmosphere. The brakes were applied to collectivization of agriculture and farmers were given somewhat greater freedom to grow produce on their own plots of land. Elsewhere, too, limited private enterprise was tolerated. Wages rose, as did living standards generally. And the Polish regime sensibly adopted a more relaxed stance towards the Catholic Church.

Gomułka was, however, no democrat. He was anxious to cement his own power as party First Secretary. And he was wary of the dangers of freedom of expression. In any case the need to keep on good terms with Moscow meant that there were strict limits to liberalization. Controls over freedom of expression in the arts and literature were tightened again by 1957. State criticism of the Catholic Church started again soon afterwards, though without undermining the Church's standing with much of the population or its increasing emergence as an oppositional subculture. And by the early 1960s, as the drive to agricultural self-sufficiency failed and living standards still lagged while party bosses enjoyed conspicuous luxury, disillusionment with Gomułka and his regime grew. There was no reversion to the Stalinism of the post-war decade. Solid and lasting improvements had been made. But coercion still underpinned the regime. Any who transgressed the narrow borders of permissible criticism felt it. For example, the thirty-four writers who signed a letter in 1964 demanding a more liberalized cultural policy and a relaxation of censorship found themselves banned from publishing or from leaving the country. And as usual legions of functionaries, the police, the security services and the army were kept loyal through a variety of sweeteners. The hold of the system was very strong. People in the main fitted into its demands and adjusted their lives accordingly. As elsewhere it amounted to tolerance of what could not be altered.

In Hungary the scale of the uprising, the brutal repression that followed, and Moscow's determination to maintain tight control, left Kádár's puppet government with little possibility of meaningful change at first. The need to improve living standards nonetheless worked eventually to Kádár's advantage. Decentralization of administrative controls in both industry and agriculture stimulated higher levels of production. Economic growth also benefited from the export of bauxite and uranium. The system stabilized. Standards of living rose and the improvements diluted the social disaffection that only a few years earlier had threatened to undermine communist rule. By the early 1960s Kádár was able to bring about a limited form of liberalization. Political prisoners were released and a wide-ranging amnesty was issued. The stringent restrictions on cultural activities and freedom of expression were somewhat relaxed, it became possible to listen to Western radio, intellectuals could cultivate limited contacts with the West, and overt police repression was reined in. 'Goulash communism' – a term depicting greater attention to consumer products than in the rest of the Soviet bloc – allowed even a limited market economy (though economic problems soon started to mount). But the security apparatus remained in place, under the party's control. Possibly a near doubling of annual suicide rates between 1955 and 1970 implied less than total contentment in János Kádár's Hungary. Hungary was even so on its way, in Western eyes, to becoming the least unattractive face of the Soviet bloc.

* * *

So Poland and Hungary went somewhat different ways. In the first case the clamp was loosened then gradually retightened, in the second sharply tightened then somewhat loosened. But in neither case could it be released fully. What bound both countries and the rest of the bloc together was that – to paraphrase what Friedrich Engels had decades earlier said of the economy – 'in the last instance' Soviet power determined matters. There was, it is true, no return to the fully fledged Stalinism that had been the norm before 1953, though some neo-Stalinist characteristics persisted everywhere.

Communism throughout Eastern Europe had in fact lost its earlier revolutionary raison d'être. Whatever the cynical propaganda about building a society infinitely superior to that of imperialist Western capitalism, the Soviet Union and its satellites had turned into merely conservative authoritarian states whose actual aims soared no higher than maintaining the system but were devoid of revolutionary dynamism or utopian ambitions. Beyond the apparatchiks who profited from the system and, doubtless, a leaven of enthusiasts and true believers, most ordinary people got on with their lives, indifferent or simply resigned to seemingly unalterable political conditions. Given a choice, most would almost certainly have opted for something other than the 'real existing socialism' that ultimately was kept in place by Soviet force. The reality was that they did not have that choice. Communist rule could have its harshest edges blunted and be amended somewhat in line with national demands in the varied satellite states. Fundamental change to the system was, however, out of the question.

There would be one further massive challenge to Soviet domination, in Czechoslovakia in 1968. That apart, after 1956 Soviet power in Eastern Europe was to remain intact and scarcely dented for over thirty years.

4

Good Times

.. Don't wait until years after to realise you have lived in a remarkable age – the age of BOOM.

Queen magazine, 15 September 1959

The coming together of the nations of Europe requires the elimination of the age-old opposition of France and Germany. Any action taken must in the first place concern these two countries.

Schuman Declaration, 9 May 1950

Prosperity was the hallmark of the new era in Western Europe. It was made possible by unprecedented rates of economic growth that lasted until the shock waves following the oil crisis of 1973. The generation born towards the end of the war, or in the post-war 'baby boom', was truly fortunate. Although at first growing up during the years of post-war austerity, amid the physical as well as psychological scars of the Second World War, they had experienced neither the misery of the Great Depression nor the horrors of the war itself. And they went on to enjoy material conditions in a peaceful Europe that their parents and grandparents could scarcely have imagined: the security blanket of the welfare state; improved housing; stable jobs amid full employment; better opportunities to benefit from education; and, gradually, money to spend on consumer luxuries, not just necessities, as well as increasing opportunities to travel to other countries. They could look to the future with optimism. They were living in good times.

For West Germans these were the barely believable years of the 'economic miracle'. But the 'miracle' was far from confined to one country.

Italians, too, saw their post-war economic recovery as nothing short of miraculous. The French looked back on the era between 1946 and 1975 as the 'glorious thirty years' ('*les trentes glorieuses*') – even if, in any other than an economic sense, some of those years were far from glorious. The British, told by their Prime Minister, Harold MacMillan, that they had 'never had it so good', spoke of 'the affluent society', though, for all the improvements, 'affluence' scarcely covered the living conditions of much of the British population. Compared with what was to come, the material improvements in people's lives were, of course, still modest. Compared with what had gone, they were massive. Understandably, the period 1950–73 came to be labelled a 'golden age'.

In southern parts of Europe it was a different story. The heavily restrictive, practically closed economies of the authoritarian regimes in Spain and Portugal – political hangovers from yesteryear – prevented those countries from benefiting fully from the material advances that were being made in north-western Europe. Notable improvement in standards of living, which remained well below the average in Northern Europe, came to Spain and Portugal only in the 1960s, as both countries belatedly took steps to liberalize their economies and Spain started to profit from international tourism. (The number of tourists visiting Spain rose eightfold between 1959 and 1973, while the money they spent rose twentyfold.) Greece, slowly recovering from civil war and where, as in Spain and Portugal, almost half of the population still worked on the land, also lagged behind, though high and sustained economic growth brought some modernization and a modest improvement in living standards by 1973. Turkey, rushing headlong to overcome its economic backwardness and dependent heavily upon foreign investment and American loans, hindered its progress by poor planning and rapidly rising national indebtedness.

The ideological determinants of the Soviet Union and its satellites in Eastern and Central Europe severely hindered the developments that brought prosperity and the emergence of the consumer society to the western parts of the continent. Communist economics and the heavy hand of state direction and planning dictated that the economy was disproportionately tilted towards infrastructural projects and military spending. The peoples of Eastern Europe and the USSR were consequently deprived of many of the rapid improvements in material life enjoyed by the population of Western European countries.

Nevertheless, even here – fully bearing in mind that the loss of personal liberties under repressive regimes has no price – living conditions, though falling way behind those in the West, were far better than they had been before the war, let alone during the horrors and devastation of the war itself. If not the 'golden age' enjoyed by Western Europe, economists feel able to describe the era in Eastern Europe as at least a 'silver age'. The standard of living did improve, if modestly compared with that of Western Europe: the gap between rich and poor was greatly reduced; social welfare (different to that in the West) brought a level of security unknown to most of the population before the war; housing accommodation was made available (if mostly mediocre to poor in quality and allocated, not chosen); there was full employment (with little or no choice in the place and type of work); and there were educational opportunities (narrowly confined in content and promoted by ideological rectitude and political patronage). For most people in the West there was nothing to envy in a lifestyle shaped almost entirely by the demands of the command economy. Younger people in Eastern Europe, too, tolerated it only because they had no choice, and frequently with growing dissatisfaction. Many of the older generation nonetheless recognized that, with all its obvious failings and immeasurable limitations, life under communist regimes did, in a purely material sense, amount to an improvement on what they had previously known.

Viewed through the prism of what went before rather than what would come later these were indeed, for much of the population of Europe, unheard-of 'good times'. Behind all the vast changes in material life that gathered pace in the 1950s and 1960s lay the extraordinary rates of economic growth, understandably viewed by many, who had previously known only misery and poverty, as a 'miracle'.

THE 'ECONOMIC MIRACLE'

Western Europe's astonishing surge to prosperity was not in the main attributable to any genius of political leaders for economic management. Economic policy in any case varied from country to country. The remarkable growth of the post-war economy was, in fact, global. All parts of the world (also the Soviet bloc of Eastern Europe) benefited, though some more than others. Japan's growth outstripped that of anywhere in

Europe. The United States and Canada also experienced high levels of growth, though slightly lower than Europe's. The striking economic growth in Europe allowed it to some extent to make up for the ground it had lost to America during the disastrous preceding decades. Europe's share of world trade increased. By 1963 France, West Germany, Italy and the United Kingdom between them accounted for nearly two-fifths of world manufacturing exports, the USA under one-fifth. Europe, and the rest of the industrialized West, could also benefit from the fall in the cost of imports of food and raw materials from the developing world, while the manufactured products they exported continued to rise in price.

The extraordinary economic growth had arisen from the unique circumstances that followed a global war, and instigated a virtuous circle that promoted prosperity and social advantages. Partly the growth was a natural business recovery from the ground lost during two world wars and the Great Depression. But it was no 'normal' recovery, no conventional business cycle. Numerous factors help to explain it. Release of stored-up demand, huge reservoirs of available labour at low cost and, not least, massive technological advances made during the war that could now be put to civilian use, all formed a big part of the reason for the explosive growth. The necessary rebuilding of ruined towns and cities provided a boost to growth. And where high levels of investment in technology and labour in the crucial manufacturing sector took place, in West Germany for example, high rates of economic growth tended to follow. Where investment in manufacturing was sluggish, as in Britain, growth rates remained stubbornly low. Investment, much of it initially from public spending on big infrastructural projects, brought growth, which encouraged confidence, led to further investment, and created a positive growth spiral. The role of the state was an important part of this, especially in the early stages of economic recovery, as the lessons of the Great Depression and deployment of Keynesian economics resulted in significant economic stimulus. In general, the public and private sectors of the economy were seen less as in conflict than in partnership with each other.

A major contributory factor in the sustained growth was the massive expansion of international trade. Measured in value, world exports doubled between 1953 and 1963 and then more than trebled in the subsequent decade, with particularly strong growth in manufactured products.

Growth in Western Europe was sharply boosted in the early phase by the liberalization of trade that accompanied the adoption of Marshall Aid and by the recovery of international markets. As price controls and other trade restrictions of the first post-war years were lifted and currencies were stabilized, enabling a market economy to function (though with the worst effects of the free market mediated by state planning and intervention), Western European countries started to export to expanding markets abroad. West Germany led the way. Its foreign trade increased by an astounding average of 16 per cent per year between 1948 and 1962. And increasingly during the 1950s, even more so once the European Economic Community had been established by the Treaty of Rome in 1957, the countries of continental Western Europe exported to each other, bringing more than a doubling of intra-European trade by the end of the decade.

The high rates of growth that lasted, with only minor and brief interruptions, until the late 1960s – when they tailed off as economic conditions began to alter, before the sudden and steep rise in the price of oil forced on the West by oil-producing Arab states following the Arab–Israeli War of 1973 – were not just extraordinary but historically unique. In the development of capitalism, this was a completely exceptional era. The quest to maximize profits was not at the cost of the welfare of society in Western European countries (though it exploited the low price of raw materials in the developing world). Sustained high rates of growth permitted profits to rise substantially (enabling enhanced investment) while wages and salaries could increase in real terms, bringing improved living standards. At the same time governments could benefit from the full employment that followed such high growth rates to gain additional tax revenue to fund social welfare programmes. And the growth was general, traversing diverse kinds of political and economic structure. The economies of Western Europe grew in that period at an average of 4.7 per cent per year, more than twice as fast as their average rates of growth since 1820 of 2.2 per cent. Southern Europe (Greece, Spain, Portugal and Turkey) grew – though from a low base – at an even faster rate (an average of 6.3 per cent a year). The planned state economies of Eastern Europe and the Soviet Union saw average rates of growth of gross domestic product per head only a little below those of capitalist Western Europe – and actually a greater improvement on the more modest historical growth rate – though this was from a low base, allowing scope for what economists call 'catch-up'.

The growth was, of course, not evenly spread. In Western Europe it was greatest (at an average of around 5 per cent a year) in West Germany – whose 'economic miracle' was crucial to resurgence far beyond its own borders – as well as in neighbouring Austria, and in Italy (especially the north). It was lowest, at only 2.5 per cent a year, in the United Kingdom. Ireland's growth was only moderately higher. Even though three times its long-term average rate, Ireland remained a backward economy. Turkey lagged behind Greece and the Iberian peninsula in Southern Europe, while Bulgaria, Romania and Yugoslavia performed best of the Eastern European economies (though also from low starting points).

As mentioned, the growth in the Soviet bloc was concentrated in heavy industry, where production output soared without being translated into the markedly higher living standards that economic growth in the West promoted. Largely cut off from burgeoning international trade, the countries beyond the Iron Curtain experienced no consumer boom. Even so, living conditions did start to improve modestly from the mid-1950s onwards for the great majority of the population. Construction of new dwellings almost trebled in the Soviet Union between 1953 and 1960 in an attempt to overcome the chronic shortage of housing and serious overcrowding, especially in cities. The situation was somewhat better in the satellite countries of Eastern Europe, though everywhere in the Soviet bloc housing was well below the standard in Western Europe.

Growth was everywhere more dramatic in manufacturing industry than in agriculture. But farming, too, was transformed in the course of the lasting prosperity. Agricultural productivity was at first generally much lower than productivity in industry. But the big drain of labour from the land across the continent in the 1950s and 1960s for higher earnings in industry prompted mechanization, more intensive farming methods and high-yield crops, innovations that saw productivity rise sharply. With less land under cultivation and a smaller agricultural workforce, Europe was turning out higher quantities of food.

It needed to do so to feed the growing population, increasingly concentrated in large towns and cities. Pre-war morbid anxieties about population decline seemed like a bad dream as Europe experienced a post-war 'baby boom' – another aspect of 'catching up', a reaction from the falling birth rates during an era of war and economic depression. In France, where population decline had appeared irreversible, there was an increase of nearly 30 per cent in the post-war decades. Large increases also took place in other European countries, east as well as west. Exceptions were poorer countries such as Greece, Portugal and Ireland, which saw actual population loss as workers, especially from rural occupations, sought employment and higher wages in booming industry in other countries. Birth rates in the more prosperous western half of the continent increased until the mid-1950s, reversing the pre-war decline, though they fell in much of poorer Southern and Eastern Europe. Child-mortality rates dropped markedly in practically all countries of both Eastern and Western Europe.

The drain from the countryside, already widespread before the war, accelerated. More than a third of the population in Western Europe had still worked in farming and related occupations on the eve of the war, in Eastern and Southern Europe often well over a half. Only in Britain and Belgium at that time were negligible proportions of the population engaged primarily in agriculture. During the 1950s and 1960s this changed dramatically. In Italy, for example, there was a drop in agricultural employment between 1950 and 1973 from 41 per cent to 17.4 per cent, in France from 33 per cent to 12.2 per cent. Equal if not even more spectacular drops were encountered across the continent. As the countryside emptied, urbanization intensified. Cities grew in size almost everywhere, but especially in previously relatively underdeveloped and peripheral regions of Europe. Belgrade, for example, more than quadrupled its population in the first post-war decades. Kiev's population increased threefold. So did Istanbul's. Sofia, Bucharest and Warsaw doubled in population, while Leningrad's population rose from 2.9 to 4.3 million inhabitants, Moscow's from 5.3 to 7.6 million, over that period. In Europe as a whole, 58 per cent of the population lived in cities of over 750,000 inhabitants by 1970, compared with 45 per cent in 1950, with the greatest percentage increases over that period in Southern and Eastern Europe.

As well as the magnet of the industrial regions attracting labour from rural areas, there was a massive increase, compared with the pre-war era, of labour movement across national borders. In the immediate post-war years most of the migration was politically driven. The war had created around 40 million refugees and led to enormous ethnic cleansing in

Eastern Europe. Germans, the prime target for expulsions from Poland, Czechoslovakia, Romania and other countries, headed west in their millions. An estimated 12.3 million Germans were expelled between 1945 and 1950, amounting by then to nearly a fifth of the West German population. Thereafter, the draw of work and its material rewards in the booming economies of Western Europe was the key element in migration.

Until the building of the Berlin Wall in 1961 closed the last exit route through the Iron Curtain, West Germany could benefit from the big exodus of labour from its eastern neighbour, a drain that was highly damaging to the East German economy. From 1961 other sources of labour were needed. At the height of the economic boom, in the early 1960s, over 300,000 migrants a year were moving to West Germany and a similar number to France. Italy, Spain, Portugal, Greece and Ireland had the greatest number of emigrants in search of work and better living conditions, though Turkey, Yugoslavia and North Africa, especially Algeria and Morocco, soon became major sources of cheap foreign labour. By 1973 some 7.5 million migrants were employed in Western Europe, 2.5 million of them in West Germany, 2.3 million in France. Few had met with a warm welcome on arrival. Many if not most had then faced deprivation and discrimination of one kind or another. The 'guest workers', as West Germany called them, were supposedly merely temporary residents and were not given citizenship rights. Elderly Germans, such as Franz Göll, a lower-middle-class pensioner in West Berlin, were often reminded by the Turks and Yugoslavs they saw, 'who have taken over the lower-paid work that German workers will no longer accept', of the 'foreign workers' they had regarded with some animosity during the war. The 'guest workers' themselves at first usually imagined that they would return in the end to their native countries, and sent a good portion of their earnings home to support the families from which they were separated by their work abroad, indirectly in this way providing much-needed foreign income to the poorer countries they had left behind.

Britain took a different route, recruiting cheap, unskilled labour from its former colonial territories in the Commonwealth. Unlike the 'guest workers' of West Germany, who were expected eventually to leave the country, the citizens of the Commonwealth had a right to permanent residence and a doorway to British citizenship – a factor that was starting to make immigration a significant political issue. The numbers of immigrants amounted in the early 1950s to little more than a trickle. Only 28,000 arrived between 1948 and 1953, half of them from the West Indies. The highest annual total during the 1950s was 46,850 in 1956. More people were actually leaving than entering Britain at that time, mainly to settle in the former white Dominions of Australia, New Zealand and Canada. Over 50,000 British people a year were leaving for Australia in the early 1950s, as many as 80,000 in 1965. In 1959 immigrant numbers totalled 21,600 (around 16,000 of them from the Caribbean, just over 3,000 from the Indian subcontinent – a number that would substantially increase during the 1960s). Total immigration then increased sharply to 136,400 by 1961. On average about 75,000 immigrants from the New Commonwealth came to Britain each year during the 1960s – far lower than the influx of immigrants, for instance, into France and West Germany.

Immigrants, encouraged to come to Britain to serve the needs of the growing economy, formed only a small part of the total population. The foreign-born population within the United Kingdom totalled about 2.5 million in 1961. France, Belgium and Switzerland had a substantially higher proportion of foreign-born residents among their population. Most of these were Europeans, not from overseas, though the number of Algerians living in France roughly doubled to around 700,000 between 1952 and 1975. By 1962, the British government, under growing pressure to act after some 230,000 immigrants from former British colonies had arrived within the previous eighteen months, legislated to restrict the numbers permitted to settle in Britain through the Commonwealth Immigration Act, which was followed by further restrictive measures in subsequent years.

The objective reality about immigration levels ran up against some ingrained racial prejudice. The rising animosity towards immigrants from the Commonwealth, most prevalent in the industrial regions of north-west England, the Midlands and London with its surrounds, was overwhelmingly directed at non-white immigrants – plainly an expression of racism. In August 1958 there were serious race riots in Nottingham and in the London district of Notting Hill, where hundreds of white youths attacked the homes of West Indian immigrants several nights running from 29 August to 5 September 1958. Six years later Smethwick, part of the Birmingham conurbation in the Midlands, became notorious at the 1964 general election for the disgraceful racist campaign run by the Conservative candidate, Peter Griffiths. The seat had been held by

Labour, but the district's white working class was suffering from factory closures and a housing shortage, and the Sikh minority faced vicious racism in which far-right groups were able to exploit economic and social resentment. Griffiths took the seat for the Conservatives, though he was subsequently dubbed 'a parliamentary leper' by the Labour Prime Minister, Harold Wilson. Labour regained the seat at the 1966 election. In the interim the local town council had overtly pursued a housing policy based on racial discrimination.

Racism again became a flashpoint in 1968 when Enoch Powell, at the time opposition defence spokesman, a Conservative of unusually dogmatic views, once a brilliant classics scholar who in 1934 had been elected to a fellowship at Trinity College, Cambridge, at the remarkably early age of twenty-two, but an anachronistic English nationalist and imperialist with a reputation as a maverick politician, addressed the question of immigration in highly emotive and provocative terms. His speech in Birmingham on 20 April 1968 at a Conservative Association meeting was actually directed at the Labour government's Race Relations Act that year, which aimed to ban racial discrimination in housing. Known for his rhetorical flourishes, Powell opened up the prospect of violent racial conflict in years to come. He referred to 'wide-grinning piccaninnies' and – a former scholar of the classics – envisaged the future in England when he cited the poet Virgil's allusion to ancient Rome's River Tiber 'foaming with much blood'. He was promptly dismissed from his post in the Conservative opposition's shadow cabinet and his political career never recovered. But an opinion poll shortly afterwards indicated that three-quarters of the British population agreed with Powell. London dockworkers marched on parliament to demand his reinstatement in the shadow cabinet. Racial prejudice, officially condemned, of course continued but, in terms of outward expression, from now on it became politically the province of fringe racist and neo-fascist movements – menacing to those in their path, but with little of a following and facing vehement opposition both from organized anti-fascist groups and from mainstream politicians of all parties. The excitable mood that Powell had aroused fairly quickly subsided, helped by the drop – already under way when he delivered his 'rivers of blood' speech – in further immigration from the New Commonwealth in the wake of the Labour government's race-relations legislation.

By this time Britain, which had begun the 1950s as the leading economy in Europe (for all its post-war austerity and national indebtedness), was well on the way towards the unenviable reputation that it gained in the 1970s as the 'sick man of Europe' because of its poor economic performance. Britain's levels of growth in the post-war decades had been mediocre by international comparison – though they were actually more than twice as high as the country's growth rates at the height of Britain's industrial supremacy in the nineteenth century. Britain was increasingly exposed as the economic potential of the grouping of six states (France, West Germany, Italy, Belgium, the Netherlands and Luxembourg), which by 1957 had come to form the European Economic Community (EEC), rapidly expanded.

Britain's relatively weak rates of growth were partly a consequence, paradoxically, of the country's wartime triumph. Especially high growth rates were, perhaps unsurprisingly, registered by the countries where war-damage had been extensive – Germany, Austria, Italy and, outside Europe, Japan – and where, consequently, there was a pressing need for massive infrastructural repair. Compared with most of continental Europe, however, the war had caused much less physical damage to Britain and had left its economic, as well as political, structures largely intact. And Britain had emerged from the war still (just about) in possession of its colonial empire – since 1931 named 'the Commonwealth'. Not only was its residual world-power status retained (if in reality strongly diminished) and still entailing a relatively high level of military spending, but its economic elites felt assured of their continued pre-eminence. But, on top of the country's huge debts (which would finally be repaid only decades later), victory in the war had left outdated methods of production, complacent management too unwilling to risk innovation, and a multiplicity of trade unions, which increasingly proved a further handicap to economic efficiency. Crucially, Britain invested less than its main competitors. And Britain's industrial relations, with a tradition of managerial authoritarianism and union militancy, were not conducive to the innovatory methods of production needed in increasingly competitive markets. The result was a steady decline in Britain's exports. The contrast between Britain's decline and West Germany's rise – a loser in the war, a winner in the post-war economic-growth stakes – was stark.

In West Germany, the paradigm of the 'economic miracle', the effort to rebuild the country was accompanied by an attempt to avoid conflict between employers and employees. Nazism, war and the post-war huge influx of cheap labour had broken not just the structures but also the mentalities of pre-war class struggle. The German Labour Front had during the Third Reich replaced the brutally destroyed independent trade unions with a single huge Nazified agglomerate. This had forcibly established a pseudo-solidarity of the workplace, sugaring the pill of coercion with improvements in leisure facilities and enhancement of workers' status within the 'people's community'. The destruction and twelve-year absence of genuine trade unionism produced, if at inordinately high human and political cost, the basis for a new start in industrial relations after the war. The urgency of rebuilding out of the ruins had stimulated greater unity in the workplace than had ever been achieved by Nazi propaganda. And the workforce itself was drastically changed, a consequence of wartime losses and the massive influx of refugees and expellees. A more pliant, individualistic workforce had emerged, content for the most part with increasing wages, better living standards and stable employment in an expanding economy. Trade unions were reconstituted along more rational lines than the unreconstructed myriad craft unions in Britain. Workers' councils, following the example of the Weimar Republic, gave workers a voice in industrial relations, and a legal stipulation in 1951 compelled the boards of large firms to involve workers' representatives in the co-determination (*Mitbestimmung*) of managerial decisions. Economists adjudge that better industrial relations and investment in vocational training to produce a skilled labour force contributed substantially to the growing gap in economic performance between West Germany and Britain.

Britain's relative decline was also a consequence of political judgement largely fashioned by the country's imperialist tradition, its former economic supremacy, and its preference for Atlanticist and Commonwealth rather than continental links. When early steps were taken to promote economic cooperation, as the ruined continent looked to recovery from the wartime devastation, Britain's encouragement to other countries was accompanied by a determination to remain aloof itself. Despite post-war austerity, economic considerations, quite apart from political priorities, pointed British policymakers towards keeping their distance. Steel and coal production in the first post-war years, for instance, far outstripped that of any other European country. Detachment rather than involvement in European cooperation seemed sensible.

Britain's attachment to the Commonwealth – which attracted three-quarters of the country's exports in 1956 – turned it away from continental Europe, but saw it anchored to declining markets. By the mid-1960s only a quarter of the United Kingdom's total trade was with the Commonwealth as its different members developed closer relations with other parts of Europe, Japan and the United States. Britain was not able, however, to benefit fully from the expanding intra-European trade. By the time Britain, slow to liberalize its external trade and its economy by now increasingly uncompetitive, realized the disadvantages of the route it had chosen and decided that it did after all want to join the EEC, it had missed the boat.

This unbroken pattern of economic growth showed the first signs of stalling in the mid-1960s. The pattern was not uniform, and national economies performed in varied ways. Italy, for instance, saw no economic stagnation. Booming exports and soaring tourism contributed to a continuation of Italy's 'economic miracle'. But indicators of difficulties were nevertheless apparent in many parts of Western Europe. Labour shortages, wage inflation and rising prices started to cast shadows. Wages had risen sharply, and faster than prices during the 1950s, largely owing to a growth in labour productivity. But in the early 1960s prices, which had been relatively stable and had only risen modestly in the previous decade, increased on average by about 20 per cent in Western Europe.

Demand for labour, in economies with full employment, was high. Trade unions, whose membership attained peak numbers in the postwar decades, were able to flex their muscles. Industrial unrest became more commonplace. Denmark, Sweden, Belgium, France and – most chronically – Britain came to experience problems with labour militancy. Deterioration in labour relations often followed or accompanied attempts by governments to curb the inflationary pressures of overheating economies. West Germany, the motor of Europe's economic recovery, saw growth slacken after 1962 but, worried about inflation, curtailed lending and tightened the labour market, measures that contributed to sharp, though temporary, recession in 1966–7. Switzerland, Sweden and Denmark were among the other European countries to introduce measures to stem rising inflation and overheating economies. France had brought in restrictive measures in 1964, which led to a temporary recession before renewed expansion in 1965–6.

Throughout Western Europe, the economic downturn in the mid-1960s was a passing interlude rather than a fundamental break in the pattern of growth that had existed since 1948. It was, however, a harbinger of the more troubled years of the later 1960s before the onset of the oil crisis in 1973 brought the long post-war boom to an abrupt end.

The 'economic miracle' had produced untold benefits for the population of Western Europe, improvements, too, in the southern and eastern parts of the continent. Surveys showed that people were in general more satisfied, happy and optimistic by the early 1970s than they had been in the 1950s. High levels of economic growth had, however, one lasting disadvantage, not recognized by many people at the time. They came at the cost of the environment. This suffered irreparably, as it had done since the Industrial Revolution, from the drive to improve productivity, and especially from the huge growth in manufacturing. At this point only a small minority were paying any attention to the long-term damage that was being caused. The 'golden age', though it brought great improvements to the living standards of Europeans, was responsible for a serious worsening of environmental damage. The swiftly growing use of pesticides and other chemicals in more intensive farming greatly improved crop yields but inflicted harm on the environment that only slowly came to be widely recognized. The huge boost in energy consumption from the 1950s reflected growing prosperity, for example in the ownership of cars and wider possibilities of travel. But it also led to new records of harmful carbon emissions (doubling in Germany, for instance, between 1948 and 1957), the scale of whose damage would become apparent only to later generations. Only from the 1970s onwards would the environment become a significant political theme – and even then have difficulty in stirring the interest of most of the population.

THE WELFARE STATE

Part of the virtuous circle of economic growth was the increased stream of revenue to governments that enabled states to spend far greater amounts on welfare provision. Tax revenue rose at unprecedented rates with the return to full employment and the big expansion of consumer spending. State budgets in Western Europe were up to twenty times higher in the 1970s than they had been in 1950. Governments were consequently in a position to spend far more on welfare programmes than ever before. Welfare provision and full employment had been the overwhelming needs of a new society – the obvious lesson of the Great Depression, and recognized by all post-war governments. In the post-war decades all political parties agreed on the need to expand welfare provision. The extraordinary economic growth allowed the fulfilment of both aims – in the east under communist regimes that forcibly created societies more equal than ever before, if at a high political price, and greatly extended welfare provision from the state, and in Western Europe under liberal capitalism that also reduced social inequalities (though to a far smaller degree than in the east) and combined market forces with the varying forms of welfare state.

Pre-war advances in social security had left many gaps. Scandinavia, Germany and Britain had made most progress with national insurance schemes, but these were still limited, while in most European countries large sections of the population had minimal insurance (or none at all) for accidents at work, unemployment and ill-health, and little or no provision for old-age pensions. The war had then massively increased the need for the state to provide for widows, orphans, refugees and, at first, still high numbers of the unemployed. So there was a general necessity to develop far more comprehensive systems of social security. This blended with the general belief in the need for drastically improved social welfare and the drive in every country to create a better and fairer society. It was not all altruistic. There was wide recognition that welfare provision was essential to ensure an effective labour force for a modern economy.

The Beveridge Plan that formed the basis of the sweeping reforms in social security introduced by the Labour government in Britain was widely admired beyond British shores. Sweden also attracted international attention for its successful extension of the national system of social security it had developed in the 1930s, based upon principles of equality. Sweden introduced a state pension of the same level for all in 1946, child allowance the following year, and began moving towards a uniform system of comprehensive education in 1950. Over the following few years nearly all Western European countries introduced national schemes, varying in detail but each of them setting out to provide a wide framework of social security for their citizens that would guarantee basic material well-being for everyone, without distinction. By 1960 most countries were spending between 10 and 20 per cent of gross domestic product on welfare, only authoritarian Portugal and Spain less than 5 per cent.

In essence, people contributed through their earnings either directly to state-administered insurance funds or through general taxation, receiving appropriate benefits in accordance with contributions. They were under such schemes legally protected from the worst hardships of unemployment, invalidity through accidents at work, or poverty in old age, while child welfare was supported by family allowances. By 1970 the overwhelming proportion of citizens in Western Europe were covered by health insurance and pension schemes. The principle that the elderly, the young, the sick and the incapacitated would have a safety net of social security, funded through the contributions of the working population, was crucial not just to providing for the most vulnerable, but also in establishing the framework of a society in which the strong helped the weak. The advances on the decade before the war were enormous. Belgium spent twelve times as much per head of the population on social security in 1957 as it had done in 1930, Italy eleven times as much, France eight times, Holland five times. Even those countries which had already in the 1930s spent relatively heavily on social security now spent far more – Sweden six times as much, Switzerland four times as much, Germany two and a half times as much, the United Kingdom – the highest spender in 1930 – a third more. The welfare state became everywhere, therefore, a major – and expanding – component of state expenditure. As long as economic growth continued, income from tax revenues was sustained, and expectations of social security remained relatively modest, the welfare state could flourish as the crowning glory of post-war Western European society.

In Europe behind the Iron Curtain the systems of social security, which before the war had resembled those in Western Europe even though less well developed, were now shaped by communist ideology, though they were never wholly unified in practice. The state completely controlled social welfare. There was no place for private insurance schemes or charitable institutions, as in Western Europe. Provision for the working population was the decisive criterion. Full employment was taken as the axiom of welfare. There was no unemployment insurance, since unemployment officially did not exist. Those regarded as unproductive – pensioners, handicapped, housewives – had lower levels of support than those in work. Anyone not employed in state-run concerns was also disadvantaged. And the principle of equality was in practice undermined by the higher benefits paid to soaring numbers of bureaucrats and a corrupt political elite. Even so, when compared with the gross inequalities and extreme poverty in Eastern Europe before the war, the communist systems of the post-war era, whatever their heavy-handed state control and restrictions of personal freedoms, did succeed in improving the welfare provision of the great majority of the population.

THE CONSUMER SOCIETY

The prosperity created by the 'mixed economy' – a restructured capitalism in which free-market competition was tempered by government intervention (what the West Germans called the 'social market economy') – opened the door to sweeping social change. Exceptional economic growth blunted the edges of the class conflict that had bedevilled Europe before the war. The spectre of mass unemployment that had plagued the Depression years seemed to have been banished forever. Full employment appeared destined to last indefinitely. Trade unions became converted from quasi-revolutionary forces of class warfare into coopted parts of a corporative triad of government, capital and labour representation that increasingly came to dominate state economic planning. Wages, both nominal and real – that is, in terms of their relative buying power – increased. West German workers, benefiting from their country's 'economic miracle', saw their real income grow fourfold over the 1950s and 1960s. That was an extreme case. But most people everywhere in Western Europe were better off.

In most countries progressive taxation led to a modest redistribution of incomes. The share of income of the top 10 per cent was slightly reduced (most notably in the Scandinavian countries, Finland and Britain), that of the lowest income groups marginally increased – though of course great disparities both in income and in wealth remained. In terms of wealth distribution, inequality was even more marked. The richest 1 per cent in

Britain still owned 45 per cent of the country's wealth in the 1950s, in Sweden the richest 1 per cent owned around 33 per cent of the wealth, though the trend – as long as high economic growth was maintained and governments still pursued mild redistributive policies – was downward, to 31 per cent in Britain in the 1960s, 24 per cent in Sweden. Statistical comparisons are not possible for other countries, though big differences are unlikely. The richest 1 per cent in Switzerland owned 43 per cent of the country's wealth in the 1960s. In West Germany 35 per cent of the wealth was in the hands of the richest 1.7 per cent of the population at the beginning of that decade. In Eastern Europe such crass disparities of wealth and income had effectively been solved by draconian expropriation, even if a new political elite was able to accumulate sufficient wealth and privilege to belie all the basic principles of communism.

As prosperity (though certainly not evenly experienced) spread across society, households needed to spend less of their income on necessities. They were finding that they had money left over and, in Western Europe at any rate, could buy from a swiftly widening range of commodities. The modern consumer society was born.

Europe – west as well as east – had been a poor continent in 1950. Housing was mostly of bad standard, often lacking hot water, a bathroom or indoor toilet; families could afford few luxuries; food was still widely rationed; and most men still had jobs entailing hard manual labour. (Relatively few women worked in paid employment, though the pattern was not uniform; the textile industry, for instance, though in decline, still employed high numbers of women.) The consumer boom that gradually gathered momentum separated Western Europe from the eastern parts of the continent. There, the modest rise in living standards was accompanied by constraints imposed by ideological priorities on the variety and availability of the type of household commodity that would soon be taken for granted in the West. Standardized products, often of poor quality, were available at low cost. But a consumer boom such as Western Europe was starting to experience was ideologically impossible in the closed economies of the east.

In Western Europe, consumerism brought the population of different countries closer together in their lifestyles, tastes and leisure pursuits. This was made easier by the increasing uniformity of commodities. Consumerism encouraged mass production of goods and standardization of products that reduced costs and cut the price to the purchaser. Small producers increasingly found it an uphill struggle to compete against the big manufacturers. Regional or local tastes and variations became less and less pronounced. Supermarkets, a new phenomenon whose dominance would become extensive only from the 1970s onwards, could buy in bulk (with bargaining power to force down prices from suppliers) and offer a wide range of goods, supplanting small shops. Food production was meanwhile expanding so rapidly that within a few years surpluses began to accumulate. Household expenditure was no longer dominated by necessities. A declining amount had to be spent on food (though still a much higher proportion of income in Eastern European countries than in the West). Severe malnutrition was a thing of the past. It would increasingly be replaced by a new form of bad diet: excess sugar and fats. Advertising became a new industry, well tuned to exploit the expanding market for a wide array of consumer products. The success of Coca-Cola across the whole of Western Europe was just one guide to the impact of new marketing techniques. Cigarette firms used ubiquitous international advertising for their products, whose serious health risks were only beginning to be acknowledged.

With prosperity came better and cheaper accommodation, aided by state subsidies and a doubling in the number of houses built during the 1950s. The quality was at first low. Given the desperate post-war housing shortage, quantity was more important than quality. New dwellings (houses and apartments) were being built at the rate of around half a million a year in West Germany, 400,000 a year in Italy and France and almost that level in Britain. Practically all buildings in north-western Europe would now be supplied with electricity and running water. However, as late as the 1960s only about half of households in Portugal, Greece and Balkan countries had access to electricity. States were commonly spending 6–7 per cent of their gross national product on house-building. And accommodation was becoming better – more spacious, less crowded, more comfortable, increasingly now with a bathroom and toilet inside and not out in a yard. What this could mean for personal dignity was graphically expressed in 1969 by an Italian peasant who lived south of Rome. Having an inside toilet instead of being forced to go out into the fields, he said, made him 'feel like a human being, like other people, not like an animal as I felt before'.

By the early 1960s, slums were being swept away in big cities. Urban planners saw new opportunities to redesign towns and cities, many of them often badly damaged during the war, to accommodate the growing workforce and rapidly increasing volume of traffic. Suburban areas were expanded, new arterial roads constructed, sometimes entirely new towns built. The thirst to discard the old and to modernize as quickly as possible consumed some of the town planners. The result was often shoddy architectural designs, housing projects that would soon degenerate into new slums, and a ready resort to civic vandalism in some cities. Industrial priorities produced some horrendous urban designs not only in Eastern European countries (where forty new cities, constructed on the basis of socialist realism, were created in the 1950s, among them Nowa Huta in Poland and Eisenhüttenstadt in the German Democratic Republic). But, mercifully, the historic centre of Prague, undestroyed in the war, was preserved, while the core of the completely ruined Warsaw and Gdańsk (formerly Danzig) was elegantly restored.

Patterns of employment started to change. Working hours were generally reduced (giving more time for leisure pursuits); the numbers working in agriculture fell sharply, those in gruelling industrial work less rapidly, though there was a significant growth in the 'tertiary sector' of white-collar work. By the 1960s, too, far more women were entering the labour market. By 1970 around a third of employees in Western European countries were women, with Denmark in the lead at just under two-fifths, though about a third of female employees had part-time work. Only the Scandinavian countries and Finland came close in the 1960s to the levels of female employment in the communist countries of Eastern Europe, especially Poland and the German Democratic Republic. And in the eastern bloc part-time jobs scarcely existed, for women as for men.

In 1950 few people had cars, tourism was still the preserve of the wealthy, and household components that later generations would take for granted – telephones, washing machines, fridges, television – remained scarce. During the 1950s the spread of prosperity began to bring such commodities within reach of ordinary families and, fired by the continued economic growth and rapid technological innovation – for instance in electronics – the availability grew during the following decade. By the later 1950s the children of the immediate post-war 'baby boom', with little or no experience of the earlier acute shortages, were starting to enter their teenage years. Most of them were soon in work and starting to develop their own consumer demands, contributing to the rapid expansion of, for instance, the clothing and record industries. Meanwhile, even the least affluent sectors of society – the economic migrants who had poured into rapidly growing towns and cities and immigrant workers from overseas former colonies or 'guest workers' – were earning sufficient to contribute to (and benefit from) the expanding consumer boom.

Expenditure on household appliances rose more quickly than any other part of the household budget. The fridge and the washing machine were increasingly commonplace in middle-class households but within two decades, as their price dropped, became accessible also to working-class families. By the early 1970s most households had a fridge, and could for the first time buy food in bulk for storage and later use. Two-thirds of families by then had a washing machine, freeing women for the most part from a significant element in household drudgery. A big status symbol in the 1950s was ownership of a television. Britain began in the lead, but when television had launched there in 1946 there had been only 1,760 subscribers. By the mid-1960s there were 13 million television sets in Britain, nearly 10 million in West Germany, 5 million in France and Italy, about 2 million in Holland and Sweden. By the end of the decade nearly every household in Western Europe had a television. For family entertainment, television had supplanted radio. But the invention of the small transistor radio and its mass production at low prices meant that during the 1960s radio ownership became available to nearly everyone, and was the medium of choice for most teenagers. Radio listening was turning into an individual, not family, form of entertainment.

More than anything else, the ownership of a car was the mark of the new age. From being a luxury attainable only by a few, the car became a mass product available even to families with relatively modest levels of income. In 1950 Britain had proportionately the most passenger cars (42 for every 1,000 inhabitants) of any European country. Spain was at that time at the bottom of the league in Western Europe (three cars per 1,000 inhabitants), at the same level as Poland and Hungary. By 1970 Britain had been overtaken in car ownership, using the same measure, by France, Belgium, West Germany, Sweden and Denmark, with Italy, the Netherlands and Norway close behind. Spain still languished in this regard among Western European countries, just ahead of Poland and Czechoslovakia.

The growth of the automobile industry after 1950 was startling. Hitler had promised Germans a 'people's car' (*Volkswagen*) in the 1930s. But it was only in the 1950s that the Volkswagen could become a symbol of Germany's 'economic miracle'. At last, under a successful democracy not a dangerous dictatorship, a car was accessible to much of the population. By the 1960s West Germany was Europe's biggest car manufacturer, producing just under three million passenger cars a year, and exporting about a million of them. Volkswagen meanwhile saw its market share decline in the face of the competition in particular from Fiat and Renault as Italian and French automobile manufacture soared to meet the rapidly expanding demand. Where villagers in central Italy had even in the late 1950s still in the main used donkeys as their means of transport, many were a decade later driving their own Fiats. Of the major industrial countries, only Britain managed, through lack of innovation and investment, abetted by mounting labour militancy, to turn its once thriving car industry into one of near terminal decline. Only the brilliantly innovative Mini, in its early years, and, at the luxury end of the market Rolls Royce, Bentley, Jaguar and Aston Martin, bucked the general downward trend, as Britain's cars gained an unenviable reputation for unreliability and lack of style. By 1965, car ownership had soared – nearly 10 million owners in France (up from 1.5 million in 1948), 9 million in West Germany (compared with 0.2 million in 1948), 9 million in Britain (compared with 2 million in 1948) and 5.4 million in Italy (against 0.2 million in 1948).

Greatly extended car ownership contributed enormously to the spread of tourism. But chartered flights and package holidays also started to become available, opening the possibility of foreign tourism at relatively modest prices for the first time to a mass market. Foreign tourism before the war had been the preserve of the wealthy. It now began to be made accessible to all. By the mid-1950s European borders were crossed by 30 million tourists. A decade later this had risen more than threefold. Traffic jams on major tourist routes every summer, throngs in railway stations and airports, were from now on an unchanging part of Europe's calendar. Tourism began to rescue Spain's backward economy, still in the doldrums after years of General Franco's dictatorship. By the later 1960s, 17 million foreign tourists were visiting Spain, swelling the state's coffers by a much-needed $1.5 billion (about 40 per cent of its foreign currency income). Italy was Europe's main tourist magnet, with 27 million visitors, France had 12 million, Switzerland, Germany and Austria around 7 million. Not everyone went abroad, of course. Domestic tourism also thrived. A fully fledged tourist industry emerged as hotels, campsites, caravan manufacturers and the myriad businesses that operated at seaside resorts flourished.

Relatively few tourists went to Eastern Europe, which in this way, too, was blocked off from the influx of Western spending. The Dalmatian coast of Yugoslavia, it is true, started to attract visitors from Western Europe, and there was a trickle to Hungary and Czechoslovakia. For the most part, however, the Soviet bloc had to rely on its own tourists, who had relatively little to spend compared with their counterparts in the West, and faced greater regulation of their movement.

As foreign tourism, and consumerism more generally, spread, the differences between the countries of Western Europe diminished. Travel exposed people – many of them of the younger generation – to other cultures, customs, foods and lifestyles. Partnerships of 'twinned' towns in different countries were established, leading to organized visits from each of the towns every year. Student or school-pupil exchanges were often set up. More people learned foreign languages. Some cultivated 'pen-friends' in other countries. The ease with which young people in general could travel abroad began to break down barriers that had seemed insuperable to their parents' generation. They often encountered similar tastes in music, dress and leisure pursuits with Europeans from different countries. European borders started to mean less. And ignorance, the ubiquitous basis of prejudice, was reduced. This all formed part of a far-reaching transformation of cultural norms in Europe that started slowly in the 1950s but then gathered pace rapidly amid the great vitality of the later 1960s.

STEPPING STONES TOWARDS INTEGRATION

Western Europe's remarkable recovery in such a brief period from the ruins of war and the legacy of austerity to a 'golden age' of prosperity brought the first, tentative steps towards integration. Each step on a long, winding and unending journey towards European union would prove tortuous. Potholes would have to be avoided, hurdles jumped, detours made. Above all and from the very outset, whatever steps were taken, small though they were at first, there was the obvious difficulty of reconciling the supranational organizations necessary even for limited economic cooperation with the reluctance of nation states to concede ground in preserving their own sovereignty.

The integration of Western Europe was from the outset at least as much a political as much as it was an economic project. The need to overcome the disastrous national economic protectionism of the interwar years and the extremes of nationalism that had led to the calamity of the Second World War was felt on all sides. What turned this general feeling into practical, if somewhat hesitant, early steps towards integration was a threefold constellation: strategic concerns, national interest and far-sighted idealism.

Even in the darkest days of the war small numbers of idealists, some of them in resistance movements, had contemplated some form of unification of Europe, and such ideas gained ground immediately after the war. Winston Churchill was one of those, in a famous speech he delivered in Zurich in 1946, who advocated unity on the broken continent, looking to a future 'United States of Europe' (though without British inclusion). At The Hague in May 1948, 750 delegates from sixteen European countries (and participants from the United States and Canada) attended a Congress of Europe that voiced ideas on European cooperation and, from some delegates, calls for political, economic and monetary union, though without tangible results.

A number of significant moves in the direction of European political and economic cooperation took place in the later 1940s without greatly advancing the cause of the integration that idealists desired. The emerging Cold War formed the background. If the impulse was at first to guard against any possible resurgence of a threat from Germany, this soon became transmuted into a defence mechanism against the perceived new menace of the Soviet Union. Still directed at Germany, the Treaty of Brussels in 1948 envisaged military cooperation between Britain, France and the Benelux countries, though it also made provision for economic, social and cultural collaboration. By 1949 Stalin was seen as the clear danger, and the extension of Western European defence provision to include the United States had resulted in the formation of NATO.

In the economic realm, the need to implement the distribution of

Marshall Aid under the European Recovery Plan of 1947 had led to the creation the following year of the Organization for European Economic Cooperation (OEEC) by sixteen European countries and the western zones of Germany, which helped to foster the idea of the interdependence of economic systems. (In 1961 this would become the Organization for Economic Cooperation and Development, now extended to a number of non-European countries to create a far wider body.) In 1949 the establishment of the Council of Europe provided a further framework for cooperation in a number of fields, most important of which were legal matters, out of which emerged the vital European Convention on Human Rights of 1950. At least in the Council of Europe a sense of *European*, not just national, values had been given institutional form. But it fell far short of integration. None of these developments, in fact, highly welcome though they were, went beyond differing levels of cooperation. None transcended, through the establishment of supranational bodies, the prerogatives of the nation states. At each step, in fact, the sovereignty of the nation states was expressly upheld. The United States had strongly backed an integrated, united Europe as a bulwark against Soviet Communism and had seen Marshall Aid as a significant step on the way. But Britain's adamant refusal to have anything to do with the integration of European economies, let alone concede anything of political and juridical sovereignty, proved an insuperable obstacle to that goal.

As the Cold War hardened inexorably between 1947 and 1949, and the Soviet Union, not a revengeful Germany, was seen as the danger to European peace, American strategic priorities forced French foreign policy to change. A revitalized West German economy now became essential to European reconstruction, while the steps that were rapidly taken in 1948–9 to create the Federal Republic of Germany reflected the centrality of the new state to the security of Western Europe, as a crucial bulwark against the USSR. To gain the support for the establishment of a new West German state from the still wary French, understandably still concerned more than all else with their country's security, the control of Ruhr coal and steel production was in 1949 placed under an International Authority for the Ruhr.

This had a council of representatives from France, the Benelux countries, the United Kingdom, the United States and West Germany (though German voting on the council was dependent on Allied approval).

Unsurprisingly, the West Germans intensely disliked the Allied control of German industrial production. At a time when the Korean War had increased the demand for steel, the International Authority was not working well and was wound up in May 1952. It was superseded by a new organization, the European Coal and Steel Community (ECSC), which would use the issue of coal and steel control to create the embryo of wider European integration. The Community's origins dated back two years, to a speech made on 9 May 1950 by the French Foreign Minister, Robert Schuman. His proposal blended together pragmatic national interest and strategic priorities – to expand the French steel industry and to make it competitive in Western Europe – with visionary idealism. It was an important milestone on the chequered route towards European integration.

Schuman proposed a new, ambitious supranational plan that would 'lead to the realisation of the first concrete foundation of a European federation indispensable to the preservation of peace'. A 'united Europe' – the ultimate goal – could only arise, Schuman stated, if at the outset the age-old antagonism of France and Germany were eliminated. He saw the pooling of coal and steel production as a start. But technical issues of coal and steel production were only a part of the far wider vision. He held open the prospects of other countries joining in a common market that could expand to other areas of production and would promote European prosperity as well as peaceful coexistence.

The ideas that Schuman presented were above all those of his fellow countryman, Jean Monnet, head of the French Planning Board, a former banker and businessman whose skills had been utilized both by the Chinese government (in the 1930s) and the US administration (during the war), and who had then played a major role in the early stages of French economic reconstruction after 1945. Monnet provided most of the idealistic inspiration to what became known as 'the Schuman Plan'. Monnet was a long-standing, convinced federalist. He envisaged a democratic supranational federation that would take shape gradually, incrementally, and over a lengthy period of time through a process of continuous reform. As early as October 1943, in Algiers as part of the French Committee of National Liberation, headed by Charles de Gaulle (whose autocratic tendencies worried Monnet) and effectively France's government-in-waiting, Monnet had declared that Europe's future social development and prosperity needed a Europe united by free trade. In

1944 he spoke of the need to rebuild post-war Europe through 'a true yielding of sovereignty' to 'some kind of central union', and a European market without customs barriers to prevent any resurgence of nationalism. He hoped the United Kingdom and France would take the lead, though evidently he doubted whether the British would be willing to participate. Four years later, writing to Schuman while on a visit to Washington, Monnet stated a 'deeply rooted conviction' of what was needed to cement the European relationship with the United States and to counter the danger threatening the West: 'Western European countries' efforts have to become a true European effort. And only a Western *Federation* is able to achieve this.' But Monnet did not see pooled sovereignty as eclipsing France's national standing. On the contrary: Monnet saw European integration as a vehicle to restore French political and economic dominance in continental Europe. After the war he put French interests first in proposing that France take over the crucial German coalfields of the Saarland and the even more vital coal and steel of the Ruhr, with a view to greatly strengthening the French economy while also leaving Germany permanently weakened.

Behind the undoubted idealism lay, therefore, pragmatic national imperatives. The key determinant – it would prove the lasting basis of the European Community (and later the European Union) – was the relationship between France and Germany. French priorities were to integrate the West Germans in a European framework under French control before they could regain any great strength, at the same time reinforcing France's hand in the production and distribution of the most vital industrial base, Ruhr coal and steel (and freeing this also from British control). West Germany, the major partner, also had overt national interests in integration. Konrad Adenauer, the Chancellor, was anxious to bind – economically, politically and strategically – the Federal Republic to the West, both as a bulwark against the threat from Soviet communism and as a platform for acquiring full territorial sovereignty at the earliest opportunity. For West Germany it was a chance to remove Allied control of Ruhr coal and steel production, prevent any further thoughts of dismantling industrial installations, establish German equal rights with other countries, and ultimately bring the major industrial area of the Saar (from 1947 onwards a 'Protectorate' under French occupation) fully back to Germany (which eventually took place after a plebiscite in 1955). The Benelux countries

(Belgium, the Netherlands and Luxembourg), which had in fact removed customs duties and set up a common external tariff already in 1948, needed little persuasion to see national advantages in the wider markets and liberalization of trade that was implicit in Schuman's proposal. Alcide de Gasperi, the premier of Italy, another European idealist, saw a chance to overcome his country's long-standing economic weaknesses and backwardness (especially in the south, the Mezzogiorno). Italy was the poorest of the six nations that would join the new organization, but de Gasperi looked to advantages in ending its traditional protectionism, despite weighty opposition from the country's steel manufacturers. He was right. By 1961 Italy's 'economic miracle' had turned the country from being economically backward into one of Europe's advanced industrial nations.

Putting the Schuman Plan into operation had faced internal opposition. This was at its most vehement in West Germany, where the Social Democrats saw the country's integration into Western Europe as an obstacle to the desired unification of the country, and in France from the Gaullists (for the Plan's limitation of national sovereignty) and the Communists (regarding it as a 'capitalists' club'). Nevertheless, the European Coal and Steel Community, confined to six countries, was established by treaty, signed on 18 April 1951, and came into effect on 23 July 1952. It brought together the vital coal and steel industries of France, West Germany, Italy, the Netherlands, Belgium and Luxembourg under a single 'High Authority'. For Jean Monnet, it was 'the first expression of the Europe that is being born'. Britain, still confident of its lead in steel and coal production and unwilling to be bound by a supranational authority, declined the invitation to join.

The High Authority, comprising nine representatives from all the member states, was the policymaking body. It was to preside over a programme aimed at the removal of tariffs and establishment of a common market (initially for coal and steel, though to be widened to other spheres). Its powers were hedged by a 'Special Council of Ministers' drawn from national governments, to ensure that national interests were upheld. A Court of Justice, to adjudicate on any disputes arising from High Authority action, was also established. But the High Authority was deliberately designed as a 'top-down' institution. There was no legislative body, nor a proper parliament. A Common Assembly, whose delegates were drawn from the national parliaments, had merely supervisory, not legislative powers. In practice, the Assembly, far from trying to confine the High Authority, promoted its moves to supranational direction of the economy. Progress in this regard was not speedy, and national protectionism by the Belgians, Italians and, not least, the French themselves, hindered progress, though gradually trade barriers started to be eliminated. In the wider aim of political integration, envisaged by Schuman, little was achieved beyond a growing awareness that the administration of increasingly interwoven economies necessarily demanded institutions and laws that had implicit, if not explicit, political implications.

By the mid-1950s there had been some real, if slow, progress towards economic integration. Politically, however, the European project as envisaged by Monnet and Schuman had stalled. This was in the main because of the failure of the European Defence Community, a project that the French (hoping to head off German rearmament) had proposed in 1952 only to vote it down themselves in 1954. Integration of European defence would have necessitated a common foreign policy. As it was, the inability to create a European army, the foreign policy to support it, and the institutional arrangements that would invariably follow, left the kernel of what had already been given a name, the European Political Community, stillborn. The ill-starred European Defence Community had been a case of trying to run before walking. It was simply asking too much of nation states with their own strong military traditions, like France (and Britain, too, which, it was initially hoped, would participate), to relinquish so soon such a key part of their sovereignty to an unknown and untried supranational entity. There was no disguising the fact that it amounted to a severe setback for those who had pinned their hopes on unhindered advancement towards European integration.

The European Coal and Steel Community was left, it was true, to linger until the Treaty of Paris, which had established it, expired in 2002. It was a slow death, noticed by few. In reality, it had lost its momentum in the wake of the collapse of the European Defence Community. An indication of its waning significance was the decision of its chief architect, Jean Monnet, not to seek re-election to the presidency of the High Authority. Western Europe seemed indeed to be retreating from integration rather than proceeding towards it. West German military rearmament, then the Suez debacle, in which Britain and France had acted like imperialist powers of a bygone age, looked like major impediments to any common cause among European nations. Curiously, however, Suez, the self-evident dominance of the two Cold War superpowers, and also the growing anti-colonial movements in Africa and Asia, were such plain signs of the diminished international standing of Europe's nation states that the one area where they could plainly benefit from closer integration, rather than separate national paths – the economy – gained new momentum. In the wake of Suez, where the Anglo-French invasion had collapsed after the Americans had merely threatened damaging financial repercussions for Britain, the French premier Guy Mollet was open to the argument of Adenauer that the only counterweight to American dominance was to be found in European unity. Mollet and Adenauer subsequently overrode doubts within their own governments to reach agreement on the free entry of French and German goods into each other's markets. It was the pivot of the wider agreement that was already taking shape on the creation of a common market between the six countries of 'little Europe' that had formed the European Coal and Steel Community.

Whatever political travails were besetting Western Europe in the early 1950s, the economy of every country was booming. The success, if still limited, in the economic sphere of the European Coal and Steel Community and the unwieldy framework of the earlier Organization for European Economic Cooperation both pointed the way towards new initiatives, most especially in creating a common market for European trade. Monnet, though no longer head of the High Authority, played a significant role in promoting the idea. But the key figure in driving forward the process was the former Belgian socialist Prime Minister and President of the Common Assembly of the European Coal and Steel Community, Paul-Henri Spaak.

Britain wanted nothing to do with the proposed common market. And the Scandinavian countries had established their own closer cooperation in the Nordic Council that had been formed in 1952. So the steps towards future closer European integration were confined from the outset to the original six members of the European Coal and Steel Community. Their foreign secretaries met at Messina in 1955, aiming to promote 'a fresh advance towards the building of Europe'. In concrete terms they proposed the establishment of a customs union leading to a common market and an integrated policy on the use of atomic energy. After Messina progress was surprisingly swift until the decisive moment in March 1957, at Rome, when two treaties were signed by the prime ministers of the six member countries, setting up a European Economic Community (EEC) and a European Atomic Energy Community (Euratom). Three years earlier, with the collapse of the attempt to create a European Defence Community, European integration looked to have run into the buffers. By 1957 it was full steam ahead. As the name of the new institution suggested, economic integration was the priority. But it was to be the start, not the finish. The long-term political objective was embedded in the Treaty of Rome itself: this was 'to establish the foundations of an ever closer union among the European peoples'.

The short- to medium-term objectives of the Treaty, which came into effect on 1 January 1958, were ambitious enough. They sought to consolidate and promote rising living standards through economic growth. There was to be free movement of labour and capital, the ending of trade restrictions, together with coordinated policies of social welfare and the creation of a European Investment Bank. The aim was to create a common market, free of internal tariffs. External tariffs, though generally reduced, were retained. And agriculture, facing quite specific difficulties, was protected. The institutional arrangements were modifications from the European Coal and Steel Community. A Commission of nine members formed an executive. Its powers were, however, limited by the Council of Ministers, drawn from the national governments and by the Parliamentary Assembly – still not a fully fledged parliament – that could recommend, but not legislate. A Court of Justice was set up to adjudicate on disputes between member states. A separate Commission and Council were set up for Euratom (and eventually merged with those of the EEC in 1965). The institutions were served by a bureaucracy of around 3,000 civil servants (and growing) by 1962.

By 1960 the EEC, covering a population of 165 million, had made impressive progress. It had hugely expanded its contribution to world trade, while total industrial production had increased by 70 per cent over the previous decade. Euratom's progress was less impressive. It faced obvious difficulties from the start – even greater once de Gaulle had come to power in 1958 – since the French were determined to uphold national security interests in such a sensitive field and were unwilling to stand by while West Germany acquired atomic capability.

The success of the EEC already in its first years forced the nation states that did not belong to it to create their own organization. The European Free Trade Association (EFTA), founded on 20 November 1959 and coming into effect on 3 May 1960, linked together the 'Outer Seven' – Great Britain, Denmark, Norway, Austria, Portugal, Sweden and Switzerland (Finland was later to join) – in a second economic area in Europe. Compared with the EEC, however, it was a far looser arrangement, purely (as the name suggested) a trading organization that demanded no dilution of national sovereignty and had no aim of ultimate political integration. It was also from the outset weakened by the deteriorating economic performance of its most important member, Britain.

The British economy had by this time not only lost the European economic predominance it had briefly enjoyed in the first post-war years, but was being overtaken by the rapidly growing continental economies. Its trading strength was diminishing, its ties with the Commonwealth waning, and its 'special relationship' with the United States largely one-sided. It was not surprising, therefore, that by 1961 Britain was reconsidering its stance and deciding to apply for membership of the EEC. For existing members two concerns predominated. The first was the problem of Britain's Commonwealth trading arrangements, which could not be accommodated. The second was the fear that Britain's almost exclusive preoccupation with free trade would hinder, perhaps even vitiate, the long-term political objectives of the EEC. Britain's application indeed came with strings attached – safeguards for British agriculture and Commonwealth ties, and agreement with the other EFTA countries that wanted to join the EEC. These were significant obstacles. Britain's application was directly to founder, however, on the rocks of opposing French national interests. In 1963 the application met with the resounding 'Non' of the French President, Charles de Gaulle, who was to repeat his veto on British entry when a second application was made in 1967.

De Gaulle's primary concern was to prevent the possibility of Britain coming to usurp France's dominance in the EEC and damage the Franco-German foundation of the Community. He also distrusted Britain's close relations with the United States, the main threat in his view to France's leadership of Europe and prestige as a great power. Quite apart from his negative stance towards British entry, de Gaulle was, however, at best an ambivalent European and his years in office as President of France were difficult ones for the cause of European integration. De Gaulle, a traditional French nationalist whose views were anchored in the need to restore France's former glory and uphold its great-power pretensions, most obviously against the dominance of the USA, was prepared to accept pragmatically the benefits that the limited forms of European integration had brought his country. What he wanted, however, was not a supranational power, but a 'Europe of the Fatherlands'. His version of European union was one in which France dominated while the Germans were willing but subordinate partners and American and British influence was kept at bay. He set his face adamantly against any significant inroads into French national sovereignty, opposed any strengthening of the EEC's Commission and consistently put the interests of France first, way beyond those of the Community.

The resulting tension brought open conflict in 1965. Matters came to a head over the powers of the Commission. The occasion was the complex issue of agriculture. Following wearisome negotiations it had been agreed in 1962 to establish a Common Agricultural Policy (CAP) with a single market for agricultural produce at fixed prices and subsidies for farmers. However, the question of financing the CAP had become embroiled in proposals to extend the powers of the Commission, which sought to gain control of the revenue from external tariffs, and suggestions that the European Parliament should be given legislative powers. This would have meant, therefore, a widening of the supranational authority of the EEC. When this became a condition of the agricultural settlement, de Gaulle – even though the CAP would benefit French farmers – posed his own conditions: unless France was offered a solution it found satisfactory, and a right of veto on the strengthening of supranational powers in the EEC, it would boycott European institutions.

For seven months France did so, after de Gaulle had ordered French representatives back from the Commission's negotiations. The resulting 'empty chair crisis', as it was dubbed, was finally resolved with an uneasy 'Luxembourg Compromise' of 1966. This provided for a veto on matters of 'very important national interest' (left undefined), qualified majority voting on agriculture, and a weakening of the Commission, whose prerogatives in some spheres were subject to approval by the Council (representing member states). The underlying problem of trying to reconcile national interests with supranational institutions, far from moving towards any resolution, had become magnified. As long as de Gaulle remained in power in France, this was unlikely to change.

By this time the 'European project' could point to some successes. Institutionally and administratively there was some streamlining when, in 1965, it was agreed to merge the EEC, Euratom and the Economic Coal and Steel Community. And economic advances, if at times stuttering, had certainly been made, particularly in liberalizing trade. The last internal customs were eliminated in 1968 and a unified external duty was introduced. The liberalization of trade, together with greater investment and technology transfer, increased competition, and economies of scale added an estimated 1 per cent to European growth rates. On the debit side, the Common Agricultural Policy remained a headache and deliberations in 1969 to try to move towards monetary union proved abortive, given the disparity in strength of national currencies (not least between the French franc and the German mark). Politically, however, union seemed as distant a goal as ever. Integration on all fronts had progressed since 1950 in a sort of European foxtrot: two steps forward, one to the side, and one back. In fact, from the outset moves towards integration had been overwhelmingly driven by *national* motives – initially to ensure French dominance, then as a platform to re-establish a German nation state. The aim of ever-closer union had in practice bolstered the system of European nation states.

The core of the six founder members of the EEC was not widened until 1973. Before then, Greece (in 1962) and Turkey (in 1964) had been given associate status – Greece's suspended in April 1967 when a military putsch abruptly ended (temporarily) democracy in the country. Malta (1971) and Cyprus (1973) also gained the status of associate members, while preferential terms on the import of a range of industrial goods were offered to a number of developing states in Africa. But de Gaulle's double veto of British membership meant that the EEC had remained a 'club' of the original Six that had founded it in 1957. Apart from France, however, the other five countries were much more favourably disposed towards British membership. Once de Gaulle had left office in April 1969, and when, in June 1970, the strongly Europhile conservative Edward Heath, after an unexpected election victory, had become British Prime Minister, the prospects of widening the European Community (as it had been called since 1967) to include the United Kingdom improved sharply.

The new French President, Georges Pompidou, was more open to British membership of the European Community than his intransigent predecessor had been. In part this was because he saw the need to counterbalance the position of West Germany, whose thriving economy and strong currency had turned it into Europe's indubitable economic powerhouse and weakened the dominance of France that the French had at first taken for granted. Moreover, the Federal Republic's Social Democratic Chancellor (since October 1969), Willy Brandt, had begun to shape a new relationship with Eastern Europe, his *Ostpolitik*, which had unknoweable consequences for the European Community and for France. From the British side, it was time to make a final attempt to join the Community. Heath, relatively cool towards America, was a European from conviction. He had been deeply moved by the devastation he had witnessed while serving in the British army after the Normandy landings. European unity was for him, as for other idealists of his generation, the only way to secure lasting peace. And from the point of view of national interest, joining the European Community seemed an attractive option. With trade with the Commonwealth in sharp decline, membership of the European Community would offer the British economy – in poor shape, suffering high inflation, and wracked by industrial unrest – the opportunity of benefiting from the far more successful Common Market that had developed in Western Europe. Following a meeting in Paris in May 1971 between Pompidou and Heath, detailed negotiations in Brussels paved the way for the United Kingdom to become a member of the European Community on 1 January 1973. Ireland and Denmark joined at the same time. Norway's application caused, however, bitter divisions in the country. A referendum in 1971 in which 53 per cent of the voters rejected membership, put an end to Norwegian expectations of joining the Community.

The expansion of the Economic Community to now nine countries introduced a new, and as it would prove, lasting difficulty: Britain's semi-detached stance. Heath belonged to a small minority of European idealists in Britain. In his own party (and beyond) there were many, especially of the older generation, who could not be reconciled with the end of empire and the fact that Britain's status had been reduced in effect to that of a European medium-power. Most of the British population were at best indifferent towards the European Community, while the left was opposed to an organization perceived as a 'rich man's club'. Those who favoured it did so generally because of its perceived economic advantages, but no more. 'Europe' was a balance sheet. The European Community was tellingly referred to, for years afterwards, as the 'Common Market'. Would Britain be better off inside the EC, or staying outside? That was the only question for most people.

They did not see Britain as part of Europe. And indeed in some significant ways its historical development had set it apart from continental Europe. The country's centuries-old parliamentary sovereignty, its traditions, ancient institutions and legal system, had not been interrupted by invasion and occupation. Its modern history had rested on overseas empire rather than European ties (other than being twice in recent memory forced to fight in European wars). Its duodecimal coinage and system of measurements (decimalized, to many people's regret, in 1971 to facilitate European trade) reminded people on a daily basis that they were not like the countries of continental Europe. The sense of distinctiveness was enhanced by Britain's geography as an island on the edge of the continent, looking across the Atlantic as much as across the English Channel. All this was subsumed more than anything else in Britain's long-standing sovereign and jealously guarded powers as a nation state whose complete independence would brook no inroads from any source. Politicians – Conservative and Labour – and the majority of ordinary citizens therefore needed a good deal of persuasion to overcome their insularity and to embrace, rather than grudgingly accept, being part of a European Community. The insularity had produced ingrained prejudice. France, just over twenty miles off the southern English coast, was seen as 'foreign'; Australia, 12,000 miles away, was not.

Over time, of course, and especially in the younger generation, such attitudes changed. But there was no avoidance of the fact that Britain was belatedly joining a European Community which, by this time, had evolved, naturally enough, in ways to suit its core membership. The Common Agricultural Policy was one area bound to cause hackles to rise in Britain, where consumers now had to pay higher food prices in order to subsidize uncompetitive continental – especially French – farmers. That already efficient British farmers should also profit substantially was no consolation to British consumers, already hit hard by rampant inflation. So the 'Common Market' began in Britain somewhat inauspiciously.

But the disadvantages of not belonging were emphasized by business and by the government. The arguments seemed convincing, whatever the misgivings. When put to a referendum in 1975, a two-thirds majority favoured Britain staying inside the European Community. Many had voted to stay in 'Europe' because they had presumed this meant belonging to a widened free-trade area, and would therefore have economic benefits, ignoring (or oblivious to) the underlying political objective of 'ever closer union' that had been enshrined in the Treaty of Rome in 1957. It was an impressive result, nonetheless, showing that most British people recognized that the country's future was best assured by closer ties with its European neighbours. A sense of Britain as part of Europe was taking hold, specifically in the better-educated and wealthier sectors of society. A residual antagonism towards everything emanating from, and associated with, 'Brussels' (the seat of the European Community's Commission) remained, however, and would continue to complicate and weaken the aim of turning economic integration into closer political union.

By 1973 the European Community had far more to worry about than any potential future difficulties in accommodating British particularist interests. Problems in the American economy, notably a rising payments deficit, were affecting European monetary stability. Britain had devalued its currency in 1967 and France in 1969, while the extraordinary strength of the Deutschmark reflected an obvious economic imbalance among European countries that had increasing difficulty in sustaining fixed rates of exchange among themselves. In 1971 the Bretton Woods system of convertible fixed-rate currencies, dating back to the international agreement of July 1944, was abandoned in favour of more flexible floating currencies. In practice this further enhanced West Germany's financial dominance among the countries of the European Community.

* * *

The real blow to the economies of Western Europe came, however, with the oil crisis of 1973. This followed the fourth and largest Arab–Israeli War – after those of 1948, 1956 (the Suez debacle) and the Six-Day War of 1967 that had brought Israel huge gains in territory. The Arab countries had, unsurprisingly, refused to accept the territorial outcome of Israel's preemptive strike in June 1967. This had taken away great tracts of land that had previously been possessed by the Arabs, enlarging Israeli territory more than threefold, incorporating the Golan Heights and Sinai peninsula into Israel while placing the whole of Jerusalem under Israeli rule. Quietly the Arab states had planned their revenge. On 6 October 1973, the Jewish holy day of Yom Kippur (the Day of Atonement), Egypt and Syria launched a huge, and at first highly successful, military attack on Israel. The Israelis hit back strongly, however, and regained much of the initiative before the intervention of the superpowers (along with a massive increase in American aid to help to rebuild a badly damaged Israeli economy) engineered an uneasy ceasefire at the end of the month.

The Arab countries turned to oil as a new and potent weapon that they were prepared to use against the West. The Middle East had produced only 7 per cent of world oil output in 1945. By 1973 the proportion was almost two-fifths. In the middle of the war Arab oil ministers, working through the cartel of OPEC (the Organization of Petroleum Exporting Countries), had agreed to raise oil prices to Western oil companies by 70 per cent, cut production by 25 per cent, and impose an oil embargo on the United States and other supporters of Israel. It marked a new departure in international conflict, and created huge problems for Western economies that had become heavily dependent upon oil consumption. The oil regime that the West had both promoted and hugely benefited from now showed itself capable and ready to defend its interests with dramatic effect. The quadrupling of the price of oil had a devastating impact on almost every economic calculation or assumption. The ensuing near panic pointed again to the limited progress of integration as the individual countries of the European Community (as well as those outside) sought their own national solutions.

The oil crisis brought severe economic recession, the first one of any seriousness since before the Second World War. In a wider sense it inaugurated a new era for Europe. The years of post-war boom were at an end. The good times were over.

5

Culture after the Catastrophe

I am no longer sure of anything.

Jean-Paul Sartre, 1951

A-wop-bop-a-loo-bop-a-wop-bam-boom!

'Tutti Frutti', by Little Richard, 1955

Culture offers a window into the soul of a society. It is a window with many panes, and each pane is coloured in different hues. Some panes are opaque – so opaque that nothing can be seen through them. Such is the variegation of cultural expression in any free society that succinct summary is scarcely possible and the search for common clear lines of interpretation extremely difficult. Yet in quite different ways culture casts light on the character of Europe in the early post-war decades. And despite the Iron Curtain and the diversity of cultural development in Eastern and Western Europe – chiefly a reflection of different levels of political control – and despite, too, the unquestionable national influences on culture in an era of nation states, a shared culture was in many respects the European continent's main defining entity.

During the 'good times' of almost uninterrupted economic growth and rising prosperity between 1950 and 1973, European culture mostly looked to the future. This reflected not just the unprecedented rapidity of economic improvement; it also accorded with the early political steps towards overcoming the deep scars of the nationalist past. There was increasing optimism, a sense that mankind could achieve practically anything it wanted. This accompanied an almost religious belief in what science could achieve. Space travel pioneered by the Soviets and

Americans seemed to underpin such faith. So did other advances in science, particularly medicine, that held out great promise for a brighter future. More than anything the cult of youth and the generational revolt that came to full expression in the later 1960s embodied a self-conscious break with the past. Pop music was its ubiquitous medium. Across Western Europe and even beyond the Iron Curtain idols such as Elvis Presley in the mid-1950s, the Beatles and the Rolling Stones nearly a decade later, represented a new era, a future that belonged to the young. A popular culture focused on the immediate present, and beyond that living in confident expectation of a better world to come, helped to influence a transformation in social values that started to change at a pace probably more rapid than at any time in history.

But although Europe confidently looked to its future, it could not forget its past. The optimism of scientists was one side of the coin. The other was a prevalent – and understandable – sense of pessimism among the literary intelligentsia in the early post-war years. George Orwell offered a compellingly bleak reason: 'Since about 1930 the world had given no reason for optimism whatsoever. Nothing in sight except a welter of lies, cruelty, hatred and ignorance.' Such unremitting despair, which despite Orwell was far less characteristic of British than continental European intellectuals, did gradually decline as economic recovery took hold, yielding to new types of social criticism, much of it levelled not at the depressing past but at the present-day shallowness of a materialistic consumer society. But the horror of what Europe had been through returned time and time again in different ways. It was an inescapable component of cultural expression. 'To write poetry after Auschwitz is barbaric,' the German philosopher Theodor Adorno (who had spent the Nazi era in exile, mainly in the USA) had remarked in 1949. This was not to be taken literally. Indeed, it was belied by Paul Celan's powerful poem, 'Die Todesfuge' ('Death Fugue'), composed by a Romanian-born Jew whose parents had been deported to their deaths and had himself spent time in a labour camp towards the end of the war. It became widely known after its publication in German in 1952, explicitly depicting the gaunt imagery of death in a concentration camp. Celan epitomized the essence of Adorno's reflection, regarding his poem as 'an epitaph and a grave'. He never fully recovered from the deportation and death of his parents, suffered repeated bouts of depression, and many years later, in

April 1970, his body was found in the Seine outside Paris. Adorno captured a sense of the difficulties for any intellectuals or those engaged in the creative arts who attempted in the post-war years to grapple with the meaning of Europe's recent calamitous plunge into the abyss of inhumanity.

For most people perspectives were different. Those born during or after the war emerged from post-war austerity and hardship wanting the pleasures and experiences of a brave new world. Many, perhaps most, of those who had lived through and fought in the two world wars, including the millions who had suffered grievous fates, did not want to dwell on the terrible past. They too in untold numbers wanted a brighter future, not to be compelled to revisit past misery. Indeed, interest in the two world wars and the Holocaust was lower in the 1950s and 1960s than it became in the last quarter of the twentieth century. Nevertheless, the shadow of the immediate past could not easily be dispelled in the early post-war decades. In culture, intellectual currents and popular mentalities, the recent past was always present; it could not be wished away.

THE SHADOW OF THE PAST

The impact of the Second World War was less obvious in the creative arts than in philosophy or history. It was there just the same. Post-war attitudes towards the music of Richard Wagner offered an obvious example. Wagner's own ideological antisemitism, Hitler's close connections with the Wagner family and the expropriation of Bayreuth (home to the annual Wagnerian festival) as a Nazi cultural shrine, posed notable obstacles to the reception of the composer's works in a world that had witnessed the Holocaust. Wagner polarized feelings like no other composer. Against the admirers of his music-dramas as unparalleled works of genius and grandeur were those who saw in Wagner and his music a crucial cultural underpinning of German nationalism, antisemitism and, ultimately, Nazism, war and genocide. After five years in which Wagner's Bayreuth theatre, the Festspielhaus, had been used for the performance of concerts and operas by other composers, the Bayreuth Festival was revived in 1951 and was soon flourishing again under the direction of the composer's grandsons, first Wieland and then Wolfgang.

Wieland's emphatic break in artistic staging marked the clear rupture with pre-war links with Nazism. Even so, the taint of the strong connection between Wagner and Nazism could never be fully eradicated.

The compositions of Dmitri Shostakovich also clearly illustrate how in classical music the past could be overtly bound up with current politics. His epic Seventh Symphony, 'Leningrad', first performed in the starving city itself during the terrible German siege between 1941 and 1943, had totemic status in the Soviet Union as a memorial to the immense suffering of the population. It represented beyond that the hope of the Soviet people gained through victory over fascism in the 'great patriotic war'. But the experimental forms of Shostakovich's music were sharply criticized by the Soviet regime both before and after the war. The composer had in fact probably been saved only by his celebrity from becoming yet another victim of Stalin's purges in the later 1930s. He continued to risk the regime's displeasure. Even under Khrushchev's 'cultural thaw' Shostakovich walked on the edge. His String Quartet No. 8, 'In Memory of the Victims of Fascism and War', composed in 1960 to commemorate the bombing of Dresden in 1945, reprised themes from his earlier compositions that had been condemned as 'bourgeois formalism'. And his Thirteenth Symphony (1962), 'Babi Yar', based upon a poem by Yevgeny Yevtushenko that recalled the massacre of 33,771 Jews – the figure is precisely known from the records of the Nazi killers – near Kiev in 1941, courted controversy by singling out the persecution of the Jews and obliquely criticizing the Soviet Union's own antisemitism.

There were by contrast few reflections of the wartime catastrophe in the post-war classical music scene in Western Europe. The past there had a different meaning. People wanted a return to normality after the disaster, not to be reminded of it. The popularity of Benjamin Britten's *War Requiem* of 1962, first performed at the consecration of the new Coventry Cathedral that year – the medieval cathedral had been destroyed in the German bombing of Coventry in November 1940 – was an exception. Nor did audiences by and large warm to avant-garde classical music – such as the experimental works of Olivier Messiaen, Pierre Boulez or Karlheinz Stockhausen. They mainly wanted the traditional, not the modern. In general, audiences flocked to hear once more the classical repertoire of the eighteenth and nineteenth centuries – Bach, Mozart, Beethoven, Brahms, or the operas of Donizetti, Verdi and Puccini, even

Wagner (despite being tainted by Nazi associations). They welcomed back famous conductors such as Arturo Toscanini, Otto Klemperer, Bruno Walter, Karl Böhm and Tullio Serafin, and rejoiced in newer luminaries like Herbert von Karajan and Georg Solti. And they thrilled at the performances of a galaxy of operatic stars such as Maria Callas, Joan Sutherland, Jussi Björling, Tito Gobbi and Giuseppe di Stefano – extraordinary singers, though performing a favourite repertoire from an earlier era. By the mid-1960s even the brilliant American composer and conductor Leonard Bernstein implied that classical music had lost its appealing inventiveness. 'Pop music,' he said, 'seems to be the only area where there is to be found unabashed vitality, the fun of invention, the feeling of fresh air.'

Other forms of creative art also reflected a tension between the past and the future, between the traditional – or at least the familiar – and the modern avant garde that sought to break with earlier forms of representation. As Europe had sunk into ashes the main innovatory impetus in painting had moved to New York. American influence – epitomized by the work of Jackson Pollock – was prominent in the shift to radical forms of abstract expressionism. This was more welcomed in Britain than in continental Europe. It was an influence even so in the spread of a bewildering diversity of abstract art that became dominant in post-war Europe. New experimental art forms, emerging by the end of the 1950s, often aimed to shock conventional sensibilities. Such forms included the Parisian group *Nouveau Réalisme*'s creation of images of urban squalor and consumer products, bearing similarities to the independently developing American Pop Art, most closely associated with Andy Warhol.

The innovations themselves drew on pre-war artistic movements. Moreover, Pablo Picasso, Henri Matisse, Marc Chagall and other luminaries of the pre-war era were still active, and attracting far more visitors to their exhibitions than did the radical younger artists. As always, artistic innovation saw itself as a revolt against traditional forms of expression – which were now seen to include much of what had been considered revolutionary before the war. But the most radical forms of abstract art struggled to appeal to wide audiences who continued to flock instead to see the works of the Old Masters. The war thus marked an artistic shift, though far from a complete break with the past.

In architecture the shadow of the past was all too visible in the ruins and devastation of Europe's great cities and towns. The war marked an obvious break. Rebuilding was an urgent necessity. But in ravaged economies it had to be inexpensive. The most characteristic style, used especially for housing or shopping complexes, government buildings, and then the campuses of new universities, was brutalism, derived from the French term for raw concrete (*béton brut*), its material base. It drew on the rationalism and functionalism of the 1930s, though it took the earlier styles to new extremes. It was seen as 'progressive' and associated with some eminent architects, including the great Swiss designer and urban planner, Le Corbusier. And it was international, spreading rapidly across the world. Its impact in Western Europe varied. Italian public architecture was better than almost anywhere else. Daring constructions were attempted, as in the extraordinary cantilevered designs of Luigi Moretti, that remained exceptional in the early post-war years.

Brutalism hardly penetrated in Italy. Elsewhere, too, there were major exceptions. One was Le Corbusier's strikingly modernist pilgrimage chapel, Notre Dame du Haut, at Ronchamp in eastern France, built for the Catholic Church between 1953 and 1955, described by Nikolaus Pevsner as a 'monument of a new irrationalism'. Another was the last work of Mies van der Rohe, the Neue Nationalgalerie in West Berlin, a building completed in 1968 that maximized the aesthetic effect of glass and steel in creating light and space. In Britain, on the other hand, brutalism became inescapable. It was visually stark and forbidding – its facades of bare concrete, glass and steel utterly denuded of any ornamentation. Its style exuded the atmosphere of post-war austerity (though it continued to be deployed when funding became less of a problem). It seemed to represent modern, solid, no-frills collective society. It had its admirers, especially in later decades – usually among those who did not have to live or work in 'brutalist' constructions. But for many, the buildings were an aesthetic affront from the outset. And for later generations the dilapidated concrete of prominent buildings in the heart of their cities was for the most part regarded as an eyesore, not an attraction.

East of the Iron Curtain, too, a type of brutalism (without the name) was welcomed as anti-bourgeois 'socialist' architecture, which in town planning concentrated on the construction of cheap and simple apartments for the working population. Drab, mass-produced, low-cost, purely functional housing to cope with the drastic shortage of accommodation was one side of socialist architecture. The other was the 'social classicism' of monumental representative buildings, intended to display the greatness of the worker state – as in Warsaw's Palace of Culture and Science (completed in 1955, 'The Wedding Cake', as locals called it, among even less flattering names), or Stalinallee (later Karl-Marx-Allee) in East Berlin, an imposing boulevard two kilometres long and almost 90 metres wide.

In the theatre the war marked a hiatus more than an outright break. But the past was an inescapable part of the theatre's post-war revival. Antifascism and biting critique of bourgeois society ran through the entire oeuvre of the great Marxist playwright Bertolt Brecht, who returned from exile to East Berlin (where he lived until his death in August 1956), attracted by the offer of his own theatre company, the Berlin Ensemble. Brecht had been famous long before the war as one of the most luminous stars in the firmament of Weimar Berlin before the Nazis had destroyed it. Much of his most important work had been accomplished during the Weimar era, when his theories of 'epic theatre' had been developed. 'Epic theatre', though Brecht invented neither the name nor the concept, amounted to a self-conscious break with the past. In his new conceptualization Brecht rejected the 'theatre of illusion', which stimulated an audience's identification with characters and created the illusory sense that it was experiencing reality, and sought to induce rational reflection through the audience's detachment or 'alienation' from action on the stage.

After the war Brecht was more active as a theatrical director than writer. But his plays were enormously popular in West Germany – second only to Shakespeare and ahead of Schiller measured by numbers of performances during the 1960s – and were well known across Europe, east and west (and beyond, especially in the USA). In East Germany, he was acclaimed as a writer of international renown who had chosen to make his home in the German Democratic Republic. But the prized citizen was not without problems. The East German leaders were cautious about granting him too much exposure, aware as they were of his limited enthusiasm for the realities of communist society – despite his public (if somewhat ambiguous) support for the crushing of the 1953 uprising, and although he had the following year received the Stalin Peace Prize (the proceeds of which, around 300,000 Swiss francs, he deposited in the Swiss bank account that he retained).

The most innovatory strand of Western theatre in the 1950s and 1960s was the 'theatre of the absurd', which became synonymous with the names of the Irishman Samuel Beckett and the Romanian Eugène Ionesco, both of whom lived and wrote in Paris. The underlying philosophy of their work was that life had neither meaning nor purpose; it was absurd. The dialogue of plays such as Beckett's *Waiting for Godot* (1953) and *Endgame* (1957) consisted of seemingly meaningless conversation by figures who parodied human existence in performances explicitly devoid of action. It was little wonder that the theatre of the absurd aroused great hostility. But the plays were also widely performed and attracted much praise, as well as inevitable, if paradoxical, discussion of what meaning was contained in meaninglessness. The theatre of the absurd drew on an artistic lineage reaching back to dadaism and surrealism after the First World War. Much of it was a theatrical representation of long-standing developments in the visual arts. But the thinking behind the theatre of the absurd also had a relevance that emanated from the more immediate past.

It was close to that of the great French writer Albert Camus, a towering figure of post-war literature, who won the Nobel Prize for Literature in 1957. During the German occupation Camus had written leading articles for the underground Résistance newspaper, *Combat*, and continued to write for the newspaper until it closed in 1948. After the war he published some of his most important novels – *La Peste* (*The Plague*) in 1947 and *La Chute* (*The Fall*) in 1956 – with oblique reference to Nazism and the Holocaust. Through Camus's writing the theatre of the absurd had a link with the immediate, terrible past. *La Peste* (in which the citizens of Oran in the French province of Algeria respond partly with fatalism, partly by opportunistic exploitation of the situation, but partly through active attempts to combat the onset of a plague epidemic) is usually interpreted as an allegory of the French experience under Nazi occupation. The arbitrary impact of the plague and random exposure to death highlight life's absurdity. But Camus, who resisted being labelled an 'existentialist', struggles to retain the belief in meaningless existence when he emphasizes through his most sympathetic characters the need not to simply accept the arrival from outside of suffering and death, but to struggle against them – and not alone, but in solidarity with other citizens for the good of the community.

Literature, more than painting or the theatre, reflected the need to search for meaning in the catastrophic events of the recent past. Perhaps unsurprisingly, this was particularly pronounced in West Germany. (In the German Democratic Republic, official doctrine determined a fairly tight straitjacket for literature as a vehicle for the all-pervasive doctrine of anti-fascism.) At a time when most ordinary German citizens sought to shut out painful memories, influential writers tried to wrestle with them. One of the first was Wolfgang Koeppen. His novel *Tauben im Gras* (*Pigeons on the Grass*, 1951), written in the style of a 'stream of consciousness', described a single day in a city where anxiety about an east–west conflict intermingle with hopes for the future and the attempt to find meaning in the ruins. Continuities with the Nazi past are not hidden, but they exist alongside paths towards a more open, pluralist society. And with his *Der Tod in Rom* (*Death in Rome*, 1954), Koeppen, who had been at least out-wardly conformist during the Third Reich, was again among the first writers to explore questions of German guilt related to the Holocaust.

A number of younger West German writers soon to establish them-selves as prominent literary figures dealt directly or allusively with the recent German past as part of their exploration of the necessary cultural and aesthetic break with that past in the self-consciously uncertain new democracy. In their work, and that of others, new beginnings and the recent past were closely interwoven. Alfred Andersch (born in 1914), who had served in the Wehrmacht, touched in his best-known work, *Sansibar oder der letzte Grund* (1957, later translated into English as *Flight to Afar*), upon themes of communist resistance, desertion from the army, persecution of the Jews and 'degenerate art' (as the Nazis had labelled avant-garde art forms). He suggested at the same time a double-edged moral duty – to help the persecuted to flee, but also to return from free choice to Germany, the land of the persecutors. Heinrich Böll, three years younger than Andersch, had viewed his war service through the eyes of his fervent Catholic belief, writing in December 1940 that 'a new spirit' had to exist in Europe and that 'it is certainly our task "to propa-gate Christianity"'. But he vehemently opposed Nazi inhumanity and militarism. *Billard um halb zehn* (1959, *Billiards at Half-Past Nine*) focuses squarely upon Nazi persecution and destructiveness, while his still earlier novel *Und sagte kein einziges Wort* (1953, *And Never Said a Word*) is critically pessimistic about the values of civilization in a newly developing society shaped only by economic priorities. His internation-ally acclaimed (though in conservative circles in West Germany heavily criticized) *Ansichten eines Clowns* (1963, *The Clown*) develops these themes, focusing on post-war morality in Adenauer's Germany, the inheritance from the Nazi past, hypocritical conservative values and, most especially, the illiberal role of the Catholic Church.

Beyond West German borders the best-known post-war author – especially after his novel *Die Blechtrommel* (1959, *The Tin Drum*) had been turned in 1979 into a film that won him international renown – was Günter Grass. The originality of the novel, his first, lay in its double perspective. The Nazi era in Danzig (where Grass had spent his early years) was portrayed both through the clear-sighted eyes of the three-year-old Oskar Matzerath and those of the thirty-year-old adult Oskar, by now confined in a mental hospital. Oskar, the child whose psychological development had been arrested, giving him clairvoyant powers, uses his prize possession, his tin drum, to intervene in adult events, such as when he joins a Nazi procession that ends up marching to the beat that he sets. Through this complex construction Grass portrays the descent of his home town into inhumanity and destruction. The device of the double perspective permits a child's revealingly naive perception of a world whose pernicious reality he is only as an adult fully able to grasp. The tin drum itself is a way of drawing attention to the individual who watches, is averse to the regimentation of mass rallies and dogmatic ideology, but is not involved in anything that could be regarded as political opposition. The work, highly controversial as its reception was in a society that was for the most part stuffily conservative and heavily religious in its dominant values, symbolized for a younger generation a critical approach to the recent past that was part of a questioning of the present.

Over his long life – he died in April 2015 – and celebrated literary career, Grass embodied in his works, and in his political engagement (as a prominent supporter of the Social Democrats), German soul-searching about the Nazi past. How complicated the relationship to that past was for those, especially, who had lived through the Nazi era was laid bare in Grass's autobiography when, only as late as 2006, he revealed that as a sixteen-year-old in 1944 he had joined the Waffen-SS and served for six months as a tank gunner.

West Germany was exceptional in the extent and depth of its literary soul-searching. Nowhere else matched it. Significant works in Italy nevertheless reflected the legacy of Fascist rule and war. Carlo Levi's poignant

Cristo si è fermato a Eboli (1945, *Christ Stopped at Eboli*) – later made into a film – was a memoir of the political exile under Mussolini's dictatorship that he spent in a remote, backward malaria-infested and 'god-forsaken' region of southern Italy. Curzio Malaparte, a one-time fascist who was later persecuted for his criticism of Mussolini's regime, used literary form to depict his experiences as a war correspondent on the Eastern Front in *Kaputt* (1944), while in *La pelle* (1949, *The Skin*) he focused on the moral as well as physical destruction in Naples as the Allies fought their way northwards after 1943. Some of the poetry of Salvatore Quasimodo (awarded the Nobel Prize for Literature in 1959) related to the injustice in the Fascist era and suffering in the war. Elio Vittorini, a communist intellectual who had at one time shown some support for Mussolini's politics, highlighted resistance in his novel *Uomini e no* (1945, *Men and not Men*). And Giorgio Bassani, in his *Il giardino dei Finzi-Contini* (1962, *The Garden of the Finzi-Continis*, later turned into a successful film) wrote about the experiences of the Jewish community in Ferrara as it faced discrimination and persecution under Fascism. But after the war most Italians did not want reminding of the Fascist past. Primo Levi struggled to find a publisher for the book that was later to make him world-famous, *Se questo è un uomo* (*If This is a Man*), about his survival in Auschwitz. When he finally did so, publication in 1947 was in a tiny print run of only 2,000 copies, not all of which were sold. It was only after more than a decade had elapsed that it was taken over by a major Italian publisher, Einaudi, and, greatly helped by translation into English, started on its path to becoming a major classic among Holocaust memoirs.

The sense of despair or fatalistic nihilism encountered in the literature of continental Europe was almost completely absent in Britain. The war had after all been won, even if the country was reduced to the verge of penury. A sense of moral victory over the evil of Nazism, combined with the expectation that the wartime sacrifices would lead to the creation of a better society, accompanied a pronounced insularity in cultural as in political and economic life. The war had produced little or no poetry to match the poignancy of that of the First World War, except perhaps the poems of Keith Douglas, and especially 'Vergissmeinnicht' ('Forget-Me-Not'). Nor did it lead to much introspection. Few were given to abstract philosophizing about the ruin of civilization. People, including intellectuals, wanted to look forwards, not back to the wartime years. Almost the only major literary work that focused squarely on wartime experience was Evelyn Waugh's semi-humorous trilogy, *Sword of Honour,* published between 1952 and 1961 – a culturally pessimistic satirical depiction of the decay of traditional institutional and social values in a world of mediocrity and emptiness. The war, for Waugh, was the triumph of dishonour, the betrayal of idealism. The war as an assault on humanity lay beyond his vista.

In terms of the international resonance of his political and social writing in the immediate post-war era, Britain's most important writer was George Orwell – the British voice of ethical socialism. Orwell castigated the values and failings of the British conservative establishment. But he retained a strong English patriotism that he rooted in long-standing traditions of equality, justice and liberty. He looked to the wartime experience as paving the way for vast and radical social change. But ultimately he was deeply pessimistic about the future, from what he had seen of the recent past. Fascism had been defeated. But what would replace it? Orwell utterly rejected visions of a communist utopia. His experiences during the Spanish Civil War had opened his eyes to the intrinsic oppression and ruthlessness of Soviet communism. The dystopian novels that made him world-famous, his satire *Animal Farm* (1945) and especially *Nineteen Eighty-Four* (whose title simply transposed the date of completion, 1948, it was published the following year), portrayed future totalitarian society in which the individual was completely subjugated to political and social domination by omnipotent and omniscient rulers. 'Big Brother is Watching You', representing the total power of the supreme leader, was a slogan that entered everyday parlance. It was a world in which language itself turned untruth into truth, where the negative became the positive, where unfreedom was converted into what was permitted to be known as freedom. Totalitarianism would become the ideological theorem par excellence in Western analysis of the Cold War. As a literary device, it was perfectly depicted by Orwell's brilliance as a writer.

In a continent split between rival political systems and rival ideologies it was inevitable that literary and intellectual endeavour would become so often overlaid with the dogmas of the Cold War. The Soviets poured money and expended much energy into subsidizing efforts to bolster anti-American sentiment among intellectuals (and others) in Western Europe. Given the levels of anti-Americanism prevalent within parts of the European left, most notably in France, the efforts were not without success.

The United States countered with its own propaganda initiatives. In terms of intellectual influence, the most important was the Congress for Cultural Freedom, set up in June 1950 and soon disseminating anti-communist views throughout Western Europe. The Congress, secretly funded by the CIA, was backed by a number of leading anti-communist intellectuals. They included the philosophers Bertrand Russell, Benedetto Croce, Karl Jaspers and A. J. Ayer, Arthur Koestler (famous for his brilliant anti-Soviet novel *Darkness at Noon*, published in 1940), the distinguished French political writer Raymond Aron and the Oxford historian Hugh Trevor-Roper. Koestler, a one-time communist now fired with the zeal of the convert, was the leading speaker at the founding conference in Berlin. But the launch did not go altogether smoothly. Trevor-Roper and Ayer, both of whom had worked during the war for British intelligence, were alienated by the shrill tone of Koestler's obsessive hatred of communism. Nevertheless, initial British misgivings about the Congress soon dissipated and in the cultural cold war anti-communism established itself as the paramount ideology among intellectuals (and others), beyond, that is, the minority still wedded to the Soviet Union.

For some leading intellectuals, as had been the case before the Second World War, Marxism nevertheless offered the only sure route to a better society – notwithstanding the revelations that emerged from Khrushchev's attack on the crimes of Stalinism in February 1956 and the crushing of the Hungarian uprising later that year. With the glories of Weimar Berlin a distant memory and the cultural riches of Central Europe destroyed through the Holocaust, dispersed through emigration, or suppressed by Soviet domination, Paris reasserted its dominance in European intellectual and cultural life. And it was not just by chance in this post-war atmosphere that the existentialist philosophy of Jean-Paul Sartre – extensively elucidated in his major wartime work *L'Être et le néant* (1943, *Being and Nothingness*), and briefly in his short tract written after the war *L'existentialisme est un humanisme* (1946, *Existentialism and Humanism*) – was eagerly swallowed.

Sartre, already before the war much influenced in his thinking – though not in his political leanings – by the German existentialist (and admirer of Hitler) Martin Heidegger, argued that mankind's only distinguishing feature was 'to be conscious of the nothingness of its being'. Existence was absurd, without meaning. Only the individual could choose a meaning for his or her own life. Choice was crucial, the redeeming feature of the philosophy. The apparent despairing bleakness could be combated by freedom and choice through which the individual created his or her own values. The war had, however, in some ways refashioned Sartre's existentialist thought. What had begun as an individualist (and non-political) philosophy was reshaped into an activist force in which individual freedom meant a responsibility to work for the liberty of all. This implied nothing less than endeavouring to bring about the radical transformation of society. His thinking now led him towards Marxism, the political philosophy of social transformation and struggle against bourgeois society. He lent his strong support to the French Communist Party (though did not join it), and to the Soviet Union. And he justified communist political violence in the interests of the goal of the revolutionary overthrow of bourgeois society, seen as the ultimate guarantee of freedom (though he attacked Soviet abuses of human rights and condemned the suppression of the Hungarian uprising in 1956).

Sartre recognized the tensions within his own thinking. To state the absurdity and 'nothingness' of existence yet aim to fight for a new and better society (did society even exist?), to be created (and imposed?) by a mass party directed by a political philosophy that claimed to rest on reason and the immutable laws of history, was an obvious contradiction. Yet Sartre seemed to many to capture the post-war mood of oscillating despair and optimism about the nature and fate of humankind. By the later 1950s existentialism was starting to lose its appeal. But Sartre, the French public intellectual par excellence, continued to magnetize the young, most especially, and to influence their anti-establishment and revolutionary views. Tens of thousands lined the streets of Paris at his funeral in April 1980.

In the early post-war years, and not just in France, Marxism linked the triumphant fight against fascism with hope for the future. For its devotees it provided a belief-system as all-encompassing as Tridentine Catholicism was for its own followers. But the readiness to overlook or explain away the crimes of Stalinism and the oppressive character of Soviet rule was severely dented by the invasion of Hungary. Many leading Marxist intellectuals left the Communist Party as a result. And when Marxism began in the 1960s to exert renewed intellectual influence, and to excite students as it was disseminated in universities, the Soviet Union was generally no longer the main model (see Chapter 6).

Beyond the Iron Curtain antifascism was the ideological glue that bound the past with the future. Fascism, which for citizens of Central and Eastern Europe was largely synonymous with Nazism, under which they had suffered so much and for so long, had been defeated by Soviet armed might in 'the Great Patriotic War'. Victory had been underpinned by the indomitable belief that the power behind the Nazi thirst for brutal conquest had to be crushed if socialist society were to be created. This belief rested in turn upon a definition of fascism, devised in 1933 and refined two years later by Georgi Dimitrov (before the war head of the Soviet-run international organization, the Comintern, and after it Bulgaria's leader between December 1946 and his death in July 1949). This defined fascism as 'the open terroristic dictatorship of the ... most imperialist elements of finance capital'. The implication was obvious: the struggle against Hitler's barbarism had been won; but what had produced fascism remained immanent in the imperialist capitalism of the West. The vision of the future – a communist utopia – could only be turned into reality by the continuation of the struggle against Western capitalism. Past and future were therefore bonded by the vision.

Some notable German writers, forced into emigration during the Third Reich, chose to return not to capitalist West Germany but to the German Democratic Republic. Bertolt Brecht, as mentioned, and his wife, Helene Weigel, were among them. Brecht's works, including his *Furcht und Elend des Dritten Reiches* (1938, *Fear and Misery of the Third Reich*) and his biting satire on Hitler's rise to power, *Der aufhaltsame Aufstieg des Arturo Ui* (1941, *The Resistible Rise of Arturo Ui*), brilliantly encapsulated antifascism and the emancipatory ideas of Marxism, popularizing them in the West at the same time as helping to legitimate the communist alternative state in East Germany. Stefan Heym was another writer who chose to live in what he called 'the better Germany' after serving in the American army and writing on resistance and persecution during the war. He was another great propaganda success for the early GDR regime, though he increasingly became disillusioned with the rigid controls and repression of the state. An even bigger catch for the early GDR was the return from exile of Anna Seghers, a committed communist whose novel about a concentration camp, *Das siebte Kreuz* (*The Seventh Cross*), written in 1939 and turned into a Hollywood film in 1944, had made her internationally famous.

Whatever their initial enthusiasm, few intellectuals worthy of the name could tolerate for long shackling themselves to an ideology that in political practice produced only censorship, restriction and narrow conformity. In the Soviet Union Ilya Ehrenburg's short novel, *The Thaw* (one of whose leading characters was a 'little Stalin' type), seemed the harbinger of new intellectual freedom when it was published in 1954. But the break with the 'frozen' past of Stalinism and the suffocating constraints imposed by Stalin's post-war cultural controller Andrei Zhdanov could not be pushed too far. Vassily Grossman's epic *Life and Fate* (1960), which in its chronicle of a Soviet family during the Second World War was highly critical of Stalinism, was confiscated by the KGB in 1961. Grossman did not live to see its later publication, to great acclaim, in the West, dying of stomach cancer three years later. The 'arrest' (as Grossman put it) of his book was an indication that literary expression in the Soviet Union retained narrow limits. The central trope of antifascism continued to frame all thinking on the past and on the future.

Outside the Soviet Union, even so, intellectual nonconformity started to show its face in the 1950s. The Polish writer Adam Ważyk, once a supporter of Stalin, registered his disillusionment with Stalinist Poland in 1955 in his *Poem for Adults*, a searing critique and lament for a Poland that had disappeared, and left the Communist Party two years later. Jan Kott, a Polish writer and theatre critic who in 1951 had been fulsome in his praise of Stalin and advocated the subordination of the theatre to the party's ideology, also reversed his stance in the mid-1950s and joined Ważyk in ending his party membership in 1957. Conformity still generally prevailed, nevertheless, and however severe the criticism of actual conditions, most intellectuals did not reject Marxist ideology. Deviation from Marxism, not Marxism itself, had, it was claimed, produced the distortions and the oppression that had resulted.

USES AND ABUSES OF THE PAST

The cultural cold war was fought out more than anywhere else on the battlefields of historical myth, memory and interpretation. In this domain the shadow of the past lay at its most starkly visible. It was only in part a clash between opposite sides of the Iron Curtain. In greater measure, it reflected contrasting stances within Western Europe – in themselves mirroring national experience and mythology about the war.

The Dimitrov definition of fascism meant that Eastern European understanding of the recent past remained relatively inflexible and monolithic. It offered an unchanging and straightforward interpretation of the disastrous course of recent history – diametrically altered through the triumph of Soviet communism – alongside a clear political message. Fascism had served capitalist interests; its leaders were the tools of big business. And since capitalism still flourished in the West, the political message – the way in which the past served the present and future – was plain to read. The past was a warning. It provided the guideline to the future struggle.

The message embellished the imagery of heroic communist resistance to Nazi rule, to the exclusion of practically all other forms of resistance. Naturally, the glorious feat of the Red Army and the Soviet people in repelling, then destroying, the fascist invaders was emblazoned in all historical writing, with little attention paid to the war effort of the Western Allies. Inconvenient facts such as the Hitler–Stalin Pact of 1939 and the subsequent Soviet annexation of the Baltic states and eastern Poland were simply ignored or at most explained away as strategic necessity because of the failings of the appeasement of Hitler by the Western powers. Not least, racism – and most especially antisemitism – was not seen as the ideological centre of the Nazi creed, as later generations would come to recognize it, but as an inexorable consequence of rapacious capitalist imperialism. Jews had of course been grievously persecuted; but so had countless others, mainly Slavs, under the Nazi jackboot. The distortions were manifold (and have subsequently been laid bare by historical research). But incorporated in an ideology that brooked no alternatives and backed by a monopoly party and the power of the state, this interpretation was unchallengeable in Eastern Europe. It was represented in countless history books. But, at its most uncompromising, it was widely displayed for the 'enlightenment' of the general public in the Museum of German History (*Museum für Deutsche Geschichte*), established in East Berlin in 1952.

Western Europe, however, had its own myths about the immediate past. Its own distortions were more nuanced and varied than the Soviet version, but they were there nonetheless. France, for instance, used wartime resistance as the foundation of post-war political legitimacy. The heroism and martyrdom of the resistance were underlined at every point, its limited effectiveness, internal rivalries and ideological conflicts played down. Resistance was portrayed as the representation of national identity, Vichy as the betrayal of all that was truly French. De Gaulle himself was regarded as the embodiment of the spirit of resistance. This version was embellished through the publication in the 1950s of de Gaulle's wartime memoirs – an important contribution both to the cult of the resistance and, especially, to his own image as France's saviour. As late as 1970 he was still seen in France to a far greater extent as the symbol of the continued fight after the defeat of 1940 and of the Liberation four years later than as the founder of the Fifth Republic.

A veil of silence was drawn, in contrast, over the extent of collaboration with fascist regimes. It would take decades before 'the Vichy syndrome' would be squarely addressed in France. A serious beginning was not made before Marcel Ophül's film *Le Chagrin et la Pitié* (*The Sorrow and the Pity*) in 1969. This lengthy two-part documentary, focusing on the town of Clermont-Ferrand in central France, opened the window for the first time on everyday collaboration during the German occupation. The sensitivity of the topic was such that, in this the final year of de Gaulle's presidency, national television was not allowed to show the film – the 'embargo' on the television showing lasted until 1981 – though this did not prevent the film from becoming a sensation in France. And it was not a French but an American historian, Robert Paxton, who as late as 1972, in *Vichy France: Old Guard and New Order, 1940–1944*, first explored the Vichy regime's own initiatives in deporting Jews to their deaths.

In Italy antifascism was one part of the essential basis of the post-war Italian state and its republican constitution. It formed a common bond that crossed the otherwise sharp political divides. The courage of resistance against fascist terror, during the last two years of the war after Mussolini had been reinstated in power by the German occupiers of northern Italy, was a cornerstone of early post-war attempts to shape national identity in the new Italian republic. Resistance, stated the widely read historian, Roberto Battaglia, in his 1953 book *Storia della resistenza italiana* (*History of the Italian Resistance*), represented the 'real people' of Italy, the heart of the nation, and in a 'national uprising' in 1945 had 'redeemed the honour of Italy which had been so vilely besmirched by the Fascists'.

The crucial part played by the communists in resistance was, however, played down. For the main ideological prop of the new Italy was anti-communism. After the Cold War had set in, Italy had received Marshall Aid, joined NATO, and been extensively funded by the United States, with the more divisive anti-communism largely displacing the unifying antifascism as the dominant ideology in a state largely controlled by the Christian Democrats (and backed by the strong influence of the Catholic Church). The Fascist past was by now largely blotted out. State television, which began transmitting in 1954, scarcely touched upon contemporary history.

Works on fascism by historians, in so far as they penetrated wider public consciousness at all, concentrated largely on the causes of its takeover of power in 1922, its repressive character, and its preparations for war. The history of Italian society under Fascist rule and the extent of support for Mussolini's regime remained unexplored themes. This was largely to remain the case until the mid-1970s, when in the third volume of his immense four-volume biography of Mussolini (published 1965–96), subtitled 'The Years of Consent', Renzo de Felice claimed that the majority of Italians had backed the aims and policies of the Fascist regime. This opened up, amid huge controversy, the whole issue of support for fascism in Italy. Whatever the merits of the arguments, it broke the convenient myth of a national identity built around antifascism.

In West Germany, as in Italy, the history of resistance helped to legitimate the new democracy. Whereas in the German Democratic Republic resistance to Hitler's regime was almost entirely accredited to the communists, in the Federal Republic – in an almost exact mirror image – the patriotism of conservative resistance, in particular of the army, was highlighted, whereas that of communists was played down. Pride of place was accorded to 'the men of 20 July 1944' – chiefly army officers spearheaded by Colonel Claus Schenk Graf von Stauffenberg – who had conspired to assassinate Hitler and paid a terrible price for their narrow failure. Led by individual conscience, ethical integrity and moral duty to overthrow tyranny, they had put their lives at stake in order to destroy a criminal regime and restore the legal order, freedom and democracy to Germany. Resistance to Nazism in this view represented 'the other Germany' – the 'true' Germany before Hitler's repressive regime had subjugated the country to totalitarian unfreedom. Nazism, in this message, was an evil interruption to what had been a positive course of German history.

Some publications did stand outside the conservative intellectual mainstream. But few beyond specialists read Karl Dietrich Bracher's exposure of the structural weaknesses of Weimar democracy, while the historical profession was itself dismissive of his work as that of a political scientist. Some outstanding pioneer research on the Nazi era was undertaken in the Institute of Contemporary History (*Institut für Zeitgeschichte*) set up specially for that purpose and astonishingly already at work by 1952, a mere seven years after Hitler's suicide in the Berlin bunker. But again little of this penetrated public consciousness, or even university curricula (where the most recent past scarcely figured). Moreover, even here emphasis on continuities with the pre-Nazi past could run into difficulties. Kurt Sontheimer, a researcher at the Institut in the late 1950s, revealed a panoply of anti-democratic views in the Weimar Republic stretching far beyond the Nazis and encompassing conservative mentalities. Uneasy with his findings, the Institut turned down his book for publication within its own series of monographs. It was later published separately and, in a more favourable climate, became a standard text.

Conservative dominance of the West German historical profession marked not just continuities in personnel and thought that had survived the Third Reich, but also matched the atmosphere of the Adenauer era. There was little appetite for exploring the past, revisiting uncomfortable memories, airing topics best forgotten. The Nazi past was simply too recent, the wounds still raw, the suffering in the last phase of the war – which left Germans with a sense that *they* had been the main victims of a criminal regime – too grievous, the complicity and collaboration in the workings of party and state too extensive to encourage the public to do any other than engage in what amounted to a conspiracy of silence, a desire to blot out the past.

Where there was not outright silence there was implicit, or even explicit, apologia. The German people had been seduced by propaganda and taken to ruin by Hitler and a clique of Nazi gangsters; most of the population had opposed the regime but had been powerless to act in a totalitarian police-state; no one other than the Nazi leaders had wanted war; the German army had fought honourably and carried out its patriotic duty to the end (a view decisively revised only decades later); the barbarous actions in Eastern Europe were those of SS criminals; ordinary Germans were not involved and knew nothing of the extermination of the Jews. The Holocaust (as it came to be known) was almost completely excluded from public debate and formed little part of historical inquiry. Only in the 1980s would it come to assume a central role in popular and scholarly interpretations of the era. Whereas in the German Democratic Republic the genocide against the Jews was simply subsumed in the wider exterminatory barbarism of fascist imperialism, in West Germany – in so far as it was discussed at all – it was attributed solely to the evil designs of Hitler and the SS leadership. The psychologists Alexander and Margarete Mitscherlich later summed up the collective response in their book *Die Unfähigkeit zu trauern* (*The Inability to Mourn*). The book signified the beginnings of a new era in the analysis of the Nazi past when it was first published in 1967, and went on to become a best-seller.

Although most West Germans wanted to enjoy the benefits of the 'economic miracle' and not to dwell upon the past, they could not altogether shut it out. In 1961 an unlikely book at first sight, an analysis several hundred pages long of German diplomatic records before the *First* World War – Fritz Fischer's *Griff nach der Weltmacht* (translated as *Germany's Aims in the First World War*) – provoked enormously bitter controversy. Fischer turned conventional historical interpretation on its head. Until then he had been little known outside professional circles – a conservative himself, who had even for a time been a member of the Nazi Party. But his book rocked the conservative establishment. For he claimed on the basis of his research into the plans, beliefs and actions of the German elites in the immediate prelude to the First World War that they had aimed at nothing less than conquest to establish Germany as a world power. In other words, Fischer purported to show that Hitler was the product of continuities in German history reaching back into the nineteenth century. His research advanced an interpretation that was difficult for many Germans to accept. While they had meanwhile come to acknowledge that their country was responsible for the Second World War, they were now told that it had also been responsible for the *First* – something which the Allies had alleged at Versailles, and which had been so ferociously denied by Germany then and ever since. Germany, it seemed in the light of Fischer's work, had long before 1914 trod a 'special path' (*Sonderweg*) among European nations. The path had led to Hitler, war, genocide and national disaster.

It was an interpretation that, once the immediate controversy had subsided, coloured German views about their own past for decades. In some ways, it inaugurated the process that from the 1960s onwards led to ever greater readiness to explore the darkest corners of the German past. The failings of an earlier generation to confront the past fed into the sense of alienation and rejection expressed in the student protests of 1968. But it would be a decade after those disturbances before serious research started to be undertaken on the myriad forms of everyday complicity in Nazi rule by large sections of the population, and even longer before the Holocaust itself took centre stage in the reassessment of the German past. Even so, in the early 1960s it became impossible for Germans to shut their eyes completely to the attempt to kill Europe's Jews. The capture in Argentina in May 1960 by Israeli agents of Adolf Eichmann, the chief organizer of what the Nazis had called 'the Final Solution of the Jewish Question', his trial in Jerusalem the following year and subsequent execution by hanging in June 1962, and then the trial in Frankfurt am Main between 1963 and 1965 of personnel who had served at Auschwitz, the biggest Nazi extermination centre, drew public attention for a time to the genocide that was an inextricable part of Germany's war. 'Death is a master from Germany,' Paul Celan had written. It was becoming ever more difficult to exclude this thought from public consciousness.

The place of the recent past in British public consciousness differed from that anywhere else in continental Europe. Britain had been unconquered, had not been occupied, and had emerged victorious. Its wartime history encouraged the creation of a national self-image built on wartime heroism. This embellished the sense – already derived from its historical traditions and institutions – that Britain was both exceptional and stood apart from mainland Europe. History, memory and myth were all brought into service to unfold a glorious episode in 'our island story', one of heroism and triumph, of good vanquishing evil. Britain had already had to fight, and win, one world war against Germany. Reluctantly, it had been forced to do it all over again. Victory over Nazi evil attained by fighting 'shoulder to shoulder' with its Western ally, the United States, embellished, furthermore, the notion of a 'special relationship' with its transatlantic cousins. Conversely, most people showed little interest in developments across the English Channel. The well-worn cliché, 'Fog over the channel, continent cut off from England', was meant as a joke; it contained a grain of truth, even so, in its self-parody of British isolationism.

Britain in the post-war era was brought up on the version of the war associated with its greatest hero, Winston Churchill. Churchill's six-volume history of the conflict, *The Second World War*, published between 1948 and 1953, established the line of interpretation. Appeasement had taken the country to the verge of disaster. In 1940, its 'finest hour', Britain had stood alone in the fight against Nazi tyranny. German invasion had been warded off by the bravery of young fighter pilots who, against the odds, had won the 'Battle of Britain' in the summer of 1940. The British people had then held out night after night as their homes were relentlessly bombed during the German 'blitz'. After the darkest night, dawned slowly the light. Through the great victories in the Desert War, by winning the 'Battle of the Atlantic' at enormous cost, and by the courage of bombing crews who nightly ran the gauntlet of German fighters to pummel enemy instalments, the corner was eventually turned. D-Day on 6 June 1944 was the culmination of bravery and triumph – the moment when, alongside our staunch American allies, victory was sealed and the path laid to the ultimate crushing of Nazism.

The heroic story was reinforced and embedded in the general consciousness through countless tales of 'derring-do' by British servicemen both in fictional accounts and in wartime recollections, and by popular films such as *The Cruel Sea* (1953), *The Dambusters* (1955) or *Sink the Bismarck* (1960), while comic strips indoctrinated countless youngsters with imagery of British heroism and German 'baddies'.

Until the 1960s, however, there was little serious interest in the history of the Second World War. The history syllabus in schools and universities still ended, as a rule, in 1914. And relatively little 'foreign history' (as it was labelled in the Oxford syllabus) was studied. With a handful of significant exceptions – prominent among them Hugh Trevor-Roper's *Last Days of Hitler* (1947) and Alan Bullock's *Hitler: A Study in Tyranny* (1952) – few major works on the Nazi era were undertaken. This was only just starting to change in the early 1960s. Even then, anti-German stereotypes were upheld in the controversial book by Britain's most popular historian, A. J. P. Taylor, *Origins of the Second World War*. Taylor's book, couched with his usual penchant for sharp epigrammatic sentences and cynical aperçus, was self-consciously revisionist. It came close to blaming British appeasers, not Nazi aggressors, for the war. It appeared in 1961, the same year as Fritz Fischer's striking revision of interpretations of German aims in the First World War. Taylor used Fischer's findings to underpin his own anti-German interpretation – he had already in 1944 published a short, strongly anti-German work, *The Course of German History* – that 'in international affairs there was nothing wrong with Hitler except that he was a German'. (Born in Austria, Hitler had acquired German citizenship only in 1932.)

The past, therefore, continued to cast its deep shadow over the European continent – though in strikingly different ways. From the 1960s onwards, encouraged by the expansion of higher education more or less everywhere, research started to gather pace on the ideologies and political movements that had taken Europe into a calamitous war and genocide. Strikingly, though, it would be only from the 1980s, as they were receding chronologically ever more into the distance, that the Second World War and the Holocaust would become a central part of European public consciousness.

BREAKING WITH THE PAST

The past, consciously or not, shaped the post-war present. But between 1955 and 1965 changes in popular culture took place that amounted to a major break with the past. Before then popular culture had followed patterns recognizable from the pre-war era. After the decade of 1955–65 it felt as if a revolution had taken place.

Most people did not care about the past. They wanted to enjoy better times. The younger generation especially, born towards the end of the war or just after it was over, lived for the present and looked to the future. 'Seize the day' was their implicit slogan. During the 1960s – though the process had begun already in the preceding decade – they stamped their indelible imprint on a transformative shift in popular culture. Generation as well as social class became a more significant social cleavage than probably in any earlier era. Gradually, but permanently, the changes altered social values and life patterns. Gradually, too, the gap between 'high' and 'popular' culture lessened. It was not that teenagers were turned into opera fans, or that pensioners worshipped hard rock; but the chances of tastes overlapping were greater than earlier in the century. Middle-class parents, infected by (or anxious not to be excluded from) the tastes of their offspring, might enjoy pop as well as classical music, or university professors attend football matches – earlier mainly the preserve of the industrial working class. It would be as well not to exaggerate the scale or speed of the change. Nor was it uniform across the continent. The Berlin Wall, it has been said with little exaggeration, was the plain illustration of the contrast between a technicolour west and a grey east, where state controls in every country beyond the Iron Curtain tried, with a fair degree of success, to restrict the availability of 'decadent' Western culture. Within Western Europe the cultural transformation was slowest where the influence of the Catholic Church was strongest. The process of change, once begun, would nevertheless continue inexorably, developing and spreading almost by osmosis for the remainder of the century and beyond. But its crucial start was in the decade between the mid-1950s and the mid-1960s.

The universal language of youth is music – popular music, that is. And here there is little difficulty in locating the seismic break with the past. In 1954 the top of the hit parade in Britain was Vera Lynn's 'My Son, My Son', a ballad by the singer who had during the war been known as 'the forces' sweetheart'. Within a year the top spot was occupied by 'Rock Around the Clock' by Bill Haley and the Comets. It marked the arrival of rock and roll – a new sensational style of music that had crossed the Atlantic from the United States with an immediate mass appeal to teenagers. Instantly, dance halls, once the preserve of the sedate quickstep and foxtrot, were given over to frenetic jiving. When Haley's spin-off film appeared in 1956, the reaction was remarkable. His fans screamed in the cinemas and rocked and rolled in the aisles. Catching the spirit of youthful rebellion, the banal story of a dance-band manager who became a success after seeing the appeal of rock and roll, sparked teenage disturbances and vandalism in towns and cities across Western Europe. The film was banned by eighty town councils in the United Kingdom. Haley was soon gone from the scene. His Comets passed across the sky and disappeared. But then came Elvis Presley.

From the mid-1950s onwards Elvis became practically a deity for much of the younger generation in the United States, but increasingly in Europe too (helped by the presence of US troops and the American Forces Network, AFN, music programmes). A string of massive hit records – among them 'Heartbreak Hotel', 'Hound Dog', 'Blue Suede Shoes', 'Jailhouse Rock' and 'One Night' – made him rock and roll's first megastar. Good-looking, with slicked-back hair, a sultry expression, and a performance style that included suggestively gyrating hips, he became a sex symbol for millions of teenagers – and a threat to morality in the eyes of many of their elders. While many older Europeans saw the phenomenon as a further dangerous debasement of genuine culture, teenagers worshipped at the shrine, not just of Elvis, but of other major American rock and roll artists. An array of them – including outstanding figures such as Jerry Lee Lewis, Little Richard, Chuck Berry, Eddie Cochran and Buddy Holly – enjoyed massive popularity in Europe as well as in the USA. The impact of rock and roll on the younger generation was explosive. For Charles White, experiencing a sheltered if not smothering education at a Catholic monastic school in the west of Ireland, 'hearing Little Richard's "Long Tall Sally" ' – released in 1956 – 'was like getting out of the Bastille after 40 years. FREEDOM, FREEDOM, FREEDOM!' For White, and for many others, rock and roll amounted to nothing less than a cultural revolution.

In 1962 the centre of this musical cultural revolution moved to England. Their first recording success, 'Love Me Do', announced the arrival of The Beatles – four fresh-faced, mop-haired Liverpool boys (John Lennon, Paul McCartney, George Harrison and Ringo Starr) who by the following spring were already a phenomenon. 'Beatlemania' swept through Britain. In 1964 rapturous crowds followed them throughout their American tour. Their music developed from the early emphasis on rock to more sophisticated sounds, reaching perhaps a high point of creativity during their 'psychedelic' phase with *Sgt. Pepper's Lonely Hearts Club Band*, released in May 1967. Their own experiments with drugs chimed with the increased use of recreational drugs among young people. That same year their song 'All You Need is Love' was performed via satellite to a global television audience estimated at 350–400 million people and became a theme of the 'flower power' peace movement and international protest against the Vietnam War. The Beatles were by now embodying the rejection of conventional values and the anti-establishment protest among young people.

Other British bands followed the trail blazed by the Beatles, reversing the earlier American dominance of popular music. Among them were The Animals, The Kinks and The Dave Clark Five, though by far the most important (and enduring) were The Rolling Stones, their popularity not far behind that of the Beatles by the mid-1960s. Their cultivated 'bad boy' image, the earthy style of their blend of rock and blues, and their appearance – long hair and casual clothes (in contrast to the initially uniformed appearance of the Beatles and most other bands at the time) – gave them an anti-authoritarian appeal that fitted well into the youth culture of the 1960s.

This culture was international, sweeping across America and Europe, penetrating even beyond the Iron Curtain as well – despite the disapproval of state authorities. Young people started to look alike. They wore similar types of clothes. During the rock craze of the late 1950s Britain's youthful rebels – sometimes modelling themselves on Marlon Brando (a motorcycle gang leader in the 1953 film *The Wild One*), or James Dean, a young American actor who gained iconic status among teenagers as the star of the 1955 film *Rebel Without a Cause* and who died in a car accident the same year at the age of only twenty-four – had worn leather jackets and 'drainpipe' trousers to set themselves apart. There were variants in West Germany, France and elsewhere. The 'Teddy Boys', 'Halbstarken' or 'blousons noir' consciously aimed to look different from the rest of society. They were, however, a rebellious (sometimes violent) minority. Early in the 1960s the styles of young people were still generally conservative, much like those of their parents. But by the end of the decade they looked different from their elders. They often wore their hair long. Their clothing was usually casual. Through inspired marketing, jeans, originally American working attire, became a uniform of youth, and in a reversal of what had happened earlier were now even worn by some of their more trendy parents. 'Hippie' appearance, starting in America and catching hold in Europe, indicated adherence to a 'counter-culture', often involving drugs and sexual liberation.

Not all young people wanted to be taken for 'hippies'. Fashion design, specifically targeting the young (men as well as women), who had more to spend on buying clothes than their parents had ever been able to afford, advertised attractive and distinctive styles. 'Youth' became big business. Carnaby Street was soon the emblem of 'swinging Britain' with an array of boutique fashion shops offering the latest 'gear' for both sexes. The British fashion designer Mary Quant was hailed in fashion-conscious Italy as 'the creator of the most with-it fashion in the world . . . She invented the miniskirt'. Jean Shrimpton and the waif-like Lesley Hornby, better known as Twiggy (described in an Italian magazine as 'the doll with the freckles'), became 'super-models', international trend-setters in female clothing. One fashion oddity was the disappearance of men's hats, even long after the war still worn by most adult males. Perhaps the greater attention that young men in the 1950s started to pay to their elaborate hairstyles, quiffed back and greased in the style of Elvis Presley, is part of the answer to this minor sartorial mystery.

The greatest single influence on the changing popular culture of the 1960s was without doubt television. This had a major impact on the culture of young people – the first television generation. But it affected all sectors of society, in all countries. Television actually began life back in the 1920s. But the onset of its triumphant march to complete supremacy as the medium of popular culture began in Europe three decades later. Britain was at the forefront of the advance. The initial major boost to television ownership came in preparation of the coronation of Queen Elizabeth II on 2 June 1953 in Westminster Abbey. Millions of families clustered around the new and exciting addition to their furniture – a capacious polished cabinet with a tiny screen – to watch grainy black-and-white pictures of the great events in London.*

The coronation was the first big televised event not just in Britain, but across Europe and further afield. Sixteen European broadcasting organizations took part. Even in Republican France the coronation was said to have been watched by a million people. But television in Europe was still in its infancy. In 1953 Dutch television transmitted three hours of programmes a week to only 10,000 receivers. Although two-thirds of American households possessed a television set by 1955, in Italy

---

* Our family was unusual in buying a television not for the Coronation but in order to view the Cup Final at Wembley one month earlier, on 2 May 1953, when Blackpool beat Bolton Wanderers 4–3 in a thrilling match that finally gave the most famous English player of the day, Stanley Matthews, a cup-winner's medal at the age of thirty-eight. Most of the people on the street, it seemed, crowded into the small living room of our terraced house in Oldham to watch the match.

television still had fewer than 100,000 subscribers. Expansion was, however, rapid from then onwards. By 1963 there were 12.5 million television sets in Britain, 8 million in Germany, 3 million in France and around a million in Italy (though only 1 per cent of Spaniards owned a television in 1960 while in Greece television only began in 1969). Still, the spread of television could not be halted, even by the rigorously controlling communist states. The gap in 1964 between television ownership in East and West Germany, for example, was fairly small: 42 per cent to 50 per cent of households. By 1970 Sweden had the greatest number of television sets proportionate to its population (312 sets for every 1,000 inhabitants) of any country in Europe, but Hungary (171 sets) was not far behind Ireland, Italy and Austria.

On 20 July 1969 the landing on the moon by the Apollo 11 spacecraft and the first steps taken by mankind on its surface by Neil Armstrong and Buzz Aldrin were watched across the globe as extraordinary pictures were relayed by satellite to the largest television audience ever recorded up to that time – an estimated 530 million viewers worldwide. Televised sport was by this time becoming an integral part of popular culture. Through satellite links the Olympic Games could now be watched across the world. In Europe, where football was the prime sport, the European Cup, established in 1955, the European Championship and the World Cup drew increasingly vast viewer audiences across the continent and, as air travel became easier and cheaper, introduced travelling fans to other countries, helping to break down – or sometimes reinforce – national stereotypes.

Unlike commercial television in America, state television networks, funded by a broadcasting fee (sometimes supplemented by advertising), were the norm in the early years. Italy, France and West Germany, for instance, had such systems by the end of the 1950s. The BBC in Britain was funded solely by a licence fee. Everywhere, television (like radio) was seen as a public service. Commercial television, wholly sponsored by advertising, had begun in Britain in 1955 when ITV (Independent Television) broke the state monopoly. It seldom, however, posed any serious challenge to the state sector in continental Europe before the 1980s. East of the Iron Curtain, television was of course rigidly controlled by the state, whose authorities took over from the Churches as the guardians of public morality and at the same time sought to block any Western influence. State television, in the West too, sought to balance entertainment with documentary and other 'educational' programmes. Audiences, at first with only a single channel and down to the 1980s only a few additional channels, were given little choice. But it was plain from the start that entertainment programmes were what viewers wanted to watch.

Television was by now supplanting radio as the dominant form of entertainment for the family. Comedies, adventures and light dramas, quizzes and sport were what people in their millions wanted above all to watch. Viewing had an impact on family life and on leisure pursuits. Families often gathered around the television set in the evening. Certain programmes were priorities, not to be missed. Mealtimes were adjusted accordingly. Going to the cinema, to a café, a pub, a restaurant, or simply to visit friends or relatives, had to be fitted into viewing patterns. Leisure, even more than in the age of radio, had come into the home. Television was the new god.

Visits to the cinema became less frequent as television spread. By the end of the 1950s cinema attendances were already declining. By the mid-1970s they had fallen in France, Italy and the Netherlands to approximately a third of their 1955 level, almost as steeply in Norway and most drastically, to little over a twelfth of that level, in Britain. A third of British cinemas closed between 1957 and 1963. Many were turned into bowling allies or bingo halls, others left as fading dream-palaces of yesteryear. East of the Iron Curtain the pattern was somewhat different and in any case not uniform – a halving in Poland of cinema attendance, but a slight rise in the Soviet Union and a substantial rise in Bulgaria. The relative absence of television was the most likely reason. As late as 1960 there were only 4.8 million television sets in the USSR. The cinema (alongside reading and drinking) was still one of the few widely available diversions from the drabness of daily life.

Given the shortage of capital, American dominance of the European cinema in the early post-war years had been inevitable. Even in the early 1960s imported American films still formed a major part of what was available in Europe's cinemas, though France and Italy were relatively resistant to the common trend. The French especially preferred their own films, and the market share of French cinema started to climb – enhanced by international successes such as Roger Vadim's *Et Dieu . . . créa la femme* (*And God Created Woman*), which in 1956 launched the career of the new sex-goddess, Brigitte Bardot. West Germany, unsurprisingly given the American military presence, was more open to imports from the United States. Some of the most popular films in the 1950s, such as *Die Halbstarken* (1956, *Teenage Wolfpack* in its English-language version), about teenage gangs, or *Sissi* (1955), starring Romy Schneider, depicting the tragic life of the wife of the Habsburg Emperor, Franz Joseph, had nevertheless been German productions.

Britain, given the shared language with America, had always been peculiarly exposed to the dominance of Hollywood. But British film production had continued to flourish in the early post-war period. Its outstanding film at that time was Carol Reed's *The Third Man* (1949), with its wonderfully evocative images of war-torn Vienna and a memorable performance by the American star Orson Welles as Harry Lime, the anti-hero at the centre of the penicillin drugs racket. Britain was exceptional in relishing war films (along with war novels, war memoirs and war comic books). Glorying in past heroics masked the sense of national decline. More than a hundred war films were produced between 1945 and 1960. Some 8.5 million people saw *The Dam Busters*, released in 1955, over 12 million saw *The Bridge on the River Kwai* (depicting Japanese cruelty towards British prisoners of war) two years later. No other European country could glorify the war in film. Where war films were made at all in continental Europe, they tended to concentrate on themes of resistance or the suffering of innocent victims. But in countries with complex, ambivalent wartime histories such films could not expect to be hugely popular. People mainly wanted escapism from the war, not being reminded of its horrors.

Just after the war Italian cinema had been totally dominated by American productions. In 1957 five of the ten top-earning films in Italy were still American. By the late 1960s, however, this had changed. Only three American productions – two Westerns and a Disney comedy – figured in the ten most popular films, though film tastes had largely migrated to Italian Westerns and comedies. It was, however, far from one-way traffic. Gina Lollobrigida and Sophia Loren, like the French sex-symbol Brigitte Bardot, became household names throughout Europe and across the Atlantic. And a number of Italian film directors made high-quality productions that were highly popular both in Italy and abroad. Prominent among them was Federico Fellini's *La Dolce Vita* of 1960. The film depicted a 'good life' that was empty, meaningless and sordid. It was a critique of contemporary morality, and of a powerful and decadent Italian upper class. Featuring (a major part of its success) the Swedish star Anita Ekberg, it included some risqué scenes that Italian television, still heavily influenced by the morality of the Catholic Church, avoided. Controversy about the film only helped its popular appeal, in Italy and even more so abroad. The film's huge international success helped to turn post-fascist Rome into a fashionable tourist attraction. And, derived from the name of one of the characters in the film, Paparazzo, it bestowed a word, *paparazzi* (intrusive, nuisance photographers), on English and other languages.

Michelangelo Antonioni's prize-winning films *L'Avventura* (1960, *The Adventure*), *La Notte* (1961, *The Night*) and *L'Eclisse* (1962, *Eclipse*), which explored emotional insecurity in modern society, won international acclaim, while his English-language film *Blow-Up* (1966), about a day in the life of a fashion photographer in 'swinging London', became a huge popular as well as artistic success, not least because of its – for the time – explicit sex scenes. Other Italian directors who gained major international recognition included Luchino Visconti. His *The Damned* (1969), about the relations of an industrialist's family with Hitler's regime, won international acclaim, while Franco Zeffirelli gained great popularity through his filming of Shakespeare's plays *The Taming of the Shrew* (1967), starring Richard Burton and Elizabeth Taylor, and *Romeo and Juliet* (1968).

Italian cinema was nevertheless exceptional in some ways. Italy had the highest number of cinemas in Europe and television was late to establish itself. Italians still in the mid-1960s spent far more on the cinema than on the theatre or sporting events. Even high-brow avant-garde films could find a large audience there. In most other parts of Europe that was not the case. Occasionally, however, an art film, such as *The Seventh Seal* (original: *Det sjunde inseglet*, 1956), by the Swedish director Ingmar Bergman, in which a knight returning from the Crusades plays chess for life or death with a black-clad grim reaper, could break the usual bounds to become both a classic and an international success.

As post-war recovery took hold and prosperity grew, film, theatre and literature had throughout Western Europe increasingly turned to social criticism. In the eyes of many artists prosperity and stability had become synonymous with materialism, hypocrisy and stuffy conservative values. The conventional lifestyle and values of middle-class society, or class-based unfairness and lack of opportunity, were frequent targets. The social criticism looked to the past in order to revolt against it. Britain and West Germany, as so often, produced contrasting responses to social and cultural change.

A 'New Wave' of literature, theatre and film in late 1950s Britain focused on the poverty, aggression, resentment and sexual values of the English industrial working class. John Osborne's *Look Back in Anger* (1956), a huge hit on the London stage, then on television, and three years later a successful film, practically inaugurated the genre and gave rise to the generic appellation of 'angry young men' (without anyone being certain what they were angry about, let alone how they intended to make things better). 'Kitchen-sink drama', as it was soon dubbed, produced a rapid succession of novels and plays that reached mass audiences when turned into hugely popular films – not least because their earthy sexual content was daring for its time – such as *Room at the Top* (1959), *Saturday Night and Sunday Morning* (1960), *A Taste of Honey* (1961), *A Kind of Loving* (1962) and *Billy Liar* (1963). They conveyed a nostalgia for 'genuine' northern English working-class life in the process of being lost. This had been the thrust of Richard Hoggart's *The Uses of Literacy* (1957), which, for a work of scholarship, had attracted a surprisingly wide readership. Hoggart had criticized the hedonism and cult of youth in a society where 'liberty equals licence to provide what will best increase sales'. He had argued that 'we are moving towards the creation of a mass culture' which, in its modern consumerism and commercialized, sensationalist entertainment, he saw as 'less healthy than the often crude culture it is replacing'. It amounted in his view to the destruction of the 'urban culture "of the people"'.

By the 1960s satire was increasingly deployed to parody the political establishment and the entrenched class system, in theatre, the press and television. Political satire was, of course, nothing new in journalism or theatrical productions. But the far bigger television audiences now exposed greater numbers than ever before to the often biting wit directed at established figures and institutions, as in the widely viewed weekly television programme, *That Was the Week That Was*, shown in 1962–3. Deference was plainly in decline.

In West Germany cultural creativity was still often connected to consciousness of the Nazi past. Rolf Hochhuth's play *Der Stellvertreter* (1963, *The Deputy*) provoked a storm of controversy by attacking the silence of Pope Pius XII during the Holocaust. Literary criticism was usually more subtle. Hans Magnus Enzensberger, for example, criticized the German mentalities of the 1960s while alluding to the recent past in his poem, published in 1964, 'Middle-Class Blues' (choosing a form that recalled American, not German, musical tradition): 'We can't complain./ We're not out of work./We don't go hungry./We eat.' Then comes the oblique reference to the past: 'The grass grows,/The social product,/ . . . We eat the past.'

An 'unmastered past' – a catastrophe built on the complicity of so many citizens that had been largely blocked out of consciousness and supplanted by the materialist values of a prosperous consumer society – produced an exceptional level of cultural disorientation and at the same time frenetic experimentation with the 'new', the avant-garde, in all art forms. The sense of alienation of West German intellectuals, from what they often castigated as a smug, shallow society that was trying to erase the past, was more acute than anywhere else in Europe. The 'new cinema' of Alexander Kluge or Edgar Reitz (and later Wim Wenders) paralleled the 'New Wave' (*la nouvelle vague*) cinema of François Truffaut, Jean-Luc Godard and others in France, which turned its back completely on conventional narrative forms and created something more like reflective essays in film. In deliberately provocative experimental theatre and painting, existing values of culture, and of politics and society, were challenged.

It would be easy, however, to exaggerate the influence of the cultural avant-garde. International influences in popular culture from 'Coca-colonization' (as the all-pervasive impact of American commercial products was dubbed) to the music of the Beatles and other major bands were almost certainly more important in the silent transformation of social values. Nevertheless, the cultural avant-garde had a disproportionate effect on the highly educated sector of the younger generation. Notions of an 'alternative culture' spread – a culture that was more democratic, more communal, less reverential of traditional forms, more self-consciously revolutionary.

BREAKING WITH THE VALUES OF THE PAST

Culture in its manifold forms of art, literature and other creative expression reflects, challenges and shapes the values and mentalities of a society. In the 1960s these values and mentalities, especially among the younger generation, were in the early stages of an enduring and intensifying transformation. The role of crucial influences on social attitudes and behaviour – prominent among them the military, work, education, religion and the family – was altering, often diminishing.

By the 1960s European societies had become largely demilitarized. The army had lost its influence as a central feature of society. Militaristic values were no longer so dominant. States spent less on defence, more on welfare. Schools and the Christian Churches were less able to indoctrinate the young with militaristic and nationalistic values than they had once done. The belief, inculcated into young men down to the end of the Second World War, that it was their sacred duty to fight and die for their country, was waning strongly. Most young men, it is true, still had to undertake compulsory military service for two years or so. But they seldom did so enthusiastically, often in fact resentfully. Military service was a lingering remnant of the time when mass-conscripted armies were necessary to fight major wars. In the era of nuclear weapons they were increasingly an anachronism – though it took most states a long time to bow to this reality. Large conscript armies composed of reluctant military novices were also largely redundant in the increasingly unpopular wars against liberation movements in soon-to-be former colonies. Most governments, acknowledging public opposition to conscription, started by the end of the 1960s to offer alternatives to military service – civilian work in hospitals or schools, for example. Whether undertaking such work, or enduring two years of pointless military drilling and parading, most of the young men forced to undertake their 'national service' could not wait to return to civilian life. The civilian world, not the army, now shaped their value-system.

The world of work, too, was altering greatly. In an era of practically full employment, unions had strong bargaining power to improve conditions for their increased membership. Assembly-line production in big factories was still ubiquitous in the 1950s and 1960s, though starting to give way to a more flexible organization of working patterns that allowed for labour to be less monotonous, more humane, and yet increasing efficiency through greater use of worker initiative. Even the demarcation lines between workers and managers were no longer as firm as they had once been. Swedish car factories were in the vanguard of experiments to reduce the divide and make production a more corporate enterprise. These changes had not gone very far by the end of the 1960s. But in the workplace, too, the old iron discipline of classic capitalist production was weakening.

Class divisions were generally becoming less rigid. By the late 1960s a third of the West German middle class had working-class origins. Another fifth had dropped down from the upper middle class. Working-class solidarity was eroded as squalid slums in city centres were cleared, long-standing communities broken up, and socially less cohesive tenement blocks or areas of social housing constructed in new areas, sometimes in suburbs at a distance from the place of work. 'On these new big clean stairways there was no fellow feeling . . . These fine new glossy doors were always shut,' an English woman recalled (though implicitly romanticizing earlier days, when most working-class housing had actually been appalling, to be replaced by new estates that were far cleaner and healthier). Better-paid skilled workers, at one time drawn to political radicalism, were, as the German sociologist Ralf Dahrendorf put it, on the way to 'embourgeoisement', exploiting their bargaining power in 'the individual search for happiness'. The trend towards 'a levelled-middle-class society' can easily be exaggerated. It was in any case stronger in prosperous West Germany (where the term was coined) than in most parts of Europe, and did not apply at all beyond the Iron Curtain. But it hinted at what was happening more widely. As the 'service-sector' drew people who at one time would have headed for industrial work towards administrative and clerical jobs, the gap in mentalities between the upper echelons of the working class and the white-collar lower middle class narrowed.

As the working week was shortened, there was more time for leisure pursuits. These were becoming a dominant interest. More than two-thirds of those asked in a West German survey of 1973 rated leisure and the family as more important than work. More people were able to enjoy holidays – often now abroad – than ever before. At home, too, the options increased for spending time away from work with the family, in the garden (as more people had home gardens or allotments), or in other myriad diversions from the dreary demands of employment. Many of the leisure pursuits were individual, not collective – part of a general trend that was still in its early stages and would progress further in later decades. But, as we have been noting, important spheres of popular entertainment – music, film and television – offered forms of leisure that crossed national borders, united large segments of youth, and shaped common interests and mentalities across Europe's frontiers, penetrating even countries beyond the Iron Curtain.

After the war secondary education rapidly expanded in most European countries, offering opportunities for advancement that had earlier been restricted to a social elite. On average in Western Europe two and a half times more pupils aged between ten and nineteen years of age attended school in 1970 than had done so in 1950. National (and sometimes regional) differences persisted, but there was a general recognition of the need to prepare a greater proportion of the population for entry into more complex forms of work, or to go on to higher education. In Eastern Europe post-war education was radically different both from that before the war and from developments in Western Europe. Private and religious schools were abolished, greater attention was paid to Russian language, literature and history, more emphasis placed upon science and technology, and all overlaid by the elucidation of the history of the labour movement and Marxist-Leninist interpretation of social and political development.

The opportunities for a university education also started to widen in the 1960s. New universities and polytechnics were founded. Where in 1950 only around 3 to 5 per cent of those aged between twenty and twenty-four attended university, by 1970 the figure was generally between 12 and 18 per cent, with Sweden and the Netherlands over 20 per cent. The trend was similar beyond the Iron Curtain, though at a somewhat lower level, ranging from 8 per cent in Albania to 14 per cent in the GDR and a high point of 16 per cent in Yugoslavia. Higher education was still largely a male preserve – more so in Western than in Eastern Europe. Only a quarter of graduates at the University of Manchester in 1965, for instance, were women (a tiny number of whom graduated in science and medicine). But more young people than ever before were exposed through university education to new or different ways of thinking. A highly intelligent sector of society was as a result able to challenge existing social conventions and political decisions precisely at a time when these were more fluid and open to serious criticism than at any time since the Second World War.

European culture had in great measure been a product of nearly two millennia of Christian teaching and since the eighteenth century the values of the Enlightenment. The spread of scientific and medical knowledge, however, together with the greater optimism in the possibilities of finding rational answers to society's problems, undermined faith in the supernatural. Church adherence had, moreover, traditionally been stronger in more closely knit communities in the countryside than in the sprawling urban conglomerates and among the industrial working class. The continued drain from the countryside to a more amorphous urban society further helped to weaken, therefore, the direct social impact of the Churches. In the cities, too, the counter-attractions to religion provided by an ever-increasing array of leisure pursuits were plain. Even during the most solemn days of the Christian calendar at Easter, young people often preferred the funfair, the cinema or a sporting event to going to church. Declining religious observance was the effect, not the cause, of the wider social changes that were affecting the Churches, as all other institutions. Yet it meant a diminished impact not just of religious teaching but also of moral values that had been the traditional domain of the Churches.

In the communist states beyond the Iron Curtain the steep fall in religious observance and professed belief was to a great extent politically driven. It could be a severe disadvantage to be a practising Christian (or Jew or Muslim). The Churches themselves had to endure political repression. The number of Orthodox priests in the Soviet Union dropped by almost a half within six years, between 1959 and 1965. Large numbers of churches, mosques and synagogues were closed, and all religious bodies closely monitored by state authorities. Privately held belief persisted beneath the surface, though just what proportion of the population continued to hold a religious faith cannot be known. In Central and Eastern Europe the trend was generally similar, though not uniform. Albania was the state most hostile to religion. When asked what the difference was between the major religions in their country, Albanians had a ready answer: 'Christians don't go to church on Sundays, Jews don't go to the synagogue on Saturdays, and Muslims don't go to the mosque on Fridays.' Poland stood at the opposite end of the spectrum. The Catholic Church increasingly came to stand for Polish national identity and posed an alternative belief system to the official state ideology. Religious observance as well as popular piety, far from declining, increased as a result. There was 70 per cent attendance at Mass each Sunday in the 1960s. By the 1980s the number of regular churchgoers would rise, especially in working-class parishes, to a quite remarkable 90–95 per cent of the population. For the communist authorities this was by any measure a disaster.

In Western Europe the long-term decline in religious observance – more marked in the various forms of Protestantism than in the Catholic Church – had been temporarily halted during the traumatic war years and their immediate aftermath. But during the 1960s ties with the Churches loosened markedly, a trend that would continue and accelerate for the remainder of the century and beyond.

Dilution of religious commitment proceeded fastest in north-western Europe, where economic modernization was most advanced, the population was relatively well educated, liberal political systems were most developed, and cultural norms subject to the greatest change. Decline was slower in the Catholic south of the continent where religion retained a stronger hold over the population than in the northern predominantly Protestant regions of Europe. The Republic of Ireland, economically a relatively backward country, where the 'special position' of the Catholic Church had been enshrined in the constitution of 1937 and Catholicism was embedded in national identity, posed an exception in north-western Europe. More than 90 per cent of the population still went regularly to Mass as late as 1960. Few if any parts of Europe could compete with that. But even in wealthier and more modernized regions such as Bavaria, allegiance to the Church remained relatively strong. And the millions who still journeyed to Catholic shrines like Lourdes in France, Fatima in Portugal, Knock in Ireland or Częstochowa in Poland (where the icon of the

'Black Madonna', symbol of the nation, resided), testified to the continued vitality of Catholic belief.

In general, throughout Europe more Catholics than Protestants were
still regular attendees of church services, though the numbers were falling. Surveys showed that most people still professed a belief in God.
Most of the population also continued to declare a nominal religious
adherence. And the offices of the Churches were still usually called upon
for baptism, marriage and funerals. The indicators are, nonetheless, that
fewer people were continuing to do so, and that religious belief itself was
contracting. Surveys showed, for instance, that the numbers of Europeans who believed in an afterlife were falling. The Churches – the
Catholic Church especially – continued to play a major role in upholding
public morality. But it was an uphill struggle.

The Churches tried to adapt to the rapid social changes. Ecumenism –
the opening to other faiths in the quest for Christian unity – started to
make headway. The meeting in 1960 between the Archbishop of Canter-
bury, primate of the Anglican Church, and the Pope was the first since
long before the Reformation. And, a sign of things to come, the first
women pastors in Europe were ordained by Lutheran churches in Denmark (already in 1948), then Sweden (1960) and Norway (1961). Some
Protestant theologians sought to define belief in novel ways. Paul Tillich
argued that faith did not stand in opposition to reason, but transcended
it. The Anglican Bishop of Woolwich, John Robinson, rejected notions
of an objective God outside human imagination. The complex writings
of these theologians were important in provoking debate within the Protestant Church. But few normal churchgoers were interested in questions
of ontological theology, most were not attracted by the idea of a God
whose existence was purely subjective, and those drifting away from the
Church were unlikely anyway to reverse their steps on account of elevated theological debate.

The Catholic Church, too, was on the threshold of epochal change.
The election in 1958 of Pope John XXIII inaugurated a significant break
with the aloof papal monarchy of his predecessor, Pius XII, and began
possibly the most transformative papacy of modern times. His crucial
decision – not welcomed by the ultra-conservative Vatican Curia (the
papal-governing apparatus) – was to call a general Council of the Church,
the first since 1870, only the second since the sixteenth century. The Pope

was responding to a strong feeling among a new generation of bishops, and below them from the grassroots of clergy and laity, that the Church needed to reform and modernize in order to prevent serious erosion of its following. Already in the late 1950s West German bishops were keenly aware of the 'habitual neglect of Sunday Mass' as a 'pastoral problem' and the 'serious concerns' of many priests about the decline in the numbers of practising Catholics. Debate on pastoral reform and renewal from below was most advanced in France, spreading to Holland, Belgium, West Germany and Italy, though the ideas had made little headway in Ireland, Britain and on the Iberian peninsula, where the highly conservative Church was the most resistant to change.

Vatican II (as it was usually called) accorded increased 'collegial' authority to the bishops, alongside the Pope (the Bishop of Rome), though any diminution of papal primacy was countered by the reaffirmation of the doctrine of papal infallibility. The Council went a good way in opening the Church to ecumenism, advocating reconciliation with other Churches. There was an apology to Jews for their suffering at the hands of Christians (and the offensive attribution to Jews of blame for the killing of Christ in the Good Friday service was removed), a call to enter into dialogue with Jews, and a denunciation of antisemitism. In 1965 the centuries-old schism with the Eastern Orthodox Church was healed. For ordinary churchgoing Catholics the most overt – and for traditionalists highly objectionable – change emanating from the Council was the replacement of Latin, the language of the Church in Western Europe since ancient times, by the vernacular language when celebrating Mass, a move designed to make the Church less remote from the people.

The changes were major, and lasting. They reinvigorated debate within the Church, among the laity as well as clergy, stirred enthusiasm among the faithful for new forms of participation in pastoral work, and widened horizons to greater awareness of social deprivation outside Europe, notably in Latin America. But the historian Diarmaid MacCulloch rightly described the outcome of the Council as only 'half a revolution'. Pandora's box had been opened, but the bishops were soon trying to push down the lid again. Moves to link the Church to political radicalism and to Latin American 'liberation theology' were blocked. Lay participation was welcomed, as long as the clergy retained firm control. The 'college' of bishops amounted to little more than verbiage as papal primacy was reaffirmed. And the Swiss theologian, Hans Küng (who had participated as an advisor in the Vatican Council), was eventually barred from teaching Catholic theology – he was a professor in Tübingen in West Germany – after publicly rejecting the doctrine of papal infallibility.

Where the reforms flowing from Vatican II most signally failed to adjust to crucial currents of social change was in the sphere of sexual behaviour. Many attending the Council had hoped that there would be at least a relaxation in the rules prohibiting priests from marrying. But celibacy for the clergy was reaffirmed by Pope Paul VI, the more conservative successor to John XXIII, who died in 1963, long before the Council he had summoned had finished its work. This almost certainly contributed to the decline in the numbers of those willing to enter the priesthood – and an increase in those leaving it to get married. A far wider problem was the continued ban on contraception pronounced by Pope Paul in his encyclical *Humanae Vitae* ('Of Human Life') in 1968. This not only led to heated protests among the Catholic clergy as well as laity; the papal ban was in practice widely ignored. Quite apart from the damage this did to papal authority, it marked the limits of Vatican II's ability to change Catholicism in ways that could significantly redress the advance of secularization and the decline in Catholic observance. With the ban on birth control, the papacy was plainly in conflict with changes in sexuality and in the family that the Church was powerless to halt.

Attitudes towards marriage, divorce, cohabitation and extramarital births were changing. The post-war 'baby boom' was over. Young people were no longer following the Churches in seeing reproduction as the prime purpose of marriage. And they were marrying later than had been usual after the war. Greater employment opportunities encouraged individuals to organize the rearing of children primarily in accordance with their own lives, desires and material circumstances, rather than the other way round. More women now sought paid employment, and wanted to control their own lives. They increasingly contested the traditional view that their place was to bear children and run the family home. In Western Europe their progress was greatest in Scandinavia, slowest in Catholic countries, where social teaching directly emphasized the duty of the wife and mother at home. Ireland even enshrined in its constitution 'that mothers shall not be obliged by economic necessity to engage in labour to the neglect of their duties in the home'. The pattern of later marriage and fewer children was also developed in Eastern Europe, though in part for different reasons. Systems of maternity support permitting full-time employment for women were far more extensive than in the West. But lack of prosperity and the wait for a suitable apartment imposed their own limitations on the readiness to marry early and have children.

Above all, better methods of contraception and changing laws on abortion meant that women were more able than ever before to determine when, or if, they were going to have children, inside or outside marriage. The crucial invention in the United States in 1960 of the contraceptive pill – soon just generally known as 'the Pill' – fundamentally changed women's lives. Women could themselves now for the first time reliably control reproduction. The Pill transformed sexual behaviour. It opened the path to the sexual freedom enjoyed by both men and women from the later 1960s onwards.

Sexual liberation began an erosion of marriage that would accelerate in the last decades of the century. Divorce rates started to rise noticeably, if nowhere near as fast as later in the century. Already by 1970 over a quarter of marriages in Sweden and Denmark were ending in divorce. By then almost a third of Swedish and Danish couples in their early twenties were choosing to live together without entering marriage, and nearly a fifth of births in Sweden were outside marriage. These were well in advance of the ratios in other Western European countries. The trend pointed nevertheless in the same direction, as it did in Eastern Europe, though Catholic countries lagged far behind. Divorce in Italy, for instance, was not legal until December 1970, in Portugal 1975, in post-Franco Spain only in 1982, in Ireland as late as 1997, and in Malta not even until the twenty-first century, in 2011.

Behind the trends lay a sexual revolution that was challenging practically all conventions on sexuality and by the later 1960s was a central part of the youth counter-culture. The Feminist Liberation Movement – Simone de Beauvoir, the partner of Jean-Paul Sartre, had been an early pioneer and her book *Le deuxième Sexe* (1949, *The Second Sex*) a vital ideological influence – played a significant part in promoting women's sexual independence. The increasing acceptance – at least in theory – of

women's equality, a major and lasting achievement of the feminist movement, amounted to one of the most important social changes of
subsequent decades and was in good measure made possible by the invention of the Pill. Its availability enabled both men and women to enjoy
casual sex without the risk of pregnancy. 'Free love' – sexual freedom to
interchange multiple partners – crossed the Atlantic from the hippie culture in San Francisco. Homosexuality, too, still generally in the 1950s
part of a furtive and criminalized demi-monde, started on the path
towards wider acceptance in society – though the path would be a long
and stony one as the detritus of deeply embedded prejudice was only
slowly trodden down.

The rapidly expanding mass media contributed hugely to the increasing social acceptability of new attitudes towards sex. Books and films
were soon challenging, and breaking, traditional taboos. In 1960 the
publication of the unexpurgated version of D. H. Lawrence's *Lady Chat-
terley's Lover* (which contained explicit descriptions of sexual intercourse
in vivid, demotic language) came before a London court, charged under
the Obscene Publications Act. When the counsel for the prosecution,
Mervyn Griffith Jones, a pillar of establishment rectitude, asked the jury
whether it was a book 'you would wish your wife or your servants to
read', he seemed to be speaking from a bygone age. Expert literary witnesses lined up to defend the book. Somewhat eccentrically, the
controversial Bishop of Woolwich, John Robinson, suggested that the
sexual intercourse luridly described by Lawrence was 'an act of holy
communion'. The publisher, Penguin Books, was eventually acquitted of
all charges. The furore predictably contributed to an explosion in sales
of the book. This British case was an early example of the impossibility
of sustaining previously rigorous censorship of sexual expression as
social values were changing so rapidly. In literature, film, newspapers
and magazines – television in its early years was still protective of public
morality – it was obvious that sex was big business.

Governments were compelled to adjust to the changing climate. Sweden and Denmark again took the lead in the accessibility of contraceptive
methods. Britain made the Pill freely available to married couples on a
doctor's prescription from 1961, and from 1968 to all women, married or
not. Following pressure from feminists, France removed its ban on birth
control in 1965. Catholic countries, in accordance with the Church's

official stance, resisted relaxation of restrictions on contraception, which were only lifted in Italy in 1970, in Ireland more than a decade later still. Abortion had been legal in the Soviet Union and among its allies since the 1950s. But laws permitting abortion – usually still with strictly applied conditions – spread within Western Europe only from the late 1960s and early 1970s onwards. Although the passage of legislation usually followed heated debate and was opposed particularly by the Catholic Church, predominantly Catholic countries too gradually moved to legalize abortion, though some countries, such as Malta, continued to hold out against the trend and would still impose a ban on abortion into the next century.

Changing social attitudes were also reflected in legislation on homosexual practice. The stance of European governments towards homosexuality had historically been varied. Official bans existed in most (though not all) communist states. Most Western democracies had criminalized homosexuality. It had been legal in France since the Revolution, however (though the Vichy regime, in common with other fascist regimes, had banned it), and in Denmark, Sweden and Iceland (though not Norway or Finland) for two or three decades. But from the late 1960s onwards, responding to growing objections to current law, governments across Europe began to liberalize legislation on homosexuality. The 'Gay Rights Movement', beginning in the United States, exerted further pressure. Gradually, though the process would extend into the 1990s, the criminalization of homosexual acts among consenting adults was brought to an end throughout Western and post-Soviet Eastern Europe. Widespread discrimination against homosexuals nevertheless continued, most plainly in Russia.

* * *

Social values had changed immeasurably in Europe since the war. Society in Western Europe had by the late 1960s in general become more liberal, more tolerant than it had been in 1950. Of course, there were counter-currents to this generalization. Racist attitudes still persisted widely, if often just below the surface. Sexist attitudes were commonplace. Women often had to contend with unwelcome sexual overtures from men who enjoyed exploiting their position of power in numerous walks of life. Feminism faced an uphill struggle to change male prejudices towards women and alter long-standing discrimination against them in education, job opportunities and in the workplace.

For some among the younger generation the liberalization was in any case too slow, and far from radical enough. They sought much faster and far more sweeping change. By the later 1960s they were posing a challenge to the social and political order, east as well as west of the Iron Curtain.

6

Challenges

It is prohibited to prohibit. Liberty begins with one prohibition:
that against harming the liberty of others.

Graffiti in Paris, May 1968

Do not be indifferent to the day when the light of the future was
carried forward by a burning body.

Daubing on the Wenceslas Statue, Prague, January
1969, following the self-immolation of Jan Palach in
protest at the Soviet occupation of Czechoslovakia

During the second half of the 1960s Europe, west and east, experienced
a period of political turbulence greater than at any time since the immediate aftermath of the Second World War. Both sides of the Iron Curtain,
in quite different ways, faced challenges to their systems of rule. In Western Europe it came to a head in the student protests of 1968. In Eastern
Europe the 'Prague Spring' in the same year sent shock waves through
the Soviet bloc. By the early 1970s the turbulence was subsiding again,
though its legacy was multifaceted and long-lasting.

The turbulence, transitory though it proved to be, mirrored profound
transformations in social and cultural values, most obviously marked
among the generation of the post-war 'baby boom', by this time in or
reaching early adulthood. The values and behavioural patterns of an
older generation, schooled in the discipline imposed by living through
world war, were by the mid-1960s being subjected to fundamental challenge. Authority, obedience, duty – these were, for the young, values
redolent of the past. The young especially became more individualistic in

their appearance, habits and lifestyles, less ready to accept the often staid conformity and authority of their elders. And in certain circumstances they were ready to rebel.

PROTEST AND VIOLENCE

Generational Revolt

In 1960 the American sociologist Daniel Bell had announced 'the end of ideology in the West'. The great ideologies, especially Marxism, that had developed in the nineteenth century and dominated the first half of the twentieth century were, he argued, over and would play no major role in the emerging technocratic society. The 1950s had seen the 'exhaustion' (as he called it) of political ideas and the redundancy of fundamentalist ideologies. Even given historically unusual, relatively high levels of political consensus in European countries, this was a peculiarly American assessment. And within half a decade it was already appearing to be a strange misjudgement.

For by the middle of the 1960s the earlier relatively quiescent domestic scene was giving way to a more disturbed political era in which the ideological clash between Marxism and capitalism played a central role. Nor was this clash solely or even mainly related to the entirely opposed social and political systems across the Iron Curtain. For the most part, in fact, it was an ideological conflict *within* Western society, between Western forms of Marxism and capitalist liberal democracy. It found articulation in the political protest, reflecting a more extensive sense of alienation in much of the younger generation, which became more widespread after the middle of the 1960s. For many participants it was an explicit generational revolt. 'We were a new generation that was seizing power' was how one former activist retrospectively described the heady atmosphere (and its inbuilt illusions). Some found inspiration in the demonstrations and protests that were having a major impact in the American civil rights movement of the 1960s. In Europe as well as in the United States the poetically lyrical music of the American singer Bob Dylan, notably 'Blowin' in the Wind', 'The Times They Are a-Changin'' and 'Masters of War', became anthems of protest for young people. Above all, the unfolding horror of the Vietnam War – the first war that could be followed on television screens – offered a cause that, transcending national boundaries, bound together vehement denunciation of unbridled materialism, imperialism, colonialism, American power and Western capitalism with idealistic notions of rebuilding society along neo-Marxist classless lines. The protest became reflected, too, in the new expressions of political violence, extreme manifestations of alienation often inchoately directed at what was regarded as the political establishment.

Protest exploded spectacularly in 1968. But unrest had been seething for some years before it reached boiling point. '1968' is the symbol for a phenomenon that straddled that year, a rejection and subversion of the underlying values of the time. Students, with educational advantages, increasingly with contacts abroad, and with the opportunities to turn the radical ideas they absorbed into forms of collective action, spearheaded the generational revolt. What has been described as a 'global protest' movement found expression in the United States and Japan, in various parts of Western Europe (even under the authoritarian regime in Franco's Spain), and it resonated, too, in certain ways – differing, however, from their manifestation in the West – in parts of the eastern bloc, notably in Poland and Czechoslovakia. Within Western Europe the protest movement was at its most acute and most dramatic in Italy, West Germany and France. It had in each case some specific characteristics, though there were also common features.

At its most basic, the protest was an outburst of student discontent at the conditions within universities. The rapid growth of student numbers in the 1960s had led to grossly overfilled lecture halls and seminar rooms. And there were not nearly enough university teachers. Professors were remote, aloof and authoritarian figures. Not for nothing were they known in Italy as *baroni*. Student numbers there almost doubled to half a million in the 1960s. The University of Rome, designed for 5,000 students, had 50,000 by 1968. Many students left without qualifications. Even those who graduated often found difficulties in getting jobs. This was just an extreme example of a general pattern in most Western European countries. In West Germany there were nearly four times as many students as there had been in 1950 – though the numbers of university teachers and the available facilities had far from kept pace with the speed of the expansion. The administration of universities was reactionary and restrictive in the eyes of many students. The soulless concrete jungles of new university campuses intensified the anomie. Social disaffection became endemic. For some it became a total rejection of existing society. 'We don't want to find a place in this society,' commented an Italian student in 1968. 'We want to create a society in which it is worthwhile finding a place.'

Although each manifestation of protest reflected specific national conditions, growing ease of communication and travel facilitated the swift transmission of grievances across borders. Anger and resentment smouldered within the student body. The tinder-box was ready to be ignited by firebrand student leaders such as Daniel Cohn-Bendit ('Danny the Red') in France and Rudi Dutschke in West Germany, who were adept at transforming specific student grievances into a challenge to all forms of authority in the 'bourgeois state'. The recent past, most plainly in Italy and West Germany, offered a ready basis to invoke continuities between the former fascist regimes and current capitalist society. Max Horkheimer's adage, that anyone not wishing to speak of capitalism should keep quiet about fascism, was frequently cited.

Antifascism was a central component of the mood of protest in West Germany and important, too, in Italy. A channelling of protest into mass fascist movements, as had happened in the 1930s, was, therefore, explicitly ruled out. Fascism was anathema. This was overtly a rebellion from the left. Marxism provided the intellectual inspiration. The 'New Left' as its adepts called themselves, seldom, however, looked to Moscow and the Soviet model – its image irreparably tarnished after the violent suppression of the Hungarian uprising in late 1956. Instead, they found their heroes, somewhat incongruously for young citizens of industrialized Western Europe, in the leaders of peasant revolutions and the guerrilla struggles in the Far East and Latin America. They looked admiringly to Mao Zedong (unaware of, or prepared to overlook, his own responsibility for immense crimes against humanity), the North Vietnamese leader Ho Chi Minh, the Cuban head of government Fidel Castro (the face of opposition to American imperialism) and, most especially, the romanticized figure of Che Guevara, the Cuban revolutionary shot dead by Bolivian troops in October 1967.

They explored Marx's early writings and admired those, like Rosa Luxemburg and, most especially, Leon Trotsky, excluded from the orthodox

Leninist canon or excommunicated from the faith. The work of Antonio Gramsci, the Marxist theorist of fascism who had died while languishing in one of Mussolini's prisons, was especially revered. They were inspired by contact with Marxist intellectual gurus in and outside Europe. These included the French philosophers Jean-Paul Sartre, Louis Althusser (an increasingly strange and mentally disturbed figure and opponent of attempts to relate Marxism to humanism) and Michel Foucault, whose work emphasized the repressive power and controlling discipline of social institutions and agencies. Among the most prominent influences on student radicals was Herbert Marcuse, the German-born American critic of 'late capitalism', who saw contemporary society as dehumanizing, advocating revolution and the total rejection of the false gods of a Western consumerist culture. Marxist ideas in different guises served to fire the imagination of the generational rebellion of a relatively well-educated and articulate social group, driven by an urge to create a better world, to produce a fairer, more egalitarian society. A political revolution was not enough in their eyes. The entire belief systems and social structures that they underpinned had to be destroyed and society created anew.

The issue that most gripped young people – and not only them – across national frontiers was the worsening Vietnam War. This polarized political and ideological differences, inflamed emotions, and turned the attitudes of many young people against the country that had since the Second World War usually been held up as the model of democratic values, freedom and prosperity: the United States.

The Americans had been increasingly sucked into a widening and intractable conflict in Indochina (comprising Vietnam, Laos and Cambodia) since the French had started to withdraw in 1954–5. The aim was to contain the spread of communism throughout Indochina. To this end, Washington had come to depend upon a corrupt, puppet government in Saigon, the capital of South Vietnam. By the early 1960s the United States was starting to pour increasing amounts of weaponry into Vietnam, without coming any closer to defeating the fight for national independence of Ho Chi Minh's North Vietnamese forces, which were intensifying their guerrilla campaigns in the south. As the danger grew that the conflict was being lost, President Lyndon B. Johnson, the successor to John F. Kennedy (assassinated in November 1963), took the fateful decision in 1965 to commit American ground troops to the fight in Vietnam.

By the end of the year there were 184,000 American soldiers in Vietnam; within two years the number had grown to 485,000. Protests at the American involvement in Vietnam had already begun at the University of California at Berkeley in 1964, and rapidly widened in the coming years, led by the Students for a Democratic Society, an organization inspired by the ideas of the New Left. In April 1967 a gathering of 200,000 people in New York protested against the war. Over the following months the war escalated, its horror epitomized by the increased use by US forces of terrible napalm bombs. Public opinion in the USA turned against the war as young Americans in increasing numbers were conscripted to serve (and die) in what seemed – and *was* – an unwinnable conflict. Many were conscripts from poor white or black families. Richer or well-connected families often seemed somehow to avoid having their sons drafted. The protests grew in size and intensity. Their message crossed the Atlantic. Major demonstrations against American involvement in Vietnam soon took place in West Germany, France, Italy and other Western European countries.

Without the growing protest against the Vietnam War, student unrest about university conditions, however well justified, might well have remained just that. As it was, Vietnam converted the disaffection into a far wider manifestation of political and social protest, sometimes involving violent clashes with the police. It turned discontented students – some of them, anyway – into would-be revolutionaries.

But in this role they were mere dilettantes – not the real thing. Only briefly, and only in France in May 1968, when some ten million workers engaged in strikes and factory occupations as forms of protest against the Gaullist state, did the established order seem seriously threatened. Once the spontaneous strike-wave in France subsided and the heady atmosphere sobered up, the intensity drained from the student protests. They gradually fizzled out with some improvements in university governance being the only tangible gain. But for many of those involved, the adrenalin flow and excitement of the action had carried them along, and left indelible memories.

The '68ers saw themselves as a 'special' generation. But much of the population either disapproved of or was indifferent towards the protest movement. The great majority of young people in European countries were not students. Many of them, indeed, already employed in hard and badly paid manual jobs, regarded students as a privileged elite – which was not far from the truth. And most of the students themselves were primarily interested in what directly affected them. Many opposed the wider aims of the left-wing protesters. The organization of conservative students in West Germany, the Christian Democratic Student League, was, for instance, only marginally smaller than the left-wing body, the Socialist German Student League. A majority of West German students in an opinion survey of 1967 favoured the emergency laws (to limit personal freedoms in a declared state of emergency) that the government wanted to introduce and which the left-wing student activists so vehemently opposed. And student views on the conservative-led coalition government were split down the middle between critics and those who approved. In any case, the minority that harboured utopian ideals of revolution to destroy capitalism completely lacked the capacity to pose a fundamental challenge to well-established and stable democratic systems, or to mobilize wide sections of society which had experienced years of full employment and unprecedented prosperity – and stood vehemently opposed to Marxism.

The Explosion of Protest

Student protest spread across Italy during 1967 in a wave of demonstrations and strikes at universities. The simmering discontent over university conditions had gathered momentum when a student of architecture, Paulo Rossi, was killed in a fight with neo-fascist students in Rome in April 1966 and declared to be 'a new victim of fascism'. There was much opposition, too, to plans for government reforms of higher education (later abandoned), which were criticized by students as the subordination of learning to the demands of the capitalist economy. By early 1968 the mood of protest had deepened. In late February the police evicted students who had been occupying buildings in the University of Rome. When the students tried to recapture one of the buildings on 1 March it resulted in a pitched battle with the police – dubbed 'The Battle of Valle Giulia'. The police baton-charged the crowd of around 1,500 students. The students retaliated by setting a number of cars on fire. By the end forty-six police and hundreds of students were left injured. Up to then the student movement had been relatively peaceful. From now on clashes with the police were invariably violent. Gradually, however, as some concessions were made to student demands, the unpopular reform legislation was dropped, and public support for the students waned, the intensity of the conflict as it related specifically to conditions within universities declined.

After 'Valle Giulia' the student movement changed its character. Spontaneous protest turned into organized revolutionary agitation. A radical minority of students who belonged to a variety of revolutionary groups, determined to learn from the swift splintering of worker and student interests in France, now turned to mobilizing the discontent in Italy's industrial working class. Many factory workers had come from the impoverished south of the country and formed a sub-proletariat. They were badly paid, frequently employed at piece-rates on production lines, exposed to soulless working conditions and authoritarian management, and unaccustomed to the discipline of trade unions and political parties. Articulate, radical students found as they went into the factories to encourage the workers to rise in protest that their message often fell on receptive ears.

Some 7.5 million workers took part in around 3,800 mainly 'wildcat' strikes from the latter part of 1968 to autumn 1969. This pushed the trade unions into action, and at the end of what was dubbed the 'hot autumn' by December 1969 they had successfully negotiated major improvements in the workplace and gained substantial pay rises – double those of other Western European industrial countries on average over the following years, though not matched by similar levels of increased productivity. Trade unions emerged greatly strengthened, and able to exert substantial power at the national level to improve conditions for the Italian working class. Worker militancy became a part of Italian life. Italy was the strike capital of Europe. Four and a half million workers participated in industrial disputes in 1972; over six million in 1973. But the unions wanted concrete material improvements, not utopian political ideas. Student radicals' hopes of a revolutionary momentum were therefore disappointed. And meanwhile the government, though frequently changing in composition, introduced between 1969 and 1971 a number of political and social reforms – the raising of pension levels, some expansion of social housing, legislation to provide the right to divorce, and the introduction of regional government – that were at best partial remedies but were sufficient to prevent social unrest from developing revolutionary potential.

As any genuine expectation of revolution evaporated, however, protest turned ugly. Radical militants – on the right as well as on the left – began to resort to extreme forms of violence, remote from the earlier conflicts between students and police, to try to destroy Italy's political and economic system. The aim, certainly from those on the neo-fascist right, was to create a permanent sense of panic that would lead to clamour for an authoritarian regime to impose order through force – thereby destroying the constitution. Someone dubbed it a 'strategy of tension' (*strategia della tensione*). It was not clear who invented the label. But it stuck.

In April 1969 dozens were injured when two bombs exploded in Milan. Bombs placed on trains in August caused injuries to a further twelve people. And in December, in the worst atrocity, four bombs (two placed in banks, one at Piazza Fontana) killed sixteen people and injured eighty-seven. A crowd estimated at 300,000 people gathered in the centre of Milan out of sympathy for the victims of the outrage, an indication of the revulsion felt by most Italians. Anarchists were swiftly held responsible and a number of them arrested for the incidents. One, Giuseppe Pinelli – subsequently cleared of any involvement in the crime – mysteriously fell to his death from the fourth floor of the Milan police headquarters in circumstances never satisfactorily clarified. Evidence later emerged that implicated with a high degree of probability not the anarchists but a group of neo-fascists who, disturbingly, had connections with a colonel in the Italian secret service. Investigations dragged on for years, amid much foot-dragging by the political establishment and judicial authorities, and the case was ultimately left unproven. Terrorist attacks by radical right-wing groups – in all around 6,000 of them, resulting in 186 killed and 572 injured – continued through the 1970s and into the early 1980s, the worst of them the bombing of Bologna railway station in August 1980 that killed 85 and injured more than 200 people.

Terrorism soon manifested itself on the left as well as on the right. The myriad revolutionary organizations that had emerged from the protest movement of the late 1960s were losing momentum, plainly failing in their hopes of destroying the capitalist state. Recognizing this, the Red

Brigades (*Brigate Rosse*) came into existence – a small but deadly organization that replaced agitation with armed struggle, based on the urban guerrillas of South America. The Red Brigades were founded in 1970 by former student activists Renato Curcio and Margherita Cagol together with Alberto Franceschini, all of whom came from committed anti-fascist and communist families, and Mario Maretti, who had emerged from a middle-class right-wing background and had taken no part in the 1968 student protests. The Brigades were soon carrying out bombings, assassinations and kidnappings. It is estimated that 336 attacks by the end of 1974 – though killing only two people – can be attributed to left-wing terrorist groups. The worst was still to come. In a campaign that punctuated the 1970s, the most notorious outrage perpetrated by the Red Brigades was the kidnapping and, fifty-four days later, murder of the former Christian Democratic Prime Minister Aldo Moro in the spring of 1978. This stung the government into tougher action. Stringent anti-terrorist laws and the creation of a specialized police unit led to the arrest of most of the terrorists by 1980. The Red Brigades continued in existence into the 1980s, though the movement, socially isolated, was in evident decline with by now no more than around a dozen active members.

Student protest in West Germany, unlike that in Italy and France, did not incite any wider unrest or gain support from industrial workers. It did not relate, in any real sense, to class conflict. It was nevertheless more ideological than anywhere else, framed in good measure by the burden of the Nazi past. 'This whole generation was of course anxious and angry about what our parents had backed,' one female activist later recalled. That Konrad Adenauer's government had effectively drawn a line under the Nazi era, and that many deeply implicated in the crimes of Hitler's regime had prospered in West German post-war liberal democracy, encouraged the view, grossly mistaken though it was, that this political system and the capitalist economy upon which it rested were actually the continuation of fascism in a new guise. The existence of big industrial firms and banks that had been mainstays of the Nazi regime and, though newly constituted since the war, had benefited from the rapacious exploitation and slave labour of the Hitler era, was taken to underline this interpretation. The apparently authoritarian tendencies of Adenauer's style of 'Chancellor democracy', the attempted inroads into press freedom in the 'Spiegel affair' of 1961, and the planned legislation for a state of emergency that seemed an eerie reminder of the descent into Nazi dictatorship in the early 1930s, all pointed in the eyes of the New Left to continuities with fascism.

The Eichmann and Auschwitz trials had highlighted the gross inhumanity of the Nazis. For one activist in the student protests this created, along with feelings of horror and shame, 'the loss of a childlike basic trust in the society from which we had come and in which we had grown up'. But a focus on the Holocaust itself – the term was not yet widely used – and the centrality of racial antisemitism to Nazi ideology would have to await a still later generation. For now, National Socialism remained largely understood by student radicals and other followers of what was generally coming to be labelled 'the New Left' as the most extreme manifestation of capitalism. ('National Socialism' was, in fact, an appellation consistently decried by the New Left, since 'socialism' was viewed purely in positive terms and therefore could not be allowed to be brought into association with the evil of the Third Reich. Instead, Nazism was invariably labelled 'Hitler-Fascism', or simply 'Fascism', to indicate that it was merely the German radical manifestation of an international phenomenon inextricably rooted in capitalism.)

Continuities with the Nazi past appeared more than ever confirmed when a former Nazi, Kurt Georg Kiesinger, who had joined the party as early as 1933 and had served during the war in Goebbels's Propaganda Ministry, became Chancellor in December 1966. Kiesinger headed a 'grand coalition' comprising the Christian Democrats, the Free Democrats and the Social Democrats (effectively, therefore, a national government), the product of the more disturbed political conditions that had followed the end of the Adenauer era. He had come to the Chancellorship at a worrying time in Germany, with exaggerated fears flowing from what amounted to a minor recession and slight growth in unemployment. These fears and discontents had led to growing support for a neo-Nazi party, the Nationaldemokratische Partei Deutschlands (NPD, National Democratic Party of Germany). Electoral support was confined to a small minority of the population. Even so, the NPD won nearly 8 per cent of the vote in the Hesse regional election in November 1966 and attained its best result, almost 10 per cent in Baden-Württemberg in April 1968, gaining seats in seven regional parliaments between 1966 and

1968. This lent further sustenance to the belief on the left that Germany might be returning to its dark past.

In the eyes of the New Left there was no possibility of meaningful parliamentary opposition to a government that represented all the major parties in parliament. In any case they saw no differences of substance between parties that could so readily enter into a coalition with one another. This prompted the founding of what was called an Extra-Parliamentary Opposition (Ausserparlamentarische Opposition, APO), led by the Student Federation (which had been excluded from the Social Democratic Party in 1960). The APO won many recruits on account of the government's declared intention to promulgate highly controversial laws that extended the executive powers of the state and limited citizens' rights in a national emergency, for which the necessary two-thirds majority could now be found in parliament. Beyond this, the Federal Republic's close relationship with the United States – prosecuting a terrible war in Vietnam and for the New Left the very face of capitalist imperialism under whose aegis Germany stood as prime candidate for nuclear annihilation in the event of a superpower showdown – served to mobilize student protest.

The visit to West Berlin on 2 June 1967 by the Shah of Iran, Reza Pahlavi, provided the flashpoint. Since a coup instigated by the CIA in order to consolidate American oil interests in the region had installed bolstered his power in 1953, the Shah had presided over a brutally repressive dictatorship. The day of his visit had already seen protest demonstrations and been filled with tension before the Shah arrived at the West Berlin opera house that evening to see a performance of Mozart's *The Magic Flute*. He was greeted by a torrent of abuse, and his entourage had to run the gauntlet of a bombardment of tomatoes thrown by a crowd of a thousand or so demonstrators, activated by the Student Federation. The West Berlin police, encouraged by their superiors to take a tough line with the demonstrators, acted without restraint in the beatings they meted out to the protesters. Then, as the crowd tried to disperse, a shot rang out and a student, Benno Ohnesorg, a bystander not a radical agitator, fell dead. The protesters now had a martyr, killed by a police bullet.

It only transpired many years later that the policeman who fired the shot, Karl-Heinz Kurras, was an informant of the East German state security service, the Stasi. No evidence of any East German order to

Kurras to kill a protester, conceivably in an attempt to destabilize West Germany, has ever come to light (though much of the documentation has meanwhile disappeared or been destroyed). The motive for the shooting remains a mystery. But it was carried out not by a proto-fascist police-man, as was presumed by the student protesters, but by a committed supporter of the East German regime.

The Student Federation had about 2,500 members at most. But some 7,000 students and their teachers attended Ohnesorg's funeral. The pro-test now became an attack on all forms of authority in what was viewed as a quasi-fascist state. A central target of student attacks was the West Berlin headquarters of the newspaper empire of Axel Springer, publisher among other titles of the *Bild-Zeitung*, the widely read daily that had castigated the demonstrators as left-wing stormtroopers, thereby deliber-ately evoking memories of the Nazi takeover of power. The Student Federation, whose leading spokesman was the charismatic sociology stu-dent Rudi Dutschke, demanded the expropriation of the Springer concern and called for 'direct action' in the struggle against the 'terror' and authoritarianism in West Berlin. But the Springer press was not alone in its condemnation of the Marxist left and the escalating radical-ization of the student movement, which was unquestionably intolerant of any critical or oppositional opinion. No less a figure than the eminent philosopher and social theorist Jürgen Habermas, who in many respects sympathized with the students, described the increasing intolerance of the student movement as 'Left Fascism'.

Over the next months Dutschke became something of a media star in West Germany, seldom out of the limelight, and constantly preaching the need for a 'revolutionary will' in a whirlwind of mass meetings. But on 11 April 1968 he was shot in the head and seriously wounded in an attack by a young neo-Nazi. He narrowly survived, but his career as a student leader and agitator was over. The attack prompted a further upsurge in violence, with the West Berlin headquarters of the Springer press, which was believed to have provoked the attack on Dutschke, a particular tar-get. Influenced by Marcuse's ideas, the question of the use of violence to accomplish revolutionary aims had already turned into a central issue of debate. Days before the attempt on Dutschke's life two department stores in Frankfurt am Main, the nerve hub of West German business, were deliberately set on fire as a protest against the 'terror of consumerism'.

Among the arsonists were Andreas Baader and Gudrun Ensslin, later leading lights in the *Rote Armee Fraktion* (Red Army Faction), an organization that specialized in the extreme violence of self-styled 'urban guerrillas'.

In this heated atmosphere West Germany's Federal government, now confident of the necessary majority support that had earlier been lacking, prepared the ground to promulgate the highly controversial emergency legislation. Tens of thousands – far from confined to the 'usual suspects' in the Student Federation – took part in a march on the government capital, Bonn, in mid-May 1968. Unlike the situation in France, however, the trade unions demonstratively distanced themselves from the student protest and held their own rally in Dortmund. It was to no avail. On 30 May more than three-quarters of the members of the Federal Parliament backed the legislation – which included, in the event of a declared state of emergency, limits on the secrecy of postal and telephone communications.

The passing of the emergency legislation turned out to be the turning point. Those on the fringes of the student movement lost interest in an extra-parliamentary opposition that on the crucial issue had proved ineffective. The continued efforts of the hardcore, in what increasingly seemed to many a pointless mission directed towards ultimate revolution for unclear utopian goals, fell ever more on stony ground. Further episodes of violent attacks on the police served only to alienate potential support. And as the Social Democrats, distancing themselves from their conservative Christian Democratic partners in the unpopular grand coalition government, started to make significant gains among students and young academics, the radical Student Federation struggled to retain its following, splitting into various factions, then eventually in March 1970 dissolving itself.

By that time, following the general election of September 1969, the moderate left under the appealing figure of Willy Brandt (who became the new Chancellor) for the first time since 1928 found itself in a position to form a government – now in coalition only with the liberal Free Democrats. An indication even so that the upheavals of the late 1960s had left their mark on West Germany's conservative middle class was the readiness of Brandt's coalition government to bow to pressure from the Christian Democrats and in 1972 to introduce a *'Radikalenerlass'*

('Radicals' Decree'). This made loyalty to the constitution a prerequisite for state employment – a broad category that included postmen and railway workers as well as civil servants and teachers. Hardly more than 2 per cent of potential employees were in practice rejected. It sent a sombre signal, even so, that the state distrusted its citizens. The legislation was abandoned by the Federal government in 1976 (though some, but not all, state governments repealed it only at later stages). By then the heady days of the student movement in West Germany were well and truly over.

But as in Italy, a tiny minority of fundamentalists, who had emerged from the disturbances of 1968 without playing any notable role in the West German student protests, turned to extreme violence and outright terrorism. What called itself the Red Army Faction but was generally better known as the 'Baader-Meinhof Group' (named after its most prominent figures Andreas Baader and Ulrike Meinhof, both of whom, like other prominent members, came from solid middle-class families), saw itself as part of an 'urban guerrilla' movement and formed links to other revolutionary formations across Western Europe and elsewhere, also to anti-Zionist organizations in the Middle East. From 1970 onwards the militants engaged in what they claimed was an 'anti-imperialist struggle' against a West German state that supported the American war in Vietnam. Over the following years they carried out numerous robberies and bombings, aimed ultimately at the overthrow of what they saw as an oppressive capitalist and fascist state.

The episodic but serious violence continued even after the arrest and imprisonment of Baader, Meinhof, and a number of other leaders of the Red Army Faction in 1972. It reached a climax in the 'German autumn' of 1977. On 13 October a Lufthansa airliner was hijacked by the Popular Front for the Liberation of Palestine and flown to Mogadishu in Somalia. The hijackers demanded the release of the imprisoned Red Army Faction leaders. However, the eighty-six hostages were freed when the plane was stormed by German counter-terrorist police troops. Within the Federal Republic itself the kidnapping and eventual murder of the leading industrialist (and former SS man) Hanns-Martin Schleyer the same month followed prior shootings of prominent victims earlier in the year. The leaders of the Baader-Meinhof Group themselves met violent ends. Ulrike Meinhof hanged herself in her cell in Stammheim Prison in Stuttgart in May 1976. And during the night of 18 October 1977, as news of the freeing of the hijack hostages in Mogadishu came through, Andreas Baader was discovered shot dead and Gudrun Ensslin hanged in their cells. Jan-Carl Raspe (another prominent member of the group) died next day of gunshot wounds and a fourth member, Irmgard Möller, survived serious stab wounds. According to official reports – though there were many doubters – there had been a suicide pact.

As in Italy, the terrorist violence deployed by the militant groupuscules in the 1970s had at most only an indirect relation to the student protest movement. It emerged even so as the most extreme expression of the deep sense of alienation felt among wide swathes of the younger generation in Europe towards the social values, the materialist culture and the military power of the Western world. According to opinion surveys, around a quarter of West Germans under the age of forty were said to sympathize with the Baader-Meinhof Group. Most young West Germans, like other members of society, were nevertheless repelled by what they saw as senseless violence incapable of altering the West German state and guaranteed, in fact, only to solidify popular backing for measures to uphold order. Most older Germans probably shared the views of Franz Göll, by this time a pensioner (born in 1899), who had earlier been employed in a number of lower-middle-class jobs. Göll valued personal freedom, as long as it did not disturb or threaten social and political order. He favoured harsh treatment of the terrorists of the Red Army Faction. 'It is as if a virus had infected their brains, blocking normal thought,' he wrote in his diary. The writer Heinrich Böll, with pardonable exaggeration, stated that the campaign of the Red Army Faction was a 'war of six [people] against 60 million'.

Curiously, perhaps, the events of 1968 in France, which more than anywhere else elevated the student revolt of that year to near legendary status in popular memory, left no legacy of terrorist violence equivalent to that in Italy and West Germany. Nor did 'Vichy' play anything like the role that the legacy of fascism did in Italy, let alone that of Nazism in West Germany. Still, it was there in the background. Hostility to a parental generation that had complied, or even sympathized, with the Vichy regime was part of the intellectual ferment stirring the younger generation in France. It was interwoven with the lingering cult of the Resistance, of admiration for those who had actively engaged in the fight to defeat fascism. There was a more direct link to the very recent

Algerian War. As one student activist later explained: 'Our parents had not risen up immediately against fascism . . . We saw fascism arriving in Algeria . . . We fought straight away and those who trained us were the generation of the Resistance.' A further ingredient was the deep antagonism towards what was perceived to be the autocratic presidential regime of Charles de Gaulle. By 1968 the atmosphere was combustible. In May that year student protest came closer than anywhere else – if only for a very short time – to undermining the power of the state.

The 'May events' in France marked the culmination of unrest that had been germinating for some years. The explosion of protest was triggered by the high-handed reaction of university authorities to student unrest about conditions in the recently established extension (for its arts and social science faculties) of Paris Nanterre University, an unappealing campus with hardly any social amenities to the northwest of the French capital. Factory-like buildings, overcrowded lecture theatres, and paternalistic forms of authority out of touch with the changing attitudes of a younger generation contributed to the potential for radicalization of a rapidly growing student population – nearly quadrupling within three years – on the Nanterre campus. Among student demands for reform was the abolition of gender segregation in student accommodation. The threat to expel the leading spokesman for this demand, Daniel Cohn-Bendit, a sociology student of German-Jewish descent who had been strongly influenced by the growing protests of the student movement in West Germany, led to student strikes and a retraction of the expulsion threat. But the problems at Nanterre continued, prompting in March 1968 the occupation by students of the administrative buildings and eventually the temporary closure of the campus in early May. By this time Paris was taking over as the centre of the disturbances.

Just possibly, the disturbances might have been confined to Nanterre but for the fact that the disciplinary hearings against eight students accused of insulting Nanterre professors were held at the Sorbonne. When the centre of the trouble moved to Paris it sparked violent clashes between students and the police, resulting in the temporary closure of the Sorbonne for the first time in its long history on the evening of 3 May 1968 and the arrest of nearly 600 students. The following week, during the night of 10–11 May, students erected barricades in the Latin Quarter of Paris. Hans Koning, an American novelist of Dutch descent who witnessed the events, described 'a wild excitement in the air', an atmosphere of elation, not fear. 'It was astounding to watch the students being unafraid of the police with tear gas and CS gas, concussion grenades, nightsticks, pistols, helmets, visors, shields, grenade rifles and the famous leaded capes . . . The fight was so unequal, the police so brutal that you had to be a very determined Law & Order person to feel sympathy for the authorities . . . When dawn came, the last barricades fell to the police, and the remaining young men, and some young women, were dragged, often clubbed, into the police vans.' Another eyewitness reported a young girl 'rushing out into the street practically naked', being mishandled by the police, 'then beaten like the other wounded students'. Public sympathies sided with the students. The sympathies of workers, particularly younger workers, swiftly translated into direct action. The wanton assault on the protesters was the signal for the trade unions to proclaim a twenty-four-hour nationwide general strike for 13 May out of solidarity. This at once turned the disturbances in France into more than a student revolt.

The clashes with authority highlighted growing anger, frustrations and grievances that had smouldered for some years, not all of them confined to students or the issue of university reform. The disturbances swiftly turned into a wave of protest across France, extending to embrace millions of workers calling for the right to manage themselves.

There had been mounting industrial unrest in 1967 as the economy temporarily slowed and unemployment rose. But the worker action in 1968 was far from any move towards organized revolution. It had a spontaneity that differed from more familiar industrial disputes and was reminiscent in some ways of the elated atmosphere in 1936 at the formation of the Popular Front government. The ultimate goal of the protesters, if they had one, was unclear. And the interests of students and industrial workers were naturally disparate. What temporarily bound them together was the rejection of traditional authority – of employers and managers who dictated rather than consulted, of university administrators keen to keep students in their place and of professors unwilling to yield power in the hallowed halls. The leaders of the French Communist Party, still closely bound to Moscow and anxious to retain their control of the trade-union movement, scorned what they saw as would-be revolutionaries – motley groups of Trotskyites, Maoists and Anarchists who lacked any coherent strategy for challenging, let alone toppling, entrenched state authority.

Yet, for a short time, the Gaullist Fifth Republic did wobble. The upsurge of demonstrations, riots, strikes, and occupation of workplaces briefly threatened the stability of the French state. The political order seemed under threat. De Gaulle himself remained imperiously aloof from the disturbances until nearly the end of the month. Apparently imperturbable, he even left for Romania on 14 May for a four-day state visit. Television showed pictures of him watching folk-dancing while France struggled to avoid chaos. However, he was sufficiently unnerved to disappear – without even informing his Prime Minister of his movements – across the German border for a few hours, on 29 May. He had gone to make sure that he had the support of his armed forces. In Baden-Baden his resolve was stiffened by the reassurance of General Jacques Massu, the head of the French forces in West Germany, that he had the military's backing. Reinvigorated, the President addressed the nation the following day in a defiant radio broadcast. He announced new elections, threatened to take emergency powers if there were to be no quick return to order, and warned that France faced the danger of dictatorship. Soon afterwards an orchestrated demonstration of half a million de Gaulle loyalists marched through the centre of Paris while de Gaulle himself warned in a televised address of the dangers of communism.

These moves did the trick – in the short term. The tide turned. Offered substantial pay increases and other concessions by the Prime Minister, Georges Pompidou, most workers returned to their places of employment (though big strikes recurred the following month and for the last two weeks of June public services were almost paralysed). The police broke up student occupations of university buildings. And urgent university reforms to widen participation in faculty management were introduced, taking the heat out of the immediate issue that had underpinned student protest. The disturbances subsided. The heady atmosphere of rebellion evaporated. Order was gradually restored. The explosive protest that had lasted for most of May was over. A month later the elections provided a massive vote of confidence in de Gaulle.

It proved a pyrrhic victory for the French President. De Gaulle proposed regionalization of government as a step towards decentralization of the state. But the move backfired. Many people interpreted it as an attempt to bolster the position of the President at the expense of parliament. When put to the test in a referendum on 27 April 1969, the proposals were rejected. De Gaulle immediately resigned. The chaos that some had predicted should he be defeated did not, however, materialize. The general's time as 'saviour' of France was over. He was the face of the past, not of the future.

Nowhere else in Western Europe did '1968' produce the level of turmoil experienced in Italy, West Germany and France, though the generational and cultural revolt that lay behind the unrest did find expression elsewhere. Already by the mid-1960s an 'alternative culture' – strongly anti-authoritarian, egalitarian, opposed to existing standards of social morality – had emerged strongly among Amsterdam's younger generation. But there it was non-violent and liberal in tone. It was also attuned to campaigning for practical social improvements – bicycles provided by the city for free public use to combat Amsterdam's traffic problems, for instance, or occupying empty property to deal with homelessness – rather than dogmatically pressing for utopian political transformation. The Vietnam War played no great role in mobilizing students in the Netherlands. Nor was 1968 an especially eventful year. Nevertheless, the pressure to improve conditions in universities – in its most direct expression through the occupation of Amsterdam University buildings in 1969 – probably had more concrete results than in France, West Germany and Italy, where the disturbances had been far greater. The government quickly responded to the pressure and in 1970 a law was passed to democratize Dutch universities and end the archaic hierarchies that had previously dominated them.

Britain, too, experienced little of the enormous unrest within universities that had formed the backcloth to the huge student-led protests of 1968. Although student numbers had rapidly expanded in the 1960s in Britain, as elsewhere, they were still relatively small and far more closely regulated than in continental Europe by a restricted system of entry. The ratio of students to teaching staff was kept remarkably low. Oxford and Cambridge students still enjoyed one-to-one tutorials in colleges that provided a privileged higher education for students who came disproportionately from Britain's elite public schools. Elsewhere, too, however, lectures and seminars were small, and contact between students and their teachers was close and frequent. There were, therefore, few objective grounds for massive discontent such as was experienced on the

continent. Sit-ins, occupation of university buildings and protest demonstrations of one kind or another did take place in some universities
(notably in the London School of Economics and, perhaps more oddly, at
the new University of Essex), though for the most part they amounted to
no more than a minor backwash of what was happening in continental
Europe. Young lecturers often sympathized with the students in their
demands to democratize the way in which faculties were run and to
dilute professorial power, and in this the protest actions attained some
success. Overall, the scale of disturbance within universities was small,
and the energies of the protest soon dissipated.

Where the protest was more marked and significant was in the political arena. Protests about the Vietnam War had taken place in universities
across Britain since 1965. The London School of Economics – distinctly
left-leaning and internationally renowned for the study of political economy, history and sociology – became the magnet for more wide-ranging
student opposition to the Vietnam War and support for liberation movements in what was then called 'the Third World'.

Opposition to the Vietnam War, however, went far beyond a student
core. It united students, religious leaders, labour organizations and –
mostly left-wing – political activists. From 1966 the Vietnam Solidarity
Campaign, with a distinct Trotskyite flavour, campaigned for the victory
of North Vietnam. Big protest demonstrations took place in London in
1968. In March tens of thousands took part in what had been a peaceful
demonstration in central London until several hundred demonstrators
broke away from the protest march and headed into Grosvenor Square,
location of the American Embassy. There they found a phalanx of police,
some on horses, waiting for them. 'It was one of the most exciting
moments of my life,' recalled *The Times* columnist, David Aaronovitch,
then a thirteen-year-old boy. 'But once we were in the square it became
more frightening than exhilarating.' The resulting clash left hundreds of
police and demonstrators injured in the worst violence on the streets of
London for decades. 'The talk among the departing demonstrators was
all of police brutality. People had been whacked over the heads with
truncheons, ridden down by horses and kicked with regulation, iron-
shod police boots. But the next day the papers were full of an image of a
policeman, bent, his face contorted as a desert-booted demonstrator
kicked him in the face.' Subsequent demonstrations, including one of an

estimated quarter of a million in October 1968, avoided a repeat of such serious violence. Protest at the war continued. But 1968 was its high point. And the scale of violence involved was very low in Britain when compared with that in Italy, West Germany and France.

The Lasting Meaning of 1968

What did '1968' in Western Europe amount to, ultimately? The protest movement had been so multifaceted that specific conclusions about its impact are not easy to draw.

Some improvements in the structures of university governance that brought a modicum of democratization were certainly made. Professorial power was to some extent curtailed – perhaps more so in Britain, oddly enough, where student protest had been mild, than in much of continental Europe. Conditions for those studying improved as steps were taken to lessen the overcrowded lecture halls and libraries. Students began to be treated as adults, not least with regard to their sexual behaviour on campus – an issue that had helped spark the disturbances in France. Universities, as part of the general social change that saw the age of majority reduced from twenty-one to eighteen in many European countries in the late 1960s and early 1970s, ceased to assume moral responsibility for students.

But the drama, excitement and memory of '1968' were not in the main evoked by the modest changes within universities. Changing the world – or at least their own societies – was the ambition that had galvanized thousands behind the protests. There had been talk of worker ownership of the means of production, factory democracy, work that made for contentment, not alienation, learning that was fulfilling, not channelled towards the needs of the capitalist economy, and above all peace, not violence.

The achievements fell well short of these lofty goals. The protesters had everywhere to come to the realization that they had underestimated the resilience of the existing state systems. Plenty of contemporaries thought the '68ers had been little more than dreamers, naive romantics whose utopian hopes were merely illusions, bound to come to nothing. Such views were understandable, and not completely unjustified. They were harsh, just the same. The legacy of 1968 was more indirect than direct. It was nevertheless real.

The huge wave of opposition to the Vietnam War in Europe was an important international extension to the more significant protest movement in the United States, which itself contributed to the growing readiness of the American administration to seek a way out of such an unpopular and unwinnable war. In a more directly tangible sense, within Europe itself the industrial unrest that had flowed from the student protests in Italy and France (though not in West Germany) resulted in substantial improvements in working-class pay and working conditions. The power of the trade unions was strengthened as a consequence. Talk of building a 'new society' was overblown. But governments, whatever their colour and with varying degrees of success, attempted to defuse industrial confrontation through corporate forms of negotiation involving management and unions. They tried, too, often again with limited success, to combine economic modernization and technological improvements with social reforms – such as improved pensions and better housing – that would improve the quality of life for the majority of citizens.

The date '1968', immediately acquiring epic status for those who had participated in the demonstrations and strikes, came to symbolize an era of changing cultural values, not just the events of a single year. Although the actual disturbances of 1968 soon faded, their legacy had no definitive end date. The anti-authoritarian, egalitarian and libertarian attitudes of the '68ers had a lasting impact. They fed into the partial democratization that some (though not all) organizations experienced in the following years. The protest movements captured and accentuated generational and emancipatory impulses that pre-dated 1968 and continued long after the drama had subsided. They were instrumental in the moves towards less authoritarian education. They also opened up moves for gender equality. Women still faced widespread discrimination in education, in the workplace, and in most other spheres of social interchange. The feminist movement was as yet in its infancy and women's liberation played only a subsidiary role in the protests of 1968. Nonetheless, the pressure for equal rights for women and racial minorities – drawing on the Civil Rights movement in the United States – and for sexual freedom (including women's rights to have an abortion) and gay rights, even if those rights only bore fruit gradually (and partially), owed more than a little to the impetus provided by '1968'.

The peace movement – the American hippie slogan 'make love not war' had crossed the Atlantic – gained new sustenance from the post-1968 atmosphere and underlay the revitalized anti-nuclear protest of the 1980s. The legacy of 1968 also helped to foster the emerging 'Green Movement' that would become increasingly voluble in defence of the environment in the later twentieth century. Some '68ers even became prominent members of the Greens. Joschka Fischer, a one-time student militant and advocate of communist revolution who had been involved in street battles with the West German police, later became a member of the Federal Parliament for the Green Party and rose to become Foreign Minister, no less. Daniel Cohn-Bendit – 'Danny the Red' – was later a member of the European Parliament and leader of the French Greens.

The '68ers retained vivid – frequently rose-tinted – memories of the heady days when they thought they were overturning the established order. They still felt many years later that they had been involved in a heroic struggle. Many of them nonetheless became conventional 'model' citizens, some – like Joschka Fischer, or Lionel Jospin, a Trotskyite in the 1960s who three decades later became Prime Minister of France – even members of the 'establishment'. Nonetheless, the young protesters and would-be revolutionaries of 1968 took their values with them as they grew older into their daily lives and into often mundane occupations. The attitudes that had shaped the revolt of the young that year had a lasting, indelible effect. Some, it is true, consciously depoliticized their lives and detached themselves from their radical past. Disillusionment with a revolutionary movement that did not produce revolution was not uncommon. But others sought to continue 'the struggle' in one way or another by deploying their reformist zeal in their adopted professions – sometimes as journalists, lawyers, human-rights activists and social workers. Those who became teachers at different educational levels often inculcated the values they had absorbed in 1968 in the new younger generation. These were the 'multipliers' who ensured that the changing values did not die with the protest movement itself.

THE OTHER '68

A spectacular challenge to the existing order – more dramatic, and with greater immediate significance than the events in Rome, West Berlin, Paris and elsewhere – was meanwhile threatening to undermine Soviet power in Central Europe. But the 'Prague Spring' – '1968' in Czechoslovakia – had very little to do with the wave of student protests that year in Western Europe. Its causes, character and consequences were quite different.

Echoes of what was happening in the West were nevertheless heard across the Iron Curtain. Student protest occurred in differing intensity in a number of countries. It entailed considerable courage to protest in the eastern bloc. The prospects of success were non-existent, and protesters had to reckon with severe retaliation by the state. Other than in the unusual circumstances of Czechoslovakia they also faced a high degree of social isolation; their shows of political non-conformity were opposed, or at any rate not backed, by most of the population – unsurprisingly unwilling to risk the venom of the regime and dependent upon the state for employment, educational prospects, housing and other necessities of everyday life. The motives for the protest also differed significantly from those in the West. One Polish activist later succinctly characterized a key difference: 'For us democracy was a dream – but for them it was a prison.' A Czech student leader in 1968 subsequently remarked: 'We wanted just freedom . . . they fought for a different type of society . . . I used to say, "Oh, please, your poverty – look at how it seems compared to our poverty."' And despite his personal magnetism, Rudi Dutschke's visits to activists in East Berlin and Prague did not result in a meeting of minds. 'The love lasted, but the problem with Dutschke was that he only talked nonsense, leftist, stupid 68er nonsense,' a GDR dissident, arrested in 1968 for protesting against the Soviet invasion of Czechoslovakia in August that year, later wrote. A Czech activist encountered similar difficulties: 'Rudi Dutschke (personally, I liked him) was not very successful with his visions of free, non-restrictive communist society, when he visited Prague this spring [1968]. The arguments of French students and their red flags hanging don't excite our students.'

Activists travelled into Eastern Europe surprisingly often in the late 1960s, while the partial liberalization of the communist systems in Czechoslovakia, Hungary and Yugoslavia permitted some movement at least in the opposite direction. Nearly 700,000 citizens, many of them students, travelled from Czechoslovakia to the West during 1968 and early 1969. The Hungarian 'Windows to the West' policy from the mid-1960s provided an exposure to Western popular music and cinema – as long as it was seen to be critical of capitalism. The German Democratic Republic was far more restrictive. After the building of the Berlin Wall the regime at first experimented with a policy of relative tolerance, but decided in 1965 that this had been mistaken and then clamped down heavily on Western cultural influences. Although they were unable to travel to the West, most East Germans could by then, however, receive Western television and radio channels, and many young people – 200,000 of them in 1968 – travelled to Prague, where the more liberal climate provided an opportunity to hear Western pop music or watch Western films. The Stasi reported in March 1968 that some East German youths were regularly receiving Western-style clothes, records and publications 'supplied by contacts in West Berlin' and then circulated among friends.

Some of the group under surveillance were later that year arrested for protesting about the Soviet invasion of Czechoslovakia. This, rather than any substantial echo of the 'May events' in France or the disturbances that had rocked West German and Italian universities, prompted spontaneous outbursts of protest in the GDR. Leaflets were clandestinely circulated and walls daubed with slogans supporting 'freedom for Czechoslovakia', attacking the Soviet Union and criticizing the GDR's leadership. Compared with some other parts of the eastern bloc, however, such protests in the GDR were small in scale. Most of the protesters were young. But relatively few students appear to have been involved. In all, 1,189 East Germans, three-quarters of them under the age of thirty, were punished by the authorities for their support for Czechoslovakia. But the vast majority were young workers; only 8.5 per cent were students or school pupils. Earlier in the year the student protests in West Berlin had left no mark of note on the other side of the Wall. State security was too tight, repression too substantial. But in addition most East German students and intellectuals, either opportunistically – with an eye on career opportunities – or from commitment, were too bound up with the regime to become involved in open dissent. And unlike the far more serious difficulties the regime had faced in 1953 there was this time no sign that the scattered and isolated protest might turn into organized opposition. Most significant of all, there was no split within the party leadership. There was just repression.

In Poland it was a different matter. Polish students and intellectuals, recognizing the climate of protest in Western Europe and the mounting demands in Czechoslovakia for a liberalization of the system, raised their hopes of greater freedom of expression, already voiced by leading writers. Their hopes were peremptorily dashed when, in March 1968, the Soviet ambassador insisted on the closure of a Warsaw theatre that was staging a play, *Dziady* (*Forefathers' Eve*), by Adam Mickiewicz, the pre-eminent national poet, which criticized the conditions in Russia in the early nineteenth century. The clumsy action sparked angry protests that reached a high point on 9 March 1968, when 20,000 students marched through Warsaw shouting 'Down with Censorship' and 'Long Live Czechoslovakia', to be met by brutal police repression. Undeterred, the students demonstrated in front of party headquarters two days later. The police response with water cannon and tear gas led to a street battle that lasted several hours. The protests spread to other Polish universities. In Cracow workers showed their support for the students before being dispersed by police dogs. But, crucially, the students failed to gain widespread support of the workers while public opinion, fed by the regime's press organs, was hostile. Repression did the rest. Parts of Warsaw University were closed by the police; a number of courses were terminated; and students made up a quarter of the 2,700 persons arrested (their teachers a further 10 per cent). Hundreds of students were conscripted into the army. A prominent figure among the academics who were dismissed from their posts was the already distinguished (later to become world-renowned) philosopher and critical analyst of Soviet orthodox communist theory, Leszek Kołakowski.

By early April the upheaval had subsided. One side-effect of the unrest had been the regime's unleashing of anti-Zionist rhetoric – claiming that 'Zionists' had stirred up protest among politically naive students. The result was the effectively forced emigration, under the pressure of the anti-Zionist campaign, of around 13,000 Jews (including hundreds of intellectuals) – most of those who had still remained in post-war Poland. The regime was assisted in its suppression of the serious Polish disturbances in 1968 by the events in neighbouring Czechoslovakia. The crushing of the Prague Spring through Soviet armed intervention concentrated minds in Poland. Władysław Gomułka was able – for now – to reassert his authority. But Poland's problems had not gone away.

Demonstrations had already taken place in Czechoslovakia in autumn 1967, sparked by the poor living conditions in Prague's student halls of residence and provoking heavy police retaliation. There, however, the protests blended into a growing pressure from wider sections of the population for more democracy and liberalization of the system. Generational revolt that played such a notable part in Western Europe was far less important in Czechoslovakia. Protest there attracted support across the social and age spectrum, largely prompted by widespread economic discontent. The Communist Party's own report, in April 1968, was a damning indictment of its own dismal record. It condemned the 'catastrophic state of housing', the stagnation of living standards, transport deficiencies, and the poor quality of goods and services. The planned economy was failing miserably to provide even basic necessities – and this in one of the most advanced industrial economies in the eastern bloc.

Most importantly, the pressure for radical reform was led not from the outside, but from within the ruling Communist Party, in fact from close to its centre. For Alexander Dubček, who became the face of the demands for change, reform was a necessity. Not just, or even mainly (at least at first), from idealistic conviction; he increasingly saw reform as the only way to ensure that the party retained its control. Western protesters (at least their most radical spokespersons) wanted to overthrow capitalist society and replace it with some utopian form of communism. Eastern European protesters, who lived under 'real existing socialism' (as their brand of communism was usually described), did not for the most part want to replace it, but to reform it. Few preferred Western capitalism; their aim was to make communism more democratic and liberal. The Prague Spring put an end to such illusions once and for all. Its ultimate lesson was that liberal freedoms and democracy were incompatible with the existence of the communist state. Where they threatened the power of the ruling Communist Party and endangered as a consequence the unity of the Soviet bloc, attempts to spread them would be crushed by armed force.

What turned into the Prague Spring had its background five years earlier, in 1963, in pressure for greater autonomy for Slovakia, which had been systematically reduced under the centralizing constitutional changes of 1960. The Slovak Communist Party was in practice subordinated to the Czech Party, which was controlled by the veteran Stalinist, Antonín Novotný, its First Secretary and, since 1957, President of Czechoslovakia. In the wake of Nikita Khrushchev's de-Stalinization measures in the

Soviet Union, Novotný felt compelled to make corresponding moves in Czechoslovakia. Symbols of the changing climate were the removal (and subsequent cremation) of the embalmed body of the former leader Klement Gottwald and the destruction of the immense statue of Stalin that towered over Prague. In early 1963 Novotný also felt obliged to establish a commission of inquiry into the show trials of Rudolf Slánský and others that had been carried out in the 1950s. The commission's report rehabilitated those convicted and exonerated them of charges of treason, though it did not restore full party membership to the Slovak victims of the purges who had been condemned as 'bourgeois nationalists'. The findings of the commission, however, posed an implicit threat to Novotný. For Alexander Dubček, a member of the commission, knew that Novotný himself had in fact supported the show-trials.

As First Secretary of the Slovak Communist Party from May 1963, Dubček – trained in Moscow and a party loyalist for fourteen years – appears to have put this knowledge to advantage to enable him to introduce greater freedom of expression and to reduce press censorship in Slovakia. He used the changes to air Slovak grievances against Prague and to demand a new commission with the aim of rehabilitating the Slovak victims of the purges entirely. Czech writers and journalists took note of the loosening of controls in Slovakia, and Novotný, under pressure because of a significantly worsening economic situation, reluctantly conceded some limited freedom of cultural expression for Czechs too. Dubček, continuing to champion Slovak grievances and even tacitly condoning the national feeling that the discontent aroused, maintained the pressure on Novotný by implying the need for reform throughout Czechoslovakia, not just in Slovakia. The further implication was that he, Dubček, was the man to lead it. By 1967 the gulf within the top echelon of party functionaries between the reformers and those opposing change was becoming unbridgeable. It was at this juncture, in October 1967, that the student demonstrations in Prague about the poor conditions in their halls of residence occurred.

Criticism of the force used by the police against the students stretched deep into the party membership, further weakening Novotný and the reactionary old guard while advertising the need for a new broom to sweep clean. The factional split within the party leadership crystallized in the mounting power struggle between Dubček and Novotný. Once the

Soviet leader, Leonid Brezhnev, withdrew his support, Novotný's fate was sealed. In January 1968 Dubček replaced him as First Secretary of the Party. Two months later Novotný also resigned as President and was succeeded, on Dubček's nomination, by Ludvik Svoboda, widely popular as a war hero and a victim himself of the 1950s purges. By this time the Prague Spring was turning into full bloom. Censorship scarcely existed, and attacks on leading figures in the party multiplied in the press – to the growing consternation of communist leaders in Moscow and in the Soviet satellite states.

The 'Action Programme', aimed at 'Socialism with a Human Face', that the Presidium of the Party approved on 5 April 1968, provided a searing condemnation of the failings of the Novotný years. From now on, it stated, the Communist Party would guarantee 'rights, freedoms and interests' and would be prepared to amend directives and resolutions to meet popular demands. Plainly, such a level of democratization was incompatible with orthodox communist belief in the 'dictatorship of the proletariat'. With the installation of a new government the following day, led by Oldřch Černík, Dubček and his fellow reformers occupied all the key positions in party and state.

The atmosphere was exhilarating. 'Suddenly you could breathe freely, people could associate freely, fear vanished,' recalled the playright Václav Havel, who two decades later would become President of Czecho-slovakia. At the May Day parade in Prague's Wenceslas Square that year flowers were thrown at the rostrum where Dubček watched in delight, cupping his hands to shout out greetings to well-wishers in the proces-sion. 'This is the spring of our new existence,' reported the party newspaper, *Rudé právo*, next day.

However, Dubček – an indecisive, uncertain individual, and unsure about the real levels of popular support for socialism – was no longer able to control the pressure for radical reform that he had been largely instrumental in unleashing. He was himself carried along on the wave of the zeal for change that had spread outwards from the party to much of the population. His own popularity posed a quandary. He had to sus-tain the momentum of reform. At the same time he had to prevent it from being seen to endanger the interests of the Soviet Union and its close allies. Weakening communist rule in one country could easily have a domino effect.

The fear that this might happen posed a grave danger to the Czech reformists. For the leaders of the Soviet Union and of the German Democratic Republic, Bulgaria, Hungary and Poland – members of the Warsaw Pact – were meanwhile becoming increasingly anxious about developments in Czechoslovakia. In mid-July they published what amounted to a warning to Prague to put an end to what it portrayed as a 'counter-revolution' against the socialist system that imperilled 'the socialist commonwealth'. In early August Brezhnev's demands to reinstate censorship, dismiss some leading reformers, and generally put the Czechoslovak party's house in order again brought some half-hearted measures to restore 'democratic centralism'. But Dubček's turn for support to Yugoslavia and Romania, the two communist countries whose own independent stance had meant an uneasy relationship with Moscow, was not guaranteed to calm nerves among the Warsaw Pact countries. On 17 August the Soviet Politburo took the critical step: it decided to intervene militarily in the domestic affairs of another socialist state in the name of 'international proletarian solidarity'. During the night of 20–21 August 1968 up to half a million Warsaw Pact troops from five countries backed by 7,500 Soviet tanks and a thousand planes began their invasion of Czechoslovakia.

On the orders of the Czech government, there was no armed resistance. But television and radio – until the stations were brought into line – carried vivid reports of the opposition to the invaders and the mass support for Dubček, soon shown in huge crowds that began to gather in Prague and Bratislava in protest at the invasion. Dubček, Černík and four other party leaders were taken into custody and flown to Moscow (where Dubček seems to have suffered a nervous collapse). Alongside President Svoboda and a number of leading figures in the party who had joined them in Moscow, they were subjected to intense pressure to denounce the liberalization programme. On 26 August they caved in and signed their agreement to accept a Soviet ultimatum, reversing the Prague Spring reforms in return for the withdrawal of the occupying forces (almost all of which left by the end of October). 'Fraternal relations' were restored – under duress. The agreement was framed under a new, ominous premise, later known as the 'Brezhnev Doctrine'. This laid down a 'common international obligation' to defend socialist countries against 'counter-revolutionary forces'. From now on, then, Warsaw Pact states had an explicit duty to intervene where any member was adjudged to be stepping out of line.

The process of 'normalization' took several months. But it was a one-way street. The Czechoslovak delegation at the 'negotiations' in Moscow returned to Prague during the night of 26–27 August. Public dismay at what was widely viewed as a capitulation in Moscow was assuaged by a moving broadcast appeal by a sobbing Dubček – like the other Prague Spring reformers still immensely popular – for the realistic acceptance of inescapable 'temporary, exceptional measures'. Inexorably, however, the pressure for 'normalization' intensified. The leaders of the Prague Spring were all gradually ousted from their positions. The process was hastened by signs of continued mass discontent. When Jan Palach, a Prague student, set fire to himself in protest at the reversal of liberalization, his funeral on 25 January 1969, organized by students, was attended by an estimated 100,000 people with a further 200,000 watching from the pavements. And huge anti-Soviet demonstrations followed the victory by the Czechoslovakian ice-hockey team over the USSR in world-championship matches in March. The disturbances swiftly led to Soviet intervention to ensure the removal from office of Dubček (replaced as First Secretary of the Czech Communist Party by another, more compliant Slovak, Gustáv Husák). He was expelled from the party in 1970 and dispatched into obscurity as a minor forestry official in Slovakia. Others associated with the Prague Spring were gradually replaced. Three sweeping purges of the party membership were undertaken between September 1969 and June 1970. Thousands of trade union officials, teachers, academics, journalists and others who worked in the mass media and cultural sphere were dismissed.

By the end of the process Czechoslovakia had been 'normalized'. 'The Russians have finally achieved what they call normalization: a nasty and brutish police state', was the bitter verdict of a disaffected Czech surgeon, Dr Paul Zalud, writing during an authorized visit to West Germany in 1969 to a British communist, Leslie Parker. Order had been restored. The advances of the Prague Spring had been reversed. Censorship, travel restrictions and unassailable rule by the Communist Party had been reimposed. The population was reduced to sullen compliance. Political nonconformity declined. A tiny number of writers and other intellectuals continued in a variety of ways to register their protest. Such 'dissidents' (as they came to be called) were, however, in the immediate aftermath of the Prague Spring little more than an irritant to the regime.

In the eyes of the West the crushing of the Prague Spring marked a further heavy blow, after Hungary in 1956, to the prestige of the Soviet Union and the 'socialist' system of rule, which once more, as was only too clear, could be sustained only by armed force. For many communist supporters in Western Europe the Soviet Union had abdicated all moral authority through its action in Czechoslovakia. None of this mattered much to the Soviet leadership. It was a small price for keeping the alliance of socialist countries intact. Soviet power had prevailed.

SHIFTING SANDS IN EASTERN EUROPE

With the threat from the liberalizing tendencies in Czechoslovakia eliminated, fundamental alteration to the structures of rule in the political systems of the Warsaw Pact states was ruled out. For the population of those countries it meant general dull public conformity, acquiescence in the confines of political orthodoxy and limited 'niche' spheres of private life beyond the prying eyes of the surveillance state and its armies of informants.

There was nonetheless movement in the communist state systems. Nowhere was a retreat to full-blown Stalinism possible. Significant differences within the Soviet bloc continued to exist. The pressures for liberalizing change were generally higher in those countries with some exposure to Western cultural influences, a sizeable intelligentsia, and an industrialized economy with an organized working class (even in the absence of free trade unions). The suppression of the Prague Spring sent a plain message that any liberalization had to be kept closely in check. But as long as there was no threat to the integrity of the Soviet bloc (as there had been in Czechoslovakia), the Kremlin was prepared to grant some latitude. The evident problems of the command economy in several eastern bloc countries, in some cases necessitating sizeable Soviet subsidies, meant Moscow was open to attempts within the system to modernize production. Especially in the more industrialized economies the Stalinist command system – which of course had originally been introduced in an overwhelmingly agrarian Soviet Union – was singularly ill equipped to satisfy basic consumer needs let alone compete with the rapid economic advances in the capitalist West. So a sort of uneasy balance had to be struck – in somewhat different ways, and with varying degrees of success – between a regimented political system under the control of a monopoly party and the innovation and competition needed to liberate economic, social and intellectual resources.

In the Soviet Union itself strong economic growth in the late 1960s meant there was no recurrence of the industrial unrest and extensive discontent of Khrushchev's last years in power. The grip of the regime was tightened and, in the wake of the Prague Spring, ideological orthodoxy reinforced. When a small group protested in Red Square after the invasion of Czechoslovakia, its members were swiftly arrested, and subsequently sentenced to three years in prison camps. Dissidence continued, and sullied the name of the Soviet Union still further in the West. But it could not remotely shake the firm hold of the regime over its own citizens.

Bulgaria was the closest of any of the satellites to the Soviet Union, and in any case its high economic dependency made it unlikely to deviate much from Moscow's line. The coercive force of the police state, a still predominantly rural population and a small intelligentsia all militated against the pressures for liberalization that had arisen in Czechoslovakia. There was much rhetoric about economic reform; but little in practice materialized. Towards the end of the 1960s there was even some retreat to rigid neo-Stalinist orthodoxy from the limited economic reforms and cultural thaw that had been introduced in the earlier part of the decade.

Hungary went in the opposite direction. Janos Kádár's 'goulash communism' permitted a level of limited exposure to market forces that gave the population the highest standard of living in the Soviet bloc. The 'New Economic Mechanism' introduced on 1 January 1968 was a genuine innovation in the economies of Soviet satellites. Central state planning was reduced essentially to long-term investment projects, fiscal policy and regulation of prices for basic essential products. Beyond this, firms could make profits and operate commercially. Foreign trade with the West increased, agricultural production was stimulated, and the shortages of basic commodities that were endemic in other parts of the Soviet bloc disappeared. Kádár also showed himself to be enlightened enough – or at any rate sufficiently ready to learn lessons from 1956 – to allow some freedom of expression and even openness to Western pop music, without loosening the reins to an extent that was likely to cause tension with Moscow. In consequence, Hungary, which in 1956 had been the most rebellious, turned into the most contented country among the Soviet satellites, with little political dissidence.

Poland, on the other hand, under the leadership of Władysław Gomułka, had become a classic case of a system that, from seeming to embrace reform in 1956, had hardened into unbending orthodoxy, alienating much of the population in the process. Gomułka's regime had kept tight controls on dissent, had ruthlessly quashed student protest, and had avidly backed the invasion of Czechoslovakia. It presided, however, over a sharply deteriorating economy. The regime's crass response was to announce in the very run-up to Christmas, with effect from 13 December 1970, an immediate increase in the price of food ranging from 12 and 30 per cent. This tipped the already welling discontent into a torrent of angry protest. Huge demonstrations, starting in the Baltic shipyards in Gdańsk, Szeczecin and Gdynia, but swiftly spreading to Warsaw and other cities, took place the following week. When a train carrying workers to the Gdańsk shipyard was attacked by armed state militia, all hell broke loose. Workers marched on party headquarters. Shops were looted. A training centre for the militia in Słupsk, near the Baltic coast, was burnt down. Militia men were physically attacked by mobs and some killed. There were big clashes with police. Tanks crushed some demonstrators. The death toll numbered 45, almost 1,200 were injured, and 300 arrested. When police opened fire on striking workers in Gdańsk, Gomułka had gone too far. He was forced to resign a week after the explosion of unrest.

His replacement, Edward Gierek, a former miner with a good sense of worker needs, immediately announced improvements in pay and conditions, then, amid continued strikes and backed by a loan from the Soviet Union, a freeze on prices at their earlier levels for twelve months. He visited the shipyards, addressing the workers directly and bluntly, admitting failings in the party. He abolished the forced deliveries to the state, detested by farmers, and increased payments for food purchases. Non-state employees were now admitted to free medical care. Censorship and restrictions on foreign travel were somewhat relaxed. Morale improved.

The first period of Gierek's leadership went down as the 'belle époque' of the communist years in Poland. Earnings rose by 11 per cent in 1971. A huge housing programme made a million more apartments available – not enough, but a big improvement on Gomułka's time. Practically everyone experienced better living standards as economic modernization was directed, in contrast to earlier years, towards consumer needs. But the economic problems had not gone away. To bring about the necessary stimulation of the economy and to repay the loan from the Soviet Union, Gierek borrowed from the West to the tune of $6 billion. This bought off the immediate problems. But he was simply storing up trouble for the future. The oil crisis hit Poland hard after 1973 and further Soviet assistance was needed to cope with it. By the late 1970s serious problems were once again mounting.

The German Democratic Republic was a special case among the countries of the Soviet bloc. The Berlin Wall, the GDR's sense of being an ideological showcase for 'real existing socialism' in competition with its capitalist neighbour, and a particularly pronounced anti-fascism provided East German society with a distinctive flavour. The building of the Wall in 1961 had given the regime new confidence and strengthened its power. A wave of arrests had followed as the ideological struggle against 'the enemy within' was enhanced. Intimidation, repression and pressure to conform were now a part of life in the GDR. However, as its leaders recognized, the system could not function on repression alone – especially if it was to attain its stated goal of overtaking West Germany economically by 1980.

The New Economic System, introduced in 1963, was an attempt to overcome the deteriorating state of the economy, which had led to shortages and indications of discontent reminiscent of those a decade earlier. Alongside levels of decentralized management and incentives to increase output – though still within the framework of a centrally imposed economic plan – went an increased propaganda effort to mobilize the active support of the population. New emphasis was placed upon technology, knowledge and rational organization, underpinned by a drive to produce a highly educated population. In 1951 a mere 16 per cent of pupils had spent more than eight years at school; by 1970 this had climbed to no fewer than 85 per cent, while entry to higher education was widened, and a number of new universities and polytechnics were built. Productivity rose by 7 per cent, national income by 5 per cent in 1964–5. The standard of living began to rise appreciably – though not as fast as was hoped, and lagged far behind that of West Germany. Still, televisions, washing machines and fridges were no longer possessions only of a small minority of the population. The signs of improvement were accompanied by a degree of cultural relaxation. Statues of Stalin disappeared; 16,000 political prisoners were amnestied.

Party leaders were, however, far from happy at yielding some of their control over the economy, which in any case was still hampered by innumerable constraints and unable to overcome an intrinsic lack of competitiveness. And once Khrushchev's reforming zeal had given way to Brezhnev's emphasis on stability, the trend towards modest liberalization ceased. More stringent controls over the cultural sphere were introduced in December 1965 and the New Economic System was revised the same month. There was a renewed emphasis on centralized planning, with disproportionate financing directed towards electronics, the chemical industry and engineering. With increased resources also provided to expand the army and security service (the Stasi), consumer industries were again neglected.

The Prague Spring offered confirmation to the GDR leadership that they had been right to quell the liberalizing cultural tendencies that could only have led to political destabilization. But the inherent problems of an economy directed by a single party with complete power over the running of the state were laid bare. Shortages and blockages in the supply of basic provisions, let alone consumer goods that were taken for granted in West Germany and shown nightly on television, once more began to cause unrest. Party bosses were increasingly uneasy about Walter Ulbricht's leadership, and the neglect of urgently needed consumer products in favour of technological projects that would only bear fruit in the distant future. In addition, Ulbricht's hopes of closer economic co-operation with West Germany ran completely counter to Moscow's wishes. Ulbricht's personal arrogance did the rest. In late 1970 a majority of the party leadership voted for a change of economic course. Soon afterwards they asked Brezhnev to replace Ulbricht as leader. Brezhnev complied, and on 3 May 1971 Ulbricht resigned. His successor, Erich Honecker, was a long-serving high functionary whose impeccable anti-fascist credentials derived from his involvement in the communist resistance movement under Hitler's regime and ten years of incarceration in Nazi prisons. He now oversaw a restructuring of the economy, with greater prominence given to consumer production. He never, however, veered from lap-dog allegiance to Moscow.

Communist rule was meanwhile developing in a different fashion in the Balkan countries. Albania, throwing in its lot with China after the Sino-Soviet split, continued its ideologically self-determined path into political isolation and dire economic poverty – the worst in Eastern Europe. Depriving itself of Soviet aid, Albania was unable to make good what it had lost through trade agreements with China. Its own version of the 'cultural revolution' that China was enduring in the mid-1960s brought attacks on intellectuals, teachers and religious belief. The split with the Soviet Union was completed when Albania left the Warsaw Pact after the invasion of Czechoslovakia – though in truth it had long been no more than a nominal member. Cutting itself adrift from Moscow, but simply too far from China to develop close links with Beijing, Albania's fossilized system remained an oddity, stuck in a cul-de-sac of its own making.

Romania, a member of the Warsaw Pact, was also increasingly going its own way, though taking care not to push relations with Moscow to breaking point. Albania's choice of China over the Soviet Union indirectly benefited Romania. The Kremlin was aware that it could not further diminish its influence in the Balkans by adding Romania to the loss of Albania and the independence of Yugoslavia. So Romania was permitted its semi-detachment. Nicolae Ceauşescu, who had succeeded the brutal Stalinist Gheorge Gheorgiu-Dej in 1965 as head of the Communist Party (and in 1974 also became President of Romania), gained plaudits in the West by opposing the invasion of Czechoslovakia and by building a form of Romanian 'national communism' – a brand of nationalism within a communist framework – that insisted upon not dancing to Moscow's tune. He was able to exploit the widening split between China and the Soviet Union to establish, against the Soviet line, foreign relations with West Germany and Israel. He cultivated Romanian national pride. And economic growth, providing sufficient supplies of foodstuffs and other necessities, sustained his early popularity. At first there was a degree of cultural loosening, too, which allowed some access to Western media (though this altered after he visited China, North Korea,

Mongolia and North Vietnam in 1971, returning to introduce his own form of cultural revolution, with new stringent ideological controls on what was permissible expression). The Romanian deviation from Soviet orthodoxy was set to continue.

Yugoslavia's brand of communism, resting on decentralization and industrial management at the base, seemed to many Western admirers to offer an attractive alternative to the stultifying Soviet system. The population benefited substantially from greater exposure to the West than any other country in Eastern Europe. The Dalmatian coast was promoted as a tourist venue in the 1960s, swelling the state coffers by millions of dollars – hard currency that helped to provide necessary imports and ensure a relatively good standard of living. Half a million Yugoslavs were meanwhile finding employment as 'guest workers' in West Germany and subsidizing the economy by the money they sent home to their families. Frequent contact with the West opened the country to its cultural influences. Yugoslavia was the most liberal of the communist countries of Eastern Europe. However, by the late 1960s the economic failings of the state were plain to see. Productivity was falling far behind the rise in average income, inflation was increasing, national debt was becoming a serious problem, inequalities were growing, and unemployment was rising sharply. This was the background to the emergence of centrifugal tendencies in the Yugoslavian state.

Croatia was the most prosperous part of Yugoslavia. But Croatians were resentful that much of the income gained from foreign tourism was distributed to less well-developed regions of the country. Croatian agitation for greater autonomy started to grow and feed into the beginnings of revitalized nationalism. An early expression was the demand, backed by 130 intellectuals in 1967, that Croatian (and not what they saw as the state-imposed language of Serbo-Croat) be used in schools. Conversely, Serbians thought economic prosperity had disproportionately benefited Croatia, and in the eyes of powerful factions liberalization – most advanced in Croatia and Slovenia – had gone too far. For students, however, it had not gone far enough. At the beginning of June 1968, prompted by events in France, the first mass demonstrations since the war took place when students in Belgrade protested about overcrowded universities, the privileges of the party oligarchy, increased consumerism, and economic conditions that forced many of them to leave the country to find employment. Marshal Tito, anxious to contain the unrest, promised to accommodate student demands. Apprehension about possible Soviet intervention following the invasion of Czechoslovakia – which provoked strong protest from the Yugoslavian government – worked in favour of the authorities and the unrest died down. It flared up again in 1971, this time in Zagreb, and posed a greater threat to the integrity of the Yugoslavian state.

What became known as the 'Zagreb Spring' built upon growing nationalist demands for greater autonomy for Croatia. Croatian party bosses, figures in the media and student representatives spoke in favour of independence. They saw national identity under threat – diluted by the loss of the large numbers of Croats who had left in search of work abroad and by the influx of Serbs and others. The Croatian party leader Savka Dabčević-Kučar expressed in 1970 her concern 'that Croatia has become more the home of Serbs and other nationalities than of Croats themselves', while Franjo Tudjman – later to become President of an independent Croatia – claimed 'the existence of the Croatian people' was under threat from assimilation. There was a widespread feeling that Croats were under-represented in the bureaucracy, the police and the officer corps of the army, and that Croatia was being bled dry economically by other parts of Yugoslavia and turned into little more than a colonial dependency of Serbia.

In July 1971 Tito, himself a Croat, summoned the leaders of Croatia to Belgrade, where he berated them for permitting the resurgence of nationalism. He warned obliquely of the danger of internal disorder that might provoke Soviet intervention. Nationalist feeling remained unabated, however, and found expression in the student occupation of Zagreb university buildings in November and calls for a general strike as thousands marched in huge demonstrations under the slogan: 'Long live the independent state of Croatia'. This time Tito acted by purging the party leadership in both Zagreb and Belgrade, expelling hundreds from the party, and having nearly 200 people arrested. Any suspected of nationalist tendencies were also removed in Slovenia, Macedonia, Montenegro and Bosnia-Herzegovina. The purges extended to those who favoured greater liberalization, while a new law in 1972 imposed greater restrictions on press freedom.

The repressive measures succeeded in calming the situation. Tito was aware, however, that repression was not enough. A new constitution of 1974 sought to accommodate reformist demands by establishing a better-balanced confederation, decentralizing power, and devolving a greater degree of relative independence to the various republics. In practice, however, the new constitution promoted, rather than undermined, nationalist and separatist tendencies, enhancing ethnic distinctions. Tito's immense authority – that of the war hero, national saviour and subsequent embodiment of unity – was the single most important entity in keeping the increasingly ramshackle foundations of the Yugoslavian state together. But Tito was eighty years old in 1972. What would be the future of Yugoslavia after his death?

THE FORWARD MARCH OF SOCIAL DEMOCRACY IN WESTERN EUROPE

By the early 1970s in Europe, east as well as west, the troubles of the previous few years were for the most part fading. The Soviet bloc had been 'normalized' again after the upheavals of the Prague Spring. Dissidence existed, but was easily contained. 'Real existing socialism' in the communist countries seemed destined to last indefinitely. In Western Europe, beyond the southern belt (see Chapter 7) where democracy existed only at the behest of the military (Turkey) or did not exist at all (Greece after 1967, Portugal and Spain), systems of government remained intact and were generally resilient. Politics, it is true, were starting to become more volatile. Political violence was more overt than at any time since the Second World War. Not just the Red Brigades in Italy and the Baader-Meinhof Group in West Germany, but nationalists in Northern Ireland and separatists in the Basque Country were using terror as an intrinsic part of their campaigns. But nowhere was there a radical, let alone revolutionary, momentum. The underlying consensus that had developed in the post-war years, on the central role of the state to provide for the welfare of the population and to ensure constantly rising living standards, still held in its essentials.

In fact, Social Democrats, the most staunch champions of the 'big state', under which high government expenditure (and taxation levels) paid for social welfare and improved living conditions for the poorer sections of society, generally gained ground in the 1960s and early 1970s. Sometimes this occurred alongside other left-wing parties, and it was usually at the expense of conservative and Church-aligned parties.

In Britain the Labour Party (representing the British variant of social democracy) had narrowly won the 1964 election and the Labour government under Harold Wilson greatly increased its ruling majority in 1966. Worsening economic problems and industrial conflict provided the backdrop, however, for a surprising Conservative victory under Edward Heath at the 1970 general election and still greater difficulties to come (see Chapter 7).

Conservatism, as already noted, had been losing ground in West Germany to rising expectations of reform since the end of the long Adenauer era in 1963. The Christian Democrats found themselves after the 1969 general election out of office for the first time since the foundation of the Federal Republic with the formation of a new coalition led by the Social Democrats under Willy Brandt, one of the towering figures of the postwar era. Brandt, a politician with great personal appeal, had impeccable socialist credentials. Born in illegitimacy as Herbert Frahm, he had fled to Scandinavia at the beginning of the Nazi era, from where he had been involved (changing his name in the process) in working-class resistance to Hitler's regime. So the shift from a government headed by a former Nazi, Kurt Georg Kiesinger, appeared to symbolize the onset of a new era. Coming on the heels of the student demonstrations and the troubled political scene in 1968, the Brandt coalition seemed like a breath of fresh air in a stale room. The atmosphere changed. There was new expectancy and hope, most of all among the young.

Neighbouring Austria also moved in the later 1960s towards reforming social democracy. There was little in the result of the 1966 election, when for the first time in the post-war history of the country the conservative Austrian People's Party won an absolute majority, to hint at what was to come. Splits within the Socialist Party, and the fears that it might be prepared to work with the small Communist Party, had been part of the background to the conservative victory. But after the leadership of the Socialists had passed in 1967 to the formidable Bruno Kreisky, who put forward a far-reaching programme of social and economic reforms, the Socialist Party started to gain ground. It became the largest party in the elections of 1970, allowing Kreisky to form a minority government.

New elections the following year saw Kreisky's party win an absolute majority and form a stable Social Democratic government that dominated Austrian politics for the following decade..

In the Netherlands a main change in the 1960s was the gradual eclipse of the 'pillarization' (vertical, mainly denominational sub-cultures and their political representation) that had traditionally shaped the Dutch form of liberal democracy. In the wake of increasing secularization, support for the Catholic People's Party dwindled, while promises of social reforms helped the Labour Party gain ground. It emerged from the 1972 elections as the largest party and the following year its leader, Joop den Uyl, became Prime Minister at the head of a coalition government. Belgian social democracy faced greater problems because of the deepening linguistic and cultural division between Flanders and Wallonia, which led to corresponding splits in the major parties. In the bewildering myriad of parties that formed Belgian governments, the Socialist Party and the conservative Christian People's Party were easily the largest, though backed in each case by little more than a quarter of the popular vote. Still, the widespread anti-conservative direction of politics was present here, too, marked by the emergence after 1968 of 'green' ecological parties.

Social democracy had been the basis of political stability and welfare reform in Scandinavia since the Second World War. It continued to enjoy the support of around 40 per cent of voters in Sweden, Denmark and Norway, though the Norwegian Labour Party's long domination suffered erosion during the 1960s not from the right, but from growing support for the Socialist People's Party on the left. Finland's politics were, as ever, complicated by the need to remain on reasonable terms with the Soviet Union next door. Governments were invariably coalitions involving numerous parties. The Social Democrats (with slightly over a quarter of the vote) formed the largest party, followed not far behind by a more radical party of the left, the Finnish People's Democratic League (dominated by Finnish communists). Together they garnered over 40 per cent of the popular vote, though the extinction of the Prague Spring in August 1968 harmed the Democratic League. It split those who continued to support the Soviet Union from those who denounced its actions and moved towards forms of communist thinking and organization seen as more relevant to Western Europe, which were gaining support especially in Italy, France and Spain and coming to be called 'Eurocommunism'.

Even where conservatism continued to dominate government, as it did in Italy and France, it had to take account of the demands of the left – though often more in rhetoric than substance.

In the morass of Italian politics there was a significant gap between the far-reaching reforms promised and those actually implemented. Some changes at the end of the 1960s in employment law, improvements to the health system, and the widening of pensions provision were steps towards a more encompassing welfare state. But much more never left the drawing board. For many on the left, for neo-Marxist intellectuals, and for the rapidly growing numbers of students, what was achieved was far from enough.

The Socialists had been incorporated in an 'opening to the left' in 1963 in Aldo Moro's government – led as always by the largest party, the Christian Democrats, though their proportion of the vote had slipped beneath 40 per cent for the first time in the election that year. The Socialist Party split over involvement in a conservative-led government, then reunited in 1966. But the real beneficiaries of the 'opening to the left' were the Communists, critical of Moscow – especially after Czechoslovakia – and, profiting from their exclusion from government, turning into a reformist, not revolutionary, party. After declining in the early 1960s, the Communist Party's membership and voter support started to increase significantly. Its proportion of the popular vote rose from 25 per cent in 1963 (compared with only 14 per cent for the Socialist Party) to 34.4 per cent by 1976, not far behind the Christian Democrats and easily outstripping the Socialists as the main party of opposition.

In France the departure from politics of the national hero Charles de Gaulle in 1969 – he died the following year – produced neither chaos nor a void, but continued conservative domination under his successor Georges Pompidou. Gaullism without de Gaulle brought no seismic changes. But Pompidou, having won a massive victory in the 1969 presidential election, was, initially at least, more reformist in his short term of office – he died, prematurely, in April 1974 – than most people had expected. The events of May 1968 had been a shock to France, and especially to French conservatism. When the turmoil died down it had left behind an urge for social change. Demands for greater rights for women – politically, and also over their own bodies – were one lasting outcome. But promises of a 'New Society' were soon exposed as mainly empty. Conservative opposition proved too strong. Modernization under Pompidou was largely directed at industrial and technological development – and was dependent, too, upon continued high rates of economic growth that were about to evaporate.

The French left, meanwhile, was changing in character. Numerous Marxist – mainly Trotskyite or Maoist – splinter groups had emerged from 1968. Their agitation and pressure for change continued. But they stood outside the mainstream, even on the left. The Communist Party, which since the war had been supported by around a quarter of the electorate and had been closely aligned with Moscow, suffered what proved to be terminal damage from the Soviet invasion of Czechoslovakia in August 1968. Accepting that it could not gain power alone, through revolution, it became more reformist, aiming at long-term transformation of society. This was bound to lead to disillusionment among its followers. But its turn towards reformism coincided with the needs of the Socialist Party, licking its wounds from its devastating defeat in the presidential election of 1969 (when its candidate, Gaston Defferre, had won a mere 5 per cent of the vote). Under its new leader, François Mitterrand, the party moved towards reformist modernization, laying out a programme to decentralize and make nationalization and state planning more democratic. In 1972 the Socialist and Communist Parties presented a Common Programme for Government, advanced as a reformist route to profound change in society. But the wind was in the sails of Mitterrand's Socialists, now starting to eclipse the Communist Party as the main party of the left.

The pluralist political systems of Western Europe had everywhere to accommodate pressures for reform in the later 1960s and early 1970s. They obviously did not adjust in uniform fashion, since politics within individual nation states were heavily conditioned by domestic agendas. But when the evident diversity is taken into account, similar patterns of change affected most of Western Europe. It was hardly undiluted harmony. There was nonetheless an extensive level of stability in Western Europe, and every expectation of continuing prosperity nearly everywhere.

* * *

There were even rays of hope in the international arena. In 1970 Willy Brandt took his country in a new direction with far-reaching consequences by reversing policy on Eastern Europe. Until now West Germany had refused to recognize the German Democratic Republic and had laid claim, in the event of reunification, to the 1937 borders of the German Reich (which included land beyond the Oder–Neisse line that since 1945 had formed part of Poland and even the western tip of the Soviet Union). Brandt's bold initiative won him the Nobel Peace Prize in 1971. His 'Eastern policy' (*Ostpolitik*), a term that Brandt actually disliked, was at first deeply divisive – applauded by the left, bitterly opposed by conservatives and representatives of those expelled from Eastern Europe after the end of the war. Brandt aimed in the first place to replace alienation by co-operation in relations with the German Democratic Republic. His strong belief was that *Ostpolitik* could only be successful if West Germany remained firmly anchored in NATO and fully integrated into Western Europe. As Brandt himself put it: 'Our Eastern policy has to begin in the West.' There were worries, at home and abroad, that *Ostpolitik* would lead to dangerous concessions to the Soviet bloc and eventually turn the Federal Republic away from its Western moorings. But it proved an increasingly popular political breakthrough.

The new *Ostpolitik* established over the following three years formal relations with the German Democratic Republic, normalized those with Czechoslovakia, and recognized in the Treaty of Warsaw in 1970 the reality of Poland's western border along the Oder–Neisse Line, which it accepted could not be changed by force, thereby in practice conceding the permanent loss of Germany's former eastern provinces. (Final, unconditional recognition of the German–Polish border at the Oder–Neisse line would come only in the process of German Unification in 1990.) The momentous shift was symbolized in December 1970 when, on a visit to Warsaw, Brandt spontaneously fell to his knees at the monument to the Ghetto Uprising of April and May 1943 in a personal show of expiation for the murder of the Jews.

Brandt's change of direction in West German foreign policy matched an apparently promising change in superpower relations. In May 1972, after talks over the previous three years, Richard Nixon, the President of the United States, and Leonid Brezhnev, the General Secretary of the Communist Party of the Soviet Union, signed an agreement arising from what was known as SALT I (Strategic Arms Limitation Talks), aimed at improving mutual security by restricting anti-ballistic missile systems. This was followed the next year by a further Agreement on the

Prevention of Nuclear War, with the ambitious objective of removing 'the danger of nuclear war and the use of nuclear weapons' altogether. The moves suited both major parties – the Soviet Union concerned about the rapprochement between the USA and Communist China (cemented by Nixon's visit to Beijing in February 1972), the USA about the diplomatic damage caused by the Vietnam War. What became generally known as 'détente' defused superpower tensions and held out the highly welcome potential of lasting improvements in relations between the biggest nuclear powers. It seemed that Europe – and the world generally – could start to breathe a little easier. That was before the economic and political repercussions that followed the oil crisis of 1973.

7

The Turn

The industrial democracies are determined to overcome high unemployment, continuing inflation and serious energy problems.

Declaration of the G-7 on economic cooperation, November 1975

Crisis? What Crisis?

Headline in the *Sun* newspaper, misquoting British Prime Minister James Callaghan, 11 January 1979

The oil crisis of 1973 was a turning point in Europe's post-war history. It ushered in a series of changes that left a profound mark on political, economic and social structures. By the mid-1980s these changes – amounting to no less than a paradigm shift from the boom of the early post-war decades – were transforming the continent. There were clear signs already in the years preceding the oil crisis that the long-lasting boom was coming to an end. Change was on the way. But the oil crisis was a massive accelerant. As a direct consequence of the cuts in supplies imposed by Arab oil producers the cost of a barrel of oil jumped within a year from $2.70 to $9.76. By 1980, after a second oil crisis in 1979, the price had soared to almost $50 per barrel. Oil had provided 8.5 per cent of Western Europe's energy supplies in 1950. Twenty years later the figure had risen to 60 per cent. For countries so heavily dependent on oil, the gravity of the crisis was obvious.

The crisis marked the end of the optimism that had characterized the previous two decades. The earlier beneficent impact of sustained growth

9. Little Richard, a star of the rock and roll craze that swept over Europe in the second half of the 1950s, during his European tour in 1962. On that tour, he performed on some dates alongside The Beatles, then a little-known group but which within months would become a global phenomenon.

10. A symbol of mid-1960s 'swinging London': the mini skirt in Carnaby Street. The ladies clothes shop next to the fashionable boutique had still not quite caught up with the latest modes.

11. (*opposite*) Mid-1960s affluence in France: a line of Citroën DS cars in a showroom on the Champs Elysees in Paris.

12. May 1968 in Paris. Police in riot gear face students during the huge protest demonstrations. For a short time the spread of unrest appeared to pose a threat to the stability of the government. Significant student protest took place in 1968 in many countries, not confined to Europe. Alongside France, Italy and West Germany saw its major manifestations.

13. (*opposite*) The Soviet leader Leonid Brezhnev is greeted with smiles and flowers in Bratislava on 3 August 1968. The President of the Czech Republic, Ludvik Svoboda, clasps Brezhnev's hand. A smiling Alexander Dubček, First Secretary of the Czechoslovak Communist Party, (*right*) waits to offer another bouquet. In the second row are (*left*) Alexei Kosygin, the Soviet Prime Minister, (*behind Brezhnev*) Nikolai Podgorny, Chairman of the Presidium of the Supreme Soviet and (*behind Dubček*), Oldřich Černík, the Prime Minister of Czechoslovakia.

14. Less than three weeks after the false show of friendship in Bratislava, troops from the Warsaw Pact invaded Czechoslovakia during the night of 20-21 August 1968. Here, two young men wave a flag on an abandoned Soviet tank in Prague, as a car burns fiercely close by. Defiance was, however, quickly crushed by military might.

15. (*below*) The West German Chancellor Willy Brandt falls to his knees while in Poland on 7 December 1970 to pay tribute at the monument in Warsaw to Jewish victims killed by the Nazis during the Ghetto Uprising in 1943. Brandt sought, through a new policy towards countries of eastern Europe (*Ostpolitik*) to improve West Germany's relations with the former Soviet bloc.

16. A Swiss poster opposing women's right to vote. A referendum on 7 February 1971 finally gave women the vote in federal elections, though it would be another twenty years before the last canton allowed women to vote on local issues.

was replaced by the negative primacy of economics. The presumption that living standards would continue to rise, a feature of the era of the 'economic miracle', was abruptly called into question. High rates of inflation combined in a new and dangerous linkage with rising unemployment, a phenomenon the immediate post-war decades had thought was conquered forever. The result was greater economic insecurity than most people had experienced since the war. It was not long before doubts were raised about maintaining the levels of spending on the welfare state itself, the very foundation of people's sense of security as Europe had recovered from the Second World War. The economic model, drawing on the theories of John Maynard Keynes, that had dominated the formation of the political economy in Western Europe since the war was now fundamentally challenged and increasingly rejected. The changed economic climate increased political volatility, while sharpened conflict in Northern Ireland, Spain, West Germany and Italy brought frightening terrorist atrocities. How did political systems in both Eastern and Western Europe respond and adapt to the drastically changed circumstances? How, indeed, did they survive intact, when they had collapsed during times of economic crisis in the 1930s?

Not everything in the years following the oil crisis evoked gloom and pessimism. The crisis itself exposed the need for structural changes to the economy to turn away from older industries already in decline. Damaging levels of inflation were eventually (and with much pain along the way) brought under control. And individual choice in lifestyles and consumerism made greater inroads into social conformism. Dictatorship disappeared from the western half of the continent. Within months of each other the authoritarian regimes in Portugal, Greece and then Spain collapsed – and peacefully, without external military intervention. A new and worrying development, however, was the steep deterioration in international relations, which had seemed on a more positive trajectory. The détente of the first half of the 1970s, which had pointed towards a limitation on nuclear arsenals and international respect for human rights, did not last the decade. By 1980 Europe was entering what is frequently referred to as its 'second Cold War' – a new and dangerous phase of superpower confrontation.

ECONOMIES IN TROUBLE

How sharply the oil crisis of 1973 marked a caesura is plainly illustrated by the rates of economic growth in Europe. Between 1950 and 1973 average annual growth rates had been 4.7 per cent in both Western and Eastern Europe and as high as 6.3 per cent in the underdeveloped economies of Southern Europe, belatedly starting to catch up. In the twenty years that followed the oil crisis growth rates were more than halved, dropping to 3.1 per cent in Southern Europe, 2.2 per cent in Western Europe, and even becoming negative, at −0.4 per cent in Eastern Europe. In Western Europe, Norway, Ireland (another backward economy catching up), Italy, Austria and West Germany had the best growth rates, the Netherlands, the United Kingdom, Sweden and Switzerland the worst. Beyond the Iron Curtain, Hungary (where increased per-capita gross domestic product belied mounting problems of mounting financial dependency on the West) was least badly affected, Romania worst. Of the countries in the south of the continent, Turkey's growth (at 2.6 per cent) was higher than anywhere else, though it was from a low base. Whatever the national variations, the general pattern in all regions was clear.

The dynamics that had produced two decades of prosperity were fading. Until 1971 the economies of the Western world had been underpinned by the fixed convertible rates of currency exchange with the dollar – itself tied to the price of gold (at a fixed value, unchanged since 1934) – agreed at the Bretton Woods conference in July 1944. The complexities of putting such a system into practice meant that the Bretton Woods system was fully implemented only from December 1958 onwards. And within a decade it was encountering difficulties. Bretton Woods had essentially been a deal worked out by the United States and the United Kingdom. It reflected the post-war dominance of the dollar as the international reserve currency in place of the earlier pre-eminence of sterling. Since then Western economies had both become far more interwoven and varied widely in strength. It had become increasingly difficult to reconcile the fluctuating economies with fixed exchange rates. Currency speculation – and the financial uncertainty that this caused – was inevitable. Increased tension in holding fixed, convertible exchange rates prompted the first moves, in the Werner Report of 1970 (named after the chairman of the committee that produced it, Pierre Werner, Prime Minister of Luxemburg), towards monetary union in Europe. (In fact, the French had made the first overtures to West Germany about currency union as early as 1964 – a move intended to enhance France's international standing and weaken German dependency on the USA. The suggestion had been quietly ignored in Bonn.) It was an idea whose time had not come. The proposals were blown away in the monetary storms that soon followed.

The continued dominance of the once-mighty dollar could no longer be taken for granted. The United States economy – the pivot of the entire Bretton Woods system – was itself running into difficulties. By the end of the 1960s the USA had a rising payments deficit and soaring trade deficit – a result of increased imports from Europe and Japan, the expansion of social spending under the administration of President Johnson, and not least profligate military expenditure on the escalating Vietnam War. Inflation was proving difficult to constrain. As the American balance of payments continued to deteriorate and both inflation and unemployment rose, it was evident that the dollar was overvalued. Speculation against the dollar in favour of the German mark and the Japanese yen was the inevitable consequence. In May 1971 the West German government – followed by Austria, Belgium, the Netherlands and Switzerland – decided that it would no longer maintain the existing parity with the dollar. This prompted a strong rise in the value of the mark and a flight from the dollar. The Bretton Woods system had been built around a fixed price of gold, 35 dollars per ounce. The weakness of the dollar fostered speculation that the price of gold would rise. It did. By the end of the 1960s gold was selling for more than double the official price. Bretton Woods was no longer sustainable. On 15 August 1971 President Richard Nixon suddenly announced a dramatic shift in American policy: amid a raft of anti-inflationary measures, he suspended the gold convertibility of the dollar.

With that move, the Bretton Woods system – the basis of the post-war economy – was dead. Floating exchange rates were the future. But they entailed further uncertainties for the international economy. How to manage them was the new problem – and would rapidly create difficulties. No patent solution was found. All proposals foundered on the issue, faced by economies of quite varying strength and not least by the central US economy, of combating the worrying rise in inflation without resorting to classical deflationary measures of such severity that they would undermine growth, hugely increase unemployment (with all its attendant social and political consequences), and perhaps plunge the world into a new great depression.

In the meantime, from December 1971 the major European industrial countries moved to construct a narrow band within which their currencies could fluctuate against the dollar, now decoupled from gold. The 'snake', as the system became known, soon proved a failure. Given the different levels of development of the European economies and their varying national strategies for coping with inflation and controlling government expenditure, the failure was a near certainty from the outset. Countries were primarily concerned to look after their own interests and to wrestle with their domestic difficulties through national polices. The United Kingdom, Ireland and Denmark had already left the 'snake' by 1972 (though Denmark soon rejoined), as did Italy in 1973 and France in 1974. The 'snake' became in practice a smaller collection of north-west European economies dominated by the German mark. Only West Germany and the Benelux countries stayed the course. On the combined initiative of the German and French governments the unsatisfactory currency 'snake' was converted in 1979 into the European Monetary System. The deutschmark became even more plainly the peg on which to hang other European currencies.

The problems of the 'snake' prompted the move to more general floating currencies. At the same time they encouraged the notion, already contemplated in 1970, of the eventual attainment of European monetary union. This was for now no more than a pipe dream. West Germany's economic dominance (and sizeable surplus) meant that it was far outstripping the weaker economies, making the coordination of diverging currencies extremely difficult. Floating currencies rather than fixed rates increasingly suited most countries that could make internal adjustments without having to contemplate politically damaging devaluations.

In essence, the currency travails reflected a deeper malaise in the Western economies even before the impact of the oil crisis. Industrial production increased, in fact, by some 10 per cent in 1972–3. But this created some industrial overcapacity at the same time that demand for imported primary products was intensifying. Economies were overheating. Monetary expansion, cheap borrowing, and growth in national money supplies in the wake of the weakening dollar led to sharp price rises. In the year before the oil crisis the price of raw materials was already soaring – a 63 per cent rise in a single year – while profitability in the industrial sector of the most wealthy countries was declining, putting obvious strains on mass production. And even before the oil crisis, inflation was reaching worrying levels – 7 per cent in West Germany, from ingrained memory stretching back to the hyperinflation of 1923, the society most paranoid about inflation.

The Keynesian approach of promoting growth by stimulating demand had been the basis of practically all post-war thinking on the economy. It had proved the tried and tested way out of economic trouble, stagnation and mass unemployment. But this remedy did not fit the conditions of the early 1970s. Two decades of high growth had produced full employment. The problem now was of rising inflation. Pumping money into the economy was guaranteed merely to add to inflationary pressures. Stimulating demand simply prompted claims for higher wages. Without increased productivity that just fed into further inflation. A large (and still rising) proportion of workers, especially in the expanded public sector, belonged to trade unions – in 1970 around two-thirds in Sweden, half in Britain, a third in West Germany (though little over a fifth in France). Unions were able to exploit virtually full employment and a labour shortage to win sometimes spectacular wage increases – 19 per cent in Italian industry in 1969 – without commensurate increases in productivity. Governments were finding it more and more difficult to cope with levels of public expenditure, especially on welfare. This accounted for 40 to 50 per cent of the expenditure of Western countries by the early 1970s, quadrupling in Western Europe on average since the end of the war and rising especially fast in Italy and France. In these circumstances, Keynesian theory offered no solutions.

In already worsening economic conditions, the shock to the Western economy from the oil crisis of 1973 was immense. Countries reacted in the main according to their national interests. France tried to make special deals with Iraq, Britain with Iran and Kuwait. Neither Britain nor France were badly affected by the embargo, in contrast to the Netherlands, the worst-affected country. In fact, the embargo was already lifted on Europe (though not on the USA) by November 1973 after the European Community had issued a statement interpreted as being relatively favourable towards the Arab position in the Middle Eastern conflict. But the difficulties of coordinating policy in the light of differing national interests persisted. When the United States and fifteen other countries established an International Energy Agency in November 1974, seen among other things as a forum for developing contingency plans on oil-sharing in the event of a new emergency, France would have nothing to do with it. The French adjudged that participation might harm its own relations with OPEC, while Britain and Norway, which had discovered their own offshore oilfields, reserved their right to take independent action.

The severe impact of the oil crisis was also felt in Eastern Europe, with long-term damaging effects. As a major oil producer itself, the Soviet Union was in fact a beneficiary of the global rise in the price of oil and greatly increased its revenues by exporting beyond Eastern Europe to developed market economies. Increased output from western Siberian oilfields paid for imports from the West. The unexpected bonanza concealed for a time the underlying weaknesses of the Soviet economy. The other socialist economies beyond the Iron Curtain, apart from Romania lacking their own oil supplies, were in a far less fortunate position. (Romania's own oil supplies cushioned the country from the impact of the 1973 crisis, but were insufficient to cover its threefold growth in demand for oil during the 1970s. Even here, therefore, oil had to be imported, greatly increasing Romania's foreign debt by the end of the decade.) The Soviet Union increased the prices (though at less than world market value) to member states within its own economic bloc (COMECON), insisting on payment in hard currency or through delivery of finished industrial goods. Supplies from the Soviet Union were certainly vital for the satellite countries. Without them their political problems might have become difficult to contain. A crucial consequence of the oil crisis, nevertheless, was that the socialist countries were compelled to look for extended loans to the capitalist West. Their state debts to Western countries began to mount alarmingly in a spiral from which there was no escape. Hungary's debts in dollars rose eighteen-fold during the 1970s and 1980s, Poland's twenty-fold, the German Democratic Republic's more than forty-fold. By the end of the 1970s growth had slowed drastically or turned negative across the region.

Yugoslavia, outside the Soviet bloc, experienced similar problems. State indebtedness rose from \$4.6 to \$21 billion between 1973 and 1981. There was at first no obvious sign of trouble to ordinary citizens. Growth continued. The state continued to spend heavily on new hotels, sports halls and roads. Living standards were maintained. But, like other socialist countries, necessary economic transformation and increased competitiveness were as good as impossible within the system. Falling growth, increased national debt, unemployment and inflation all gathered pace. By 1984 living standards had fallen by 30 per cent. The economic disparities between the Yugoslavian republics widened – by the end of the 1970s, for example, Slovenia was nine times wealthier than Kosovo – intensifying the potential for ethnic conflict. It was perhaps no surprise that Tito's death in May 1980 was soon followed by an outburst of ethnic violence in Kosovo between Albanians and Serbs – a harbinger of worse to follow.

In Western Europe there was no escaping the immediate consequences of the oil crisis. Governments took emergency measures to deal with the oil shortage, often resorting to rationing of petrol and heating oil, restricting non-essential use of vehicles (especially on Sundays) and imposing speed limits to lessen consumption. (People started to buy smaller, more fuel-efficient cars in order to spend less on petrol.) The British population was exhorted by the government to heat only one room in the house even during the cold winter months. Dutch citizens were threatened with prison sentences for exceeding their ration of electricity usage. The panic soon abated, once the embargo was lifted.

But the quadrupling of the price of oil was much more harmful. By the second half of 1974 it led to a serious recession, reduced industrial production, and brought a fall in gross national product. Balance of payments problems were hugely exacerbated by the dramatic rise in the price of oil imports. Commodity prices rose across Europe by over 13 per cent in 1974, driving up the already rising inflation. Compared with the years 1950–73, consumer prices were on average more than twice as high in the decade 1973–83, more than four times higher in the Mediterranean countries. As always, those on fixed incomes were especially badly hit by inflation. The price increases were invariably passed on to the consumer, resulting inevitably in wage demands to meet the higher cost of living, further intensifying inflation where they were met – as they usually were, given the strength of trade unions. But the rising costs of employment led to redundancies. More than 7 million people in Western Europe were soon out of work. Unemployment leapt from an average of 2 to 4 per cent between 1950 and 1973, to 12 per cent over the subsequent decade. Worst hit were the old, labour-intensive industries – mining, steel, shipbuilding, textiles – where there were huge drops in production (exacerbated by growing competition from rapidly expanding Japanese industrial output) and high levels of unemployment.

Rising unemployment alongside rising inflation was a phenomenon that confounded classical economic analysis. Early attempts to combat the economic downturn by reflationary measures to boost demand just made things worse. 'Stagflation', as it became known, varied in accordance with economic strength and industrial structures. The most buoyant economy, that of West Germany, was relatively successful in coping. Inflation was held under 5 per cent between 1973 and 1981, unemployment below 3 per cent. The disruption to the economy, still registering growth of around 2 per cent, was relatively minor. In the worst-affected countries, Britain and Italy, it was much more severe. Italy's economy was still growing solidly, but inflation was running at 17.6 per cent. Britain had the worst growth rate of only 0.5 per cent between 1973 and 1981, while inflation averaged around 15 per cent.

By the early 1970s Britain, once the world's industrial powerhouse, was in a sorry state. Long years of insufficient investment, archaic trade union structures, poor management, and political failings in economic planning and policy by successive governments had significantly weakened Britain, economically and politically. The Labour government's attempt to reform the trade unions had been a dismal failure. The Conservatives, coming to power under Edward Heath in 1970, fared even worse, both in managing the economy and in handling industrial disputes. Prices and wages had continued to spiral upwards, merely fuelling inflation. In 1972 prices rose by 7 per cent, but industrial earnings by 16 per cent. Capitulating to a miners' strike that year, the first national coal strike since 1926, the government had conceded a pay rise more than double the rate of inflation. A policy of stimulating growth through reductions in taxation had meanwhile been introduced. Although the rate of growth sharply (and temporarily) rose, the boom merely added fuel to the flames of inflation, which the government then vainly sought to control by imposing limits on wage rises. And all this was before the oil shock.

The gathering crisis in industrial relations, as the economy reeled from the impact of soaring energy prices, came to a head in 1974 after the National Union of Mineworkers – the most powerful trade union in the country – had demanded a big pay rise, well in excess of the wage restriction recently introduced by the Conservative government. This led to a state of emergency, the rationing of electricity usage, and a three-day week for industry. There was panic-buying. One London factory was producing a million candles a day as people feared power cuts. Astonishingly, manufacturing output hardly fell – an indictment of the lack of productivity on the normal five-day week. Eventually, it came to a show of strength between the government and the union at a general election in February 1974 specifically called by Edward Heath on the issue of 'who governs Britain?' The electorate gave its answer: it was not the government.

The new Labour administration under Harold Wilson acceded straightaway to the miners' pay demands. Predictably this sparked a wages explosion. Earnings rose by 24 per cent in 1975. But inflation reached 27 per cent while unemployment rose to over a million (double the level of any year for over two decades). Government spending was out of control as public expenditure soared to 46 per cent of gross domestic product. The balance of payments deficit had more than trebled since the start of the oil crisis and stood at a record height. The Bank of England raised the lending rate but could not prevent continued speculation against sterling. In 1976 the British government suffered the humiliation of having to go with a begging bowl to the International Monetary Fund to obtain a loan of $3.9 billion, the highest in the Fund's history. The inevitable spending cuts, now introduced by a Labour Chancellor of the Exchequer, Denis Healey, and falling heavily upon housing and education, brought a small reduction in the deficit and slowed inflation, while reducing state revenues from taxation. But holding down wages to 5 per cent, well below the cost of living, meant inroads into the standard of living that the trade unions, especially dominant in the public sector, were not prepared to accept. The number of days lost in industrial disputes rose alarmingly to a post-war peak by 1979, a level as bad as any in the century. The notorious 'winter of discontent' of 1978–9 saw bodies left unburied because gravediggers were on strike, rubbish piling up in streets because the refuse collectors were on strike, children locked out of schools because caretakers were on strike, and the sick not admitted to hospitals because their ancillary workers were on strike.

This was the background to the resounding victory of the Conservative Party, now led by Margaret Thatcher, in the general election of 3 May 1979. It was also a turn to neo-liberalism that signalled a radically different approach to the problems that had bedevilled British governments during the 1970s.

At least in Britain oil from the North Sea was starting to flow in 1975 and by 1980 was exceeding the output of Iran or Kuwait. Italy, however, had no oil, but oil supplied 75 per cent of the country's energy needs. Along with Britain, Italy had an adversarial tradition of industrial relations, in contrast to the more corporate systems in Scandinavia, West Germany, Austria, Switzerland, the Netherlands and Belgium. Industrial conflict was endemic. And the severe economic problems of the early 1970s formed the backdrop to the rise in political violence carried out in the campaigns of the Red Brigades and other militant factions (see Chapter 6). Amid continued high inflation and a rapidly rising balance of payments deficit, Italy was compelled to take big loans from West Germany and from the International Monetary Fund, bringing severe deflationary measures and restrictions of the money supply in their wake. The resulting recession brought stagnation in production, rising unemployment, and an increase in public spending to 55 per cent of gross domestic product by 1982 – a higher proportion than in any other major Western European country. Only Italy's sizeable 'black economy' prevented a worse decline. Between four and seven million Italians are reckoned to have profited from this 'unofficial' side of the nation's economic life, which by 1979 accounted for up to 20 per cent of the economy.

Britain and Italy remained in the doldrums in the later 1970s. In general, though, there was a slow and fragile recovery from the worst of the crisis. This was spurred on by the strong European economies of West Germany and Switzerland and, outside Europe, of Japan. It was helped, too, by the 'petro-dollars' that flowed from the oil-rich countries of the Middle East into Western economies, often in orders for capital infrastructure or military weapons.

The tentative recovery in the later 1970s had no sooner begun than it shuddered to a halt in a second oil crisis in 1979. This followed the revolution in Iran in January that year when, following months of massive unrest that even the brutality of the secret police could not bring under control, the Shah of Iran had been deposed. Little more than the puppet of the United States, the Shah's power had been shored up in 1953 following successful machinations by the CIA and the British MI6 to depose the democratically elected government. The regime was detested by most of the population. The exiled spiritual leader of the Shiite opposition to the Shah, Ayatollah Khomeini, was received by rapturous crowds in Teheran on 1 February on return from exile in France and proclaimed an Islamic republic. This inaugurated new and lasting great political turmoil, not just in the region but across the world.

A consequence of the upheavals was a sharp drop in Iranian oil production. Although Saudi Arabia increased production, memories of the previous crisis were enough to cause a new panic. The big drop in production from both Iran and Iraq, as these two major oil-producing countries began a war in 1980 that was fought with great ferocity and would last for eight years, did nothing to calm nerves. The price of oil tripled again between 1979 and 1981, now standing more than ten times higher than it had been in 1973. It was once more a global crisis, with the worst impact felt by the poor countries of the developing world. Western Europe was in a better position, as North Sea oil started to flow in significant quantities and the development of nuclear power gathered pace. But the European economies were less strong than they had been at the outset of the 1973 crisis. The recession after the second oil crisis was in some ways, therefore, more serious. Morale was already damaged. Anxieties had risen. Governments had proved unable to find solutions to the problem of 'stagflation'. A new economic philosophy, discarding the Keynesian imperatives that had held the ring since the end of the Second World War, was coming to be seen as the only way to combat the malaise.

The theoretical work that was beginning to find new converts especially in the United States and in Great Britain was *Capitalism and Freedom*, published in 1962 by the eminent economist Milton Friedman, a leading figure in the Chicago School of Economics. It amounted to a frontal rejection of Keynesianism. State intervention in the economy to stimulate demand was ruled out in this thinking. So was state regulation of markets through fiscal policy. Friedman advocated instead an economy self-regulated by the forces of the free market. He argued that the supply of money determined the price level. If money supply were kept in close tandem with gross national product, inflation would cease to be a problem. As it was, money supply had greatly outstripped production. Tightening the money supply was, therefore, the necessary remedy to bring inflation under control, even at the cost of higher unemployment. This monetarist philosophy was the core of what was widely coming to be called 'neo-liberalism' (though 'monetarism' was a more accurate term for the theory, and preferred by its exponents).

'Neo-liberalism' had a lengthy intellectual pedigree. The Austrian economists Ludwig von Mises and Friedrich Hayek were among its early proponents. The influence of Hayek, especially, was considerable. Hayek had been born in Austria in 1899, but had emigrated to England in 1938 and eventually taken British citizenship. He belatedly acquired guru status, largely because of the book he had published in 1944, *The Road to Serfdom*. This linked socialism (which he saw as inseparable from coercive intervention aimed at creating equality) and state-planning with servitude. Only the competitiveness of the free market liberated from state controls, argued Hayek, was compatible with democratic freedom. Hayek wrote in forceful language, understandable not just by other economists. It turned economic theory into a fully fledged social and political ideology. This would pose a fundamental challenge to the entire precepts that had underpinned the post-war consensus on the welfare state, which had presumed high levels of taxation and centralized government control of an economy resting on partly nationalized industry and a large public sector.

In reality, governments would continue to mix parts of Keynesianism with monetarism. But the breakthrough of monetarism to official recognition as the new orthodoxy in two countries, Britain and the United States, was close. In January 1980 Ronald Reagan took up office as President of the United States, and his economic policy – what was soon dubbed 'Reaganomics' – incorporated an adaptation of monetarism (though neo-liberal dogma was ignored when it came to the stratospheric increase in military spending and a tripling of the national debt).

Only Britain, among Western European leading economies, was an early and avid convert to neo-liberalism. Practically all countries were gradually forced in the 1970s to introduce deflationary measures to stabilize their economies. Fear of inflation galloping out of control had become a dominant theme of politics. But while deflation was a strategy, neo-liberalism was an ideology. Deflation was, in fact, not the aim of neo-liberalism – though it usually formed part of the armoury deployed to reduce state expenditure and indebtedness. Rather, neo-liberalism sought to produce long-term growth through low taxation, deregulation, privatization of industry and public services, and reduction in the size of the public sector. The overall aim was to replace the state by the market as the driving and controlling force of the economy.

The severity of Britain's economic problems in the early 1970s, the worsening industrial relations that brought the government in headlong conflict with large and powerful trade unions, the cultural affinities of Britain with the principles of American economic and social liberalism and, not least, the personal role of Margaret Thatcher in driving through a new economic agenda against much opposition, account for British exceptionality in embracing the monetarist framework of neo-liberalism. The United States and Britain spearheaded the 'neo-liberal turn' – which with a widening ripple effect would have a major impact on the lives of millions of ordinary people. Neo-liberalism was resisted across the rest of Western Europe, where there was a far greater attempt to retain the consensual basis of economics and politics that had yielded such rich post-war dividends and to protect important national industries from the most harmful effects of severe and rapid restructuring. But from the 1980s onwards privatization, deregulation, cutting the size of the public sector, and attempts (not always successful) to curb trade unions and workers' rights became part of the agenda of most governments.

RECESSION POLITICS

The drastically changed economic conditions framed by two deep recessions, following the two oil crises of 1973 and 1979, inevitably had an impact on the political systems of countries on both sides of the Iron Curtain. There was, however, a fundamental difference in their capacity to adapt. Management of the economy shifted throughout Western

Europe by the mid-1980s away from Keynesianism towards neo-liberalism. This had painful consequences. Many people saw their livelihoods destroyed or badly damaged as unprofitable branches of industry were closed down. Tens of thousands were made unemployed. The potential for conflict was magnified. But liberal democratic systems, if put under greater pressure, were able to cope.

The countries of the socialist bloc of Eastern Europe faced more serious difficulties. Their state-run economies – inefficient, uncompetitive, technologically dated, too dependent on heavy industry – were inflexible. They could not be fundamentally changed without changing the political systems that controlled them and the unbending ideology that determined those political systems. They had scarcely any room for manoeuvre without undermining the very basis of Marxist-Leninist polity. With great difficulty the communist states surmounted the turbulence of the 1970s. There was no sense at the start of the following decade that it would be the last in the history of those states. Yet they emerged from the crisis years of the 1970s significantly weakened. And their weakness was the Achilles heel of the Soviet Union itself. Should one state within the bloc crumble, the danger of a domino effect was real. Poland had often appeared to be the weakest link in the chain. And it was indeed in Poland that the gravest threat to the stability of the entire Soviet bloc manifested itself.

Poland's debts to Western countries were eight times higher in 1975 than they had been five years earlier. Food prices were kept low only through heavy state subsidies – even in a country where almost a third of the population still worked in agriculture. The government's attempt in 1976 to combat the spiralling debt by a big increase in food prices – 50 per cent for butter, over 60 per cent for meat, a doubling for sugar – led to strikes by tens of thousands of workers and eventually a withdrawal of the price rises. Harsh repression against the protesters followed. But this led to the formation of protest groups among intellectuals, prominent among them Jacek Kuroń, co-founder with Antoni Macierewicz of a Workers' Defence Committee (*Komitet Obrony Robotników*, KOR) aimed at providing legal representation for those arrested and circulating reports of their trials.

The Catholic Church, too, which called for the release of arrested workers, was becoming a more prominent voice of national opposition to the regime. This was hugely bolstered in October 1978 by the election of the Archbishop of Cracow, Cardinal Karol Wojtyła, as Pope John Paul II. The Polish leader, Edward Gierek, immediately foresaw trouble for the regime. He was right. A third of the Polish population – around 12 million people – turned out to welcome the Pope when he made an emotional return to his homeland in June 1979. It was a visit that Gierek thought he could not prevent, despite the Kremlin advising him to do just that. The exultant crowds were a clear sign that any ideological hold of communism over the Polish people was by now wafer thin. Kazimierz Brandys, a prominent Polish writer and one-time member of the Communist Party until he became estranged from the regime, witnessed the elation when the Pope went to Warsaw. 'I think that in such moments,' he wrote in his diary, 'everyone must have seen in John Paul II the spiritual embodiment of the national history.' The Pope's visit to Poland was to prove the catalyst to the events that rocked the regime during subsequent months.

By the following year Poland's economic crisis had deepened. Nearly all the earnings from exports were by now going simply to service ever-rising debt. Rationing, power cuts and, once again, increased food prices were the government's response. And once again the Polish working class responded angrily, now with organized big strikes across the country. In August 1980, led by Lech Wałęsa, a thirty-seven-year-old electrician, the strike committee in the Gdańsk shipyards demanded free trade unions, the right to strike, and press freedom. It also sought representation of the 'authentic' interests of the working class by independent trade unions – a direct challenge to the assumption that the Communist Party was the sole representative of the working class. As the strikes spread the government felt compelled to negotiate – and on 31 August to concede practically all of the strikers' demands. On 17 September an independent federation of free trade unions was formed, with Wałęsa as its chairman. It was given the name *Solidarność* (Solidarity) that had been adopted by striking workers the previous month. Within months it had 9.5 million members. The official communist unions had by then lost 8.6 million members. Solidarity sought reform within the existing system, not to overthrow it. What it had unwittingly done, however, was to introduce as a matter of principle the right to free association – something intrinsically incompatible with the communist state system.

Alarmed that this was the thin end of the wedge, some communist leaders – prominent among them Erich Honecker, head of the German Democratic Republic – urged the Soviet Union to intervene. Leonid Brezhnev held back. He had been warned by the new party leader in Poland, Stanisław Kania (Gierek had resigned in early September, allegedly on health grounds), that an invasion like that in Czechoslovakia twelve years earlier would prompt a national uprising. The Polish leadership was advised to put its house in order itself. A sign that it was preparing to do just that was in February 1981 the elevation of the Defence Minister, General Wojciech Jaruzelski, a somewhat sinister-looking figure behind his trademark dark glasses, to the post of Prime Minister. When new mass protests at food shortages, rationing and empty shops took place in the summer, Jaruzelski was put under great pressure from Moscow to act. The pressure intensified in September after Solidarity issued an appeal to the workers of other socialist countries to establish their own free trade unions. After some dithering Jaruzelski eventually, on 13 December 1981, declared martial law. Solidarity was banned, around 10,000 of its members were arrested (Wałęsa spent over a year in jail, though in privileged confinement), the freedoms that had been granted were retracted, and the initial spontaneous protests at the draconian measures violently repressed. The West – the United States in the lead – reacted with economic sanctions, though there was relief that the Soviet Union had not intervened militarily. Martial law was eventually lifted – followed by the ending of Western sanctions – on 21 July 1983 (a first stage had taken place in December 1982) after a second visit to Poland by Pope John Paul II, again evoking rapturous adulation from millions of Poles. Not all restrictions disappeared. Solidarity remained banned but, partly through secret assistance from the CIA, survived in illegality as potentially still a huge dissident movement. Its moment was still to come.

Nowhere else in the eastern bloc mirrored the events in Poland. Superficially, a veneer of stability was sustained. To the outside world the old order seemed as intact as ever, and likely to continue into the indefinite future. The courage of prominent dissidents attracted great admiration in the West. They included the writer Alexander Solzhenitsyn (stripped of his Soviet citizenship and expelled from the Soviet Union to West Germany in 1974); the nuclear physicist, Nobel Prize winner and human rights activist Andrei Sakharov (sent into internal exile within the Soviet Union, in Gorky, in 1980); the singer-songwriter Wolf Biermann (stripped of his East German citizenship and expelled from the GDR in 1976 while on a concert tour of West Germany); and in Czechoslovakia the playwright Václav Havel, the writer Milan Kundera (deprived of Czech citizenship in 1979), and the 243 signatories to the intellectuals' protest movement, Charter 77. Their treatment by repressive communist regimes was loudly and repeatedly condemned. But nothing suggested that their opposition was much more than a pinprick to such regimes. The mounting economic problems behind the scenes were a far more serious challenge. Just how serious they were could, however, scarcely be grasped from the outside. The sense of monolithic solidity, backed by the power of the Red Army, made it almost impossible for most Western observers to see the growing problems of maintaining the system of rule in the eastern bloc. Through judicious use of sticks and carrots the regimes seemed capable of sustaining their power. For the present, it looked as if the danger to the system had been contained, even in Poland.

Fundamental change could only come about from the very top – from the leadership of the Soviet Union. At the end of the 1970s such a prospect seemed highly unlikely. The Soviet economy, its structures ossified, incapable of reform and renewal, was creaking, in the view of some observers facing chronic decline. But there seemed no obvious danger to the existence of the Soviet system of government. Could it not continue indefinitely? And where might change come from?

In Western Europe a general rule was that the stronger the economy before the crisis struck and the greater the level of political consensus, the better were governments able to handle the difficulties. Conversely, governments had a far harder task where the crisis struck more strained economies and less consensual politics. Initial attempts to use Keynesian techniques to boost the economies gradually gave way to retrenchment and deflationary methods, even under Social Democratic governments. There was increasing acceptance, even reaching into supporters of left-wing parties, of the need for a new economic course. Most significantly, democracy proved resilient during its worst crisis since the Second World War. Nowhere was it threatened as it had been so disastrously during the Great Depression of the 1930s.

This owed something to the international cooperation that had been so patently lacking during the Great Depression, when countries had been left to their own devices and economic nationalism had been part of the spiralling aggression that led to war. During the 1970s, in contrast, there were attempts to work together and to coordinate responses to crisis. The European Council established from 1975 onwards regular meetings of the heads of government of the European Community's member states. The same year, on the joint initiative of the French and the West Germans, the heads of state and government of the leading six Western industrial countries (West Germany, France, Great Britain, Italy, the USA and Japan) met at the Château de Rambouillet in north-central France as the G6 – to become in 1976 with the addition of Canada the G7 – to seek common ways of working towards economic recovery and monetary stability. Summits were from now on a normal component of international economic management. And, though unpopular on account of the tough conditions attached, sizeable loans from the International Monetary Fund – an institution that, of course, had not existed during the Great Depression – bailed out the floundering economies of Italy, Britain and Portugal before the end of the 1970s.

International cooperation played its part in upholding stability. Even so, individual countries had largely to adjust to the crisis based on their national potential and their traditions. Social Democratic parties usually had trouble in retaining their support. Their ideological premises – commitment to the welfare state, state regulation of the economy, a belief in redistributive taxation to create equality – were all now questioned. Even in Scandinavia, where they had been dominant for so long, the Social Democrats were under pressure in the years following the oil crisis. In Sweden the Social Democrats found themselves in 1976 in opposition for the first time in forty years as a government centre-right coalition took office. The Norwegian Labour Party was dependent on the left-wing Socialist Party for support in a minority government after 1973. The Social Democrats had problems, too, in Denmark (where the Conservatives achieved their best result in 1984) and in Finland, though they held on as new protest parties emerged, making the formation of stable coalitions more difficult.

For the most part the trend in Western Europe was towards the conservative right. The fragmentation of 'pillarization' that down to the 1960s had been the hallmark of the Netherlands and Belgium continued. This produced a number of new political parties but it led by the 1980s to the election of centre-right coalition governments committed to tackling the economic problems through variants of deflationary politics. In Austria, Bruno Kreisky's thirteen years as Chancellor came to an end when the Socialist Party lost its absolute majority at the 1983 general election. Corruption scandals had undermined the party, even though the economy was stable. It remained in office as a minority administration propped up by the still tiny Freedom Party (*Freiheitliche Partei Österreichs*, FPÖ), which would soon move sharply towards the far right of the political spectrum. The main gainer from the 1983 election was, however, the conservative Austrian People's Party. In Switzerland, government continued throughout the crisis of the 1970s to be formed from coalitions between the four major parties (the Social Democrats, the Free Democrats, the Christian Democrats and the Swiss People's Party). The rightward trend was less prominent here than elsewhere, given Switzerland's sustained financial strength and stability, though in the federal elections of 1983 for the first time since 1925 the Social Democrats failed to emerge as the largest party. As the social basis of support for the political left (and trade unionism) weakened, the liberal and conservative centre-right gained ground and the influence of market forces strengthened.

The sharpest turn to the right was in Britain. Without Britain's specific experience of the crisis there, it is unlikely that Margaret Thatcher, who had replaced Edward Heath as leader of the Conservative Party in February 1975, would have become Prime Minister. As one of her biographers, Hugo Young, put it: 'It was her good fortune to be propelled into the leadership when the party was ready for a return to fundamentalist Conservatism of a kind she was most at ease with. The party wanted something they could believe in, and she was only too pleased to supply it.' The first British female Prime Minister (though distinctly not a feminist) stamped her personal imprint on government as no other post-war Prime Minister had done. Mrs Thatcher was greatly aided by the weakness and divisions within the Labour Party, which in November 1980 turned sharply to the left under a new leader, Michael Foot, widely viewed as hopelessly ineffective. In 1981 a faction among those who felt the party was in danger of becoming a Marxist-led organization, which could only appeal to a minority of the population, broke away to form the Social Democratic Party (SDP). Facing a fatally divided opposition, Thatcher's government had unusually wide scope to radicalize its economic policies.

Mrs Thatcher brought a striking simplicity to her judgements that resonated with some of the public, while repelling many others. She was admired and loathed in almost equal proportions. She found the libertarianism of 'that third-rate decade, the 1960s' repugnant, and sought a return to upstanding 'Victorian values'. On economics her views were redolent of nineteenth-century liberalism rather than of the 'one-nation' conservatism of other post-war Conservative leaders. Free trade and the regulatory forces of the market, not government intervention and control, were for her the way to national prosperity and strength. Governments had to live within their means just as the housewife had to manage the family budget. The welfare state, in Mrs Thatcher's view, diminished self-reliance and the initiative of the individual. There was no such thing as 'society', she averred, only individuals and families. She was an archetypal conviction politician, increasingly difficult to overcome in debate, largely closed to ideas that she did not instinctively favour at the outset, though highly responsive to those ideas that fitted her pre-existing leanings.

The first years of Thatcherite economics were hardly a resounding success. Inflation fell. So did the deficit. Unemployment, however, had risen to over three million by 1983, most of the job losses falling in manufacturing industry. Much of what had been the distinctive character of the British economy and its workforce vanished. Public expenditure actually rose. So did taxation, instead of being reduced as the Conservatives had hoped. Austerity was the backdrop to serious riots in twelve of Britain's largest cities in 1981. Mrs Thatcher adamantly refused to alter course. The *Guardian* newspaper now predicted that the time had come to write the 'obituary of Thatcherism'.

The Argentinian invasion in April 1982 of the disputed Falkland Islands far away in the south Atlantic (long claimed by Argentina, though with a population overwhelmingly wedded to Britain) came to her rescue. The invasion was an affront to British national pride. Mrs Thatcher spoke for much of the country in her refusal to submit to blatant aggression. By the middle of June 1982, in a last hurrah of colonial-style expeditions that baffled much of Europe, British forces had retaken the

Falklands. For Thatcher, it proved that Britain was no longer a nation in decline. She herself gained new confidence from leadership in war. Politically, her own approval ratings, and those of her government, soared. The recession had meanwhile ended, growth had picked up, inflation had fallen, though unemployment remained stubbornly high. The corner seemed to have been turned. The general election of June 1983 produced a much-enlarged Conservative majority, while Labour slumped to the party's worst result since 1931 with a mere 28 per cent of the national vote. Thatcherism was triumphant – and triumphalist.

Crucial to restoring British greatness, in Thatcher's mind, was to break the power of the trade unions. She now prepared to take on the National Union of Mineworkers, the most powerful of the unions. Once again she was greatly aided by the inept leadership of her opponents. Under militant Marxist leaders, Arthur Scargill and Mick McGahey, the miners' union was thirsting for a showdown with the government. In April 1984 Scargill called the miners out on strike to prevent further pit closures in an already declining industry. But he refused to ballot the miners on strike action. The union split as miners in some parts of the country voted to continue working. A second tactical error was to attempt a coal strike in the summer months, and after the government had built up coal stocks.

The strike was an extraordinarily bitter confrontation. The scale of violence between striking miners and police reached levels not previously seen in Britain in the twentieth century. At Orgreave, a coking plant in south Yorkshire, a pitched battle raged on 18 June 1984 as police – later acknowledging that excessive violence had been used – charged on horseback into thousands of strikers. Television news that day carried scenes of police officers beating miners with truncheons, though no policeman was called to account for the excessive violence used. Dozens of miners were arrested on charges of rioting, which were later dismissed on grounds of unreliable police evidence. The strike petered out in early 1985, ending in March as the miners, their families suffering from the months without pay, were driven back to work. Over 11,000 arrests had been made in all. The strike hampered economic recovery. But from the government's point of view, it had been worth it. The National Union of Mineworkers lost half of its membership. The power of the unions was broken. Coal mining went into steep decline. In 1980 there had been 237,000 miners working in Britain. A decade later there were only 49,000.

After the Falklands War the miners' strike was a second major milestone in the Thatcher era. There was no middle ground. Mrs Thatcher polarized the population as no other post-war Prime Minister had done. She mirrored as well as articulated Britain's deep social divisions, anchored in traditions of class conflict. She gave voice to middle-class frustrations and resentment at the strongly felt national decline. But she engendered extraordinary alienation and hatred in much of the industrial working class that saw itself as the target of Conservative class-driven politics. The relatively well-off south of England provided her bedrock of support. The industrial regions of the north, Scotland and Wales were largely hostile territory. She never came close to winning the support of even half of the voting population in elections. And most people were repelled by her nineteenth-century values. The notion that the poor were a product of their own lack of effort was rejected by an overwhelming majority – in fact, by more people in the 1980s than during the previous decade.

What no one, friend or enemy, denied was that she was a politician of personal courage as well as remarkable determination. Both were prominently on display on 12 October 1984 when an IRA bomb exploded at the Grand Hotel in Brighton where ministers were staying during the Conservative Party Conference, coming close to killing her and much of the government, leaving five colleagues dead and others maimed for life. But Mrs Thatcher insisted that the Conference proceed as usual.

The IRA terrorist campaign was the most violent face of the complex problem of Northern Ireland – whether, as most of the majority Protestant population wanted, it should remain part of the United Kingdom, or whether, as the mainly Catholic minority of republican nationalists insisted, it should become part of a united Ireland. 'The Troubles', as they became known, had re-emerged in the late 1960s and descended the following decade into brutal ideological intransigence punctuated by horrific violence perpetrated by paramilitaries on both sides. By the time of the Brighton bomb, both Conservative and Labour governments had tried in vain to resolve, or at least contain, the problem. It continued to defy solution, also by the Thatcher government.

By the mid-1980s, at considerable cost to the social fabric and widening inequality, inflation had been controlled and the trade unions were weakened. What remained of the Thatcherite neo-liberal agenda was the crusade to shrink state expenditure, privatize nationalized industries, and cut welfare spending. Her large parliamentary majority provided the platform for Mrs Thatcher to tackle the underlying aim of her strategy: to rebalance Britain's economy and restore its national prestige.

Outside Britain the political consequences of the economic downturn were most serious in Italy. The country was simultaneously beset by the dramatically worsened economic situation, chronic governmental instability, continuing industrial conflict, widespread disaffection, and the worrying outbreaks of terrorist violence of revolutionary movements (notably the Red Brigades). Fears of a shift back towards the fascist right were behind the move by the leader of the Communist Party, Enrico Berlinguer, to forge a 'historic compromise' between the Communists, the Socialists and the Christian Democrats. Such an anti-fascist grand alliance would, he imagined, overcome the country's endemic difficulties and provide a new start for the country. Any such venture depended in part on the Communists themselves adapting to changed times. Berlinguer consequently led his party to turn its back on Moscow in favour of a new-style (if somewhat vague) 'Eurocommunism', which rejected both the Soviet model and the Social Democratic acceptance of the capitalist system. In practice, however, Eurocommunism tacitly acknowledged the need to work within capitalism to engineer a democratic road to a socialist society. It was an appealing message to many, especially in northern cities.

Seemingly en route to becoming Italy's largest party, the Communists made big gains in 1976. And since there was no prospect of a government of the centre-right, the Christian Democrats were compelled to look to left-wing parties. Berlinguer himself dismissed notions of a left-wing coalition of the Communists with the smaller Socialist Party since this might prompt the very swing to the extreme right that he was anxious to avoid. He was also wary of incurring the hostility of the United States, anxious at the advances of communism in Italy. He preferred, therefore, to enter an informal political alliance with the Christian Democrats. This lasted, despite intrinsic tensions, until the murder by the Red Brigades in May 1978 of the former Christian Democratic leader and Prime Minister, Aldo Moro (who had favoured the alliance).

Under the alliance the economy started to show signs that it was over the worst (in part owing to a greater level of cooperation between employers and unions), some significant improvements were made in welfare provision, and the framework for a national health service (replacing the earlier fragmented and uncoordinated provision) was instituted in 1978, though it did not function at all smoothly in practice. Not least, and no mean achievement given the opposition of the Catholic Church, abortion was legalized.

But cooperation with the Christian Democrats did the Communist Party little good. When it lost votes heavily in the elections of 1979 for the first time since the Second World War, the Communists returned to opposition. The Christian Democrats relied instead on coalition with the small, left-leaning Republican Party and with the Socialists whose leader, Bettino Craxi, eventually became Prime Minister in August 1983. Governmental instability was to remain a hallmark of Italian politics. But Craxi's strong personality and tactical adroitness enabled his administration to last for four years – longer than most.

And by the mid-1980s Italy's 'second economic miracle' was under way. This had looked anything but likely at the start of the decade, with inflation still at 21 per cent and minimal economic growth. But the steep economic recovery in the United States, the drop in the oil price, the decline in terrorism, and Craxi's firm government inaugurated a remarkable turnaround. This also owed more than a little to the increasing security felt in business circles after the powerful metalworkers union had been forced in 1980 to end its big strike and capitulate to aggressive tactics by their FIAT employers. Economic growth returned. Industrial losses turned to profits as exports benefited from the spreading international boom and domestic demand was fuelled by savings that people had made during the bad years from the 'black economy'. Neo-liberal precepts were introduced, as elsewhere. Privatization of unprofitable parts of industry began. Industrial restructuring reduced labour costs through extensive redundancies, and a climate of business enterprise replaced earlier collectivist values. Italy's national debt remained unhealthily high, however, while northern Italy benefited disproportionately from the growing economy, leaving the south, as ever, far behind.

The governments of Western Europe's other two biggest industrial nations, West Germany and France, navigated the economic storm-waves with fewer traumas than did either Britain or Italy. They faced similar economic problems as energy prices soared. But they handled them better. They benefited from strong economies that could cushion the worst of the oil shock. Their governments were also under highly competent new management. Helmut Schmidt succeeded Willy Brandt as Chancellor of West Germany on 16 May 1974 following the revelation that one of Brandt's closest aides, Günter Guillaume, had been spying for the East German intelligence services. Only three days later, Valéry Giscard d'Estaing, head of the centre-right Independent Republicans, narrowly defeated François Mitterrand in the French presidential election. Both men had solid experience and expertise in economic affairs, Schmidt as Brandt's Minister of Finance between 1972 and 1974, Giscard as Finance Minister to de Gaulle between 1962 and 1965. Schmidt – good-looking, relaxed, chain-smoking, confident bordering on arrogant – exuded an air of cool competence. Giscard – aristocratic in demeanour, telegenic, the very image of the modern technocrat in complete command of his brief – seemed the face of the future after the long paternalistic reign of Charles de Gaulle and his successor, Georges Pompidou.

West Germany's economy had continued to grow impressively, by almost 4 per cent a year on average between 1976 and 1979. Structural problems, many of them shared with other European countries, were, however, becoming more evident. Old industries such as coal mining and steel, employing huge numbers of workers, were becoming less competitive in world markets. Large-scale redundancies occurred as pits and steel-mills closed their gates. There were protests and strikes in industrial regions, though the traditions of corporate industrial relations, the willingness of trade unions to work constructively with government, and generous government subsidies to mitigate the social consequences in the worst afflicted areas, avoided the damaging conflicts that occurred in Britain and Italy.

Export-oriented industries suffered from the strength of the German mark. A way of adapting was to turn from mass production to specialized production. But modern technologies placed a high premium on expertise, based on skills and training. Unskilled workers accordingly found themselves disproportionately disadvantaged in the labour market. The trend in employment, as elsewhere in Western Europe, towards white-collar work in the service sector could not make up for the scale of the losses in industry or accommodate most of the unskilled employees who had lost their jobs. Nor did newer, upcoming, and rapidly growing branches of the economy in the service industries need large labour forces. Increasing unemployment was the inevitable result – a worry, especially for older Germans who still had vivid memories of the 1930s. Germans had an even greater fear of inflation. So the tripling of inflation rates to over 6 per cent per annum by the mid-1970s, if low by the standards of neighbouring countries, was a cause of anxiety. In West Germany, as elsewhere, there was no agreed recipe for dealing with 'stagflation'. But if no new economic model was plainly in view, it was clear that the old Keynesian solutions were out of date.

The second oil shock of 1979 was more damaging to the West German economy than the first, of 1973, had been. Economic growth slumped to only 1.9 per cent in 1980, minus 0.2 per cent in 1981 and minus 1.1 per cent in 1982. Unemployment reached post-war record levels – two million by 1983 (nearly a tenth of the workforce). Inflation at 6.1 per cent in 1981 remained stubbornly high. Wages, for those still in work, fell in terms of what they would buy. With rising state expenditure – partly because of the costs of high unemployment – and falling taxation revenues, state indebtedness increased; by 1982 it had more than quadrupled since 1970. Helmut Schmidt was by this time under pressure from the left of his party. The sharp economic downturn and growth in unemployment formed only part of the reason. Even more important were the mounting fears about nuclear power, which had been extensively developed in the 1970s to replace the dependency on oil, more voluble protest at the environmental damage caused by industrialization, and above all the resurgence of great anxiety about the likelihood of nuclear war as renewed tensions between the superpowers marked the end of détente and the inauguration of the 'second Cold War'.

In this climate the voices were becoming louder in the SPD's coalition partners, the Free Democratic Party (which spoke for many industrial leaders) for a change of economic direction – and a change of government. The breaking point of the coalition came when the Free Democrats published an analysis that proposed what amounted in effect to a turn towards neo-liberalism. This included cuts to unemployment pay and pensions, tax reductions, greater deregulation, higher investment, and more reliance on market forces than state intervention. It invited a collision with the trade union wing of the SPD, which remained set upon state intervention and close government steerage of the economy. The coalition had evidently reached the end of its life. Leaders of the FDP arranged to change coalition partners. On 1 October 1982, in a contrived move, Schmidt was replaced as Federal Chancellor by the Christian Democratic leader for a decade, Helmut Kohl. The FDP, the eternal survivor despite its small minority of voter support, remained in government.

West Germany – and Europe – had been fortunate to have Helmut Schmidt, 'the crisis Chancellor' (as the historian Heinrich August Winkler called him in one of the many glowing tributes that followed his death in November 2015) at the helm during the deeply troubled years of the 1970s. In temperament the cool, pragmatic Schmidt had been the opposite of his charismatic, visionary predecessor as Chancellor, Willy Brandt. But in dealing with the impact of both oil shocks and with the growing international tension at the end of the 1970s, Schmidt's expertise and judgement had been invaluable – and not just to his own country.

The political system had remained, in fact, extraordinarily stable during the economic turbulence of the 1970s. Both the major affiliations, the Social Democratic Party and the Christian Union (representing the twin parties of the Christian Democratic Union and the smaller Bavarian wing, the Christian Social Union), saw their membership swell in the 1970s. But by 1980 disenchanted Union voters, who found the right-wing candidate for Chancellor, Franz-Josef Strauss – highly popular in Bavarian bastions of Catholic conservatism, but distinctly less so elsewhere – an unappealing choice, had swung to the Free Democrats. They were the chief beneficiaries of the election that year, increasing their voter support to 10.6 per cent from 7.9 per cent in 1976. The Union was the loser, dropping to 44.5 per cent of the vote, while the SPD remained stable at 42.9 per cent. With the defeat of Strauss, the more moderate Kohl remained unchallenged as leader of the opposition. The result provided the framework for his stepping into government two years later.

Helmut Kohl's government followed the general course of Western European governments under the impact of the second oil crisis in steps to curtail government expenditure (and especially limit the growth of social spending), while increasing economic competitiveness through deregulation, a more flexible labour market, tax incentives and privatization. Although this naturally alienated the left and brought about political protests, the government, keen to avoid an abrupt alteration of course, steered clear of any incisively radical change of direction. There was no attempt to turn back the clock on the social improvements made during the era of Brandt and Schmidt, or to interfere with the rights of trade unions. State subsidies for old and struggling industries (most notably coal mining and steel) actually rose, despite the government's proclaimed intention gradually to remove them, in order to cushion the social hardship in traditional big industrial regions like the Ruhr or the Saarland. Continuity, certainly with the later phase of the Schmidt government, was more marked than any sharp break. West Germany avoided the intensely heated social conflict that the Thatcherite government had provoked in Britain. And the economy started to improve – helped greatly by the worldwide improvement as oil prices fell and the American economy grew sharply.

The combination of strong environmental concerns and acute nuclear fears – a sharper blend of protest than elsewhere in Europe – led by the early 1980s to the emergence of the first major new political movement in West Germany since the immediate post-war period, the creation of the Green Party. Already in the 1983 general election the Greens made their mark, coming from nowhere to win 5.6 per cent of the vote and gain twenty-eight seats in the Bundestag (the Federal parliament). Four parties, not the earlier three, from now on became players in the contest for political power. More important was that West German democracy, which many people still felt was insecure, had come through the first big economic downturn – one that had seen a rise in both unemployment and inflation – completely unshaken. It had been a remarkable post-war success story.

The equivalent post-war French success story of the 'thirty glorious years' seemed in grave danger of hitting the buffers when the first oil crisis struck. The long years of continuing boom had come to be seen as normal and permanent. After 1974 the pattern familiar from elsewhere set in. Inflation rose to over 15 per cent, while unemployment doubled to a million and growth plummeted to minus 0.3 per cent. President Giscard d'Estaing combined initial social reforms (for instance, liberalizing abortion and divorce laws) with a turn by 1976 to economic austerity. He replaced his main rival and increasingly disgruntled Prime Minister, the

Gaullist leader Jacques Chirac (elected Mayor of Paris the following year), with Raymond Barre, a highly experienced economist, though a technocrat rather than a skilled politician. Barre's brief was to balance the budget and modernize the economy. He acted to stabilize the franc, cut government expenditure, reduce labour costs and increase taxation.

The austerity measures naturally raised hackles on the Socialist and Communist left, still just about united around their 'common programme' of 1972. But Giscard also faced opposition from the right by the Gaullists, reshaped by Chirac in 1976 as the Rally for the Republic (*Rassemblement pour la République*, RPR). There were conservative objections to Giscard's social reforms. Personal rivalries and political bitterness were, however, more important than ideological divisions in separating the Gaullists and Giscard's restyled centre-right grouping, the Union of French Democracy (*Union pour la Démocratie Française*, UDF). Together, the Gaullists and the UDF won the 1978 parliamentary elections by a surprisingly large margin. They had been greatly helped by new divisions on the left. Municipal elections had pointed towards a victory for the left, as Barre's austerity measures began to bite. But the Communists, under Georges Marchais, retreated to more hard-line Marxism, fearing they were about to be overtaken in popularity by Mitterrand's Socialist Party, which had moved further towards reformism rather than outright rejection of a capitalist market economy. The Socialists won only slightly more of the vote (23 per cent) than the Communists (20 per cent) in 1978, but the wind was in their sails, all the more so since the Communist Party subsequently descended into bitter infighting.

Barre's reforms had meanwhile had some effect in stabilizing the economy. But the electoral success emboldened Giscard and Barre to move further towards economic liberalism. Competition, deregulation of prices and exposure to the free market were encouraged. There were, however, no great steps as yet towards the privatization of major industries. State direction of the economy, a long-standing tradition in France, was maintained. Heavy state subsidies continued to be central to planning in aviation, the telephone network, railways, the car industry and, not least, the building of nuclear power stations. As was the case in other Western European countries, the French steel industry was struggling to stay competitive in the face of imports from Asia and parts of Eastern Europe, where production costs were much lower. The state intervened to take over some of its debts and fund retraining schemes, though closing the most unprofitable steel-mills, with huge job losses amid heated protests in the stricken communities in the north and in Lorraine.

Business profitability returned, helped by reductions in corporate taxation and lower wage bills. But Barre had overestimated the speed and strength of recovery. And the strong franc was an obstacle to exports. The second oil crisis of 1979 then blew the deflationary programme completely off course. Inflation rose again, to 14 per cent. Unemployment, too, increased, reaching 1.5 million in 1980 and moving upwards. There was much public sympathy for the distress in the industrial regions worst affected. Barre became more unpopular than ever. The Socialists and Communists, for all their divisions, gained ground with their promises of job creation and state intervention to stimulate the economy. More, not less, state socialism was seen as the route to economic recovery.

Such promises of national renewal after years of an increasingly unpopular and fractured governing coalition took François Mitterrand to victory in the April–May 1981 presidential election with 51 per cent of the vote. After twenty-three years of continuous power, the Gaullist stranglehold on French government was over. The joy on the left was undiluted. It was further amplified when the Socialists took command of the National Assembly only a month after Mitterrand's triumph. The new government took immediate steps to reverse the deflationary policy. Keynesianism was restored to favour. Wages, pensions and child benefit were increased. The retirement age was lowered. The working week was reduced. Funds were provided for building new homes and the creation of 150,000 jobs. A youth employment scheme was introduced. Taxation of the most wealthy was increased. Extensive nationalization was planned. Export industries were encouraged by devaluation of the franc.

The policies were an unmitigated failure. Growth was far lower than anticipated. The balance of payments worsened as foreign imports grew. Inflation remained high (in stark contrast to neighbouring West Germany, where it fell). And unemployment continued to rise. Mitterrand was forced within less than two years into a complete reversal of his promised economic policy. A price and wage freeze had already been introduced in June 1982. The following March the franc was devalued for the third time within eighteen months. Public expenditure cuts – notably on social security – followed, taxes were increased for much of the population, but reduced for business, and the first moves towards privatization of nationalized industries were taken. The results of the 180-degree shift were modest. Within two years inflation had fallen, as had the balance of payments. Unemployment, on the other hand, still stood at over 10 per cent of the working population, while growth was only 1.9 per cent in 1985. When the Gaullists returned to government in March 1986 they found that their socialist predecessors had paved the way for the further moves towards neo-liberalism.

An ever-repeated mantra of Thatcherism across Western Europe was that, as far as the economy was concerned, 'there is no alternative'. Was this true? Deflation had been a painful but necessary remedy everywhere, given the double recession after the two oil crises. The turn to forms of neo-liberal economics was general by the mid-1980s, whatever the colour of the government. Mitterrand's experiment in France was the clearest demonstration that the old Keynesian recipes no longer worked in the face of a global economic downturn that had produced stagflation. His volte-face demonstrated to an entire generation of politicians that international conditions had severely narrowed the economic options of national governments. Yet West Germany, France, and also the more unstable Italy had shown that even within deflationary economics and the politics of recession there had been alternatives to the ideologically driven and conflict-ridden extreme neo-liberalism adopted only by the Thatcher government.

DEMOCRACY TRIUMPHS

While Western European democracies struggled to adjust to the effects of the oil crisis there was good news to the south. The authoritarian regimes of Greece, Portugal and Spain collapsed within months of each other in 1974–5. Was this simply coincidence? Or were there deeper causes of the transformation?

Before the Second World War pluralist parliamentary democracy had, apart from a cluster of countries in north-western Europe, been a contested system of government, rejected both by powerful elites (especially in the military) and by wide swathes of the population. By the early 1980s it was welcomed everywhere in Western Europe – with the partial exception of Turkey, the most peripheral country in the western bloc, where the military remained the determining force in politics. It amounted to a remarkable and lasting transformation, a triumph for democracy.

Political change in Greece, as in much of the rest of Western Europe, had appeared in the early 1960s to be moving towards the left. The conservative right wing which, backed by the military, had run Greece since the end of the civil war of 1946–9 in what was little more than a facade democracy, had become increasingly unpopular and was ousted in elections in 1963. But the military viewed the new government's proposed liberal reforms as a Trojan Horse for the return of communism. When King Constantine II forced the government out of office in 1965 it prompted a constitutional crisis and rising popular unrest. To forestall new elections in May 1967 right-wing army officers headed by Colonel George Papadopoulos, fearing steps in a left-leaning government to bring the army under civilian control, purge the leadership, reduce military expenditure and terminate the American presence in Greece, staged a coup on 21 April.

The king failed in a badly executed attempt to wrest control back in a counter-coup and fled into exile in what turned out to be a permanent end to the Greek monarchy. The 'rule of the colonels', as it became known, was quickly consolidated. A junta of twelve colonels, the 'Revolutionary Council', was established. Papadopoulos was from the start, however, the dominant figure, eventually combining the positions of Prime Minister and other key ministries – notably foreign affairs and defence – with the regency that was set up after the king's attempted counter-coup. Political parties were dissolved, thousands of left-wing sympathizers were arrested (and many tortured in prison), civil rights were suspended, and rigorous censorship of the media was imposed, while numerous opponents fled abroad. The regime worked closely with industrial leaders, supported agriculture, backed tourism, and started a number of big construction projects. Economic growth was at first strong, though it started to sag badly in the early 1970s. Greece's image abroad suffered as criticism of the regime's assault on human rights mounted. But the regime was propped up by support from the United States, concerned more about its vehement anti-communism than its appalling human rights record. Nor was there any united opposition to

the regime by the Western European democracies. While the Netherlands and the Scandinavian countries were forthright in their hostility,
Britain and West Germany voiced criticism of the regime's brutal practices but tacitly backed a country seen as vital to NATO interests.

More significant in the growing crisis of the colonels' rule was internal
opposition which, despite the repression, could not be silenced. The
problems became apparent of trying to install a neo-fascist regime in a
Western European network of countries wedded to the principles of liberal democracy and human rights. When Papadopoulos sought in
lukewarm fashion to hedge off trouble by introducing minor liberalizing
measures (including the partial lifting of censorship and release of some
political prisoners), all that he succeeded in doing was to embolden
opposition while antagonizing a hard-line faction within the regime. The
army was sent in to suppress a big student demonstration against the
regime in Athens Polytechnic in mid-November 1973, resulting in a number of deaths and many injuries, but the unrest prompted Brigadier
Dimitrios Ioannidis, head of the dreaded Military Police, to overthrow Papadopoulos days later and restore order by the reimposition of
martial law.

The rule of Ioannidis was only of short duration. His own downfall
came after his regime had sponsored a bungled attempt by the Cypriot
national guard to overthrow the president, Archbishop Makarios, with a
view to incorporating Cyprus into Greece – a long-standing desire of the
Greek right. Makarios managed to escape and eventually make his way
to Britain. But the failed coup prompted a Turkish invasion and occupation of northern Cyprus in July 1974, forcing around 200,000 Greek
Cypriots to flee south. The Greek Junta tried to mobilize armed retaliation, though in vain, since it had lost the backing of the army. The
colonels' regime no longer had its crucial prop.

The military that had overthrown democracy in Greece in 1967 now
took steps to reinstate it. A faction of officers withdrew support for Ioannidis. The former conservative Prime Minister, Konstantinos Karamanlis,
was summoned back from his exile in Paris and promptly began the
return to civilian democratic government. His coalition government
restored the constitution of 1952 and freed political prisoners. Elections
in November 1974, the first for ten years, gave New Democracy, the conservative party led by Karamanlis, an absolute majority. One measure

introduced by the colonels' regime survived its demise, for in 1973 the Junta had abolished the monarchy. In December 1974 a referendum rejected its restoration. Greece was from now on a republic, with a new constitution (introduced in 1975) and a democratic system of government. Confirming the break with the past, the leaders of the Junta were later tried and sentenced to lengthy terms of imprisonment.

Greece remained, however, desperately poor, its economy grossly inefficient, and its clientelist political system riddled with corruption. Despite such evident weaknesses, Western Europe's democratic leaders were anxious to prevent any possible reversion at some point to authoritarianism. They swiftly moved to accept Greece back into the Council of Europe, which it had left during the colonels' rule. Before the colonels took power, Greece had enjoyed associate membership of the European Economic Community – suspended during the years of the Junta – and had been promised sizeable financial aid to modernize its economy. After his return to office Karamanlis began a new drive for Greece's membership. He saw this as essential for the country's prosperity, which in turn would go far towards consolidating its democracy. European Community leaders saw the weight of the argument. Entry negotiations began already in 1976. Within five years, earlier indeed than anticipated, on 1 January 1981 Greece became the tenth member. It was, however, much weaker economically than the other nine. Political not economic priorities had been behind its admission.

A lingering oddity and, as would prove, insoluble legacy of the colonels' rule was the division of Cyprus. The situation rapidly became stalemate. Greece withdrew from NATO (eventually returning in 1980) in protest at its failure to condemn Turkey's invasion. Turkey refused the demands of the United Nations to withdraw its troops. Makarios returned as President to the Greek part of the island, though of course without Turkish recognition. The smaller Turkish part of the island was in contrast recognized solely by Turkey. With a 'green line' down the middle of the island, presided over by a United Nations peacekeeping force, the division of Cyprus was set to remain for the rest of the twentieth century – and beyond.

On the Iberian peninsula the long-standing dictatorships of Portugal (since 1926) and Spain (since 1939) still stood semi-detached from the rest of Western Europe. But their rulers were old and infirm. Portugal's political system had been almost preserved in aspic under its longest-serving Prime Minister, António de Oliveira Salazar. Its economy, too, was unmodernized. As part of EFTA since 1968, Portugal had started to benefit modestly from improved trade relations but was still economically backward. Tourism, unlike in Spain, was still not a major entity. Many thousands of Portuguese had to leave home each year to work abroad (sending home important subsidies, which supported the domestic economy). But the big drain on the economy was the colonial empire – an increasingly expensive anachronism that required nearly half of government expenditure going on the military, and compelling unpopular conscription to the army for young Portuguese needed to repel the guerrilla warfare of anti-colonial movements in Angola, Mozambique and Guinea-Bissau. Opposition to the colonial wars grew. It was even voiced by sectors of the Catholic Church, which had traditionally been such a staunch ally of the authoritarian state but now reflected the more liberal stance that had developed since the Second Vatican Council (1962–5).

When Salazar, who had ruled since 1932, suffered a bad stroke in 1968 and died two years later, it marked the beginning of the end. The creaking system continued, only marginally liberalized, under his successor, Marcello Caetano, though it was living on borrowed time. A brief consumer boom funded largely by borrowing abroad soon petered out. Economic unrest was widespread, not just among poorly paid workers. Inflation in the wake of the oil crisis was as high as 30 per cent by 1974. The most dangerous development for the regime was the disaffection of young officers, who were angered not only by their low pay but also at fighting bitter and dangerous colonial wars in an evidently lost cause. The military had brought the regime into existence in 1926 and long been its essential prop. Once a section of the officer corps turned against it, as they did in a putsch during the night of 24–25 April 1974, it was doomed.

What would follow the successful coup d'état was unclear. It was far from evident that democracy would emerge triumphant. At first a military council, the National Salvation Junta, took control under the putschist leader General António Spínola – former deputy head of the army's general staff. But it was unable to bring stability. Spínola was eventually ousted and fled to Spain. The uprising spread, both within the military and in the civilian population. There was enormous euphoria at what was dubbed 'the carnation revolution' (after the flowers on the uniforms and in the rifle muzzles of the insurgents). 'The red carnations decorate tee-shirts and glasses,' noted the British politician Judith Hart, during a visit to Portugal in the summer of 1975. 'The posters proclaiming freedom and democracy and the power of the people are everywhere.' Turbulence continued for two years. Six provisional governments came and went; and two coups were attempted, one from the right, the other from the left. The country remained mired in unrest. Strikes, factory occupations, land seizures and flights of capital were manifestations of bitter political and ideological divisions. The Communists appeared to be the strongest political force. However, elections to the Constituent Assembly in April 1975 showed that popular backing for communism was in fact weak. The Socialist Party, under Mário Soares, gained most support, with 38 per cent of the vote. The Liberals won just over 26 per cent. The Communists trailed with only 12.5 per cent of the vote.

As their hopes of power diminished, left-wing radicals in the military – riven by numerous factions – attempted another coup, in November 1975. It proved their swan song. The rising was put down by the state-supportive forces under General Ramalho Eanes. Army reforms were swiftly put in place and the power of the military was curbed. The radical left lost influence in the military. Communism was meanwhile forced to the political fringes. A new constitution in April 1976 established the framework for civilian government and, following new elections later in the month (in which the Socialist Party again emerged victorious), a measure of calm descended upon the disturbed political scene. General Eanes, popular after repelling the putsch attempt the previous November, was elected as President with the backing of all parties except the Communists, who from now on were excluded from power. Eanes provided the necessary symbol of national unity. Soares, supported financially by the West German Social Democratic Party, was the key political player in the early stage of Portugal's transition to parliamentary democracy. But it was still a rocky road.

Portugal's colonial empire had been wound up during the year after the 'carnation revolution'. With that, the last of the major European colonial empires was gone and the era of colonial imperialism was finally over. But it was a bloody ending. The Portuguese left their former possessions in a terrible state. There was no smooth process of decolonization. East Timor was seized by Indonesia. Angola was wracked by civil war. Mozambique also soon descended into civil war, while revolutionary forces turned Guinea-Bissau into a one-party state that took violent revenge against former supporters of the colonial regime. Across Africa hundreds of thousands of Portuguese colonial settlers fled, leaving behind all that they had owned, returning home to add to the burdens of Portugal's struggling economy.

Land reforms, already set in place, started to reverse the expropriations that had taken place after the revolution and bring an end to the inefficient collective farms. But in 1977–8, amid continuing unrest, high unemployment and heavy state indebtedness, with average per-capita income little over half of the average in the European Community countries, Portugal was forced to seek financial aid from the International Monetary Fund. It came, though with strings attached. Austerity measures were introduced, gradually reducing the high debts of the state through reductions in expenditure and more balanced budgets, but at the cost of prolonging the high unemployment and continued economic backwardness of the country. Governmental instability continued, with nine governments in seven years between 1976 and 1983. Soares was ousted in 1978. The executive powers of President Eanes, elected to office but still commander-in-chief of the armed forces, to intervene in national politics (which he frequently did), were curtailed only by constitutional changes in 1982. A genuinely civilian presidency with limited powers was only instigated with the narrow victory, by direct suffrage, of Mário Soares in a two-stage election in 1985–6. Only by that stage could the democratic system in Portugal be regarded as solidly based.

Soares himself had in 1977 instigated the approach to the European Community that would develop into formal negotiations on Portugal's entry the following year. The country's economic problems meant that membership could not be achieved overnight and complex negotiations dragged on until 1984. In 1986 the step was finally taken: Portugal had come in from the periphery to become a member of the European Community. It was by this time a settled Western European democracy, its long years of dictatorship a fading memory.

The progress of the 'carnation revolution' was closely followed across the border by Portugal's near neighbour as the long rule of General

Franco drew to a close. There was apprehension among would-be reformers at the turbulence in Portugal and, especially, the advances on the communist left.

Much-needed reforms, introduced in 1959, had opened Spain's backward economy to international markets, bringing growth at over 7 per cent per year during the 1960s. Rural Spain, the regime's backbone, started to empty as labour drained to the cities or to the rapidly growing tourist resorts. In the wake of growth, too, came demands for higher wages and better working conditions in expanding industries. Working-class unrest, especially in the industrial regions of Catalonia and the Basque Country, intensified. Trade unions were still banned and strikes were illegal, but workers nonetheless formed collective bodies that organized protests, strikes and demonstrations. And the number was rising. There were 1,595 strikes in 1970, 2,290 in 1974 and 3,156 in 1975 (resulting that year in the loss of 14.5 million working hours). In the Basque Country the unrest fed into separatist politics that in turn in 1968 had spawned an armed nationalist movement, ETA (*Euzkadi Ta Askatasuna*, Basque Homeland and Freedom), which began a prolonged and bitter terrorist campaign against the regime and its successor.

As the Francoist regime visibly faced growing and insurmountable challenges, the iron fist was almost its only response. As late as 1974 some 6,000 Spaniards languished in jail awaiting trial on political charges. Torture was commonly used in the jails. Prisoners were deprived of legal support. There was also a return to the use of the death penalty as part of a military crackdown. No executions had taken place between 1963 and 1974 as Spain had tried to show its best face to the world. But there were five executions only a month before Franco's death in November 1975.

Meanwhile, the beaches of the Costa Brava guaranteed sunshine, and cheap package holidays had already by the 1960s started to attract millions of tourists each year. They exposed Spaniards to external cultural influences that inevitably clashed with the traditional values of Catholic Spain. These values were in any case being eroded in the aftermath of the Second Vatican Council. In fact, even the Catholic Church, since the civil war the ideological bulwark of Francoism, was turning away from the regime. By 1970 far more priests sympathized with socialism than with the state's official falangist ideology, while the Church hierarchy defended human rights and spoke out in favour of political neutrality.

Young people, especially, found the regime's moral rigidities stifling. A slight relaxation of censorship in 1966 did not go nearly far enough. In 1968 a minority of young, well-educated people courageously showed that they were not prepared to accept authoritarian rule. Student demonstrators in Madrid and other Spanish university cities, inspired by what was happening in other parts of Western Europe, motivated by their strong opposition to the Vietnam War and to American bases in Spain, and hostile to a dictatorship resting on political repression, faced the wrath of Franco's regime. Some were sentenced to long imprisonment for their defiance. The gulf between the repressive state and the demands of a society looking for liberalization and democratization was immense.

Some in the state bureaucracy recognized, in fact, that liberalization was necessary, and that this would open the door to closer relations with the European Economic Community, which in turn would offer greater prospects of prosperity and modernization for backward Spain. The unbending Francoist dictatorship, dependent in its workings upon the military, the security services, and entrenched oligarchies in the bureaucracy and business, stood in the way of any such moves. But the regime faced the obvious question of who or what would follow Franco. His close entourage had in December 1968 regarded it as a sign of the dictator's impending mortality when he interrupted a cabinet meeting to go to the toilet – something, impervious to the discomfort of his ministers with less iron bladder control during interminably long meetings, he had never done before. It had been the 'triumph of the continent over the incontinent', one of them had later quipped. Franco held on, in fact, for a further seven years, though his long life – he celebrated his eightieth birthday in December 1972 and was in poor health – was obviously drawing to a close.

He had addressed the problem of the succession in 1969 by turning back to the vacant monarchy and anointing Prince Juan Carlos as his heir – thus retaining power while preparing his successor to take over the authoritarian regime. A staging post was evidently foreseen in the appointment as Prime Minister in June 1973 of Admiral Luis Carrero Blanco, among Franco's most long-standing and diehard supporters, who held many of the levers of power in his hands. Carrero Blanco, it was imagined, would secure the continuity of the authoritarian regime.

Such plans literally went up in smoke when Carrero Blanco was killed by a bomb planted by ETA terrorists on 20 December 1973. Even had he lived and succeeded Franco as head of state, it is questionable whether the creaking authoritarian regime could have survived much longer. As it was, both Franco and the regime he ruled entered their death-throes. The predictable reversion to overt repression after Carrero Blanco's assassination only served to increase Spain's international isolation as a pariah nation. And the country's economic woes had meanwhile been intensified by the price rises in the wake of the oil crisis. Only Franco's mortality, it seemed, blocked the route to inevitable change.

Richard Nixon's Secretary of State, Henry Kissinger, had commented during a visit to Madrid in 1970 that Spain was 'waiting for a life to end so that it could rejoin European history'. Five years later the wait for the life to end was over. Franco's health had deteriorated sharply during 1975 and on 20 November the last of the pre-war European dictators died, by then a physical wreck. The only head of state present at the funeral was the Chilean dictator, General Augusto Pinochet (whose repressive regime, following the overthrow of Chile's elected government of President Salvador Allende in 1973, would have met with Franco's approval). Foreign dignitaries demonstrably turned up, however, four days later for the coronation of King Juan Carlos. Pinochet was this time not invited.

The king's coronation symbolized the beginning of a new era. But no one knew how that would turn out. Would the king preside over some continuing form of authoritarianism? Would there be another bloodbath? Or would there be moves to introduce democracy? Not least: how would the army, the mainstay of the regime's power and suspicious of the king, react to the demise of the dictator? There was widespread rejoicing at the end of Francoism. But there were also fears for the future. It was an uncertain one for a country that had torn itself apart so recently and was still living with the consequences. Crucially, though not plainly to be foreseen, the king, if at first cautiously, placed the weight of his popular legitimacy as the monarch on the side of the forces pressing for democratization. He was no instinctive democrat. But he recognized the way the wind was blowing. The huge demonstrations and mass strikes that had taken place in the immediate aftermath of Franco's death had convinced him that this was the only way forward. As in Portugal, parties, factions and movements, though still officially proscribed, started to take shape. But decisive change came from within the structures of the old regime. In effect, the Francoist state gradually dismantled its own power structures.

Beyond his support for democratic forces, a vital step was the king's replacement of the hard-line and unpopular Arias Navarro as Prime Minister by Adolfo Suárez in January 1976. It was no abrupt change to a democratic champion. But it proved a crucial choice. Suárez, a Falangist who had held a number of positions in Franco's government, had earlier been seen as a reactionary. His contacts with reformist groups within the Franco regime had convinced him, however, that Spain's future lay with democracy, and that the popular legitimacy of the monarchy, and Juan Carlos's own commitment, offered the surest route to that goal. A revolutionary break with the regime could risk renewed civil war. A transition had to be negotiated with the left.

Speed was of the essence, before the Francoist establishment could react. Suárez offered a referendum on political reform and elections by June 1977. He skilfully courted the Socialists – themselves recognizing that constitutional government, not violent revolution, was the best way to remove the remnants of the regime – while using his support from the king to placate army leaders, neutralize the moderates on the right, and isolate hard-line Francoists. Remarkably, through financial inducements and promises of future advancement, Suárez persuaded the deputies of the National Movement, the single party in the Cortes (the Spanish Parliament), to vote in favour of the reforms as the only way to prevent serious conflict. In a rare case of turkeys voting for Christmas, the members of the Cortes accordingly voted themselves out of existence.

In the referendum on 15 December 1976 an overwhelming 94 per cent of voters backed the changes. On 15 June 1977, for the first time in over forty years, pluralist elections were held in Spain. The old parties of the left, including the Communists, had meanwhile been legalized – earning Suárez the enmity of the Francoist diehards. Suárez's Union of the Democratic Centre (*Unión de Centro Democrático*) – a coalition of centrists and the reformist right, patched together by much backstairs wheeler-dealing – proved victorious, with 34 per cent of the votes, but the Socialists gained 29 per cent. The vote overall gave a strong imprimatur to constitutional parliamentary democracy. Radical parties, left and right, did badly. The Communists, with only 9 per cent, gained far fewer votes than had been expected, while the various factions of the neo-fascist radical right could only between them manage under 2 per cent of the vote. A little over a year later, on 31 October 1978, a new, democratic constitution was approved in parliament and ratified by the population in a referendum on 6 December.

But the problems were soon mounting for Suárez. By 1977 he had to contend with rampant inflation, sharply rising unemployment, and shrill demands for autonomy in Catalonia and the Basque Country (echoed, if less vigorously, in other regions). The grant of limited devolved powers by no means quelled the demands. The Basques, especially, pressed for independence from Madrid. Acts of terrorist violence carried out by ETA would continue for years to cause fear and revulsion within the Spanish population.

Under increased pressure, his popularity plummeting, Suárez resigned as Prime Minister on 25 January 1981. A month later, the fledgling Spanish democracy had to withstand a last attempt to derail it by hard-line Francoists. On 23 February Lieutenant-Colonel Antonio Tejero of the Civil Guard and around 200 of his men stormed into the Cortes and proceeded at gunpoint to hold the members of parliament hostage. The attempted coup collapsed only after King Juan Carlos had addressed the people on television, declared his support for the constitution, and ordered the troops back to their barracks. Three days after the coup's failure – Tejero later served fifteen years in a military prison for his part in the debacle – three million people demonstrated in Spanish cities in favour of democracy, one and a half million in Madrid alone. Democracy was safe.

After the elections of 1982 the Socialist Party, which had turned its back on its earlier Marxist programme, returned to political power in Spain for the first time since 1936. It was to remain in office for the next fourteen years. Felipe Gonzáles, the new socialist Prime Minister, pushed ahead with the process of reforming internal structures of the civil service and military. He also used his popular backing and parliamentary majority to implement an economic austerity programme using monetary and fiscal measures to reduce high inflation and a heavy deficit in government spending. Wages were pegged below inflation levels. Greater flexibility in the labour market was promoted. Spending on social security was lowered. Some moves towards privatization of state-owned industries were initiated, but there was no consistent privatization policy and the public sector remained large (though possessing many businesses that the private sector did not want). Elements of neo-liberalism were thus incorporated in the programme of a socialist government. It was a further sign of the economic trend across Western Europe.

The government reversed the earlier opposition by the Socialist Party to Spain's membership of NATO (which it joined in May 1982), though it also insisted on reducing the number of American bases in Spain, a policy supported by a popular majority in a referendum in March 1986. Just before then, on 1 January, Spain had been admitted, alongside Portugal, to the European Community, ending a process that had begun in 1977. With that move, Spain had finally rejoined European history.

The emerging new democracies in Greece, Portugal and Spain completed the post-war triumph of democratic pluralist systems of government throughout Western Europe. There were obviously significant differences between the preceding three dictatorships, and the way in which they collapsed. And there were indeed undoubted elements of coincidence. Greece's rule of the colonels was a recent and brief (if for its victims seemingly endless) interruption of pluralist government, however imperfect Greek democracy had been. Its collapse had been triggered by the external events of the Turkish invasion of Cyprus. The authoritarian systems in Portugal and Spain, in contrast, had been built over decades and had established far deeper roots than had the Greek dictatorship. The fates of both systems were closely entwined with the personalities and ideologies of their long-standing rulers, Salazar in Portugal, Franco in Spain. Unsurprisingly, therefore, the physical decline then death of these dictators ushered in the disintegration of the regimes. The regime in Portugal was the only one whose problems were closely linked to the liberation struggles in a colonial empire. Its collapse led to more prolonged turbulence than in the other two countries. And of the three regimes, only Spain restored the monarchy, which itself – somewhat unpredictably – became the most vital stabilizing factor in the consolidation of democracy.

Beyond the coincidental and contingent, however, there were more deep-lying reasons for the termination of the three quite different dictatorships. Crucially, the authoritarian regimes were all deeply out of tune with an increasingly internationalist, libertarian and strongly anti-militaristic culture that had spread rapidly since the mid-1960s, especially among younger people. Youth protest was a significant feature of the gathering opposition to authoritarianism in each of the three countries.

The rigidly repressive attempt to uphold nationalistic cultural values that seemed to belong to the unattractive face of bygone times could not hold back the liberating tide that was with extraordinary speed crossing national frontiers despite the desires of the rulers.

Nor could economies any longer be run as closed systems based on ideas of national autarchy. Greece, Portugal and Spain could not escape the vagaries of global capitalism any more than the Western democracies could, and their economies were less well equipped to cope with the oil crisis. The three countries were in fact already experiencing fundamental social and economic transition. All had been partially transformed by the industrialization that had gathered pace in the two decades or so before their collapse – Spain by mass tourism as well. This had greatly reduced the size of the rural population and served to undermine traditional structures of the family and Church. The countryside had earlier provided much of the base of support for authoritarianism. The modernizing changes in the economy greatly weakened this support, while strengthening the industrial working classes, with their predominant ideological base in socialism and communism, still capable of mobilizing mass backing despite long years of repression. Not least, in the European Community, Western European democracies offered a stark, and successful, alternative to the backward dictatorships – one rooted in international cooperation and liberal democracy. It had brought prosperity to other parts of Europe that Greeks, Portuguese and Spaniards could only dream of as long as their authoritarian regimes remained in place. Almost the first thing that the leaders of the democratic forces did, once authoritarianism had been ousted, was to make overtures to the European Community with regard to their entry. Greece joined in 1981, Portugal and Spain five years later. It was the ticket, as their new governments had foreseen, to previously unimaginable prosperity and liberalization.

Cultural and economic transformation meant that dictatorship, resting heavily upon the backing of the military, was an outdated and dysfunctional, as well as grossly inhumane, form of government. As stable democracies had been consolidated in most of Western Europe and the prospect of conventional war in the region had all but disappeared, societies had increasingly come to be dominated by civilian, not militaristic, values. The military, between the two world wars such a baleful force in politics for the most part, and invariably supportive of authoritarianism, by now played no central role in domestic politics. Only in Greece and on the Iberian peninsula (apart from Turkey, on Europe's fringes) had the military still remained the dominant political force. But its power was now largely directed at internal repression to bolster authoritarian regimes. Spain's military had no role outside the country, Portugal's only an increasingly reluctant one in fighting attritional colonial wars, while Greece's had shown itself incapable of preventing the Turkish occupation of northern Cyprus. In each case, the military had lost much of whatever prestige it had once had. It was justifiably viewed by much of the population as no more than a repressive, reactionary force that stood in the way of freedom and progress. And the best guarantee of attaining these, as most people recognized, was by pluralist parliamentary democracy. The era of the one-party state, which had claimed to be the only means of national defence against threats from the enemy within as well as external enemies, had had its day in a peaceful, prosperous and liberal Western Europe.

In none of the three cases did dictatorship, for all its travails, simply implode or evaporate. Nor was it just swept away by economic problems, severe though these were. Powerful forces had upheld authoritarian rule. Their dominance could only be ended when the social and cultural pressures that had built up coincided with the evident weakness of the regimes, and found agencies within the ruling echelons that were prepared to support reform, change and progress towards democracy. Precisely this constellation emerged in Greece, Portugal and Spain by the mid-1970s. The dramatic changes altered the prospects permanently for the people of those countries as they were brought into the European fold. By then, within only a few years, democracy in all three countries had been consolidated, and had gained the backing of the overwhelming majority of the population.

THE COLD WAR RETURNS

While Europe, east and west, had been submerged in economic crisis during the 1970s, the international scene had paradoxically brightened considerably. With the United States bogged down in a costly war in Vietnam – it would end with the withdrawal of American troops and the entry of the North Vietnamese army into Saigon in April 1975 – and the Soviet Union keen to avoid a deepening rapprochement between America and China, the prospects arose of a reduction in international tension through putting the brakes on the dangerous escalation in nuclear weaponry. The American–Soviet agreements reached in 1972–3 were a beginning. So was the attempt to provide a firmer base for international relations in the Conference on Security and Cooperation in Europe (CSCE) held in Helsinki during July and 1 August 1975. Thirty-five states were represented, including the superpowers, Canada, and all European states other than Albania (which refused to take part). The Soviet Union had initiated the Conference in the hope of gaining ratification of the post-war territorial settlement in Eastern Europe. The Helsinki Final Act (Helsinki Accords) of 1975 did not fully meet these hopes since it accepted the inviolability of frontiers and banned annexation of territory under international law. It did, however, allow for peaceful change of borders – widely viewed as a diplomatic victory for the Soviet Union.

What amounted to something of an own goal for the Soviet Union, however, was the commitment, enshrined in the agreement, to respect 'human rights and fundamental freedoms'. Soviet leaders viewed the commitment cynically. They could decide what this amounted to within the Soviet Union. 'We are masters in our own house,' Andrei Gromyko, the Soviet Foreign Minister, reminded his colleagues. This was to underrate the loss of moral ground internationally when the Soviet Union and its satellites continued to lock up thousands of dissidents while paying lip service to human rights. Nevertheless, Soviet political and military strength could withstand moral condemnation. And the defusing of international tension, to which the Helsinki Accords had contributed, bolstered rather than undermined that strength.

Détente, however, was never more than partial. It provided in fact a fig leaf for the military of each of the superpowers behind which they could continue their nuclear weapons programmes, striving for superiority. President Jimmy Carter had indeed pledged during his election campaign in 1976 to seek cuts in the nuclear arsenal. But his emphasis on human rights – including welcoming Soviet dissidents to the White House – unsurprisingly encouraged Brezhnev to drag his feet on the planned follow-up to the original SALT I agreement of 1972 to limit nuclear arsenals. Eventually, SALT II was signed by Carter and Brezhnev in Vienna, amid much pomp and ceremony, in June 1979, with the aim of reducing and limiting nuclear weaponry. Carter declared it 'a historic contribution to world peace'. But it was a dead letter from the start. The US Congress was unhappy about parts of the treaty. Then the Soviet invasion of Afghanistan in December destroyed any hope of ratification. 'There goes SALT II,' Carter remarked as news of the invasion came through. By the end of the year détente had collapsed.

In 1977 the USSR had begun stationing new intermediate-range SS-20 nuclear missiles in East Germany as well as in the Soviet Union. With a range of 5,000 kilometres they did not fall within the criteria of the SALT agreement. But they posed an obvious and direct threat to Western Europe. The West German Chancellor, Helmut Schmidt, devised a bold response. President Carter (whom Schmidt held in barely concealed contempt) had initially opposed the move before finally yielding to German pressure. In January 1979 Western leaders agreed to Schmidt's proposal to counter the threat by stationing American intermediate-range missiles in Western Europe, mainly in West Germany. In December NATO reached a 'twin-track resolution': to deploy, mainly in West Germany and Britain, hundreds of cruise and Pershing II missiles (capable of reaching Moscow within ten minutes), while at the same time continuing to work with the Soviet Union towards nuclear arms control.

The clouds were already darkening by this time. The Islamic revolution swiftly swept over Iran after the deposition of the Shah and return of Ayatollah Khomeini in 1979. Its consequences would be felt, in Europe and the world beyond, for the rest of the century and beyond.

So would what happened in Afghanistan, washed over by outlying waves from the Iranian revolution. An Afghan communist leader, Mohammed Taraki, had seized power in Kabul in April 1978 and set up a communist government. Taraki was himself murdered by a rival, Hafizulla Amin, in September 1979. But support for the communist regime was shallow – more or less limited to the small, educated sector of a largely illiterate population. Amin's control rapidly disintegrated. Events in Iran fired up Afghan opposition to the planned reforms – which included secular education and women's rights. In backward rural areas, tribally run and impenetrable to modernizing forces, religious leaders helped to stir resistance to the 'infidel'. In near civil-war conditions, and given it had helped to establish a communist regime, the Soviet Union's leaders considered intervention to restore order. The move was necessary, it was thought, to protect the southern borders of the USSR and to head off any possible internal destabilization as a result of Islamic influence on its own large Muslim population in the Central Asian republics.

In December 1979 the fateful decision was taken to send in troops. Soviet leaders thought the intervention would last a month or so. A cursory reading of history would have told them how easily invaders invariably became trapped in the intractable terrain of Afghanistan, and how they had been repelled for centuries. According to remarks much later by Zbigniew Brzezinski, formerly the hawkish National Security Adviser of President Jimmy Carter, the CIA had been secretly fomenting the opposition since July 1979 in the very hope of inducing the Soviets to get sucked into their own 'Vietnam'. Precisely that happened. The Soviets found themselves for the next nine years sucked ever deeper into an imbroglio – costly in manpower and resources, increasingly unpopular at home, and unwinnable. At the same time the seeds of later horrors were sown as opposition to Soviet occupation drew in jihadists from Algeria to Pakistan, fighting alongside Afghans as the *Mujahideen*, largely financed by Saudi Arabia, backed too by economic and military assistance from the CIA.

The United States responded by reheating the Cold War. President Carter ratcheted up the anti-Soviet rhetoric, calling Afghanistan, with notable hyperbole, the greatest threat to peace since the Second World War. A partial embargo was placed on exports to the USSR, including high technology. The SALT II treaty was not ratified. And America boycotted the 1980 Moscow Olympic Games – a largely pointless exercise, except in preventing athletes who had been training for years from experiencing what for many would have been the climax of their careers. Most Western European countries, in fact, ignored the boycott. Nor was the trade embargo an unqualified success. France and West Germany did not impose their own sanctions and indeed benefited from the trade gap left by the Americans. It was nonetheless plain: there was nothing left of détente. The 'Second Cold War' had begun.

For the next five years superpower relations worsened. The new American President, Ronald Reagan, a former B-movie actor whose folksy manner combined with firm conservative principles proved a winning formula in the election of 1980 after the widely viewed failure of the Carter presidency, set the tone. He was avidly backed by his most assertive ally, Margaret Thatcher. Part of restoring prestige after the Vietnam debacle was to demonstrate American strength through a readiness to confront the Soviet Union, which by 1983 Reagan was describing as 'an evil empire'. The nuclear arms race escalated that year. The first Pershing missiles were stationed in Western Europe in November. The Soviets responded by breaking off new negotiations on long-range missiles. Strategic Arms Reduction Talks – START for short – were stopped before any start had taken place. Earlier in the year Reagan had announced a new nuclear programme, the Strategic Defence Initiative (SDI), dubbed 'Star Wars' since it aimed at a comprehensive anti-missile defence system located in space. It threatened to tip the nuclear balance decisively in America's favour. The Soviets did not have the resources to match it. But when they tried to ensure that restrictions on it be included in talks on nuclear arms limitation, the Americans refused. Mutually Assured Destruction (MAD) remained much as it had been. It provided its own perverse brand of security of a sort.

Not that this was how ordinary people saw it. Fear returned. The new Cold War brought new anxieties about a nuclear holocaust. These were not at the same pitch as they had been during the Cuban Missile Crisis of October 1962. They were real and acute nonetheless. Peace movements, particularly in Britain and West Germany, gathered even greater strength than they had possessed in the 1950s. In Britain the Campaign for Nuclear Disarmament (CND), which in 1979 had a membership of only 5,000, grew to twenty times that number by 1985. Women set up a 'peace camp' outside the American base at Greenham Common, which became internationally as well as within Britain a symbol of the new movement of protest at the stationing of Pershing and cruise missiles and the intensified threat of a nuclear war in Europe. West Germany, where most of the missiles would be based, was the epicentre of the protest. Two and a half million people signed a petition drawn up in November 1980, the 'Krefeld Appeal', that demanded an end to nuclear weapons in Europe. Around 1.3 million took part in October 1983 in demonstrations in German cities against the stationing of the missiles. This went ahead nonetheless with the support of the governments of Helmut Kohl in West Germany and Margaret Thatcher in Britain.

The escalation in the nuclear arms race came at an unimaginable financial cost. The United States, its national debt soaring into the stratosphere, could cope. For the Soviet Union, it was a far more difficult burden to shoulder. It has been estimated that from a Soviet gross domestic product around a sixth as large as that of the United States, some 15–17 per cent was spent on defence, about three times as high as the American proportion. This level of military expenditure could not be sustained indefinitely. The Soviet Union was not on the verge of internal collapse. It could have limped on for years to come, despite an underperforming economy, a geriatric leadership, and serious problems in the satellite countries. But it urgently needed internal reform and restructuring. And it needed visionary leadership to bring that about. It was not easy to see where it would come from.

The Soviet Union went through three seriously infirm leaders within as many years. Leonid Brezhnev had for years been propped up by a diet of sleeping tablets (to which he was addicted), alcohol and cigarettes. After a number of strokes he was barely mobile and noticeably slurred his speech. On his death in November 1982 Yuri Andropov, the former KGB chief, became head of the party, introduced some needed changes, but was too much of a traditionalist to offer hope of fundamental reform. In any case, in poor health from kidney disease he lacked the necessary stamina. He lasted barely more than a year, dying in February 1984. He was replaced as General Secretary by someone older, less competent and even frailer, suffering badly from emphysema. Konstantin Chernenko was plainly a stop-gap, a non-entity backed as party chief by other members of the gerontocracy, keen to hold on to their posts and to head off planned inquiries into corruption. He died on 10 March 1985. There was general agreement in the upper ranks of the party that the much-needed inner renewal and exterior strength of the Soviet Union depended upon a leader who was relatively young, energetic, resourceful and dynamic.

Waiting in the wings was just that man. Mikhail Gorbachev, the unanimous choice of the Politburo as next General Secretary of the Communist Party, was only fifty-four years old – almost a juvenile when compared with the previous three leaders. He had been Andropov's protégé, and had effectively run affairs while Chernenko had been nominally in charge. Gorbachev was about to step out of the wings and onto centre stage, not just in the Soviet Union but in world affairs.

8

Easterly Wind of Change

We know that our road is difficult. However, the choice has been made and we have paved the way for perestroika.
Mikhail Gorbachev, speech to the Soviet people at New Year
1989

We now have the Frank Sinatra doctrine. He has a song, 'I Did It My Way'. So every country decides on its own which road to take.
Soviet Foreign Ministry spokesman Gennadi Gerasimov,
October 1989

Hardly anyone, whether in Eastern or in Western Europe, foresaw what was coming. Radical change in an apparently ossified Soviet bloc seemed unthinkable. That it could come from within the Soviet Union itself was unimaginable. Nor did Mikhail Gorbachev have any idea, when he became head of the Communist Party of the Soviet Union on 11 March 1985, that within six years his actions would utterly transform world history. He wanted to reform the Soviet Union; he ended up destroying it. It was, of course, not his work alone. But without him it would not have happened. Between his accession to power in 1985 and spring 1989 the strong easterly wind of change under Gorbachev gradually gathered hurricane strength until it was on the verge of destroying all in its path and upturning the roots of the old order in Eastern Europe.

PERESTROIKA

The word, untranslated, went round the world. It meant 'reconstruction' and entered circulation with a speech delivered by Gorbachev in Leningrad in May 1985, when the new General Secretary of the Communist Party announced: 'Obviously, we all of us must undergo reconstruction . . . Everyone must adopt new approaches and understand that no other path is available to us.' What 'reconstruction' amounted to in precise terms, how its meaning and consequences would change over time, and the levels of opposition it would encounter were all unclear. What it initially meant to Gorbachev, and to those in the party who gave him their enthusiastic support, was the renewal and revitalization that they saw as essential to restoring the ideals of the Revolution of 1917.

Gorbachev was an insider. He had come to prominence within the regime. There was no need to imagine that whatever reforms he might seek to introduce would damage that regime – its structures of power within the Soviet Union or its domination of Eastern Europe. Gorbachev himself, a dyed-in-the-wool communist, had no intention of doing so. Although it faced growing problems in the economy and in relations with non-Russian nationalities, the USSR was stable when Gorbachev assumed office. It had low levels of foreign debt, did not face serious internal disorder, and could rely upon the loyalty of the armed forces and security services. There were no concerns about political destabilization either among those – a small minority – who wanted to introduce necessary reforms or among the ultra-conservatives, the dominant force in the Politburo, who wanted to stop them. The Soviet Union could have staggered on, in sclerotic fashion no doubt but without fear of imminent collapse, for the foreseeable future without the disintegrating dynamic of perestroika.

Born in March 1931 to a peasant family in Stavropol in the northern Caucasus, a region with a strong ethnic mix though mainly inhabited by Russians, Mikhail Gorbachev had experienced poverty and the persecution of family members under Stalinism before he began his rapid rise through the party to membership of the Politburo by 1980. His organizational skills, dynamism and decisiveness had gained recognition. He was seen as an emerging notable talent. He came to prominence during the short period of Andropov's leadership. Andropov acknowledged the need for reforms (within narrow constraints) and looked to promote a number of younger party loyalists. He regarded Gorbachev as his leading protégé and gave him extensive responsibilities over much of the economy, especially agriculture. Gorbachev sometimes chaired the Politburo when the ailing Andropov was absent (though this task usually fell to Konstantin Chernenko). The death of Andropov and succession of the conservatives' choice, the already ailing Chernenko, in February 1984 proved only a temporary setback.

Chernenko's illness meant that Gorbachev for much of the time ran the Politburo and Party Secretariat. He was by now number two among the leadership of the Soviet Union. When Chernenko died in the evening of 10 March 1985, Gorbachev summoned the meeting of the Politburo, later that night, which already in effect predetermined that he would be elected next day, unopposed, as General Secretary. It was not because he had radical ideas for reform that he was elected. Gorbachev himself lacked precise plans. He simply felt that change was necessary. His mainly conservative Politburo colleagues were certainly uninterested in far-reaching reform that might threaten the system that guaranteed them rewards and privileges. Not all of them, by any means, were enamoured of Gorbachev. But no alternative candidate stood out. After the demise in quick succession of three near-decrepit leaders there was the feeling that younger, more dynamic leadership was vitally necessary. And Gorbachev's energy and drive were impressive.

It is not at first sight obvious, even so, how Gorbachev could introduce increasingly radical change when he was the sole reformer in the Politburo, completely surrounded by conservatives. One reason is that Gorbachev was extremely persuasive and forceful. In contrast with his predecessors, he did not rely upon the authority of his office but on the power of argument. Politburo meetings were longer than they had been in the past. There was extensive debate. Sometimes Gorbachev would amend his initial position. But through compelling argument and the force of his personality he proved adept at gaining approval for his policies. And in the early stages, especially, he was anxious to keep the conservatives in the Politburo in line behind the steps he advanced.

He was greatly helped by the fact that the conservatives had no clear alternative strategy to offer in place of reform. Gorbachev had no difficulty in highlighting the poor state of the economy, which had worsened during the later 1970s and early 1980s. Economic growth had been declining. The budget showed a big deficit. There were shortages, a flourishing black market, low productivity, rampant extortion and corruption, and one of the lowest standards of living even among socialist countries. Military spending had, as usual, been sustained, but at the expense of the standard of living. He had seen at first hand the mounting problems of agriculture, was well aware of the deficiencies in industrial production and severe lack of investment, and recognized the growing burden of foreign debt. The conservatives might not want change. But they could not find ways of breaking the economic stranglehold simply by leaving things as they were. Gorbachev had the advantage, therefore, in pressing for change; there was no obvious alternative. The conservatives were from the outset on the defensive.

It was much the same with regard to foreign policy. Gorbachev could point to the growing gap with the United States in technological development. This was made all the more evident once the Soviet Union had to contend with President Reagan's Strategic Defence Initiative ('Star Wars'), announced in 1983. The response in the Soviet Union had been the usual one: step up military expenditure. Gorbachev, too, at first thought that the Soviet Union had to increase its military spending substantially, which would enable it to catch up with the USA and overcome the deficiency in, especially, information technology. But he quickly grasped that another way of approaching the problem would be to work for a fundamental alteration in international relations with the United States. He envisaged extensive nuclear disarmament. This would persuade the Americans that their expensive Strategic Defence Initiative was wholly unnecessary. Faced with the obvious problem that a substantially greater budget for defence when the civilian economy was already under strain would severely limit the possibilities of improving the standard of living of Soviet citizens, Gorbachev was able to persuade the Politburo to try his alternative approach. The conservatives had nothing with which to counter his arguments except persevering with policies – tried, tested and failed – that would make matters worse. Moreover, they were worried about what Andropov, only a few years earlier and still at the time head of the KGB, had emphasized as Reagan's reckless unpredictability, fearing that he was planning a surprise attack on the Soviet Union. They had come close to panic in 1983 when Soviet intelligence mistook a NATO military exercise as a sign of imminent nuclear attack – the most dangerous flashpoint since the Cuban Missile Crisis of 1962, though hushed up at the time. Finally, they realized that the stationing of the SS-20 missiles in Eastern Europe had been a failure, which – apart from the exorbitant cost – had merely provoked the West into retaliating by the deployment of the superior Pershing II missiles, against which the Soviet Union had no effective protection. So the conservative military establishment was open to change. Again, the weakness of the conservatives was Gorbachev's strength.

Beyond his own eloquent persuasiveness and conservative weakness, Gorbachev was able to pursue his reformist agenda by strengthening his own position within the Politburo and in other leading organs of the party. Although he always had to cope with a majority in the Politburo who did not share his embrace of reform, he quickly introduced changes in personnel that strengthened his hand, especially in foreign affairs. He promoted a number of former fellow protégés of Andropov, who favoured reform, at the expense of the remaining conservatives. These included those who had manoeuvred behind the scenes on his behalf to ensure his seamless election as General Secretary: Nikolai Ryzhkov was given charge of the economy and made Chairman of the Council of Ministers; while Yegor Ligachev, who had handled the party's Organizational Department under Andropov, was elevated to membership of the Politburo and given charge of ideological matters in the Secretariat. An important ally, supporting radical reform, was Alexander Yakovlev, now brought in to the party's Secretariat. Eduard Shevardnadze, the Georgian party boss, who avidly shared Gorbachev's view that change was necessary, was appointed Foreign Minister, while the conservative die-hard Andrei Gromyko was removed by nominally promoting him to Chairman of the Supreme Soviet Presidium, the head of state. Ryzhkov and Ligachev – also Boris Yeltsin, the party leader in Sverdlovsk (later returned to its Tsarist name of Yekaterinburg), now appointed as head of the Secretariat in Moscow – would be among those who later distanced themselves from Gorbachev and became his critics. In the early stages of reform, however, they were important allies against the traditionalists who wanted to drag their feet at any prospect of change. At lower levels, too, Gorbachev brought in party officials who would be sympathetic to reform. Beneath the surface of the sclerotic Brezhnev regime a new leaven of well-educated economic managers and technical experts had come to see that change was necessary. They, and middle-ranking party officials, had to tread carefully. But many of them were open to reformist ideas and, given a lead from above, ready to embrace them. By mid-1986 two-thirds of party secretaries in the provinces were new appointees.

Finally, Gorbachev was able to steer his reformist path in an ever more radical direction because, as his position strengthened, his own views on reform changed fundamentally. He began as a communist; he ended as a Western-style social democrat. He gradually came to the realization that reform was not enough. By 1988 he had reached the point where he recognized that the Soviet system had to be completely overhauled and transformed. In the process of his personal metamorphosis he carried the Soviet leadership with him – some more willingly than others, some trying in vain to apply the brakes, like trying to stop a runaway juggernaut. As reforms gathered pace it was increasingly difficult for Gorbachev's opponents to obstruct, let alone reverse, them. It was far too late to resort to Stalin's methods of nationwide terror. Drastic repression would have been much more difficult to implement than it had been in the 1930s. Soviet society had changed since those days. People for the most part liked Gorbachev's reforms. Between 1985 and 1990 the General Secretary enjoyed immense personal popularity. In the intelligentsia, too, Gorbachev found much support for his radical proposals (though local party functionaries often dragged their feet).

Nor could the clock be turned back to the full-scale command economy of yesteryear. The serious economic problems of the Soviet Union could not be combated by such an approach. And the pressures to loosen, not tighten, the reins were meanwhile building up in the peripheral, non-Russian nationalities of the Soviet Union. So the reforms developed their own dynamic. One conservative, Vitaliy Vorotnikov, who later regretted being carried away by the power of Gorbachev's arguments, lamented that 'the train of pseudo-democracy had gathered such speed that to stop it was beyond our powers'. He was right: as long as Gorbachev was Soviet leader, the pressure for change could not be halted. It carried Gorbachev along with it. When faced with the question of halting or radicalizing his reforms, his answer was predictable and consistent. 'I'm doomed to go forward, and only forward,' he is reputed to have said. 'And if I retreat, I myself will perish and the cause will perish too!' But the radical change that 'going forward' involved proceeded inexorably in one direction: that of eroding, and ultimately undermining totally, the power structures of the Soviet state.

However serious the problems of the Soviet Union were when Gorbachev became party leader, they could have been sustained for some years to come. There were those at the time, and subsequently, who in fact argued that the Soviet Union could have successfully followed the example, adopted in China in 1979 under the leadership of Deng Xiaoping, of combining economic reform with the continuation of strong, authoritarian political control. Such a strategy of undertaking economic reform and only then attempting political transformation, they claimed, would have preserved the Soviet Union indefinitely. Gorbachev disagreed. He judged such views to be naive. He thought economic reform in the Soviet Union without accompanying significant political change would have been doomed to failure. (For his part, Deng apparently thought Gorbachev was 'an idiot'.) As it was, the structural problems allowed Gorbachev to build up what became an unstoppable momentum for radical change. But without Gorbachev's personal input, his own unquenchable and intensifying thirst for reforming the ossified power structures of the Soviet Union, that momentum would not even have started. This undiluted will for change was what, in the transformation of the Soviet Union, its satellite states and ultimately the whole of Europe, amounted to 'the Gorbachev factor'.

Although economic reform seemed the initial focus of Gorbachev's attention as General Secretary, for months few concrete measures followed the rhetoric. His starting point – aimed in good measure at placating the almost wholly conservative Politburo – was in fact to work for improvement within the strategic framework laid down under Brezhnev. His policy, he said in his first speech after his election as General Secretary, was one 'of accelerating the social and economic development of the country and seeking improvement in all aspects of the life of our society'. It was a singularly vague statement of intent. Although convinced of the urgent need for reform, Gorbachev had no clear plan in mind. He was able to persuade even conservatives that economic management had to be decentralized. But the precise steps to that goal, implementing change, turning statements of intent into practical reality, were a different matter.

He was treading in a political minefield. For all his impatience for change, it could not be brought about overnight. Months of avid persuasion, replacement of diehards by those open to reform, and bold moves to build a climate for change were necessary before the process of reform could take hold and gather pace. And all the while Gorbachev himself was learning, and changing. He gradually gathered confidence about the possibilities of radical reform. He was, too, carried along on the stream of the reforms that he had already instigated.

He soon realized that economic reform could only take place on any significant scale if it were to be preceded, not followed, by political restructuring. He was soon, therefore, pushing for *political* reform. And this, from starting as the platform for subsequent economic and social reform, gradually became an end in itself. 'In the heat of political battles we lost sight of the economy,' Gorbachev later admitted.

Visits to different parts of the Soviet Union in the summer of 1985 reinforced Gorbachev's withering assessment of the state of the economy. But what really shook him, and convinced him more than ever that limited reform and administrative adjustments would far from suffice to remove the malaise, was the terrible nuclear disaster at Chernobyl, in Ukraine, about a hundred kilometres north of Kiev, on 26 April 1986. The overheating of a reactor at the nuclear power station had led to a catastrophic explosion. The radioactive fallout, far worse than that at Hiroshima and Nagasaki after atomic bombs had devastated the Japanese cities in August 1945, was carried by high winds over wide areas of Eastern, Central and Northern Europe. Exposing millions to the effects of radiation, it was immediately recognized as an international, not just Soviet, disaster. It left a major imprint on the anti-nuclear and environmental movements in Western European countries.

For Ukrainians in the region at the epicentre of the explosion it was an unmitigated calamity. But neither the scale nor the nature of the disaster was immediately recognized, since the authorities at first left the local population in the dark about what exactly had happened. One eyewitness, the pregnant wife of a fireman who fought the blaze but did not survive, described the chaotic scene of the horror:

> There were these tall flames. Lots of soot, terrible heat . . . They beat back
> the fire, but it was creeping further, climbing back up . . . They didn't

have their canvas suits on, they left just in the shirt they were wearing. Nobody warned them. They were just called out to an ordinary fire . . . He begged me: 'Get out! Save the baby!' . . . There were soldiers everywhere . . . Nobody said anything about radiation. It was just the soldiers who were wearing respirators . . . On the radio, they announced: 'The town is being evacuated for three to five days. Bring warm clothes and tracksuits. You'll be staying in the forests, living in tents' . . .

At least twenty people were killed. The numbers of those who later died as a result of the explosion are estimated as running into the tens of thousands. Health problems arising from exposure to the high levels of radioactivity were felt for many years. The atmosphere was polluted, the ground contaminated. It was impossible to live in the area. Around 135,000 citizens were forcibly resettled.

For Gorbachev the disaster revealed not just an obsolete technology but also 'the failure of the old system'. He later remarked that 'Chernobyl shed light on many of the sicknesses of our system as a whole'. There had been incompetence, attempts to hold back vital information, hushing-up of bad news, irresponsibility, carelessness, widespread drunkenness and poor decision-making. It added up to a further 'convincing argument in favour of radical reforms . . . We had to move perestroika forward.'

A second Russian word entered the international vocabulary soon afterwards: glasnost – 'transparency' or 'openness'. It was an essential component of Gorbachev's desire to spur public debate on his changes, in this way spreading their popularity and making them irreversible. It was not intended to introduce unlimited freedom of speech or free access to information, let alone Western-style liberal democracy. Nonetheless, in Soviet terms the move was extraordinary and the consequences were incalculable. A sign that Gorbachev was drawing a line under the repression of nonconformist opinion was his recall from exile in Gorky of the most famous dissident in the Soviet Union, the atomic physicist Andrei Sakharov, in December 1986.

Over the following year Gorbachev's ideas on restructuring evolved further. The draft Law on State Enterprise that he presented in June 1987 envisaged the election of works managers, a level of decentralization of production and – in echoes of Lenin's New Economic Policy of the 1920s – the existence of a small private sector in services and industry.

Within two years the initially small private sector had expanded substantially, though remaining small. In the state sector, still hugely bigger, it became possible to make workers redundant and to shut down loss-making concerns. In a further move away from the state-controlled command economy, land and even publicly owned factories could be privately leased for up to fifty years. Gorbachev had meanwhile, in November 1987, demanded the introduction of the rule of law and a new political culture as the basis of Soviet society. Astonishingly, too, and a complete break with Leninist class ideology, he wanted a foreign policy that rested on 'common human values' with other countries.

In line with the change of policy in international affairs that he had successfully persuaded his Politburo colleagues to accept that ending the nuclear arms race was directly in the interests of the Soviet Union, Gorbachev had lost no time in meeting President Reagan with a view to seeking out an agreement. The previous year, before taking office, Gorbachev had already made a positive impression on Reagan's prime ally, Margaret Thatcher, during a 'charm offensive' in Britain. Although he was well aware that she was a hardline anti-communist, he saw her as 'the shortest way to send a message to Washington'. When he and his wife Raisa had lunch at Chequers, the British Prime Minister's country residence, on 16 December 1984, Gorbachev had broken the ice by assuring Mrs Thatcher that he was 'not under instructions from the Politburo to persuade you to join the Communist Party'. Mrs Thatcher visibly relaxed at the joke and later, picking up the words of one of her advisers, remarked: 'I like Mr Gorbachev. We can do business together.'

Gorbachev and Reagan also established a good personal rapport when they met in Geneva in November 1985. At a second summit, in Reykjavik in Iceland, on 11–12 October 1986, Gorbachev took Reagan completely by surprise in proposing a 50 per cent reduction in strategic nuclear arsenals on both sides, then, when the Americans hesitated, suggesting the complete elimination of intermediate-range missiles in Europe. The proposal foundered when Reagan refused to contemplate restrictions on testing for the Strategic Defence Initiative. A third summit, in Washington between 7 and 10 December 1987, achieved greater success. Gorbachev and Reagan this time signed the Intermediate Nuclear Forces Treaty, committing the Soviet Union and the United States to the destruction of all ground-based missiles within a range of 500 to 5,500 kilometres.

Gorbachev and Reagan met again between 29 May and 3 June 1988, this time in Moscow, where they discussed human rights and the removal of Soviet troops from Afghanistan, which had been announced in April – Gorbachev drawing a line under the disastrous episode of the Soviet Union's 'Vietnam'. Perhaps most importantly, the meeting reflected a changed climate – one of greatly improved relations between the super-powers, prompted in no small measure by the personal chemistry between Gorbachev and Reagan and by the bold initiatives in reducing the prospect of nuclear conflict that the General Secretary had taken.

Addressing the United Nations General Assembly in New York on 7 December 1988, Gorbachev announced that he was unilaterally reducing the Soviet armed forces by half a million men and would be withdrawing six armoured divisions from the German Democratic Republic, Czecho-slovakia and Hungary by 1991. He referred to a 'common goal' for humanity in establishing a peaceful world. Class struggle was not mentioned. He was turning his back on the tenets of Marxism-Leninism. He had come far in a short time.

Problems in the Soviet Union were meanwhile, however, mounting in worrying fashion. Glasnost had prompted people to speak out about their grievances, not least about the corruption of local officials, which government publicity had itself castigated. In the non-Russian republics this easily gained an ethnic dimension, manifesting itself in resentment against Russian functionaries, seen as outsiders given advancement instead of locals. There were ethnic disturbances in Kazakhstan and Azerbaijan, but more ominous signs of rising breakaway nationalist feel-ing, seeking autonomy from Moscow, in the Baltic republics of Latvia, Lithuania and Estonia. Gorbachev had opened Pandora's box. The lid could not be pushed down again.

By late 1988 it was plain, too, that the economy was failing. Gor-bachev's reforms had made the situation worse, not better. All the indicators showed that the economic performance was sharply deterio-rating. The Soviet Union's financial deficit was growing alarmingly. The sale of vodka was vital to tax revenues that propped up the tottering budget. Income from exports – especially of oil and gas – was dropping. For such a huge country, rich in natural resources, it was remarkable that a high proportion of hard currency, gained from exports to the West, had to be used to import food. Rationing of staple food products – including meat and sugar – was widespread by the end of 1988. Hospitals reported a shortage of medicines. Within a year many everyday commodities – milk, tea, coffee, soap, meat – had disappeared from the shops. Unsurprisingly, the anger of countless ordinary citizens was palpable. Strikes broke out in several parts of the country. And amid the growing economic crisis and huge popular discontent, elections were due.

The elections in March 1989 – the first free election in the history of the Soviet Union – to the Congress of People's Deputies (a new body, of 2,250 members, replacing the former Supreme Soviet as the highest legislative body in the land) produced sensational results. These were not multi-party elections, as in Western democracies. Candidates had to be members of the Communist Party. The novelty was, however, that more than one candidate could contest each position. This was the compromise – some freedom of choice within a continuing one-party state – necessary to placate conservatives. It was, if an imperfect arrangement, an important move towards democracy. The sensation was that some 20 per cent of the candidates endorsed by the party were rejected by the electorate. In each of the biggest cities in the Soviet Union – Moscow, Leningrad and Kiev – the candidate backed by the party was defeated. In Moscow, Boris Yeltsin (who had resigned from the Politburo in 1987), opposed by the entire party apparatus, won almost 90 per cent of the votes.

It was the worst electoral defeat for the Communist Party since 1918. It opened the path to further political turbulence. In the Congress itself around 300 reformers – Yeltsin prominent among them – pressed for further democratization and more radical change. At the same time the Baltic republics were more stridently demanding autonomy from Moscow, while there were protests leading to bloodshed in Georgia in support of national independence. Rebelliousness and inter-ethnic conflict, bringing in their train rioting and violence in the Caucasus, reflected the fraying bonds of the non-Russian republics. And all this was against the backdrop of continued, and mounting, economic crisis. Gorbachev remained popular, as he would do until the summer of 1990. Yet his popularity and his power were at their peak. They would soon start to wane.

But for Gorbachev himself there could be no retreat. What had started as evolutionary reform was starting visibly to become revolutionary change. And the implosion was not only affecting the Soviet Union. Inexorably, it had momentous implications, too, for the satellite states of what had, until now, formed the Soviet empire in Eastern Europe.

MOMENTUM FOR CHANGE

How significant was 'the Gorbachev factor' in the collapse of the Soviet bloc? The question has to be addressed in the light of the grave structural weaknesses that were blighting the socialist states. It raises once more a central issue of interpretation: how important is the role of individual agency in effecting major historical change? And to what extent is that role itself conditioned by structural determinants?

The structural problems of each of the Soviet satellites had deepened in the wake of the oil crises of the 1970s (see Chapter 7). The gap in levels of growth between the Soviet bloc and the Western economies was expanding, not shrinking. State indebtedness in Eastern Europe by the mid-1980s was reaching alarming levels. A large proportion of hard-currency earnings was used up in servicing debts to Western banks so that a way out of the vicious circle became well-nigh impossible. Gorbachev's advisors told him that Eastern Europe was an economic burden to the Soviet Union, not a strategic necessity.

Romania showed that a route out of state indebtedness was not completely impossible. It was hardly, however, a route to commend itself. The International Monetary Fund had in 1982 imposed stringent conditions on Romania in return for rescheduling repayment of its huge (and still growing) national debt. In response, Nicolae Ceaușescu adopted a radical strategy: to pay back the debt completely, and within a very short time. The debt was in fact eliminated by 1989. This was only possible, however, by imposing horrendously draconian cuts in consumer spending. The cuts – including a 'rational eating programme' to reduce the intake of calories by up to 15 per cent – condemned citizens to lives of abject misery. Imports were drastically pared back, leading to chronic shortages of the most basic foodstuffs. Electricity consumption fell by 1985 to only 20 per cent of its 1979 level, while gas consumption in Bucharest in the winter of 1987 was fixed at two hours per day.

As Romanians starved and froze, Ceaușescu increasingly resembled a latter-day Nero, luxuriating (with his wife Elena) in a lifestyle of brazen extravagance and relishing a personality cult that plumbed depths of servility and absurdity rare even by the standards of authoritarian regimes. Signs of megalomania were unmistakable. Grandiose prestige projects swallowed fabulous sums of money. Around 40,000 inhabitants were turned out of their homes to make way for the 'House of the Republic' in Bucharest, stylistically reminiscent of the worst excesses of Stalinist architecture. In 1988 Ceauşescu announced a scheme entailing the destruction of 8,000 villages in order to build 'agro-industrial complexes'. Villagers who would not destroy their own homes received no compensation. The Hungarian minority were to be 'Romanianized'. Women suffered disproportionately as contraception and abortion were banned and the age of marriage reduced to fifteen. Tens of thousands of children were removed from poor families and placed in orphanages.

Ceauşescu's regime was truly monstrous. But the sheer scale of cronyism and corruption of the ruling elite, and the fearful repression of the 'Securitate' – the dreaded state security organization (estimated to have 24,000 active officers), backed by a huge surveillance network of possibly hundreds of thousands of informers – did much to ensure only muted opposition, however little genuine popularity the regime enjoyed. As yet even those Romanians who in private were critical could scarcely contemplate any exit route from Ceauşescu's rule. But Romania, whatever the specific character of its brand of communism, could not escape the climate of change that was starting to affect the entire communist zone.

The despotic tyranny in Romania stood out plainly, in fact, from the rest of the socialist bloc. Although part of the Warsaw Pact, Ceauşescu had increasingly gone his own way since the invasion of Czechoslovakia in August 1968. That he had distanced himself from the Soviet Union in developing a form of Romanian national communism, and had consequently opened up a rift within the Warsaw Pact countries, had encouraged Western countries to court such a repulsive dictator. In 1978 Ceauşescu had even been invited to make a state visit to Britain and had dined with Queen Elizabeth II. Although Ceauşescu made overtures to Gorbachev, since Romania needed Soviet economic aid, a meeting of minds was impossible. Indeed, their meeting in May 1987 prompted strong criticism from the Soviet leader. Romanian and Soviet paths were set to diverge further. But the more Gorbachev clarified his radical approach to change within Warsaw Pact countries, the more Ceauşescu's absolutist rule in Romania became endangered.

The other Warsaw Pact countries were sharply divided in their attitude towards Gorbachev's reforms. The regimes in Bulgaria (traditionally unwavering in its loyalty to Moscow), the German Democratic Republic and Czechoslovakia looked on the changes under way in the Soviet Union with disapproval, apprehension and foreboding. Resistance to the new climate under Gorbachev equated to the defence of the structures of power in their own countries on which their authority depended.

Todor Zhivkov, leader of the Bulgarian Communist Party as well as head of state since March 1954 and still clinging to power, was unlikely to be impressed by Gorbachev's reforms in the Soviet Union. An attempt in 1982 to boost the flagging economy, and in particular to improve the supply of consumer goods, had failed. The country's economic problems worsened when the Soviet Union, faced with falling revenue from oil exports, reduced its oil supplies to Bulgaria (and its other Eastern European satellites). Bulgaria's economy, Gorbachev later noted, was kept alive by the 'artificial respiration' of foreign capital. Faced with ballooning foreign debt and an economy deemed to be 'on the verge of a heart attack', Zhivkov diverted attention by intensifying discrimination against the Turkish minority – about a tenth of the population. As 'restructuring' proceeded in the Soviet Union, relations with Moscow became more strained. Zhivkov paid lip service to reform in a half-hearted 'Bulgarian perestroika' introduced between 1986 and 1988. He was even taken to task – at least nominally – by Gorbachev in 1987 for adopting a line that might ultimately threaten the communist monopoly of power in Bulgaria, and for surrounding himself with advisors who favoured an orientation towards the West. But Zhivkov's stance contained no small dose of hypocrisy. For he had no intention of weakening, let along surrendering, his hold on power. In 1987 the Politburo of the Bulgarian Communist Party expressly rejected perestroika as inapplicable to Bulgaria.

So did Erich Honecker for the German Democratic Republic, which he had led since 1971. With loans from West Germany and payment extracted for use of the transit route to West Berlin and crossing the Wall from West to East Berlin, the GDR was able to sustain reasonable standards of living – high for the eastern bloc, if far below those in Western

Europe – even though, here too, beneath the official optimism the economy was in decline and state indebtedness sharply increasing. Political dissidence was more widespread than it had been a few years earlier. It found expression, despite the limits of public debate and the constant threat of punitive action by the coercive forces of the state, in the peace movement which, as in West Germany, had been prompted by the stationing of nuclear weapons on German soil in the escalating 'Second Cold War'. By 1986 there were an estimated 200 peace groups in the GDR. Protestant clergy played a major part in articulating opposition on the nuclear issue, and also stirring strong feelings, especially among young people, about environmental damage. None of this posed an existential threat to the stability of the regime, which as it always had done, was prepared to resort to strong shows of force in repressing public demonstrations of disaffection. Honecker saw no need to change course. Unsurprisingly, the new broom sweeping clean in the Soviet Union under Gorbachev was not welcomed. Reform, mistakenly at first imagined to be little more than cosmetic, was regarded as wholly unnecessary in the GDR. Honecker stated explicitly in January 1987 that the path of perestroika did not suit East Germany. 'If my neighbour decides to change his wallpaper, that doesn't mean that I have to do the same,' was the GDR's stance, as voiced by Kurt Hager, the regime's chief ideologist.

In Czechoslovakia, far more than was the case in the GDR or Bulgaria (not to mention Romania), the advent of Gorbachev opened up the gulf between the regime and wide sectors of the population (above all intellectuals) – a breach that had never been healed, even if not openly apparent, since the crushing of the Prague Spring in August 1968. Since then, using Timothy Garton Ash's apt metaphor, Czechoslovakia had been like 'a lake permanently covered by a thick layer of ice'. Beneath the glacial surface, there was movement. Most people had for long been bought off by relative plenty in the shops. By the mid-1980s, however, economic growth had stalled and national indebtedness increased. The economic prognosis made depressing reading. Political stability had been sustained by ritual conformity of the many, ruthless repression, and surveillance of the dissenting minority. But persecution had failed to silence the dissidents completely. The signatories of Charter 77 had, in fact, seen their goal not as active opposition but as maintaining a dissenting voice simply by refusing to remain silent. By the mid-1980s the signatories to

Charter 77 had risen in number from the original 240 to 1,200. Hundreds of illicit publications had reached a wider, if still small, readership, inside the country and abroad.

Supporters of Charter 77, and many other citizens of Czechoslovakia, saw Gorbachev as a breath of fresh air and warmly welcomed the early signs of change in the Soviet Union. The Soviet leader was rapturously received by a crowd of some 50,000 people when he visited Prague in April 1987. For Gustáv Husák, the Czech leader since the 'Prague Spring', and for the rest of the Czech leadership, that was a deeply worrying sign – another reminder of 1968. They had make lukewarm noises of support for Gorbachev's programme of reforms, though the General Secretary was in no doubt that they were unmoved in their opposition to any changes that might loosen their hold on power. Any hope that Husák's resignation as party leader in December 1987 – he remained head of state – would open the door to substantive change was swiftly dashed. His replacement, Miloš Jakeš, was another hardliner.

The stance of Bulgaria, the GDR and Czechoslovakia towards Gorbachev's reforms stood in sharp relief to the situation in Poland and Hungary. Both countries had already in the 1950s shown themselves to be the least compliant of the satellite states. Brutal Soviet intervention in Hungary in November 1956 and the threat of similar action in Poland had forced the two countries into line at that time. But both countries had continued to tread the tightrope of adherence to Moscow while pursuing limited deviation in their national development of communist rule. Hungary especially had partially veered away from the heavy constraints of the command economy with its variant of 'goulash communism'; the growing unrest in Poland in the late 1970s had resulted in the birth of the independent trade union Solidarity (*Solidarność*) and signs of emerging liberalization before the promise had been snuffed out by the imposition of martial law in December 1981.

Both Poland and Hungary had already experienced, beneath the imposed conformity of the system, the emergence of forms of 'civil society'. Intellectual discourse flourished just below the surface. Independent associations, discussion groups and publications had gained support in both countries. Thousands of them had sprouted like mushrooms from the soil in Hungary during the 1980s. The same was true, if anything even more so, in Poland. There, indeed, burgeoning democratic opposition extended far beyond the intellectual circles that were its bed-rock in Hungary. Support among workers for Solidarity had been suppressed under the martial law decreed in December 1981; but it was far from destroyed. Opposition, in the form of strikes, demonstrations, the circulation of illegal publications and other forms of civil unrest, continued (partly funded by the CIA) despite thousands of arrests. And the Catholic Church provided an institution that had come to represent ideological opposition to the state, providing a powerful alternative to the regime in popular legitimacy and loyalty.

Courageous intellectuals in Poland continued to defy repression to make the view heard that 'the party has deprived itself of its mandate to govern, and no one can do anything to change this'. From an internment camp in 1982, the writer and dissident Adam Michnik cited the novelist and poet Czesław Miłosz (who had broken with the Communist regime three decades earlier and taken refuge in the West). Miłosz had commented that the avalanche that would sweep away the repression 'depends on the stones over which it rolls'. Michnik added, 'And you want to be the stone that will reverse the course of events.'

In both countries the arrival of Gorbachev on the scene now gave legitimacy to the reformist opposition while substantially undermining the already weakened leadership of the regime. The trajectory of change in the two countries differed. In Hungary the drive to reform came largely from above, from within the Communist Party itself; in Poland, the regime's leadership acted under pressure from below, from a mass movement demanding reform, as articulated by Solidarity. In both countries reformist forces had taken shape in response to growing structural problems. But the new wind blowing in Moscow was responsible for turning reformist tendencies into mounting and ultimately irresistible pressure for regime change.

In Hungary the long-standing formula of unwavering loyalty to Moscow and the Warsaw Pact in return for tolerance of a domestic loosening of economic constrictions and ideological relaxation became neither necessary nor applicable once Gorbachev had established power in the Soviet Union. As Hungary's economic problems worsened from the mid-1980s onwards and national debt rose by 1987 to the highest level within the Soviet bloc, the popularity of the government waned. Inspired by what was happening in Moscow, reformers within the party saw their chance to push for more radical change than had previously been possible. János Kádár, still party leader three decades after assuming power following the uprising of 1956, had for long steered Hungary's cautious path towards internal change. But in the altered climate he feared the dangers involved in Gorbachev's push for rapid reform. His failing health served as a useful pretext to justify his forced resignation as General Secretary of the party in May 1988 when he was 'elevated' by those less hesitant about embracing change to the newly created – purely ceremonial – post of Party President. His replacement, both as party leader and already, since June 1987, head of government, Károly Grósz, a pragmatic conservative who favoured liberalizing economic reforms but also the retention of a communist monopoly of power, did not last long. He was himself ousted in November 1988 as head of government by Miklós Németh, backed by a reforming cabinet, which declared the need for a multi-party system.

Months beforehand oppositional groups had been openly demanding political pluralism and a free press. Between September 1987 and March 1988 they formed a number of organizations – the 'Hungarian Democratic Forum', the 'Network of Free Initiatives' and FIDESZ (the Alliance of Young Democrats). With different emphasis, each of these rejected the communist one-party state in favour of pluralist politics, market-orientated economics, and the pursuit of overtly national interests. The pace of change accelerated. In November the Alliance of Free Democrats was founded as a political party, arising from the Network of Free Initiatives. Once obsolete pre-war parties – the Independent Smallholder Party (in November 1988) and the Social Democratic Party (in January 1989) – were resurrected. An independent trade union organization (though attracting only minority worker support) was established in December 1988. The foundation of a Christian Democratic People's Party followed in March 1989. By then the ruling Communist Party had accepted – an important symbolic move – that the uprising of 1956 had represented a true struggle for independence, 'a popular uprising against an oligarchic rule that had debased the nation'. A vital step, legitimizing what was by now well under way, had already been taken several weeks earlier, in January 1989, when parliament had decreed that Hungary would become a multi-party state, and the Communist Party had formally accepted the end of its one-party rule. The revolution in Hungary was far from complete. But by the early months of 1989 it was unstoppable.

In Poland the rapidly deteriorating economic position – as an attempt to follow the Hungarian model of a limited market economy failed, debts to the West continued to mount, inflation remained high, and standards of living fell during the early 1980s – pushed General Jaruzelski's regime by the middle of the decade to seek a form of rapprochement with Solidarity. The readiness to compromise was further prompted by a significant flashpoint: the kidnap and murder in October 1984 by members of the state security police of thirty-seven-year-old Jerzy Popiełuszko, a Catholic priest who had publicly voiced his support for the trade-union opposition, and been a prominent thorn in the side of the regime. The wave of anger that swept the country following the killing boosted the opposition and worried the regime. An estimated quarter of a million Poles, including the Solidarity leader Lech Wałęsa, attended Popiełuszko's funeral on 3 November. A period of sullen, superficial calm followed. But the atmosphere remained tense. The tentacles of the police state were still as long as they had been at the height of Stalinism. However, the regime recognized that it had to make concessions to the public mood. A partial amnesty in November 1985 for members of Solidarity was followed in July 1986 by a complete amnesty for all the political prisoners arrested since 1981 (martial law had itself been formally lifted in July 1983). Among those released was the vociferous activist on behalf of Solidarity and internationally known intellectual Adam Michnik. The political situation was, however, only temporarily and partially stabilized.

Living conditions continued to deteriorate. Early in 1986 the government had been forced to increase weekly working hours and prices for foodstuffs. Soundings by the regime indicated that trust in the government had fallen to its lowest level since the 1950s. The state leadership played for time. It had hoped to preserve communist rule through the introduction of radical economic reforms to open up the economy more than ever before to private enterprise. A referendum at the end of November 1987, however, produced insufficient backing for the reforms, leaving only deep disaffection about the price rises that had already been introduced. The government was rapidly losing control of events.

By the spring and summer of 1988 the ensuing unrest resulted in another wave of strikes, at the Lenin Shipyard in Gdańsk and in mining areas. These in turn prompted the government to enter into talks in August with what it termed 'the constructive opposition'. Supporters of Solidarity were themselves divided: some sectors of the movement favoured negotiation with the regime, others a more radical stance. The internal division weakened Solidarity at this juncture – as the limited participation in the summer strikes had shown – and predisposed it towards a compromise with the government. For its part the government suffered public embarrassment when it invited Lech Wałęsa as a 'private individual' to a television debate with the leader of the official trade union, Alfred Miodowicz – a debate that Wałęsa won hands down. Following this media debacle, the government was again prepared to enter into talks with the Solidarity leader.

On 18 December 1988 Wałęsa established a Solidarity Citizens' Committee to orchestrate pressure on the government to democratize. In January 1989, aware that stabilization of the country demanded a new basis of understanding with Solidarity (a move favoured by Gorbachev), Jaruzelski, threatening his own resignation, gained acceptance of the trade union's re-legalization. This paved the way for the formal Round Table negotiations that began in February. Even at this stage the Minister of the Interior, Czesław Kiszczak, told the Polish people on television that 'socialism would remain the system of government'. In reply, Wałęsa declared that 'the time of political and social monopoly of one party over the people was coming to an end'. When the Round Table talks ended in April, it was with an agreed compromise to hold elections in June in which 35 per cent of the seats in the lower house of parliament (the Sejm) were to go to independent candidates. Wholly free elections would be held for the newly created, and less important, upper house, the Senate, while the position of President as head of state – a post destined, it was presumed, to be held by Jaruzelski (until now Chairman of the Polish Council of State) – was restored. Even now, the government felt satisfied with a deal that it thought would guarantee continued communist control. It soon proved to be a further miscalculation. By the spring of 1989 the attempt to resist the mounting pressure for democratic change was like trying to hold back the surging tide.

General Jaruzelski had been a strong supporter of Gorbachev's reforms. Indeed Gorbachev acknowledged that Polish moves towards economic reform, even under martial law after 1981, had been well in advance of the position in the Soviet Union. Like Gorbachev, Jaruzelski had seen reform as necessary, but as taking place *within* the existing system in order to preserve communist rule, not to destroy it. Like Gorbachev, he had not foreseen the inexorable corrosion of the system that flowed as the consequence of substantive reform. Unlike Gorbachev, however, whose aims evolved with the radicalization of the reforms, Jaruzelski came only with great reluctance to accept the political changes that had been forced upon him and the regime.

In every country of the Soviet bloc the structural crisis was palpable by the time Gorbachev came to power in March 1985. What had at its root an inability within the system to overcome worsening economic conditions had grown to become a crisis of legitimacy of the respective regimes of the satellite countries. These had handled the problems in different ways, most (like Bulgaria) by introducing as little change as possible, others (notably Poland and Hungary) by a willingness to reform, while still attempting to hold the essence of communist rule in place. The pressure for change from within the system had meanwhile intensified greatly in Hungary and Poland especially, and had in intellectual circles (and in Poland within sectors of the suppressed Solidarity movement) given rise to radical demands for greater political as well as economic liberalization that threatened the communist monopoly of power.

It is easy, however, to pre-date, in the light of later events, the inevitability of collapse of the communist states. However grave the internal problems, the Soviet bloc looked far from being on the verge of collapse in March 1985, when Gorbachev assumed power in Moscow. Earlier Soviet leaders might well have reacted very differently to the difficulties in the satellite states. The iron fist had, after all, been the response in East Germany in 1953, Hungary in 1956 and Czechoslovakia in 1968. Moscow had been allergic to a threat within any part of the imperium that had the potential to undermine the entire foundation of the system. The 'Brezhnev doctrine', formulated immediately after the suppression of the 'Prague Spring', if never officially enunciated, had defined the ideological basis for intervention. 'A socialist state that is in a system of other states constituting a socialist commonwealth', it averred, 'cannot be free of the common interests of that commonwealth.' Common socialist interest, in other words, justified military intervention to suppress anything that threatened it.

The leaders of the Soviet satellites were still in the early 1980s more than conscious of the continuing veiled threat of military intervention. They could not be sure that the Soviet leadership had turned away from such a strategy. Some, indeed, took comfort from this possibility. General Jaruzelski in fact later justified the declaration of military law in December 1981 precisely on the grounds that he was heading off such an eventuality (though minutes of the Soviet Politburo indicate that Yuri Andropov, head of the KGB at the time, had discounted the possibility, even should Solidarity win power in Poland, and had persuaded Brezhnev not to intervene). Absolutely crucial, therefore, was Gorbachev's renunciation of the 'Brezhnev doctrine'.

When the General Secretary informed the assembled leaders of the Warsaw Pact countries at their first brief meeting in the Kremlin after Konstantin Chernenko's funeral in March 1985 that future relations would respect the sovereignty and independence of each country, their reluctance to accept his affidavits at face value was understandable. The fear of intervention only slowly diminished. Gorbachev repeated his message a month later at a meeting of the leaders of the Warsaw Pact countries in Poland. His private remark, 'Let's not force anyone. Let each country decide what it should do,' became more widely known. To Polish observers, however, nothing pointed to what was to come. The rituals of Gorbachev's visit were no different from those of previous decades. In November 1986 in Moscow he made Eastern European leaders more formally aware that 'the Brezhnev doctrine' was obsolete. In Prague in April 1987 he declared the Soviet Union's acceptance of the right of each socialist land to determine its own future in the light of national interest. The following year Gorbachev again plainly stipulated that the states in the Soviet bloc had 'the right to choose'. The Soviet Foreign Ministry spokesman, Gennady Gerasimov, later wittily remarked that the 'Brezhnev doctrine' had been replaced by the 'Sinatra doctrine' – letting the Eastern Europeans do it their way.

So there would be no future resort to Soviet armed might in Eastern Europe. Leaders of the satellite countries had to recognize that no rescue was forthcoming from the Soviet Union if they failed to satisfy the demands of their peoples. They were not over-anxious to pass the message on to their peoples, since their own power depended upon them continuing to believe that Soviet intervention remained a possibility.

Indeed, Gorbachev himself did not publicly renounce 'the Brezhnev doctrine' when challenged by a Polish intellectual to do so in Warsaw in June 1988. Only gradually would the light dawn for ordinary people. When it did, in the course of 1989, the end of communist rule quickly followed.

Gorbachev's entirely new approach to relations between the Soviet Union and its satellite states in Eastern Europe, no longer regarding it as an absolute priority to hold a country at any cost, was decisive in establishing the platform for peaceful evolution to national independence and the introduction of pluralist democracy. No one in March 1985, when Gorbachev was elected General Secretary of the Soviet Communist Party, even experts far more aware than the general public of the structural crisis running through the Eastern European states, could imagine that these would collapse within five years. More than a year and a half after Gorbachev had become Soviet leader, in October 1986, one of the foremost experts on central Europe, Timothy Garton Ash, citing Václav Havel's long-term 'ideal of a democratic Europe as a friendly community of free and independent nations', commented: 'Hard to dissent from that; still harder to imagine its achievement.' Even as late as January 1989 Garton Ash was still more than doubtful that the division of Europe would be overcome. But from then on the political – no longer just economic – crisis of the entire Soviet bloc was starting to run out of control at an accelerating speed.

The magnitude of Gorbachev's personal contribution to the dramatic change, not just in the Soviet Union itself but throughout Eastern Europe, can scarcely be exaggerated. His was a classic case of Karl Marx's dictum that men do indeed make their own history, but 'under circumstances which they find before them' (and, it might be added, with consequences that they did not foresee). Of course, Gorbachev was able to act as he did because of the gravity of the structural problems in Eastern Europe. And of course, as in the Soviet Union, there were in every country – if in some more than in others – reformers who were prepared to support his reforms, and to press for more radical change. But without Gorbachev's singular readiness to embrace change, whatever the obstacles, history would have been different. How different is impossible to say. Probably at some stage the system would have imploded. But that might have taken years to happen, if at all, and under different conditions. That the collapse came so quickly, so decisively, and with so little violence and bloodshed, is to a great extent the personal achievement of Gorbachev.

BUSINESS AS USUAL: WEST EUROPEAN PREOCCUPATIONS

Few people in Western Europe were fully aware of the momentous changes that were shaking the foundations of the eastern half of the continent. Close interest in the internal development of the countries behind the Iron Curtain did not extend far beyond intellectual circles. The name 'Gorbachev', however, was soon familiar to anyone in the West who took the slightest notice of world affairs. The Soviet leader was indeed soon more popular throughout Western Europe than he was in his own country. That his changes promised greater freedom for the peoples of Eastern Europe and the Soviet Union accounted for some of his popularity. But overwhelmingly Gorbachev was popular because of the promise he held out for an end to the Cold War – for an end to the threat of nuclear annihilation that had hung like a sword of Damocles over the entire world for four decades.

Gorbachev's meetings with Western leaders – European leaders as well as Ronald Reagan – during his first years in power laid the ground for his growing popularity. His rapport with Margaret Thatcher, though they were ideologically polar opposites, continued to develop along the positive lines that had started when they had first met. The initial scepticism among Western European leaders about the genuine intentions of the new Kremlin chief was gradually assuaged. Through his engagement with their concerns and through force of personality, Gorbachev was able to persuade them that he was serious about nuclear disarmament and about trying to turn his notion of Europe as a 'common home', east and west, into reality. Early meetings with President Mitterrand and Mrs Thatcher did not go entirely smoothly. But alongside the airing of serious differences, a basis of mutual appreciation and understanding – a novelty in east–west relations in the Cold War – was created.

Gorbachev further built trust through talks on the complexities of disarmament with leading figures from NATO countries – Denmark, the Netherlands, Norway, Iceland and Italy, as well as Great Britain – after the

setback of the Reykjavik summit in October 1986. His first meeting, in October 1988 in Moscow, with Helmut Kohl, the West German Chancellor, also
struck a highly positive note. Kohl impressed Gorbachev with his earnest
desire for close cooperation in the interests of pan-European peace. Agreements on economic, scientific, cultural and environmental cooperation were
signed. The good personal relations between the two leaders played a crucial
role in establishing the platform for constructive long-term relations.

In a television age meetings between major political figures reached a
wide audience. Gorbachev had, soon after coming to power, taken part
in a live, critical interview by a group of Western journalists on French
television, the first time that a Soviet leader had been willing to engage
with the public in this way. Through news broadcasts his face soon
became well known to countless millions throughout Western Europe.
People warmed to his open personality – a complete contrast to the grim
visage of earlier Soviet leaders. And they responded well to his emphasis
on peace, nuclear disarmament and European unity.

Cheering crowds greeted him and his wife, Raisa, when they came to
London in April 1989. The reception was if anything even more rapturous when Gorbachev visited Bonn in June that year. West Germans, in
the firing line should it come to nuclear war, were unsurprisingly especially elated at the initiatives Gorbachev had taken towards disarmament.
'I will never forget our encounter with the citizens of Bonn in the Town
Hall Square,' he later wrote. 'We were literally overwhelmed by manifestations of goodwill and friendship, the cheering crowds expressing their
support and solidarity.'

It had taken time to reach this point. For all the positive tone of their
encounters, and the mutual trust that was gradually built up, there had
been serious stumbling blocks in the way of harmonious relations, above
all on the central question of nuclear disarmament. The three major
Western European powers at the heart of the nuclear debate – Great Britain, France and West Germany, the first two themselves nuclear powers,
the third in the front line of any nuclear confrontation in Europe –
brought their own national interests directly into play in reacting to
Gorbachev's initiatives. Thatcher and Mitterrand both disliked Reagan's
'Star Wars' programme, out of scepticism over its long-term effectiveness, from fear that it would undermine the entire notion of nuclear
deterrence, and, not least, because any ensuing nuclear disarmament

would directly affect their own international status as members of a very restricted 'nuclear club'.

Talk at the superpower summit in Reykjavik in October 1986 about removing all mid-range nuclear weapons from European soil did not go down at all well with Mrs Thatcher. The following month in Washington, President Reagan's openness to the idea of nuclear disarmament worried Thatcher, who feared that it would bolster the lobby for unilateral disarmament in Britain. 'We must not get into a situation where people were told that nuclear weapons were wicked, immoral and might soon be rendered unnecessary by the development of defensive systems,' she argued. It was important to retain popular support in Europe for the deployment of cruise and Pershing missiles, as well as to modernize Britain's own nuclear arsenal. The Americans, she asserted, should warn Moscow that if the Soviet Union did not reduce nuclear arms, the 'Star Wars' programme would proceed. She won assurance that the NATO strategy of deterrence would remain in place.

Mitterrand's position did not vary in essentials from that of Thatcher. Kohl's welcome for 'Star Wars' was also muted, though from a different perspective. He was not convinced that the system would work. He doubted that it was either technologically or financially feasible. And above all he worried that a nuclear shield would in practice be deployed to protect the United States, while leaving Europe more vulnerable to nuclear attack. This worry was not fully assuaged even by the real progress Gorbachev and Reagan made on arms control, since the agreement they eventually reached in Washington in December 1987 on intermediate-range missiles, significant breakthrough that it was, did not cover tactical nuclear weapons with a range of under 500 kilometres – exactly the type of weapon that, it was feared, would be used in a superpower battlefield confrontation on German soil.

At the same time Kohl came to believe Gorbachev's sincerity in aiming to end the nuclear arms race. This had not initially been Kohl's position. The Bonn government had been sceptical about the true aims of the new Kremlin chief. In an interview in October 1986 Kohl had even insultingly (and absurdly) compared Gorbachev's mastery of the media with that of the Nazi propaganda minister Joseph Goebbels. The Soviet press naturally responded furiously. In the West, too, where disarmament talks were at an early and sensitive stage, Kohl's clumsiness went down badly. It was, however, in the interest neither of Bonn nor of Moscow to dwell on the faux pas. Kohl apologized to Gorbachev, putting the blame on the press. Influenced by his experienced and diplomatically agile Foreign Minister, Hans-Dietrich Genscher, who quickly recognized that it was directly in West Germany's advantage to work actively to support Gorbachev's initiatives, Kohl became convinced of the new opportunities for close cooperation. His decision in October 1987 to remove Pershing missiles from West German soil signalled German readiness to adjust as rapidly as possible to the new climate.

Hope of lasting improvement in relations between the West and the Soviet Union had grown markedly by that time. Hardly any Western European leader, however, even then could anticipate the speed of developments over the coming year, or believe that by the end of 1989 the Berlin Wall – symbol of the Cold War – would have come down. When President Reagan, standing in front of the Brandenburg Gate in West Berlin on 12 June 1987, demanded 'Mr Gorbachev, tear down this wall!', the sentiment was applauded but the demand itself seemed no more than a rhetorical flourish. The Wall appeared destined to last into the indefinite future and indeed, ran some arguments, it remained a welcome source of stability, permanently putting the 'German Question' on hold. A month later, when he met the impressive West German President, Richard von Weizsäcker, who tentatively raised the issue of German unity, Gorbachev remarked that 'history would decide what would happen in a hundred years'.

Beyond the promising developments in international relations, the people of Western European countries were largely preoccupied with their own concerns, which were utterly detached from the dramatic shifts taking place east of the Iron Curtain. Europe was still a continent of two quite separate halves.

The social, economic and cultural transitions that had taken root in Western Europe during the 1970s intensified during the subsequent decade. The term that seemed to capture the spirit of the age was 'postmodernism'. What it precisely meant no one could define. It was generally taken to imply a transition from a society dominated by industry to a computerized world shaped by information technology, and from 'high' Westernized culture to global mass culture. It also signified divergence, dissonance, a pluralism of interpretations, the absence of any claim to an authoritative voice, to cultural superiority or predominance. Perhaps the very vagueness of the concept helped its appeal. From philosophy to the visual arts, through literary criticism to historical understanding, it voiced a pervasive sense of scepticism, relativism, uncertainty and fragmentation. Notions of progress, of rationality, of truth, of any single comprehensible way of grasping where society had come from and where it was going, evaporated under the lens of postmodernist critique. The rejection of any 'objective reality' favoured a splintering of cultural interpretation into a myriad of individualist, subjective approaches or 'discourses', none of which could claim superiority over others. Although cultural unity had always been a chimera, the extent to which postmodernism penetrated intellectual understanding during the 1980s and afterwards did reflect in oblique ways the increasing breakdown of the collective and the dominance of the individualistic in society.

The decline in a sense of society as a collective concern and responsibility was enhanced as a greater focus on individual choice and individualist lifestyles caught hold. Advertising agencies, and the attractions of consumer choice brought nightly to the attention of much of the population through the spread of commercial television, played a big role in this trend. Consumer spending had not been seriously interrupted during the downturn of the 1970s. And as economies recovered from their earlier travails consumerism reached new heights. Shopping 'malls', an import from the United States, started to spring up in town centres or as enormous cathedrals of consumerism on the outskirts of city centres. People could shop there to their heart's content, under cover, with free parking facilities and an array of cafés that allowed them a moment's relaxation to ponder what they had bought and what they needed to buy before rejoining the hurly-burly. The spread in the use of credit cards encouraged people to spend now and pay later. 'Shopping' was no longer a matter of acquiring daily necessities. It became a leisure pursuit in itself – a pleasurable search for the latest bargains or fashions. Some trendy clothes carried a designer's logo – a brilliant way of obliging the wearer to provide free further advertising. The choice of clothing became in itself one of the most distinctive indicators of the new individualism – a way for all to see of demonstrating individual taste and highlighting the wearer as a beacon of fashion-consciousness.

Leisure was also becoming more individualized. Personal computers – another major influence from across the Atlantic – made their entry into

European society. Computers were still limited in what they offered. But what they did offer was by now expanding hugely. During the 1980s development of the microchip (an invention of the 1950s) made a quantum leap, enabling ever larger memory capacity on tiny integrated electronic circuits. By the end of the decade a single microchip could incorporate over a million interconnected transistors allowing a vast expansion of memory and the application of computer technology to more and more everyday commodities. Governments recognized that computer skills would be vital in the future and began introducing them into school classrooms. Young people, though, embraced computers first and foremost because of the electronic games that they could now play in their own living rooms – shooting down as many 'space invaders' as possible in what could become an obsessive and endless solo activity. The American company Atari, the Japanese enterprise Nintendo and Binatone, founded in Britain, led the boom in electronic games during the 1980s.

Popular music (in its widest definition) also reflected fragmentation. The still enormously expanding commercial potential of popular music promoted ever varied innovation. Subcultures of popular music such as punk rock, heavy metal or hip-hop, spreading from the United States during the 1970s and producing derivative offspring well into the next decade, developed cult followings. Other subgenres, including new wave, synthpop or dance-rock, also vied for popularity among young people and established their own clienteles of passionate followers. More wide-ranging in their appeal, with millions of fans worldwide, were British bands such as Duran Duran, Spandau Ballet and Culture Club (whose star singer, Boy George, became famous in his own right), individual artists like the hugely talented and inventive David Bowie, or the long-established but still flourishing West German band Kraftwerk. The computer revolution made a major contribution to the musical experimentation and popular success of these and many other artists, who could benefit from the rapid development of electronic synthesizers. A television channel dedicated to popular music, MTV (an American channel available on the rapidly spreading cable and satellite networks), and the new potential offered by video recordings, meant that these and countless other musicians were able to reach huge audiences, almost exclusively among the young. But listening to music – beyond live concerts – was increasingly a personalized experience. The Walkman, a

Japanese invention of the late 1970s, became an emblematic accoutrement for teenagers during the following decade. The tiny stereo cassette-player let people take their music with them, wherever they went, listening to audiotapes on headphones, cut off from the world as they sat engrossed in their music on buses, underground trains, in cars or in their own rooms at home.

The younger generation was at the forefront, as it had been since the 1960s, of liberalizing social values. Feminist values were far more widely upheld by both sexes, although equal rights for women remained an elusive goal, not least in the workplace. Sexual freedom became far more socially acceptable than it had been only a few years earlier. The 1980s discovered, however, that there was a terrible, unexpected aspect to the expanded sexual freedoms. A new killer disease, discovered in the United States in 1981, was, it was established, spread by sexual contact. 'Acquired Immune Deficiency Syndrome', or AIDS as it swiftly became universally known, had no cure (though over time medical treatment was able to slow down the progress of the disease that, as the name implied, aggressively attacked and eventually destroyed the body's immune system). Although AIDS resulted from heterosexual as well as homosexual sex – and also seemingly innocent blood transfusions in hospitals – it was during the 1980s heavily associated with homosexuality, leading to an upsurge in discrimination and intolerance towards gay men, who were left reeling by this devastating illness. By the mid-1990s reported AIDS-related deaths reached a high point in Europe of nearly 20,000 people a year. Some other parts of the world, notably the African continent, were far worse affected. Worldwide it has been estimated that HIV (Human Immunodeficiency Virus), which if untreated leads to AIDS, has claimed the lives of about 35 million people since the 1980s.

The decline of state ownership of industry and moves towards privatization, which accelerated sharply during the 1980s, in some ways accorded with the shift away from collective values. Privatization, spasmodic during the 1960s and 1970s, now became routine. Western European states profited from privatization – at least in the short term – by some $150 billion by the late 1990s.

Britain, the closest European country to the American ideals of deregulated capitalism that had been emphatically reinforced under Ronald Reagan, led the way. Margaret Thatcher was, in fact, more single-minded in her zeal for deregulation than the American President, and privatization was a central component of her determination to reduce the size of the state. By 1986 the British financial sector was largely deregulated. This bolstered the primacy of the City of London in the British economy, turning Britain more sharply than anywhere else in Europe into heavy dependence on its service and, especially, its financial sector. The rapid shrinkage of Britain's manufacturing base was the opposite side of the coin.

The Labour movement of course strongly resisted policies of privatization. But the Labour Party suffered resounding electoral defeats in 1983 and 1987, while the trade unions were weakened and losing members. Beyond ardent Labour supporters, and including many within the working class, privatization was in fact popular. Millions of individuals, including thousands of employees of nationalized companies, became shareholders in privatized companies as state assets were sold off. Inevitably, of course, most shares were swallowed up by big investors, many of them in time non-British, who actually controlled the companies. Traditional patrician conservatives sometimes lamented the trend that was so welcomed especially by the young, upwardly mobile middle classes – the 'Yuppies' as they were contemptuously dubbed by the left. The former Prime Minister Harold Macmillan, by now well into old age, famously criticized his successor, Mrs Thatcher, remarking that she was 'selling off the family silver'. It was to no avail. Two-thirds of the once state-owned British industries were in private hands by 1992, including some of the most crucial parts of industry such as gas or telecommunications.

Alongside privatization went de-industrialization. This was a European-wide trend that had set in during the 1970s. But it went farthest and fastest in Britain. West Germany had done much in the 1970s to cushion the blow on communities of the demise of the old coal and steel industries, as well as protecting newer industries, upholding a large manufacturing sector, and sustaining high levels of technological and engineering skills. The following decade Britain, on the other hand, closed down at breathtaking pace much of its old manufacturing base. Coal, steel and shipbuilding were soon little more than a part of Britain's industrial past. Little was done to mitigate the social damage done as tens of thousands of workers lost the main source of their livelihood. No alternative employment was available that could easily or adequately compensate for the final closing down of a factory that had once provided work for an entire community, while towns were now left demoralized, without an economic raison d'être, their local institutions and social cohesion undermined. Entire swathes of the country – the old industrial heartlands in South Wales, in the Clyde Valley of Scotland, and in the north of England – were alienated (and would remain so into the indefinite future) by government policy that they saw as favouring only commercial and banking interests, above all the City of London.

For all the widespread animosity towards Thatcherism in Britain's industrial regions, many in the working class were themselves ready to profit from policies that redistributed ownership from the state to private individuals. Some 1.7 million tenants of council houses, built at state cost over decades for the less well-off, accepted the government's offer to buy the property they lived in at heavily subsidized prices. It was touted as the route to a 'property-owning democracy'. And the sales produced £24 billion for government coffers, contributing to the ability to lower taxation. But these were one-off gains. The council houses, once sold, could not be resold by the state. And if the state was not going to replenish the supply of council houses – as, it was obvious, the Thatcher government had no interest in doing – the long-term consequence was likely to be a housing shortage and a transfer of rental profits to private landlords.

The pattern of de-industrialization and privatization in Britain in the 1980s was extreme. Labour legislation meant that employees on the continent were often better protected than was the case in Britain, making changes in working practices more difficult to achieve. Modernization of industries and investment in training as well as capital was much more significant, especially in West Germany and France. Belief in the role of the state and its support for public services was also stronger than in Britain. Resistance to privatization was, therefore, substantial in instances where it was widely felt that key public services were threatened. Still, the economic forces that had provided the impetus for the British government to grasp the nettle of privatization with both hands affected every country to a varying extent. In France, where the socialist President Mitterrand had to 'co-habit' by 1986 with a conservative National Assembly (and a Gaullist Prime Minister, Jacques Chirac), the privatization of banks and branches of industry offered, as in Britain, the opportunity for ordinary people to become shareholders. That the demand for shares outstripped the supply indicated the popularity of the move. West

Germany, too, was by the mid-1980s in the process of deregulating financial services, energy, and its commercial television and radio channels. By the end of the decade commercial parts of the postal services were also privatized. Among the largest European economies Italy was the country where privatization made only partial headway in the 1980s. Some big companies such as Alfa Romeo and state-owned banks, for instance the commercial bank Mediobanca, indeed shifted from the public to the private sector. But the bulk of heavy industry, most of the major banks and insurance firms, radio, television and the health service remained (before a second wave of privatization in the 1990s) within the public sector. But the Italian economy, which had earlier thrived, was by now lacking in innovation, inefficient and bloated in manpower, leaving it increasingly uncompetitive.

As the numbers employed in industry dropped – over a fifth of industrial jobs were lost on average in advanced economies between 1979 and 1994 – the character of the working class changed, and with that the nature of class politics. The old monolithic industries had gone, or were going. The close-knit class identities that these industries had spawned were dying. Ever more young people from working-class backgrounds had individual interests and pursuits not available to earlier generations. They had little or no experience of the collective interests that had come from sharing the same type of work, similar mentalities, similar lifestyles. They had grown up with privatization, had no expectation of (or desire to) follow their fathers and grandfathers to work down coal mines or into steel mills, had moved away from deadened communities to more prosperous areas (or sometimes abroad) often to find employment in white-collar occupations, or had benefited from rapidly expanding opportunities to study at university and moved up the social ladder.

The changing structure of employment, and gradual shifts in social culture, did offer some new prospects to women. Feminist values were far more widely upheld by both sexes, especially the younger generation, than had been the case only a decade earlier. But if equal rights for women remained an elusive goal, not least in the workplace, job opportunities, advancement or pay, women could nevertheless benefit from the rapidly changing conditions. Thousands, no longer bound to the home or work in a nearby office or town, were able to move to newly expanding cities to find employment in administration, hotels, health occupations, marketing or, for a growing minority with university education, in the professions and management. Women with children were entering the labour market far more often than had been the case even in the recent past. As the proportion of men in employment declined somewhat, the proportion of women rose – though most of the increase was in part-time work. Women's fight for equality would continue. But the changes that were altering women's lives and opportunities militated, as they did with men, towards greater self-assertion, individualism, and away from old, more collective lifestyles, identities and interests.

The backbone of Europe's Social Democratic and Labour parties was weakened in the process. Socialist traditions were dissolving. And among young people, even those on the left, there was no great appetite for the high-taxation regime that had been the staple of social democracy's welfare state. Low taxation to maximize the amount retained in wages and salaries for consumer spending on individualist tastes was increasingly preferred to financing public services through high taxation. But as Social Democratic parties were able to offer no viable or sustainable economic alternative to the widely adopted policies of rationalization, enhanced competition in the globalized market and privatization, they started to be seen in the eyes of many – often those who had been disadvantaged by globalization and de-industrialization – as little different in essence from Conservative or Christian Democratic parties.

The erosion of class-based parties was still only partial and limited. Indeed, in some countries it was still barely perceptible. It was only the beginning. But the trend towards movements of national or regional identity, though still not of major significance, was certainly discernible in some parts of Europe. Nationalist parties started to gain support in Scotland, Catalonia and Flanders. In each case growing economic prosperity – in Scotland mainly related to the still expanding oilfields in the North Sea – enhanced people's feelings that they were disadvantaged by policies of their central governments, whether these were based in London, Madrid or Brussels. Disaffection in Austria at the duopoly of the Conservative and Social Democratic parties that had run Austria since the end of the war brought a trebling of support (to nearly 17 per cent of the vote by 1990) for the right-wing nationalist programme of the Austrian Freedom Party (FPÖ), under its flamboyant leader Jörg Haider, whose populism was tinged with approving comments about the Third

Reich. In France the National Front, drawing on support from disillusioned conservative middle-class voters but also making inroads into the working class, regularly attracted around 10 per cent of French voters during elections in the 1980s, while the party's populist and racist leader, Jean-Marie le Pen (a veteran of the Algerian War), took as much as 14.4 per cent of the vote in the 1988 presidential election that was won by Mitterrand and the Socialists.

Growing awareness of environmental damage from industry and from modern consumer demands formed another emerging element in the changing political constellation. These were global concerns, reflections of the impact on every part of the world from a globalized economy. The international organization Greenpeace, founded in Canada in 1971, drew worldwide attention to the destruction of the environment, sometimes through spectacular actions that won media attention, such as blocking Rhine shipping for three days in 1980. Recognition that great, perhaps irreparable, damage was being done to the environment started to seep more deeply into people's consciousness. The seriousness of what was taking place was undeniable. Various reports showed the damage from carbons produced, for example, by refrigerators, hairsprays and other domestic aerosols to the ozone layer (which filters out ultraviolet radiation from the sun); the poisoning of fisheries through outpourings of industrial chemicals; the 'acid rain' from chemical emissions that was destroying vegetation and polluting water supplies; the dangers of lead in petrol; the loss of Amazonian rainforests to produce timber for the developed world; and the immense harm to wildlife caused by huge spillage from oil tankers that ran aground (such as the Exxon Valdez in Alaska in March 1989, leaking ten million tons of crude oil and killing immense numbers of birds). Western governments could not ignore the warnings indefinitely. The environment was becoming a political issue.

Green parties, reflecting the widening anxieties about environmental damage, started to proliferate. By the mid-1980s they had been established in most Western European countries. Beyond West Germany (where the Greens had formed a political party in 1980 and won sufficient votes to enter the federal parliament three years later) they had not as yet entered the political mainstream. Even so, they were making progress. In 1984 the first Green members of the European Parliament were elected. The shock of the Chernobyl disaster of April 1986 gave

environmental politics, particularly in northwestern Europe, a significant boost. The Swedish Greens, founded in 1981, were by 1988 the first
new party for seventy years to enter the Swedish parliament. In Finland
the Greens, founded in 1987, won ten seats in parliament four years later.
Elsewhere, environmental movements remained peripheral in parliamentary politics, but were gradually able to influence traditional parties into
growing interest in ecological matters.

Increased awareness of environmental issues was matched during the
1980s by enhanced sensitivity towards racism. Neo-fascist and racist parties and organizations were regarded as abhorrent by most of the
population. Racial tolerance was coming to be seen generally as the
plainest hallmark of a civilized society. Race hatred was, accordingly,
viewed as the absolute negation of all standards of humanity. Racism of
course did not disappear. But politically, culturally and socially it had
become taboo, its outward expressions suppressed as unacceptable. As
immigration into most Western European countries increased, societies
had to try – and did so with varying success – to adjust to the challenges
of multiculturalism. But sensitivity towards race was conditioned not
just by current concerns.

The ghosts of the past were returning to haunt the present. Until the
end of the 1970s the terrible events during the Second World War that had
culminated in the Holocaust – the term was only just starting to be universally used to signify the German planned extermination of Europe's
Jews – had not penetrated far into general public consciousness. Historians had, of course, written about it. But their scholarly analyses had not
reached a wide public. This was about to change – though not, primarily,
as an outflow of the work of historians. The Holocaust was about to
become a touchstone of historical consciousness in Western Europe.

The change partly arose from conscious attempts within the Jewish
community in the United States to foster a sense of identity centred on the
Holocaust. It was not simply a matter of preserving historical memory,
important though this was. 'Moral capital', it was felt, could unify 'collective memory', and could help to bolster support for policies favourable
to Israel. Symptoms of the changing climate were the foundation in 1977
of the Simon Wiesenthal Center in Los Angeles, named after the celebrated Nazi-hunter (himself a Holocaust survivor) Simon Wiesenthal,
and, even more important, the decision two years later to establish a

Holocaust Memorial Museum in the heart of Washington D.C. Holocaust memorials and commemorative days began to proliferate. Teaching on the Holocaust in American schools and universities started to spread. In 1978 the major breakthrough into general consciousness of US citizens came with the showing on prime-time television of a four-part series simply entitled *Holocaust*, which was watched by nearly 100 million Americans. The fictional drama that followed the lives of a Jewish family, exposed to the full horrors of the Holocaust, and an SS man who rose to a leading position in the implementation of the extermination programme, captured the imagination in ways that scholarly literature could never do. Jewish organizations maximized the subsequent publicity opportunities presented by the success of the series to spread awareness of the Holocaust still further, both in Jewish and non-Jewish communities.

In West Germany a year later the showing of the series was a sensation. *Holocaust* was watched by around 20 million viewers (around half of the West German viewing population), who were transfixed by the personalized and highly emotional dramatic depiction of persecution and extermination. People empathized with the victims and recognized the monumentality of the crime as they had never done before. 'A nation is shocked' was the verdict of one scholarly analysis of the impact of the film. '*Holocaust* has shaken up post-Hitler Germany in a way that German intellectuals have been unable to do,' commented the widely read weekly *Der Spiegel*. More than three decades after the end of the war an American film, criticized by some as reducing the destruction of the Jews to the level of a 'soap opera', had opened up the sense of national guilt. The following year the Federal Parliament (the Bundestag) abolished the statute of limitations on war crimes, permitting further legal prosecution of perpetrators of the Holocaust. The film was widely seen as playing a significant role in the decision.

From this point on, West German historical writing as well as public awareness focused on the Holocaust as never before.* In 1985 the fortieth anniversary of the end of the Second World War (publicized in the mass

---

* I was present in 1979 at a major conference of German and British historians on the Nazi state. Remarkably, not a single paper was devoted to the Holocaust. Only a few years later that would have been unthinkable. The first West German conference

media far more extensively than on any previous anniversary) kept the Holocaust, and other German wartime atrocities, in the public eye. The visit by President Reagan, on the invitation of the West German Chancellor, Helmut Kohl, to a war cemetery at Bitburg in May 1985 as part of the commemoration of the end of the war, backfired when it transpired that the cemetery held graves of SS men. Kohl was by this time trying to reconcile German responsibility for the Holocaust with the attempt – seen as important to preserve positive relations between the Federal Republic and its most important ally, the USA – to emphasize the positive transformation of his country since the end of the war and to acknowledge that it had broken the shackles of the past.

This played its part in the rancorous dispute about the Holocaust, involving practically all West Germany's leading historians, that occupied the pages of the country's leading newspapers for weeks during 1986. At the core of the dispute was the question of how the Nazi past – and above all responsibility for the Holocaust – fitted into present and future West German consciousness. Should guilt for Nazism's crimes give way to a more positive sense of national identity, as was forcefully argued by Michael Stürmer, a prominent historian and speechwriter for Helmut Kohl? Or was Auschwitz essential to West German identity, as the eminent social philosopher Jürgen Habermas claimed? Was the Holocaust, in fact, no worse than the crimes of Stalinism? Such issues – and above all the question of the uniqueness of the Holocaust – preoccupied West German intellectuals in 1986. Much of the general public naturally had little interest in the historians' dispute. For many people it was time to move on from obsessing about the Nazi past and being consumed by guilt for events in which they themselves had played no part. Even so, the resonance of the dispute showed that the Holocaust had become a lodestar of West German consciousness.

Beyond West Germany a concatenation of separate events caught the public imagination throughout Western Europe and beyond, and drew international attention to the Holocaust. Claude Lanzmann's *Shoah*, released in cinemas in 1985, a searing documentary based on the eyewitness testimony of victims, graphically illustrated the horror of the

---

specifically related to the Holocaust did not take place until 1984, almost four decades after the end of the war.

extermination camps. The trial of Klaus Barbie, the former Gestapo chief in Lyon (extradited in 1983 from his Bolivian exile to France), which exposed his role in the torture of the resistance hero Jean Moulin, and the deportation of over 200 Jews, kept the Holocaust in the public eye in France. And the 'Waldheim Affair' in 1986, in which the elected President of Austria and former Secretary-General of the United Nations, Kurt Waldheim, was forced to admit that he covered up the truth about his wartime service in Yugoslavia and Greece, where his unit had perpetrated serious atrocities, shone the international spotlight on Austria's reluctance to acknowledge its part in the Nazi catastrophe. In one way or another the Holocaust was by now seldom out of the attention of the mass media – and, consequently, of substantial parts of the population. The Second World War started to be seen in a different light, with emphasis increasingly placed on racial policy, Nazi barbarity on the Eastern Front, and above all the genocide against the Jews.

Whatever the reshaping of the social and cultural landscape, economically and politically Western Europe remained stable in the later 1980s. The economic turmoil of the previous decade had been surmounted. Politically, there was much continuity. Helmut Kohl's government was re-elected in West Germany in 1986, Margaret Thatcher's in Britain the following year, and François Mitterrand – whose economic policy had retreated far from its earlier socialist programme – won a second term in office as French President in 1988. Following elections in 1987 in Italy, the Christian Democrats returned to head the government, replacing the socialist-led administration of Bettino Craxi, while the Communist vote had slumped. The late 1980s seemed a time of optimism in Italy, too, though behind the scenes corruption and escalating state indebtedness were worrying developments.

The European Community also looked with renewed optimism to the future. After some years of stagnation, 'Eurosclerosis' as it was dubbed, 'The Single European Act' of 1986 – the first time that the Treaty of Rome of 1957 had been substantially amended – breathed new life into the Community. The Act aimed to establish by 1992 a single market to allow for free movement of goods, services, capital and people within the borders of the European Community without national barriers or constraints. The driving force behind the innovation was the dynamic, newly appointed President of the European Commission, Jacques Delors. But

Delors wanted to use the Act as a step towards attaining *political* union. In the summer of 1988 Delors told the European Parliament that he wanted to see 'the beginnings of a European government' within ten years. This put him on a direct collision course with Mrs Thatcher, and much of the British population. Thatcher had, in fact, played no small role in pressing for the Single Market. But she saw the European Union, as did much of the British political class and, led by them, most of the population, as little more than an economic entity, a free-trade zone. In contrast to Delors she fundamentally ruled out the aim of European political union. 'We have not successfully rolled back the frontiers of the state in Britain, only to see them re-imposed at a European level with a European super-state exercising a new dominance from Brussels,' thundered the British Prime Minister in a speech in Bruges on 20 September. The speech marked the beginning of sustained 'Euroscepticism' – opposition to British membership of the European Community – in Britain, with Mrs Thatcher as its champion (even though she had plainly stated at Bruges that Britain's 'destiny is in Europe as part of the Community'). By 1990 'Europe' was dividing her party, and her government. It contributed signally to Mrs Thatcher's resignation as Prime Minister on 22 November 1990. And it was set to remain a festering sore at the heart of British politics. Beyond that, the clash between Delors and Thatcher reflected the crucial underlying tension in the European Union, one that had been present ever since the early ruminations on future European unity by Jean Monnet back in 1950: the tension between supranational objectives and national sovereignty. It was an issue that would continue to bedevil European politics.

* * *

By the time of Mrs Thatcher's downfall, Europe itself had been transformed. During the 1980s Western and Eastern Europe had continued to follow different trajectories. In 1989 this altered dramatically. From the spring of that year Western Europe looked with new interest, excitement and astonishment at what was happening east of the Iron Curtain as Gorbachev's winds of change, by now a hurricane, uprooted the structures of communist domination that had been in place for over forty years.

9

Power of the People

No one has yet witnessed a society with nationalized property, a planned economy, and a democratic and pluralistic political structure.

Adam Michnik, *Letters from Prison and Other Essays*, 1985

By 1991 the Cold War was over, the Iron Curtain confined to the past. 'The end of an era' is a common cliché. Here, the term is accurate. What happened between 1989 and 1991 was no less than a European revolution – and, amazingly, unlike earlier revolutions it was (largely) free of bloodshed. How was that possible?

Without Mikhail Gorbachev it might not have been. It is possible in retrospect to see the structural reasons behind the collapse of the Soviet Union and its satellite states in Eastern Europe. But without Gorbachev there is no reason to presume that the collapse would have come when it did, would have taken the course that it did, or would have had the consequences it did. His role was indispensable.

Even so, another force was necessary to bring about the revolution in Eastern Europe: the power of the people. Emboldened by what they were seeing in the Soviet Union the peoples of Eastern Europe rebelled against the communist masters who had held them in thrall for over forty years. A prelude had taken place in Poland in 1980 when popular opposition to communist rule had led to the formation of the Solidarity movement and had shaken the existing regime to the core. The following year, however, the ruling forces in Poland had struck back. Solidarity was banned, the opposition suppressed, the pressure for change blocked. Once the new wind blew in the Soviet Union in the later 1980s Solidarity was revitalized. In neither Poland nor elsewhere was it expected that the end of communist rule would come quickly. But in late 1989, in an avalanche of change, the existing regimes were overturned. In each country the people sought, and won, their freedom. The revolution from above that Gorbachev had instigated had turned into a revolution from below as the people realized their rulers stood on ground that was trembling. In one country after another, they took power into their own hands. Finally, the change that had commenced there swept back in an unstoppable force over the Soviet Union itself. What had stood, seemingly indomitable, for nearly seventy years, was demolished in two.

THE SATELLITES DROP OUT OF ORBIT

Poland, as it had done since 1980, led the way. The elections held on 4 June 1989 brought a landslide victory for Solidarity, which by now had morphed from a trade union – where it was, in fact, much weaker than it had been in 1980 – into, effectively, a political party. The modest turnout of only 62 per cent probably reflected a high degree of mistrust for elections that many believed would change nothing. But the result could not have been plainer. In the first round Solidarity won 92 of the 100 seats in the Senate and 160 of the 161 seats open to it in the Sejm (the lower house of parliament). Mingling with the exhilaration was fear. On the very afternoon of the election television had brought pictures of tanks rolling into Tiananmen Square in Beijing where hundreds of students, demonstrating for democracy, were mown down by government troops. How would the Polish government react to the opposition victory at the polls? In fact, the regime accepted the verdict of the people. Forty years of communist domination were over – almost, but not quite.

Government was still in the hands of the Communists, and General Jaruzelski was duly elected to the new post of Executive President. The second round of voting on 18 June confirmed, however, the rout of the communist establishment. Around 65 per cent of the votes cast went to Solidarity, though at only 25 per cent the turnout was miserably low. Jaruzelski's offer to Solidarity to participate in a grand coalition was refused. On 7 August Solidarity's leader, Lech Wałęsa, proposed a government led by Solidarity, backed by smaller parties that had earlier been mere puppets of the Communist Party (by now a minority party in the Sejm). By 24 August Poland had a leading member of Solidarity, Tadeusz Mazowiecki, an intellectual with a long history as a political dissident, as its new Prime Minister – appointed by the communist President Jaruzelski and approved by nearly all the communist deputies in the Sejm. During the following months the foundations of the communist state were systematically dismantled. Poland became simply a republic, no longer a People's Republic; police and army were depoliticized; the constitution eliminated the leading role of the Communist Party; and the party dissolved itself (re-emerging in January 1990 as the Social Democratic Party). But with the end of the common enemy went any unity among the opposition.

During 1990 pressure built on Jaruzelski to step down as President. But when he did so the leaders of Solidarity belied the name of their movement. The recently re-elected Chairman of Solidarity, Lech Wałęsa, declared his own candidacy, directly challenging Mazowiecki, formerly one of his closest advisors. Impatient for faster change, imperious in manner, but with a sure populist touch that enabled him to give unique voice to the spreading discontent, Wałęsa was resentful at the way he felt the intellectuals in the movement, such as Mazowiecki and Adam Michnik, had sidelined him. Elections in November (with a second round in December) resulted in defeat for the intellectual and overwhelming victory for the electrician and former trade union leader, who was sworn in on 22 December 1990. By this time Solidarity itself had splintered, losing support to new parties that had emerged in the new Polish democracy. Poland was rapidly turning into a recognizable pluralist society. A remarkable political transition had taken place democratically and without bloodshed.

Economically, the early experience of pluralist democracy was less successful. 'Shock therapy', known from the name of the new Finance Minister, Leszek Balcerowicz, as the 'Balcerowicz Plan', was applied to the state-controlled economy, which from the beginning of 1990 was abruptly opened up to market forces. The swift consequence of extensive deregulation and currency devaluation was soaring inflation. Exports rose while those of other parts of Eastern Europe languished. But by the time of Wałęsa's election as President the rate of inflation had reached nearly 250 per cent, there was nothing to buy in the shops, production had fallen drastically, and there was a sharp rise in unemployment. Average real incomes dropped by a third. Relief of much of the debt to foreign countries and stringent conditions for support from the International Monetary Fund gradually formed the basis of economic recovery over subsequent years. By then the privatization of Poland's economy was well under way. In economics as well as in politics, Poland was fast learning what it meant to be a 'Western' country.

On 16 June 1989, less than a fortnight after the election in Poland that had ushered in the end of communism there, came the Hungarian moment. An enormous crowd, around 200,000 people, had assembled in Heroes' Square in Budapest for the televised ceremonial reburial of the hero of the 1956 uprising, Imre Nagy – hanged by the communist regime after a farcical show trial in 1956. The previous year police had violently broken up a demonstration to mark the anniversary of Nagy's execution. Now, a year later, Heroes' Square was draped no longer with the hammer and sickle banner but with the national flag. The last speaker to pay tribute to Nagy's memory was Viktor Orbán from the Young Democrats. Orbán drew rapturous applause when he declared: 'If we can trust our souls and strength, we can put an end to the communist dictatorship.' The steps to that end followed rapidly, one after the other. And, as in Poland, they proceeded peacefully.

János Kádár, who was responsible for Nagy's execution, did not live to see the demise of the state that he had presided over for so long, dying of cancer on 6 July 1989. A month earlier the Communist Party had agreed to talks with the Round Table of oppositional groups that had been set up in March. But much of the summer was taken up by disagreements within the oppositional groups, while the Communists – themselves divided – continued to run the government. In a confused and confusing situation, the trajectory was nonetheless plain. Free parliamentary elections were agreed on 18 September, though other aspects of the transition to democracy, especially the question of whether parliamentary elections should precede elections to the presidency, were still matters of dispute among the oppositional groups. Early the following month the Communists dissolved their party and changed its name – officially, it had been the Hungarian Socialist Workers' Party – to simply the Hungarian Socialist Party. On 23 October, the anniversary of the 1956 revolution, the new Hungarian Republic – as in Poland, no longer a 'People's

Republic – was proclaimed to an enormous crowd gathered outside the parliament building in Budapest. The long-delayed parliamentary elections – marking the return to pluralist politics – eventually took place in March and April 1990 and produced an unwieldy coalition of mainly liberal and centre-right conservative parties.

A summer of much inertia followed, during which the economic situation sharply deteriorated. Although Hungary's economy had for many years been more open to limited forms of private enterprise than any other Soviet-bloc state, and had recently moved further in that direction, full exposure to the vagaries of the market introduced Hungarians to the harsh realities of Western capitalism. But heavy indebtedness to the West and inflation that was threatening to run out of control meant, as in Poland, that there was little alternative to seeking Western support, however difficult the transition might be. IMF financial aid helped Hungary overcome the difficult transition – though only after new austerity measures had been introduced in July 1990. That autumn, too, the government introduced a big programme of privatization. As elsewhere in the former Soviet bloc, neo-liberal economic ideas, largely imported from the United States, were dominant. Opinion surveys indicated that by that time there was less public confidence in the recently elected democratic government than there had been in the previous communist administration. Meanwhile, Soviet troops, once numbering around 100,000 in Hungary, were withdrawing, the last of them leaving in March 1991. This was the most visible sign that Hungary had in effect pulled out of the Warsaw Pact and was turning to the West. The decisive moment had in fact already occurred in the summer of 1989.

That August, Hungary had agreed, in return for substantial financial aid from West Germany, to open its border to Austria for East Germans. With this single move Hungary not only turned its back on the obligation to return anyone seeking to leave a fellow socialist country to their land of origin; crucially, it created a hole in the Iron Curtain. When the border was opened, on the night of 10–11 September, thousands of East German citizens voted with their feet, crossing through Hungary into Austria, first into holding camps, then from there into the Federal Republic of Germany. By the end of October 50,000 had left.

They also took refuge in embassies of the Federal Republic in Budapest, Prague and Warsaw. On 30 September 1989 the West German

Foreign Minister, Hans-Dietrich Genscher, announced on television that he had successfully negotiated with Moscow and East Berlin to transfer 60,000 GDR citizens to the Federal Republic. Thousands standing on station platforms, and millions more watching on television, jubilantly greeted the sealed trains that transported the refugees west.

Even seasoned observers of the German Democratic Republic had not foreseen such rapid or radical change. GDR leaders themselves were certainly unprepared for it. The East German leader Erich Honecker had recently remarked that he could envisage the Berlin Wall standing in a hundred years' time. There had, indeed, been a growth in opposition to the regime across the summer, much of it articulated by Protestant pastors. But intellectuals, unlike those in Poland and Hungary, had largely been in the regime's pocket. Political nonconformism up to this point had posed no great threat to the regime. The regime's leaders, for their part, showed no willingness to make concessions. Local elections in May 1989 had been blatantly rigged. Party hardliners backed the Chinese massacres of the students in Tiananmen Square; regrettable, but necessary to protect socialism, was the tenor of the justification. And the Stasi – the feared state security service – still retained its vice-like grip over society.

Outwardly, the regime continued to exude confidence. Preparations were in full swing for the celebration of the fortieth anniversary of the founding of the GDR on 7 October. Behind the mask, however, there was mounting panic. There had been an effusive welcome for Gorbachev by cheering crowds as the Soviet leader attended the celebrations in East Berlin. The GDR leaders, above all the utterly intransigent Erich Honecker, could not mistake the huge gulf separating them from Gorbachev. The words that Gorbachev used privately in speaking to the East German leaders were swiftly made public: 'Life punishes harshly anyone who is left behind in politics.'

Demonstrations against the regime, inspired each Monday evening by prayers for peace in the Church of St Nicholas in Leipzig, had grown in size – a few thousand in early September, around 20,000 a month later, perhaps 70,000 by Monday, 9 October 1989. Two days earlier, during the fortieth anniversary celebrations, the police had acted with their usual brutality against demonstrators. There were public intimations – Tiananmen Square was still in people's minds – that the security forces would resort to arms against the Monday evening demonstrators in Leipzig. Rumours circulated that the regime was ready to crush the protest by force. A showdown was expected. Kurt Masur, the internationally known conductor of the Leipzig Gewandhaus orchestra, was among those – also including three local party functionaries – who led an appeal to avoid violence. It was uncertain whether the appeal would carry weight. Honecker had instructed the Stasi on 8 October to prevent any disturbances. That sounded ominous. Then Moscow intervened: there must be no bloodshed in Leipzig. The message got through to the party and police in the city. Even so, demonstrators could not be sure. They had to reckon with the possibility that the police might use live ammunition against them. To march that evening took courage. In the event, the demonstration passed off peacefully. It was a decisive moment. People realized that the police would no longer intervene, that it was safe to demonstrate. On 4 November around half a million citizens took part in a vast demonstration, broadcast live on television, in Alexanderplatz in the centre of East Berlin. They demanded free elections, free expression, resignation of the government, legalization of oppositional groups, and the end of the communist claim to leadership of the country. 'We are the people,' they chanted.

The revolt of the masses was about to reach its climax. On 3 October, smarting from the embarrassing scenes of East German refugees fleeing to the West, the GDR authorities had banned travel to Czechoslovakia without a visa. The route to Hungary was thereby closed off. But as the protests against the regime grew, it became impossible to sustain this highly unpopular measure, which effectively walled in the entire population. On 1 November the restriction was withdrawn. Between 3 and 5 November more than 10,000 citizens crossed the Czech border, en route into West Germany. With this effective permission to depart for the West, showing only a passport, the Berlin Wall had actually become pointless. However, leaving the GDR still meant completing cumbersome formalities to explain the reason for any journey. In any case, the Wall still stood – though not for much longer.

Travel restriction had been a major cause of grievance. By 9 November the regime had prepared a decree, to be made public the following day, permanently permitting travel on all routes directly into the Federal Republic, and into West Berlin, without any formality. The party's newly appointed media representative, Günter Schabowski, had evidently not digested the content of the new directive that had just been passed to him when he proceeded to read it out at the press conference that evening, 9 November. When journalists asked him when the directive would become effective, he replied without hesitation: 'Immediately, straightaway.' Further questioned, he said this also applied to Berlin. At this, thousands of GDR citizens, who had been watching keenly on television with growing amazement, jumped into their Trabants, Ladas and Wartburgs and simply headed for the Wall. By mid-evening there were huge throngs at all the Berlin border-crossings, pressing to enter West Berlin. The border guards, for decades such a menacing presence, uninformed of any change, tried at first to prevent people leaving, then they attempted to stamp passports to indicate that the holders were leaving the GDR and not coming back. But, completely overwhelmed, they soon gave up wondering what they were expected to do. Left sometimes with lipstick on their cheeks and their hats askew, they simply waved the masses through. 'Freedom at last,' some shouted.

West Berliners also rushed with frenzied jubilation to their side of the Wall. They were soon singing, dancing, embracing strangers, plying their euphoric but still bewildered fellow Germans from the east with flowers, chocolates – and bananas (like all fresh fruits not readily available in the GDR). Next day border guards lined the Wall. They were soon replaced, however, by thousands of young people who clambered on top of what had for nearly thirty years been a symbol of division and suppression.*

---

* My two (then teenage) sons, David and Stephen, who were with me while I lived in West Berlin during 1989–90, were among them. I had entirely missed the world-historical events the previous evening. An American student had rung me to ask whether I would meet him to discuss his doctoral thesis. So I spent the evening of 9 November in a West Berlin pub, oblivious to what was taking place a mile away. When I returned to our flat, Stephen told me the Wall had come down – Mum, he said, had telephoned from England and had seen everything on the BBC's *Nine O'Clock News*. On the morning of 10 November a West German friend rang me to ask whether I fancied going to East Berlin to see what was going on there. We went, passing through the stringent border controls at Friedrichstrasse, still functioning as usual, only to find that nothing much was happening, so decided to return to West Berlin. As I left the S-Bahn – the suburban railway – at Bahnhof Zoo, back in West Berlin, a man rushed up to me and clasped me in a great bear hug. 'Herzlich willkommen im Westen,' he greeted me, excitedly. 'Wo kommen Sie denn her?' ('A warm welcome to the West. Where are you from?') When I replied 'Manchester,

Bits of the Wall were chiselled out – as souvenirs, but also as destruction of a hated monument to tyranny. The next days were one long party in West Berlin. Crowds of Berliners, from east and west, milled around the city centre. A Coca-Cola regional executive was soon afterwards rewarded with quick promotion for his initiative in ordering cans of Coke to be handed to the East Germans entering West Berlin, ensuring that his product had massive free advertising exposure on television. The Underground was at times so full that trains went through stations without stopping. Banks opened exceptionally on the Saturday morning to dole out the 'welcome money' of 100 German marks. East Germans had no difficulty in spending it. Starved for so long of Western consumer commodities, they could often be seen carrying newly bought ghetto-blasters along with bunches of bananas or bags of oranges.

By then the East German regime was plainly on its last legs. The shambolic way in which the opening of the Wall had taken place showed a government no longer in control. Without the option of Soviet backing for maintaining power through military force against its citizens the regime was effectively powerless. And had it used force it would have lost all prospect of financial aid from West Germany, without which its economy would have struggled to survive. As it was, its political disintegration was imminent. Honecker had already on 18 October been deposed from all his party and state offices – officially on health grounds. But his successor, Egon Krenz, a somewhat sinister-looking arch-apparatchik, had been a close acolyte of the deposed leader and was cut from the same cloth, down to defending the Tiananmen Square massacres. His attempts to pose as a new-model reformer were doomed from the start. By early November most of the other GDR leaders, including Erich Mielke, head of the Stasi, had gone. (The dismantling of the organizational framework of the Stasi quickly followed.) On 2 December the crucial clause in the East German constitution, declaring the GDR a socialist state run by the communist Socialist Unity Party was removed. Krenz, and the rest of the Politburo and Central Committee of the Party, resigned two days later. By 6 December Krenz had also quit his position as head of state. The power of the people had by then ensured that the GDR was

England', he dropped me as if I had bubonic plague and dashed off to inflict his bear hug on the next arrival.

well on its way – confused though the path would remain for some months – to the full embrace of pluralist democracy. The people's peaceful revolution – thanks to their own courage, but in no small measure, too, to the external backing of Gorbachev – had triumphed.

The opposition groups – New Forum, Democratic Awakening, Democracy Now, and many others (around 300 to 325 in all, though most of them with no more than around twenty members) – that had sprung up during the summer and autumn of 1989 had spearheaded the revolution. They all wanted democracy, with free elections as a start. Beyond that their leaders, many of them intellectuals or idealists whose principles were rooted in their Protestant faith, naturally enough often differed in their precise objectives – in so far as they had these. Unsurprisingly there was much uncertainty. They wanted to be rid of the oppressive state communism that they had all experienced. And there was intense anger among the swelling masses of their supporters at the corruption of the leaders who had preached socialist equality but enjoyed luxuries and privileges that were a gross abuse of power and a betrayal of the sacrifices they demanded of those who had trusted them. 'Real existing socialism' was seen to have been a lie. But there were many still idealistic communists among the protesters, including some who had been party members. None of the leading advocates of radical change looked to Western capitalism as a model. Nor did they want unification with capitalist West Germany.

These views mirrored those of East Germans generally. According to opinion surveys soon after the opening of the Wall, 86 per cent of the population favoured 'a path towards a better, reformed socialism'. They harboured hopes, soon to be proved illusory, of a 'third way' – something like the type of 'socialism with a human face' that had been crushed by Soviet force in Prague in 1968. They were soon finding, however, that their hopes were being overtaken by rapidly growing demands by ordinary people for precisely that which they had not at first sought: unification with West Germany and the satisfaction of their desire for consumer commodities that they briefly glimpsed on their short stays in West Berlin. Where the cry in the autumn had been 'we are the people', it was by the end of the year changing to 'we are one people'. Even more striking was the new slogan catching on: 'United German Fatherland'. Surveys showed that just below 80 per cent of the East German population now wanted unification. Popular pressure was starting to build up, alongside diplomatic initiatives among political leaders, that would within months culminate in German unification.

The opening of the Berlin Wall was the symbolic moment that told the world the Soviet bloc was finished. Already, the other dominos were tumbling. The end of the remaining communist regimes in Czechoslovakia, Bulgaria and Romania came quickly – though in each case, unlike Poland and Hungary, those in power were not ready to yield it.

Intellectuals in Czechoslovakia, at their head Václav Havel, and backed by large numbers of students, had for months become more vociferous in their opposition to the regime. Some 10,000 people had demonstrated on 28 October 1989 on the anniversary of the foundation of Czechoslovakia in 1918. A petition put together by Havel (who had been released from prison in May) and a number of associates, entitled 'A Few Sentences', seeking the introduction of democratic rights, attracted around 37,000 signatories by November. The pressure for change mounted rapidly. The dramatic events in the West German Embassy in Prague showed that change was possible, and on the way. The fall of the Wall was its most spectacular manifestation. But the regime in Czechoslovakia was not ready to capitulate. Riot police wielding truncheons brutally attacked student demonstrators on 17 November. Far from deterring the demonstrators, the police violence encouraged further, much larger demonstrations. Within days the numbers of demonstrators demanding an end to the communist dictatorship had swollen to 200,000. By 24 November three-quarters of a million protesters assembled in Wenceslas Square. Half of the country's workforce supported the two-day general strike that followed. Opposition groups had meanwhile, on 19 November, organized themselves in a 'Civic Forum', led by Havel, to demand democratic change. The discussions in its headquarters, the bowels of Prague's Magic Lantern Theatre, were often inchoate, rambling and confused. But, both prompting and also being driven by the huge popular groundswell of opposition, the Civic Forum orchestrated the 'velvet revolution' that swept away the tottering remnants of communist rule.

Before the end of November the entire party leadership resigned and the party's pre-eminent position was erased from the constitution. The government tried, in a major reshuffle on 3 December, to keep control in the hands of the communists. It was too late for that. Threatened with a general strike a new cabinet, most of whose members were drawn from Civic Forum, was sworn in on 10 December. The great survivor from 1968 and embodiment of the old regime, the President, Gustáv Husák, at last conceded defeat and resigned. On 29 December 1989, just before the end of a year so rich in momentous events, Václav Havel took the oath as the new head of state. In a profoundly symbolic move the hero of 1968, Alexander Dubček, had been appointed a day earlier to the essentially honorific position as Chairman of the Federal Assembly. Soviet troops began withdrawing from Czechoslovakia in late February 1990. Elections in June 1990 (and Havel's re-election as President the following month) confirmed Czechoslovakia's successful transition to a liberal democracy.

The basis of a 'civic society', which developed in the interstices of communist rule its own forms of pluralist political thinking and debate in opposition to the party's monopoly of power, scarcely existed in Bulgaria. So the breakthrough came not from below but from above, through a coup d'état within the party leadership. Popular pressure for democracy followed, rather than preceded, change at the top. Todor Zhivkov's belated attempt in November 1989 to head off his critics in the party leadership by purporting to embrace reform was to no avail. Eastern Europe's most long-standing party leader, who had come to power only a year after Stalin's death, was toppled from within, forced out of his party and state offices on 10 November 1989. The man who metaphorically wielded the knife, and Zhivkov's successor as party boss, Petăr Mladenov, was, however, himself a member of the old guard, had served as Foreign Minister since 1971, and, as it later transpired, had as late as December 1989 considered turning tanks on demonstrators. He himself would be ousted as head of state in July 1990.

Before then, nonetheless, as Gorbachev had initially done in the Soviet Union, Mladenov introduced the first substantial reforms as a long overdue step towards (as he hoped) sustaining, not breaking, communist power. He was prepared by late December 1989 to enter negotiations about a programme of reform with oppositional groups, several of which had earlier that month come together as the Union of Democratic Forces. Transformation of the state took place over 1990. It was far less dramatic, more laboured, and more piecemeal than in the other former eastern bloc countries. But it was no more stoppable. Party and state were formally separated in January; in March strikes were made legal; the Communist Party restyled itself the Bulgarian Socialist Party in April; and elections were held in June, when, however, the former Communists won the largest share of the vote (47.2 per cent). Weak coalition government, divided in its views about how to cope with seriously mounting economic problems amid widespread unrest, staggered on through the second half of 1990. An end began to come into view only after a non-party lawyer, Dimitar Popov, had agreed on 7 December 1990 to form a provisional government on the basis of an Agreement Guaranteeing a Peaceful Transition to Democratic Society made by the three largest parties. Rebuilding the shattered economy – as elsewhere, backed by support from the IMF and the World Bank, and on the basis of market reforms and privatization – could only now begin in earnest, though recovery was slow to take effect.

In five of the six countries in the Soviet bloc the revolution in 1989 was astonishingly peaceful. The regimes had at first either used violent means, or at least contemplated using them, but had been deterred by the realization that they would not be backed by the Soviet Union. The 'Gorbachev factor' was decisive. Regime leaders had then tried to placate the population by belated and piecemeal attempts at reform, actually with the aim of retaining power. But popular opposition, realizing that, without Soviet backing, the leaders of their countries were as exposed as the emperor with no clothes, had been increasingly emboldened to voice their demands for democratic change. The power of the people grew exponentially in the autumn of 1989. The leaders of the communist regimes were discredited, exposed and increasingly helpless.

But if peaceful revolution was the normal pattern, in one country the regime came to a violent end. It was predictable that if the balloon were to go up with a bang anywhere, it was likely to be in Romania. The monstrosity of Nicolae Ceauşescu's tyranny ruled out negotiation, compromise, gradual reform and peaceful transition, such as took place elsewhere. Opposition, activated by the climate of change inaugurated by Gorbachev, was certainly stirring beneath the surface. But it had little impact until late autumn 1989 in the face of continued harsh repression and brutality by the regime. Revolutionary change in neighbouring Hungary encouraged the opposition in Romania, though the regime responded by erecting a wire fence in the summer of 1989 to prevent an exodus across the Hungarian border – 20,000 had left since 1987.

For weeks the regime seemed to be weathering the storm that had swept across the rest of Central Europe. The deluge began to overtake Romania, however, on 12 December 1989. On that date the state police, the feared Securitate, tried to deport a priest, Lászlo Tökés – for some time a thorn in the side of the regime – across the Hungarian border from the city of Timişoara in western Romania, but found their action blocked by hundreds of protesters. Over the following days the protest escalated dramatically. The regime responded in the way it knew best – by resorting to extreme violence. On 17 December the army fired shots into a crowd, killing several protesters. But despite the violence, by now the protest was gaining unstoppable momentum. When Ceauşescu, returning prematurely from a visit to Iran, addressed a rally in the centre of Bucharest at lunchtime on 21 December, the television coverage had to be broken off. Instead of the usual rapturous applause of organized claques, the unthinkable happened. The 'Leader' was booed and whistled. That evening the army, militia and Securitate used truncheons, water cannon and live fire against a huge crowd but failed to quell what had by now escalated into a full-blown revolution.

Ceauşescu was again forced to retreat from a hostile crowd, which he had tried to address from the balcony of party headquarters on the morning of 22 December. Fearing that the crowd was about to storm the building, Ceauşescu and his wife, Elena, were airlifted from the roof by helicopter. Their hopes of a safe refuge, however, proved short-lived. They were arrested that evening not far away in Târgovişte in southern Romania by units of the army, now responding to the orders of the National Salvation Front that had seized power in Bucharest. On Christmas Day the Ceauşescus were peremptorily sentenced to death by a rapidly improvised court martial, taken outside and executed by a firing squad. Only once the death of the former dictator became known did the violence that had continued for five days and cost over a thousand lives subside. Overall it has been estimated that around 10,000 people were killed during the Romanian revolution.

In Romania there was no speedy transition to democracy. A country with a small intelligentsia and middle class – largely bought off by the regime – and an acutely repressive police state was in no position to construct any basis of functioning 'civil society', even in clandestine form, until the dictatorship had ended. Unlike Poland or Czechoslovakia there was no government in waiting. Those who now wielded power in the provisional government in Romania had themselves for the most part been members of the former ruling party. They took their opportunity in the chaos of December to grasp the reins hastily dropped by the departing dictator.

At their head, named as provisional head of state, was Ion Iliescu, who had earlier been a prominent member of the Ceauşescu regime. Concessions were made to pluralism. But much of it was little more than a facade. A plethora of new parties took shape; some old parties were reborn. But as elections in May 1990 showed, the new-old guard in the National Salvation Front held all the levers of power. The Securitate infiltrated all the significant avenues of social control. Opposition was met by mob violence – with the police nowhere in sight – deliberately incited by the government against any seen as dissidents, opponents, 'deviants' or foreigners. Only slowly, across 1990, did the enormous turbulence in Romania, sustained by unrest fostered by economic misery, begin to settle down. By the end of that year Romania finally had a widely approved democratic constitution. State ownership of the economy was by then starting to be opened up to privatization. But the transition to a functioning pluralist political system and to a capitalist economy remained a slow process. Democracy in Romania continued to be a lengthy and imperfect work in progress.

THE UNEXPECTEDLY RAPID ROUTE TO GERMAN UNIFICATION

In Poland, Hungary, Czechoslovakia, Bulgaria and Romania transition to democracy was essentially a matter – apart, of course, from the scarcely negligible factor of loosening the bonds with the Soviet Union – of satisfying the needs of the citizens of those countries. The path to this end was winding and often strewn with thorns. But it took place within established national borders. In all but Czechoslovakia these borders remained unaltered. And even after the subsequent 'velvet divorce' in 1993, when Czechoslovakia split into the two states of the Czech

Republic and Slovakia, the external borders remained those of the former united country. Here, too, the transformation from a communist regime to a liberal democracy, dramatic though it was, raised no issues that demanded intervention by international powers to approve and confirm a major alteration to Europe's geopolitics. That there was no revival of the territorial claims and conflicts – between Germans and Poles, or Hungarians and Romanians, for instance – of the kind that had been so poisonous between the wars itself showed how far Central European borders had become settled since 1945.

The case of the German Democratic Republic was different. As one of two states within the German nation it owed its very existence to the fundamental alternative it offered to its larger and more prosperous capitalist neighbour. Even more crucial: the creation of the two Germanies had been a direct product of the conditions imposed by the victorious Allies at the end of the Second World War. Any change in the status of the GDR, therefore, had major international consequences.

It was barely possible after the opening of the Wall to keep up with the rapidity of the change that was taking place in the GDR, and, above all, in Berlin. The city was still formally divided, still formally controlled by the wartime Allies. In practice, however, it was witnessing by the day changes that in practical terms were ending the city's division. The oppressive border controls were quickly dismantled (though they were officially abolished only on 1 July 1990). What was left of the Wall began rapidly to disappear. Another symbolic moment came on 22 December 1989, when a huge jubilant crowd cheered Helmut Kohl as he spoke at the reopening of the Brandenburg Gate. For the first time in more than a quarter of a century it became possible to walk beneath the Brandenburg Gate, the emblem of Berlin, which until then had stood just to the east of the Wall and, surrounded by its 'death strip', had epitomized the division of the city. Crowds of people passed through the Gate in pouring rain that night and progressed in festive spirits down the beautiful boulevard, Unter den Linden, into the heart of East Berlin. In the capitalist West dozens of street vendors would have rapidly materialized to set up their stalls and take advantage of the readiness of the throngs of people to part with their money. But in East Berlin there was a dearth of stalls, cafés or pubs open on Unter den Linden. Celebrations of the first walk under the Brandenburg Gate remained necessarily sober. To move from the

Kurfürstendamm, the main shopping boulevard in West Berlin, to Unter den Linden in the east was still to move between two economically separate systems. But this, too, was quickly changing.

The economic imbalance between the two parts of what had once been the same country was a decisive factor. It had been there before the Wall was built, when the drain of labour to the prospering West Germany could not be countered, short of walling in the people of the German Democratic Republic. The material allure of the West had then for forty years been out of reach, though increasingly visible as West German television programmes advertising the attractions of Western consumerism became accessible to much of the East German population. The opening of the Wall now meant that citizens of the GDR could, at least in theory, begin to take advantage of the far greater prosperity of West Germany. And the swelling chorus of 'German, united fatherland' by East German protesters had indicated that most of them did not see West Germany as a foreign country; that they felt an identity with the people of the larger, western part of what had in living memory (at least of older citizens) been a single country. Among West Germans this feeling was even stronger. Already according to opinion surveys in late November 1989, 60 per cent of East Germans but 70 per cent of West Germans favoured reunification.

East Germans remained, however, poor by Western standards. Their currency, the (East) mark, would buy them little or nothing in the West. And their 'welcome money' of a hundred (Western) marks was soon gone. As long as the value of the East German currency remained unaltered it would be impossible to improve the standard of living of the population, or to rebuild the structural foundations of a rotted economy. But any alteration depended upon the relationship between the Federal Republic and the German Democratic Republic. Political change had to precede economic restructuring. Momentous decisions were necessary. And this meant involvement of the former wartime Allies. The stance of the post-war superpowers, the United States and the Soviet Union (most especially the latter), was a critical element in a highly complex equation.

Still, the decisive role was played by the Germans themselves. The key initiatives came from West Germany – in particular from the West German Chancellor, Helmut Kohl, a politician who seemed constantly to be underrated, but who played a major personal role in the transformation of his own country, and of Europe too. Neither Kohl nor anyone else had thought of speedy unification even after the opening of the Wall necessarily called for a new basis of relations between the two German states. Nor, once the prospect of unification emerged, was it imagined that it would happen so rapidly. What followed was unexpected. It took Kohl, too, by surprise. But he, more quickly than others, saw and acted upon the opportunities. He was pushed along by the tide of events. But he surfed that tide, diverting the waters – at times against weighty advice – into channels that flowed only in one direction.

The East German government at first wanted nothing to do with thoughts of unification. The newly appointed Prime Minister, Hans Modrow, a moderate reformer who had earlier been party leader in the Dresden district, rejected outright what he described on 17 November 1989 as 'unrealistic and dangerous speculation' about unification. He favoured what he called a 'contractual community' between the two German states. Whatever it meant, this term did not last long. It was subsumed by 28 November in a new term, 'federation', which Helmut Kohl used in a speech to the Bundestag, outlining a 'ten-point plan' to develop ways towards German unity. He did not even tell his own cabinet what he was going to say. He indicated areas of close cooperation, resting on the precondition of democratization in the GDR. He emphasized that any fundamental transformation in relations between the two countries had to fit 'the future architecture of Europe as a whole', ending by stating that the political aim of the Federal government remained 'reunification' – the return of Germany to a single state. But that was no more than a reiteration of what had been the West German aspiration ever since Germany had been divided. Kohl was still in early December implying that even the 'federation' that he had spoken of in his 'Ten Points' would take years to mature. During the course of December, however, it became ever clearer that popular pressure in both West and East Germany was driving a rapidly accelerating process towards unification that Kohl was happy to steer and that other European leaders could, even where they wished to, do little to prevent.

'I love Germany so much that I'm glad there are two of them' – the old saying attributed to the French writer François Mauriac – was a thought that must have crossed the minds of more than one politician during those days. At any rate, the prospect of unification at first caused much consternation among Western European leaders, and also, unsurprisingly, in Moscow. Only President George Bush, the successor to Ronald Reagan in 1989, spoke from the outset in positive terms about the prospect of early German unification, as long as the new united Germany remained within NATO. But precisely such a notion alarmed Moscow and prompted initial sharp rejection of any idea of unification.

A summit meeting of Bush and Gorbachev held in stormy seas on board a Soviet ship off the coast of Malta on 2–3 December 1989 produced a highly welcome agreement to build upon good relations and cooperation between the two superpowers. The meeting of the superpower leaders was momentous in marking the symbolic end of the Cold War. But in their news conference neither leader held out expectation of early moves to German unification. 'Any artificial acceleration' of the process of unification, stated Gorbachev, would hinder change in Eastern Europe (indirectly referring to the still sensitive question, especially in the eyes of those who had been expelled from the former East German provinces, subsequently part of Poland, of whether the Oder–Neisse line, established by Soviet fiat back in 1945, should remain the eastern border of Germany). Bush, despite his private acceptance of German unification, hinted for his part that 'a concept of permanent borders' still existed – a comment capable of differing interpretation, but seemingly suggestive of retaining the territorial status quo, by implication within Germany itself.

Over the following days Mitterrand and the prime ministers of Italy and the United Kingdom, Giulio Andreotti and Margaret Thatcher, continued to voice their opposition to German unification – Mrs Thatcher more stridently than anyone – as did the Dutch Prime Minister, Ruud Lubbers. At a meeting with Thatcher in early September 1989, Mitterrand had argued that, following unification, only the European Union with a common currency could contain the power of an enlarged, more populous Germany, which would be substantially bigger than any other Western European country. Mrs Thatcher replied that it would be 'insufferable' to have both German unification and a single currency. For her, and for some other British politicians of her generation, the Second World War had been fought to destroy German power. Unification threatened to revive it. Other European leaders were more open to the prospect of German unification, as long as existing frontiers (beyond the inner-German border) and security arrangements were guaranteed. With this prerequisite, they took the view that it was hard to argue against national unity, should that be the freely determined will of the people of both parts of the divided country.

The breakthrough came, as in a sense it had to, in the basis of agreement between the two countries that had from the beginning formed the core of the moves towards European integration, France and West Germany. When Mitterrand and Kohl met at the Strasbourg conference of leaders of the European Community on 8–9 December 1989, agreement seemed unlikely. Mitterrand, like other European leaders, had been taken aback by Kohl's peremptory announcement, without consultation, of his Ten-Point Plan just over a week earlier. Unification was a sensitive topic. Anxieties among the European leaders were evident. Kohl did much to defuse the situation by confirming that German unification would be embedded in further moves towards European integration. The Chancellor declared his readiness to take practical steps in a conference of heads of government before the end of 1990 to meet President Mitterrand's wish to move towards European economic and currency union. By April 1990 Mitterrand and Kohl had even reached agreement on an ambitious plan to convert the European Community into a European union with a political identity by 1 January 1993 (though this would fall well short of the fully fledged political union that Kohl was willing to establish).

Mitterrand was anxious to bind Germany into an integrated Western Europe. Kohl, a true disciple of Adenauer, saw the obvious advantage for Germany in continuing to be bound in to the West, both to defuse any international tensions and to head off any incipient German nationalist revisionist tendencies. As the price and in order to bring about European currency union he was even prepared to sacrifice the Deutsche Mark (D-Mark, DM), the very symbol of West Germany's post-war prosperity and economic standing.

Events now, east and west, carried Kohl, Modrow and the leaders of all the major powers along in their wake and soon ensured that unification would be a proximate goal not a distant dream. A sign of the pressure building from below was the tumultuous reception that Kohl received from a huge crowd that gathered in the centre of Dresden on 19 December

1990 to hear him and Modrow speak. It was not the nebulous idea of a 'contractual community' that set the crowd alight. What did so was the prospect of unification. 'Germany united fatherland,' the crowd shouted, amid a sea of West German flags. Kohl responded by declaring his aim to be, 'if the historic hour permits it, the unity of our nation'. The Chancellor left Dresden convinced that this 'historic hour' was now close.

Signs of irreversible collapse in the German Democratic Republic were by this time plain to see. In the first days of December the clause upholding the leading role of the Socialist Unity Party (the East German Communist Party) was struck from the constitution, Erich Honecker and other former prominent figures in the regime were expelled from the party (and charged with corruption and misuse of power), the Politburo resigned en masse, and the subordinate, only nominally independent, parties aligned themselves with the western Christian Union and Free Democrat parties. A newly formed East German Social Democratic Party entered similarly into close cooperation with its West German sister party. Elections to a newly constituted pluralist parliament were envisaged for May 1991, though eventually, under the pressure of events, they were brought forward to March. Meanwhile, a sizeable exodus from the terminally stricken state was under way. Nearly 120,000 East Germans left for the West between the opening of the Wall and the end of 1989.

By the end of January 1990 Gorbachev, following a meeting in Moscow with Modrow, had changed his mind on German unification. This was decisive. President Bush had essentially been in favour from the beginning. But Gorbachev faced different sensitivities in his own country, which had suffered so grievously and so recently at the hands of a united Germany. A united Germany would inevitably once more look eastwards as well as to Western Europe. So for the Soviet leader to embrace the idea of German unification required an act of political courage. From now on, even so, Gorbachev acknowledged the right of Germans, east and west, to come together as a single state. Modrow's own report on the situation within East Germany had changed Gorbachev's mind. The great majority of the population simply no longer supported the idea of two German states, the East German leader told Gorbachev. The pressure in favour of unification was so strong that it was impossible to preserve the German Democratic Republic. 'If we do not take the initiative now', Gorbachev recalled Modrow saying, 'the process will become uncontrollable and we won't be able to influence developments in any way.' Gorbachev concurred. He and his closest advisors had already reached the same conclusion: 'German unification should be regarded as inevitable.'

The by now realistic prospect of early unification again raised the obvious question of whether a newly unified Germany could belong to NATO. The Soviet Union had earlier rejected such a notion outright. This remained Gorbachev's position in February 1990. But circumstances were changing fast. This was the most important single issue. It dominated diplomatic negotiations that month. The formula of 2+4 – the two German states and the four former occupying powers – was agreed as the basis for the negotiations. Britain and France more or less made up the numbers in these negotiations. So did the East Germans. The main players were the Federal Republic, the United States and the Soviet Union. The key actors were Kohl and Gorbachev, with an important though lesser role played by Bush.

The East Germans wanted military neutrality for both parts of Germany as they moved towards a federation. There was no question of that in the eyes of the Western former occupying powers. At first, there was general acceptance among the Western powers of the suggestion, first made by the German Foreign Minister, Hans Dietrich-Genscher, that NATO would continue, as currently, to have bases in the Federal Republic but they would not be extended to the territory of the former German Democratic Republic. This, according to Gorbachev's recollection, was categorically stated as the American position by the US Secretary of State, James Baker, when he visited Moscow on 9 February. Gorbachev was still not ready to concede even this arrangement. Towards the end of February, however, the Americans changed their tune (though it was almost certainly what they had wanted all along) and now insisted – in agreement with Chancellor Kohl – that NATO had after all to be extended to former GDR territory if the security of Germany as a whole were to be guaranteed. While, it is true, there had been no earlier formal promise not to extend NATO, the alteration nevertheless explicitly contradicted an earlier understanding on all sides. It later prompted ill-feeling in Russia (and also to some extent in Western Europe) – a sense that the West had not acted in good faith and had reneged on its promises.

The reality in any event was that Gorbachev, still not expecting the rapid collapse of the Warsaw Pact, had been completely outmanoeuvred. In May 1990 he conceded under American pressure that a united Germany should choose for itself which alliance it wished to join. It was a move that the Soviet Union before Gorbachev could never have contemplated, let alone accepted. That Gorbachev now did so was an indication not just of his own unique contribution to the process of German, and European, transformation, but also of the rapid weakening of the Soviet Union. The Soviet economy urgently needed Western financial aid. Germany was ready to offer the required financial credits in return for Soviet cooperation over reunification.

That a united Germany would be free to belong to NATO was confirmed, and became public Soviet policy, when Kohl visited Moscow in July 1990. In return the Soviet Union was given guarantees that Germany would forever renounce possession of nuclear, chemical and bacteriological weapons and would retain no more than 370,000 men under arms. There was also the little matter of covering the cost of Soviet troop withdrawal from the territory of the GDR and relocation to the Soviet Union – an expensive bill of DM 12 billion with a further DM 3 billion credit, which Kohl, after much haggling with Gorbachev on the telephone in September 1990, eventually agreed to pay. For Kohl it was a settlement that he could scarcely have dreamed of only a few months earlier. For Gorbachev it amounted to a deal to cement long-term good relations between the Soviet Union and Germany, which he saw as crucial for Europe's future. For Gorbachev's enemies at home – who were rapidly increasing in number – it was an unforgivable betrayal of the interests of the Soviet Union.

The other sensitive issue that lingered over the 2+4 negotiations was that of the East German border. The Federal Republic had never formally abandoned the ultimate aim – however unrealistic it had become – of a return to the borders of 1937 (which included western parts of what had become post-war Poland). The representatives of the ethnic German population who had been forced to flee or had been expelled from those provinces just before and after the end of the war had formed a substantial lobby, mainly within the parties of the Christian Union, which could not be ignored. And there had been no international treaty, as had been the case in 1919, to bring the war to a formal end – and to confirm the

Polish western border. As late as July 1989 the West German Finance Minister, Theo Waigel, had told a big rally of Silesian expellees that in his view the lost eastern provinces beyond the Oder–Neisse Line were still part of the 'German Question'. This represented the view of a small minority. By this stage, in fact, 90 per cent of West Germans accepted this line as a permanent frontier. But in order to placate the expellee lobby Kohl himself remained until the spring of 1990 evasive on this issue. Eventually, on Genscher's initiative, the matter was addressed in early March when the West German parliament, the Bundestag, solemnly renounced any claim to the former eastern provinces and confirmed the East German border as the Oder–Neisse Line – to be ratified later (and finally accomplished in October 1991) in a treaty between Poland and a government representing the whole of Germany.

Unification was by this time emerging as an imminent likelihood. Not much earlier still viewed as a mid-range prospect at best, the time frame had shrunk visibly under the pressure of events. West German strength and East German weakness were now proving so evident that the eventual outcome was no longer in doubt. The Federal Republic was already exerting gravitational pull. It took overt economic form. In mid-February 1990 it was made plain that the Federal Republic would no longer provide financial aid to the GDR. Without that aid the East German economy, already moribund, was doomed. At much the same time Kohl persuaded his government to endorse a currency union with the GDR. In other words, despite the evident huge disparity in economic strength between the two states, the West German D-Mark would become the currency in both.

A currency union on these terms contained self-evident risks and entailed major economic disadvantages. The West Germans would be bailing out indefinitely at inestimable but doubtless enormous cost an effectively bankrupt East German economy. From the opposing perspective, there would be drastic economic and social effects. Many East Germans would lose their jobs as wholly inefficient state-run industries were closed down. (Industrial output indeed fell by an astonishing 51 per cent between August 1989 and August 1990.) Those favouring a generous exchange ratio of the D-Mark to the East Mark of 1:1 ratio were mainly in the ranks of the Social Democrats and trade unions. The expert advice, from the Bundesbank and Kohl's Finance Minister, Theo Waigel, was that a 2:1 ratio was necessary to avoid destroying any prospect of competitiveness from the East German economy and inflicting a heavy burden on West Germany's finances. Kohl had at first agreed. But politics had primacy. With an election looming in the autumn and his popularity sagging in the Federal Republic but soaring in the east, the Chancellor came to see the advantages of bowing to the pressure to agree to the 1:1 ratio. Politically, it was an irresistible proposition.

West Germany was by this time making all the running. On 8 March the government decided against dissolving the Basic Law (the Federal constitution of 1949) prior to the creation of an altogether new constitution for a united Germany. Article 146 of the Basic Law had in fact made provision for such an eventuality. Instead, it was determined that the German Democratic Republic would be directly incorporated into the Federal Republic as five new *Länder* (like the Saarland had been in 1956) under Article 23 of the Basic Law. This was undoubtedly the easiest and quickest route. But it implied a takeover rather than a merger. And indeed, once the dust had settled on unification, complaints began to be heard that the former German Democratic Republic was being treated much like a colony of West Germany. However unjustified, the feeling was in some ways understandable. It became more pronounced with the wholesale dismissal of teachers, scientific researchers, university lecturers, and others in the professional middle classes who were adjudged to have had connections with the Stasi or had otherwise been too closely involved with the East German regime; or when West Germans were brought in to preside over the restructuring of politics and the rebuilding of the economy. Many East Germans came to see themselves as second-class citizens in their own country.

The East German elections to the 'People's Chamber' (the GDR parliament) on 18 March 1990 – brought forward from the original date of 6 May – gave the plebiscitary imprimatur, however, to the West German initiatives and the fast route to unification under Article 23. East Germans voted for the abolition of their own state. The attractiveness of the D-Mark was the decisive factor. West German political leaders – Helmut Kohl, Willy Brandt and Hans-Dietrich Genscher – played major roles in the election campaign. Brandt, in particular, enjoyed enormous personal popularity. The result was nevertheless a triumph for Kohl. It was in truth a triumph for the D-Mark. The conservative 'Alliance for

Germany' (in effect the newly formed East German manifestation of the Christian Union), which promised the introduction of the D-Mark and rapid unification, won the day with 48 per cent of the popular vote (on a turnout of 93.4 per cent). The Social Democrats lagged behind on 21.9 per cent. The Party of Democratic Socialism (PDS), the successor to the Socialist Unity Party (the East German Communist Party), managed only third place with 16.4 per cent – though it gained an impressive 30.2 per cent in East Berlin, the old communist heartland.

With this result any lingering hopes of a 'third way' to a better social-ism, harboured by many of the intellectuals who had led the popular uprising against the state in the GDR the previous autumn, were dead and buried. The courageous individuals who had spearheaded the pro-test movements of differing kinds in the autumn of 1989 now felt ignored by the established parties and organizations of West German capitalist liberal democracy. 'Socialism has not delivered what it promised' was the lapidary verdict of one worker who doubtless spoke for multitudes as they looked back, often resentfully, at a regime that they felt had betrayed their hopes for four decades. He and millions of others thought they saw the future – and it was not the failed system of Marxist-Leninist socialism they had lived under in East Germany. Prosperous West Ger-many, with its liberal freedoms but above all its successful economy, was the magnet.

From the March elections in East Germany to unification was a short and fairly straight road. The key step was the establishment of the cur-rency union – meaning the introduction of the West German D-Mark as the only legal currency in both parts of Germany – on 1 July 1990. The agreed exchange rate of 1 East Mark to 1 DM (in fact, the old compul-sory official rate at the Berlin border crossing) was an extraordinarily generous arrangement since the true rate was far higher – probably at least 8 to 1 (the earlier black-market exchange rate). It applied to GDR citizens in employment, with pensions or with savings (up to 4,000 marks or 6,000 marks for those over sixty years old). Even larger savings and company debts were exchanged at the rate of two to one. In the short term, those who had savings would now be able to enjoy foreign travel or buy commodities that had earlier been unavailable to them. Within a short time the material trappings of Western life indeed became a novel but increasingly frequent sight in eastern parts of Germany. But for many the cushioned though modest lifestyle provided by the communist system was now abruptly ended, despite massive subsidies from West Germany.

Employment, for instance, had been guaranteed under communism, however unproductive. But employees and their families were now exposed to the vagaries of the market. Within a year three million East Germans were unemployed. And the East German economy was almost wholly uncompetitive. Only about a third of industry was viable without subsidies, according to estimates (which proved optimistic) in May 1990. Thousands of formerly state-owned East German firms were privatized over the following four years. They were first transferred to an agency set up to implement privatization, the *Treuhand* ('trust fund'), which took over more than 13,000 companies, employing four million people. Most of the former state-owned companies became subsidiaries of West German firms. But in their current condition many of them were of little value. Sale prices were commensurately low. Making the companies profitable was a slow business. The Treuhand ended up losing more than 250 billion marks. Private investment, almost all of it West German, was sluggish. And it was far from enough. The West German state had to bear much of the financial burden of unification. A colossal investment programme was required. The infrastructure – including roads, railway, bridges, also a dilapidated telephone system – needed urgent renovation. In addition, there were the huge social costs of unemployment pay and welfare provision. The West German government spent an estimated 350 billion marks (nearly £120 billion at the exchange rates at the time) on East Germany in the three years following unification. This naturally meant a big increase in the state debt of the Federal Republic, and an increase in borrowing costs – not just for Germany.

Much like Poland, the transition in East Germany amounted to a sharp economic shock. This was guaranteed by the terms of the currency union and the scale and speed of privatization. The former East German economy was exposed after unification to the most rapid and radical liberalization of any former Soviet-bloc country. But at least the East Germans, unlike the citizens of any other former Soviet-bloc country, could rely upon huge subsidies from their far wealthier neighbour. From 1991, indeed, a 'solidarity subsidy', partly to help finance the transition in East Germany, was deducted from West German pay packets. (It also comprised West Germany's contribution to the costs of the first Gulf

War, and was such a useful addition to the revenue of the Federal government – eventually totalling around 15 billion Euros a year – that it was retained indefinitely, to the increasing irritation of most of the population.)

The economic and social complexities of unification were recognized as truly daunting even before it took place. The psychological problems of adjustment would prove over time perhaps even more challenging. But there could be no turning back. Nor did the will exist to do so either within Germany, or internationally – despite the misgivings in Paris and London. By the end of September the last political difficulties had been surmounted. A treaty between the two German states to resolve legal and administrative technicalities involved in unification was signed on 31 August 1990, ratified by both the People's Chamber of the German Democratic Republic and the Federal Parliament on 20 September, and came into force on 29 September. On 24 September the German Democratic Republic, in agreement with the Soviet Union, left the Warsaw Pact. A week later the four occupying powers brought their old rights and responsibilities to an end (though ratification – the nearest thing to a treaty to end the Second World War, if over forty years late – only took place in stages over the following months). On the stroke of midnight on 3 October 1990, amid a huge celebratory street party in Berlin, the Federal President Richard von Weizsäcker pronounced the unity of Germany and the country's wish to work for global peace in a united Europe. For Helmut Kohl, the 'unity Chancellor', it was an extraordinary triumph.

It was unquestionably a moment of unique historical significance, not just for Germany, but for the whole of Europe and, in its implications, for international relations more generally. It marked the symbolic end of an era in which the German nation state had first inflicted unimaginable suffering and destruction on Europe, then, divided for forty years, in its western part at least, had contributed greatly to building the foundations of a new Europe resting on peace, prosperity and stability. What the future would bring might be uncertain. For now, however, there was widespread rejoicing in Germany – if still some foreboding among Germany's neighbours.

THE LONG DEATH THROES OF THE SOVIET UNION

While the drama in its former satellite states in Central Europe and in the Balkans had been unfolding, the Soviet Union itself was imploding. The process that had essentially begun in 1985, when Mikhail Gorbachev had embarked upon his structural reform programme – intended to keep the Communist Party in power, not to break its power – had for four years, like a brewing great ocean storm, gathered force. From spring 1989 onwards, for the following two years and more, the storm raged, reaching hurricane strength in the summer of 1991, when it finally blew the Soviet Union away.

During this period Gorbachev's international stardom contrasted with the ebbing away of his power within the Soviet Union itself. Until the summer of 1991 he was still, without question, the towering figure in Soviet politics. But he was increasingly buffeted by the gale-force winds of change that he had unleashed. He no longer controlled events. Instead, he was their captive. Within the Soviet Union itself, as had been the case in the former satellite states, the power of the people was making itself felt, most obviously in the mounting displays of serious unrest and increasingly shrill nationalist demands for independence in the non-Russian republics, especially in the Baltic and the Caucasus. But also in Russia itself from 1990 onwards Gorbachev's once unassailable popularity was collapsing. He was more and more seen as the cause of all the woes besetting the once-mighty Soviet Union – the loss of the former satellite states, the deterioration in living standards at home, the separatist pressures of the outlying republics, the unmistakable decline of what had until recently been a superpower. Politically, he was attacked both by hardline reactionaries, who saw him as a traitor responsible for the destruction of all that had been great about the Soviet Union, and by radical reformers, who wanted to go further and faster than Gorbachev himself.

Prominent among the latter was the person who emerged as his most dangerous opponent and who would eventually supplant him: the impulsive, domineering, flamboyant, unpredictably wilful but shrewdly effective political operator Boris Yeltsin. In the 1980s Yeltsin had been the First Secretary of the Moscow Communist Party, but frustrated by the slow pace of reform he had – an unprecedented step – resigned in 1987 from the Politburo, had strongly criticized Gorbachev, and had a few weeks later been sacked as party boss in Moscow. He never forgave Gorbachev for the demotion. His election as a non-party delegate, with massive popular support, to the Congress of People's Deputies of the Soviet Union in March 1989 then gave him a new platform from which to launch forthright attacks on Gorbachev. Yeltsin's heavy drinking provided opportunities for the controlled press to smear him. But the attacks did not dent his popularity. For Russians, he, not Gorbachev, seemed to offer hope for the future. And increasingly this meant for ordinary people the chance to improve their lives through access to the goods and commodities that Westerners took for granted. A sign of things to come was the opening of the first McDonalds fast-food outlet in Moscow on 31 January 1990, when the queue of thousands of Muscovites preparing to spend precious roubles on their first taste of a 'Big Mac' snaked around the block. For most non-Russians, meanwhile, the future lay in independence from Moscow. They increasingly looked to nationalist movements that sought total autonomy from the Russian-dominated Soviet Union.

Centrifugal forces were now threatening to tear apart the highly centralized states system of the Soviet Union. The perimeter was endangering the centre. The system was being eroded from the outside in. There was trouble in early April 1989 when the police and soldiers turned on a rally of around 100,000 backers of independence in Tblisi, the Georgian capital, leaving nineteen civilian protesters dead. Troops were sent to Estonia, Latvia and Uzbekistan to head off the possibility of similar demonstrations. But the pressure for greater autonomy could no longer be held back by sheer coercion.

The anti-Soviet mood, growing fast, was particularly pronounced in the Baltic. Older inhabitants could still remember the years of independence before Estonia, Latvia and Lithuania were annexed by the Soviet Union in 1940. There was resentment at the influx of ethnic Russians. And access to Scandinavian television gave people a sense of the Western prosperity they were missing. In the Baltic republics the elections of March 1989 had seen strong support for candidates who favoured independence, and now won seats in the Congress of People's Deputies. On

11 March, Lithuania went so far as to declare its independence. The old national flag was reintroduced and the Soviet Hammer and Sickle flag disappeared overnight. Moscow rejected the Lithuanian declaration as invalid. A fortnight later Soviet tanks were sent in and rumbled past the Lithuanian parliament building in Vilnius, though, following this threatening demonstration of force, they withdrew after a few hours without opening fire. There was to be no repeat of Hungary in 1956. But Lithuania was subjected to economic blockade, and had its oil supplies cut off for a time. And this was not the last attempt by the Soviet government to prevent Lithuania's secession.

Elsewhere, too, the Soviet Union faced worrying problems. It had from the 1920s been a federation, dominated by Russia, of nominally autonomous republics, built around the main ethnic population of a region. Ethnic tensions were now an indication of the fraying fabric of the federation. Serious ethnic unrest flared in Uzbekistan in June, when hordes of Uzbek youths set on the Turkish-speaking Meshketian minority. According to official figures ninety-five were killed, hundreds more injured, a good deal of property destroyed, and thousands were forced to flee from Uzbekistan. Across the summer there were further outbreaks of violence in the Central Asian republics and demonstrations in favour of national independence in Georgia. The weakening of Soviet rule was also shown by huge strikes about living conditions by miners in western Siberia and Ukraine (estimated to number 300,000 men) in July, which led in October to the Supreme Soviet conceding the right to strike – an upturning of the principle that the Communist Party and its official trade unions could alone determine the interests of workers. In August an extraordinary million-strong human chain stretched through Estonia, Latvia and Lithuania in protest at the Nazi-Soviet Pact of 1939, which had preceded their annexation by the Soviet Union the following year. By September 1989 the signs of disintegration were coming closer to the heart of the Soviet Union when a movement seeking Ukrainian autonomy, the Ukrainian Popular Front, held its inaugural congress in Kiev.

The deployment of the Soviet army could not prevent tensions and violence continuing in the Caucasus and Central Asian republics in 1990. There were serious ethnic clashes, in which around fifty people died, between Azerbaijanis and Armenians in Baku, the capital of Azerbaijan, in January 1990 over the disputed region of Nagorny Karabakh.

When Soviet troops were sent in to quell the disturbances they met fierce resistance from activists of the Ajerbaijani Popular Front. By the time they had restored order about 130 civilians had been killed and several hundreds more left injured.

In the Baltic, too, there was no lessening of the momentum towards autonomy, amid signs of growing animosity towards the ethnic Russian minority population. In May 1990 the nationalist-dominated parliaments in Estonia and Latvia had followed Lithuania's example over a year earlier in voting for independence. During the summer moves to autonomy took place in many parts of the Soviet Union. Even the most important, Ukraine and Russia itself, declared their sovereignty, though for the time being they saw this as compatible with continued membership of the Soviet Union. There was, however, little doubt that the Soviet Union, if still in existence, was by now on a life-support machine.

The struggle for independence in the Baltic republics posed a particularly acute problem. The Soviet Union was, however, not yet ready to concede defeat. Soviet troops based in Vilnius and Riga, the capitals of Lithuania and Latvia respectively, attempted in January 1991 to overthrow the elected governments and crush the moves to independence. But the show of Soviet force was met by huge popular protest in both countries. There was bloodshed. Fourteen Lithuanian and four Latvian civilians were killed and hundreds injured in the ensuing disturbances. In Moscow itself there were big protests at the violence. Yeltsin publicly supported the moves towards autonomy. The violence could not stop what had become inevitable. Over 90 per cent of Lithuanians supported independence in a referendum in early February. Similar plebiscites in Latvia and Estonia in early March saw three-quarters of voters supporting independence. Perhaps in an earlier era Soviet armed might would have crushed even such overwhelming displays of popular feeling. But by 1991 the Soviet Union was no longer prepared to defy the will of almost the entire population and to try to hold down the Baltic countries simply by force.

The erosion of the system was meanwhile spreading to the centre of Soviet politics. As the state, run by its monopoly party, lost its grip, factions increasingly jockeyed for position. The gulf between the reformers and the reactionaries was wider than ever. Gorbachev was far from radical enough for those who wanted to go much farther and faster that he did himself in dismantling the Soviet Union. The reformers were not united in their aims, which were in any case still inchoate. Some wanted the introduction of capitalist markets. Others were nationalists who wanted greater power and independence for the republics. Yeltsin himself straddled both groups, though as yet he did not clearly reveal where he stood. Gorbachev's conservative opponents at the opposite extreme increasingly detested him and the disastrous trajectory of damaging change (in their eyes) that he had inflicted on the Soviet Union, though they were not strong enough to topple him. He had even so to tread carefully. He remained tactically nimble. But he could satisfy neither wing of his serious critics. His desire to sustain the integrity of the Soviet Union while accepting, even welcoming, political and economic changes that in practice undermined it, was a basic weakness. Did he actually still want reformed communism – his initial aim? Or did he want Western-style social democracy and capitalist economics? Unquestionably he had moved towards the latter. But apart from what was tactically advisable to say in public, his private stance was not categorically clear. He remained within the Communist Party, still its General Secretary, even when reformers were urging him to leave it and when the political choices he made were more obviously those of a social democrat. He still did not confront the contradictions of attempting fundamental reform within the political straitjacket of the Soviet system. His position was increasingly at risk. He was endangered from both sides.

He was still powerful enough in the spring of 1990, however, to surmount any challenge from within, and could count upon the backing of the large reform factions in the Supreme Soviet and Congress of People's Deputies. By April 1990 the Congress had ratified the dramatic constitutional change that Gorbachev had successfully engineered in the Supreme Soviet in February, abolishing the political monopoly of the Communist Party and recognizing multi-party politics. On the surface his position even appeared strengthened after he had been elected in mid-March for the newly created post of President of the Soviet Union. As Chairman of the Supreme Soviet he had already been *de facto* head of state, but the new office gave him extended executive rights since the Congress had decided to disempower the Politburo. In reality, however, his position was becoming significantly weaker, especially once Boris Yeltsin had in March 1990 been elected Chairman of the Russian Supreme Soviet – the head of easily the largest and most important of the Soviet republics, comprising three-quarters of the entire Soviet territory. He gave Russian interests clear priority over those of the Soviet Union. A drastic reduction in the Russian contribution to Soviet tax revenue significantly weakened Gorbachev's position. Yeltsin gained popular support from Russian nationalists, and elite backing from economists attracted by neo-liberal thinking on the free market (and hopes of large-scale American aid). The Russian nationalists saw the other republics (with the exception of Belarus and Ukraine) as peripheral, non-Slavic entities, whose independence would enhance and strengthen Russia itself. As Gorbachev's popularity plummeted in the wake of the calamitous economic conditions, for which he was personally held responsible, Yeltsin's star as the Russian people's champion was plainly in the ascendancy.

The next months saw the disintegration of the Soviet Union played out against the backdrop of looming complete economic collapse. Compared even with 1990 – itself a year of misery – production fell drastically in 1991 and the budget deficit rose equally alarmingly. There were shortages of consumer goods and fuel. Food prices doubled. Unsurprisingly, popular support drained away from an increasingly hapless Gorbachev, whose plan for economic recovery had proved a sorry failure. Well over half of Soviet citizens, according to an opinion survey in autumn 1990, said their lives had become worse under Gorbachev; only 8 per cent thought they had improved.

Gorbachev's bitter conservative enemies were meanwhile marshalling their energies in an organization calling itself *Soyuz* (Union), founded in October 1990. And the most evident threat to Gorbachev was still the ominous rise of Yeltsin, who had left the Communist Party that summer and the following June won a personal mandate in the Russian presidential elections. While Gorbachev looked more and more like a defeated man presiding over a fractured Soviet Union, Yeltsin was building an unassailable base of support in Russia. Nearly quarter of a million citizens of Moscow defied the strong presence of security police to demonstrate in favour of Yeltsin in March 1991. Amid the tottering foundations of a once mighty edifice, they warmed to a rhetoric that exuded confidence in Russia's future and they liked the image of strength that he conveyed.

Yeltsin was still not in a position to challenge Gorbachev for supremacy. In the spring of 1991 he in fact saw tactical advantage in working alongside Gorbachev, despite their differences, in advocating a new Union treaty, to be signed on 20 August, ostensibly to increase the powers of the Soviet republics, creating a 'Union of Sovereign States' in which little more than economic policy and military affairs would remain Soviet prerogatives. In reality, Yeltsin was only genuinely interested in bolstering the power of Russia itself – and, with that, fortifying his own position.

Meanwhile, Gorbachev's conservative enemies were stirring. On 23 July 1991 twelve prominent Soviet figures – mainly party functionaries, if not of the highest ranks, the leader of *Soyuz*, and also two army generals – signed 'A Word to the People', published in the press, which passionately denounced the 'enormous, unprecedented misfortune' to have befallen 'the Motherland, our country, the great state entrusted to us by history, by nature and by our glorious forebears', which was 'perishing, being broken up and plunged into darkness and oblivion'. Other opponents of Gorbachev almost certainly knew of the composition of the letter and stood behind its sentiments, even if they remained in the shadows. The Americans had warned Gorbachev in June of a conspiracy brewing against him. But he had heard it all before from leading reformers at home. Undaunted, but gravely underestimating the danger, he put Yeltsin temporarily in charge in Moscow and left in early August for a much-needed holiday in the Crimea.

The plotters launched their coup on 18 August. At his holiday dacha Gorbachev discovered that his telephone connections had been cut off. Three of the conspirators turned up to advise him to hand over power temporarily to his Vice-President, Gennadi Yanaev. Gorbachev refused outright. Back in Moscow the leaders of the putsch – Colonel-General Vladimir Kryuchkov (head of the KGB, the Soviet State Security service), Boris Pugo (Minister of Internal Affairs), Valentin Pavlov (the Prime Minister), Marshal Dimitri Yazov (Defence Minister), and Vice-President Yanaev – formed a State Committee that would run the country following the state of emergency they planned to announce on 19 August.

In fact, they bungled practically every move, failing even to block the telephone network, prevent satellite television from operating, or arrest Yeltsin and others still loyal to Gorbachev. They further miscalculated in putting in charge of military operations in Moscow Pavel Grachev,

Commander of Soviet Airborne Ground-Forces, who transpired not to be a supporter of the coup at all. With Grachev's tacit backing, Yeltsin was able during the morning of 19 August to rally support. It took courage and boldness. In the most memorable moment of the drama that was swiftly beamed around the world on television, he climbed onto a tank outside the Russian Supreme Soviet headquarters (known as the White House) to denounce the coup. The next day and a half were tense. The State Committee had not given up, and ordered tanks to move in on the White House. But once more the power of the people played an important part. Crowds of citizens, many of them young Muscovites, defied the display of force in anti-coup demonstrations that gathered strength on 20 August. Three protesters were killed. By that evening, however, the coup was crumbling. The plotters were divided on their course of action and military commanders were refusing their orders. By early afternoon on 21 August the coup was over. The plotters were arrested. Two of them committed suicide. Next morning Gorbachev arrived back from the Crimea. He had remained resolute throughout the crisis. But he had understandably been seriously weakened by the coup. The following days would plainly show how rapidly his power was draining away. The hero of the hour had been Boris Yeltsin.

The end for the Soviet Union was quickly approaching. Any prospect of renewal through the new treaty envisaged by Gorbachev was by now dead. On 23 August 1991 Yeltsin suspended the Soviet Communist Party within Russia (and would later, on 6 November, go on to ban it altogether). And he announced a new cabinet, with himself as Prime Minister, which would instigate a programme of sweeping economic reforms built upon principles of a liberal market economy.

The other republics were meanwhile also going their own way. Nearly all of them had opposed the putsch. Once it failed they exploited the evident weakness of the floundering Soviet Union to press home their own claims to independence. The Baltic states led the procession. Yeltsin recognized their independence in the name of Russia on 24 August. Over the following three days Ukraine, Belorussia (now calling itself Belarus), Moldavia, Azerbaijan, Uzbekistan and Kyrgyzstan all proclaimed their independence from the Soviet Union. A number of other republics followed suit in September. The Soviet Union was left comprising only Russia and Kazakhstan. The final nail in its coffin was when 90 per cent of Ukrainians backed the declaration of independence in a referendum on 1 December. A week later, on 8 December, Russia, Ukraine and Belarus agreed to dissolve the Soviet Union and to form a Commonwealth of Independent States, a loose formation in which any semblance of unity was restricted to economic and military matters. Eight further republics joined them on 21 December. The three Baltic states and Georgia, which like Lithuania had declared its independence as early as March 1990, refused the invitation to membership in order to go their own way.

Gorbachev had already on 24 August resigned as General Secretary of the Soviet Communist Party, the key post that since Stalin had been the fount of power in the Soviet Union. He remained for the time being President, though this was by now a largely empty title for an office devoid of real power or purpose. In a television address on 25 December, Gorbachev stepped down from this office too. That evening he formally transferred all his powers to Yeltsin, the Russian President, who entered the Kremlin in the early morning two days later and celebrated with his closest supporters over a bottle of whisky.

In his final television address to the country, Gorbachev defended his record. His reforms, he declared, were historically necessary and justified. They had, he stated, dismantled totalitarianism, which had inflicted poverty on the country, and had brought the breakthrough to democratic transformation and liberal freedoms. And through the ending of the Cold War the threat of another world war had been eliminated. The message was more likely to receive a warm welcome in the West than among the citizens of the dying Soviet Union. Among the latter Gorbachev sharply divided opinion. He had paved the way for their new-found independence, for democratic pluralism, and for freedoms impossible to contemplate as long as the Communist Party held monopoly power. But for many among his critics, however fine democratic principles and aspirations were, Gorbachev had worsened their living standards. And he had ended the Cold War only by capitulating to the West and reducing what had once been a mighty superpower to humiliating inferiority. 'We had an empire when he took over the Kremlin,' recalled a Moscow taxi-driver bitterly years later. 'By the time he left six years later, it was all gone. He sold us off to the West. He just caved in.' Gorbachev himself continued to feel enormous regret for the demise of the Soviet Union. 'I regret that a great country with huge possibilities and resources

17. A huge workers' demonstration in Lisbon on 1 May 1974. A few days earlier, on 25 April, the 'Carnation Revolution' had peacefully ended the authoritarian rule that had lasted for almost half a century in Portugal.

18. Turks in 1980 in the large steel-producing city of Duisburg, in the Ruhr District of north-west Germany. Large numbers of Turkish *Gastarbeiter* ('guest workers') had started to come to West Germany in the 1960s to fill labour shortages in the booming economy. But the early expectation that they would eventually return home was misplaced. *Gastarbeiter*, like immigrants in other parts of Europe, faced prejudice and discrimination, especially in the early years.

19. (*right*) A woman anxiously treads through the rubble in the centre of Belfast, Northern Ireland, on 21 July 1972 following an IRA bomb attack. That day the IRA detonated no fewer than twenty-two bombs in the city, killing nine people and injuring a further 130.

20. A vast crowd in Warsaw on 6 February 1979 attends the celebration of mass by Pope John Paul II on his homecoming to Poland. The Pope's visit greatly strengthened the links between Polish national identity and Catholicism, substantially weakening allegiance to the Communist regime in the process.

21. (*above*) Lech Wałęsa (*centre*) among workers on strike at the Gdańsk shipyard in August 1980. The action was in support of demands for free trade unions, the right to strike, and press freedom.

22. (*right*) The French President François Mitterrand and the West German Chancellor Helmut Kohl symbolically demonstrate reconciliation and friendship as they stand on 25 September 1984 in homage before the monument at Douaumont that commemorates those who fell at the battle of Verdun in 1916.

23. The Soviet leader, Mikhail Gorbachev, in discussion with Margaret Thatcher, the British Prime Minister, during her visit to Moscow at the end of March 1987. Despite their ideological differences, they got on well and had enjoyed a good working relationship since their first meeting in London in 1984.

24. Hundreds of thousands demonstrate against the East German regime in the rain in Leipzig on 6 November 1989, three days before the fall of the Berlin Wall. The Monday Demonstrations in Leipzig had grown massively since they began in early September and exerted increasingly irresistible pressure for radical change on the regime.

vanished,' he told an interviewer long after the events. 'My intention was always to reform it, never to destroy it.'

On 31 December 1991, sixty-nine years after its foundation, seventy-four years after the Russian Revolution that had led to its creation, the Soviet Union was dissolved. There were no fanfares; there was no dramatic ending. At the last, it just fizzled out. Even so, it was an epochal date – the end of a momentous episode in history, the point of failure of probably the most remarkable political experiment in modern times. The Soviet Union had been central to the era of catastrophic conflict that culminated in the terrible bloodshed of the Second World War. Since emerging victorious, if at enormous cost in human lives and untold devastation from the titanic showdown with Hitler's Germany, it had attained domination over the eastern half of Europe, developed into a superpower, and indelibly shaped not just European but global affairs. The edifice built on violent struggle by Lenin and his followers during the Russian Revolution of 1917 and the subsequent horrific civil war in Russia had promised a coming utopia built on equality and justice.

It proved, however, a construction that could only work – and even then at unimaginable human cost – within a vast, undeveloped country which was converted through extraordinary levels of coercion into a mighty force that could withstand four horrific years of war against Nazi Germany, then turn into a superpower in possession of a huge nuclear arsenal. The model was not transferrable to other parts of Europe that had far different social, economic, political and cultural structures. Nowhere, either in the Soviet Union itself or in any of its post-war satellite countries in Central and Eastern Europe, did the majority of people choose communism in free elections. Although Soviet rule was backed by many (if over time a declining number) idealistic true believers in communism, and many more opportunistic fellow travellers, it proved capable of sustaining its ever more plainly empty promises only through the tight clamp of extreme coercion and suppression of freedom. Gorbachev had loosened that clamp to the point where the peoples of the Soviet Union could force it apart completely. And without the clamp there was nothing left.

A NEW ERA

Some on the left mourned the end of the Soviet Union. They regretted the failure of what at one time had seemed an optimistic face of the future, an alternative to the damaging inequities of capitalism. The sense of loss was not confined to the former apparatchiks and beneficiaries of the system, nor those who lamented the loss of empire and decline of a great power. The great historian Eric Hobsbawm, a convinced Marxist since his youth, was far from alone among left-wing intellectuals in recognizing the systemic failings of the Soviet system, acknowledging that he would not have wanted to live under it, but still lamenting its demise. Hobsbawm admired Gorbachev (though he wished there had been a 'less ambitious and more realistic reformer'), but was gloomy about the post-Soviet future. When the Soviet Union foundered, he wrote, 'the losers, in the short and medium term, were not only the peoples of the former USSR, but the poor of the world'.

Regrets did not extend in the West, however, far beyond the shrivelled minority – even among Western communists – of those who had clung to their belief in the superiority of the Soviet system to the end. Liberals and social democrats shed no tears, while those on the conservative right, in Western Europe and even more so in the United States, congratulated themselves on winning the Cold War. They applauded President Reagan's hardline stance (abetted by his British acolyte, the 'Iron Lady' Margaret Thatcher) on communism, revelling in what they saw as the vindication of the 'Star Wars' programme and levels of military spending that had demonstrated Western economic superiority and exposed Soviet weakness. They did not conceal their sense of triumph at what they paraded as the victory of liberal capitalism over state socialism, of freedom over serfdom.

Most people, though, refrained from outright triumphalism. Relief was more apparent – relief that the Cold War was finally over and, consequently, that the danger of nuclear conflict had been eliminated. This mingled with satisfaction at the collapse of a system built upon oppression and unfreedom and the sense that Western values had triumphed. In Central and Eastern Europe the relief, though echoing similar sentiments, had a different tone. People there above all felt relief that the long years of subjugation to the heavy hand of communist rule, backed by the interests of the Soviet Union, were finally over. They could start to reclaim their own national identities. And they could hope in due course to benefit from the prosperity that Western Europe enjoyed.

There was, even so, little prolonged rejoicing. The former Soviet satellites were already exposed to the difficult problems of adjusting to the brave new world they had entered. Fleeting euphoria was swiftly tempered by new hardships. And for the people of Western Europe the collapse of the Soviet Union had been too protracted, the actual end too undramatic, for any explosion of joy at the death of the old ideological enemy. Other issues were already occupying attention, not least war in the Persian Gulf in 1990–1 in the wake of the crisis precipitated by Iraq's invasion of the neighbouring Arab country of Kuwait. In the West the real moment of euphoria about the downfall of communism had been earlier, in November 1989, when the Berlin Wall fell – the symbolic moment when the Soviet clamp on Eastern Europe was broken. What followed had amounted to a long coda.

There was, even so, widespread recognition that the death of the Soviet Union marked a historic caesura, a major turning point in history. Writing in *The Guardian* on 27 December 1991, Martin Woollacott echoed a commonplace sentiment: 'The twentieth century came to an end at 7pm Moscow time on December 25, 1991' – when Gorbachev had broadcast his resignation as leader of the Soviet Union. 'It is as if the business of our century is over ahead of the calendar. The two enormous conflicts which have characterised it, that between capitalism and communism, and that between the old empires and the new powers – struggles that have interacted through the decades – have ended. "Bolshevism", as Winston Churchill in 1918 demanded it should, has finally "committed suicide".'

Three years later, in his celebrated *Age of Extremes*, Eric Hobsbawm also portrayed the demise of the Soviet Union as the end of the 'short twentieth century', an era that had come to a close, one defined by the contest between capitalism and communism. From a conservative perspective, the American political scientist Francis Fukuyama even went so far as to claim that it marked 'the end of History'. In his book, *The End of History and the Last Man*, published in 1992, he drew upon a widely read and controversial essay he had published three years earlier, as the sweeping changes in Eastern Europe were taking hold. Fukuyama was not making the patently absurd claim, as some critics naively presumed, that events would not continue, that history in this sense would cease. Rather, he was arguing in philosophical terms, drawing in part on ideas adumbrated by the famous early nineteenth-century German philosopher Georg Wilhelm Friedrich Hegel, who had seen the victory of the principles of liberty and equality, spread after the French Revolution, as the final stage of history. Fukuyama argued that with the triumph of liberal democracy over its only serious challenger, communism, ideological development had reached the peak of its evolution, and with that 'History' (with a capital 'H') had therefore come to an end. After the demise of communism, wrote Fukuyama, 'liberal democracy remains the only coherent political aspiration that spans different regions and cultures around the globe'. As 'the doctrine of individual freedom and popular sovereignty' liberal democracy was left as the sole 'competitor standing in the ring as an ideology of potentially universal validity'. In the huge debate that ensued, this bold thesis unsurprisingly attracted heavy criticism. It was not just viewed as erroneous. It was also widely regarded as the reflection of triumphalist American neo-conservatism.

The subsequent course of world history has indeed done little to uphold Fukuyama's argument. The cultural and political rejection of the principles of liberal democracy in large parts of the world casts doubt on the teleological presumption of the 'end of History'. The Chinese model of economic liberalism and political authoritarianism, which successfully produced extraordinary growth in China, has posed a serious challenge to those, not just in the West, who long presumed that a market economy would inevitably lead to liberal democracy. The future is as unpredictable as it was when Hegel first determined that 'History' had reached its end. The upheavals in Europe between 1989 and 1991 that culminated in the collapse of the Soviet Union and the alternative to capitalist liberal democracy that it had represented for nearly three-quarters of a century, did not amount, even in Fukuyama's philosophical terms, to the end of 'History'. They were nevertheless a political earthquake with seismic consequences for the entire world, and quite specifically for Europe. After 1991 Europe was a new place.

The new Europe was no longer split down the middle by the Iron Curtain. But the end of the decades-old bifurcation of the continent did not signify the approach of unity. Rather, Europe was now divided into four distinguishable groupings. A fundamental ideological split, it is true, no longer existed, but the differences between the groupings were scarcely insignificant.

The first grouping comprised the countries of the Commonwealth of Independent States – Russia, Ukraine, Belarus and eight other former Soviet Republics – formed in the last days of the Soviet collapse. These countries had no traditional basis in pluralist democracy, legal autonomy, or the institutions (including Churches, trade unions, an independent press) that in much of the rest of Europe had over time given rise to extensive realms of civilian freedom from state control. In the turmoil that followed the breakdown of a regime that had dominated this part of Europe for some seventy years, it was unsurprising that these former Soviet republics would look to strong figures as presidents, such as Yeltsin in Russia, Leonid Kravchuk in Ukraine or Aleksandr Lukashenko, the dictatorial President of Belarus from 1994 onwards, ostensibly to uphold order. History, as well as geography, separated this part of Europe from most of the remainder of the continent. It would continue to follow a separate path.

At the other end of the spectrum were the countries of Western Europe. For them the end of the Soviet Union, following German unification, meant that the potential for European unity beyond the traditional boundaries of Western Europe and the existing confines of the European Community had suddenly opened up. The question of European integration had to be rethought. This was necessary not just to make sure that Germany was inextricably bound to the West, but also to take account of the aspirations of the countries freed from Soviet control (though at no point was it seriously imagined that integration would extend to Russia and other parts of the former Soviet Union). How could the new, but poor, democracies of Central and Eastern Europe be incorporated within the project of European integration? And what were the geopolitical implications of the new Europe? How far, for instance, should the Western defence alliance, NATO, stretch into Eastern Europe? Or was NATO now even redundant since there was no longer an Iron Curtain and the Warsaw Pact (disbanded in 1991) had ceased to exist?

The third loose grouping were the countries that had formerly been bracketed together in Western eyes as 'Eastern Europe', themselves far from a unified bloc. Some of them – notably Poland, Czechoslovakia and Hungary – could look back to a pre-communist past in which there had been a pronounced sense of national identity and it had involved some experience, however chequered, of pluralist democracy. They had also, even under communist rule, created or nurtured important elements of a culture that existed beyond the tentacles of the state. Moreover, Czecho-slovakia and Hungary, less so Poland, had never seen themselves as part of 'Eastern Europe'. They had always regarded themselves as the core of *Central* Europe, a geographically vague entity but one that had enjoyed strong cultural links to Austria and Germany – links that extended for the most part westwards rather than in the direction of Moscow. They now saw the opportunity to rebuild their national identities, democratic traditions and cultural vitality. They also, not least, felt the strong gravi-tational pull of Western European prosperity. Economically and culturally, the countries of Central Europe sought to rejoin a Europe from which they had been cut off for so long.

The Baltic countries – Estonia, Latvia and Lithuania – though geo-graphically part of Eastern Europe, also shared with the Central European countries long-standing traditions of national independence, even if their fragile interwar democracies had been of short duration. They harboured bitter resentment at the Soviet annexation in 1940, had vehemently fought to re-establish their independence among the dying embers of the Soviet Union, and now looked to the West – to NATO and to the European Community – for protection against any future Russian encroachment, and to the prosperity that they saw bound up with West-ern democracy. Naturally, the Russians looked askance at any such extension of NATO's scope.

In south-eastern Europe the post-Soviet world left yet another constel-lation. The collapse of communist rule in Bulgaria and Romania had been replaced by what amounted to little more than facade democracies. There had been too much corruption, poverty ran too deep, and there had been little development of the intermediary structures of civil society to allow a smooth transition to a well-functioning liberal democracy. When the dust began to settle after the enormous upheaval, power still lay dispro-portionately in the hands of those who had been part of the old regimes. These countries, too, envied the prosperity of the European Community. But joining the Community was at best a distant aspiration. This was even more true of Albania, where the communist regime staggered on until it finally fell in March 1992, but where, in this poorest of all the for-mer European communist states, corruption, criminality and the legacy of decades of authoritarian rule meant that the transition to anything genuinely resembling democracy, and one that could harbour hopes of integration into the European Community, would be a lengthy process.

Yugoslavia had never belonged to the Soviet bloc. There, the tensions that had mounted since Tito's death in May 1980 amid serious and growing economic problems had exacerbated emerging ethnic conflict. And, as Yugoslavia started to disintegrate in 1989, these played out with terrible consequences.

Finally, the end of the Soviet Union, and of the Cold War, not only reshaped Europe. It also changed global politics. Mikhail Gorbachev had ensured that in its last years the Soviet Union had acted in collaboration with the United States to defuse a number of long-standing bitter conflicts on the African continent – in Ethiopia, Mozambique, Angola and Namibia. He also helped to impress upon the African National Congress in South Africa a new readiness to come to terms with the presiding apartheid regime it had fought for so long. The last head of state of apartheid South Africa, President F. W. de Clerk, also became ready to negotiate with the African National Congress once it was deprived of Soviet backing and the threat of communist revolution in southern Africa had consequently receded. The release from prison, where he had been incarcerated for twenty-seven years, on 11 February 1990 of Nelson Mandela, internationally lauded as the face of opposition to the racist apartheid regime in South Africa, was symbolically the moment of new hope for the future. But with the demise of the Soviet Union a number of African states – and, in Latin America, Cuba – lost a protector (of sorts) and a source of financial support. The way ahead for them was not one of rapidly increasing prosperity but of further exposure to the rapacious demands of the swiftly expanding globalized economy.

Not least, the collapse of one of the two superpowers of the post-war world had opened up the prospect, and for a time the reality, of American global dominance, of unipolar power in world affairs. Over time China would come to challenge that dominance, as would a resurgent Russia. Meanwhile, however, American neo-conservatives rejoiced at the prospect of hegemony: the United States had won the Cold War, the future under a *pax americana* looked bright. The first years of the new post-Soviet era would soon put that proposition to the test, and in Europe itself. For war was about to return to the European continent.

10

New Beginnings

I don't think Europe quite realizes the potential for violence in Yugoslavia, and it could be about to start any time now.
Srđa Popović, Yugoslav human rights lawyer, June 1991

I asked the Polish historian Jerzy Jedlicki when before in its history Poland had been so well placed. Scarcely hesitating, he replied, 'Probably the second half of the sixteenth century.'
Timothy Garton Ash, November 1995

The end of the Cold War gave rise to great expectations. It was a time of new beginnings in Europe. This was most obviously true of the former communist countries, where liberal economic systems and democratic government started to take shape. But Western Europe, too, saw important new departures in the establishment of the European Union and moves towards the creation of a common currency. Hopes of lasting peace were meanwhile encouraged by the dissolution of the Warsaw Pact's military structure in March 1991. And as political leaders turned their intention to strengthening European integration, the potential of a Europe united by a common interest in peace underpinned by democratic government and guaranteed by shared prosperity seemed realizable. More than anywhere else hopes were high among the peoples of Central and Eastern Europe that following the collapse of communism they would soon begin to enjoy the prosperity already widespread in the western half of the continent.

The years of transition in the first half of the 1990s were, however, to prove more difficult than anyone amid the early euphoria had anticipated. Only after the middle of the decade would the picture look encouraging. And even as people at the beginning of the 1990s dared to dream that a better world was imminent, a great shadow was falling once more over the continent. At the very beginning of the decade war returned to Europe.

ETHNIC WAR

The war in Yugoslavia – or rather a series of wars – that lasted from 1991 to 1995 was a major shock to the new Europe. A dreadful term, 'ethnic cleansing', came into use to epitomize the character of the war. Forcible expulsions and mass killing of people in order to make the disintegrating Yugoslavia more ethnically homogeneous caused the rest of Europe to shudder. The European Union wrung its hands, but its attempts to resolve the complex issue could do nothing to stop the terrible conflict. The United Nations sent peacekeeping forces that failed to keep the peace. Ultimately, Europe proved again incapable of ending a war on European soil and establishing a durable post-war settlement without, yet again, relying upon American intervention.

Ethnic war in Yugoslavia was not, as many in the West unthinkingly presumed, just the Balkans reverting to type – a modern version of age-old conflicts. It nonetheless had a crucial historical background, if a recent one. This was the channelling of disaffection at the growing failings of communism in Yugoslavia during the 1980s into ethnic nationalism. In his long rule, Tito (who died in May 1980) had ruthlessly suppressed ethnic grievances, ruling Yugoslavia with an iron fist and strong personal authority, which he deployed to sustain a careful balance of interests in the complex state. Grievances – together with some deep animosities that lingered from the Second World War – had, however, bubbled beneath the surface and emerged strongly as communism failed to provide answers to mounting, and comprehensive, economic and social distress. The ethnic divisions of Yugoslavia formed the crucible in which the tragedy of that country was to unfold.

The post-war communist state comprised six republics – Bosnia-Herzegovina, Croatia, Macedonia, Montenegro, Serbia and Slovenia – whose populations varied in size. Serbs (nearly eight million) greatly outnumbered Croats (the second-largest ethnic group, under five million). At the other extreme, Montenegro's population was only some 600,000. The distribution of population did not for the most part correspond to the borders of Yugoslavia's constituent republics, leaving an ethnic mix that reflected differing cultural traditions, language and religion. While Slovenia in the north-west was almost entirely mono-ethnic, in other parts of the federal state Serbs, Croats, Muslims, and other ethnicities were not separated by neat borders. Many Croats lived in Serbia. There were Serbian enclaves in Croatia, and both Serbs and Croats lived in Bosnia-Herzegovina, cheek by jowl with two million Muslims, as they had done, generally peacefully, for hundred of years. Montenegrins, Macedonians and Albanians formed other parts of the ethnic patchwork of Yugoslavia, alongside other ethnic minorities. Tito's ruthlessly imposed balancing act ensured that each of the republics had benefited (if not equally) from the rapidly growing economy in the post-war decades and in so doing helped to defuse underlying ethnic tensions.

From the economic downturn of the 1970s onwards, however, rising discontent started to be voiced in terms of cultural difference and identity. These gained further emphasis when the gap between the more prosperous and the poorer republics widened as Yugoslavia plunged by the middle of the following decade into a full-scale economic crisis – huge, unpayable international debts, plummeting standards of living, soaring inflation and mass unemployment. Through the ethnic lens there was a double distortion: the poorer republics were viewed by the richer ones as parasites, the richer by the poorer as the beneficiaries of a federal system that was set up to serve their interests.

Slovenia, already in the early 1980s the most Westernized, culturally tolerant and economically advanced republic, was by 1989 far and away the most prosperous part of economically struggling Yugoslavia, followed at some distance by Croatia. At the opposite pole were Bosnia-Herzegovina and, easily the worst off, Kosovo. The increasing social and economic disparities fostered disaffection, which in turn fuelled ethnic prejudice and animosity. Slovenes and Croats became more resentful at some of their relative prosperity being siphoned off to benefit less productive parts of the country. Serbs looked enviously at the better standard of living among Croats and Slovenes. Kosovans looked to the Serbs to protect them from discrimination by Albanians.

Expatriate nationalists who worked abroad or had been forced into exile helped to promote ethnic resentment back home.

Plainly aware of the traumas that were afflicting the Soviet bloc, Yugoslavs too wanted change. Political crisis loomed as the communist system, incapable of offering any remedy to the country's woes, lost legitimacy. By 1986 as many as 88 per cent of Slovenians and 70 per cent of Croats were expressing unwillingness to join the Communist Party. Even in Serbia, the dominant republic in the federal state, the figure was as high as 40 per cent. The waning hold of communist ideology brought a revival of religious belief – a divisive element as Orthodox Serbs, Catholic Croats and Bosnian Muslims began to see religion as a sign of ethnic identity.

Ethnic nationalism was rapidly becoming the main replacement ideology. Most young adults (though less so among Croats and Slovenes), according to a survey in 1985, still put their Yugoslavian identity ahead of ethnic identity. Other surveys nonetheless pointed towards worsening ethnic relations. So did some elements of popular culture. Football fans turned matches into symbolic displays of aggressive ethnic rivalry – waving banners to advertise their ethnic identity, singing old Second World War refrains of Chetnik Serbian nationalists, or, on the Croat side, giving the fascist salute of the Ustaše, who had been guilty of unspeakable wartime crimes. Football hooliganism – a feature of the 1980s in a number of European countries (especially Britain) – acquired in Yugoslavia an outright ethnic dimension. When Dinamo Zagreb played Red Star Belgrade in 1990, 1,500 Croats and Serbs engaged in a pitched battle. The leader of Red Star Belgrade's 'Ultras' was Arkan, the nickname of the violent criminal Željko Ražnatović, soon to spearhead the most notorious Serbian paramilitary force.

History became reinterpreted in accordance with the emerging ethnic divisions. From the mid-1980s onwards a more liberal climate permitted public discussion in books, literature, film and in the mass media of topics that had long been taboo. The Second World War became a topic of discussion, beyond the traditional Yugoslav extolling of the partisan army. Tito himself was far from exempt from criticism. Previously the untouchable national hero, he was increasingly portrayed as a decadent autocrat whose personal luxurious lifestyle stood in sharp contrast to his publicly avowed socialist principles. His wartime role was revised as the Chetniks, for long officially decried as monarchists and reactionaries (if not outright fascists), were rehabilitated by the Serbs. This in itself amounted to reducing the part played by Tito's communist partisans. By the beginning of the 1990s streets and squares in Tito's honour were being renamed. His mausoleum was closed.

A crucial element in the use and abuse of history in promoting an aggressive and intolerant sense of ethnic identity revolved around the terrible atrocities perpetrated by the Ustaše fascist militia of the Independent State of Croatia during the Second World War. The Ustaše had killed, often bestially, hundred of thousands of (mainly) Serbs, Jews and Roma. The numbers killed were, however, bitterly contested by both Serbs (who hugely exaggerated them) and Croats (who grossly reduced them). Franjo Tudjman, soon to become President of Croatia, was among those strongly playing down the scale of the Ustaše killings (and bizarrely blaming the persecution of the Serbs largely on Jews, whose numbers murdered in the Holocaust he also claimed to have been wildly exaggerated). Croats emphasized their own grievous suffering at the hands of Serbian partisans after Croatia had capitulated at the end of the war. The collective Serbian memory of the Ustaše atrocities, on the other hand, bolstered the rapidly spreading view that only in a Serbian state would the people be free from the threat of any recurrence.

No unifying figure capable of transcending the underlying, and mounting, ethnic tensions had succeeded Tito, the war hero and symbol of national unity. The unwieldy constitution of 1974, in attempting through decentralization to provide ethnic balance to the governance of Yugoslavia, merely compounded the growing centrifugal tendencies and political problems of the country. Institutional power, in Tito's last years of deteriorating health, was shared among an eight-member presidency (from the six republics and Serbia's two provinces, Vojvodina and Kosovo), one of whom on an annual rotating basis would serve as head of state and commander-in-chief of the army. Yugoslavia had a federal parliament, six parliaments of the republics, two for Serbia's provinces, and ten communist parties (including one for Yugoslavia as a whole, and one for the army). Unsurprisingly in this complex balancing act, regional parties and governments became more important than the federal entities. The major exceptions – large ones – were the army and the security police, which remained under federal control.

Still, there was as yet no sign of imminent explosion. This was before

Slobodan Milošević, a skilful political tactician who had progressed assuredly upwards on the path of career advancement to become the leader of the Serbian Communist Party, realized that exploitation of ethnic nationalism, not the promotion of communism, was the way to attain the aggrandisement of his own power, and that of Serbia.

Milošević lit what would prove to be the touchpaper to widening ethnic conflict when he delivered an incendiary speech in Kosovo on 24 April 1987. Kosovo held a special place in Serbian mythology. It was seen as the cradle of the Serbian nation, where in 1389 the Serbian aristocracy, vanquished in battle with the Turks, had heroically chosen death rather than capitulation. By the late twentieth century the Serbs formed a deeply resentful minority of the population in Kosovo – grievously persecuted in their own land, as they saw it, by the Albanian majority (around 85 per cent of the total). Milošević went to Kosovo as a high-ranking communist functionary. He returned a fêted nationalist. Responding to an angry crowd of Serbs who were claiming that they had been assaulted by the Albanian Kosovan police, he had told them, in a televised speech, 'This is your land' and 'No one should dare to beat you', immediately unleashing a night of anti-Albanian violence. He had poured petrol on the flames of Serbian nationalism, and not just in Kosovo. It also gave him the platform soon afterward to manoeuvre successfully to become Serbian President. It marked the beginning of Yugoslavia's long death throes.

In the three years after Milošević's baleful Kosovo speech things went from bad to worse. The federal state increasingly struggled to keep a hold over its constituent parts as the economy collapsed. Mirroring what was happening across Central and Eastern Europe, pressure grew for democratization and autonomy within Yugoslavia. In 1990 communist rule in Yugoslavia came to an end. But in pluralist elections that year, the first in over four decades, nationalist parties were the winners everywhere apart from Serbia and Montenegro (little more than a Serbian puppet). And even there the communist parties were becoming by now effectively vehicles of Serbian nationalism. The federal state of Yugoslavia was already struggling for survival.

Franjo Tudjman, who in 1989 had founded the nationalist Croatian Democratic Union Party and became President of Croatia following the next year's election, was by now appealing to the unity of ethnic Croats, inside and outside Croatian borders. Ominously, he referred to Bosnia as a 'national state of the Croatian nation', in which Muslims were seen as merely Islamicized Croats. His party spoke of defending Croatia at the River Drina, the border of Bosnia and Serbia. As President he pressed increasingly for Croatia's independence (while initially paying lip service to the notion of a loose Yugoslav federation). Croatian national assertiveness rapidly became worrying for the Serbian minority in Yugoslavia's second-largest republic. The red-and-white chequered flag that almost overnight fluttered from so many buildings reminded them of the wartime Croatian state, run by the dreaded Ustaše. The Croatian language became the only one permitted in administrative arrangements. Signs were changed to use only the Croatian Latin characters, discarding the Serbian Cyrillic script used by Serbs. (In Belgrade the reverse happened. The Latin script was degraded, replaced everywhere by Serbian Cyrillic.) The cautious ethnic balance of the state administration was disturbed as Serbs were dismissed and replaced by Croats. Worst of all, Serbs were also removed from the police, unfailingly conjuring up the spectre of the return of the fascist Ustaše.

The fears of the Serbian minority in Croatia were to spark the beginning of four long years of war in Yugoslavia. The war fell into a number of phases, bewildering to outsiders in their complexity. During the first, in 1991–2, after Slovenia had, following a ten-day 'phoney war', been allowed to secede from Yugoslavia, Croats were with great brutality driven out of those parts of Croatia that were inhabited mainly by Serbs. The second phase was the first part of what amounted to the core of the war: the three-cornered murderous conflict of Serbs, Croats and Muslims in Bosnia that lasted from 1992 to 1995, as Serbs and Croats waged ethnic war against the Muslims – the main victims of the dreadful unfolding of ethnic cleansing. The Serbs at this point had behaved worst and gained most. In the third phase – the latter part of the Bosnian war – however, the Croats, having built up their army, saw it in their own interest to ally with the Muslims, and now turned the tables on the Serbs, expelling them from areas they had formerly occupied. In this last phase the Serbs were the main losers, and victims of extensive Croat and Bosnian Muslim brutality.

Serbian fears at the outset were especially pronounced in the Krajina (an ancient word denoting a frontier or borderland, a long rim along the western and northern border of Bosnia-Herzegovina), where they formed about 12 per cent of the population. Milošević inspired their hopes of protection in a Greater Serbia and inflamed aggression towards neighbouring Croats. Serious trouble was already brewing in 1990. Once Croatia declared its independence on 25 June 1991 – the same day as Slovenia – the trouble boiled over. Milošević, the key player at this stage, saw Slovenia's secession from Yugoslavia (which followed a brief armed conflict with few casualties) as no great loss to his ambition to bring about Greater Serbia. He had bigger fish to fry. His attention could now switch to the question of the Serbs who lived on Croatian territory.

Milošević had already in March 1991 admitted that 'Yugoslavia is finished'. What would replace it was unclear. But when he met Tudjman for secret talks later in the month, there was discussion of both Croatia and Serbia benefiting from the partition of Bosnia-Herzegovina. Croatian and Serbian expansion were both on the agenda. Before any attention could be turned to Bosnia, however, Tudjman's ambitions to establish an ethnically homogeneous Croatian state and Milošević's schemes for a Greater Serbia were bound to clash over the issue of the sizeable Serbian minority living on Croatian territory.

The British journalist Misha Glenny was shocked at the level of mutual hatred between Croats and Serbs he encountered when travelling in the Krajina even prior to the Croatian declaration of independence. 'Croats and Serbs argued endlessly with me,' he recorded, 'as to why Serbs and Croats, respectively, were congenital monsters. They would cite history, religion, education and biology as reasons.' The visceral hatred struck him as new, a product of the enormous upsurge of nationalism in the dying embers of the Yugoslav communist state – the flames deliberately fanned by state-sponsored media in Belgrade and Zagreb. Young men from mixed ethnic areas and border territories, soaked in male machismo, were drawn to paramilitary units – and once there to a pervasive climate of whipped-up ethnic hatred and glorification of violence. Old fears and handed-down memories were now embedded in recently inflamed hatreds – Croat fears of the return of the Second World War Chetniks, Serbian fears of the revival of the Ustaše. As violence spread, spawning counter-violence, the murderous mentality widened to previously peaceable parts of the population.

When Serbs killed and mutilated the bodies of several Croat policemen in a village near Vukovar in the north-east of Yugoslavia in May

1991, it lit the fuse to an explosion of violence across the Krajina, chiefly perpetrated by Serbian paramilitaries backed by the units of federal (in practice largely Serbian) Yugoslav army units under the command of a highly able – and utterly ruthless – Colonel (soon to be General), Ratko Mladić. Between August and December 1991 around 80,000 Croats were expelled and forced to flee – many more would follow over subsequent months – from predominantly Serbian areas. Areas outside the Krajina were also attacked as the violence spread. The beautiful Dalmatian resort of Dubrovnik, once visited by countless tourists, was bombarded, besieged and much destroyed – with scant military rationale. The port of Split on the Adriatic also suffered. All this took place in view of journalists and television cameras. Worst of all was the terrible violence in the pretty Danubian town of Vukovar, where thousands of civilians were caught up in a three-month siege and bombardment. As the world looked on in horror, hundreds were killed and many more wounded before the siege ended with the fall of the town to the Serbs on 20 November 1991.

This phase of the war ended in January 1992 (following negotiations conducted by a special envoy of the United Nations, the former US Secretary of State Cyrus Vance). An armistice, to be supervised by a United Nations peacekeeping force of around 12,000 troops, was agreed. It could do nothing, however, to ensure that expelled Croats felt safe enough to return to the designated 'Protected Areas', or to prevent the Yugoslav army, on its withdrawal over subsequent months, from leaving much of its weaponry with Serbian militia and security forces. About a third of Croatia had by then fallen under the control of the rebel Serbs.

Hopes, faint though they were, of an overall political solution to Yugoslavia's troubles, rested on the efforts of Lord Carrington, formerly British Foreign Secretary and subsequently Secretary General of NATO. These were torpedoed when Germany – echoing strongly anti-Serbian public opinion at home – put strong pressure on other countries in the European Community to recognize Croatian independence. There were direct consequences for Bosnia-Herzegovina.

This central Yugoslav republic – of its population 44 per cent were Muslim, 33 per cent Serbian and 17 per cent Croat – now faced an unenviable choice: declaring its own independence, or remaining in a Yugoslavia dominated by Serbs. The Bosnian Serbs were led by Radovan Karadžić, a former psychiatrist convicted in the mid-1980s of embezzlement and fraud, whose wild mane of hair would soon make him instantly recognizable to a global television audience. Karadžić refused to contemplate Bosnian independence, which stood in complete opposition to the aim of unifying all Serbs in a Greater Serbian state. For Karadžić and his followers, a Bosnian declaration of independence meant war. On 3 March 1992, following a referendum held on 29 February and 1 March, in which nearly two-thirds of voters supported independence, the Bosnian President, the Muslim lawyer and intellectual Alija Izetbegović, who had served five years in prison during the 1980s for his opposition to communism, issued precisely that declaration.

On 7 April, the day after the European Community had recognized the state of Bosnia-Herzegovina, Bosnian Serbs declared their own independence in what they were before long calling the Serbian Republic (*Republika Srpska*). Already in preceding weeks Muslim civilians had been wantonly killed and assaulted in north-eastern Bosnia by Serbian paramilitaries. By the end of April, Sarajevo, the ancient and beautiful capital of Bosnia-Herzegovina, for centuries the home of an ethnically and religiously mixed population, was besieged by thousands of troops from the Yugoslav army (overwhelmingly Serbs) and Bosnian Serbian police and paramilitaries. The diary entries of a twelve-year-old girl, Zlata Filipovic, offer a taste of the daily fears of Sarajevo citizens during the siege: 'It's dangerous to walk around town. It's especially dangerous to cross our bridge, because snipers shoot at you. You have to run across. Every time [my mother] goes out, Daddy and I go to the window to watch her run . . . You run, and you run, and you run, and there's no end to the bridge.' The siege was set to last for almost four years, and cost the lives of nearly 14,000 people, thousands of them (including over 1,500 children) civilians, and a further 56,000 people (nearly 15,000 of them children) injured.

Ethnic hatred did not consume everyone. Two twenty-five-year-old lovers, killed as they tried to escape Sarajevo in May 1993, had been sweethearts since school days; he was a Serb, she was a Muslim. But they belonged to a dwindling minority. For a terrible spiral of atrocities in the escalating ethnic war by now engulfed the entire region. Milošević and Tudjman looked on from Belgrade and Zagreb respectively. As they had recognized in their secret talks in 1991, they stood to gain. War for them was a rational business.

Each side committed atrocities. The worst, however, were inflicted on the Muslims. Killing, rape, beatings, robbery and destruction of property (houses, shops, mosques and other community buildings) were all part of a systematic use of terror that successfully drove the Muslim population above all from their homes and 'ethnically cleansed' entire areas. Terrified Muslim women and children were put into train wagons in Banja Luka, in northern Bosnia, and ferried away, like Jews who half a century previously had been deported to Auschwitz. Men were rounded up and put into modern-day concentration camps, redolent of the horrors of the Second World War. Columns of refugees walked for days on roads and through mountain passes to escape the terror, but were themselves subjected to horrific violence – abuse, intimidation, pillage and often murder – as they fled. It was estimated that a minimum of 20,000 women were raped.

By the time the Bosnian War ended in 1995 the dead, according to the most reliable calculations, numbered over 100,000. Over 60 per cent of those were Bosnian Muslims, who also comprised the overwhelming majority of the civilian deaths. Their fate contributed to the deepening process of radicalization in the Islamic world. Serbs made up 25 per cent of those killed, Croats 8.3 per cent. Around 2.2 million had been forced to flee their homes. No conflict since the Second World War had left so many dead or displaced.

The worst single atrocity came last. By 1993 the town of Srebrenica in eastern Bosnia had become a Muslim enclave in Serbian-controlled territory – grossly overcrowded by refugees fleeing from murderous ethnic cleansing in nearby villages. The town was placed under United Nations protection as a 'safe area' in April that year. The Serbs were nonetheless determined to take the enclave. Their blockade of food and even medical supplies caused conditions to deteriorate alarmingly. Fewer than 400 Dutch soldiers, as part of the United Nations protection force, were left to defend the 'safe area' by the time Serbian troops, almost four times greater in number, commanded by General Mladić, began their offensive to take the town on 6 July 1995. Within five days Srebrenica was in Serbian hands. From 12 July the Serbs began to separate the men and boys from the women (who were transported by force to Bosniak territory). Around 8,000 of them were taken into the woods and systematically massacred. It was the grimmest episode in the entire grim war, a stain on

European civilization. Europe, and the wider world, was reminded of a horror it thought had been eradicated for good. Finally, the West was stirred into a concerted effort to end the conflict.

A number of attempts had been made, the most promising (as it seemed for a time) by Cyrus Vance and the former British Foreign Secretary David Owen. But proposals for territorial division had invariably fallen foul of one belligerent side or the other. By 1995, however, the war was becoming counter-productive for Serbia – badly affected by UN sanctions, internationally isolated, and under the threat from the United States – despite European reluctance – that it would arm the Bosnians (whose plight had gained them wide international sympathy). Moreover, the Bosnian Muslims and Croats had stopped fighting each other in March 1994. So Serbia stood friendless and alone. Milošević decided that the time had come to hold on to what he had – and at the expense of the Serbs who lived outside Serbia itself, precisely those he had promised to protect by incorporation in a Greater Serbia. For Milošević the intransigent Bosnian Serbs had become no more than a hindrance.

The two decisive steps in 1995 were interlinked: the end, under American pressure, of the Croat offensive against Muslims in Bosnia, and the new determination of the United States to find a territorial solution to the Bosnian War, which the Europeans (and the United Nations) had failed to achieve. The enormous bloodletting and huge destruction had occurred in a part of Europe with the Europeans looking on. In Srebrenica the Dutch UN soldiers had helplessly stood by while the Muslim men and boys were led out to their execution. Timothy Garton Ash, visiting Bosnia in 1995, castigated 'the external policy of that thing called Europe, which looked so bright and hopeful just four years ago'. The hubristic claim by Jacques Poos, the Luxembourg Foreign Minister, in 1991, that 'the hour of Europe has dawned', seemed four blood-soaked years later like a sick joke.

The Americans now brought new urgency to the search for a peace settlement. Military cooperation between Zagreb and Washington was offered as the bait to Tudjman to stop hostilities against the Bosnian Muslims and make territorial gains at the expense of the Serbs. The stick to match the carrot was that if Croatia did not comply, the country would face international isolation, sanctions, and most likely indictment of its leaders for war crimes. Recognizing where his interests lay, Tudjman was ready to comply. In the late spring and summer of 1995 the Croats, having built up their armed forces in the meantime, turned the tables on the Serbs in the Krajina, inflicting their own ethnic cleansing of Serbian areas. The Serbian uprising against Croat rule had begun in 1990 in the Serb-inhabited town of Knin, about forty miles inland from the Dalmatian coast. By 1995, the 'ethnically cleansed' town was Croatian. Where once 37,000 Serbs had lived, the town had been reduced to an empty shell with a population of just 2,000.

The balance of power had by now completely shifted. Tudjman, the loser in 1991, had turned out to be a winner. Milošević, triumphant early in the war, was now on the defensive. And without the support of Milošević, who had cut off their arms supply, the Bosnian Serbs themselves faced the prospect of losing all their gains. The chances of ending the conflict were greater than they had been since its beginning. But there was still some way to go before the warring parties might reach a settlement – demanding reluctant compromise on all sides – that could hold.

The thorny path to any potential deal was trodden by the tough, no-nonsense American negotiator Richard Holbrooke, a former US Assistant Secretary of State with extensive diplomatic experience. By late September 1995, Holbrooke had pressed Tudjman and, more unwillingly, Izetbegović into accepting the basis of a settlement in which Bosnia-Herzegovina would remain a sovereign state, but as a federation in which Bosnian Serbs would control just under a half (almost all in the Republika Srpska) and the Croats around a fifth. This was the essence of the deal that was eventually agreed at a conference held in Dayton, Ohio, in November 1995 (later formally signed in Paris on 14 December). The agreement was to be implemented by a NATO force of 60,000 troops. It was an uneasy, fragile arrangement – as all sides acknowledged, far from perfect. But the pragmatic settlement, despite continuing tensions, proved surprisingly durable.

The issue of Kosovo, which in a way had sparked the entire conflict, remained unresolved. Serious, endemic ethnic violence had not ceased. Much of it was carried out by the Kosovo Liberation Army. This guerrilla organization of Albanians who had turned to armed struggle for Kosovan independence had hardened criminals among its members, though most had been radicalized by their maltreatment at the hands of the Serbian police. A lesson the Kosovans had drawn from the Dayton

Agreement was that violence pays. The West had bowed to the realities of armed might in Bosnia but had forgotten, it seemed, the demands for autonomy of the overwhelmingly Albanian majority in Kosovo. Milošević's response to the violence was to unleash a Serbian campaign of ethnic cleansing against Albanian villages. Over the following two years an estimated 10,000 Albanians were killed, and over half a million took flight into neighbouring countries. When brutal Serbian reprisals against the supporters of the guerrilla army were stepped up in 1998, they prompted what amounted to an armed rising by the Kosovans – backed by weaponry they had looted from arsenals in Albania itself. For the West the circulation of pictures of the bodies of forty-five Albanians, victims of a Serbian police action, on 15 January 1999, in a village south of the capital city of Priština, was the decisive moment. It brought a reminder of Srebrenica, anxiety that another Bosnia was in the making, and a determination this time to act before it was too late.

The Bosnian War helped to persuade the West to adopt what became known as the doctrine of liberal (or humanitarian) interventionism – the belief that Western democracies needed to act against misrule to protect the human rights of those menaced by regimes. The Contact Group (as it called itself) – the USA, Russia, Britain, France and Germany – that had earlier fruitlessly sought a settlement in Bosnia met again at Rambouillet, near Paris, on 6 February, but despite threats of military action Milošević rejected their peace plan, since it involved stationing NATO troops on Serbian territory. The day after talks were finally broken off on 19 March the Yugoslav army – Yugoslavia by now was reduced to Serbia and its puppet, Montenegro – began an offensive in the north-west of Kosovo, carried out with much violence. Milošević still refused to negotiate. On 24 March major NATO air strikes, with the United States in the lead, began against Yugoslavia. More than a thousand planes inflicted extensive damage on the country's infrastructure, destroying many buildings in the capital, Belgrade, itself, and killing hundreds of civilians. The air strikes were carried out without any mandate from the UN Security Council – the Russians and Chinese had indicated that they would use their veto – thereby calling their legality into question. Many in the West were appalled. Those in favour of the West's new doctrine of humanitarian intervention claimed, however, that in such an emergency, where human rights were being trampled on but where political interests were certain to impose a veto in the Security Council, a higher morality had to prevail. Lessons from the past – not just the most recent past in Yugoslavia – were invoked. Germans compared inhumanity in Kosovo with Hitler's crimes. The British spoke of the dangers of appeasing dictators.

Serbian forces in Kosovo intensified their offensive in retaliation at the air strikes. By now more than three-quarters of a million Kosovans had taken flight, mainly towards Albania and Macedonia. It took eleven weeks before Milošević finally backed down on 9 June 1999. Air strikes were halted the next day. Kosovo became a United Nations Protectorate within Yugoslavia, to be guaranteed by a NATO peacekeeping force. The final status of Kosovo was left unresolved. But the Serbs had had enough of their one-time champion Slobodan Milošević. In the wake of huge popular protests following (disputed) presidential elections Milošević yielded to the pressure and on 7 October 2000 was replaced as President of Serbia by the lawyer Vojislav Koštunica, leader of the Serbian Democratic Party. A year later Milošević was handed over to the International Criminal Tribunal for the former Yugoslavia, set up in The Hague in the Netherlands in 1993 to prosecute the perpetrators of serious crimes committed during the Yugoslav wars.

Kosovo staggered on, its internal violence by no means ended, most directed at the Serbian minority. In 2008, opposed by Serbia and without United Nations backing, Kosovo's parliament unilaterally declared independence, which promptly gained international recognition. Two years earlier Montenegro had terminated its union with Serbia and itself became fully independent. With that, the state of Yugoslavia, which had arisen from the upheavals of the First World War, survived the Second, and then successfully defied Stalin, had ceased to exist – a victim of its own internal enmities.

The judicial reckoning was still to come. Slobodan Milošević was one of 161 persons indicted before the International Tribunal in The Hague. Most were sentenced to a lengthy period of imprisonment. Milošević died during his trial in 2006. Radovan Karadžić (belatedly indicted after years in hiding) was eventually sentenced to forty years, in March 2016. Ratko Mladić also evaded justice for many years. He was finally convicted in November 2017 of genocide, war crimes and crimes against humanity, and sentenced to life imprisonment. The interest of the world had moved on long before the trials approached their conclusion. For the three million whose lives had been ruined and for the hundreds of thousands who had seen loved ones killed or maimed by four years of bitter fighting, the verdicts of the court, while no doubt welcome to most, were scant compensation for the torment and suffering.

The fall of Yugoslavia had shown that even in the new Europe armed might could still ride roughshod over the rule of law. Violence had paid off. The power of the gun had again proved decisive. Bosnia and Croatia had been ethnically cleansed. The new nation states that had arisen from the wreckage of federal Yugoslavia reflected a pattern in Europe's twentieth century: they had borders based on high levels of ethnic homogeneity. Most Europeans, sickened to the core by the daily television bulletins on the horror as Yugoslavia disintegrated, shut out of their lives what was actually happening in another part of their own continent. Yugoslavia was a reminder, even so, that the past still cast a long shadow over Europe. Expectations after the demise of communism that unity and peace would spread across the continent had been no more than an illusion.

MISPLACED HOPES

Yugoslavia's disaster was a profoundly negative reversion to the type of ethnic and territorial conflict that had once afflicted much of Eastern and Central Europe. And the failure of the rest of Europe to prevent it was deeply depressing. Nevertheless, the tragedy should not hide the fact that, whatever the initial disappointment and at times disillusionment, the states of the former Soviet bloc did not return to earlier forms of authoritarian nationalism. The pull of the European Union, reflecting the principles of democracy and the rule of law, was the strongest counterweight to any such tendencies.

The euphoria felt by much of the population of Central and Eastern Europe was so great in 1990 that disenchantment was bound to follow during the early years of difficult transition to completely new economic and political systems. Massive disruption to people's lives was unavoidable during the double transformation from communist states with state-controlled economies to democratized political structures and liberalized economies. Living standards often suffered in the early years, though economic growth saw them start to improve significantly during the later 1990s.

The path adopted (with numerous variants) in the process of fundamental economic restructuring followed neo-liberal theories that by now had almost entirely displaced Keynesianism as orthodoxy. A programme, dubbed 'the Washington Consensus', originally devised in 1989 for Latin American countries, was widely deemed to be the way forward in the formidable task of transforming the moribund state-owned economies of Eastern and Central European countries. It gave outright priority to fast liberalization of the economy through deregulation, privatization, and opening up to the freedom of the market. This required the quickest possible abolition of state controls and ownership in favour of market competition. For the people of the former communist countries to reach the broad sunlit uplands of prosperity enjoyed in the West, they would first have to pass through a vale of tears. Emerging on the other side, the journey – it was presumed – would have proved worthwhile.

The neo-liberal approach was welcomed by Central and Eastern European leaders as the best way to align their countries in the shortest possible time with the more economically advanced Western Europe. Copying the West was, so it was thought, the key to 'rejoining' Europe. Poland's Finance Minister, Leszek Balcerowicz, and the Czechoslovakian Finance Minister (later Czech Prime Minister), Václav Klaus, were the most ardent European supporters of 'shock therapy', as it was labelled, a term associated with the Harvard economist Jeffrey Sachs. But in one form or another neo-liberalism dominated the strategy to convert socialist to capitalist economies as rapidly and thoroughly as possible.

New laws deregulated the economy as the straitjacket of socialist planning was removed. Market prices replaced price controls. Currencies were made convertible. Foreign trade was liberalized by reducing or eliminating tariffs to allow free movement of goods and capital. Banks, stock exchanges, and a whole panoply of financial laws had to be speedily introduced. Privatization of state concerns gathered pace. It was more successful at first for small and middling-size concerns than for big enterprises, for which major foreign investment proved initially difficult to attract.

The International Monetary Fund helped to subsidize the transition, providing a total of $27 billion by 1997, though in loans not grants. Poland was singularly fortunate to have its debts effectively written off by

1993 – a reward for being the 'shop-window' country of the 'shock therapy', and also on account of its size and strategic importance. Assistance also came from the European Economic Community (soon to be renamed the European Union). This at first targeted Poland and Hungary, but soon became a wider programme. The amounts were, however, much lower in relative terms than the Marshall Plan of 1947, which had been so important to Western Europe's post-war rebuilding, and less generous in their stipulations.

For millions of citizens of the countries of the former Soviet bloc the impact of the economic changes during the first years of such rapid and draconian transformation was dire. The former German Democratic Republic was exceptional in benefiting from largesse amounting to billions of marks from West German coffers. Nevertheless, here as elsewhere living standards at first fell as unemployment rose steeply and industrial production plummeted to little more than a quarter of what it had been in 1988. At least East Germans could, and did, vote in large numbers with their feet by joining the drain to the more prosperous Western Germany where they could find work in their own country. Around 600,000 (nearly 4 per cent of the population) left in 1989–90, though the numbers dropped thereafter to around half that level before increasing again in the later 1990s. Nowhere else did people have that option. Elsewhere, too, the blight on the living standards was generally even harsher. At a time when income was rising in Western Europe, it was dropping by 20 to 30 per cent in Central and Eastern Europe. Unsurprisingly, only a small minority of citizens in Bulgaria, the Czech Republic, Slovakia, Hungary, Poland and Romania felt (according to opinion surveys in 1993–4) they were better off than they had been before the fall of communism.

Gross domestic product dropped in all post-communist countries in the first years of transition. Industrial production in Poland fell by nearly a third in 1990–91, the country's gross national product by almost a fifth. By 1992, 13.5 per cent of the working population – 2.3 million people – had no job. In the famous Gdańsk shipyard, birthplace of Solidarity, the number of employees dropped from 17,000 to 3,000 by the mid-1990s, and financial losses became unsustainable. The pattern was similar across most of Central and Eastern Europe. Compared with 1989, Albania's industrial production had declined by 1993 by a staggering 77 per cent. In Romania industrial output dropped by 22 per cent in 1992 alone. In Czechoslovakia and Hungary the decline between 1989 and 1993 was over a third. It was similar in the Baltic countries, Estonia, Latvia and Lithuania. Unemployment soared in each country, while purchasing power was eaten away by rocketing inflation. Rural areas also suffered badly. Agriculture slumped in some countries to only a half of its output before the collapse of communism. The population drained away since agricultural employment was in steep decline (though still far higher than in Western Europe, especially in the Baltic countries, Poland and, above all, the Balkans). The privatization of former collective farms was slow and piecemeal, affected by disputes over ownership and lack of capital. The mainly small farms that came into being were poorly mechanized and unprofitable.

By the mid-1990s, however, and already as early as 1992 in Poland, the worst was over. Growth, averaging almost 4 per cent (much faster than in Western Europe, though from a far lower base), began to gather pace across the region. Unemployment rates started to come down, as did inflation (though not in the still deeply troubled economies of Bulgaria and Romania). By the turn of the millennium, benefiting from global growth, Central and Eastern Europe, taken as a whole, had almost recovered to the level of 1989 – and now had completely restructured economies. Although the price had initially been high, and although there were substantial variations in the levels of success achieved, they had taken major steps towards ending state monopolies, extending private ownership, and building functioning, liberalized market economies. By the end of the decade prospects were looking far brighter for the former 'eastern bloc' countries.

Had the pain of such an abrupt transition from socialism to capitalism been necessary? On this, the opinion of eminent economic experts differed at the time, and it continues to differ diametrically. Advocates of the 'shock therapy' remain convinced that the bitter medicine offered the best and quickest possible route to economic health. Critics claim that the medicine need not have been so nasty; similar, if not better, results could have obtained by more gradual acclimatization to the demands of economic change. A slower transformation, they argue, which placed greater store on modifying market forces through a (modernized) state sector, would have produced growth without countries first having to undergo such drastic decline (and the accompanying social distress).

Hungary, where steps towards partial liberalization of the economy had already been taken well before the fall of communism, is usually highlighted as showing the merits of a more gradual approach. However, by 1995 Hungary was struggling to combat its high level of foreign debt and compelled, under pressure from the International Monetary Fund and the World Bank, to introduce severe austerity measures. The economy slumped as a result, and nearly a third of the population were classed as falling below the poverty line. There was much disillusionment at the rise in unemployment, the impact of privatization, and cuts in state welfare. Moreover, Poland, the paradigm of successful 'shock therapy', in fact soon diluted the worst effects of its chosen strategy. Steps were taken to moderate the speed of reform and in particular to defer privatization. In addition, as mentioned, it was alone in benefiting from debt remittance. The Czech Republic, the other prime example of the remedies of 'shock therapy', actually still heavily subsidized large enterprises and anyway did not avoid financial crisis by the mid-1990s. (The two halves of the former federal state of Czechoslovakia, unable to agree on a political direction, decided on an amicable divorce in 1993, creating the separate states of the Czech Republic and Slovakia.) The interpretational debate is unresolved. Beyond the often arcane debates among economists, however, the reality was that every path from socialism to capitalism was strewn with thorns. There was no easy way through the thickets.

Those countries fared best that had good prerequisites for making the painful transition. Within the former Soviet bloc (leaving aside the abnormal case of the German Democratic Republic), Poland, Hungary and the Czech Republic had strong industrial bases, rapidly developing commercial sectors, relatively good transport infrastructure and emerging civic cultures, and held attractions for Western investment. Slovenia, easily the most advanced Yugoslav republic, fell broadly into this pattern. So, in most respects, did the Baltic countries. Romania, Bulgaria and Albania, on the other hand, lagged far behind in every regard, while much of Yugoslavia was consumed by war.

Whether or not the strong dose of neo-liberalism was the right medicine, by the arrival of the new millennium there had been growing levels of convergence with Western economies. Societies, too, for so long separated by the Iron Curtain and forced to follow differing trajectories, were starting to come together. Ease of communication and travel, television, popular culture and sport all played their role in helping to unify what had still so recently been divided. Cities, benefiting most from the advantages of freedom of travel and ease of communication, fared best. Prague and Warsaw were examples of rapidly booming cities. There was a big gap, though, between the showcase capitals and the provincial towns and rural areas, which witnessed a population drain (especially of young people) away to expanding conurbations. Regions turned into wastelands by de-industrialization were also left behind. But even here, once the worst of the drastic economic adjustment was overcome, membership of the European Union served as a hope for future prosperity.

That route was not open to the European successor states to the Soviet Union – Russia itself, Ukraine, Belarus and Moldova. For these countries there was, and could be, no turn to the West. This was the new dividing line in Eastern Europe. The prerequisites for successful, if arduous, transition that generally existed in Central Europe were wholly lacking in an economic zone dominated by Russia. The basis for state regulation of a commercialized economy was as good as non-existent. There was little attraction for foreign investment. The infrastructure was poor. And there were no traditions of the rule of law, pluralist democracy, and a civic culture independent of the state. What emerged in Russia was robber-baron capitalism. Corruption on a colossal and endemic scale transferred many of the state resources, including the enormous profits from oil and gas, into the hands of unscrupulous oligarchs who invested much of their vast wealth in the West, ostentatiously flaunting their untold riches in luxury Mediterranean yachts or palatial houses in London and other Western European cities. Industrial production in Russia meanwhile plummeted, state debt soared, and by the late 1990s the Russian Federation was bordering upon economic collapse while much of the population endured a miserable standard of living. Most people thought they had been better off under communism and lamented the decision to dissolve the Soviet Union.

Ukraine, possessing some of the most fertile land in Eastern Europe, underwent prolonged economic crisis during the 1990s, experiencing rocketing inflation and deep depression. Gross domestic output fell to under a half of what it had been before the fall of communism. Hundreds of thousands of Ukrainians were forced to seek work abroad to provide meagre subsidies for families at home. The city of Lviv, for example, saw its population dwindle by nearly a fifth over the 1990s as people left for work elsewhere. Poverty levels in backward rural areas were profound, average incomes far lower, for example, than in Turkey.

Belarus and Moldova, both of which, like Ukraine, were highly dependent on Russia, also suffered a prolonged deep economic depression during the 1990s. The response in Belarus after 1994, to restore price and foreign-exchange controls and restrict private enterprise, could not halt the economic decline. Moldova's abrupt turn from a planned to a liberalized economy in 1992, with an infrastructure unprepared for such a drastic shift, produced huge inflation and unemployment, leaving much of the population in poverty and the country languishing among Europe's poorest. Both countries, together with Ukraine and Russia itself, took a decade to recover from the economic shock that accompanied the fall of communism. High rates of growth (from a low base) were experienced after the turn of the millennium. But corruption was deeply ingrained, poverty (compared with Central and Western Europe) extensive, and economic instability entrenched.

Politics in Russia and the other Soviet successor-states were turbulent and only superficially democratic. The tendency was towards strong executive powers vested in a president. If in a new guise, a revival, or continuation, of authoritarianism incorporating significant elements of the Soviet heritage, was the norm. The dominant figure in Ukraine turned out to be Leonid Kuchma, whose rule was characterized by corruption and close relations with powerful oligarchs linked to criminality. In Belarus, Alexander Lukashenko, President from 1994, soon sharply curtailed the powers of parliament and ruled in autocratic fashion. In Russia itself President Yeltsin's impulsive and autocratic tendencies, not helped by his copious alcohol consumption, were an outright provocation to his many enemies, inside and outside parliament. An attempt to overthrow him in 1993, after he had overstepped his constitutional powers, failed, however, amid bloodshed in central Moscow.

In the aftermath Yeltsin took steps to shore up his executive powers by a new constitution that was backed by the electorate in a referendum and parliamentary elections, though low turnout and strong suspicions of manipulation showed the weak legitimacy of his position. Yeltsin's popularity suffered in subsequent years from ubiquitous and scandalous corruption – reaching into his own family – and from the continuing disastrous finances and economic state of the country. The rapidity of the moves in 1992 to liberalize the economy and deregulate prices had brought rampant inflation that had wiped out the savings of countless citizens. And privatization, beginning the same year, had simply placed huge state assets for a fraction of their true value into the hands of a small number of super-rich oligarchs, the bosses of newly constituted big private concerns. Organized criminal gangs used extortion, blackmail and even murder to force through the process of privatization and consolidation of enormous wealth. Russia, within the space of only a few years, became a criminalized society.

Yeltsin's attempts at liberal reform were, unsurprisingly, widely condemned not just as an outright failure but as a scandalous destruction of the national economy. By the late 1990s there had been some economic recovery. But the living conditions of most Russians were still miserable while the gross corruption and blatant abuse of power were all too evident. It was little wonder that many looked to the country's former glories. What were seen as Yeltsin's pro-Western leanings provoked desires to restore 'true' Russian values.

The pre-selected heir, when Yeltsin suddenly announced his resignation on 31 December 1999, was Vladimir Putin, who had begun his career in the Soviet security police, the KGB, and had been Prime Minister since August. Yeltsin, by now in poor health, had singled out Putin, regarded as a firm loyalist, as his desired successor – doubtless on assurances that he and his family would be protected from all charges of corruption (which indeed followed through Putin's very first presidential decree on the day he took office). Rumours, backed by considerable circumstantial evidence, that Putin's succession had been engineered in sinister fashion have never fully subsided. According to these claims, a number of bombings in Moscow in September 1999 that killed and injured hundreds of people and were blamed on Chechen terrorists were in fact the work of the Russian state security services, the FSB (successor to the KGB). The presumed purpose was to gain support for retaliatory war in Chechnya, to be directed by Putin, which would boost the new president's popularity. This, indeed, turned out to be the case. Whether or not the conspiracy theory holds, the fact was that Russia was ready for a new 'strong man' – without Yeltsin's obvious flaws – to take the reins.

Whatever the variations in national cultural and political traditions in Central and Eastern Europe beyond former Soviet republics, there were some general features in the transition to liberal democracy. Despite the immense difficulties of adjustment, there was no turning back to one-party rule. Pluralist forms of politics established themselves every-where during the 1990s. People overwhelmingly liked the freedom – of expression, to travel, to live without fear of arrest, to practise religion – that had been denied under communism. The end of the snooping society of informers (usually to gain some material advantage or avoid disadvan-tage), reporting on and often denouncing other citizens – which was a common feature of all the communist states but found classical represen-tation in the shadowy omnipresence of the Stasi in the German Democratic Republic with its 170,000 or more 'unofficial collabora-tors' – was as good as universally welcomed. Democratic government, in principle and in (often chequered) practice, became accepted.

According to opinion surveys undertaken in eight countries in Central and Eastern Europe during 1993–4, a majority of citizens favoured the *principle* of a number of parties competing for the power of government. The lowest ratings, between 40 and 49 per cent, were found in Ukraine, Russia and, surprisingly, Poland, with a middle range, from 51 to 57 per cent, in Estonia, Hungary, Bulgaria and Lithuania. Remarkably, though from its singularly awful experience of communism not altogether surpris-ing, Romania recorded by far the highest proportion in favour – far above the norm at 81 per cent. Those opposed in principle constituted about a fifth of those questioned – in the main presumably former committed com-munists. When it came to democratic *practice* (though what that meant was left undefined), it was, however, a different story. The highest propor-tion of those with a positive attitude again, surprisingly, occurred in Romania, where 30 per cent of those questioned approved. (This may well have reflected approval for the early steps taken by the post-communist government of Iliescu to eliminate the most repressive measures of Ceauşescu's regime.) In the other seven states surveyed, the range stretched from 29 per cent in Estonia to only 12 per cent in Ukraine. Although these levels of dissatisfaction with democracy in practice were higher than in Western European countries, there too a good third of citizens had essen-tially negative attitudes towards the practice of democracy. Political parties were widely regarded as little more than a necessary evil.

Jaundiced views about the practice of democracy in Central and East-ern Europe were understandable. Corruption had been rife everywhere under the communist regimes. In their early years the new democracies offered no improvement. No country was immune. But in some countries the rule of law – the basis of genuine democracy – barely operated. Romania, Bulgaria and Albania were in the vanguard of inbuilt corruption and clientelism, not far behind Russia and Ukraine, especially in the process of privatization. Slovakia, too, was deeply corrupt. Even in the economically more advanced Czech Republic rampant corruption in the privatization process contributed to the fall of the government in 1997.

Ambivalence about the new democratic politics was also shaped by the continuities in personnel with the former regimes. For those who had detested (and often suffered under) communism, it was often galling to see that many who had served communist regimes were able to make a political 'comeback' in different colours as democrats.

In the early phase of the transition the actions of former communist functionaries, especially members of the security police, were systematically evaluated only in Germany. But the former East Germany had by now, of course, been incorporated into an already well-established liberal democracy. The speedy dismantling of the institutional framework of the former communist regime, and the acquisition of most of the state security files that revealed the extent of the 'Stasi-State', made thorough evaluation possible. Elsewhere, the picture was much more chequered. Investigation in Hungary and Czechoslovakia was largely confined to responsibility for the Soviet invasions in 1956 and 1968, and in Poland to the imposition of martial law in 1981. Otherwise, only Czechoslovakia, where memories of 1968 and its aftermath were still vivid, introduced in 1991 what it called 'lustration' – a 'cleansing' – to exclude all former communist functionaries from high public office. It was to be a further six years before Poland, in 1997, followed with its own lustration law.

Political disillusionment and economic hardship brought an increased readiness to turn back to former communist politicians, who could often continue in political life, usually by joining post-communist successor parties. As members of new Social Democratic parties, now operating within democratic pluralism, they returned to government in Poland, Hungary, Lithuania and Bulgaria in 1993. Adam Michnik called the process in Poland 'the velvet restoration'. In Romania the dominant figure during the 1990s was Ion Iliescu, who had earlier been a prominent communist (though he had distanced himself from the worst outrages of Ceauşescu's regime). Many other former communists could find a home in the party he led, the Social Democratic Party of Romania, as well as in the Socialist Labour Party. In Poland the great hero of Solidarity's opposition to communism, Lech Wałęsa (by now a more authoritarian, nationalist-leaning figure), was astonishingly – in the eyes of the outside world – defeated in the 1995 presidential election by the former communist minister, Aleksander Kwaśniewski.

Although pluralist systems of government were generally stable, governments themselves were not. The assault on living standards across the whole of Central and Eastern Europe during the 1990s produced much volatility. Social tensions grew as millions were thrown out of work, and as high inflation and currency devaluation destroyed savings. Every government that tried to deal with the daunting economic and social problems invited dissatisfaction with its policies. Having sought pluralist elections, many citizens thought it pointless to vote in them. This was partly a legacy of communist times when elections had been little more than farcical acclamation in a single-party dictatorial system. But it also reflected disillusionment with what had taken the place of communism. Turnout in elections fell in consequence, and was often extremely low. Governments, held responsible for unpopular policies or for being unable to alter them and bring about substantial improvement, generally met the wrath of the electorate and were overturned at the next election. Heads of government seldom lasted long. The average term of office of a prime minister in the former Soviet bloc was under two and a half years.

Leading politicians often turned to nationalism and anti-foreigner sentiment to improve their sagging popularity. Amid widespread social distress it was easy to find scapegoats among foreigners or ethnic minorities. The Prime Minister of Slovakia, Vladimír Mečiar, who presided over a corrupt, semi-authoritarian regime that rigidly controlled the mass media and intimidated political opponents, had evoked a separate sense of Slovak national identity and culture in pressing for autonomy. Stirring anti-Hungarian feeling – the Hungarian minority constituted just over a tenth of the population – was a convenient part of his political armoury. In Hungary itself there was a rise in nationalist feeling and in animosity to ethnic minorities during the 1990s. Sinti and Roma were made scapegoats here, while discrimination against Hungarians in Slovakia and Romania was exploited to shore up nationalist feeling. FIDESZ, once a liberal movement, became, under its forceful leader Viktor Orbán, strongly national-conservative and increasingly authoritarian in tenor. In Bulgaria the Turkish and Roma minorities were singled out. In Latvia and Estonia there was legal discrimination against the large Russian minorities – less so in Lithuania where the Russians formed only a small proportion of the population.

Whatever their manifold and serious deficiencies, the new democracies of Central Europe, unlike the interwar fragility that had seen nearly all of them turn to authoritarianism, were fairly well consolidated by the end of the 1990s, helped by the significant economic growth that followed the early years of calamitous decline. Another factor was of major importance in ensuring that progress towards stable democracy and economic prosperity would continue: the prospect of membership of the European Union. Despite the disillusionment engendered during the first years of democracy, this prospect offered hope for the future. By the end of the decade the hope was starting to become realizable for the Central European and Baltic states. The Balkans, however, were still desperately poor. The Dutch writer Geert Mak, visiting Bucharest in 1999, described the thousands of homeless children (and the endless packs of stray dogs) roaming the streets. Economic backwardness, high levels of corruption, inadequate basis of the rule of law, and limited progress towards consolidated democracy meant that Romania, and Bulgaria too, faced a lengthy wait before they might contemplate entering the European Union.

Hungary had in 1991 along with Czechoslovakia and Poland signed an agreement in the Hungarian town of Visegrád aimed at promoting their mutual cooperation and advancing their hopes for European integration. With the creation of the Czech Republic and Slovakia two years later, the original three had become four states. By 1996 all had submitted applications to join the European Union. The attractions of doing so, and pressure to meet the entry criteria, encouraged moves to deepen the hold of democracy and the rule of law. The prospect of 'rejoining Europe' was, for instance, a strong inducement to the Slovak electorate, and to the elites, to reject Mečiar's facade democracy in 1998, end the direst aspects of his rule, rein in the worst of the cronyism, and introduce significant legal, democratic and economic reforms.

By the turn of the millennium the citizens of Central and Eastern European countries had endured a turbulent decade. Dreams of an early great improvement in the quality of life based upon a better Western model of liberal democracy had rapidly faded. But new hopes had gradually replaced them – of future benefits they could foresee as members, before too long, of the prospering European Union.

HOPES OF UNITY

As Yugoslavia collapsed into bloodshed and ruins, and as the citizens in Central and Eastern Europe saw their lives turned upside down by the harsh transition to capitalism, the leaders of Western European countries assembled, still in somewhat self-congratulatory mood following the fall of communism, in the Dutch city of Maastricht in December 1991 to plan further steps towards 'ever closer union'. The advances made towards introducing the Single Market (to be launched on 1 January 1993) made the time seem propitious to press forward with the process of integration. And an increasing majority of Europeans, according to opinion polls in 1991, viewed the European Community favourably and supported efforts to unify Western Europe.

The deliberations were anything but straightforward. But on 7 February 1992 the path-breaking Treaty of Maastricht was signed by twelve leaders from the European Community, to take effect in November the following year. That was the easy part. The pursuit of unity would prove to be bedevilled with problems. Much would indeed be achieved in the remainder of the decade and beyond. The attainments of what, henceforth, was to be called the 'European Union', were significant, and of great importance. But hopes of overcoming deeply entrenched national interests to create a genuine political union underpinned by commitment to a European identity were impossible to fulfil.

In fact, the ambitions of the Maastricht conference fell far short of any attempt to create a political union in Europe. At best this remained a distant and nebulous vision. Helmut Kohl had for some years been among the strongest proponents of political union. So had his Foreign Minister, Hans-Dietrich Genscher. For them, political union was the ultimate objective. But what it meant was left open. And even in Germany strong voices – most notably that of the President of the Bundesbank, Hans Tietmeyer – argued that currency union should *follow*, not precede, political union.

The concept of political union was neither at this point nor in the future clearly defined. It was actually little more than a rhetorical device, an implied direction of travel that might be acceptable in principle to most (though not all) members of the European Community as long as there was no attempt to turn it into reality. In practice, political union might well have looked like Germany on a European scale – a federal 'united states of Europe' – with some powers residing in the nation states, but crucial powers transferred to a central European government. Resting on common values, much of the sovereignty of nation states – including economic, social and security matters – would be located at the European level and upheld by a parliament that would ensure the representation of full democratic rights. But federal Germany, if that was indeed the implied model, comprised constituent parts that shared the same history, traditions and culture. Its strongest bonds were national. The same was true of the United States of America, the other model sometimes cited. Forging a single political union out of the disparate histories, traditions, cultures and languages of Europe's numerous nation states was, however, a different matter altogether. Few if any would have been prepared to make the extensive surrender of sovereignty necessary to create a genuine political union to replace a much looser confederation of nation states. The very prospect of Germany, after 1990 far and away the most populous state with the strongest economy, coming to dominate any future political union, was in itself not likely to encourage moves towards that goal. And although they were among the most enthusiastic pro-Europeans, even Germans, as Kohl was well aware, would have been unwilling to concede too much sovereignty to a European government based in Brussels.

However noble the vision, itself in good measure a reaction against Germany's dark past and a reflection of Kohl's strong personal commitment to ruling out forever the nationalist demons that had led into the abyss, it never had the slightest chance of becoming reality. Kohl himself soon acknowledged that the opportunity (if indeed there had been one) had passed. His willingness to embrace the idea of European political union had been part of the price for unification: a readiness to bind a new Germany, like the old West Germany, inextricably into the liberal values and democratic structures of the West. No other Western European country, let alone France, Germany's chief partner in building the European Community, or Britain, more sensitive still to any implied surrender of national sovereignty, had a similar background or could contemplate the political union envisaged by Kohl. For François Mitterrand, in fact, political union was far from a priority. Following the introduction of the Single Market, the French President saw Economic and Monetary Union as the most promising vehicle of sustaining the momentum of European integration. He was cautious, however, about advancing too rapidly down the route of political union, foreseeing great difficulties in pushing the British, especially, too far in this direction, and concerned not to offer a hostage to French nationalists at home. In Kohl's dealings with Mitterrand, therefore, as German unification (with all the fears that prospect held for the French) became an imminent certainty, the goal of European political union faded from view. Currency union – an idea with a long pre-history, dating back to the plan proposed by Pierre Werner, the Luxembourg Prime Minister, in 1970 – replaced it as a more attainable goal (and vision) to bind Europe together, and, in French eyes, to constrain any future German power ambitions.

This was the compromise agreed at the Maastricht Conference. A single currency, not yet with a name, would be introduced (at a date later stipulated as 1 January 1999). Much of the strategy for the new currency followed German thinking. The German Finance Minister, Theo Waigel, remarked with satisfaction in December 1991 that the treaty on Economic and Monetary Union 'bears the German hallmark. Our stability policy has become the Leitmotif for the future European monetary order.' A European Central Bank – it eventually came into being in June 1998 – would supervise monetary policy and oversee price stability. Countries preparing to enter the single currency had to meet 'convergence criteria' and join an exchange-rate mechanism (ERM) to hold currencies steady and interlinked. Government debt was not to exceed 60 per cent, annual deficits were to be no more than 3 per cent of gross domestic product. Targets were set for low inflation and low interest rates.

Currency union without political union was a risk. It had not been tried before. The United States offered no model, since America was in essence a federated nation state with a central government. Without historical precedent, Europe would have to build its institutional arrangements and political framework for its planned single currency from scratch. Political leaders were aware that success was not guaranteed. Helmut Kohl himself, addressing the Bundestag, the German federal parliament, only a month before the European leaders met in Maastricht, had unambiguously outlined the risk. 'The idea of maintaining in the long run an economic and a currency union without political union is mistaken,' he had declared. He went ahead, nevertheless, despite his own evident misgivings and the warnings of numerous German economic experts.

Beside the crucial agreement on currency union, Maastricht took steps towards tightening European integration in significant areas. A new legal entity, 'The European Union', was formed, integrating the European Economic Community and the Atomic Energy and Coal and Steel Communities and substantially widening inter-governmental cooperation to areas of foreign, security and judicial policy – though cooperation was left far short of anything resembling a central government in these spheres. The Maastricht Treaty also introduced the status of citizenship of the European Union, additional to citizenship of member states.

Maastricht was a major step in the direction of European integration. But divisions were plain even as the European leaders were deliberating. The United Kingdom, despite being a strong advocate of the Single Market and of widening EU membership, the leader as ever of the 'awkward squad' in matters of closer European integration, negotiated an exclusion, or 'opt-out', from the proposed currency union. It also attained a further opt-out from a protocol (the 'Social Chapter') added to the Treaty, which aimed at improving living and working conditions through a wide range of social policies. Denmark was the other country most reluctant to accept the Maastricht provisions. It was a severe jolt to the European establishment when, as part of the ratification process, Danish voters rejected the Maastricht Treaty in a referendum on 2 June 1992. With that, the Treaty could not come into effect. Significant exemptions (from defence and security commitments, certain aspects of internal affairs and, most notably, the single currency) had to be made before Danes were prepared to accept the Treaty in a second referendum in May 1993.

Before then, France, such a key player from the beginning in the 'European project', had in a referendum in September 1992 backed ratification only by the narrowest of margins. In Britain there was no referendum, but Conservative 'Maastricht rebels' had joined forces with Labour opponents of the exemption from the 'Social Chapter' in May 1992 to cause great difficulty for the Conservative government before the bill to accept the Maastricht Treaty eventually gained parliamentary approval. Even in Germany, the European country par excellence, there was great opposition to the decision to replace the beloved D-Mark, emblem of post-war prosperity, by a new European currency. And it took a decision in October 1993 by the Federal Constitutional Court to establish that the provisions of the Maastricht Treaty did not breach German democratic rights laid down in the Basic Treaty (or constitution) of 1949.

Their specific national cultures and histories had made Britain, France and Denmark, too, particularly averse to further concessions of sovereignty. Maastricht's provisions were, in fact, not wholly welcomed anywhere. The other member states, however, had fewer misgivings on the question of sovereignty. Germany, Italy and the Benelux countries had long accepted that the pooling of elements of national sovereignty was vital to peace, prosperity and stability in Europe. Spain, Portugal and Greece had seen membership of the European Community not just as the pathway to prosperity, but also as the obstacle to any regression to dictatorship. They accepted that the limited merging of sovereignty was a necessary and positive step towards attaining those goals. For the Republic of Ireland membership of the European Community had already brought substantial economic benefits, a reduction in dependence on the British economy, and a less nationalist perspective on the unresolved and thorny issue of relations with Northern Ireland. In most member states of the European Community, therefore, Maastricht was welcomed as a logical progression from the previous developments towards greater integration (though the complex and abstract nature of the Treaty meant that outright popular enthusiasm was limited).

After such a difficult birth, the Maastricht Treaty finally came into effect on 1 November 1993. Subsequent amendments, revisions and extensions were made in the Treaties of Amsterdam (October 1997) and Nice (February 2001), but Maastricht had been the decisive juncture. It had converted an essentially economic entity, the European Community, into the European Union – something indeed well removed from a federal 'united states of Europe', but nonetheless a construct with indubitable political dimensions and ambitions. As Maastricht's difficult passage in Denmark, France and Britain illustrated, these ambitions stirred much animosity in those countries. The opposition would become more shrill early in the next millennium, when further proposed constitutional changes would struggle to gain acceptance.

By the later 1990s, however, the early turbulence that had accompanied the ratification of the Maastricht Treaty had settled down. Economic growth had contributed from the middle of the decade to a sense of material well-being and progress across most of Western Europe. The feeling among citizens of continental Western European countries that the European Union was bringing tangible benefits was boosted by the implementation in 1995 of an agreement initially reached at Schengen in Luxembourg a decade earlier allowing people to travel throughout much of Europe without border controls. Only Britain and Ireland of the member states remained outside the Schengen zone.

Meanwhile, negative attitudes towards the forthcoming introduction of the Euro (as, it was agreed in 1995, the single currency would be called) had become less strident. When it was eventually launched, successfully, on I January 1999 as an exchange currency only – notes and coins were to be in circulation only from 2002 onwards – the currency union comprised eleven states (Belgium, the Netherlands, Luxembourg, France, Italy, Germany, Ireland, Spain, Portugal, Austria and Finland). Nevertheless, there were powerful voices prophesying trouble ahead. 'The Euro is coming too soon', warned a declaration by 155 economists in 1998. The worries about sustaining a common currency among disparate economies without fiscal or political union were reasonable. The launch had taken place in a good climate. And there was still fair weather. But how would the Euro stand up to a serious crisis? It remained an open question. After all, from the very beginning the Euro had been in the first instance a political project. What had counted above all else was the drive to European integration.

This raised the obvious question in the early 1990s: what was to be done about widening the European Union? The big issue was the integration of countries that until very recently had belonged to the Soviet bloc, with very differently structured economies, and which were now undergoing enormous difficulties in converting to capitalism and liberal democracy.

The whole matter of widening the European Union was far from straightforward. There were those who argued that deepening the existing structures should come first and only afterwards their extension. France, under President Mitterrand, especially wanted to deepen Western European bonds and to offer a confederation rather than full membership to states in Central and Eastern Europe. Worries that extending the European Union to Eastern Europe would ultimately strengthen Germany's position played no small part in Mitterrand's thinking. The weighty counter-arguments, advanced among others by Germany, Britain and Denmark, gave priority to widening over deepening. Again political determinants carried the day. The baleful history of Central and Eastern Europe after the Versailles Treaty of 1919 carried an obvious lesson. A repetition of the calamitous collapse into fascism and authoritarianism had at all costs to be avoided. Geopolitics, too, came into it. Squeezed between Western Europe and the Russian sphere of influence, questions of the future security of the countries of Central and Eastern Europe were also of paramount importance. Yugoslavia's descent into war at precisely this juncture concentrated minds.

In June 1993, therefore, the decision was taken in Copenhagen to welcome new member states from Central and Eastern Europe, provided that they met stringent criteria on democracy, the rule of law, respect for human rights, protection of minorities, and a well-functioning free-market economy. In 1994 Hungary became the first of what would eventually be a long queue of further states to seek admission to the European Union. Already before the Copenhagen agreement arrangements were under way to admit Finland, Sweden, Norway and Austria to membership. These countries had no difficulty in fulfilling the criteria and all but Norway, where a majority (as in 1972) voted in a referendum in 1994 against membership, became members of the European Union on 1 January 1995. The obvious economic and political gulf with member states of the European Union meant, however, that Central and Eastern European countries had to wait far longer.

The reasons for widening the European Union were cogent, and the prospects of joining helped both stabilize and democratize Central and Eastern European countries. But it would not be easy seamlessly to integrate over 70 million people from countries with far less well-developed economies and political cultures than those of Western Europe. There would in due course be a price to pay in a more unwieldy, less cohesive and less economically balanced European Union.

DISPIRITING GOVERNANCE
IN WESTERN EUROPE

Although a majority of Western Europeans, according to opinion surveys, were well disposed towards the European Union, Europe seldom
preoccupied the minds of most citizens during the 1990s. Usually they
had other concerns, close to home. Nevertheless, some of the problems
that they faced had a European, not simply a national, dimension. They
flowed in part from the recession in Europe (overlapping with the American recession of 1990–91) that set in during the early years of the decade.
The effects from the impact of the costs of unification on Germany left
wide ripples. Whether they stood on the moderate political left, like the
French President François Mitterrand, or on the conservative right, such
as the German Chancellor Helmut Kohl or the successor to Mrs Thatcher
as British Prime Minister, John Major, the issues they had to confront
were similar. Among them were questions – none of them new, but none
of them mastered – of the competitiveness of national economies, increasing demands for social spending and control of inflation, levels of
unemployment and state indebtedness. Wrestling with these issues in the
changed conditions after the end of the Cold War usually made for political unpopularity, which in turn often led to new governments that then
still had to struggle with the old problems. There was, of course, a pronounced national flavour to the specific impact of the problems in
European countries. But the sense of malaise went beyond any single
country.

In Germany the burdens of unification played the most significant
part. Helmut Kohl had in 1990 rashly awakened expectations of 'blos-
soming landscapes' in eastern Germany within three or four years. The
Chancellor had not been alone in grossly miscalculating the extent of
what needed to be done to replace antiquated infrastructure and wholly
rebuild the economy.* Instead of a swift climb to the promised prosperity, the whole of Germany was by 1992 suffering an economic malaise

---

* I recall being surprised when, at a meeting I attended in West Berlin in May 1990, leading bankers and businessmen expressed confidence that the economic problems in East
Germany would be overcome within five years.

that was to last for the best part of a decade – though East Germans paid by far the higher price. In 1993, with the economy in recession, gross domestic product fell by 2 per cent, a steeper decline than at any point in the history of the Federal Republic. By 1995 the German state debt was twice as high as it had been in 1989 (partly, however, because of government investment in infrastructure).

A worrying side effect of the economic downturn, and a sign of what would become a growing trend across much of Europe, was the animosity shown towards 'asylum-seekers'. Over three-quarters of all the 'asylum-seekers' in the European Union sought out Germany on account of its generous asylum laws – themselves a reaction to the inhumanity of the Nazi era. In 1992, accentuated by the wars in Yugoslavia, the number seeking asylum reached 438,000 (though under 5 per cent were actually classed as fleeing from political persecution). Some horrifying incidents of neo-Nazi attacks on immigrants, mostly though not only in eastern parts of Germany, shocked Germans and the outside world.

Helmut Kohl was re-elected Chancellor in October 1994 in spite of the stuttering economy. The introduction of a popular health-care insurance scheme had helped him in election year. So did divisions in the Social Democratic opposition. And there was still something of an afterglow attached to the Chancellor of German Unification. But Germany's economic malaise continued during the following years. Unemployment rose beyond four million by 1996 – a figure that in a different age had caused tremors for German democracy – while the economy, coping with high labour and welfare costs, was struggling to stay competitive. Kohl, once the hope for the future, was heckled at election rallies in eastern Germany by disillusioned voters. The government seemed to have run out of steam. Many people simply felt, as they sometimes do in democracies when a government has been in office for a long time, that 'it was time for a change'. The issues that dominated the 1998 election were almost entirely national – the high level of unemployment above all. European integration, which eight years earlier had been so central to Kohl's vision of the future, hardly figured. When the votes were counted, Kohl found himself out of office after sixteen years as German Chancellor, defeated by Gerhard Schröder of the Social Democratic Party.

Germany's economic problems in the 1990s had an impact on other countries in Western Europe. Over 10 per cent of France's working population, a record high of three million people, were unemployed by 1993, while the rising costs of social welfare – a large proportion of state expenditure – were driving the already worrying budgetary deficit still higher. Attempts to rein in state spending and privatize parts of the economy were predictably unpopular. Governments that introduced unpopular policies usually lost at the polls. France was no exception. The Socialist Party, the mainstay of the government, lost heavily in the March 1993 general election. The parties of the conservative right under Jacques Chirac were the victors. Two years later, at the end of Mitterrand's second term of office, the Socialist president – ill with cancer and also unable to stand again according to the constitution – was succeeded by Chirac, who defeated the Socialist candidate Lionel Jospin. Two features of French politics had wider currency across Europe: allegations of financial malpractice (which led to the suicide of the former Prime Minister Pierre Bérégovoy); and significant popular aversion to immigration (reflecting in part the influence of the Front National, whose leader, Jean-Marie Le Pen, won 15 per cent of the vote in the 1995 presidential election).

Immigration was not yet a significant issue in Italy. Corruption, however, certainly was. Italy, Europe's fourth-largest economy (after Germany, France and Britain), was already facing serious economic difficulties in the early 1990s. Some flowed indirectly from the consequences of German unification. When the German federal bank, the Bundesbank, sharply increased the lending rate in 1992, it put pressure on weaker economies with high rates of inflation. The upshot was that in September Italy was forced out of the exchange rate mechanism of currencies banded together within a restricted range of fluctuation (and in effect shadowing the D-Mark, against which the lira promptly lost 24 per cent of its value). Italy's fundamental problem was its level of debt – 120 per cent of gross domestic product, twice as high as that permitted under the Maastricht criteria. Almost 40 per cent of tax revenue went each year simply to pay the interest on the debt. Higher taxes, cuts in public expenditure and privatization were a remedy not likely to win much popularity for the government, headed by the Christian Democratic leader, Giulio Andreotti.

But conventional politics were put in the shade in 1992, just before the general election, when an enormous corruption scandal – nicknamed

'Tangentopoli' (loosely meaning 'bribery city', or 'bribesville') – was exposed. Politicians from all the main parties at the highest level (as well as some major Italian firms) were implicated. The corruption ran through the entire political system. All the major parties lost votes in the parliamentary general election two years later. But the fallout from what emerged as a huge web of corruption and criminality of politicians and public officials went much further than electoral losses.

A thousand politicians and almost 1,500 civil servants and businessmen were accused of taking bribes. Some, including Andreotti, were strongly suspected of collaboration with the Mafia. The former Socialist Prime Minister Bettino Craxi was later sentenced in absentia – he had fled to Tunisia in 1994 to avoid punishment – to twenty-eight years of imprisonment. Andreotti himself, following a decade of trials (including complicity in a murder carried out by the Mafia), was finally in 2002 given a sentence of twenty-four years of imprisonment, only to be acquitted finally on appeal of all charges. The Italian public had had enough. The scandal brought down the political establishment that had presided over the country's fortunes since the Second World War. The Christian Democratic Party, the dominant force in Italian politics for almost half a century, was dissolved in March, the Liberal Party in February, the Socialist Party in November 1994. The Social Democratic and Republican parties were reduced to insignificance. The Communist Party had already disbanded in 1991 and split into two successor parties, neither of which enjoyed as much popularity. Party politics had to begin almost anew. The old party blocs of left and right from the Cold War era were finished. Italy became the first Western European country to turn to new 'populist' politics.

The outcome was not altogether reassuring. Into the vacuum stepped the flamboyant media tycoon Silvio Berlusconi, at one time closely connected with Craxi and rumoured to have entered politics to gain immunity from arrest for suspected corruption. The party that he had founded from scratch in November 1993, Forza Italia, backed by his media empire, and heavily dependent on Berlusconi's own forceful personality, promised a new start for Italy ('a new Italian miracle', as the party leader himself put it). The style was populist and anti-establishment. Berlusconi portrayed himself as an 'outsider', free of the taint of the old, corrupt party politics, who would use the talent that had made him such a successful businessman to reinvigorate Italy. Forza Italia was set up like a business, with neo-liberal economic objectives. But Berlusconi was confident that his popular appeal would win support from the large reservoir of right-leaning, anti-communist voters who were left without a political home. Would it, however, turn out to be more than old wine in new bottles?

The political right, in fact, had started to splinter even before the Tangentopoli scandals. The collapse of communism had robbed Christian Democracy of its ideological cement. And there were new forms of identity politics. In northern Italy the Lega Nord (Northern League), led by Umberto Bossi, demanded regional autonomy and an end to subsidies for the poorer south. In the Mezzogiorno, the Alleanza Nationale (National Alliance), led by Gianfranco Fini, had blended together neo-fascists and remnants of Christian Democracy in a right-wing conservative movement that still drew oxygen from its opposition to organized socialism. Berlusconi, Bossi and Fini joined forces to win almost 43 per cent of the vote in the elections in March 1994, well ahead of the 34 per cent that went to the left-wing 'Progressives', formed from the two successor parties to the communists. Their shaky coalition government fell apart, however, nine months later, forcing Berlusconi out of office. It would prove, though, to be far from the end of his political career, and he would return to lead Italy's government on two future occasions. Nor was it the end of the chronic instability of Italian governments that since 1948 had lasted on average less than a year. And if in a new guise, with numerous and at times bewildering variations, the divisions between left and right and north and south remained the main fault lines in Italian politics.

In Britain, Mrs Thatcher's successor as prime minister, John Major, had defied most predictions by winning the general election in early April 1992 – the fourth election victory in a row for the Conservatives – if with a much reduced majority. But he led a weak and divided government, riven above all by 'Europe' (shorthand for Britain's chequered relationship with the European Union). His administration never recovered from the humiliation of Britain's ignominious withdrawal from the European Exchange Rate Mechanism on 16 September 1992 – 'Black Wednesday', as it was quickly dubbed – after the government had drastically raised the bank rate and spent over £3 billion in vainly trying to prop up sterling. From then on, as the British economy struggled against recession,

Major was a wounded Prime Minister, tormented by his party's Euro-sceptic wing, parodied in the mass media, and damaged by financial scandals (though minor by Italian standards) involving prominent Conservatives. He was weakened beyond repair as head of government.

By the mid-1990s Britain's economy was beginning to recover strongly. But the recovery did little to help Major. Tony Blair, elected Labour leader in May 1994, presented the sharpest of contrasts to Major's grey image. The highly articulate, ever-smiling and charismatic Blair seemed to embody what was soon being dubbed 'cool Britannia'. He offered the prospect of a new, dynamic Britain – outward-looking, pro-European, modern, progressive, tolerant, inclusive. He advanced the vision of a 'third way' that would transcend the traditional class barriers and social divides. His party, now relabelled 'New Labour', rejected the commitment to nationalization of the economy, built into its constitution since 1918, and looked to embrace market forces, tempered by social justice. At the general election of 1 May 1997 the Conservatives were crushed as Blair – at forty-three the youngest Prime Minister since William Pitt the Younger in 1783 – swept to power with Labour's largest ever majority, of 179 seats. After eighteen years of Conservative government it seemed like a new start, a 'nation reborn' as the prominent political journalist Andrew Rawnsley put it.

Blair had been inspired by the US President, Bill Clinton, who had succeeded George H. W. Bush in 1993. And in turn Blair offered a model that some other European leaders sought to emulate. An unspoken 'third way' seemed in operation in France under the socialist Lionel Jospin, appointed Prime Minister in 1997. Jospin linked classic socialist policies – improved social security, health-care provision, greater financial assistance for the poorest in society, better representation for women in politics, and a thirty-five-hour working week – with tax reduction and privatization of state-owned concerns, policies associated with neo-liberalism. Germany was soon also following a variant of the 'third way'. Gerhard Schröder, the telegenic, energetic Social Democrat, who in the 1998 German elections had defeated Helmut Kohl, ending a period of conservative government stretching back to 1982, was among Blair's most prominent admirers in continental Europe. Schröder, like Blair, offered a modern image of Social Democratic government. Conservatism seemed, if not everywhere, on the retreat in the mid-1990s.

Social democracy in its new, modern guise – combining social advances with the gains to be made from a globalized market economy within an integrated European Union – seemed to many Europeans to offer hope for a better future. Yet within only a few years it would lead, despite notable achievements on the way, to widespread disappointment and disillusionment. In celebratory mood during the night of his election triumph in 1997, Blair declared that 'a new dawn has broken'. Instead of a new dawn, it turned out to be the start of a long sunset for European social democracy.

Old certainties, both on the conservative right and on the social democratic left, were crumbling. An uncomfortable component of the more fractured politics, in which protest movements often finding voice in nationalist, green and regional parties were an increasingly significant presence, was the growing appeal of anti-immigration as a political issue. By the end of the 1990s Jean-Marie Le Pen's Front National was attracting the support of nearly five million French citizens (over 15 per cent of the electorate), compared with 2.7 million in 1986. The Dansk Folkeparti had become the third-largest parliamentary party in Denmark, backed by 12 per cent of the population. In Switzerland the Swiss People's Party, led by the industrialist Christoph Blocher, increased its vote by 12.6 per cent – a record in Swiss electoral history – to attain 22.6 per cent of the vote in the federal elections of 1999 and become the country's largest party. And in Austria the Freedom Party of Austria, under Jörg Haider, whose penchant for fast cars combined with remarks that hinted at pro-Nazi sympathies, rose from under 10 per cent of the vote in 1986 to as much as 27 per cent in 1999. Common to the success of all these movements, with counterparts in other European countries, was strident opposition to immigration. Since mainstream parties supported immigration, as did the European Union, anti-immigrant nationalist protest could also be marketed as anti-establishment and Europhobic politics. The sizeable protest element beyond the core base support for anti-immigrant parties meant that the level of backing was unstable. Nevertheless, beyond influencing the programmes of the mainstream parties of left and right, they ensured that immigration was an item of growing importance on the political agenda in the years to come.

The 1990s had been a chequered decade in Western Europe. Much of the bright new promise had proved illusory. By the middle of the decade there was a palpable sense of disappointment and dissatisfaction in much of the population. The steps towards European integration, though in themselves significant achievements, remained for most people detached from their daily lives. But as economic growth returned the second half of the decade became far brighter. By the end of the decade, with, surprisingly, 'cool Britannia' setting the trend, Europe – east as well as west – seemed on the verge of a more exciting era. At the New Year celebrations in 2000, as Europeans joined the billions around the world to celebrate the start of the new millennium, Tony Blair captured the mood, wishing that the 'confidence and optimism' could be bottled and kept forever.

*   *   *

In September 1990, still in the glow of the end of the Cold War, President George H. W. Bush proclaimed the beginning of a 'new world order' that would be 'freer from the threat of terror, stronger in the pursuit of justice and more secure in the quest for peace'. It was to be 'an era in which the nations of the world . . . can prosper and live in harmony'. They were fine words. But the vision all too rapidly turned out to be an illusion.

There were certainly some encouraging developments. The swift and decisive defeat of Iraqi forces that had invaded Kuwait in early 1991, by a big American-led multi-national coalition under a United Nations mandate, seemed to end the menace of the Iraqi leader, Saddam Hussein, in the Middle East. The agreement by the United States and Russia to dismantle two-thirds of their nuclear warheads under the second Strategic Arms Reduction Treaty (START II) in January 1993 still further reduced the threat of nuclear conflagration. The bitter Arab-Israeli conflict appeared after many long years to have real prospects of eventual resolution under the somewhat improved relations of what was euphemistically called the Oslo Peace Process (though the continuation of serious violence was ominous). And under the aegis of the United Nations there was – though on paper more than in reality – growing recognition of the urgent need to limit the emission of greenhouse gasses that were contributing to the global warming and environmental damage which threatened the future of the entire globe.

But a depressing debit side of the ledger had to be set against these positives. Despite pious utterances by world leaders about eradicating world poverty and upholding universal human rights, there was little or no discernible improvement. Poverty, already searing, was getting worse, not better, in sub-Saharan Africa. Somalia was among the countries wracked by famine and civil war, collapsing into near anarchy. Cultural and religious differences in many parts of the world as well as hard economic interest combined to block any real progress on human rights. Worst of all, at a time when awareness of the Holocaust was greater than ever in European countries, another genocide was raging in Rwanda and taking a toll, within a mere three months, of over a million lives. The hapless 'international community', unable to act to prevent the slaughter, showed itself again to be little more than a hollow phrase.

Europeans could watch the horrors taking place in distant parts of the globe nightly on the television news. They were appalled by what they saw. And many were generous with donations to charity organizations such as UNICEF, the Red Cross, Oxfam or Médecins Sans Frontières. But along with the general sense of helplessness there was the feeling – where people were not numbed into indifference by the constant reminders of appalling suffering – that the terrible events were far away, of little direct relevance to their own lives. Relief that Europe had overcome its own disastrous past and was now spared such horrors – conveniently forgetting Yugoslavia – was a frequent, if usually unspoken, sentiment.

The complacency was soon to be shattered. Realization that Europe was inextricably part of an ever more closely interconnected world, that it could not be hermetically sealed off from the terror that was commonplace in more disturbed regions of the globe, and that this terror had connections with its own imperialist past, was driven remorselessly home in a single moment. And it came not from an event in Europe itself, but over three thousand miles away, in New York – and quite literally out of a clear blue sky. In the early afternoon (European time) of 11 September 2001 – a date soon known universally simply as '9/11' – in a carefully planned and orchestrated spectacular act of terror, two hijacked planes deliberately flew within minutes of each other into the towers of the World Trade Center in New York. A third hijacked passenger plane was directed into the Pentagon (the headquarters of the US Department of Defence), while a fourth plane, heading towards Washington D.C., crashed into a field in Pennsylvania after passengers had courageously grappled with the hijackers. The scenes of the disaster as the twin towers crumbled into rubble remained etched in the minds of the millions who watched the scarcely imaginable horror unfold live on television. Around three thousand people lost their lives – including those on the planes – in the atrocity, many of the victims jumping to their deaths from the burning skyscrapers; and twice that number were injured. Unbearably poignant last messages were passed to loved ones by mobile telephone. The perpetrators, it was soon established, were members of the Islamic terror organization Al-Qaeda. There were European connections. The mastermind behind the attack, Osama Bin Laden, was one of the fifteen terrorists involved who originated in Saudi Arabia, America's, and much of Europe's, most important ally in the Gulf. The plot, moreover, had been hatched on German soil, in Hamburg, where five of the terrorists, including the pilot of the first plane to strike the World Trade Center, Mohamed Atta, of Egyptian birth, had been part of an Al-Qaeda cell.

The devastating attack on New York – the first foreign aggression on American soil since Pearl Harbor in December 1941 – was not just an immense shock and tragedy. It marked a frontal assault on 'Western' values, exactly as its perpetrators had intended. European leaders immediately declared their solidarity with the United States in the defence of those values. Within days President George W. Bush announced a 'war on terror' – even, oblivious to the negative resonance of the word in the Middle East, calling it a 'crusade' – that would not stop at Al-Qaeda. It would be a struggle to protect Western civilization against the Islamist ideology that had set out to destroy it. Tony Blair quickly went further than any other Western leader in offering Britain's unconditional support for the USA.

The date '9/11', more than the calendar date of 1 January 2000 a year earlier, marked the real beginning of a new century. Before then the western world had only been dimly aware of the growing problem of Islamic fundamentalism. The next years, however, would see Britain and other European states embroiled in a widening conflict against this rising force. European soldiers would find themselves fighting unwinnable wars in Muslim countries. Islamist terror would soon scar Europe's cities, affect multicultural relations, and pose liberal democracy with new dilemmas of trying to reconcile freedom and security. Europe could less than ever shut out the problems of the outside world.

11

Global Exposure

States like these and their terrorist allies constitute an axis of
evil, arming to threaten the peace of the world.
President George W. Bush, State of the Union Address, 2002,
referring to North Korea, Iran and Iraq

Of course, Europe's exposure to global influences was nothing new.
There had been trade with the Far East in the Middle Ages. Gold and
other commodities had been shipped across the Atlantic following the
conquest of the Americas in the sixteenth century. After Ottoman rule
had been established in the Balkans and southern parts of Hungary,
Turkish invasions, seen as an alien threat to Christian Europe, were
repulsed in Malta in 1565 and near Vienna as late as 1683. The Dutch
established a trading base in the seventeenth century in what would eventually become Indonesia. The East India Company began the British
colonization of India the following century. Wars were fought in the
Caribbean in the eighteenth century. European imperialist expansion
into Africa, Asia and other parts of the world followed a century later.
And what is often referred to as 'the first globalization' set in from the
middle of the nineteenth century as the telegraph and telephone, steam-
ships and railways helped to foster a huge expansion of trade to all parts
of the world. Then came the most brutal exposure – in two world wars
separated by a global economic depression during the first half of the
twentieth century. The long post-war recovery after 1945 saw Europe,
eventually Central and Eastern as well as Western Europe, opened to the
interests of American foreign policy, and to the dominant economic and
cultural influences from across the Atlantic.

Even so, there was – and was felt to be – something new about the European global exposure in the early years of the twenty-first century. Conceivably, greater numbers of ordinary people in Europe were more aware of the intrusion of the rest of the globe into their lives than ever before in peacetime. The spread of the internet in the 1990s, above all, had made the world seem smaller. The new millennium ushered in highly accentuated forms of European global exposure. And one difference was of notable significance. In earlier centuries, quite especially in the era of imperialism, Europe had exported violence to other continents. In the first decade of the new millennium Europe had its initial taste of how violence could strike back.

The attack on the World Trade Center in New York on 11 September 2001 was not just a devastating introduction to Islamist terrorism for the United States but marked a caesura for Europe as well. The impact on the continent in the coming years was profound. This in turn had major consequences for attitudes towards immigration and multiculturalism – the attempt to integrate those from other cultures who had migrated to Europe – which became acute political as well as social issues. The potential for a dangerous cultural clash between Western values and those of Islam, as forecast by the American political scientist Samuel Huntington in the 1990s, seemed to loom larger.

A second new, or at least greatly altered, form of exposure came from the globalized economy and its pervasive effect on everyday life. Although partly an intensification of trends already long under way, the 'second globalization' was more than just a continuation of well-established developments. The communications revolution that flowed from the inordinately rapid spread of computer technology and the vast expansion of a deregulated financial sector ensured that in the scale and depth of its impact, quantitative change amounted to a qualitative shift. Connections across the globe became not just easier, but almost instantaneous. Not only business was transformed. Europe, like the rest of the world, was interconnected and interdependent as never before. The internet, mobile telephones and e-mail permeated practically all aspects of society. What would have been unthinkable half a century earlier had become reality.

THE 'WAR ON TERROR'

On 20 September 2001, little more than a week after the attack on New York, President George W. Bush declared a 'war on terror' that would only end when 'every terrorist group of global reach' had been defeated. States had historically declared war against other states. What war meant in such instances was usually plain. War against an abstraction, on the other hand, lacked clear definition. But the rhetorical value of a 'war on terror' was unquestionable. It captured the mood in America, and in most of the Western world, in the immediate aftermath of the atrocity. It was a mood thirsting for revenge.

The attack on America had been planned in Afghanistan, a fractured, lawless, ultra-violent country, wracked by civil war since the end of the Soviet occupation in 1989. In the preceding decade, the United States had provided the local warlords and tribal leaders in Afghanistan, the Mujahedin, with weapons and finance to fight against the Soviets. Once the Soviets withdrew, the USA lost much of its interest in the region. But Pakistan did not, and the Mujahedin continued to thrive, now with Pakistani sponsorship. The warlords controlled their own domains. The writ of the government in Kabul did not run, unless the warlords permitted it to do so. And the Mujahedin were not just anti-Soviet; they were anti-Western as well. This was the soil in which the seeds of terrorism directed at the West, and directly at the United States, could germinate.

Osama bin Laden, scion of an exceedingly wealthy Saudi family who had founded the loose organization of Al-Qaeda in 1988 in order to fight a 'holy war', had located his base in Afghanistan when he moved there from Sudan in 1996. One of the ringleaders of a foiled plot to blow up the Word Trade Center in New York in 1993 had received some of his training in an Al-Qaeda camp in Afghanistan. In 1996 the Taliban, initially a small group of militants, originally formed in Pakistan, who avowed the most extreme, fundamentalist form of Islam, and were responsible for countless atrocities in their fight against Afghanistan's corrupt and widely unpopular government, seized the capital city, Kabul. They had been supported militarily by Pakistani intelligence and had gained financial backing from wealthy sources in Saudi Arabia. They were soon able to extend their vicious rule over more than two-thirds of the country.

After moving to Afghanistan, Bin Laden linked forces with the Taliban leader, Mullah Mohammed Omar, and declared war on the United States and the West. He was behind attacks on three American embassies in Africa in 1998, and according to information that the CIA passed on to President Clinton was planning future attacks in the USA itself.

So both Bin Laden and Afghanistan as the base of Al-Qaeda shone brightly on Washington's radar screen long before the atrocity of 11 September 2001. Once the terrible blow had fallen, it was obvious that armed American retaliation would swiftly follow. Within three days Congress had authorized the President to use whatever force he thought necessary to destroy both the organizations responsible for the attack and the state that had sponsored the terror. That plainly meant, once the Taliban leadership had refused to hand over Bin Laden to the Americans, an invasion of Afghanistan with the primary aims of destroying Al-Qaeda (capturing or killing Bin Laden in the process) and crushing the Taliban. 'Operation Enduring Freedom', the assault on Afghanistan, commenced with a bombing campaign by American and British forces on 7 October 2001.

The participation of British forces had been a certainty from the outset. The British Prime Minister, Tony Blair, had (he wrote later) immediately on hearing the news of the outrage of 11 September viewed the attack on the Twin Towers in Manhattan as 'in a very real sense, a declaration of war' by Al-Qaeda not just on America but on all the civilized world. That very evening he declared on television that Britain would stand 'shoulder to shoulder with our American friends in this hour of tragedy, and we, like them, would not rest until this evil is driven from our world'.

Other European leaders were more circumspect. Germany, for instance, decided in mid-November by only a single vote in the Bundestag to send nearly 4,000 Bundeswehr soldiers to Afghanistan. There was nevertheless wide international solidarity with the American objectives and the country's right to defend itself after the attack on New York. France, Italy and Russia were among the many countries that offered active support to the United States. 'France,' President Chirac declared, 'will not stand aside' in what had been an attack on all democracies. He added, prophetically: 'Today it is New York that was tragically struck, but tomorrow it may be Paris, Berlin, London.'

At first the war went well for the Western coalition forces. The Afghan anti-Taliban forces (calling themselves the United Front or the Afghan Northern Alliance). which controlled about a third of the country, under-took the ground fighting and, supported by the heavy air strikes, retook Kabul in November 2001. By early December they had forced the Taliban out of Kandahar in the south, their last stronghold. A small International Security Assistance Force was set up under the aegis of the United Nations later in December – soon to be supported by over twenty countries – to defend Kabul and to help establish a transitional government to be headed by Hamid Karzai, under the aegis of the Americans and the British.

By December 2001 it looked as if the worst was over. In fact, it was only just beginning. The Taliban had retreated. But they were far from eradicated and were soon rebuilding their strength. And Osama Bin Laden, together with many of his closest supporters and much of the Al-Qaeda terroristic network, had managed to escape into the remote mountainous tracts of western Pakistan. So the Western powers were unable to accomplish conclusively either of their primary objectives. Without any obvious plan for securing the peace once they had van-quished the Taliban, they were left supporting an unstable, corrupt regime and trying to pacify a large, intensely violent and unruly country. It would be another thirteen long years and cost the lives of many tens of thousands of people – about 4,000 of them from the coalition forces, but far more from the Afghan population – before, in 2014, the British ended their combat role, the Americans announced they were withdrawing all but a residual force, and NATO (which had become involved in Afghan-istan in 2003) pulled out, transferring responsibility to the Afghan government. Few objective observers could by then claim that the long stay of the Western powers in Afghanistan had been an undiluted suc-cess. Events were to justify this pessimistic conclusion: the Afghan government was to prove incapable of halting renewed advances by the Taliban, leading to Washington's reversal of the earlier decision to with-draw and announcement in 2017 that thousands more American soldiers would be sent to Afghanistan.

What had begun primarily as American retaliation had drawn into the war a global coalition of forces from as many as forty-three countries, mostly NATO members. European countries were heavily involved. Of over 130,000 foreign troops based in Afghanistan at the height of the conflict in 2011, about 90,000 were Americans. Most of the remainder were European. The largest European force, some 9,500 troops, was from the United Kingdom, but sizeable contingents also came from Germany (around 5,000), France (4,000) and Italy (4,000). Poland, Romania, Turkey and Spain made further substantial contributions to NATO forces, while numerous other European countries provided smaller contingents.

As the British had learned in the nineteenth century and the Soviets in the 1980s, Afghanistan was forbidding territory for occupying forces. That proved to be the case once again in the early years of the twenty-first century. Partly this was because the overall aims of the war in Afghanistan were not clearly specified. Were they simply to destroy Al-Qaeda and eliminate the Taliban, in which case, whatever the misleading initial signs of success, they plainly failed? Or was the goal a far wider one – as Blair insisted, no less than that of reconstructing Afghanistan as a viable democracy? 'We were in the business of nation-building,' he later wrote. Of course, the two goals were interlinked. It was felt that, in order to remove the incubus of terror, a firm basis of modern government had to replace the failed state in Afghanistan. But in the understandable desire for the swiftest retaliation against the perpetrators of 9/11, the difficulties involved in the wider goal had been gravely underestimated. Planting Western-style liberal democracy in such infertile ground was a thankless, largely impossible task. It had mostly proved a failure in much of Europe after the First World War. In Afghanistan the prospects were even more daunting. It would, with the greatest optimism, be a task for generations, not for a few years. But the forces sent to destroy the Taliban and Al-Qaeda, once there, had no easy means of extricating themselves from a rapidly worsening situation. Terror, it rapidly became plain, was here to stay – and not just in Afghanistan.

This was a second major miscalculation in embarking on the Afghan War. The Americans and their European allies had underestimated the novelty, character, scale and sheer menace of the threat they faced in international terrorism. The phenomenon was not altogether new; it had been around in the Middle East and known to Western intelligence services for about three decades. And of course, a number of European countries were no strangers to internal terrorism. The violence of the

447

IRA had seriously afflicted Northern Ireland (and to a lesser extent also the British mainland) since the late 1960s. Spain had an equivalent problem with the Basque separatist organization, ETA. Both West Germany and Italy had had to contend with serious home-grown terrorism during the 1970s. But, although each of these manifestations of terror had killed and maimed extensively, the Islamic terrorism of the twenty-first century was essentially different in character and posed an infinitely greater threat. Earlier terrorist organizations had had limited goals. They had targeted nation states. They had wanted to acquire national independence (like the IRA and ETA) or attack capitalism in specific states (like Baader-Meinhof in West Germany and the Red Brigades in Italy). Their terror had aimed primarily at the representatives of the states and systems they were assailing – politicians, soldiers, police, business leaders. Many innocent bystanders were certainly killed in their atrocities. But the numbers of casualties would have been far greater had not (usually) coded warnings of bombings been given. Moreover, the terrorists themselves had mainly sought to escape with their own lives from the horror they were inflicting on others.

With Islamist terrorism all this altered. It operated globally, not nationally. It was decentralized and international in its personnel, its targets, its acquisition of weapons, and its use of modern mass media to disseminate its propaganda. Its exponents – a major change – were willing, even anxious, to kill themselves in carrying out their terrorist acts, seeing themselves as martyrs in an apocalyptic cause. And this cause was utterly unlimited: the destruction through worldwide Islamic revolution of all Western, liberal values and their replacement by the 'true' values of fundamentalist Islam. The culture to be destroyed was epitomized by the United States and its allies. Israel, too, and Jews more generally, who (in a variant of age-old conspiracy notions) were taken to stand behind the power of the West, were also slated for destruction. To attain these chiliastic goals Islamist terrorism did not just accept that there would be civilian casualties. It actively sought to maximize the numbers of innocent civilians killed. The greater the shock, ran the thinking, the more the impact of terror was felt, the more the power of the West would be corroded, and the closer the aims of the terror would come.

There was widespread understanding in Europe for the American-led war in Afghanistan – certainly in its early stages. The aim of destroying the Taliban and Al-Qaeda was hugely popular. Before 2001 many Europeans might even have struggled to name the capital of Afghanistan. But soon names such as Kandahar, Helmand Province, Hindu Kush or Kashkar Gah became widely familiar from television news bulletins. Those frequent bulletins, often giving doleful reports of Western soldiers killed or the numbers of innocent victims caught up in suicide bombings, themselves made plain that the war was dragging on interminably. They offered the clearest indication that the enemy was far from defeated. And gradually, but inexorably, the initial popularity of the war evaporated.

In any case, interest in Afghanistan was soon overtaken by a second strand of the 'war against terror'. The invasion of Iraq in March 2003, undertaken by an American-led force again predominantly supported by the British, was a far more divisive issue than Afghanistan had been, encountering from the outset heated opposition and rapidly proving disastrous in its consequences.

For Europeans, a war against Saddam Hussein's Iraq was an entirely different matter from the war to uproot and destroy Al-Qaeda and the Taliban in Afghanistan. Nothing connected Saddam with Bin Laden's plot to attack America. So, unlike Afghanistan, there was no cause for retaliation. If the case were to be made at all, it had to be on entirely different grounds. These would prove highly contentious. Beyond other considerations, any attack on Iraq raised acute questions of legal justification. And its wider ramifications were incalculable. It would amount to a dangerous extension of the 'war on terror'. The issues raised by the war domestically split both governments and families across Europe.

Saddam, few doubted, was a brutal dictator who, backed by his loyalist Ba'ath party and a fearsome security apparatus, ruled Iraq with a rod of iron. He terrorized his own people and – as his invasion of Kuwait in August 1990 had most plainly demonstrated – was a threat to the whole region. Torture, summary executions, and other grave violations of human rights were commonplace under his regime. He had used chemical weapons in the war against Iran and against the Kurds in northern Iraq. Political, ethnic and sectarian killings – the last of these mostly inflicted on the majority Shia population of Iraq by the Sunni-dominated government – probably accounted for over quarter of a million victims, not counting the dead from the wars against Iran in the 1980s and the Gulf War of 1991. Partly as a consequence of the broad economic sanctions imposed upon Iraq in 1990 by the United Nations following the invasion of Kuwait and remaining in place throughout the decade but also through brutal repression, Saddam had reduced much of the population of his once wealthy country to poverty. It was an appalling record of a detestable regime and a hateful dictator. But did it give Western countries, with the United States in the lead, the right to take military action to depose Saddam from power?

Iraq was already in the 1980s classed by policy advisors in the United States as a 'rogue state', which definition included the aim of building 'weapons of mass destruction'. A number of prominent 'neo-conservatives' (as they were coming to be labelled) – ideologically committed to utilizing American military hegemony to impose an international *pax americana*, and who would later occupy positions of importance in the Bush administration – were urging President Clinton as early as 1998 to take military action to topple Saddam. In July 2001, three months before the attack on the Twin Towers, the Defence Ministry, headed by a forceful 'neo-con', Donald Rumsfeld, had already prepared concrete plans for military intervention in Iraq. On the day after the fateful events in New York, the Bush cabinet deliberated the issue. Afghanistan had at this point evident priority. But that was soon to change.

In his address to Congress on 29 January 2002, speaking only a month after the deposition of the Taliban when final victory in Afghanistan seemed assured, President Bush singled out Iraq as part of an 'axis of evil' that, through the acquisition of weapons of mass destruction, threatened world peace. It would become obvious over the following months that American attention was turning towards Iraq as the next stage of the 'global war on terrorism'. Bush's 'axis of evil' speech was hugely popular in the United States. Public opinion had been drastically affected by 9/11. It overwhelmingly favoured the President's all-out assault on what were seen as the sources of global terror. There was cross-party support, too, for action. Already in December 2001 Republican and Democratic senators had jointly reminded the President that his policy was 'regime-change', and called for the removal of Saddam. Iraq was by now plainly high on the American agenda.

European government leaders – and the citizens of their countries – were mostly far more hesitant. They were worried about the growing likelihood of war in Iraq and its possible consequences. They did not see any real link between the agreed threat of Al-Qaeda and Iraq. Tony Blair was the outright exception in the alacrity with which he offered British support to President Bush. Blair, like Bush, was from the outset moved by a fervent emotional conviction of the urgent need to eliminate by force the grave international existential danger that he saw presented by an Iraq in possession of weapons of mass destruction. By the time he visited President Bush at his Texan ranch in April 2002 he had already reached the conclusion 'that removing Saddam would do the world, and most particularly the Iraqi people, a service'. He had seen the effectiveness of Western intervention to protect the population in Kosovo in 1999 and had ordered British troops to intervene – which again they did successfully – in the civil war in Sierra Leone (once a British colony) the following year. Most recently he had seen the Taliban expelled (for good as was thought then) in Afghanistan. So Blair endorsed the aim of 'regime change' in Iraq with almost missionary zeal. British support for the United States could not, however, as he acknowledged, rest upon the destruction of Saddam as a tyrant, however welcome that might be. It would not suffice in international law. And it would not be enough to win the backing of the British people for war. The crucial issue, he stressed, was the possession of weapons of mass destruction.

Saddam was believed by American and British intelligence to be rebuilding Iraqi stocks of biological and chemical weapons that the United Nations had forced him to destroy in 1991 after the first Gulf War. With great reluctance, and under threat of attack for non-compliance under United Nations Security Council Resolution 1441, Saddam allowed a team of United Nations weapons inspectors, headed by the Swedish diplomat Hans Blix, into his country in November 2002. When Blix's team reported on 7 March 2003, it was to state that they had found nothing. By then, however, the findings were secondary. The American administration had already made up its mind. The President had told Rumsfeld and Secretary of State Colin Powell two months earlier that he was determined on war against Saddam. Blair, too, had made up his mind, long since. The previous July he had written a private and confidential note to Bush. 'I will be with you, whatever,' he had assured the President.

What followed the decisions already, in principle, taken to go to war was the process of convincing the American and British public that

Saddam did indeed threaten the West with weapons of mass destruction, despite the negative findings of the weapons inspectors. Both the Bush administration and the Blair government continued, in the face of grow-ing public scepticism, to insist that the weapons would eventually be located, seizing upon imperfect, unfounded and speculative reports from their intelligence agencies to advance a case in public that was, in reality, deeply flawed. Secretary of State Powell told a plenary session of the United Nations Security Council on 5 February 2003 that 'there can be no doubt that Saddam Hussein has biological weapons and the capability to rapidly produce more, many more'. Blair had continued to stress to the British public in 2002 that the objective in Iraq was disarmament, not regime change. But in September 2002 and February 2003 his govern-ment had released dossiers to prepare the public for armed intervention in Iraq, claiming that Saddam possessed weapons of mass destruction, was building a nuclear capability, and would soon have the capacity to attack London within forty-five minutes. It was an alarming scenario – but, as it proved, wrong.

Such statements from political leaders nevertheless did the trick. In November 2002 Congress gave President Bush a free hand to act against Iraq as he thought appropriate to defend the security of the United States. Only about a third of the members of the House of Representatives and of the Senate (overwhelmingly Democrats) withheld support. The pro-portion of the public opposed to military action was smaller still – only just over a quarter of Americans according to opinion polls in February 2003. The majority thought action against Iraq justified, though prefer-ring it to be backed by a mandate of the United Nations. The public, it was plain, had been persuaded by the statements of the President and Secretary of State. Most of them had indeed, opinion surveys demon-strated, swallowed the belief that Iraq was behind 9/11.

The British House of Commons on 18 March 2003 backed an invasion of Iraq by an even larger majority than the American Congress had done (412 to 149 votes). No more than a quarter of Labour members were opposed, and only two Conservatives. Public opinion was less sup-portive of action than in the United States: 54 per cent favoured it, with no more than 38 per cent opposed, and the indications were that public support was fragile and on the verge of waning rapidly. As in the USA, the British public (and Parliament) had, however, been sold the case for war on a false prospectus. It was almost certainly not the case, as later often claimed, that Bush and Blair had overtly lied in arguing for war. But they had both, from different ends of the political spectrum (a Republican President and a Labour Prime Minister), misled their people. They had used knowingly unverified and flawed intelligence to construct arguments that rested, ultimately, on little more than their own unshakeable belief – whatever the findings by Blix's team of inspectors – that Saddam did indeed possess weapons of mass destruction. Both were determined on 'regime change' in Iraq, though they – Blair more than Bush – hid this motive behind the need to eliminate the imminent menace Saddam posed to the world. And both – this time Bush far more than Blair – were prepared to act, if necessary, without sanction from the United Nations.

There had been massive protests against a war in Iraq in Britain and all across Europe the previous month. Around a million people, one of the largest protest rallies in British history, demonstrated in London on 15 February 2003. Huge anti-war demonstrations also occurred in Germany, France, Greece, Hungary, Ireland, the Benelux countries, Portugal and in other European countries, the largest being in Italy (around 3 million) and Spain (1.5 million). More than 10 million people worldwide were estimated to have joined in demonstrations.

The prospect of war against Iraq divided Europe more sharply than at any time since the fall of the Iron Curtain. While the British perception of its 'special relationship' with America encouraged Blair, as over Afghanistan, instinctively and uncritically to stand 'shoulder to shoulder' with President Bush, France, under President Chirac, took a diametrically opposite view. France had, of course, from Charles de Gaulle's time, built a strong anti-American strain into its foreign policy. But Chirac's stance towards war in Iraq had little or nothing to do with traditional French anti-Americanism. His well-founded objections were that war in Iraq would inflame Muslim anti-Western feeling. He made clear in January 2003 that France would not join in any military action. Gerhard Schröder, head of Germany's coalition government of Social Democrats and Greens, was also resolutely opposed to the war. Germany, in fact, went even further than France, declaring that there would be no German participation even in the event of a United Nations mandate. Belgium and Luxembourg backed the French and German line. But the European Union itself was riven. The Netherlands, Italy, Spain,

Portugal and Denmark and all the states that had once been behind the Iron Curtain, had subsequently joined NATO and were preparing to join the European Union, supported the war. Not only did the split run through the European Union; it was the most serious crisis of NATO since its foundation in 1949. Some NATO countries joined the coalition; others did not. NATO itself took no part in the planned invasion, though its forces provided defensive support for Turkey (which felt threatened by neighbouring Iraq).

The 'coalition of the willing', as the Americans dubbed those countries prepared to support the military intervention, enjoyed nothing like the level of international backing (especially within the Middle East) that had been behind the first Gulf War of 1991 – generally seen as a legitimate intervention to block obvious Iraqi aggression against another country. When the invasion did take place, only the United Kingdom and, in small numbers, Poland and Australia provided combat troops alongside those of the United States.

The neo-conservative right in America responded to the deep divisions in Europe by stirring anti-European feeling in the United States. Defence Secretary Donald Rumsfeld denounced France and Germany as representatives of 'Old Europe', praising in contrast Central and Eastern European countries which, in putting themselves on the side of the USA and Britain, constituted the 'New Europe'. The French came in for particular opprobrium. One press article in 2002 had already disgracefully dismissed them (with the capitulation in 1940 in mind) as 'cheese-eating surrender monkeys'. 'French fries' were renamed 'freedom fries' in the cafeterias of the American Congress (though most Americans in fact thought the gesture was silly, and the French Embassy pointed out that French fries had actually originated in Belgium). Behind the absurdity lay some serious reflections on the divergence of American and European approaches to war. 'On major strategic and international questions today, Americans are from Mars and Europeans are from Venus: they agree on little and understand one another less and less', was the view of Robert Kagan, author of an influential book *Paradise and Power*, published in 2003. 'American leaders,' Kagan concluded, ominously, 'should realise that . . . Europe is not really capable of constraining the United States.'

Resolution 1441 of the Security Council in November 2002 had given

Saddam Hussein 'a final opportunity' to comply with demands for weapons inspection. But the implied threat had not specified that failure would result in military action. Nor was it clear that Saddam was avoiding full compliance. Blix himself was ambivalent, though by February he was indicating there was greater cooperation. Saddam hardly helped his own case. As a bluff to deter military action he had never categorically denied the charge of possessing such weapons. It was a perverse and fatal mistake. Blix had reported no findings of weapons of mass destruction. But were they still hidden somewhere?

In March 2003 it was plain that the French and the Russians would veto any further resolution by the United Nations Security Council to approve military action in Iraq. Was a new resolution, however, strictly necessary? The Americans, by this stage evidently impatient with the United Nations, were already determined to act, with or without a resolution. In London the highly dubious legal advice given to the government by the Attorney General, Lord Goldsmith, was that action was covered by Resolution 1441 (though he had initially taken a diametrically opposite view). With that the British government – apart from the Foreign Secretary, Robin Cook, who resigned – was on board. War would go ahead without a mandate from the United Nations. It consequently lacked international legality. The United States had effectively decided itself, without regard for international law, how and when to prosecute war.

The invasion of Iraq started on 20 March 2003. Saddam's forces were plainly no match for the (mainly) American invaders and within three weeks the military campaign was won. Baghdad was taken by 12 April and fighting ceased. Coalition casualties were minimal. The pictures of the statue of Saddam being toppled by crowds in the city centre went round the world on television. Saddam himself had fled, though it was presumed only a matter of time until he was captured. (He would indeed be discovered in November 2003 near his hometown of Tikrit and was later tried by an Iraqi court for crimes against humanity, sentenced to death, and hanged on 30 December 2006.) With the war over and the dictatorial regime ended, there was a sense both of relief and of self-congratulation. In a scene of extraordinary hubris on board the American aircraft carrier USS *Abraham Lincoln* on 1 May, President Bush, attired in a flying uniform, addressed sailors (and the watching world on television) under a banner reading: 'Mission Accomplished'. In fact, the descent into long years of chaos and horrific bloodshed in Iraq, with lasting consequences for the United States and its allies, was just beginning.

President Bush had spoken before the invasion of building a democratic Iraq. But Iraq was not Germany in 1945. The occupiers showed scant awareness of the problems they were facing, or the sensitivities of Iraqi culture and politics. The administration of occupied Iraq under the American diplomat Paul Bremer proved utterly incompetent, its disbanding of the Ba'athist Party and the Iraqi army being enormously damaging own-goals. The Shia-dominated government installed by the Americans even intensified the gathering sectarian conflict by blatant discrimination against the Sunni minority – reduced from the former ruling elite to second-class citizens. Even worse was the torture and degrading treatment of Iraqi prisoners by their American captors in the Abu Ghraib jail, which was exposed to a worldwide television audience in 2004. The reputation of the United States had already been dragged through the mire by the treatment of several hundred prisoners, mainly from Afghanistan, suspected of terrorism and interned without trial in the detention camp at Guantanamo Bay in Cuba that had been created in January 2002. Now it hit rock bottom. Abu Ghraib made a mockery of the values of humanity and justice that the United States – and the rest of the Western world – claimed to represent. Whatever good will initially existed towards the USA and Britain for ending the tyranny of Saddam Hussein, it was replaced by widespread and growing hatred of the occupiers of Iraq as political anarchy and uncontrollable violence became the hallmarks of everyday life. Saddam had been terrible. But what replaced him, thanks to the ill-conceived and badly executed occupation that lacked any coherent concept of post-Saddam order, was in the eyes of many worse. The disastrous consequences ran far beyond Iraq itself.

The invasion, the treatment of Iraq by the conquerors, and the power vacuum that replaced Saddam Hussein's dictatorship were a gift to international jihadist terrorism. After the Iraq War incidents of worldwide terrorism, already growing in the second half of the 1990s, soared stratospherically. Some 500 incidents in 1996 had grown to 1,800 in 2003; by 2006 there were around 5,000. By far the worst-affected area was the Middle East itself. There were an estimated 26,500 terrorist attacks in Iraq alone in 2004. The number of Iraqis killed in opposing the occupation and in internecine conflict within the country after the invasion has been put at half a million. The Western world suffered relatively little. Between 1998 and 2006 jihadi targets in Britain are estimated to have accounted for 4 per cent of the total, Spain 2 per cent, Turkey 4 per cent, Russia 11 per cent (related chiefly to the conflicts in the Caucasus, especially Chechnya) and the USA 2 per cent. Nevertheless, after the Afghanistan and Iraq wars Europe could not avoid increasing exposure to international terrorism.

Britain, as the most important ally of the United States (and as a former imperialist power), was particularly threatened. Its close connections with Pakistan offered good opportunities for the cross-fertilization of jihadist ideas and recruitment to terrorism from within the population of Pakistani origin. But jihadist networks, many linked to or inspired by Al-Qaeda, were also uncovered by intelligence services in several other European countries, including Germany, France, Italy, Spain, the Netherlands, Belgium, Poland, Bulgaria and the Czech Republic. The spread of the internet was the great facilitator of jihadist indoctrination, inside and outside Europe. Pro-terrorism websites increased in number from about twelve in 1998 to over 4,700 by 2005.

Intelligence gleaned by security services about potential attacks offered the main defence against terrorist outrages. But it did not always work. On the morning of 11 March 2004, bombs planted on busy commuter trains in Madrid killed 192 people and injured about 2,000 others. Bin Laden had threatened retaliation against America's European allies. The government run by José María Aznar's conservative Partido Popular Party in Spain had supported the war, highly unpopular though this had been among most Spaniards. The outrage in Madrid had a direct political motive. In the general election that took place three days after the bombings Aznar paid the price. Many voters, according to surveys, switched support after the bombings to the Socialist Party, which had opposed the war. On winning the election the new Prime Minister, José Luis Rodríguez Zapatero, promptly withdrew Spanish troops from Iraq.

A year later terror struck Britain. On 7 July 2005 three bombs on Underground trains in London and a fourth on a bus in the city centre were detonated by Islamist terrorists, killing 52 people and injuring a further 700. The suicide bombers were all British citizens, unknown to the security services. They claimed that they were acting as soldiers of Islam and in retaliation for British oppression of Muslims in Afghanistan, Iraq and elsewhere. Britain had experienced a major terrorist attack connected with the Middle East once before, in December 1988, when a Libyan bomb placed on an American passenger plane exploded over Lockerbie in Scotland, en route from London to New York, with the loss of all 259 crew and passengers (and a further 11 victims when parts of the plane struck them as it hit the ground). Retaliation against the United States for American airstrikes against Libya during the 1980s had been the apparent motive. But in contrast to Lockerbie, the 2005 July bombings took place in the heart of the capital city, and were targeted not at America but directly at Britain itself. The wars in Muslim countries had indeed rebounded on Europe.

Subsequent years would demonstrate that no European country would be safe from Islamic terrorism. France and Germany, despite their opposition to the Iraq War, would not be spared. Islamist fundamentalism would strike where it could do so most effectively – against easy targets with maximum loss of life and the greatest possible publicity. It was not restrictive in its enemies. It amounted to an attack on Western civilization as a whole.

Although the resurgence of Islam as a widening source of Muslim identity dated back to the 1970s, the wars in Afghanistan and, especially, in Iraq gave it a huge boost. The fateful intervention in Iraq and the complete mishandling of the early phase of the occupation fertilized the growth of multiple terrorist organizations that would come in the following years to haunt the West. Some of the most deadly formed along the sectarian fault lines that widened immeasurably after the Iraq War. The deepened split between Sunnis and Shias now added its own big contribution to the growing problem of Islamist terrorism. It affected the complex geopolitics of the Middle East, which were further destablized by Iran supporting Shias and Saudi Arabia the Sunnis. Since Iran was closely linked with Russia while Saudi Arabia, where the Salafist form of fundamentalist Islam predominated, was a major ally of the United States, Britain and other European countries, Europe was certain to remain highly exposed to the continuing traumas of the Middle East.

GLOBALIZATION'S JANUS-FACE

The end of communism gave a great boost to a globalized economy. In the early 1990s (as indicated in the previous chapter) the former eastern-bloc countries struggled under its impact. But in the second half of the decade they started to profit from global economic growth, as Western Europe was doing. Between the mid-1990s and the abrupt end of growth in 2008 Europeans – both east and west – enjoyed the benefits of a booming economy. At least, most of them did. Globalization provided material advantages that earlier generations could scarcely have imagined. There was new economic dynamism. World trade flourished as goods flowed across borders as never before. By the end of the first decade of the twenty-first century trade was six times higher in volume than it had been at the time of the fall of the Berlin Wall. Europe's proportion of the world economy had in fact been in long-term decline since the 1920s. That is, Europe's economy had grown in size, but other parts of the world had grown faster. In 1980 Europe had still accounted for around a third of world trade, but three decades later it was only about 20 per cent. The creation of a major trading bloc in Europe was, however, of great importance. Without the steps towards European integration the relative decline would almost certainly have been greater. For the widened European Union had by the turn of the millennium become the largest trading bloc in the world, ahead of the United States and China in volume of exports and imports.

Production and distribution of goods had over recent years become international on an unprecedented scale. Enormous multinational firms (and, increasingly, technology giants) were the great beneficiaries. Components for car manufacture were increasingly put together in more than one country, and assembled in yet another. Japan, among the world's largest car manufacturers, had big components factories in several European countries; Toyotas, Hondas and Nissans were among the most popular cars on Europe's roads. Consumers took globalization for granted. They could buy a cornucopia of products from across the world at often astoundingly cheap prices. Consumer spending soared. Electronic goods, children's toys, clothing and a plethora of other commodities flowed from countries in East Asia that were undergoing unprecedentedly high rates of economic growth – the 'tiger economies' of South Korea, Singapore and Taiwan – but above all from China, whose economy was emerging as the largest after that of the United States. Europe provided expanding markets, too, for goods and expertise in computer software from India, another fast-growing economy. The shelves of European supermarkets bulged with staggering choices of foodstuffs from every part of the globe. Fruit and vegetables, once available only seasonally, were imported from distant warm countries. Myriad choices of Mediterranean and Middle Eastern dishes, innumerable kinds of pasta, oriental spices and other food products catered for practically every individual taste. Wines came not just from all over Europe but also from Australia, New Zealand, California, Argentina and Chile, available at low prices that would have been unimaginable a generation earlier.

As manufacturing continued its long-term decline in European countries, services replaced it almost everywhere as the dominant economic sector. By the end of the twentieth century, services accounted for two-thirds to three-quarters of employees in most European countries. Only a minority now worked on farms or in big factories. Most employees were engaged in administration, organization, or the commercial arrangements of production, not in the actual manufacture of products. Logistics – the organization of the flow of goods around the world – turned into a booming sector of industry and commerce. The number of transnational firms more than doubled between 1990 and 2008. There was an even faster growth in the number of subsidiary companies. 'Outsourcing' – contracting out parts of a business, whether administration, manufacture or distribution of products to a subsidiary, sometimes based abroad – had become a key element of a globalized economy. Governments outsourced public services to private firms to cut back on state expenditure. But most outsourcing was done by private firms themselves. Tax burdens could be minimized by relocating to countries with a low taxation regime. Moving production overseas to countries where labour was cheap, while retaining a European headquarters, could boost profits – a process that had been gathering pace for decades. Three-quarters of the labour force of Dutch multinational companies, for instance, had already been employed abroad in the 1970s. Outsourcing often meant, too, handing over elements in the production and distribution chain to self-employed people, thereby enabling firms to avoid cumbersome and costly obligations under labour law, although this often meant transposing onerous work practices on to the self-employed in small businesses.

Communications and transnational relations were by the first decade of the twenty-first century utterly transformed. The rapid spread of the internet, especially after the creation of the World Wide Web (invented in 1989 by Tim Berners-Lee and made available to the general public two years later), spearheaded a revolution that was changing the possibility of communications and availability of knowledge and information at breathtaking speed and in previously unimaginable ways. Goods could be ordered from overseas to be delivered to the front door with astonishing rapidity at the touch of a computer key. People could contact each other by e-mail across the world in seconds (drastically reducing postal services in the process). Financial transactions and transfer of capital could be completed just as fast. Total European foreign direct investment abroad overtook that of America for the first time since the Second World War. Foreign investment in Europe itself was by the end of the century almost double that in the United States. Once the Euro had been introduced in 2002, currency transactions in Europe were greatly simplified. Business benefited. So did foreign travellers.

Travellers could enjoy remarkably cheap air travel that allowed easy access, for business or pleasure, to far-flung destinations. Even after 9/11 had brought fortress-like changes to airport security the thirst for foreign travel (and the ease of undertaking it) was scarcely affected. International tourism was big business. People moved from continent to continent as never before. Travel to international conferences and business meetings expanded. Students, under the European Union's Erasmus programme, could study without difficulty in countries outside their own, transferring their qualifications from one university to another beyond national borders. It had also become far easier, with European citizenship, to move jobs or homes from one country to another. Millions of Europeans now willingly, not just from economic necessity, lived outside their country of birth. Culturally, Europeans across the continent had lost many – though certainly not all – of the differences that once had separated them. There were remarkably similar tastes, transcending national boundaries, in music (popular and classical), film, theatre and art. East and west Europeans were now indistinguishable from the clothes they wore. International news channels carried a significant proportion of very similar stories (with, of course, national or regional slants).

In these, and in many other ways, globalization was rapidly transforming – and improving – people's lives. It was in countless respects an enormous boon, extending material comforts to ordinary citizens that had less than half a century earlier been the preserve only of small, relatively wealthy sectors of society. The trends in globalization, though not in themselves new, were thanks mainly to the communications revolution massively accelerated. The huge benefits nevertheless came at very considerable cost. Globalization was plainly ambivalent – a phenomenon with a Janus-face, partly good but also partly negative. It was impossible to have one without the other.

Globalization had many losers as well as winners. One striking feature of its impact was the rapidly widening disparities of income and wealth. Inequalities had been reduced in the first two post-war decades, but then had started to rise again in a trend that accelerated as the twentieth century approached its end. The income of the top tenth of the population, even more strikingly of the top 1 per cent, rose significantly faster in most countries than that of the bottom tenth. A highly educated, technologically highly skilled managerial class was able to benefit disproportionately – the higher up the ladder, the greater the disproportion. There was a crassly widening gulf between the often grotesque salaries, bonuses and equity stakes of top executives of big companies and financial institutions, and the earnings of the vast majority of the employees of such concerns. Those who were most skilled at exploiting financial markets were best placed of all to earn sky-high incomes.

At the other end of the spectrum was a new proletariat, earning poor wages in precarious forms of employment, often living in sub-standard accommodation, with little or no surplus from their earnings and disproportionately prone, not surprisingly, to falling into debt. Women, often compelled to combine family commitments with meagre earnings potential from part-time or insecure employment, were particularly disadvantaged. So were the unskilled, the poorly educated, those who lacked the requisite qualifications in literacy and numeracy. Notably disadvantaged were immigrant or seasonal workers, driven to accept low-paid, insecure and unattractive jobs and poor housing conditions while also frequently having to contend with overt or more subtle forms of discrimination. As globalization provided a reservoir of immigrant and transient labour to meet the swelling demand, less scrupulous employers were able to push their labour costs down. This in turn alienated trade unions and the workers they represented, who felt migrant labour was depressing their wages.

Globalization worked heavily in favour of big business, while small concerns often struggled. Big supermarkets, for example, could control food markets through massive bulk buying. Small food stores, unable to compete, went to the wall in droves. Bookselling was another branch that favoured large-scale operations. Small bookshops, unable to match the holdings, marketing capacity or discount possibilities of the big booksellers, frequently went out of business. Even some big concerns faced major problems in competing against Amazon, which had begun as an online bookstore in the United States in 1994 before expanding throughout Europe, using computer technology to revolutionize book availability and speed of delivery (and within a number of years diversifying its output to a huge range of other products).

Deregulation of finance encouraged the transfer of capital to areas that offered the highest returns on capital investment. 'Hot money' could flow across borders in an instant with little or no constraint. Financial markets were global, no longer subject to restrictions imposed by national governments. Speculation in financial markets could swiftly bring extraordinary riches – or bring crushing losses, such as followed the collapse in 2001 of the 'dot-com bubble' in the wake of huge, but hazardous, investment in new firms established to exploit the rapid growth of the internet sector. Those who accumulated new-found wealth, or had inherited it, were able to increase it by lodging it securely and unobtrusively in banks outside the country of their residence, where they could take advantage of very low rates of taxation. Luxembourg, Switzerland, Andorra, the Channel Islands and the Isle of Man offered such provision within Europe.

Not surprisingly, then, in the boom years of globalization between the mid-1990s and 2008, not just income but wealth disparities widened sharply. Property-owners saw their wealth increase effortlessly as the price of property soared. Many belonged to a middle class of relatively modest income but owning houses whose value had increased exponentially. In some of Europe's major cities – London was the prime example – rich foreign investors bought much of the most desirable property. The majority of ordinary citizens, however, found themselves priced out of the market. Young people especially, unless they inherited wealth, often had no hope of ever earning enough to buy even the most modest family home. Unsurprisingly, resentment simmered.

Crass inequality of income and wealth was less acute in Scandinavian countries. These had traditionally favoured higher taxation and more even social distribution than had Britain, which aimed more closely to follow the American neo-liberal model of a low-taxation highly deregulated economy. Most continental Western European countries – France, Germany, Italy and the Benelux countries prominent among them – had not followed the Scandinavian route, but had nonetheless developed strong political traditions since the Second World War of tempering the market through social welfare policies. These also tended to mitigate to differing degrees growing income inequality, which was far more marked in the former eastern-bloc countries and also in much of Southern Europe. In the 'good years' of the late 1990s and early 2000s the growing inequalities were, if recognized, largely ignored or regarded simply as the price to pay for the wider benefits of globalization. Should the 'good years' run out, however, the potential for social unrest and political challenges to the existing system was evident.

Economic growth and rising income, while self-evidently important, did not entirely accord with how people assessed their 'quality of life'. Differing statistical indicators tried to arrive at comparative indications of what was plainly a complex and highly subjective concept. Criteria included economic well-being, political liberties, levels of employment, and stability of family and community. Whatever caveats might be attached to attempts to quantify 'quality of life', the results obtained by one of the most sophisticated evaluations, undertaken in 2005 by the London-based magazine *The Economist*, offered some indication of the place of Europe in world rankings. Top of the charts was the Republic of Ireland, where doubtless the recent transformation in the standard of living and the rapid growth in the country's economy had been decisive. Western European countries generally fared well. Nine of the top ten countries surveyed across the world were in Western Europe, though

France, Germany and Britain lagged some way behind – possibly an indicator that 'quality of life' was less easy to build and sustain in large, complex and varied economies. Most of the Central and Eastern European countries fell well behind Western Europe, some (including Bulgaria, Romania, Serbia and Bosnia) were placed still further back, while Ukraine, Belarus, Moldova and Russia entered the table lower than Syria and not too far ahead of the last countries in the list, Nigeria, Tanzania, Haiti and Zimbabwe.

Major regional as well as national disparities in wealth had always existed in Europe (not to mention between Europe and other parts of the globe, such as Africa or South America). How they were affected by globalization varied. Political stability, existing infrastructure, the quality of educational systems, and flexible social values offered preconditions in which globalization was likely to make a positive impact. Western Europe for the most part provided such preconditions. Some Mediterranean countries that had earlier lagged behind now took big strides to catch up. Spain and Portugal had higher growth rates than the core of Western Europe, while Ireland, once so backward, turned into a Western 'tiger economy'. Finland, too, after undergoing severe recession in the early 1990s, recovered strongly, especially after joining the European Union in 1995, experienced strong economic growth, and developed into a leading exporter of electronic equipment, exploiting especially the rapidly expanding demand for mobile telephones.

But there were losers from globalization, too, even in relatively prosperous Western Europe. The considerable financial assistance provided under the European Union's European Regional Development Fund helped to mitigate some of the worst regional disparities. Nevertheless, the long-standing structural problems of some areas were impossible to overcome. The age-old disparity between the poor regions of the Mezzogiorno and far wealthier northern Italy widened as the north proved much more attractive to foreign investors. Even in prosperous Germany, there were major divides between Bavaria and Baden-Württemberg in the south, flourishing regions that could attract the booming new technologies and were centres of car manufacture, and the old industrial region of the Ruhr in the north-west, or the relatively poor, largely agricultural region of Mecklenburg in the north-east. In Britain the old industrial regions of the north-east and north-west, Clydeside in

Scotland and the Welsh valleys, could not make up for the long-term decline of their staple heavy industries, while London and the south-east, buoyed by the growing dominance of the financial sector in the City of London, thrived. Northern Ireland showed the importance of political stability to inward global investment and prospects of prosperity. Having languished for three decades during 'The Troubles', the end to decades of violence in 1998 brought much-needed growth.

Where there was political instability or poor infrastructure – Romania, for example, had only five personal computers per thousand inhabitants in 1995, compared with 250 in Western Europe – or where there was widespread corruption and a poorly educated population (with Romania again a paradigm case), countries struggled to take advantage of globalization. By the year 2000 gross national product per head in Central and Eastern Europe remained only half that of Western Europe. Central European countries were themselves pulling away from those in the Balkans and those closely tied to Russia. Political stabilization and infrastructural reforms meant that globalization, partly through inward investment that could take advantage of low labour costs, enabled Central European countries to improve their economic position and make some headway towards catching up with Western Europe in the early years of the new century. Russia, too, started to recover. High energy prices and rich reserves of oil and natural gas helped the country emerge from the doldrums of the 1990s as the economy grew at 7 per cent a year between 2000 and 2008. The reinvigoration was helped by moves under President Putin to restore state control and regulation of important parts of the economy, as well as providing strong government (demonstrated by popular steps to depose, and even on occasion imprison, some of the most corrupt oligarchs), eliminating some of the worst aspects of Russia's kleptocracy, and encouraging inward investment. Inequality remained extremely high in the country, though it had, at any rate, stopped widening.

The massive economic stimulus that flowed from globalization was, not least, damaging to the environment, adding greatly to the dangers of pollution and global warming. But the need to meet rising expectations of higher living standards usually meant that environmental protection enjoyed a lower priority than continued economic growth. The fear of being outstripped in the race for growth played its part. The rapid expansion of globalization was unstoppable. Countries that did not move to embrace and adapt to it as swiftly as possible were left behind.

During more than a decade of dynamic economic growth since the mid-1990s the difficulties seemed manageable. But what problems would arise from globalization if the financial institutions that underpinned it were suddenly to be thrown into turmoil? No one gave the prospect much consideration. The growth that set in during the mid-1990s seemed set to continue indefinitely. The British Chancellor of the Exchequer, Gordon Brown, repeatedly claimed in the years after Labour had taken power in May 1997 that he had produced lasting stability in the British economy and that there would be no return to 'boom and bust'. The words would soon haunt him. But Brown was far from alone in failing to foresee that the very engines of global growth were driving the instability which would threaten it, that the globalized economy was heading straight for the edge of the cliff.

POLITICAL CHALLENGES OF GLOBALIZATION

How European governments met the challenges of globalization depended heavily upon national circumstances. But three general problems were plainly visible even in the boom years.

The first arose from hugely intensified economic competitiveness. This led to great pressure to lower wages, sustain high rates of employment, keep inflation down (helped by the low costs of imported goods from China's booming economy), and reduce the tax burden. It was often dubbed a 'race to the bottom'. The ease of international capital transfers meant that high tax regimes and forms of protectionism that had worked in the past were unsustainable. Governments had to exploit globalization while finding ways at the national level of combating its harmful side effects. How to balance these problems with maintaining social cohesion, upholding the civilized values that Europe's democracies saw as their very essence, and sustaining high levels of social welfare in the face of increased expectations and an ageing population, was a major challenge to all governments. None found easy or entirely palatable solutions.

A second problem was the impact on the home population of

increasing migration as people from poorer economies exploited the possibilities of moving to higher-wage economies where vibrant growth produced a great demand for their labour. This was a scale of mobility that it had been impossible to foresee at the creation of the Single Market in 1986. Attempts, in varying ways, to integrate migrants and develop multicultural societies frequently gave rise to social tensions and promoted political fragmentation by fostering the appeal of 'identity politics' represented by minority parties. The problem, far from new, would become more serious in the second decade of the twenty-first century. But, often beneath the surface, population migration and multiculturalism were viewed with deepening concern even in years of relatively buoyant economies and global growth.

The third serious problem, of increasing importance following the Iraq War and the attacks in Madrid and London, was the threat of terrorism. Spain and the United Kingdom had long experience of dealing with localized terrorism. The terrorism of ETA and the IRA had been deadly and of long duration. But, silently acknowledging that their goals could not be attained through armed struggle, both organizations edged towards political rather than military operations. The 'Good Friday Agreement' of April 1998 marked a crucial point in the process of bringing to a close a thirty-year tragic phase in the history of Northern Ireland, which had caused the deaths of about 3,500 people. The Basque separatist struggle in Spain had cost the lives of around a thousand individuals since the 1960s. But here too terrorist violence was in decline. After a number of truces and a 'permanent' ceasefire in March 2006 proved to be temporary, lasting only until December, ETA would announce a 'definitive cessation of its armed activity' in January 2011. IRA and ETA terrorism, deadly though it was (and the number of its victims was very large, compared with that caused by Islamist terrorism in Western Europe during the first decade of the twenty-first century), had been specific in its goals and localized in its implementation. Islamist terrorism was a different matter altogether. This would become a more acute issue in the second decade of the twenty-first century. But already it posed high demands on the security services of individual countries and on the development of closer cooperation through networking of intelligence across the Western world to combat an obviously growing menace.

The dramatic changes experienced in Europe at the start of the 1990s had fed into an intangible readiness in Western European countries to embrace substantive reform. The aim of undertaking major structural reform of European institutions had been behind the Maastricht Treaty in 1992. Individual states, too, had to adapt to changed circumstances. The need to 'modernize' in a 'new Europe' became a political mantra. In much of Western Europe this favoured electoral shifts towards social democracy. Britain elected the Blair government with a landslide majority in 1997. Gerhard Schröder became German Chancellor in a coalition government with the Greens the following year. The French had also moved towards the left in the parliamentary elections of 1997. Social Democrats formed the predominant force in coalition governments in the Netherlands, Sweden, Denmark, Austria, Italy, Portugal and Greece in the later 1990s. The trend was general, though there were exceptions – Spain, for instance, turning towards conservatism in 1996 after a lengthy period of socialist government. But far from establishing a long-term shift in political allegiances towards the centre-left, social democracy had entered upon what proved to be an Indian summer. It found itself generally on the retreat in the early years of the twenty-first century.

A reverse trend towards centre-right conservatism was soon characteristic of an altered mood in Western European electorates. Between 2001 and 2006 Social Democrats lost power in France, Germany, the Netherlands, Portugal, Finland, Denmark and Sweden. Again, there were exceptions to the trend. Italy, where the ineffable Berlusconi returned to office at the head of a right-wing coalition in 2001, moved back towards the centre-left in parliamentary elections in 2006, while Spain had elected a socialist government two years earlier following the terrorist attack in Madrid.

The two paradigm countries of new-style social democracy as Europe entered the twenty-first century were Britain and Germany. Both the governments of Tony Blair in Britain and of Gerhard Schröder in Germany offered what in their early years seemed a welcome advance on the tired policies of their predecessors. But the path of reform that both took, attempting to combine pro-market policies with remodelled notions of social justice, proved highly controversial – not least among the supporters of their own parties. By 2005 both the Labour Party in Britain and the Social Democrats in Germany were seeing their support evaporate.

Blair's promise to modernize the country under 'New Labour' (as he was now calling his party) had in 1997 sounded attractive to millions of voters. But his great electoral victory that year owed not a little to a negative factor – voters turning their backs on the divided and ineffectual Conservative government of John Major. Blair and his advisors had recognized that it was no longer possible to win sufficient electoral support by adhering to traditional Labour policies. De-industrialization had brought fundamental changes to the working class. Trade unions – the backbone of Labour – were far weaker than before the Thatcher era. And the class rhetoric of bygone years seemed outdated as individual consumer habits and lifestyles crossed class boundaries. So Blair set out to win over 'Middle England' – middle-class voters from far beyond Labour heartlands.

The programme of Blair's government attempted to blend social democracy with neo-liberal economics. Blair's critics derided it as Thatcherism with a human face. It broke with some long-standing Labour traditions and aims, for which many in the party faithful never forgave him. Equality of opportunity replaced the elimination of material inequality as Labour's goal. The commitment to nationalization of the economy, in the party's programme since 1918, was discarded. Instead of 'inefficient' public ownership, New Labour looked to control and utilize the wealth creation of a competitive free-market economy to provide a framework for social justice.

Under New Labour there was strong economic growth – which had already begun under the Conservatives in the mid-1990s (themselves benefiting from the upward swing in the global economy). Aided by further deregulation, the City of London consolidated its position as Europe's (and by some measures the world's) financial capital. Gordon Brown, an astute Chancellor of the Exchequer, made funds available to enable Blair's government to finance much-needed improvements in schools, universities and hospitals. Many among the poorer sections of society certainly benefited. Changes in taxation and welfare benefits saw the incomes of the poorest rise by 10 per cent. Child poverty was reduced. And as the economy continued to thrive, there was a pervasive sense of material well-being among much of the middle class.

But a lot of this depended on a consumer boom, financed mainly by the availability of cheap credit that in turn fuelled high levels of personal debt. Inflation in property prices, too, pleased home-owners while increasing inexorably the gulf between those who possessed property and the many who could never afford to acquire any. Under New Labour the rich got richer. One of the masterminds behind the party's rebranding, Peter Mandelson, had said in 1998 that he was 'intensely relaxed about people getting filthy rich as long as they paid their taxes' (which many managed to avoid doing). But the vain hope that wealth would 'trickle down' from top to bottom of the social ladder proved misplaced.

Blair's legacy included the devolution in 1998 of significant powers from London to a Scottish parliament and a Welsh assembly. His most important single achievement (building upon the substantial progress already made under his predecessor, John Major) was to broker the Good Friday Agreement of April 1998, which drew a line under the violent conflict between Republicans and Unionists in Northern Ireland. Despite these lasting successes and whatever the material benefits from economic growth under New Labour, the Iraq War cast a deep shadow over Blair after 2003.

It put New Labour firmly on the defensive. Many on the centre-left, completely alienated by the Iraq War, drifted to the Liberal Democrats, while others who had earlier turned away from Conservatism returned to their traditional habitat. Nevertheless, Blair won his third election in a row in May 2005, a unique record for Labour. His own personal magnetism had not been altogether eroded. More important was the continuing strength of the British economy. But the positive result for Labour could not hide the fact that the party's popularity was waning. It had won only 35 per cent of the popular vote – the lowest proportion ever attained by a majority government in Britain – and Labour's parliamentary majority fell by almost a hundred seats.

The attacks in London in July 2005 were a searing reminder of the dangers for Britain that the Iraq War had intensified. Blair's response was to propose new security measures. In this, however, he encountered much popular opposition; in the eyes of many the proposed measures threatened to undermine British liberties. When his government pressed for new anti-terrorist laws that extended the period of detention without trial from fourteen to as long as ninety days, forty-nine Labour Members of Parliament were among the majority in the House of Commons that inflicted Blair's first parliamentary defeat since coming to office in 1997.

(It was eventually agreed to increase the period of detention without charge to twenty-eight days.) Pressure built within the leading echelons of the Labour Party, especially among supporters of Gordon Brown, for Blair to step down. And sure enough in June 2007 the most successful leader in Labour's electoral history resigned as Prime Minister, leaving Parliament soon afterwards. The Iraq War had lastingly sullied his reputation. His notable achievements as Prime Minister were as a consequence widely overlooked or played down.

Gerhard Schröder did not have the luxury of the large majority that the British 'first-past-the-post' electoral system presented to Blair in 1997. The Social Democrats won the German election the following year, though with only slightly more of the popular vote than the Christian Union parties. The government Schröder was able to form, in coalition with the Greens (who were backed by a mere 6.7. per cent of the electorate), nonetheless embarked on an ambitious programme of social reforms. These included tax changes to prioritize clean energy, a law to end discrimination against homosexuality, and a significant alteration of citizenship that in 2000 made residence not ethnicity the main criterion. But the serious economic problems inherited by the Schröder government posed a big challenge.

Remarkable as it would seem only a few years later, Germany was described by *The Economist* in June 1999 as 'the sick man of Europe'. Economic growth, the magazine wrote, was lower than in the rest of the newly created Eurozone, unemployment remained stubbornly high, German exports had declined as its big markets in Asia and Russia had collapsed, and the continued costs of unification remained a burden. The morale of business leaders was poor and they feared the worst from the new left-leaning government. The analysis outlined fundamental problems that needed structural surgery to bring about economic revival. It offered neo-liberal remedies. Levels of corporate taxation were far too high, and were hampering investment. They had to be cut if German firms were not to move their operations to Central and Eastern Europe (which some were in fact doing). Germany was still 'smothered in regulations'. Commerce had to be deregulated to stimulate consumer spending. Above all, Germany's labour costs were too high, relative to what was produced, and welfare costs had swollen, encouraging firms to shed workers and add to the unemployment numbers. Germany, the article argued, had to 'restructure in response to globalization' by enacting 'radical structural reforms'. It was necessary to slash top rates of corporate and income tax and 'defuse Germany's welfare time bomb' by cutting benefits, encouraging private pension provision, deregulating services and speeding up privatization. Unless these structural reforms were undertaken, the article concluded, 'Germany is unlikely soon to shed its title as the sick man of Europe.'

Social democracy had, in other words, to make the economy globally competitive while not undermining the welfare provisions that had been built up over the years to protect citizens and improve their lives yet were now proving costly and restrictive to economic enterprise. Blair's government, which Schröder admired, was seeking in its own way to address the issue in Britain. But at least Blair had the advantage over Schröder that he could build upon the incisive changes to the economy (and inroads into the welfare state) that had already been made by the Thatcher government. Nothing comparable had been done in Germany. Schröder had to try to hold the left together while introducing reforms that were bound to be unpopular across wide sectors of his own party.

Almost immediately his modernizing aims ran foul of his Finance Minister and the Chairman of the Social Democrats, Oskar Lafontaine, who favoured a traditional programme that looked to Keynesian remedies for Germany's economic ills. These seemed, however, in arguing for stimulation of demand through higher wages, increased social spending and low interest rates – all of which would have meant higher public debt – to offer solutions from an earlier era that were out of tune with current needs. In March 1999 Lafontaine resigned his government and party positions. Schröder was the plain victor of the internal test of his authority and his policy direction.

His real problems grew from the announcement in 2003 of what was labelled 'Agenda 2010' – the programme to reform labour relations and social welfare in order to reduce unemployment and promote economic growth, which had been no more than 0.1 per cent in 2002. Social security contributions by employers and employees were meanwhile taking up on average over 40 per cent of gross salaries. 'Either we modernize,' declared Schröder, 'or we will be modernized, and by the unconstrained forces of the market.' Agenda 2010 was an attempt to align changes in welfare with the needs of a globally competitive economy – and was predictably highly unpopular. It bore some resemblance to what was happening in Britain under Blair (who in turn had been inspired by the example of President Clinton in the United States). In the interests of greater economic flexibility and competitiveness, adjustments (in reality cuts) were made to unemployment benefits, sickness payments and state pensions. It was made easier for firms to make employees redundant. The changes amounted to the greatest inroads in German social security since the establishment of the 'social market economy' over half a century earlier.

These were welcomed by business and the liberal-conservative right. But they were detested on the left. Gradually, the reforms did indeed help to reinvigorate the German economy, partly by reducing the proportion of wages and salaries in the gross domestic product. But they were not unalloyed improvements. Unemployment was soon falling. However, as in Britain and elsewhere, this disguised a rise in part-time, temporary, and other forms of precarious work that people were effectively obliged to accept. The numbers of people living in poverty increased. Inequality of incomes grew. While wages and pensions were held down, the salaries of top business managers soared.

Schröder's popularity never recovered. In September 2005 he paid the price for his reform programme in electoral defeat. Even so, the parties of the Union (the Christian Democrats and their Bavarian partners the Christian Socialists) won only narrowly. Forming a coalition from left- or right-wing groupings proved impossible. All that remained was a 'grand coalition' of the Union and the Social Democrats. Under the new Christian Democrat Chancellor, Angela Merkel, the government followed broadly the economic direction that had been laid down by Schröder. The depiction of Germany as 'the sick man of Europe' soon looked bizarre. But German social democracy, in the eyes of increasing numbers of voters, had meanwhile come to seem little distinguishable from its conservative coalition partners. The main parties, not just in Germany, were starting to look alike. In the long run that was not good for democracy.

THE EUROPEAN UNION'S CHALLENGES

Blair and Schröder were wrestling with problems that, whatever their national nuances, flowed from the acceleration of globalization and affected the whole of Europe. For the European Union this meant adapting its structures to meet the challenges that arose from the decisions in the early 1990s to introduce the Euro and to widen the EU to incorporate countries from Central and Eastern Europe. Both decisions would lead to new difficulties.

With the accession of ten new countries on 1 May 2004, the European Union increased its membership from fifteen to twenty-five countries. Eight of the new entrants (the Czech Republic, Estonia, Hungary, Latvia, Lithuania, Poland, Slovakia and Slovenia) had once stood behind the Iron Curtain. The ninth country, Cyprus, despite being split into two parts since the Turkish invasion of July 1974, gained admission after Greece had threatened to veto the accession of the former communist states. Its political problems remained unresolved. Malta was the tenth new entrant – tiny, politically split with Labour opposed to joining, with modest gross domestic product, but under its nationalist liberal-conservative government keen to benefit from the economic advantages that membership of the European Union would bring.

In geopolitical terms the widening was welcome. But the economic imbalance of the European Union was now a problem since the new countries were far poorer than existing members. The per-capita gross domestic product of the new entrants in 2004 was less than half of that of the existing members. Estonia and Slovenia were best placed among the former communist countries. But Poland, the largest country in Central Europe, had a lower than average gross domestic product even among the new entrants. Slovakia's was lower still. The average wage in Latvia was only an eighth of the average in the pre-2004 member states.

The economic disparities within the European Union became an even bigger problem when Romania and Bulgaria were admitted in January 2007. Gross domestic product per head was only a third of the average of existing member countries (an average already brought down by the last round of new entrants). Neither country came close to meeting the criteria for membership that had been agreed at Copenhagen in 1993. They were far from models of liberal democracy or the rule of law. Corruption and organized crime were still rampant. Former communist functionaries dominated the political scene and ran the security services. And in economic terms, both countries languished at the bottom of the prosperity league table of members of the European Union. Despite their evident deficiencies, they became the European Union's twenty-sixth and twenty-seventh member states. Following the Yugoslavian wars it had been felt imperative to stabilize the European 'periphery'. The hope was that, once admitted, political and economic reforms would be accelerated.

Understandably, many from Eastern Europe sought to improve their living standards and those of their families by seeking work in wealthier Western European countries. Just as unsurprisingly, there was concern in Western European countries, notably in Germany and Austria which bordered the new entrants, about the impact on the labour market of an influx of cheap workers from Central Europe. The principle of free movement of citizens across national borders had not been a significant issue when the European Union consisted of countries that had attained a very broadly similar level of economic development. Now it started to be questioned. In 2001 the European Union had allowed member states to restrict access to the labour market for the expected migrants from Central and Eastern European countries for an interim period of up to seven years to provide time for adjustment. The United Kingdom, Ireland and Sweden were the only countries not to introduce such restrictions in 2004. Sweden alone did not do so when Romania and Bulgaria were admitted three years later.

The numbers of migrants in 2004 from Central and Eastern Europe seeking work was higher than predicted even in countries that imposed restrictions. But the restrictions did amount to some deterrent. Those imposing no restrictions were, by contrast, particularly attractive to migrants. Britain's thriving economy made it a magnet. The British government anticipated an influx of some 15,000 people a year from the new member countries. Between May 2004 and June 2006, however, 427,000 work applications were approved, more than half of them for Polish migrants. In 2001 Poles in Britain numbered 58,000. A decade later the figure was 676,000. In a very short period of time Poles became Britain's largest body of foreign citizens.

A continuous rise of migrants to Britain from all eight of the former communist member states occurred between 2004 and 2007. This trend then subsided somewhat during the subsequent economic recession when many – often young – migrants returned to their countries of origin. Because of the imposed restrictions (due to last until 2014), the numbers of Romanians and Bulgarians granted work permits in the United Kingdom averaged only around 25,000 a year after 2007, though this formed part of an overall continuing steep rise in overall immigration from both inside and outside Europe.

The influx of migrant labour, most analyses concurred, was broadly beneficial for the British economy. Estimates vary considerably, depending upon the basis of the calculations, but some suggest that European migrants contributed in one form or another around £20 billion to the British economy in the first decade of the twenty-first century. In crucial areas they were indispensable. The National Health Service could scarcely operate without migrant labour; almost a fifth of those it employed were from outside Britain. The predominantly young and frequently well-educated migrants, drawn to work far from home, filled labour shortages, often in low-skilled jobs, and made relatively few demands on welfare support. However, complaints soon arose – and did not subside – about downward pressure on wages and difficulties in housing and social services in areas with high concentrations of migrants. Perceptions were frequently not in accord with realities. But perceptions became a form of reality themselves. The speed and scale of the migrant influx from the European Union quickly turned this into a political issue of growing importance. Shrill opposition, some of it thinly veiled racism, to seemingly unstoppable high levels of immigration, mostly fostered by the right-wing media, became more voluble, and not only on the political far right.

'Immigration' in Britain (unlike the terminology in most of Europe) bracketed together people coming to Britain from the European Union and immigrants from outside Europe (often from countries of long-standing immigration to Britain, especially Pakistan and India). 'Immigration' also included rising numbers of young people both from within and – three-quarters of them – from outside the European Union coming to the United Kingdom to study. A minority of them, mainly non-EU nationals, remained after completing their studies, generally offering much-needed skills and expertise.

There was a crucial difference between the categories of migrants from within and outside the European Union: freedom of movement meant that no limitation was possible on the number of migrants coming from the EU. Migrants from those countries comprised on average just under a half of total net immigration (which over subsequent years would come close to averaging more than 300,000 people a year). That made migration from the European Union, within the wider framework of increasing opposition to immigration, a particularly sensitive political issue.

This was a feature of British immigration that was not generally mirrored in other countries of the European Union. The widespread use of English globally helped to make Britain uniquely attractive. Migration was, however, in every country a fact of modern life – an inexorable by-product of globalization. European countries such as Italy or Ireland, which before the Second World War had exported people, especially to the United States, had now become countries of immigration. It was easier to move for work (or to seek refuge from war and tyranny) than it had once been. The numbers of people on the move in the search for a better life was a general phenomenon throughout Europe.

By 2010 the European Union included 47 million people (9.4 per cent of the population) who had been born outside their country of residence. Germany, France, the United Kingdom, Spain, Italy and the Netherlands had in that order the largest numbers, measured in absolute terms (ranging from Germany's 6.4 million to the 1.4 million of the Netherlands). As a proportion of the total population Austria (15.2 per cent) followed by Sweden (14.3 per cent) headed the list. These proportions were even higher than that of the United States, the traditional target for immigration. Apart (marginally) from Belgium, the proportion of those born in a non-EU state was higher than those born within a country of the European Union.

As in Britain, migrants frequently met with hostility, as in the highly negative attitude towards the rapidly increasing numbers of Romanians in Italy (which were ten times higher in 2008 than they had been seven years earlier). Age-old racist attitudes towards Roma played no small part in the aversion to Romanian migrants. In Austria, where immigration had continued to increase despite much restrictive legislation, antipathy was directed heavily towards those coming from former Yugoslavia and Turkey, traditionally the largest sources of migrant labour.

Most hostility was directed towards migrants from outside the European Union, particularly those from different cultures and often specifically towards Muslims – whose families had been domiciled in Europe for decades and were by now sometimes in their third or fourth generation. Tolerance towards Muslims, especially, was in sharp decline – partly spurred by the growth of Islamic fundamentalism. This was mirrored by a growth of anti-Western feeling, greatly exacerbated by the wars in Afghanistan and Iraq, among Muslims in Europe. In big cities especially, deep resentments among young Muslims were growing. A sense of discrimination and economic deprivation, of alienation and intense anger at Western intervention that had brought such suffering to Muslims in the Middle East, encouraged those at home to define their own identity in distinction to that of the majority populations among whom they lived. A small minority, particularly among disaffected young people, were drawn by the allure of Islamic causes. Amid intensifying mutual antipathy the strenuous efforts made by politicians and community leaders to promote multiculturalism and integration faced an uphill struggle. Communities, far from integrating, seemed to be growing further apart. Multiculturalism increasingly described communities with in practice near irreconcilable cultural difference – not integrating, but merely existing uneasily side by side.

Sometimes the tension broke out into violence, as in the anti-Muslim riots in 2001 in several poor northern British industrial towns. More generally, the antagonism simmered beneath the surface. In France there was much antipathy towards Muslims of North African origin, many of whom had lived there since the Algerian War nearly half a century earlier and whose families had actually been French citizens even before that. Serious riots in 2005 in socially deprived parts of French towns and cities with a large immigrant population fostered anti-Muslim feeling. Animosity was growing, too, in other EU countries such as the Netherlands, and in the non-member state of Switzerland. Right-wing political parties with a strident anti-immigrant (and anti-Muslim) platform were gaining support in many countries. Even though they could not yet capture the political mainstream, their message sometimes became incorporated in the demands of establishment parties to restrict immigration.

In this climate, any ambitious future enlargement of the European Union was in practice suspended, if not discarded in theory. Croatia, following earlier agreement, joined in 2013. Its gross domestic product was by then higher than that of some already existing member states. It was nevertheless allowed to join despite continued extensive organized corruption and criminality. Political considerations were once more decisive. It was felt important to send encouraging signals to Balkan states. But 'Catholic' Croatia had long been viewed as more Western than other Balkan countries. In contrast, Albania, Macedonia, Montenegro and Serbia would have to wait more or less indefinitely, while there was little prospect of Kosovo or Bosnia-Herzegovina (where the tensions of the 1990s had subsided but far from disappeared) joining in the foreseeable future.

The largest country on the waiting list was Turkey, a member of the Council of Europe since 1949, of NATO since 1952, and a recognized candidate for EU membership since 1999. Following limited improvements in civil rights and political freedom, Turkey was actually said in 2004 to have fulfilled the entry criteria. The process of negotiating Turkey's entry began in 2005, only to be suspended a year later over the failure to resolve the thorny issue of the division of Cyprus. Germany, France and, especially, Britain strongly supported Turkey's membership, predominantly because of the country's strategic significance as a bridge between Europe and the Middle East. Austria, the Netherlands and Denmark led the opposition. One objection was that Turks did not 'culturally' belong in Europe. Such a large Muslim country of 70 million, which still lagged far behind acceptable standards of liberal democracy and the rule of law, would inexorably, the critics of Turkey's accession argued, alter the character and balance of power of the still overwhelmingly (if largely nominally) Christian European Union. There were also substantial fears about large numbers of Turkish migrants seeking work in far more prosperous Western European countries, significantly adding to the existing problems of absorbing migrants and retaining social and political cohesion.

Turkey remained after 2006 a country waiting to join. In practice, that prospect was receding fast, and would recede even further in coming years. And as the prospects dimmed, Turkey itself was meanwhile moving gradually away from the secularism that Atatürk had prescribed as the basis of the country's identity at its foundation in 1923 and instead in an Islamist direction in which national identity was closely bound up with religion. How far Turkey's rejection by the EU contributed to this, or whether its internal development meant it was an inexorable consequence, is unclear. The result, in any case, was that Turkey came to be seen less as a candidate for joining the EU.

The European Union was meanwhile facing significant structural problems that were in no small measure a consequence of its extension. In 2002 a European Convention, headed by the former French President Valéry Giscard d'Estaing, had met in Brussels to draw up new constitutional arrangements for a European Union that was on the verge of major expansion. After lengthy wrangling over its precise terms, the text of a treaty establishing a Constitution for Europe was finally signed by all twenty-five members states of the by now enlarged European Union on 29 October 2004. The draft constitution modified arrangements for qualified majority voting, provided for the Commission to be elected by the European Parliament, and for an elected chair of the European Council to replace the existing six-month rotating chairmanship. The Parliament had to approve the budget and would have legislative powers alongside the Council. There would henceforth be a European Minister for Foreign Affairs.

The changes were far from the radical steps towards a federal Europe favoured by the German Foreign Minister, Joschka Fischer. They nevertheless went too far for some: in spring 2005 voters in France then in the Netherlands rejected the proposals. With that, the Constitution was dead. Some of the more significant changes were nevertheless in amended or watered-down form incorporated in the Treaty of Lisbon of 2007. This itself was only finally ratified after Irish voters had at first rejected it, then, after a number of opt-outs for Ireland had been introduced (that the Treaty would not infringe Irish sovereignty regarding taxation, family policy and neutrality), finally accepted it in a second referendum.

Despite such shocks for pro-Europeans, there was, in fact, much positive feeling towards the European Union across the continent. According to the standard *Eurobarometer* survey of opinion in 2000, only 14 per cent of citizens disapproved of their country's membership of the European Union whereas 49 per cent approved (though this number had fallen worryingly from 72 per cent in 1991). The highest satisfaction rates were in Ireland, Luxembourg and the Netherlands, the lowest in the United Kingdom. Forty-seven per cent of Europeans thought their country had benefited from EU membership, again a significant drop since the early 1990s, with the most favourable ratings in Ireland and Greece, the least in Sweden and, at the bottom of the table, again the United Kingdom.

To many Europeans the European Union seemed labyrinthine, impenetrably complex and elitist – a bureaucratic organization remote from their daily lives. National governments directly or indirectly enhanced this image. They did little to advertise, for instance, the substantial funding for poorer regions or infrastructural projects from the European Union. This funding was not enough to restore to former prosperity areas suffering badly from post-industrial blight. But used wisely it could make a difference. However, national governments were only too pleased to trumpet economic and political successes as their own while conveniently blaming 'Brussels' and EU bureaucratic interference to divert from failures closer to home.

Whatever the reasons, as it widened its membership and intensified its efforts towards closer as well as more extensive integration, the European Union was losing touch with large numbers of Europeans. Every election to the European Parliament since 1979 showed a further decline in the number of citizens bothering to vote. In 1979 participation had been 62 per cent. By 2004 it was down to 45.5 per cent. In 2004 itself, a year of economic growth, when the European Union was preparing its new Constitution and about to undergo its greatest single moment of expansion, 43 per cent of Europeans, when asked how they would feel should the European Union collapse the following day, were indifferent. Thirteen per cent said even they would be 'very relieved'. Only 39 per cent indicated that they would very much regret it. What opinion surveys plainly demonstrated was that people's own nation was overwhelmingly the strongest point of identity. By contrast, emotional association with a European identity was extremely weak.

The European Union could nevertheless point to significant achievements. A framework of international cooperation, the extension of the rule of law, the upholding of human rights, the establishment of a security network, and the creation of a single currency for a majority of member states, had all helped to widen prosperity and to dilute the nationalism that had once poisoned Europe, to strengthen civil society and to build solid democratic foundations.

Beyond the borders of the European Union and the countries in

Central and Eastern Europe that aspired to belong to it (and were meanwhile part of an expanded NATO) it was a different story.

THE 'PUTIN FACTOR'

During the 1990s it looked as if Russia under President Yeltsin was moving closer to the Western democracies. In 1996 the country became a member of the Council of Europe, signing up to the European Convention on Human Rights, and the following year reached an agreement on partnership and cooperation with the European Union. Hopes were expressed in Moscow at this time of Russia in due course becoming a full member of the European Union.

Much, however, stood in the way of closer integration. The question of human rights was one obstacle. After Chechnya's attempt to establish its independence in 1991, Russian troops had perpetrated serious violations of human rights between 1994 and 1996 and again in 1999–2000. Another obstacle was the deep unhappiness in Moscow at the expansion of NATO into parts of Eastern Europe – itself a plain sign of Russia's weakness. The climate started to change once Putin had replaced Yeltsin as President of the Russian Federation on the last day of 1999. From then onwards there was a consistent emphasis on Russian national values and invocation of the country's status as a great power. Putin started to put an end to the widespread feeling of humiliation at the drastic diminution in the standing of the country after the collapse of the Soviet Union, to give people back their proud Russian identity, and to make them believe in the country's future and a return to former glory.

His forceful advocacy of Russian interests in international dealings, especially with the United States, and his readiness to uphold them by military force if necessary, enhanced Putin's prestige at home. His popularity was boosted when, in August 2008, Russian armed forces entered Georgia (independent since 1991) to support the pro-Russian rebels seeking independence for the provinces of Abkhazia and South Ossetia.

The shift towards authoritarianism bothered Moscow intellectuals but not the masses in distant provinces. After the collapse under Gorbachev and the national weakness under Yeltsin's unstable governance, the great majority of Russians supported Putin's restoration of strong state authority. For some he was little less than a national saviour. That Russia's economy was able to recover strongly by exploiting high market prices for oil and gas helped the sense of a new start, even if the underlying serious economic problems and relative poverty of large sections of the population were far from overcome. Corruption remained endemic, but most Russians took it on board as long as their standard of living was improving. The facade of a democratic system was retained. But presidential power was reasserted, former KGB associates were granted increased political influence, the judicial system was subordinated to political imperative, the mass media brought under control, public opinion orchestrated, potential for opposition restricted, and over-mighty oligarchs seen to pose any political threat cut down to size (while those close to Putin were co-opted by massive material inducements). Putin's own dominance relied heavily on a modern-day version of medieval feudalism – on keeping the upper echelons of the state security service, the heads of the state bureaucracy, and top business leaders content through allowing them the trappings of power, advancement and wealth. No systematic ideological doctrine underpinned 'Putinism'. A strong state and a forceful foreign policy aimed at restoring Russia's status as a great power sufficed.

The growing assertiveness of Putin's Russia and the critical stance of the European Union and the Council of Europe towards its breaches of human rights, inroads into judicial independence, and hardening of anti-democratic tendencies meant increasing mutual alienation rather than greater cooperation. The Partnership and Cooperation Agreement between Russia and the European Union, signed in 1997, was not renewed a decade later. Putin emphasized 'the historical distinctiveness of the European civilizations' and warned against trying to impose 'artificial "standards"' on each other. He diverted discontent into resentment towards the West, increasingly portrayed as a threat rather than an ally.

Encroachment by the West on what Russia still thought of as its 'sphere of influence' was viewed with great unease. Following the expansion of NATO in the 1990s came the widening of the European Union in 2004. Even in what had once been parts of the Soviet Union itself the danger of penetration of the European Union could not be discounted. The pro-Western stance of the Georgian government – not least its bid to join NATO – under its new President, Mikheil Saakashvili, after the ousting in 2003 of President Eduard Shevardnadze (a close ally of Gorbachev and the last Foreign Minister of the Soviet Union), formed part of the background to the eventual Russian military intervention in Georgia in 2008. Of great concern, from Russia's perspective, was the possible extension of Western influence into Ukraine. With the 'Orange Revolution' (named after the orange scarves worn by protesters) in Ukraine in 2004 this prospect loomed large.

Opposition, especially among young Ukrainians, to President Leonid Kuchma's grossly corrupt, incompetent and highly brutal regime in Ukraine finally had a chance to express itself in elections at the end of October 2004. Kuchma (first elected in 1994) had served two terms in office. Constitutionally, he could not stand again. So he backed his Prime Minister, Viktor Yanukovych, who was declared the victor on 21 November (and warmly congratulated by Putin). The result was so obviously falsified – the true winner was plainly the popular Viktor Yushchenko, who had survived being poisoned (almost certainly by Kuchma's security service) shortly before the election – that hundreds of thousands of people travelled to Kiev and defied the bitter cold to protest peacefully for a fair election. Their continued vigil, before the eyes of the world's media, eventually forced a re-run of the election on 26 December, this time resulting in undisputed victory for Yuschchenko, who was installed as President the following month.

Putin watched with concern. 'Russia cannot afford to allow defeat in the battle for Ukraine' was the view expressed in one journal with good connections to the Kremlin as the Orange Revolution unfolded. The fear was that Western-style democracy would spread to Russia itself. The Kremlin spent hundreds of millions of dollars in trying to ensure the election of Yanukovych. The United States poured funds into support for Yuschchenko, who had openly declared his intention to apply for Ukraine's membership of the European Union. Putin had little choice but to grind his teeth and accept the outcome of the Orange Revolution. But the lines of potential future conflict had been drawn. Would Ukraine look for its future to Western Europe, or to Russia?

Kuchma's election in 1994 had firmly pointed Ukraine towards unity with Russia. But most of his support had come from the eastern parts of the country, those with especially close ties to Russia. Nowhere was his support higher than in Crimea, whose population was overwhelmingly

Russian. Crimea had been transferred to Ukraine by Nikita Khrushchev in 1954, though the Russian parliament, forty years later, had actually voted to cancel the cession – not that the vote had practical consequences. From the Ukrainian side Crimea had been lent upon in 1992 to rescind a parliamentary vote to declare independence from Ukraine. Crimea was the sharpest point of the division that ran through Ukraine, between a western half that in earlier times had been culturally aligned with Poland, Lithuania and Austria, and now looked to Western Europe for its future, and an eastern half that had culturally always fallen within the Russian orbit. The fissure was not healed by the outcome of the Orange Revolution of 2004. It would continue to fester.

* * *

By 2008 the traumas produced by the wars in Afghanistan and Iraq, prompted by the devastating terrorist attack on New York seven years earlier, had receded in Europe. And over the almost two decades since the fall of the Berlin Wall had symbolized the end of the division of the continent, Europe, east and west, had come closer together. Globalization had brought new levels of convergence, economic and political. The huge economic problems of Central and Eastern European countries during the transition to capitalist economies had significantly diminished. That substantial difficulties remained, and that the standard of living lagged behind that of prosperous Western Europe, did not contradict the great improvements in living conditions that had been made since the end of communism. Few, given a choice, would have voted to return to those times. And, meanwhile, the Euro had since its introduction in 1999 (and in actual monetary circulation since 2002) replaced national currencies in twelve Western European countries. The early years of the new currency had been encouraging. It was an important sign of an ever more closely interconnected Europe.

Politically, too, there were grounds for optimism. Millions in the former eastern bloc were now enjoying personal freedoms that had been denied them for over four decades. Whatever the obvious problems of adjustment, the European Union and the values that underpinned it had been greatly extended through the incorporation of the new member states in 2004 and 2007. The relative success of the spread of Western European values of liberal democracy and the rule of law contrasted starkly with the conditions in the zone dominated by Russia. The future looked bright.

Any veneer of self-satisfaction was, however, about to crack. Few Europeans were greatly alarmed in 2007 when news crossed the Atlantic that a number of big American investment banks were in trouble because of over-extending their high-risk credit on the purchase of properties, known as 'sub-prime', which buyers taking out big loans could have difficulty in repaying. An early sign of worry in Europe was the panic in Britain in September 2007 when depositors queued outside the branches of Northern Rock building society to withdraw their savings, forcing the British government to nationalize the faltering bank in February 2008. The panic quickly subsided. But so globally interdependent had the networks of investment and credit become that a crisis in the United States was bound to have consequences for the banking and finances of other countries, and for the world economy.

The moment when the crisis struck globally can be precisely determined. It was the filing for bankruptcy of the giant American investment bank Lehman Brothers on 16 September 2008. Within a month the European banking system faced imminent collapse. The optimism was over. A crisis-ridden era of austerity was about to dawn. The financial crash left Europe a changed continent.

12

Crisis Years

When the capital development of a country becomes a by-product of the activities of a casino, the job is likely to be ill-done.

John Maynard Keynes, 1936

Fear of migrants has been coupled with likely exaggerated fears that radical Islamic jihadists will mix with the migrant flow and bring terrorism into a borderless Europe. Together with the long and unfinished euro crisis, these concerns are feeding right-wing and populist parties in Europe and undermining the credibility of the European Union . . .

The New York Times, 29 August 2015

From 2008 onwards a combination of crises shook Europe's foundations. The worst financial and economic crisis since the 1930s imposed mountainous debts on European states, threatening to undermine the Eurozone. Huge flows of refugees fleeing from war in the Middle East accentuated political divisions and tensions. An increase in terrorist attacks in Europe intensified dangers to security. Crisis in Ukraine opened up the prospect of a new cold war between Russia and the West. And the European Union faced its own existential crisis as one of its member states, the United Kingdom, voted to leave it. What had long been presumed intact and solid seemed all at once to be crumbling. How had this multifaceted general crisis in Europe come about?

MELTDOWN AVERTED

The 'Great Recession', as it came to be known, was made in the United States, though with willing European accomplices. In no small measure its roots lay in the greed within the financial sector that overtook all sense of responsibility during the boom that preceded the crash. The banking crisis fed into a more wide-ranging crisis of public finances in almost all European countries. This in turn drove the economy into prolonged recession. The impact of such a sharp downturn in economic performance, of varying duration and severity in European countries, was to be felt for years to come.

The refusal of the US Federal Bank to provide any state funding to rescue Lehman Brothers in September 2008 ensured that the shock waves from the crash would trigger a global financial crisis. Banks had stopped trusting each other. The lending system was seizing up. The Americans had let Lehman Brothers go under, in accordance with the cut-throat logic of market economics. The colossal ensuing damage resulted, however, perversely for neo-liberal ideologists, in widespread recognition in Europe that the state had to step in to save ailing banks and prevent financial Armageddon. The unpalatable truth was that Europe's major banks were too big to be allowed to fail. The top four British banks had combined assets in 2008 worth almost four times the gross domestic product of the United Kingdom. It was a similar story, with variations, in a number of other European countries.

The worst-affected countries in Europe were those that had tacked most closely to the winds of neo-liberalism and become most reliant upon a large deregulated banking sector. Britain stood in special peril. On 6 October 2008 the Royal Bank of Scotland, which had in the space of a very few years become one of the largest banks in the world, was within hours of complete collapse. British officials worked through the night to create a huge financial rescue package to avoid economic meltdown in Britain and, given the international operations of the bank, across the world. The package, aimed at protecting depositors and helping to stabilize the banking system, involved government loans totalling around £500 billion. Days later the Royal Bank of Scotland was effectively nationalized, as the United Kingdom government bought more than four-fifths of its shares and over 40 per cent of the shares in two other banks, the large HBOS and smaller Lloyds TSB.

France, Germany, Italy, Spain and Switzerland were among the European countries that in general terms followed the British model in making funds available for vulnerable banks. Ten banks in Central and Eastern Europe received financial support. Like Britain, many governments also offered guarantees for savers. Governments in Switzerland, Portugal, Latvia and Ireland took a controlling interest in several banks – in the Swiss case, the enormous UBS bank, which had turned into an over-extended global investment bank. In Denmark the Roskilde Bank, facing collapse in 2008, had to be taken over by the Danish National Bank.

Iceland faced especial difficulties. Proportionate to its size, its banking crisis in 2008 was bigger than anywhere else in Europe. Iceland had gone far towards tilting its economy towards banking and had deregulated in 2001. Its three major banks, Kaupthing, Landsbanki and Glitnir, had grossly extended their foreign debt which by 2008, as the trust of investors evaporated, they found themselves unable to finance. Iceland's government did not have the resources to save the banks, which were effectively liquidated and new banks set up, backed by government funding to replace them. Domestic savings were guaranteed, but foreign investors and savers (also in foreign subsidiaries of Iceland's banks) suffered losses. The impact on Iceland's economy was profound, plunging the country into serious recession that only saw the first shoots of recovery in 2011. The volcanic eruption in Iceland in April 2010, spouting an ash cloud so wide-ranging that it paralysed international air traffic for several days, seemed to symbolize the damage caused by Iceland's reckless, deregulated banking system.

Massive government intervention to save the banking system had meant a large-scale transfer of wealth from taxpayers to the banks. People had put their savings, and their trust, in banks, presuming that their money would be safe. Instead, they had seen that the banks had operated as little more than gambling casinos. Unsurprisingly, confidence in banks fell in the process to an all-time low. Anger and disgust were palpable, and wholly understandable, when people with very modest incomes and lifestyles watched those who had presided over the debacle walk away with no criminal actions against them and huge pay-offs. In one of the most blatant cases, the chief executive of the Royal

Bank of Scotland, Fred Goodwin, who had steered the bank via huge expansion straight onto the rocks, was able to leave with a pension finally *reduced* to a mere £300,000 a year – decent compensation, perhaps, for eventually having to forfeit the knighthood bestowed on him in 2004 for 'services to the banking industry'.

In 2007, according to official statistics, the public finances in the European Union had been at their strongest for decades. At 57.5 per cent of gross domestic product average government debt in the twenty-eight countries of the European Union was below the Maastricht guideline of 60 per cent. Only Greece (103.1 per cent), Italy (99.8 per cent) and Belgium (87 per cent) had unduly high levels of debt. Within two years the average government debt (otherwise called 'sovereign', 'national', 'state' or 'public' debt) for the twenty-eight member states of the European Union had risen to 72.8 per cent of gross domestic product and was still rising. The debt level of Greece, Portugal, Ireland and Italy, especially, had become alarmingly high. By 2009, as economic growth shrank by 4.2 per cent on average in the countries of the European Union, Europe fell into deep recession.

The Eurozone was in a specially difficult position. The early years of the Euro, framed by global economic growth, had been successful. But when the barometer pointed to stormy weather, its underlying structural problem was plainly exposed. Chancellor Kohl's warning, back in 1991, that currency union without political union would in the long run be unsustainable, began to sound ever more prescient. Eurozone countries, their economies of widely varying strength bracketed together by the single currency, were in a bind when economic crisis struck. Currency devaluation in order to improve export competitiveness was not possible for member states. But nor was there a central government, as in the United States, that could direct economic policy, regulate taxation throughout the Eurozone, and – apart from subsidies provided through the EU's Regional Development Fund – transfer funding to struggling, depressed areas.

The logic of the Eurozone pointed to greater banking, economic and political union, implying a central federal government with fiscal powers within a federation of nation states, analogous to the framework of the United States. But precisely this option was ruled out by the deepening popular opposition to any moves towards a federal European state. Any national government intent on active pursuit of such an aim would have invited prompt rejection at the ballot box. As the grip of economic recession tightened, the historic European heritage of national identities became strengthened rather than weakened. So Eurozone countries were left with both their economic and their political room for manoeuvre extremely limited. A return to national currencies, which was likely at least in the short term to prove calamitous for the standard of living, was desired only by a minority. Fear of worse was a motive in itself for clinging to the Euro. But avoiding collapse in the most badly situated countries depended upon bailouts agreed by the European Central Bank, the International Monetary Fund and the European Commission (none of them elected bodies), with the most stringent and incisive conditions attached.

By spring 2010 the debt crisis had carried some countries into dangerous waters. Ireland's banks had financed huge spending on property, but when the property bubble burst and defaults on loans mounted, government guarantees to the ailing banks massively increased state debt. Spain, too, had to bail out banks that had suffered big losses from a housing bubble. Portugal's mismanagement of public funds over many years and bloated public sector left the country with soaring public debts once its economy slumped in 2009. When doubts about capacity to repay grew and interest rates were accordingly increased, governments resorted to swingeing reductions in public spending – with obvious harmful consequences for the standard of living of citizens, and inviting a deflationary spiral of falling revenues from tax and rising debt.

Nor was their plight simply a matter for these countries alone. Together they constituted only 6 per cent of the total gross domestic product of the Eurozone. But the currency union meant that their looming insolvency threatened the stability of the entire Eurozone. These worst-afflicted countries had no means of escaping from their crushing financial difficulties without major help from other countries (Germany above all), channelled through the European Central Bank and the International Monetary Fund. At least, in contrast to the 1930s when each country was effectively left to deal with the Great Depression through its own devices, there was a basis of international support (though with tough conditions attached) throughout the Eurozone shown towards the plight of its member states.

Greece was a special concern. The country's debt was deemed by

Standard and Poor's rating agency in April 2010 to have 'junk' status. Greece stood on the brink of defaulting on its debts and could not borrow on international money markets. It duly therefore became the first country to ask for, and receive, major financial assistance from both the European Union and the International Monetary Fund.

Over the following years a number of consecutive large assistance packages (or bailouts) were made available to Greece and smaller ones to Ireland, Portugal, Spain, Cyprus, Latvia and Romania. The bailout funding arrangements started as emergency rescue measures that were somewhat clumsily labelled as the European Financial Stability Facility (EFSF), then the European Financial Stabilisation Mechanism (EFSM). But they were soon turned into a more permanent bailout fund with yet another similar name, the European Stability Mechanism (ESM). These eased the crisis without solving the underlying structural problems.

Meanwhile, Europe had fallen into deep recession (officially defined as two consecutive financial quarters of negative growth). By May 2009, 21.5 million citizens of the European Union were out of work, nearly a quarter of them aged between fifteen and twenty-four. In Germany, Austria, the Netherlands, Denmark, Britain and a number of other countries unemployment remained relatively low. Elsewhere the situation was often dire. Spain, Greece, the Baltic countries and Ireland were the worst hit, with extremely high levels of unemployment, especially among young workers. Nearly one in five Spaniards were unemployed, double that ratio among young workers. Around two-fifths of Greek youths were unemployed. In Estonia the numbers of the unemployed quintupled in 2008–9, and tripled in Latvia and Lithuania. High unemployment remained the norm in these countries over the following years. In the Eurozone a second surge of unemployment occurred in 2011 just as the initial steep rise had begun to tail off.

By early 2012 one in three Greeks lived below the poverty line. Wages were cut – even the minimum wage was reduced by 22 per cent – as were pensions, and thousands of public-sector workers made redundant. Over 20,000 were homeless. Behind the statistics lay countless personal tragedies. A fifty-five-year-old plasterer who had lost his job outlined his own path from employment to homelessness. 'From one day to the next,' he recounted in February 2012, 'the economic crisis hit me. Suddenly I was fired without any compensation ... Two months later I couldn't even afford my rent. All my savings had gone on paying medical bills for my late wife.' He was evicted from his flat and for four months slept in his battered Toyota. Then he could no longer afford petrol for his car. He had to seek refuge in a shelter for the homeless. 'It was a big step asking them for a bed,' he remarked. 'I felt very ashamed.'

The picture, if not so bleak as in Greece, was gloomy in many parts of Europe. In Italy, where production fell by almost 25 per cent, the recession damaged the economy for over five years – the longest recession since the Second World War. The Baltic states, too, were particularly badly hit. Their previously high growth rates slumped overnight. Latvia had negative growth of −17.7 per cent in 2009. Other Eastern European economies – Lithuania, Ukraine and Estonia to the fore – were not far behind. Recovery to 2008 levels was years away.

Not everywhere suffered greatly from the recession. Countries that had during the preceding boom years managed their economies prudently and had strong infrastructures withstood the buffeting from the storm with minimal damage and recovered fairly swiftly. The German economy soon bounced back. By 2010 growth had returned to a more than healthy 4 per cent. The controversial and painful reforms introduced by the Schröder government a few years earlier were now paying dividends. There had been no big credit bubble, and state finances were sound. Germany had retained a big manufacturing sector. Spurred by reorientation of its major export industries towards new markets, especially in China, and by big reductions in corporate taxes to make business more competitive, Germany was by early 2011 back to pre-recession levels of gross domestic product.

The Nordic countries – affected in different degrees by the economic downturn – also recovered relatively quickly, apart from Iceland. Denmark, though badly affected by the financial crisis, had earlier enjoyed large budget surpluses. The country's fiscal position, with government debt below the EU-recommended level of 60 per cent of GDP, was fundamentally sound. And the Danish government promptly introduced measures to stabilize the financial system. By 2009 the economy was growing again and by 2011 it was recovering strongly. Norway was helped by its major oil exports, which even gave it a sizeable budget surplus. But its financial management before the recession had also been sound. Unlike Britain, which had profligately frittered away most of its windfall (amounting in today's values to well over £160 billion) from North Sea oil on cutting national borrowing, industrial restructuring and tax cuts, Norway had prudently put it into a separate investment fund during the boom years, and reduced public spending while still providing an extremely high standard of living for its citizens. Sweden also recovered quickly and strongly from the global downturn and within two years could register high growth rates (twice as high as in the USA, for instance, which by then was also recovering). Like Norway, its relatively large public sector was sustained through support for the labour market, and there was increased, not reduced, spending on infrastructure, education and social security, health care and unemployment support. Moreover, Sweden had learned lessons from its own financial crisis of the early 1990s and had built a resilient, stable economy that created a healthy budget surplus in good years, affording some freedom of manoeuvre during the recession. It moved quickly to address financial problems, boosting demand through extremely low interest rates and penalties for banks that did not lend. The changes gradually introduced were consonant with those across most of Europe – privatization of former state monopolies, budgetary restrictions, somewhat greater flexibility in the labour market, and less generous welfare provision (notably pensions). But they remained moderate, not radical, and did not break with the long-standing framework of a state based upon a strong guarantee of a high level of social security for its citizens. Like Norway, Sweden could reckon with a high level of consensus across political divides for its economic strategy and implementation. The 'Scandinavian model' (with variations) that had its origins in the 1930s was, however, impossible to replicate for much larger, far less homogeneous nations where the political and social divisions ran far deeper.

Poland was exceptional among Central European states in avoiding the economic downturn. Bank lending there had been low, the property market was very small, and the government had not racked up debt. Moreover, as other countries fell into recession and working conditions deteriorated, two million migrant workers returned home, bringing their savings with them. And Poland was able to increase government expenditure and devalue its currency – remedies unavailable to the Eurozone. So Poland escaped a recession. Slovakia, which had drastically reformed its economy since it had been mired in corruption during the Mečiar era and had successfully attracted much foreign investment, also weathered the storm well.

By mid-2012 the worst was generally over. The Eurozone's fragility had greatly diminished. Psychologically, an important moment came with the crisis still in full flow when the President of the European Central Bank (ECB), Mario Draghi, announced in July 2012 that 'the ECB is ready to do whatever it takes to preserve the Euro'. Under a scheme entitled Outright Monetary Transactions, the ECB announced its readiness to buy government bonds issued by Eurozone member states that had been granted bailouts but regained access to private lending markets. The scheme was of further psychological value in underpinning the ECB's determination to prevent the Eurozone from collapsing. No claims were in fact made under the scheme, since by 2013, apart from Greece and Cyprus, the Eurozone was on the way to a tentative recovery. By then well over 500 billion Euros (more than the annual gross domestic product of all but the largest and richest European countries) had been disbursed to the troubled economies, about a fifth coming from the International Monetary Fund, most of the remainder from the European Central Bank. The lion's share had gone to Greece. But several countries were as late as 2015 still running worryingly high levels of public debt and had sizeable deficits. Greece remained the worst trouble spot, with a ratio of debt to gross domestic product at 177.4 per cent (60 per cent being the maximum theoretically permissible in the Eurozone), and aid was set to continue for years to come.

Other countries, too – Italy (with a government debt of 132.3 per cent of gross domestic product, and no indication of prospective decline), Portugal (129 per cent), Cyprus (107.5 per cent), Belgium (105.8 per cent), Spain (99.8 per cent), and even France (96.2 per cent, and not declining) – still gave cause for concern. The sovereign debt crisis was by this time far less acute than it had been – though only slowly improving.

The Eurozone had survived an existential crisis intact. But was it fundamentally healthy? Could the Eurozone survive another major economic shock that might lead to potential financial crisis in one of its bigger economies, such as Italy's? Was the Eurozone, in fact, from the start a flawed project in its lack of a central fiscal authority? And was its rescue medicine likely to make the patient more ill rather than better? On these issues opinions among economists varied. The Nobel

Prize-winner Joseph Stiglitz was the foremost among those economists who doubted that the Eurozone had a long-term future unless it introduced fundamental structural reforms. Among them he included replacing the economics of austerity by expansionist policies directed at growth, the mutualization of debt, converging economies by removing surpluses to the benefit of deficit countries, and using expanded credit facilities by the European Central Bank to invest in productive enterprise to stimulate the economy. So far, the political will to introduce such change has been lacking.

The Eurozone crisis had, in fact, led in the opposite direction to that advocated by Stiglitz. Vast amounts of money were certainly poured into the economy, though most of it went to save the banks, not directly to stimulate recovery. Further immense sums were spent by the Bank of England (£375 billion between 2009 and 2012) and later the European Central Bank (1.1 trillion Euros in 2015–16) in creating new electronic money to buy government bonds in order to increase the money supply – the method known as 'quantitative easing'. This was a central part of monetary policy once interest rates had been reduced to almost zero, and was aimed at preventing *deflation* turning the recession into a disastrous depression, as had happened in the 1930s. In this aim the method could claim success. The recession would have been very much worse without it. But it was less successful in reviving the economy, largely because banks remained unwilling to lend and anxieties about the economy meant that people were reluctant to borrow. So most of the stimulus remained within the banking sector and did not pass down to the great majority of citizens. The quantitative easing was a sort of neo-Keynesianism, though primarily just to aid the banks. But little else followed neo-Keynesian methods. Once the recession had set in, the remedies largely followed neo-liberal prescriptions – retrenchment rather than expansionism. Debt reduction through austerity was the main message.

Whether that deepened and prolonged the recession has been much disputed by economists and remains an open question. Despite austerity, most countries actually saw their debt, proportionate to gross domestic product, increase during the recession and then only gradually decline. So had there been an alternative? A genuinely neo-Keynesian approach would certainly in the short run have increased public spending and indebtedness. However, investment in productive enterprise, skills, education and training could eventually have produced faster growth and lasting benefits. Where such methods were at least partially implemented, in Sweden, Norway and Denmark, they were effective. But there were special features to these Scandinavian economies, which enjoyed big surpluses before the economic downturn and a wide-ranging political consensus that was difficult if not impossible to replicate elsewhere. The financial room for manoeuvre of these Nordic countries was almost non-existent elsewhere.

Some leading economists argued forcefully, nonetheless, that spending cuts instead of an economic stimulus could only worsen and prolong a recession by throttling demand and reducing taxation revenues, thereby necessitating further cuts and perpetuating a vicious circle. There were, though, obstacles to pumping money into an ailing economy, even if the will had been present. The European Union's own agreed rules on the highest permissible levels of government debt and deficits – even if they were massively breached during the worst of the recession – constituted a barrier to the adoption of an expansionist economic policy in most of Europe. And the EU's pivotal country, Germany, anxious as always to avoid any risk with inflation, was the strongest advocate of sound finance. Germany had introduced the necessary structural reforms several years earlier to put its own house in order, ran the central argument. It expected other countries to adopt similar structural reforms. The Treaty of Fiscal Union, signed in March 2012 by leaders of all the countries in the European Union except for the United Kingdom and the Czech Republic, was forged by Germany and aimed to impose strict, legally enforceable limits on the size of national debt and deficits in accordance with the German financial model of rigid budgetary discipline.

Beyond these constraints on the introduction of neo-Keynesian policies there was another formidable obstacle: the confidence of ratings agencies in a country's financial state. Credit Ratings Agencies based in the United States – the most important of them Standard and Poor's, Moody's and Fitch – could immediately inflict huge damage on a country's financial standing through adjustment of its valuations of credit-worthiness. Adding to already high public debt through increased public spending ran the big risk of incurring the wrath of these agencies, making it more difficult to borrow on international money markets and thereby further undermining the potential for recovery. So containing debt through austerity carried the day in almost all government treasuries.

AUSTERITY POLITICS

As politicians struggled to master the daunting economic and social challenges during the recession, politics became more volatile. The political landscape started to be reshaped. Political fortunes hinged in each country, as usual, on a myriad of national issues. But among them practically everywhere was the question of how the government was handling the recession. Three *general* patterns (though there were exceptions) emerged. The first was that the political party in power, whether on the left or the right, when the recession set in was likely to suffer defeat at the next election. The second was that protest movements outside the mainstream 'establishment' were likely to gain support as trust in the political system was eroded. Millions felt intense anger at the mismanagement of the economy by their own governments, but also at the faceless power of globalized finance capitalism that had inflicted such misery on them. As so often, this manifested itself in the search for scapegoats – usually to be found among immigrants – and in nationalism that offered a sense of identity and belief in an ability to regain control that had been surrendered to international bodies.

A third common trend was that, with a handful of exceptions, governments of whatever colour adopted austerity measures. Government autonomy over a country's economy was severely constrained. Real power lay, it seemed, beyond any individual state with the anonymous manipulators of international finance, the holders of government bonds, the rating agencies, and the institutions such as the International Monetary Fund and the European Central Bank that determined levels and conditions of support for ailing economies.

Although the economic crisis affected every country in Europe, those countries with pre-existing solid economic structures and stable political systems generally came out of recession quickly and without political upheaval (though Britain's high dependency on its flawed banking system was its Achilles heel). This was the case in Germany, Austria,

Switzerland, the Netherlands, Denmark, Norway, Sweden and – among the countries that had recently joined the European Union – Poland and Slovakia. Although economic turbulence naturally played some part in shaping electoral preferences, it figured alongside other factors and was not decisive in these countries. In fact, where governments already before the recession had gained some approval for their handling of the economy, their leaders could be seen by large sectors of the population as the best guarantee against major disturbance. The continued support in Germany, Europe's most important economy, for the Chancellor, Angela Merkel, who conveyed a strong impression of calm control and solid assurance, and her able if rigid Finance Minister, Wolfgang Schäuble, who symbolized economic solidity, was one instance of this. Not only conservative parties such as the Christian Union in Germany continued in power; in Norway, for instance, the Labour Party remained the dominant political force.

Even where political stability prevailed, new political parties or older radical parties that had previously been on the fringes attracted greater popularity. Some felt betrayed by social democracy's adoption of economic policies that they associated with the neo-liberal ideas of conservatism and turned to the more radical left. But the chief gainers were the populist movements on the right. In Germany the unpopularity of Schröder's reforms still rankled among Social Democrats, who lost support to the more radical left-wing party Die Linke, while the Alternative für Deutschland, a new party on the right that opposed the Euro and the bailouts for Greece, soon started to gain eye-catching support. In Finland the major hallmark of the 2011 elections was the breakthrough of the Finns Party, a nationalist party that gained support for its opposition to a bailout for Portugal and its attempt to combat the harmful globalization that it associated in good measure with the politics of the European Union. The financial crisis in Iceland led to widespread popular protests that saw the liberal-conservative Independence Party lose a third of its support in the 2009 elections and fall from office after eighteen years in government. In Belgium the economic downturn exacerbated the long-standing and deepening linguistic and cultural differences between the wealthier Flemish and poorer, former industrial Walloon (French-speaking) regions, leading to further political fragmentation and an inability for almost a year in 2010–11 to form any national government at all.

Among some of the newer member states of the European Union in Central Europe the recession encouraged a reversion towards forms of authoritarianism, whether of the right or the left. In Hungary the election in April 2010 saw big losses for the Socialist Party. Viktor Orbán's conservative Fidesz party returned to power with a large enough parliamentary majority to push through a nationalist agenda and constitutional changes that cemented Orbán's hold on power, restricting a number of liberal freedoms and making inroads into the independence of the judiciary. An alarming accompaniment was the rise to nearly 17 per cent of the vote of Jobbik, a party of the extreme right that prompted strong echoes of the fascist past in its antisemitism and hostility to Roma.

Poland, too, was moving towards authoritarianism of the national-conservative right. The crisis in Europe gave long-standing political rivalries dating back to the post-communist transition a new, sharper edge. Both of the new parties founded in 2001, Civic Platform and Law and Justice, had arisen from the legacy of Solidarity, though with very different agendas. The liberal, free-market orientated and strongly pro-European Civic Platform had won most votes in the elections of 2001 and 2007. But its bitter rival, the strongly national-conservative, anti-liberal, Law and Justice Party, dominated by the twins Lech and Jarosław Kaczyńsky, widened the earlier base of support (extensive especially in eastern Poland) for its reactionary social programme in 2011 and went on to make big gains as the victor of the 2015 general election. Beata Szydło became the new Prime Minister.

Conspiracy theories contributed to the party's success. In April 2010 Lech Kaczyńsky, then Poland's President, had been killed in an air crash when flying to Smolensk in western Russia to commemorate the murder of over 20,000 Polish officers by the Soviet secret police seventy years earlier. Bad weather conditions and pilot error were to blame for the crash. But the Law and Justice Party continued to claim that the President had been deliberately killed by the nebulous forces of liberalism, communism or a weird amalgam of both. The claim was incorporated in the party's growing assault on Poland's liberals, hostility towards free-market capitalism and a more critical attitude to the European Union – all part of a heavy emphasis on 'true' Polish values. The migrant crisis fitted into the new climate. The surviving twin, Jarosław Kaczyńsky, the strongman of Law and Justice, spoke before the 2015 election of the danger of migrants carrying cholera to Europe and spreading 'various parasites'. Authoritarian tendencies were unmistakable. Since becoming the governing party, Law and Justice has taken steps to curtail media freedom, to limit gay rights, and to increase political control of the judiciary.

In Romania the trend, following big protests about austerity policies and the fall of the conservative government held responsible for them, was also towards more authoritarian government, though here it was on the left, under the nominally social democratic Prime Minister, Victor Ponta. Under his aegis the powers of the constitutional court were weakened, the legal system was subjected to greater political influence, former members of the security services were retained in important positions, and corruption continued to flourish unabated. The key problem in Bulgaria was not authoritarianism, but government weakness, with widespread mass demonstrations against austerity politics and against the continuing unbridled corruption and organized criminality.

Parties presiding over austerity could also expect electoral rejection in the biggest western countries in the European Union. In Italy, Silvio Berlusconi's government introduced cuts in public expenditure in autumn 2011 but proved incapable of offering anything that resembled a coherent programme for recovery. Berlusconi resigned in November and was replaced by a 'technocratic' government under Mario Monti, a financial expert and former European Union commissioner, who introduced further incisive spending cuts and tax rises. But the state of the economy worsened, mass protests (based upon the 'Occupy Wall Street' movement that had begun as an American protest at the financial crisis) grew, and Berlusconi announced that he was going to return to politics. Monti lasted only a year before resigning in December 2012. He had been backed by leaders of the European Union and by the International Monetary Fund. The German government, the key player in the European Union, also strongly supported Monti. Among the Italian public it was a different story. Monti had been persuaded to stand at the head of a new party, Civic Choice, but won only 10 per cent of the vote at the election in February 2013. That ended his brief spell in the limelight.

The election produced a political stalemate, leading some Italian commentators to remark that the country was ungovernable. Its most striking feature was the sudden rise, to garner a quarter of the vote, of a completely new protest party led by the comedian Beppe Grillo. That a comedian should gain such political prominence seemed a fitting commentary on Italian politics. After lengthy negotiations an unstable coalition under Enrico Letta, from the Democratic Party, who promised an end to austerity and a turn to policies of growth, was finally formed. Gunshots fired at the Prime Minister's office on the day the cabinet was sworn in did not augur well. Silvio Berlusconi's party, People of Freedom, lost heavily compared with the election of 2008; but it still won almost a third of the seats in both chambers of parliament. There would this time, however, be no further comeback for the great survivor. Convicted of tax fraud in August 2013, Berlusconi's age – he was seventy-five by this time – saved him from prison. But he was barred from public office and expelled from the Senate.

France was no exception to the rule that those held responsible for the crisis were dispatched from power. Between 2008 and 2012 unemployment rose to worrying levels, poverty grew, the debt climbed continuously, as did the trade deficit, while growth scarcely crept above zero, consumer spending fell, and tax revenue declined. Failure to halt the economic malaise was the main reason for the narrow defeat in the presidential election of 2012 of President Nicholas Sarkozy, an increasingly divisive figure discarded after only a single term in office following his election in 2007.

The victory in the presidential election of 2012 of François Hollande, leader of the Socialist Party, was accompanied by optimism, among the 52 per cent of the electorate who had supported him in the second round of voting on 6 May 2012, that he would revitalize the economy. When the Socialist Party gained ninety-four seats in the National Assembly in parliamentary elections a month later, a new approach to the crisis seemed certain. But modest state intervention to try to stimulate the economy did nothing to dent the worsening malaise. A super-tax of 75 per cent income of more than a million Euros a year was abandoned after two years. It had raised too little to affect the economy, but was criticized for alienating the top innovators and entrepreneurs that France needed.

Emmanuel Macron, who subsequently became Hollande's Economics Minister (and in 2017 would be elected as President), warned that it would turn France into 'Cuba without the sun'.

By then, much like his Socialist predecessor François Mitterrand had done in the early 1980s, Hollande had effectively reversed his economic strategy, moving in January 2014 to a more business-friendly, partially neo-liberal agenda of reducing labour costs and cuts in public spending. But Hollande was able neither to improve his own dwindling popularity, nor turn round the fortunes of a still worsening economy. As his hapless presidency dragged on and anger at the lack of improvement in the country's plight mounted, Hollande became the most unpopular president in the history of the Fifth Republic. By November 2016 his approval ratings stood at a record low of 4 per cent. On 1 December he became the first French president to announce that he would not be standing for re-election.

In run-down former industrial regions of France's north and east, and in poor parts of the south, many voters were meanwhile finding appeal in the nationalist, anti-Brussels message of Marine le Pen. She endeavoured with some success to detoxify the racist, neo-fascist image of her father, Jean-Marie. Her party, the Front National, won the highest proportion of the votes – almost 25 per cent – of any French party in the election to the European Parliament in May 2014. It was a sign that French politics would continue to be deeply unsettled.

In Britain the Labour Party, in office since 1997, paid the price for presiding over the banking debacle. As the lasting consequences of the banking crash became clear and Britain faced long years of recovery from such a severe economic recession, the Conservatives made great capital out of blaming Labour for the crisis, even though it was obviously global not national in its causes. And both state debt and the deficit on spending had been at manageable levels before the crisis. But the charge stuck. Another effective criticism was that Labour had failed to impose sufficient regulation on the banks, thereby encouraging the speculative bubble that led to the crisis. There was more substance to this charge. However, the Conservatives favoured deregulation even more than the Labour government had done, and had indeed themselves abruptly deregulated financial markets in the so-called 'Big Bang' of 1986 that had turned the City of London into such a vital centre of global finance. And, like Labour, the Conservatives would have felt compelled to rescue the banks in order to protect savers.

The undeniable reality, even so, was that the crash had happened under a Labour government. And since the initial financial crash the budget deficit had doubled while the level of government debt had also sharply increased. The increasingly beleaguered Labour government under Gordon Brown suffered defeat at the general election of 6 May 2010 and after an absence of thirteen years the Conservative Party, led by David Cameron as Prime Minister, returned to power, though only as the major force in a coalition with the Liberal Democrats and their leader Nick Clegg. Under the direction of the Chancellor of the Exchequer, George Osborne, the new government promptly embarked upon an austerity course to bring the deficit and government debt under control. The deficit did gradually and continually fall over the next four years, from 10.8 to 5.1 per cent of gross domestic product, though this was still well over Maastricht guidelines. Government debt, on the other hand, rose every year from 2010 to 2015, when it stood at 87.5 per cent of gross domestic product.

Recovery was painfully slow. Britain in recession was paying the price for tilting its economy since the 1980s so strongly away from manufacturing towards finance. Unlike the countries of the Eurozone, Britain had control over its own currency. It moved rapidly towards monetary easing. But despite the fall in value of the pound sterling by around a quarter between 2009 and 2013, exports remained sluggish and investments levels low. Unemployment fell, but many of the jobs available were poorly paid and insecure. Britain after 2010 had introduced the most severe fiscal consolidation of any of the large advanced economies but took longer to recover than any apart from Italy. When, finally, in 2013 modest growth started to return, it was in good measure dependent upon a buoyant housing market, consumer spending – much of it increasing private debt – and state expenditure which, despite austerity, it had proved impossible to cut as much as the government had initially intended.

The social cost of austerity politics was high. Most of it was paid by the poorer sections of society. Funding cuts in public services, largely passed on to local government, resulted in the closure of youth services, children's centres, libraries, and other important facilities that sustain social cohesion. The recession magnified social divisions. The fact that several members of the cabinet, including David Cameron and George Osborne, had been educated at some of England's most expensive public schools, burnished an image of a political elite that was completely detached from ordinary people who, as austerity started to bite, often struggled to make ends meet. The gulf in income and wealth widened. Some 13 per cent of overall income went to 1 per cent of the population – double the level in the Netherlands, for instance. Leading business executives had earned forty-seven times the average income of their staff in 1998; by 2014 this had grown to 143 times as much. And their income was increasing at a rate more than four times faster than the average earner. The median pay of top executives was now £4.4 million a year. Median earnings of the population was £26,000 per annum. Household income measured by what it would buy was nearly 6 per cent lower in 2013 than it had been in 2010. Average income for the worst-off 20 per cent of households lagged far below levels in the Netherlands, France and Germany. Yet in the most desirable parts of London property values were rising by more than 20 per cent a year, and the weekly rent for a luxurious house in plush Mayfair could cost more than most individuals would earn in a year.

Fewer people were able to buy their own homes and were compelled to live in often sub-standard rented property with too little protection from unscrupulous landlords. The neglect of house-building by successive governments over many years – and the absence of any social housing programmes to replenish the stock sold off since the Thatcher era – made itself acutely felt during the recession. Britain was one of the wealthiest countries in the world, but increasing numbers of citizens did not even have a roof over their heads. Those forced to sleep on the streets more than doubled in number in London between 2010 and 2017, and increased sharply in other major cities. The use of food banks to provide meals for the destitute rose by 1,642 per cent over the same period.

Riots in some cities in 2011 reflected anger and frustration – as well as criminal opportunism – among some of the most deprived sectors of society, including many youths from immigrant families living on desolate housing estates, who saw no future for themselves. They were at the social extremes. But as economic conditions worsened, attitudes hardened. Scapegoats were sought. Immigrants and the European Union were among them. They neatly joined together to offer a basic message to the

growing numbers who were turning to UKIP, the United Kingdom Independence Party – essentially the British (actually in the main *English*)
form of a nationalist, anti-globalization party of which versions could be
found in many parts of Europe. 'There's Poles and Nigerians moved into
this street,' said one woman, a supervisor at a London supermarket on a
very modest income but with a house that had nearly quadrupled in price
since she and her husband had bought it back in 1997. 'Nice people, work
hard, buy their homes. But why are they here when we need the homes
and the jobs? If we were out of Europe, we could put a stop to it.' Here
was the germ of the growing hostility towards the European Union:
'Euroscepticism', still a minority view in 2005, that was turning into outright 'Europhobia' and spreading.

The countries worst hit by the Great Recession – Portugal, Spain, Ireland and, more than anywhere else, Greece – saw establishment parties
struggle as they contended with grave and mounting economic crisis.
The Socialists, who had proposed spending cuts and sought a bailout,
were ousted from government in Portugal, amid widespread anger and
mass protests, in 2011. But the replacement government, led by the
centre-right Social Democrats, imposed its own severe austerity measures as Portugal's plight went from bad to worse. It paid the price in turn
at the election of October 2015, when the Socialists returned to head an
unstable minority government. In Spain the Socialist Party, compelled by
deepening crisis to introduce austerity policies despite its early intention
to provide a financial stimulus, lost almost four-fifths of its support at
the November 2011 election. After imposing still harsher austerity, and
beset, too, by corruption scandals, the conservative government that succeeded it paid the price in the 2015 election, losing a third of its
parliamentary seats. But the Socialists were also rejected by the electorate. Two outsiders, the left-wing *Podemos* protest movement, and the
centrist Citizens (*Cuidadanos*) party, between them won a third of the
popular vote – an indication of the anger felt at the politics of austerity,
which had undermined both of Spain's major parties. Ireland experienced its own political earthquake when, at the February 2011 general
election, the dominant centre-right Fianna Fáil party, held responsible
for the country's financial plight, suffered its worst defeat since the 1920s.
Its main rival, the liberal-conservative Fine Gael, became the largest
party in parliament for the first time in its history, which stretched back

almost eighty years. An indication that the long-standing supremacy of these two parties was seriously weakened were the significant gains too for the Irish Labour Party and the nationalist Sinn Féin.

The level of government turbulence in Greece was exceptional – mirroring the scale of the economic disaster. Elections in 2009, with the economy already contracting sharply, brought defeat for the conservative governing party, New Democracy. Within weeks the new socialist PASOK government under George Papandreou announced that Greece's public debt was far higher than had previously been admitted. The country did not have the resources to repay loans that were becoming due. The ratings agencies then heavily downgraded Greece's credit-worthiness, making borrowing more expensive – if lenders could be found at all. The government responded by introducing draconian austerity measures. Salaries of civil servants were reduced, state pensions frozen and taxes increased. It was not enough. In April 2010 Papandreou requested an international bailout – the first in a series, as it would turn out. The Troika (as the representatives of the International Monetary Fund, the European Central Bank and the European Commission became known) agreed within a month to a loan of 110 billion Euros, though on condition of further severe austerity measures and restructuring of the country's finances. Parliament reluctantly agreed to the demands.

On the streets of Athens huge protests registered public anger. Within a year the protests grew, organized in Athens and other cities by the Indignant Citizens (*Indignados*) anti-austerity movement. Violent clashes with police, who responded to demonstrations with brutal shows of force, increased. Some of the anger was directed towards Germany, seen as the power behind the Troika. Posters of the German Chancellor, Angela Merkel, with a Hitler moustache were a visible sign of the antagonism – absurd as they were.

Support for the main political parties dwindled. Papandreou was forced to resign in November 2011, to be followed by a shaky and in-effective coalition. Inconclusive elections in May 2012 necessitated still further elections only a month later. PASOK, the dominant party in Greece since the 1970s, only attained third place. Second, behind New Democracy (which led the new governing coalition), now came SYRIZA, a radical left-wing party, led by the charismatic Alexis Tsipras. Ominously, on the extreme right, the neo-fascist party Golden Dawn won twenty-one seats in parliament. As some sectors of the population sought scapegoats for their misery, Golden Dawn was able to stir resentment against the growing numbers of immigrants, a good number of them illegal, who had been arriving since the middle of the decade, mainly from Africa and the Middle East.

The remorseless cuts to living standards – falling overwhelmingly on the poorest – continued after a second bailout of 130 billion Euros was agreed in February 2012. The budget for health care was reduced by 21.7 per cent (contributing to a steep rise in infant mortality). The education budget was sliced by over a third of its pre-crisis level. Despite the external help, Greece defaulted on its debt repayments in March 2012. The national debt was restructured, and 107 billion Euros were written off. But it brought little relief. Practically all of the bailout funding was, in fact, necessary to service existing debt – only to incur new. Years of unrelenting and increasing austerity produced ultimately a debt mountain that was greater than when the crisis began.

Citizens were paying a high price for decades of badly run government. Greece had long had a bloated public sector, its bureaucracy was grossly inefficient, and tax avoidance came close to being a national sport. Benefit fraud was endemic. Thousands of Greeks were able to claim pensions for dead relatives. Restaurants demanded cash only as payment. Doctors did not declare a good portion of their earnings. Assets were hidden from view as a matter of course. Nearly a third of the gross domestic product, it was estimated, came from a shadow economy. And Greece's expenditure on pensions, growing more than twice as fast as Germany's or Italy's and allowing most Greeks to retire early from their employment, was running out of control. So Greece certainly had to put its house in order. The rapidity and severity of the austerity was, however, politically and socially hardly bearable.

Even so, still further austerity measures were introduced in 2013. Thousands of public-sector jobs were axed in 2013 and further wage cuts made. By the beginning of 2014 the government could announce that for the first time in many years the budget was in surplus. The news was cold comfort to Greek citizens. In elections in January 2015 they threw out their government yet again. The once-mighty PASOK was by now reduced to a mere 4.7 per cent of the vote. A big swing to the more radical left brought victory to SYRIZA. Tsipras headed the new government (though he needed the coalition support of the small nationalist Independent Greeks party). His winning programme had been to reject outright a third bailout – entailing further cuts – that the Troika deemed necessary, even though there had been modest signs of the start of a recovery. He advocated a fundamental restructuring of Greece's debt and an end to the politics of austerity. His recommendation to turn down a new bailout was backed by voters in a referendum in July 2015.

His Finance Minister, Yanis Varoufakis, whose extrovert personality soon made him well known to television audiences throughout Europe, argued vehemently for a new policy of restructuring debt – meaning in practice debt relief for Greece – and turning away from what, with some justification, he saw as a self-defeating cycle of austerity. But soon after the referendum Tsipras reversed his position and reluctantly accepted the terms of a third bailout – a loan of between 82 and 86 billion Euros to be paid in instalments until 2018. He thought it the best deal that Greece could achieve. Any alternative, he claimed, would have been 'suicide'. Varoufakis, unable to implement the changes he thought imperative, had already resigned in July. The resignation of Tsipras, his popularity falling like a stone and faced by rebellions within his own party, followed in August.

A month later, after it had proved impossible to find an alternative government, new elections took place but brought no substantial change in the constellation, and Tsipras was called upon to head the government again. In May 2016 the initially anti-austerity Prime Minister was forced to introduce new austerity measures. Greece officially ended years of recession in 2014. In reality, however, the country's woes were set to continue.

Had there been an easy way out of Greece's unenviable situation, it would have been taken. As it was, every exit route was blocked off. As Varoufakis found out, fundamental debt relief – surely necessary for Greece's ultimate recovery – faced opposition from creditors who themselves (as in the USA and the rest of Europe) absolved themselves of all blame for making the loans. Mutualization of the debt through the creation of 'Eurobonds' was firmly rejected by Germany and a number of other countries. German savers would not have tolerated the idea and, in any case, it might well have been regarded as incompatible with the German constitution. Keynesian-style government spending aimed at stimulating growth was impossible as long as the debt remained so high and borrowing so costly. And an orderly debt default in order to leave the Eurozone and return to the former national currency, the drachma, though advocated by some economists, ran the risk of devastating economic and political consequences, at least in the short term. Opinion surveys showed that Greeks wanted to retain the Euro. This was almost certainly less out of fondness for the new currency that, after early years of plenty, had been synonymous with enormous national misery, than from fear of what an alternative might mean.

Eight years after the beginning of Greece's woes, in June 2017, after more than six months of wrangling over the terms, the Greek government accepted a further bailout of 8.5 billion Euros to avoid the country defaulting on its debts. The terms included the introduction of some liberal market reforms. But the worst impact of the agreement would fall upon poorer pensioners. Pensions, reduced twelve times since the start of the crisis and by 40 per cent since 2011, were scheduled to be cut by a further 18 per cent by 2019. The expectation was of strikes, demonstrations and political turbulence to follow. The only light at the end of a long, dark tunnel was that, finally, there was an expressed readiness on the part of lenders to take the necessary steps to reduce Greece's mountain of debt and to ensure that it was sustainable in the future. Only then could Greece begin to look to the future with any equanimity.

The worst recession in eighty years had wrecked economies, toppled governments, and brought turmoil to the European continent. But Europe had survived it – if at a great cost, with much difficulty, and with some lasting fragility. There had been no collapse of democracy, no lurch into fascism and authoritarianism (though some of the trends in Central Europe gave much cause for concern, and support in many countries for anti-establishment populist parties, mostly on the nationalist-xenophobic right, would manifest itself over coming years). Civil society, despite the traumas, had proved resilient. And, whatever the policy weaknesses and failings, there had been a willingness to work together to tackle the problems of failing economies in ways that had been missing in the 1930s. There was certainly no room for plaudits. But in economic terms cautious ground for optimism was starting to return within a few years. Politically, the volatility was set to remain. And before the economic crisis was surmounted, or even held at bay, Europe faced another set of crises, this time emanating from the disastrous course of events in the Middle East. And here the limits of transnational cooperation in Europe were rapidly reached. Countries behaved almost entirely in their own national interest.

THE MIGRANT CRISIS

An 'international migrant', according to the United Nations, is 'a person who is living in a country other than his or her country of birth'. In 2015 there were an estimated 244 million migrants in the world, 76 million of them in Europe. They had moved and resettled (for the most part legally) for a wide range of reasons: to avoid conflict, discrimination and violation of human rights; also to escape unemployment, poverty or famine in search of a better life; or simply for new job opportunities. Most migrants are not classified as 'refugees'. The total number of refugees was far smaller, worldwide some 19.5 million in 2014 (about 8 per cent of migrants). An indeterminate number of the migrants to Europe in 2015–16 were driven solely or mainly by economic motives. But Europe's migrant crisis was first and foremost a refugee crisis – of persons fleeing from war, persecution and forced uprooting from their homes, seeking asylum in European countries. Many, indeed, had already acquired the status of 'refugee' before travelling to Europe. Reports on the refugee crisis tended, therefore, to use the terms 'asylum seeker' and 'migrant' interchangeably.

By 2006 the number of those seeking asylum in the European Union had fallen to below 200,000. But from 2007 onwards the numbers increased gradually and reached crisis point in 2015, when the annual figure totalled around 1.3 million. More than half of the asylum-seekers came from three countries, Syria, Afghanistan and Iraq, each of them suffering grievously from war – for which the West bore a significant part of the responsibility.

Hugely overblown Western hopes in 2011 that popular uprisings against authoritarian rule in the Middle East – quickly labelled the 'Arab Spring' – would bring freedom, democracy and peace to this most turbulent part of the world, had quickly evaporated. Some powerful rulers – President Zine al-Abidine Ben-Ali in Tunisia, Colonel

Muammar al-Gaddafi in Libya, and President Hosni Mubarak in Egypt – had indeed been toppled. But Libya descended into prolonged political chaos and in Egypt, under the former head of the armed forces, Abdel Fattah el-Sisi, the military were soon back in control. It seemed for a time that huge protests in Damascus and other Syrian cities would bring about the fall of the regime of President Bashar al-Assad (who had succeeded his father, Hafis, in 2000 as head of state). The West took it for granted for a time that Assad would be ousted. But the regime he headed was far from ready to crumble. And meanwhile, out of the chaotic descent into wholesale violence following the Western invasion of Iraq in 2003, promoted by American mismanagement of the country after the fall of Saddam Hussein, had emerged a singularly barbaric terrorist organization, Daesh, known in the West as the Islamic State of Iraq and Syria (ISIS, usually shortened to IS), a global jihadist movement of unprecedented brutality which by 2015 had extended its terrible rule over large tracts of Iraq and Syria. Millions had fled from the horror. Most found refuge in makeshift camps in neighbouring countries – Turkey, Lebanon and Jordan. But a surge of refugees now also made long and often perilous treks to Europe. By the end of 2015 the numbers reaching Europe in one way or another were more than twice as high as they had been the previous year.

Most refugees passed through the eastern Mediterranean and the Balkans, or through North Africa. Many gave the last money they possessed to unscrupulous traffickers who ferried them across the Mediterranean to Greece and Italy in dangerously overcrowded flimsy vessels. One of them, Ali, fleeing from Iraq with his four children, paid smugglers in Turkey 8,000 Euros for five places on a big sea-going yacht to bring them to safety in Greece. When they turned up at the isolated beach, however, there was no sign of the impressive-looking yacht. Instead, they were forced at pistol point to climb on board a small boat already laden with another eleven people. Halfway across to the Greek island of Kos the engine failed, the boat started to gather water and eventually sank. Greek coastguards were able to rescue some of those on board. But two of Ali's children were not among the survivors; he could only watch as he lost them to the dark waters of the Aegean. This was only one of the countless human tragedies of the refugee crisis. In 2015 alone no fewer than 3,600 migrants were drowned as they tried to get to Europe. And over the vast area of the Mediterranean and Aegean the people smugglers invariably stayed one step ahead of policing operations.

Syrians attempting to reach Europe by boat joined large numbers of migrants from war-torn regions of Africa, and thousands of economic migrants trying to escape from poverty in Bangladesh, passing through Libya (where migrant smuggler networks could exploit the anarchic lack of control over Libya's ports) to cross from North Africa to Italy and Greece. In 2015 these two countries – Greece still suffering greatly from the impact of the economic crisis – saw close to a million migrants land on their shores. Given the numbers, there was no way to check systematically the legality of those claiming refugee status. Most migrants wanted to head northwards. Germany and Sweden were their most favoured destinations. But they would soon discover big barriers in their way.

Border controls, dismantled in much of Europe since the creation of the Schengen Area back in the 1980s, returned to Europe – at least temporarily. In autumn 2015 in Central Europe, on the main migrant passages from the Balkans, Austria set up controls on its borders with Hungary and Slovenia while Hungary began construction of a high fence along its border with Serbia and also blocked its border with Croatia. Slovenia, after vain attempts to stop migrants entering the country from Croatia, also erected a fence. Slovakia set up temporary border controls with Hungary and Austria, Germany with Austria, the Netherlands with Germany. In Northern Europe, too, border controls were reintroduced – by Denmark, on its border with Germany, and by Sweden on its border with Denmark. Following an agreement reached between France and Britain in 2003 by which border checks were carried out on the French side of the English Channel, around 7,000 asylum-seekers who were trying to get to Britain, after travelling through the Schengen Area, found themselves cooped up in squalid, insanitary and inhumane conditions near Calais in a detention centre dubbed 'The Jungle'. Harrowing reports about the appalling existence in 'The Jungle' and the desperate attempts, sometimes resulting in loss of life, of migrants to board lorries crossing to England, were broadcast almost daily on television. The French authorities eventually cleared the camp in October 2016, dispersing the remaining migrants to other locations within France. But by summer 2017 more than a thousand migrants had once more found their way to

Calais, living there without access to toilets, running water or shelter, again prepared to take great risks to get to Britain.

'The Jungle' did much to protect Britain, not bound by the European Union's policy on asylum (agreed in the Lisbon Treaty), from the refugee problem. Aware of the acute sensitivity of the immigration issues – and in the media and public consciousness immigration and asylum were easily conflated – the British government preferred to spend considerable sums of money (claimed to be £1.1 billion since 2012) on humanitarian aid in safe zones close to Syria rather than on giving refugees asylum within Britain. Only around 5,000 Syrian refugees were granted asylum in Britain between 2011 and 2016. The British government agreed to take a further 20,000 more by 2020. It was a less than generous response, given the magnitude of the crisis.

Hungary's stance was especially intransigent. The country felt it was in the eye of the storm as some 50,000 migrants arrived during August 2015 – though the vast majority aimed to travel on to Germany. The Prime Minister, Viktor Orbán, warned of a 'Muslim threat' to Christian culture, a view shared by much of the population. By early September chaotic scenes on the border with Austria and at the railway station in Budapest persuaded the heads of government in Germany and Austria, Angela Merkel and Werner Faymann, to announce without prior warning that they would allow free passage of the refugees into their countries. Angela Merkel had already indicated that Germany expected to have received around 800,000 refugees by the end of the year (the actual figure, in fact, reached 1.1 million), and had said – to much amazement in other parts of Europe – that there was no upper limit. But she struck an upbeat tone. 'We'll manage that', was her confident message.

Indeed, the early response was highly encouraging. Austrian well-wishers brought food, clothing and water to railway stations in Vienna and Salzburg. Crowds cheered the refugees as they poured from the trains arriving at Munich's main station. Germany swiftly undertook to provide temporary accommodation, give each refugee a small sum of money, and make arrangements for them to learn German. The warm welcome had been stirred in part by the many heart-rending stories of suffering by the refugees, in their homeland and while fleeing from the horror of war. Humanitarian instincts were awakened when a lorry on the Austrian border had been found to contain the bodies of seventy-one refugees, or when photographs circulated in the world's press of the body of a small Syrian boy who was washed up on the Turkish coast. But the long shadow of the German past unquestionably also helped to condition the country's response, which amounted to a complete upturning of the values that had produced the catastrophic inhumanity of the Nazi era.

Opening the door to such a large influx of refugees practically overnight was bound to create enormous problems for overstretched authorities as they struggled to provide even emergency arrangements let alone organize more permanent integration. It was certain not only to raise hackles with many inside Germany, but also to alienate the leaders of other European countries who felt Merkel's unilateral move, made without consultation, had subjected them also to intense pressure from the refugee crisis. Some of the strongest condemnation within Germany itself came from the more conservative, strongly Catholic sister party to Merkel's Christian Democratic Party, the Christian Social Union in Bavaria, where around 25,000 refugees had arrived the previous weekend. The head of the party, Horst Seehofer, bitterly criticized the peremptory decision to admit so many refugees, saying that no society could sustain in the long run the numbers that Germany was accepting. Sure enough, the initial warm glow that had greeted the first wave of refugees gave way in part of the population – especially among the older generation – to coolness and often outright hostility. There was a sharp rise in the number of violent attacks on migrants, including 222 arson attacks on hostels where migrants were being accommodated.

A boost to anti-migrant feeling, and to the extreme right that was ready to exploit it, arose from events in Cologne on New Year's Eve 2015 when large groups of young men, some of them newly arrived refugees from Syria, Iraq and Afghanistan, molested and sexually abused women who were enjoying the revelry. The disturbances prompted an immediate spike in hostility towards migrants, as a torrent of abuse on the internet demonstrated. And on the right there were characteristic voices of doom. One leading figure in the emerging anti-immigrant party, Alternative für Deutschland, spoke in alarmist tones of the events as a 'foretaste of our country's impending cultural and civilizational collapse'. The authorities (which had mismanaged policing in Cologne that night) swiftly took steps to prevent any recurrence of the criminal disturbances. Although the drama subsided and tolerance – outside right-wing circles – was generally sustained, the episode showed the shallowness of the liberal values that had appeared to be well ingrained in European societies and how quickly prejudice and animosity towards migrants could surface – and not just in Germany.

The limits of European solidarity in dealing with the refugee crisis were demonstrated by the unwillingness to accept proposals by the European Union for an equitable distribution of refugees. At the height of the crisis in September 2015, Jean-Claude Juncker, the President of the EU Commission, had presented a plan for a quota system in accordance with relative size of population. But the Visegrád countries (Hungary, Poland, Slovakia and the Czech Republic) refused to have anything to do with it, and within a year the proposed quota system had been abandoned. Nor was there much solidarity when it came to raising funds to aid people caught up in the Syrian conflict. The European Commission announced that it was prepared to spend 9.2 billion Euros to assist the handling of the refugee crisis. Member states were committed to match the funding from their national budgets. Few did so. A United Nations appeal to raise $9 billion in aid to the millions displaced by the Syrian War – estimated to be over 12 million people since 2011 – also fell well short.

The moral high ground that Angela Merkel had occupied in September 2015 was soon eroded when, pressed by the strong criticism of her 'open-door' policy and the need to stem the flow of refugees, she travelled the following month to Ankara to meet the Turkish President, Recep Tayyip Erdoğan, to broker a deal between the European Union and Turkey – itself the recipient of far more refugees from Syria than any country in the European Union. The gist of the arrangement was that Turkey would take in migrants returned from the European Union in return for a cash sweetener of three billion Euros, assurances on provision of visa-free travel by Turkish citizens, and active steps towards Turkey's eventual membership of the EU. The 'Joint Action Plan' that followed led to an agreement in March 2016. 'Irregular' migrants crossing from Turkey to the Greek islands would henceforth be returned to Turkey, which would do everything possible to block sea or land routes for migrants hoping to enter the European Union. For every Syrian returned to Turkey from the Greek islands, another Syrian would be settled in the EU. And beyond the initial three billion Euros a further three billion would be provided before the end of 2018.

There was more than a whiff of hypocrisy about a deal that alleviated pressure on Europe through bribing a country which fell far short of standards of human rights and legal protection expected within the European Union. A year later tens of thousands of migrants were still languishing in dire, inhumane conditions in detention centres on Greek islands or on the mainland. Charity organizations registered increased numbers of refugees suffering not only traumatization from experiences in Syria or during flight, but depression, intense anxiety and even suicidal tendencies. By then fewer than 3,500 from around three million refugees in Turkey had been transferred to the European Union. From the perspective of the European Union that made the deal with Turkey successful.

The numbers of migrants trying to reach European countries dipped only slightly in 2016 from the high point of the previous year. Germany's attractiveness as the destination of choice remained undiminished – 60 per cent of asylum seekers in the European Union headed there, slightly more in fact than in 2015. But a number of other countries – among them Sweden, Finland, Denmark, Hungary, Austria, the Low Countries – saw big decreases ranging between 53 and 86 per cent. The migrant crisis started to recede in Germany too. The numbers crossing from Libya to Italy remained high, however, though they fell sharply in the summer of 2017 following the introduction of a tougher Italian and Libyan stance towards traffickers but also a less liberal approach to rescue organizations. Possibly, the worst of the refugee crisis was over. European countries had to recognize, even so, that mass migration – if not in the critical and uncontrolled dimensions of 2015–16 – was here to stay. This was not just because Europe constituted a peaceful haven for those whose lives had been ruined by war and devastating political violence; it was also because the crass economic disparities that had become ever more glaringly obvious in the process of globalization had themselves ensured a population transfer from poor to rich countries which needed labour and whose own birth rates were low or even in decline.

A price that the European Union had to pay for its deal with Turkey was that it became unhealthily dependent upon a country that had played a part in aiding jihadists in Syria, had a dubious record on human rights and legality (as witnessed by the mass arrests in 2016 of tens of thousands of citizens following an attempted military coup against President Erdoğan), and was becoming both more authoritarian and gradually more Islamic. As relations between the European Union and Turkey worsened during 2016 – there was talk of economic sanctions against Turkey because of arrests and limits on press freedom after the coup attempt, and of freezing access negotiations – Erdoğan threatened to open the border gates to let the refugees travel to Europe. It did not happen, and, although Turkey remained in theory a candidate for eventual entry to the European Union, the protracted negotiations to that end had in reality stalled. The refugee crisis had, even so, strengthened Turkey's hand and weakened the position of the European Union.

THE THREAT OF TERRORISM

The daily horror in Syria, filling the news channels each evening, intensified the thirst for revenge among an alienated, deeply disaffected small minority within the Muslim communities of Western European countries against societies whose values they utterly rejected and which in their eyes had inflicted such harm on the Muslim world. Consistent Western backing for Israel (despite the illegality of its settlement policy in the eyes of most of the international community) and lack of support for the Palestinians in the unending conflict had for long fed the growing alienation. The recent invasions of Afghanistan and Iraq had significantly added to it. Then there had been the intervention in Libya. The Syrian War came on top of all this. The internet provided a potent vehicle for spreading messages of hate. Some potential jihadists travelled to Syria and returned as hardened veterans ready to carry out terrorist attacks or equipped to indoctrinate malleable individuals to do the work for them. Some, whose numbers alarmist voices were swift to exaggerate, mingled among the refugees finding their way to Europe.

But the majority of those prepared to carry out terrorist attacks were home-grown, often radicalized by their personal experiences in the poor suburbs of big cities, sometimes from immigrant families which had endured discrimination for decades in the countries that had become their permanent homes. The primary motivation for terrorist attacks was usually impossible to determine with any precision, beyond the obvious purpose of instilling fear and attempting to turn communities against each other in mutual hatred in order to promote a 'clash of civilizations' that would undermine the foundations of Western liberal society. The perpetrators saw their ghastly actions as part of a perceived cosmic struggle between 'believers' and the 'godless'. In perverted logic, they could adjudge the killing of innocent bystanders, even children, to be retaliation for the deaths of innocent Muslims through Western weaponry during wars in the Middle East.

France suffered more grievously than any other country in Western Europe. The Algerian War had left lasting scars of division and discrimination. And France's uncompromising insistence on compliance with the secularized values of the Republic were a particular provocation to many Muslims. The imposition in 2011 of a ban on covering the face in public places was not confined to Muslims, but it affected Muslim women disproportionately. So there were specific grounds for resentment in France that did not apply in other countries. In addition, the socially deprived *banlieus* of Paris and other big cities provided fertile soil for hatred to germinate, spawned by the barely concealed racism of a sizeable sector of the population. Beyond these social grievances, the disastrous course of events in the Middle East offered a fertilizing agent.

On 7 January 2015 two gunmen from the Yemeni branch of Al-Qaeda entered the building in Paris of the satirical magazine *Charlie Hebdo* and opened fire with automatic rifles, killing twelve (including the editor-in-chief Stéphane Charbonnier) and injuring another eleven people. The gunmen, born in Paris of Algerian immigrant parents, were themselves shot dead by police, though not before they had killed another four people and injured several others in the aftermath of their initial attack. On the evening of 13 November 2015 coordinated terrorist attacks were perpetrated in Paris in cafés and restaurants and outside the Stade de France football stadium, when suicide bombings and mass shootings left 130 people dead and hundreds injured, including eighty-nine people killed while attending a rock concert at the Bataclan theatre in Paris. And on 14 July 2016 France experienced a new kind of horror when a heavy lorry was deliberately driven into a crowd of people in Nice as they celebrated Bastille Day, killing eighty-six people and injuring 434 others. A horrifying attack of a different kind took place on the morning of

Tuesday 26 July when two terrorists burst into the Catholic church in a quiet suburb of Rouen, in northern France, and, shouting praise to Allah, cut the throat of an eighty-five-year-old priest as he celebrated mass. The shock waves from these attacks ran through the entire continent – and the wider Western world.

Whatever the specific components of France's exposure to terrorism, the menace was a general one. Brussels suffered horrific attacks at the airport and an Underground station on the morning of 22 March 2016, when thirty-two innocent people (and three suicide bombers) were killed and 340 people left injured. Visitors enjoying a Christmas market in Berlin in December 2016 were the victims of an indiscriminate attack, reminiscent of the summer devastation in Nice, when a lorry drove at speed into the crowd, killing twelve and injuring another fifty-six people. Using the similar crude method in Stockholm, a lorry was driven on 7 April 2017 by a rejected asylum-seeker and ISIS sympathizer from Uzbekistan, into a crowd of shoppers, killing five people and injuring fifteen others.

The United Kingdom, with closely controlled borders, was less open to terrorists entering from abroad than the countries of continental Europe. But the deadly bombings of July 2005 had come from within. So did a lethal attack near the Houses of Parliament in London on 22 March 2017 when a car was driven into pedestrians, killing five people and injuring a further fifty. The perpetrator, who also fatally stabbed an unarmed policemen guarding Parliament, was again British – a fifty-two-year-old man who had lived under a number of identities, spent time in prison for violent crime, had worked for a while in Saudi Arabia, and at some point had converted to Islam. Although ISIS claimed responsibility, police believed that he had acted alone. On 22 May 2017, in the worst atrocity in Britain since 2005, a home-made bomb filled with screws and bolts intent on causing maximum casualties, exploded at the end of a pop concert in Manchester, killing twenty-two people (as well as the suicide bomber) and injuring fifty-nine others – many of them teenagers and children. It was carried out by a young Manchester man of Libyan origin, whose recent conversion to Jihadism had apparently occurred during visits to Libya through links to terrorist organizations that had flourished in the post-Gaddafi chaos. And in a third terrorist attack in Britain in less than three months, three young men from east

London drove a van into pedestrians on London Bridge on the evening of 3 June then stabbed several people nearby, killing seven and injuring dozens more, reportedly shouting 'This is for Allah'.

The simple but deadly method of intentionally driving a vehicle into pedestrians was used once again on 17 August 2017 when a van careered down one of the most popular tourist streets in Barcelona, killing thirteen people (another victim died in a subsequent attack in the coastal town of Cambrils) and injuring over 130 others in the Catalan capital. According to police reports, the terrorists had initially been preparing a bigger attack, which they had only abandoned after accidentally blowing up their stockpile of explosives.

Terrorist incidents occurred in Europe with greater frequency after 2014. No country was immune from the possibility of a terrorist atrocity. Not all terrorism was related to the disaster in the Middle East. Nor were all terrorist attacks carried out by Muslims. An abomination in liberal, peaceable Norway that had killed seventy-seven young Norwegians in 2011, most of them as they enjoyed a summer youth camp, was perpetrated by a deranged fascist and racist, Anders Behring Breivik. Many terrorist attacks in Russia had their origins in the war in Chechnya, the worst of them back in 2004 the massacre by Chechnyan separatists of 330 hostages (more than half of them children) in a school in Beslan in the northern Caucasus. However, the perpetrator of the more recent suicide bombing of the St Petersburg Underground on 3 April 2017, which left fifteen dead and forty-five injured, was a Russian citizen from Kyrgyzstan in Central Asia who did have links with jihadist organizations and was said to have spent time in Syria.

Numerous other planned terrorist attacks were foiled by timely police interception or prevented by surveillance from security services. Internet communications were a vital part of the new terrorism, inviting copycat attacks and enabling individuals or groups living in different parts of Europe to coordinate action. The open borders in much of Europe allowed easy transit to venues singled out for attack (and sometimes escape to other countries afterwards). And, whether or not there was actual contact with ISIS or Al-Qaeda, these organizations acted both as a spur to homespun terrorists to carry out attacks and afterwards used them in jihadist circles to advertise their own strength, usually claiming responsibility even where the assailants were acting alone and not under instruction. The major terrorist attacks, appalling and shocking as they were, lacked any potential to destroy Western civilization. They left a profound mark on Europe, nonetheless, adding feelings of physical anxiety to the sense of cultural insecurity that had spread during the migrant crisis. It was an alarming thought that significant numbers of people in Europe wished destruction on the peaceful communities in which they dwelled. In Britain alone, according to estimates of MI5, the inland security service, there were no fewer than 23,000 jihadist sympathizers. Nowhere felt safe from a potential attack.

In reality, large-scale atrocities – though almost a daily occurrence in parts of Iraq or Syria – were rare. Acts of terrorism had been statistically responsible for more deaths between 1970 and 1990 than from 1990 to 2015 (though the numbers, especially related to Islamist extremist violence, have been rising since 2011). So in numerical terms Europe had become more, not less, secure from terrorist attacks. It did not, however, feel like that. The random nature of the devastating attacks – often where crowds had gathered for innocent pleasure – was meant to heighten the sense of insecurity, and did so. The impact of terrorist attacks, preoccupying the mass and social media at inordinate length for days after any major incident, was enormous. Security services and politicians had a vested interest in emphasizing the threat. It was politically more astute to exaggerate a threat than to underplay it and then possibly experience a devastating attack. So the fear of being on some future occasion among those who were simply in the wrong place at the wrong time was greater than the genuine likelihood of becoming the victim of a terrorist attack. Even so, whether through 'threat fatigue', scepticism about the dire scenarios of security services, or simply 'carpe diem' fatalism, civilians rapidly recovered from the momentary shock of a terrorist attack and daily life returned to normal with astonishing swiftness. And an uncomfortable truth had to be faced: in a free and open society it was impossible to provide total security from acts of terrorism. For the foreseeable future, in globalized societies terrorism would be part of the price of freedom.

Two consequences of the migrant crisis and enhanced terrorist threat were of lasting significance. The first was that intensified security diminished civil liberties. Freedom to go places, see things, or move freely was in a variety of ways impaired. Security precautions, warnings, ubiquitous surveillance cameras or physical manifestations such as unsightly blocks of concrete outside public buildings exposed to possible ramming by vehicles became a regular part of everyday experience. Long queues at airport security checks or passport controls were accepted as the unfortunate but necessary price to pay to ensure safe travel. Attending any big public event or even visiting a museum also required patience to pass through security controls. All the precautions could be tolerated; freedom was limited, not destroyed. But life had become far less pleasant.

A second major consequence was that parties of the extreme right gained a fresh headwind. In Central Europe – Austria and Hungary, most notably – where the passage of migrants was most visible, the perceived threat to national culture through Muslim immigration benefited the right. But opposition to immigration was a potent factor in the increased support for nationalist parties also in much of Northern and Western Europe. UKIP won 26.6 per cent of the British vote, the largest proportion of any party, at the 2014 election to the European Parliament. (UKIP had far less success in the British general election the following year, winning only a single seat in parliament on the first-past-the-post electoral system though still gaining 12.6 per cent of the vote.) The Front National was backed by around a third of the French electorate. Alternative für Deutschland (founded only in 2012 and turning from initial Euroscepticism to an anti-migrant party) saw its support rise to more than 20 per cent of the electorate in a number of state elections during 2016. In the Netherlands the Party for Freedom led by Geert Wilders, who sought to have the Koran banned in the country and campaigned against what he called the 'Islamization of the Netherlands', became for a time the most popular party in the country during the migration crisis. Denmark, Sweden, Austria and Switzerland were among other countries in Western Europe to see a notable rise in support for parties focusing on what they saw as a threat from Islam to national culture. Nowhere did the nationalist parties win a majority of voter support. But their xenophobic rhetoric was not without effect on more mainstream parties. Europe, under the impact of the refugee crisis and increased terrorism, was unquestionably moving politically to the right.

The continent was changing. Long-standing liberal values were increasingly coming into question. The seemingly inexorable progress towards greater tolerance over the previous half a century or more was in danger of being reversed. There was some ambivalence, or even outright contradiction in attitudes. On the one hand, people saw the need for collective, transnational action to face Europe's crises. An overwhelming proportion of people, for instance, according to opinion surveys, approved of the European Union's role in providing humanitarian aid and thought individual countries lacked the resources to respond adequately to emergencies. On the other hand, citizens usually looked to their national governments for protection, while the migrant crisis and threat of terrorism contributed to the strengthening of negative attitudes towards the European Union. Open borders – signifying the freedom at the heart of the European project but allowing migrants to pass without hindrance across much of the continent – were now seen by many as a curse, not a blessing. The European Union stood for integration, international solidarity, tolerance and cooperation. But perceived as lacking solidarity, cohesion or effective strategies for dealing with the migrant crisis, the European Union seemed to many to be losing its raison d'être.

PUTIN'S AGGRESSION

While Europe was struggling to cope with the flow of migrants and simultaneously facing an increased threat of terrorist attacks, a different crisis was emerging in the east of the continent. On 18 March 2014 President Putin announced the annexation to Russia of Crimea – ratified by the Duma, the Russian Parliament, three days later. Apart from the invasion and occupation of the northern part of Cyprus by Turkish forces in 1974, it was the only instance of territorial annexation in Europe since the Second World War. Not only did this mark a serious escalation in the troubled relations between Russia and Ukraine: it brought Russia into direct confrontation with the NATO powers of the West. Anxiety spread among Russia's neighbours, especially in the Baltic countries, that Russia was intent on further expansion. The spectre of a new cold war – or even worse – arose. Fear was once again palpable in Eastern and Central Europe.

The annexation of Crimea followed the outbreak of further great instability in Ukraine. The divisions and conflicts in a country that had not known independence before 1991 and had no uncontested sense of national identity had been far from resolved by the outcome of the 'Orange Revolution' of 2004. By 2010 the victor of the disputed presidential election six years earlier, Viktor Yushchenko, had forfeited practically all his support as a consequence of factional conflict, political disputes and allegations of gross corruption. But under the new president, Viktor Yanukovych, the endemic corruption and cronyism in Ukraine even worsened. As in Russia, a number of oligarchs made colossal fortunes by expropriation of property, often attained through bribery, threats or violence. Yanukovych's son, Oleksandr, was among those who made rapid and immense gains. In foreign relations Yanukovych tried to steer a narrow path between the European Union and Russia. Moscow, however, looked unfavourably on Yanukovych's stated ambition to take Ukraine into the European Union, the country's professed long-term aim. And Russian objections could not be taken lightly; for Ukraine was dependent upon its powerful neighbour for its gas supplies. In November 2013 Yanukovych abruptly cancelled Ukraine's planned Association Agreement with the European Union and advocated instead membership of the Eurasian Customs Union with Russia, Belarus and Kazahkstan. It is hard to imagine that he took the step without Russian pressure. It proved a fateful move. It provoked huge protests by hundreds of thousands of people, especially in the Maidan (Independence Square) in Kiev. In their wake violence escalated and government repression intensified. On 21 February, under pressure from the West, Yanukovych was toppled, a new provisional government was installed, and presidential elections were brought forward. Yanukovych fled by helicopter to eastern Ukraine and from there to Russia.

Putin was unlikely to take such a humiliation lying down. Crimea offered a convenient target for a Russian display of strength. It had been part of Ukraine only since 1954, Russians formed a majority of the ethnically mixed population, and it was home to Russia's Black Sea Fleet – the harbour in Sevastopol was leased from Ukraine. Intervention in Crimea would both punish Ukrainian leaders for their anti-Russian stance, and win nationalist plaudits for Putin in Russia. It was inconceivable that the West would risk world war on account of Crimea. The inevitable economic sanctions were a price that could be borne. Such was Putin's calculation.

Within days of the deposition of Yanukovych (now on poor terms with

Putin though still regarded in Moscow as Ukraine's legitimate president), armed men – though without national insignia – occupied the Crimean regional parliament building in Simferopol. A request to Russia for protection of Russian citizens of Crimea duly followed and was granted by Moscow. Over the following days Russian forces entered Crimea. The regional parliament proclaimed Crimea's independence, then on 6 March expressed the wish to join the Russian Federation. This was allegedly backed by almost 97 per cent of the electorate in a referendum held on 16 March 2014. A formal parliamentary request to Moscow followed next day and was met by Putin's announcement on 18 March of the incorporation of Crimea within the Russian Federation.

Diplomatic efforts by Western leaders to find a political solution to the Crimean crisis predictably came to nothing. Nor was Russia deterred by United Nations condemnation. All that remained, short of unthinkable escalation to the point of nuclear war, as retaliation for a plain breach of international law, was the resort to sanctions. Foreign accounts of Russians were frozen and travel bans imposed, but the European Union was limited in its actions by its dependency upon gas and coal from Russia. The sanctions were not likely to bother Putin unduly. And he could live with the suspension of Russia from membership of the G8 group of world leaders. Russia was isolated. But there was no likelihood of Crimea again being detached from Russia. At home, Putin's popularity soared. Russian media trumpeted the 'return' of Crimea as a great national triumph. Even Mikhail Gorbachev said he would have acted no differently than Putin, had he been placed in the same position. Putin's power-politics, a vestige of earlier times, had paid off.

Violence had meanwhile spread to eastern and southern Ukraine (centred on the Donbass industrial region), where ethnic Russians, who had migrated from the Moscow region in large numbers since the late nineteenth century to work in the coal fields, comprised much of the population. Surveys conducted by respected international opinion-research organizations showed that, while pro-Russian feeling was unquestionably stronger in those regions than it was in western Ukraine, only a small proportion of the population supported separatism while the great majority favoured a unitary Ukrainian state. Russian intervention in Donbass was opposed even by a large majority of opinion in eastern and southern Ukraine, and by a majority of Russian speakers.

But opinion counted for little when Moscow was prepared to supply armed assistance to the separatists in eastern Ukraine. And, unquestionably, there *were* activists in local communities of the Donbass who were ready to fight to detach their region from Kiev and incorporate it in Russia. The insurgents were not simply marionettes dancing to Putin's strings.

Pro-Russian protest demonstrations rapidly escalated from March 2014 onwards into armed conflict between separatist insurgents, increasingly backed by Russian arms and paramilitaries, and the Ukrainian government. The violence was unstoppable as long as it had Moscow's support. Separatists stormed and occupied government buildings. The Donetsk airport was shelled. Heavy artillery, rocket launchers, helicopters and armoured vehicles were deployed in fighting that already by the autumn had cost hundreds of lives. In an appalling, related tragedy, a Malaysian Airlines plane was shot down by a Russian-made missile on 17 July, most likely by insurgents who mistook it for a Ukrainian military plane, with the loss of all 298 people on board.

Numerous international attempts to end the conflict, involving the United States, the European Union and the Organization for Security and Cooperation in Europe, including, too, the leaders of Germany and France and the newly elected President of Ukraine, Petro Poroshenko – one of Ukraine's richest oligarchs – produced no significant breakthrough. There would be in all eleven separate ceasefire agreements between 2014 and 2017, none of long duration. The most significant attempt, the Minsk Protocol of 5 September 2014, reduced the fighting temporarily though there were almost immediate violations of the ceasefire that within a few weeks was a dead letter. A second Minsk ceasefire after talks between the leaders of Ukraine, Russia, France and Germany on 11 February 2015 fared little better. Despite the occasional glimmer of hope, Putin, certain of support back home for his stance on Ukraine, remained for the most part unbending, seemingly set on destabilizing the whole of Ukraine and preventing it from being drawn into the orbit of the West.

Poroshenko's aim ran in precisely the opposite direction. His hopes of Ukraine joining the European Union were never likely to be fulfilled in the foreseeable future. The levels of corruption, economic and political mismanagement in Ukraine, and the need for major reforms before any prospect of membership could be entertained, were simply too great for the European Union to entertain the prospect. But the revitalized Association Agreement between Ukraine and the European Union reached on 16 September 2014 (though only scheduled to come into effect two years later) was an indication that Putin's strategy of drawing Ukraine closer to Russia had backfired.

Within Ukraine itself, the forces in the conflict had quickly become well entrenched. Both sides were unbending. In September 2014 the Ukrainian Parliament, in the teeth of nationalist opposition, bowed to reality by granting rights amounting to near-autonomy for the Donbass. Elections held in most of Ukraine on 26 October 2014 brought victory for parties with a pro-Western stance, but separate elections (recognized only by Russia) in the Donbass on 2 November produced, unsurprisingly, overwhelming support for pro-Russian separatism. For the foreseeable future there was no obvious way to overcome Ukraine's territorial division.

Still, Putin would not, and probably could not, back down. He could not jeopardize his standing at home, where, naturally, support for the separatists in eastern Ukraine was presented by Russian media as a matter of national prestige. Anyway, once opened, Pandora's box of Russian-backed separatist violence in eastern Ukraine proved impossible to close – even assuming that Putin wanted to close it. Sanctions imposed by the European Union, gradually ratcheted up at each further display of Russian intransigence in Ukraine, had at first made no significant impact, though after September 2014, when they were extended to finance, energy and armaments as well as blocking accounts and bans on travel, they started to bite, contributing to a worsening of the Russian economy. The West's only other option was to strengthen NATO's presence in Central and Eastern Europe. Troop numbers were increased in Poland and the Baltic countries, and in 2016 military exercises in Poland were carried out. With Russia also carrying out military exercises – if within its own borders – relations between Russia and the West became more tense than at any time since the end of the Cold War.

By March 2017 nearly 10,000 people had been killed (a quarter of them civilians), many further thousands injured, and over a million people had been displaced by the fighting. In the intense propaganda war, truth was an obvious casualty. But there seemed little doubt that Russia had been the main instigator of the conflict. And without Russian backing – even though blatant attempts were made to conceal its extent – the separatists would have been unable to sustain their armed struggle. For Putin, the conflict was nevertheless far from a complete success. True, the Donbass had become largely an autonomous region. But Putin had driven most of Ukraine towards, not away from, Western Europe and strengthened Ukrainian national feeling in the process. Without Ukraine, his plans for a Eurasian Economic Union (as the Eurasian Customs Union had become – an intended counterpart to the European Union) amounted to little. Russia's economy was meanwhile suffering significantly from the sanctions (and from the fall in oil prices). And Putin had perhaps irrevocably damaged Russian relations with the West. So why had he fostered the war in Ukraine, on top of the annexation of Crimea? What was his strategic aim?

The simplest explanation is the most plausible. In essence, Putin sought to restore Russia's lost prestige and standing as a great power. A former KGB officer, he had spoken of the collapse of the Soviet Union as the greatest geopolitical catastrophe of the twentieth century. In his eyes (and the eyes of many of his countrymen) it had drastically diminished Russia's status in the world and its pride as a great nation. Russia's leaders continued to look upon the former Soviet republics as part of Russia's own sphere of influence. But the fall of communism had inflicted humiliation on a once-mighty power in the eyes of many. While the United States bestrode the world as the single remaining superpower, Russia had descended into a mafia state run by powerful oligarchs who enjoyed the wealth of Croesus while most Russians suffered from an economy on the verge of collapse. It had been too weak to prevent the extension of NATO into what had formerly been the Soviet sphere of influence – even into the Baltic states, on Russia's very doorstep. Although in Western eyes NATO was a benign organization, Russians saw it as a danger. NATO's intervention in Kosovo in 1999, viewed in the West as a humanitarian act, had caused outrage in Moscow where it was seen as an abuse of NATO's defined role as a defensive organization to protect member states. But Russia had been unable to stop it. Russia was, in sum, a former great power suffering during the 1990s from a profound sense of national humiliation.

Putin had certainly restored much national pride and internal strength. The conscious invocation of nationalism at every turn provided him with a solid base of popular support – a counterweight to widespread economic discontent. Ukraine and Crimea, part of the Russian empire since the eighteenth century, had been integral to Russia's status as a great power, and later crucial components of the Soviet sphere of influence. Putin had spoken in 2012 of the task of reintegrating post-Soviet space. But the deposition of Yanukovych in 2014 vitiated the aim of cementing Ukraine's dependence on Russia. The response was the decision to 'return' Crimea to Russia as part of the wider aim of destabilizing eastern and southern Ukraine and ultimately the whole country. In this broader aim Putin miscalculated. He had bound himself without an obvious exit route to the forces he had unleashed in eastern Ukraine. Impossible to back down, impossible to go forward, Putin had bogged down Russia for the indefinite future in the quagmire of eastern Ukraine. This probably caused Putin few sleepless nights. He could at least be satisfied that, as long as eastern Ukraine was controlled by Moscow, there could be no unified nation state of Ukraine that might seek to join the European Union and NATO.

At home Putin had won plaudits for his confrontation with the West. The Syrian War gave him a further opportunity to re-establish a dominant role for Russia on the world stage. The Russian military intervention in 2015, the country's first outside the borders of the former Soviet Union since the end of communism, marked not only a crucial step in the terrible Syrian conflict, but also a new stage for Putin to attempt the restoration of Russia's status as a world power.

The confrontation between Russia and the West over Crimea and Ukraine sent fear of a return to the dark past coursing through Central and Eastern Europe. Would it lead to world war? Would Russia annex other parts of Eastern Europe, and perhaps beyond? The fears, especially in the Baltic states that had suffered annexation by the Soviet Union within living memory, were understandable, though perhaps exaggerated. Crimea and Ukraine had left Putin with his hands more than full. Why would he wish to multiply his problems by trying to annex and hold down by force the Baltic states, whose very pronounced sense of national identity was (unlike in eastern Ukraine) in good measure driven by opposition to Russia? Nor was there any evidence that Putin had wider expansionist plans in Europe beyond what he had already undertaken. Intervention in Syria, meanwhile, was a case of Putin exploiting the weakness of American policy to demonstrate Russian strength and influence in the international arena in support of Russia's traditional allies of Syria and Iran. But there is no indication that Russia harboured ambitions for a world role comparable to that of the Soviet Union. Its resources alone would not suffice for that. And restoration of Russian state power scarcely constituted an ideological aim likely to appeal to non-Russians.

The crisis in Ukraine had meanwhile subsided into a disturbing stalemate but posed no significant threat to world peace or to Europe's wider stability. Whether, however, the European Union, for so long an essential pillar of that stability, could itself be sustained, came directly into question, however, as a consequence of a further strand of the continent's general crisis: 'Brexit' – the decision by Britain to leave the European Union.

BREXIT

The fateful referendum on 23 June 2016 primarily, of course, affected Britain. But the impending departure of a member state – the first time that had happened – marked a critical moment in the evolution of the European Union, already under pressure from economic, migrant and terrorism crises, and tense relations with Russia.

'Europe' had been a running sore in British politics for more than two decades, and Britain had long been the European Union's most awkward member state. Even so, the road to Brexit was a short one. A direct line can be drawn from the financial crisis, through the austerity politics and the impact of the refugee and terrorism crises, to Brexit.

Attitudes measured monthly between 2004 and 2016 showed, amid much fluctuation, an average of 44.7 per cent of respondents approving of membership of the European Union and 42.9 per cent disapproving. Disapproval rose sharply from 2010 onwards in the wake of the Eurozone crisis, even though Britain – to widespread sighs of relief – was not a member of the Eurozone. And as many in Britain saw their standards of living stagnate or even fall after the financial crisis, the United Kingdom Independence Party (UKIP) proved increasingly capable of winning support even in diehard Labour areas by linking the economic difficulties of white working-class voters who felt 'left behind' by globalization to 'uncontrollable' immigration from the European Union. A Bank of England analysis at the end of 2015 lent some credence to the claims of UKIP that immigration could depress wages for low-skilled British workers.

On top of this came the refugee crisis. Most British voters felt that the government should be able to control immigration, and that successive governments had failed to do so. This attitude hardened markedly once Angela Merkel had opened German doors – and therefore those of the European Union – to over a million refugees. And it was easy to use immigration to engender concerns about national security. Terrorists who had travelled through Europe alongside refugees were reportedly among the perpetrators of the horrific attacks in Paris in November 2015. Nigel Farage, UKIP's leader, warned that Britain's continued membership of the EU threatened the country's security since 'ISIS promises to flood the continent with jihadists'. A UKIP poster during the referendum campaign pictured a long line of Syrian refugees at the borders of Slovenia en route to Britain accompanied by the slogan: 'The EU has Failed Us All'. This was the extreme end of the 'leave' propaganda, to be sure. But it was not without impact. Nearly half the population agreed that the risk of terrorism would be greater if Britain remained in the European Union. The need to control immigration was meanwhile seen as a priority by a far wider constituency than just UKIP supporters.

So the all-important issue as the referendum campaign began was the reduction of immigration from the European Union. As many as 69 per cent of Britons thought immigration from the European Union was 'too high'. Immigration was coupled with a desire for restriction of welfare benefits to immigrants. It was not difficult for opponents of the EU to link immigration to the mounting pressure on the National Health System, the most treasured British institution, which, they claimed, was being 'bled dry' of resources by 'health tourists' and 'creaking under the strain' of unsustainable current levels of immigration.

This was the unpropitious background to the rash promise of David Cameron, the British Prime Minister, to hold a referendum on Britain's membership of the European Union should the Conservatives form a majority government after the election of 2015. Cameron wanted primarily to blunt the edge of the anti-European lobby within his own party and halt the drain of support to the stridently Europhobic UKIP. He probably reckoned that in a likely post-election continuation of coalition government the strongly pro-European Liberal Democrats would block the holding of a referendum. The unexpected absolute majority that the Conservatives won in the 2015 election meant, however, that he thought he had no choice but to go ahead with the commitment to a referendum. A party-political tactic had become a gamble on the nation's future.

It was a gamble that Cameron, supremely confident in his own powers of persuasion, was sure he would win. He was certain that, as in the referendum in September 2014 on Scottish independence (when Scottish voters had rejected independence for Scotland by 55 to 45 per cent), the electorate would ultimately choose the status quo. Most experts agreed. Cameron staked much on the outcome of a renegotiation of Britain's terms of membership. But to most British voters the outcome, in February 2016, of his discussions with the leaders of the other twenty-seven member states was distinctly underwhelming. People quickly saw through Cameron's claims that the negotiations had brought 'substantial change' to the terms of Britain's membership, particularly on the critical issue of immigration. The European Union had adamantly upheld its key principle of freedom of movement of individuals. Cameron gained only the concession that access to in-work benefits could be restricted for up to four years and even then only for a seven-year period. That was minimal. The widely read tabloid, the *Sun*, rendered its verdict on the deal: 'It stinks'.

Three-quarters of members of the House of Commons favoured remaining in the European Union. Cameron threw all his weight behind the 'Remain' campaign. But important members of his cabinet were given free rein to support 'Leave'. Prominent among them were the Justice Secretary Michael Gove and the former Mayor of London Boris Johnson – a toff with the common touch, whose instantly recognizable mop of unruly blond hair and well-honed combination of buffoonery and verbal dexterity made this product of one of England's most exclusive public schools (Eton) one of the most popular politicians in the land (if a highly divisive figure). Johnson was to play no small part in tipping the balance of the keenly fought contest towards a victory for 'Leave'. Conservative 'Brexiteers' emphasized the restoration of sovereignty and reversion of democratic rights from Brussels to Britain. UKIP's one tune was the populist refrain about immigration. But sovereignty and immigration were just two sides of the drive for Brexit. The arguments pushed in the same direction.

Only a handful of Labour politicians actively favoured leaving the European Union. But the 'Remainers' in the party often trod warily, well aware that many of their constituents were 'Leave' supporters. And a major weakness in Labour's campaign was that the party leader, Jeremy Corbyn – for many years at best lukewarm about the European Union – was distinctly unenthusiastic, if not silent, in his support for 'Remain'.

The mood in the country was fairly evenly split. The 'Remain' side posited almost everything on the likely negative economic effects of leaving the European Union, and the consequences this would have for the living standards of ordinary citizens. A formidable array of economics experts, business leaders, bankers and politicians from all parties except UKIP painted a dismal picture of the impact of Brexit on the British economy. The Chancellor of the Exchequer, George Osborne, conveyed the impression that drastic measures would be needed to combat certain economic collapse in the event of a vote to leave. But 'Project Fear', as the 'Leave' side dubbed it, had little effect. Many simply disbelieved it or regarded it as overblown propaganda. Their scepticism was encouraged when Michael Gove remarked during a television interview that people 'have had enough of experts' who claimed they knew what was best but were 'consistently wrong'. It was a measure of how poorly many people viewed the European Union that the 'Remain' camp never sought to show the benefits of being in the EU. Most crucial of all, the 'Remain' campaign had no rhetorical weaponry to combat the key element of the 'Leave' case: control of immigration from the EU.

The slogan 'Take Back Control' hammered home by the 'Leave' campaign offered a simple and powerful message. And it was not just negative. Alongside the complete rejection of the European Union, it implied a brighter future. It combined in three words the vision of restoration of national sovereignty and the renewal of democracy with the power to halt unwanted immigration.

The 'Leave' campaign resorted to its own scare tactics – on the numbers of refugees likely to come to Britain, the threat of terrorism, the loss of national identity, and the damaging pressure on public services. Some of its claims were blatant untruths: that Britain was sending £350 million a week to Brussels which, when membership of the EU ended, would go to the National Health Service; or that Turkey might join the European Union by 2020, resulting in over five million extra people entering Britain. Neither the BBC, anxious to display even-handedness, nor the mostly anti-EU press did much to counter the lies.

When the votes had been counted and the result was announced on 24 June 2016, Britain was heading for the European Union's exit door. Of the 72.2 per cent of those who went to the polls, 51.9 per cent voted to end Britain's membership, only 48.1 per cent to remain. Scotland and Northern Ireland voted to remain; Wales and, by the largest margin, England, to leave. Older and less well-educated voters predominantly favoured leaving the EU, whereas younger and better-educated voters wanted to remain. A majority of those who described themselves as 'White British', but only a quarter of the ethnic minority electorate, voted to leave. London was overwhelmingly for remaining. So were big university cities (apart from Birmingham and Sheffield). But almost three-quarters of Conservative parliamentary constituencies and 63 per cent of Labour's voted for Brexit. Outside the big cities, England was a Brexit country.

In the immediate aftermath of the referendum, David Cameron resigned as Prime Minister. After a brief power struggle within the top echelons of the Conservative Party, Theresa May emerged as the new Prime Minister. She had been Home Secretary for six years and, as such, responsible for immigration – an issue that remained of central importance to her. She had passively rather than wholeheartedly supported 'Remain'. Once in office, she swiftly showed the zeal of a convert. Her task, she outlined, was to implement 'the will of the people'. 'Brexit means Brexit' was her vacuous mantra. Three arch-Brexiteers were placed in charge of preparing the ground for the negotiations to leave. Boris Johnson, to widespread surprise, was elevated to the post of Foreign Secretary (once a high office of state associated with exemplary skills of diplomacy that few accredited to the new incumbent). Liam Fox, a long-standing militant opponent of the European Union and strong, neo-liberal advocate of free trade, was given the remit of winning new trade deals around the globe to compensate for the potential effects of a fall in trade with the European Union – Britain's biggest trading partner by far. And David Davis, a bluff former contender for the leadership of the Conservative Party and strong supporter of the 'Leave' campaign, was appointed Secretary of State for Exiting the European Union, giving him chief responsibility for negotiating the deal to leave.

In January 2017 Theresa May announced the framework of Britain's departure. It would involve leaving the Single Market (which Mrs Thatcher's government had done much to set in place) and, probably, the Customs Union as well. On 29 March 2017 the Prime Minister formally notified Donald Tusk, President of the European Council, of Britain's intention to leave the European Union. It meant lengthy negotiations with the other twenty-seven member states on the terms of Britain's exit. Most neutral commentators thought the outcome was likely to be damaging to Britain. Even the future of the Union of Great Britain and Northern Ireland was at stake. Scotland's First Minister, Nicola Sturgeon, angered at having Brexit forced on a country that had voted against it, posed the probability of another independence referendum which could break up the union with England that had existed since 1707. And the question of the border between the Republic of Ireland (a member state of the European Union) and Northern Ireland (about to leave the EU) was a thorny one with the potential to reopen the vexed nationality question throughout the entire island of Ireland.

There was shock and sadness expressed throughout the European Union at the British decision to leave. But far more than mere regret was at stake. The departure of one of its most important member states meant the need for serious soul-searching in the EU. What had gone wrong? Had Britain's vote to leave reflected deep faults within the Union? Had Britain been at least in part pushed towards the exit door by centralizing policies and rigid principles that were also alienating citizens in other parts of Europe? How, if at all, could the fundamental structural reforms that so many observers saw as essential for the long-term survival and good health of the European Union be devised, let alone implemented, given the variety of different and often competing interests of member states? Brexit had obvious, if unclear, consequences for the rest of the European Union, as well as for Britain itself. Britain, whatever irritation it had at times prompted among its European partners, had been a leading trading partner over more than four decades, and an important contributor to the EU's coffers. The European Union was, moreover, in far from good health, rocked by major crises since 2008 that had dented its self-confidence and stability.

The crucial need, in reluctantly acknowledging the British decision, was to reinforce the solidarity and unity of the European Union. There was to be no 'punishment' of Britain (as some sectors of the Europhobic British press claimed). But the interests of the EU as a whole would, it was plain, be upheld at all costs. The Union had to be strengthened, not weakened by Britain's departure. Its future had to be consolidated in order to face crises – including that of its own existence – that went far beyond Brexit. As Britain, its negotiating team led by David Davis, and the European Union, whose chief negotiator, Michel Barnier, had long experience as an EU Commissioner and French minister, prepared to begin their complex work in the summer of 2017, a long period of uncertainty for both sides beckoned.

*   *   *

Economic crisis, migration and terrorism were global, not specifically European, problems. The Ukrainian crisis had international repercussions. Even Brexit, as Britain attempted to reshape its global trading relationships, was far from simply a European, let alone just a British, concern. The collective crises over almost a decade had shaken – though not destroyed – the foundations of European civilization. By the summer of 2017 Europe had weathered the crises. They had been checked. But they had not been overcome. Nor could they have been. Since the crises were immanent to Europe's exposure to globalization in all its manifestations, a process that had accelerated so sharply in the preceding three decades, there could be no neat or finite end to the threat they posed to Europe. Economic recovery remained far from robust, high levels of migration were inevitable, there was no patent solution to the acute problem of terrorism, and the potential for great-power conflict had been heightened since the election, in November 2016, of the impulsive, unpredictable Donald J. Trump as President of the United States. Europe's exposure to global turbulence was certain to continue for many years, perhaps generations, to come.

Since 2008 much of what had been taken for granted in modern Europe had been called into question. The stability, prosperity, even the peace that had marked the attainments of decades, were no longer guaranteed. The bonds with the United States, so vital to Western Europe since the Second World War (and since 1990 to most of Eastern Europe, too), were loosening already under President Obama and were directly called into question under his successor. Liberal and democratic values, long fought for, were under challenge. Europe in 2017 was in a fragile state, facing lasting uncertainty and insecurity – greater than at any time since the aftermath of the war. Would it find paths to better times? Or were the ghosts of the past likely to return to haunt the continent?

Afterword: A New Era of Insecurity

*Out of the crooked timber of humanity no straight thing was
ever made.*

Immanuel Kant, 1784

Europe's history since the end of the Second World War has been a heady
mixture of great achievements, severe disappointments and even disas-
ters, as the crises of recent years have graphically demonstrated. It has
indeed been in many respects a roller-coaster ride of ups and downs,
increasing speed from the 1970s, accelerating sharply after 1990, and
careering almost out of control in the new century. There have been
many negatives as well as positives along the twisting route between the
insecurity of the early Cold War and the insecurity of the multifaceted
crisis that has gripped Europe over the past decade. So what might constitute a balance sheet of Europe's history over the last seventy years?

With every caveat, any reasonable appraisal would surely highlight the
massive advances that have been made. The merest glimpse at Europe in
the first half of the twentieth century – a continent torn apart physically
and morally by war and genocide as imperialist and would-be imperialist
powers fought for mastery – shows how far Europe has come since then.
Most Europeans now live in peace, in freedom, under the rule of law and
in relative prosperity. Overt racism is illegal, even if racist attitudes are
far from eradicated. Women's rights to equality with men are accepted in
principle, if often flouted in practice. Gay men and women no longer face
official discrimination, even if old prejudice dies hard. Whatever the
qualifications, these and other cultural changes amount to momentous
progress.

'Only those who have lived in a police state can know what it is like not to live in one,' were the words of the distinguished British historian Peter Pulzer – a child in Vienna at the Nazi takeover of Austria in 1938 before fleeing with his family to England the following year. At that time, even before the war, at least two-thirds of Europeans lived under authoritarian rule, subjected to the arbitrary power of the police. For four decades after the war, Europeans beyond the Iron Curtain experienced life in police states under communist rule. Authoritarian rule still exists in parts of what used to be the Soviet Union. Turkey is turning to authoritarianism. Hungary and Poland are using democratic forms to undermine democratic substance. Still, most Europeans live today in freedom, in democracies, and under the rule of law. It is a huge advance that millions of present-day Europeans no longer have to fear the tyranny of a police state.

To Peter Pulzer's comment could be added that only those who have experienced outright destitution really appreciate what it is like not to be poor, and that only those who have witnessed at first hand the horrors of war fully understand what it means to live in peace.

The European continent is today prosperous as never before. Its material well-being (together with its freedom and relative safety) is what makes it such a strong magnet for so many migrants from war and extreme poverty in other parts of the world. Of course, prosperity in Europe is far from evenly spread. The gap between rich and poor has even widened, not narrowed. Some countries or parts of countries remain relatively poor. Even within rich countries there is poverty. Food banks for the destitute in wealthy Western European countries are a scandal. Even so, the searing, widespread poverty of pre-war Europe no longer exists.

For the wartime generation, the most remarkable development of post-war Europe has been its lasting peace. Today this is often taken for granted. In the early post-war decades, especially, the preservation of peace seemed far less certain. It goes without saying that of course not everywhere has remained peaceful: Yugoslavia was torn apart by war in the 1990s; there has been extreme violence in the Caucasus; and, in the most recent years, eastern Ukraine has been beset by armed conflict. Terrorist violence from within was, in addition, at times a serious blight in Northern Ireland, Spain, West Germany and Italy. Moreover, though Europe has been generally peaceful, the retreat of European countries from empire inevitably left a trail of violence, for instance in Algeria, Kenya and Angola. And the export of European weapons has made no small contribution to turning other parts of the world into hellholes. Still, there has been no general, European war such as destroyed the continent twice within a generation during the first half of the twentieth century. That has been the greatest blessing of all for post-war Europeans.

So the generalization has validity: the rapid and profound change over the past seven decades means that today's Europe is more peaceful, more prosperous and more free than at any time in its long history. Globalization and technological change have contributed greatly to the material benefits felt by today's Europeans. But, as preceding chapters have shown, there have also been substantial negative consequences. Globalization has paved the way for turbo-capitalism. Global investment banks, big corporate concerns and information-technology giants have established their power beyond the control of nation states, and in 2007–8 a bloated and irresponsible finance sector took the international financial system to the brink of collapse. A new 'precariat' of unskilled, often migrant, labour has emerged, taking up poorly paid jobs, able only to afford sub-standard accommodation, and living with constant material uncertainty. The sense of physical insecurity has also intensified as the incidence of, especially, Islamist terrorism – a legacy in good measure of Europe's involvement in wars in the Middle East, and of its imperial past – has increased. It has become ever clearer that what happens abroad can no longer be detached from daily life at home.

If, nonetheless, despite significant downsides change in Europe over the past seventy years has been substantially positive, this derives in no small measure from two post-war developments: NATO and the European Community. A third element – the 'mutually assured destruction' of nuclear weapons – was perhaps most important of all in deterring any descent into another major conflagration in Europe.

The shield of NATO and active American engagement were essential guarantees of the post-war order in Western Europe. Especially since the Vietnam War there has been widespread – often justified – hostility in Europe towards American foreign policy. The image of the United States abroad has often clashed with the benign American self-image of the land of the free as the international safeguard of freedom. But the growth of anti-Americanism does not detract from the indispensable role played by the USA, above all in the early post-war decades, in retaining a strong military presence in Europe. Without it, the western half of the continent would have been less stable, consolidation of liberal democracy less likely, and the maintenance of peace more precarious.

The second vital component was the establishment of what, over time, would turn into the European Union. The complicated pre-history of the EU unfolded less by strategic design than in improvised accretions and adjustments prompted by largely unforeseeable events. The organizational labyrinth that grew exponentially, complex economic arrangements which frequently – not least over farming subsidies – proved divisive, and fears of growing ambitions to build a supranational state, gave rise to much criticism and increasing animosity. But whatever the failings, mistakes and weaknesses the European Coal and Steel Community and then the European Economic Community not only provided the framework for the rapidly expanding prosperity that underpinned political stability: they also, crucially, paved the way for lasting peace by cementing Franco-German bonds of friendship, thereby removing the cancerous enmity that had played no small part in unleashing two world wars. As the pursuit of European integration widened to include the former dictatorships of Greece, Portugal and Spain, and later countries that until 1990 had lain behind the Iron Curtain, the European Union extended democratic principles, the rule of law, and the framework of international cooperation to much of Southern, Central and Eastern Europe. For the countries of those regions that had long been among the poorest in Europe but could now experience substantial material progress, and had lived for decades under dictatorial rule but were now able to develop pluralist democracies, this amounted to enormous progress.

What the European Union has been unable to accomplish is the creation of a genuine sense of European identity. For a continent of forty or so countries, each with an individual sense of identity, culture and history, embracing over sixty separate languages, this is in itself hardly surprising. Perhaps for some EU idealists it has been disappointing. But the obituary of the nation state was, in fact, written prematurely. The European Community, built on economic pragmatism more than political idealism (though for a time the two went neatly together), resulted, as Alan Milward cogently argued, not in the demise but in 'the rescue of the nation-state'. National identity continued to supersede any sense of European identity and has in recent decades arguably even intensified rather than diminished. Crucially, even so, the dangerously aggressive, chauvinistic nationalism that had spawned two world wars scarcely exists any longer. It has been diluted and countered by the gradual increase in transnational cooperation and interdependence.

If a sense of European identity has remained largely an idea and aspiration rather than a reality, it has nonetheless acquired a form of political content. 'Europe', in the eyes of most of its citizens, has come to be largely synonymous (positively or negatively) with the European Union. 'Europe' demarcates the countries of the EU as an interwoven community of nations from those on the European continent – mainly Russia and former members of the Soviet Union – that stand outside it. This 'Europe' is neither the 'Europe of the fatherlands' favoured by Charles de Gaulle (and others), nor the supranational entity that was associated with Jacques Delors; rather, it stands as a unique entity somewhere between. Some continue to look to an ever-widening 'Europe' incorporated in a federal European state as a utopian future. Others, increasing in number, regard 'Europe' with distance and even hostility as a foreign body impinging upon their sovereignty and integrity as nation states. Although in the first post-war decades the need to prevent any possibility of another war was the central ambition of the emerging European Community, that message has inevitably faded over the course of time. This has left the 'Europe' of the European Union in the eyes of many of its citizens as little more than an opaque and detached organization embodying rules and regulations that affect most people's lives, but are beyond their capacity for active political engagement. That opens the door to the politics of nationalist and separatist movements, capable of rousing an emotional attachment that is impossible to construct for the European Union. 'Europe' means for most of its citizens, then, a European Union that they might, or might not, favour. But in reality, their main emotional allegiance is not to 'Europe', but still to their national state or region (or in some cases to would-be independent nation states).

Any attempt to create a meaningful European identity seems destined to face continuing insuperable obstacles. The decline of religious allegiance and the growth of immigrant minorities mean that Europe can no longer be identified with Christianity (which has in any case for centuries been more divisive than genuinely unifying). History, too, will divide more than unify. Multicultural societies mean that Europe has no historical understanding common to all its peoples. In any case, there was never any *European* historical understanding (or mythology). This was invariably national, and even then usually contested by different parts of the population (as the lingering deep legacy of the Spanish Civil War more than eighty years after it began and more than forty years since Franco's death vividly illustrates). The Second World War (far more than the First) and the Holocaust have with the passage of time dominated public consciousness of recent history. Commemoration of neither, however, is conducive to a sense of common European identity. Perhaps the illusive search for a European identity is in any case unnecessary as long as citizens of Europe's nation states are committed to upholding in individual countries the common key European principles of peace, freedom, pluralist democracy and the rule of law; to sustaining the level of material well-being which underpins that commitment; and to striving to strengthen wherever possible the bonds of transnational cooperation and friendship.

But at this point, the assessment of Europe's recent past reaches its finite end. What remains are questions about Europe's future. How will Europe face the major challenges ahead? Will the advances of the past come to be viewed as a largely positive episode that preceded subsequent decline? How far has the project of 'ever closer union' to go when in recent years the popularity of the European Union has diminished rather than grown? And are those parts of Europe – Russia and the countries under its aegis, Turkey and the Balkan states – that lie beyond the borders of the EU and have for centuries never fully identified themselves (or been identified by external observers) with 'Europe' destined to drift further away from 'core Europe'? Not least: can the European Union 'reinvent' itself to overcome current difficulties and stimulate anew the enthusiasm for the 'European project' that was once present but has to such a large extent evaporated? The challenges are substantial.

* * *

'Study the past'. The advice of Confucius adorns one of the portals of the National Archives building in Washington. 'What's past is prologue', runs the quotation from Shakespeare's *The Tempest*, inscribed on the other portal. Studying the past permits the historian to follow Europe's often turbulent trajectory to arrive at the present. But to what is the past a prologue? In a strict sense, there is no present, only past and future. The past is a reasonably well-illuminated path (if with numerous murky corners and diversions into dark thickets) that is then blocked by a large, forbidding gate marked 'Future'. Through a few narrow openings in the gate it is possible to glimpse a number of dimly lit paths leading off and rapidly disappearing into the twilight. Perhaps one of the paths looks a little broader, a more likely way forward than the others. But this is not certain. It is impossible to tell. In any case, that path, too, leads after a short distance only into the impenetrable gloom.

The destination from there is unclear. Structural patterns of development in the past – demography or socio-economic trends, for example – can offer imprecise indicators to how in general terms coming decades might be shaped. But the future is always open. History offers only the most indistinct guide to what cannot be foreseen. Not just long-term structural processes but unpredictable events can produce momentous changes. It is easy to underestimate the role of contingency in historical change. Yet history is replete with issues that have a dramatic impact but hinge upon contingency – the outcome of a battle, unexpected political upheaval, the personality of a ruler, for example. The answer attributed (perhaps apocryphally) to the former British Prime Minister Harold Macmillan to the question asked by a journalist about the greatest difficulties faced by a government – 'events, dear boy, events' – pithily encapsulated future unpredictability, and the difficulty for historians (as for anyone) in turning from interpreting the past to guessing at the future.

By the time this book ends, in 2017, Europe was entering these uncharted realms. The continent faced greater uncertainty and insecurity than at any time since the aftermath of the Second World War. Worries continued about the stability of the banking system and the possibility of another crash. Greece's economy remained in a parlous state. Germany's trading surplus still left the Eurozone imbalanced. France faced challenging, probably unpopular, measures to make its economy more competitive. Poland and Hungary had taken worrying turns towards authoritarianism. Britain was immersed in highly complex negotiations to leave the European Union. The migrant crisis had merely abated from its high point in 2015–16, but was unending and posing especially great strain on Italy and Greece. This was one important strand of the global political problems – prominent among these the legacy of the horrific war in Syria – that were far beyond Europe's scope to resolve. Terrorist attacks in Europe were on the increase and in open societies that placed a premium on democratic liberties could never be completely prevented. International relations were worrying. The Middle East remained a powder keg, liable to explode at any time. Relations with an assertive Russia were still more strained than at any time since 1991. Turkey – deeply involved in the Syrian War – was crucial to Europe's management of the ensuing migrant crisis but was becoming an authoritarian state, moving away from the principles of European liberal democracy and away from its own secularist roots. And the emergence of Chinese power was still an incalculable factor in the equation of Europe's future relations with the outside world.

Since 2008 Cassandra voices had been heard prophesying the beginning of the end of the Eurozone, and of the European Union, the reversion to a continent of rival nation states, a return to the fascism of the 1930s and reawakening of the spirits of Europe's dark past, the danger of revived Russian power, the decline of Europe's influence in the world, an end to peace and prosperity, perhaps even a nuclear war. Donald Trump's unexpected election in November 2016 as President of the United States brought an impulsive, unpredictable figure into the White House – moreover one who had made no secret of his detachment from Europe and its dominant values. His early months in office were deeply unsettling – and not just for Europeans. A potential return to protectionism and even trade wars in the wake of a strongly assertive policy of 'America First' posed a worrying prospect of economic disturbance. But European apprehension went further. Since the Second World War, the United States, especially through its commitment to NATO, had been the guarantor of the freedoms enjoyed by Western Europe, and after the collapse of communism by most of the continent. Even though Trump backed away from his description, during his election campaign, of NATO as 'obsolete' – alarming to European ears – he remained far more ambivalent towards the crucial framework of European defence policy than any previous American president since the war. Europe's place in the post-war order that had lasted since the later 1940s was as a consequence uncertain.

Trump's election also offered encouragement to nationalists and right-wing populists throughout Europe. Their appeal was certainly a matter of deep concern to liberal Europeans, posing a threat to the values that had seemed to be well rooted as the essence of modern European civilization. But Trump's presidency caused anxiety that went beyond even such worries. Possibly most harmful of all, and not just for Europe, was his astonishing dismissal of overwhelming scientific evidence for global warming. How to protect the planet from destroying itself through irreparable damage to the environment from carbon emissions was (and remains) the single most important question facing future generations. This gravest of problems is shared by Europe with the rest of the world, But in his quixotic determination to protect and rebuild American carbon-producing industries, Trump announced on 1 June 2017 the withdrawal of the United States (second only to China in carbon-dioxide emissions) from the Paris Accords on climate control, which had been agreed only two years earlier by nearly 200 countries following lengthy and difficult negotiations. The international agreement had been potentially a major breakthrough in protection of the environment. Trump had driven a coach and horses through it.

Still, peering through the slits in the gate marked 'Future' in the summer of 2017, the pathways ahead did not seem completely enveloped in deep gloom. There were some flickers of light. In the months following the American election, Europe, too, was the scene of a number of vital elections. These gave rise to hopes – though short-lived, as it turned out – that the threat to long-established liberal democratic values from the populist right had passed its high point. Against expectations, Austria elected as its president in December 2016 (in a re-run election from the previous May, which had been annulled on grounds of voting irregularities) a strongly pro-European former leader of the Green Party, Alexander Van der Bellen, and rejected the far-right candidacy of Norbert Hofer from the Freedom Party. In the Dutch general election on 15 March 2017 the far-right anti-Islam and anti-immigrant candidate Geert Wilders did less well than expected – though his party nonetheless won 13 per cent of the vote, and the strong feeling on the migrant issue pushed the existing Prime Minister, Mark Rutte, in order to draw support from Wilders, also into engaging in anti-immigrant rhetoric. In the crucial French presidential election (in two rounds, on 23 April and 7 May 2017), the leader of the far-right Front National, Marine le Pen, who had been gaining strong support for her programme of restoration of national sovereignty, immigration control and exit from the Eurozone, was roundly defeated. Victory went to a fervent pro-European centrist, Emmanuel Macron, who stood for a new start for French – and European – politics. The party he had created from scratch, La République En Marche, still only in embryonic form at his election as president, then remarkably won an absolute majority in elections in June to the French National Assembly.

France appeared to have achieved almost the impossible: a revolution of the centre. Macron's early moves to form a close bond with the German Chancellor, Angela Merkel, with a view to substantial reform of the European Union all at once offered new hope – a way out of the crisis-ridden previous years, and promise for Europe's future. Whether the early promise will be sustained will only become clear over time. The signs are not altogether encouraging.

The British election on 8 June 2017 itself had important European implications. The unexpected loss of seats of the Conservative Party and strong gains for Labour weakened the chances of Theresa May's government pushing through the most radical form of break with the European Union (though this remained a possibility, ardently desired by some Conservatives). At the same time it became unclear exactly what the government (or the Labour opposition) ideally wanted to emerge from the complex negotiations that began on 19 June. Almost as a sideshow, the bubble of UKIP's brand of right-wing populism popped. From being the largest British party at the European elections three years earlier, UKIP failed to win a single seat in the United Kingdom's new Parliament. The vote to leave the EU had removed much of UKIP's reason for existence. The British population remained, however, utterly riven by the issue of its membership of the European Union. Increasingly, it seemed, the rationality – never apparent, in fact – of most likely making the country poorer and weakening its international status in order to obtain probably minimal reduction of immigration (much of which, in any case, is economically advantageous) was being called into question. The rest of the EU looked on with increasing bewilderment at what was generally seen as an unprecedented case of national self-harm. But support for leaving remained strong. How the negotiations on the most desirable new relationship between Britain and the European Union would develop, given such deep divisions both among the British population and within the governing elites, was impossible to forecast.

25. A man holds a Romanian flag with the Communist symbol cut from its centre on a balcony in Palace Square, Bucharest, in December 1989. The tanks in the square are an indication that in Romania the revolution of 1989 was far from peaceful.

26. Opposition to the Maastricht Treaty in Provence in 1992.
In a referendum in September, the French voted only by a
narrow margin to ratify the Treaty.

27. Shells from Serbian forces hit houses in the suburbs of
Sarajevo on 6 June 1992. Thousands of civilians were killed
and injured during the siege of the city that had begun in April
and was to last for almost four years.

28. (*opposite*) The Russian Prime Minister, Vladimir Putin, (*left*) hands President Boris Yeltsin a bouquet of flowers at a farewell ceremony in the Kremlin on 31 December 1999. Yeltsin had suddenly announced his immediate resignation and designated Putin to serve as acting president until elections in March 2000. Putin swiftly decreed that Yeltsin and his family would not have to face any charges of corruption.

29. A huge crowd in Madrid on 13 March 2004 protests at the failure of the Spanish government to blame Al Qaida, rather than Basque separatists, for the attacks on commuter trains two days earlier that killed nearly 200 people and injured around 2,000. The placards demanding peace were directed at the conservative government that had taken Spain into the Iraq War. A general election the following day brought defeat for the government. Before the end of April the new Socialist-led government pulled Spanish troops out of Iraq.

30. (*below*) A violent clash between police and angry demonstrators during a one-day general strike in Athens on 24 February 2010. The strike was staged in protest at draconian austerity measures introduced by the government to try to contain the country's crippling financial crisis and avert economic collapse.

31. An estimated 200,000 Ukrainians, protesting at the government's decision to cancel a planned Association Agreement with the European Union, light electric torches and phones during a mass demonstration on Independence Square in Kiev on 31 December 2013.

32. A Turkish police officer gently lifts the body of a Syrian child, three year-old Aylan Shenu, from the sea in Bodrum, southern Turkey, on 2 September 2015 after a boat carrying migrants sank while trying to reach the Greek island of Kos. Around the world, the picture was seen to symbolise the terrible human tragedy of the refugee crisis.

During the summer of 2017 there were cautious signs that Europe was emerging from its crisis-ridden decade. The Franco-German axis, the historical basis of what became the European Union, seemed likely to gain new momentum as a result of the victory of Emmanuel Macron in France and the probable re-election of Angela Merkel, widely regarded as a pillar of certainty in uncertain times. The prospects for reform of the European Union appeared better than they had been for years. And, meanwhile, the Eurozone was finally once more recording reasonably impressive levels of economic growth. With luck, it appeared, Europe could still be guided to a bright future.

The important German elections on 24 September 2017, however, dampened expectations and brought a further sharp reminder of how quickly the political outlook could change. Frau Merkel was duly re-elected, but the most striking feature of the election – mirroring a trend throughout Europe – was that the establishment parties lost voters while an 'outsider' party, Alternative for Germany (*Alternative für Deutschland*, AfD), gained significant support. The parties of the previous governing coalition (the CDU, its Bavarian sister party the CSU and the SPD) between them lost 105 seats in the Bundestag. The CDU/CSU's vote fell to only 33 per cent of the vote, 8 per cent lower than in 2013 and its lowest share since 1949. The SPD, whose vote fell by 5 per cent to only 20.5 per cent, also attained its worst result since the war. One 'insider' party, the pro-business Free Democrats (FDP), returned to the Bundestag with 5.9 per cent of the vote. And small gains were made by the Greens and the socialist party, *Die Linke* (The Left). But the sensation was the break-through made by the right-wing anti-immigrant party, the AfD, which earlier in the summer had appeared to be losing support but in the general election won 13 per cent of the vote, giving it 94 seats in the Bundestag. It was the first time in over sixty years that an outrightly nationalist party had won seats in the Federal Parliament. In good measure the AfD's success was a sign of the negative response of a sector of the electorate to the government's policy during the refugee crisis of 2015–16. How the result would affect the prospects for reforming the Eurozone (and the EU more widely), which Macron's election some months earlier had opened up, remained to be seen. It was unlikely to enhance them.

The last major European election of 2017, the Austrian general election of 15 October 2017, showed a further continuation of the trend towards the right and also reflected the lasting impact of the migrant issue, which formed a major theme in the election, more so than had been the case in Germany. In this, Austria resembled less Germany than its neighbour to the east, Hungary, and other countries in central Europe. The big gains in the election went to the parties of the right, the conservative Austrian People's Party (ÖVP), which won 31.5 per cent of the vote, and the far-right Freedom Party (FPÖ), with 26 per cent. Between them they increased their proportion of the vote by 13 per cent. Both parties had strongly criticized the influx of migrants from the Balkans during the campaign. The People's Party, led by the youngest head of a political party in Europe, the telegenic and charismatic thirty-one-year-old Sebastian Kurz, itself moved rightwards to address the migrant issue, attacking 'political Islam' and promising to end illegal immigration. The Freedom Party's rhetoric was utterly uncompromising. Its leader, Heinz-Christian Strache, declared that he did not want 'an Islamization of his homeland'. On 18 December Kurz and Strache reached agreement to form a right-wing coalition government. Protests were muted. Austria was moving in step with the trend to the anti-immigrant right that was common to much of Europe.

Of course, all national elections have specific features. But as 2017 drew to a close, the German and Austrian elections accorded in their own distinctive ways to a pattern that could be seen across Europe, and in the United States in Donald Trump's election. This pattern, worrying for future social and political stability, was the rise of populist 'outsider' movements (mainly of the right). They were able to exploit the rage felt by wide swaths of voters against what they saw as an inept, inadequate or sometimes corrupt mainstream parties. Whether this serious challenge to the 'establishment' will lastingly refashion the political landscape, or will gradually subside if economic conditions improve, is unclear.

* * *

Elections that momentarily capture the headlines often turn out to be of transient importance. What will remain, to preoccupy whichever politicians are in power, and inevitably to have a vital impact on future European generations, are the consequences of the long-term interwoven trends that are the legacy of Europe's recent past and of wider global developments. These trends suggest that the new era of insecurity could last a long time.

Arguably the greatest challenge, though at a global not just European level, is to halt the self-destruction of climate change. Something approaching international unity on slowing, and ultimately stopping, further long-term damage with potentially devastating consequences – a task of generations – was finally reached in the Paris Accords of 2015, only to be sabotaged by President Trump two years later. Possibly reason will prevail, even if only at the end of Trump's term of office, and perhaps the United States, such a vital partner, will return to the convention on climate control to play a major part in protecting the environment. Even without American participation, progress – if at a slower pace – will be made, most likely with China profiting from the vacuum left by the USA. The wealthier European countries are already at the forefront of attempts to counter climate change. They will surely do more to develop (and benefit economically) from renewable energy. The transition to a low-carbon economy is not optional. It is imperative to the future well-being of society. But it is a race against time to prevent further damage to the continent (and the planet) in the interests of coming generations.

If sources of renewable energy are not developed quickly, the problem of energy is likely to become an ever greater problem for European governments, and potentially give rise to conflict. Coal, the staple of the Industrial Revolution, now plays only a minor role in supplying energy in most European countries. But oil is heavily dependent upon production in the Middle East, one of the most war-torn and unstable regions of the world. The West's continued support for Saudi Arabia, despite its terrible human-rights record and financing of terrorism, is largely because the country – one of the few in the Middle East as yet (this could change) not to suffer any devastating internal turmoil – is crucial to the global distribution of oil. For some parts of Europe (including Germany) dependency on oil and gas rests unhealthily on the doubtful goodwill of Russia. Atomic energy, following the catastrophes at Chernobyl in the 1980s and, more recently, in March 2011 at Fukushima in Japan, has lost much of its early allure, and is outrightly rejected by the citizens of some major European countries. Meanwhile, the more recent introduction of fracking (following its development in the USA) to extract gas and oil from shale rock deep below the earth's surface is highly controversial on account of its potential damage to the environment and the possible increased likelihood of earthquakes. European countries are proceeding with energy policies in different ways and according to national priorities. But individually and collectively they all face the problem of ensuring future energy supplies if old sources fail, or are ruled out politically, and new sources of renewable energy are not found and rapidly promoted. It is one of Europe's most urgent future tasks.

Demographic change affects every country but is not subject to government control. It cannot be stopped; it has to be managed. But that poses major problems for the future. Decades of low or falling birth rates have meant that in most of Europe population levels necessary for growing economies can only be sustained through immigration. A younger workforce is necessary to sustain the revenue from taxation necessary to pay state pensions for far longer than was initially envisaged when welfare states were established as people live longer and enjoy lengthier periods of retirement. Life expectancy has benefited from the extraordinary advances in medical science in recent decades, while the completion of genetic mapping in 2003 will probably permit in time the elimination of still further causes of early death. Ageing populations, however, place greater demands on health and social welfare services, which become ever more costly, putting national finances under strain. As states seek ways to contain government spending, public services deteriorate, providing grounds for greater social dissatisfaction or unrest.

Migration, for economic reasons mainly from the poorer south and east to the richer north and west, has increased exponentially in recent decades, especially in the wake of the fall of communism and greatly intensified globalization since 1990. Refugees fleeing from war in the Middle East and parts of Africa have greatly swollen in numbers in recent years, not least through the botched NATO intervention in Libya. With such crass imbalances of wealth and living standards, and given the far greater ease of movement across continents, there is no likelihood of migration diminishing in importance as a challenge to future generations. In fact, as populations grow in poorer parts of the world while the indigenous European populations decline in relative terms, the migration pressure is likely to intensify significantly in future decades. It could, indeed, prove the most serious of all challenges to the cohesion of European societies.

Multiculturalism need not lead to the dangerous 'clash of civilizations' controversially predicted by Samuel Huntington in the 1990s. But over the next decades the possibility of at any rate an unsettling clash of cultures cannot be ruled out. More recently, Ivan Krastev has suggested that the migration crisis that struck so forcefully in 2015–16 threatens to result in the disintegration of the European Union. In the wake of the migration crisis, he claims, 'Europe is suffering from an identity crisis in which its Christian and Enlightenment legacies are no longer secure.' Whatever the reality of the assertion, it is likely that the challenge from migration to a sense of historically rooted European identity (and, within Europe, identity of individual nation states) will grow immeasurably. Intolerance, particularly towards those of other colours and cultures, is likely to grow as well. The prospects for social harmony and cohesion will as a consequence look less rosy.

The potential for social unrest will expand, too, if a further major challenge to European societies is not met: the vast and growing disparity of wealth and income. Every indicator demonstrates how the income gap has widened in recent decades. The rewards from globalization were enormous. But they were neither evenly nor fairly spread. While some, most obviously in the financial sector, could hugely increase their earnings, the unskilled especially fell to the bottom of a widening pile of those who lacked the requisite abilities, skills or talent to benefit. And while economic success was becoming more cut-throat, societies were losing the sense of collective responsibility for the less well-off. Increased economic competitiveness, endeavours to reduce the role of the state, and cuts in public expenditure, largely to pay for the fallout from the financial crisis, have all contributed to undermining the sense of communal experience, responsibility and ownership that was more prevalent in the early post-war decades.

Globalization has greatly increased individualism, a trend under way since the 1970s at the latest. Individual choice in commodities to purchase, in patterns of expenditure, and in lifestyles has widened immeasurably. In many ways (looking aside from the scope for manipulation of consumer tastes and purchases by sophisticated advertising) this is greatly to be welcomed. But a sense of obligations to a community beyond the individual has weakened in the process. There is no prospect at all that this trend will be reversed. Traditional forms of class society, related to industrial labour and production, barely exist any longer. Nor do the *general* levels of poor or mediocre living standards that pushed people together rather than apart as Europe recovered from the Second World War. Post-industrial individualism still requires much of the state (especially when things go wrong). At the same time it wants to reduce the role of the state and generally favours cutting taxes rather than subsidizing the less well off through higher levels of taxation. Only Scandinavia (which has some of the most stable, contented societies) broadly adheres to a model of high taxation and extensive redistribution of income. It is a model, for all its success in Scandinavian countries, that evidently does not travel well.

The problem of future social cohesion will most probably be exacerbated by a further major challenge that impinges upon many of the other serious issues facing Europe in future decades: the spread of automation. Computer technology has had a revolutionary impact on Europe (as on the rest of the world), especially in the past quarter of a century or so. It has in the main been of unimaginable benefit to society. But in most forms of employment it is going far towards making human labour at least partly redundant. In every sector of the economy, the intensified competition promoted by globalization leads to the cutting of costs through use of automation. This applies to the service sector, which has expanded so much since the 1970s, as it does to finance, construction and manufacturing industries. Banks can drastically cut back on the numbers they employ, for instance, because computerized cash dispensers and online banking have reduced the need for branches that were once so visible on every high street. Airports expect passengers to use computer technology to acquire boarding cards and check in their luggage, reducing the need for airport staff. The car industry once had plants that employed tens of thousands. But modern cars can be produced with a fraction of the labour needed before the technological revolution and robotics. Such examples will multiply and intensify in years to come. In many spheres of the economy robots will be cheaper to employ than humans. How gainfully to employ large parts of the population is likely to loom as a major political, social and economic problem in decades to come. Rises in productivity will have to be impressive to sustain populations working fewer hours, living longer, and making greater demands on reduced social services. Politicians have as yet barely begun to contemplate how to square that particular circle.

A final immense challenge, looming ever larger in recent years, is that of security. National security was once almost entirely a matter of *national* concern. The first task of a nation state was the protection of its citizens. But globalization, ease of travel, speed of transport and, more than anything else, computer technology have turned national security into a matter of prime *transnational* importance. Frontiers pose no barrier to international terrorism. So security measures have equally to cross the borders of nation states. Combating crime on an international level is, in fact, nothing new. It began in earnest with the foundation in the 1920s of Interpol (which was re-established at the end of the war and now has almost 200 members). But as international crime and terrorism networks have spread and become inordinately more sophisticated in their methods, not just the enhanced work of Interpol but also the regular transfer of security data between intelligence services has become imperative. The orchestration of terrorist attacks through social media via the internet has become a central issue for intelligence services in every European country. Another is the increasing prevalence of cyber-attacks that endanger the basis of civilization by blocking, shutting down or destroying vital installations such as energy networks or health systems, or penetrating highly sensitive military security data files. Cyber-crime of whatever kind can only be prevented or fended off by international cooperation on intelligence-sharing on an unprecedented level.

Inevitably, security scares have led to a huge expansion of surveillance of ordinary citizens by intelligence networks. There is an obvious tension in free societies between degrees of security necessary to protect citizens, and the inroads into the privacy and confidentiality of those citizens by intrusive methods of surveillance. How to protect data from being unnecessarily collected and misused, or hacked by criminals, and how individuals can protect themselves from computer algorithms that can detect where they are, who their friends are, and what lifestyle choices they make, are major issues in which freedom runs up against the surveillance techniques of the modern state – and of big computer firms. Everyone wants security. Yet what price in loss of privacy is society prepared to pay for it? One way or another, the Big Brother surveillance society of George Orwell's *1984* has come much closer.

* * *

How ready is Europe to face this barrage of weighty problems? 'Europe' in this sense essentially means the European Union. Russia and Turkey have their own priorities and will pursue independent policies. Britain, for better but most likely for worse, is about to forge its own path. Other states outside the European Union, for example in the Balkans, will face the problems without major international support networks. Each of the massive challenges demands a response that relies upon a high degree of international cooperation. The nation state, the political form that emerged as triumphant from the nineteenth century and came close to destroying itself in the first half of the twentieth, is not equipped to manage the problems at an individual level. But the European Union, which gradually emerged from the recognized need for greater cooperation, integration and unity, is itself still a work in progress – a major achievement, certainly, but an institution with many flaws and weaknesses. As things stand at the end of 2017 it is in less than optimal condition to cope with the major challenges ahead. There is at least the hope that France and Germany will provide the necessary dynamism to implement major structural reforms. And the imminent departure of Great Britain, however regrettable other member states found the decision to leave, may in practice have the effect of consolidating the EU and accelerating reform.

But what shape will reform take? The flywheels and crankshafts of the great 'compromise factory' grind slowly. The system is not made for speed or dynamism. It is designed to prevent any single power dominating. Germany has evolved by default into the leadership position, but is reluctant to lead. The smaller countries are suspicious about conceding power to Germany, and view with some unease the likely renewal of the Franco-German powerhouse. Since the creation in 1974 of the European Council of heads of government or state of the member countries, the representatives of the nation states have become the most potent body in the European Union, though their centrifugal tendencies are constrained by the centralizing leanings of the Commission and the Parliament. The difficulties of arriving at a solution to equip the European Union for the challenges ahead while satisfying the often contradictory demands of the twenty-seven member states are daunting.

In theory a potential solution would be what has long been talked about but never seemed realistic: a federal United States of Europe, with a central government and parliament, its own defence and foreign policy, and full budgetary and fiscal powers, analogous to the arrangement of the United States of America. However, that seems exceedingly unlikely to come to pass, certainly not in the foreseeable future and probably never at all. The states of Europe are simply not like the states that make up the federal union in America. Each of them in the end – though there is seldom a total contradiction – values its own national interest and identity more than its Europeanism. This is true also of the most power-ful and influential country in the European Union, Germany. The EU and the Eurozone at its heart suit Germany very well in their current form. Germany has benefited more than any other country from the Eurozone. And it is the dominant player in the complex politics of the European Union. For all the talk of much-needed reform that has risen in crescendo since the onset of the financial crisis in 2008, it is questionable whether Germany genuinely seeks fundamental reform, and whether this would be possible anyway, given the varied and often conflicting interests of the member states.

The legacy of the past – overwhelmingly still the memories of the war, occupation and the Holocaust – plays a crucial role in shaping national identities in ways that have no equivalent in the United States. So the European Union, probably for the indefinite future, will have to remain a looser form of polity, while nevertheless developing greater collective powers, and speed of decision-making, to confront both immediate and longer-term crises. Possibly, as has often been suggested, a two-speed or multi-speed Europe, or European Union of concentric circles of differing levels of integration, might eventually take shape, though such a propos-ition faces its own daunting problems of implementation. A reasonable speculation is that over the next decade, perhaps longer, the EU will in essentials bear a fairly close resemblance to its current appearance.

The external pressures around Europe put a premium on closer inte-gration and speed of action in foreign and defence issues. The German Chancellor, Angela Merkel, hinted at this at the end of May 2017 when, following a meeting of the G7 leading industrial nations attended by

President Trump, she commented that 'we Europeans must really take our fate into our own hands', adding that 'the era in which we could fully rely on others is over to some extent'. Although cautiously worded, this points towards greater integration in foreign and defence policy. A modest attempt to revive a combined European military capacity (more than half a century after the previous plan for a European Defence Community was proposed but then vetoed by the French) is taking shape, designed to complement NATO's continuing role in European defence. A European Foreign Minister, with greater powers than currently possessed by the High Representative of the Union for Foreign Affairs and Security Policy (whose remit in practice is limited since foreign policy is jealously guarded by the individual member states), will probably follow in time.

The legacy of the Second World War together with the experience of decades of peace and prosperity, guaranteed for Western Europe in the crucial post-war decades by American military might, has made Europe an essentially pacific continent. Britain and France, the old imperialist powers, are the countries most ready to engage in overseas conflicts (though both have substantially reduced their armed forces in recent years and are only equipped to take part in multi-national operations). Most others are extremely slow and reluctant to contemplate the use of armed force. This has been a highly welcome development. No one envisages a major war among European democracies breaking out. Civil values have replaced militaristic values. A return to the belligerence and aggression within Europe that led to two catastrophic world wars is today unimaginable. The shock of the explosion of military violence in eastern Ukraine was, therefore, all the greater. It was a reminder that, while war was exceedingly unlikely to come to Europe from within the countries that comprise the European Union, it could come from outside. How superpower rivalries in a post-Cold War era will develop cannot be known. But future relations between the United States, China and Russia hold the potential for conflict, perhaps even nuclear war, which might at some point engulf Europe. The Korean peninsula, where the first Cold War confrontation took place, could be the flashpoint for a future global conflict. At the very least, the European Union needs to develop the capacity to respond quickly and with unity towards external dangers that may arise.

Whether the historically rooted vested interests of the individual member states will permit far-reaching structural change within the European Union remains to be seen. 'More Europe' – that is, moves towards greater political union – may logically be what is needed. Whether it is politically feasible is another matter. European policy-making has more than ever come to be seen as the business of elites detached from the concerns of the mass of the population. Corruption scandals have helped to undermine trust in politicians. Child-abuse scandals have eroded trust in the Christian churches and other institutions. Cover-up scandals involving the police have damaged trust in law-enforcement agencies. Not surprisingly, respect for those in positions of authority has shrunk. Trust in the major pillars of democratic life is probably at an all-time low. The spread of social media has provided a potent vehicle for the expression of popular anger towards 'the establishment' or 'the system'. Democracy (and the division of powers on which it rests) is endangered in the process. Moves to give the government far stronger executive powers – as seen in Hungary, Poland and Turkey, for example – utilize pluralist democracy itself to undermine democratic foundations. The use of referenda to determine policy is itself a reflection of a trend away from representative towards plebiscitary democracy. The scope for manipulation, for appeals to emotion over rationality, is thereby greatly enhanced.

The rise of nationalist xenophobic parties or regional separatist parties reflects in good measure the move from institutional 'elite' politics to grass-roots political mobilization. It marks, too, the rise in the politics of identity, an increasingly recognizable trait in Europe since the 1980s. This phenomenon, which has gained in momentum since the financial crash of 2008, is unlikely to diminish in importance. Its expression is not confined to parties of the right, as shown by the democratic support, much of it left wing, for Scottish independence, and, in autumn 2017, the vote (deemed illegal by the Spanish government and others) in favour of Catalan independence. In these cases, the historical existence, if long ago, of independent nation states offers a basis of identity that nationalist politicians can exploit to press for autonomy and in the hope of economic advantages. The political and economic fallout from the financial crisis has enhanced that opportunity. For the most part, even so, identity politics are the preserve of the right. The reservoirs of extremist nationalist support remain large. The rising incidence of crime sparked by racial hatred and the detestable xenophobic content that pours out daily on the internet are testimony to the prevalence of mentalities which, if those of a minority of the population, nevertheless pose a threat to the liberal values on which modern democracy has in recent decades come to rest.

Europe has changed dramatically over the course of the seven decades since the Second World War. It has become a continent of democracies – even accepting that some of these are little more than a facade for forms of authoritarianism. It has turned into a continent of civil societies in which, contrasting diametrically with the first half of the twentieth century, the military play little role in domestic politics – greatly enhancing the potential for democratic stability. It has learned, whatever the difficulties, tensions and frustrations, to cooperate and negotiate, not resort to armed force, to resolve problems. And it has at its centre, as its most powerful and influential country, a peaceful, internationalist Germany – the starkest imaginable contrast to the Germany that in the 1930s and 1940s trampled human rights into the dust and almost destroyed European civilization. Europe has fought for and won freedom. It has acquired prosperity that is the envy of most of the world. Its search for unity, and for a clear sense of identity, goes on.

What will happen in the decades to come is impossible to know. The only certainty is uncertainty. Insecurity will remain a hallmark of modern life. Europe's dips and turns, the ups and downs that have characterized its history, are sure to continue.

Select Bibliography

The approach follows that which I adopted for the bibliography of *To Hell and Back*. I have confined this list to works that have helped me in the writing of this book. Other than in a few exceptional cases, I have omitted specialized research monographs, essays in learned journals and works of fiction. An asterisk indicates works on which I have drawn for brief quotations.

*Aaronovitch, David, *Party Animals: My Family and Other Communists*, London, 2016.

Abelshauser, Werner, *Wirtschaftsgeschichte der Bundesrepublik Deutschland 1945–1980*, Frankfurt am Main, 1983.

Acemoglu, Daron and Robinson, James A., *Why Nations Fail: The Origins of Power, Prosperity and Poverty*, London, 2013.

Adenauer, Konrad, *Erinnerungen*, 4 vols, Stuttgart, 1965–8.

Ahonen, Pertti, *After the Expulsion: West Germany and Eastern Europe 1945–1990*, Oxford, 2003.

*Ahonen, Pertti, *Death at the Berlin Wall*, Oxford, 2011.

Aldcroft, Derek, *The European Economy 1914–2000*, London (1978), 2001.

Aldcroft, Derek and Morewood, Steven, *Economic Change in Eastern Europe since 1918*, Aldershot, 1995.

*Alexievich, Svetlana, *Chernobyl Prayer*, London (1997), 2013.

Anderson, Perry, *The New Old World*, London, 2009.

Annan, Noel, *Our Age: Portrait of a Generation*, London, 1990.

*Applebaum, Anne, *Iron Curtain: The Crushing of Eastern Europe, 1944–1956*, London, 2012.

Arblaster, Paul, *A History of the Low Countries*, Basingstoke (2006), 2012.

Aron, Raymond, *Mémoires*, Paris, 1983.

Arrighi, Giovanni, *The Long Twentieth Century: Money, Power and the Origins of our Times*, London (1994), 2010.

Ascherson, Neal, *The Struggles for Poland*, London, 1987.

Aust, Stefan, *The Baader-Meinhof Complex*, London, 2008.

Aust, Stefan and Spörl, Gerhard (eds), *Die Gegenwart der Vergangenheit. Der lange Schatten des Dritten Reichs*, Munich, 2004.

Bakewell, Sarah, *At the Existentialist Café*, London, 2016.

Baring, Arnulf, *Im Anfang war Adenauer. Die Entstehung der Kanzler-demokratie*, Munich, 1971.

Bark, Dennis L. and Gress, David R., *A History of West Germany, 1945–1988*, 2 vols, Oxford, 1989.

Barzun, Jacques, *From Dawn to Decadence: 500 Years of Western Cultural Life: 1500 to the Present*, London, 2000.

Bayly, Christopher and Harper, Tim, *Forgotten Wars: The End of Britain's Asian Empire*, London, 2007.

Beck, Ulrich, *What is Globalization?*, Cambridge, 2000.

Beck, Ulrich, *World at Risk*, Cambridge, 2009.

Behm, Margarete, *So oder so ist das Leben. Eine Jahrhundertfrau erzählt*, Reinbek bei Hamburg, 2004.

*Békés, Csaba, Byrne, Malcolm and Rainer, János M. (eds), *The 1956 Hungarian Revolution: A History in Documents*, Budapest and New York, 2002.

Bell, Daniel, *The End of Ideology: On the Exhaustion of Political Ideas in the Fifties*, Glencoe, IL, 1960.

Bell, P. M. H., *The World Since 1945: An International History*, London, 2001.

Bell, P. M. H., *Twentieth-Century Europe: Unity and Division*, London, 2006.

*Berend, Ivan T., *Central and Eastern Europe 1944–1993: Detour from the Periphery to the Periphery*, Cambridge, 1996.

Berend, Ivan T., *An Economic History of Twentieth-Century Europe*, Cambridge, 2006.

Berend, Ivan T., *From the Soviet Bloc to the European Union: The Economic and Social Transformation of Central and Eastern Europe since 1973*, Cambridge, 2009.

Berend, Ivan T., *Europe Since 1980*, Cambridge, 2010.

Berg, Nicolas, *Der Holocaust und die westdeutschen Historiker. Erforschung und Erinnerung*, Göttingen, 2003.

Berghahn, Volker R., *Modern Germany: Society, Economy and Politics in the Twentieth Century*, Cambridge, 1982.

Berghahn, Volker R., *The Americanisation of West German Industry 1945–1973*, Leamington Spa, 1986.

Bergin, Joseph, *A History of France*, London, 2015.

Bernstein, Serge and Milza, Pierre, *Histoire de la France au xxe siècle, vol. 3, 1958 à nos jours* Paris (1992), 2009.

Bittner, Stephen V., *The Many Lives of Khrushchev's Thaw: Experience and Memory in Moscow's Arbat*, Ithaca, NY, and London, 2008.

*Blair, Tony, *A Journey*, London, 2010.

Blanning, T. C. W. (ed.), *The Oxford Illustrated History of Modern Europe*, Oxford, 1996.

Blyth, Mark, *Austerity: The History of a Dangerous Idea*, Oxford, 2015.

*Bobbitt, Philip, *Terror and Consent: The Wars for the Twenty-First Century*, London, 2009.

Borodziej, Włodzimierz, *Geschichte Polens im 20. Jahrhundert*, Munich, 2010.

Bosworth, R. J. B., *The Italian Dictatorship: Problems and Perspective in the Interpretation of Mussolini and Fascism*, London, 1998.

Bracher, Karl Dietrich, *Die Auflösung der Weimarer Republik*, Stuttgart/Düsseldorf, 1955.

Bracher, Karl Dietrich, *The German Dilemma: The Throes of Political Emancipation*, London, 1974.

*Brandt, Willy, *Erinnerungen*, Frankfurt am Main, 1994.

*Brandys, Kazimierz, *Warschauer Tagebuch. Die Monate davor 1978–1981*, Frankfurt am Main, 1984.

*Brenan, Gerald, *The Face of Spain*, Harmondsworth (1950), 1987.

*Brendon, Piers, *The Decline and Fall of the British Empire 1781–1997*, London, 2007.

Brenner, Michael, *Nachkriegsland. Eine Spurensuche*, Hamburg, 2015.

Broadberry, Stephen and O'Rourke, Kevin H. (eds), *The Cambridge Economic History of Modern Europe. Vol. 2: 1870 to the Present*, Cambridge, 2010.

*Brown, Archie, *The Gorbachev Factor*, Oxford, 1997.

*Brown, Archie, *Seven Years that Changed the World: Perestroika in Perspective*, Oxford, 2008.

*Brown, Archie, *The Myth of the Strong Leader: Political Leadership in the Modern Age*, London, 2014.

Brown, Gordon, *Beyond the Crash: Overcoming the First Crisis of Globalisation*, London, 2010.

Brown, James Franklin, *The End of Communist Rule in Eastern Europe*, Twickenham, 1991.

Brüggemeier, Franz-Joseph, *Geschichte Grossbritanniens im 20. Jahrhundert*, Munich, 2010.

Brüggemeier, Franz-Joseph, *Schranken der Natur. Umwelt, Gesellschaft, Experimente 1750 bis heute*, Essen, 2014.

*Bruhns, Wibke, *Nachrichtenzeit. Meine unfertigen Erinnerungen*, Munich, 2012.

Buchanan, Tom, *Europe's Troubled Peace 1945–2000*, Oxford, 2006.

Bulliet, Richard W. (ed.), *The Columbia History of the 20th Century*, New York, 1998.

Burg, Steven L. and Shoup, Paul S., *The War in Bosnia-Herzegovina: Ethnic Conflict and International Intervention*, New York, 2000.

Burke, Jason, *The New Threat from Islamic Militancy*, London, 2016.

Burleigh, Michael, *Sacred Causes: Religion and Politics from the European Dictators to Al Qaeda*, London, 2006.

Butler, Michael, Pender, Malcolm and Charnley, Joy (eds), *The Making of Modern Switzerland, 1848–1998*, Basingstoke, 2000.

Calic, Marie-Janine, *Geschichte Jugoslawiens im 20. Jahrhundert*, Munich, 2010.

Cannadine, David, *Ornamentalism: How the British Saw their Empire*, London, 2002.

Cannadine, David, *Margaret Thatcher: A Life and Legacy*, Oxford, 2017.

Clark, Martin, *Modern Italy 1971–1982*, London, 1984.

*Clarke, Harold D., Goodwin, Matthew and Whiteley, Paul, *Brexit: Why Britain Voted to Leave the European Union*, Cambridge, 2017.

*Clarke, Peter, *Hope and Glory: Britain 1900–1990*, London, 1996.

Clogg, Richard, *A Concise History of Greece*, 3rd edn, Cambridge, 2013.

Clogg, Richard and Yannopoulos, George (eds), *Greece under Military Rule*, London, 1972.

Cockburn, Patrick, *The Rise of Islamic State: Isis and the New Sunni Revolution*, London, 2015.

Cohen, Stephen F., Rabinowitch, Alexander and Sharlet, Robert (eds), *The Soviet Union since Stalin*, Bloomington, IN, and London, 1980.

Conan, Eric and Rousso, Henry, *Vichy, un passé qui ne passe pas*, Paris, 1996.

Conway, Martin, 'Democracy in Postwar Western Europe: The Triumph of a Political Model', *European History Quarterly*, 32/1 (2002), 59–84.

Conze, Ekart, Frei, Norbert, Hayes, Peter and Zimmermann, Moshe, *Das Amt und die Vergangenheit. Deutsche Diplomaten im Dritten Reich und in der Bundesrepublik*, Munich, 2010.

Coppolaro, Lucia and Lains, Pedro, 'Portugal and European Integration, 1947–1992: an essay on protected openness in the European Periphery', *e-journal of Portuguese History*, 11/1 (2013), 61–81.

Costa Pinto, António (ed.), *Modern Portugal*, Palo Alto, CA, 1998.

Couloumbis, Theodore A., Kariotis, Theodore and Bellou, Fotini (eds), *Greece in the Twentieth Century*, London, 2003.

Crampton, Richard J., *A Short History of Modern Bulgaria*, Cambridge, 1987.

Crampton, Richard J., *Eastern Europe in the Twentieth Century – and After*, London, 1997.

Crouch, Colin, *Social Change in Western Europe*, Oxford, 1999.

*Dąbrowska, Maria, *Tagebücher 1914–1965*, Frankfurt am Main, 1989.

Dahrendorf, Ralf, *Society and Democracy in Germany*, London, 1968.

Darling, Alistair, *Back from the Brink: 1,000 Days at Number 11*, London, 2011.

Darnton, Robert, *Berlin Journal 1989–1990*, New York, 1991.

*Davies, Norman, *God's Playground. Vol. 2: A History of Poland*, Oxford, 1981.

Davies, Norman, *Europe: A History*, Oxford, 1996.

Deletant, Dennis, *Ceaușescu and the Securitate: Coercion and Dissent in Romania, 1965–1989*, London, 1995.

Deletant, Dennis, *Communist Terror in Romania: Gheorghiu-Dej and the Police State*, London, 1999.

Dobson, Miriam, *Khrushchev's Cold Summer: Gulag Returnees, Crime and the Fate of Reform after Stalin*, Ithaca, NY, and London, 2009.

Dobson, Miriam, 'The Post-Stalin Era: De-Stalinization, Daily Life and Dissent', *Kritika: Explorations in Russian and Eurasian History*, 12/4 (2011), 905–24.

Doering-Manteuffel, Anselm, 'Nach dem Boom. Brüche und Kontinuitäten seit 1970', *Vierteljahrshefte für Zeitgeschichte*, 55/4 (2007), 559–81.

Doering-Manteuffel, Anselm and Raphael, Lutz, *Nach dem Boom. Perspektiven auf die Zeitgeschichte seit 1970*, Göttingen (2008), 2012.

Doering-Manteuffel, Anselm, Raphael, Lutz and Schlemmer, Thomas (eds), *Vorgeschichte der Gegenwart. Dimensionen des Strukturbruchs nach dem Boom*, Göttingen, 2016.

Dols, Chris and Ziemann, Benjamin, 'Progressive Participation and Transnational Activism in the Catholic Church after Vatican II: The Dutch and West German Examples', *Journal of Contemporary History*, 50/3 (2015), 465–85.

Duchêne, François, *Jean Monnet: The First Statesman of Interdependence*, New York, 1994.

Duggan, Christopher, *The Force of Destiny: A History of Italy since 1796*, London, 2008.

Dülffer, Jost, *Europa im Ost-West-Konflikt 1945–1990*, Munich, 2004.

Dyson, Kenneth and Featherstone, Kevin, *The Road to Maastricht: Negotiating Economic and Monetary Union*, Oxford, 1999.

Eder, Jacob S., *Holocaust Angst: The Federal Republic of Germany and American Holocaust Memory since the 1970s*, New York, 2016.

Eichengreen, Barry, *The European Economy since 1945*, Princeton, NJ, 2007.

Eichengreen, Barry, *Hall of Mirrors: The Great Depression, the Great Recession and the Uses – and Misuses – of History*, Oxford, 2015.

Eichengreen, Barry, Landesmann, Michael and Stiefel, Dieter (eds), *The European Economy in an American Mirror*, Abingdon, 2008.

Eley, Geoff, 'Nazism, Politics and the Image of the Past: Thoughts on the West German *Historikerstreit* 1986–1987', *Past and Present*, 121 (1988), 171–208.

Eley, Geoff, *Forging Democracy: The History of the Left in Europe 1850–2000*, New York, 2002.

Ellwood, David W., *Rebuilding Europe: Western Europe, America and Postwar Reconstruction*, London, 1992.

Engelhardt, Marc (ed.), *Die Flüchtlingsrevolution. Wie die neue Völkerwanderung die ganze Welt verändert*, Munich, 2016.

Espinosa-Maestre, Francisco, *Shoot the Messenger? Spanish Democracy and the Crimes of Francoism*, Eastbourne, 2013.

Evans, Richard J., *In Hitler's Shadow: West German Historians and the Attempt to Escape from the Nazi Past*, New York, 1989.

Fanon, Frantz, *The Wretched of the Earth*, Harmondsworth (1961), 1967.

Fäßler, Peter E., *Globalisierung. Ein historisches Kompendium*, Cologne, 2007.

Ferguson, Niall, *The Cash Nexus: Money and Power in the Modern World 1700–2000*, London, 2002.

Ferguson, Niall, *Empire: How Britain Made the Modern World*, London, 2003.

Ferguson, Niall, *The Great Degeneration: How Institutions Decay and Economies Die*, London, 2012.

Ferguson, Niall et al. (eds), *The Shock of the Global: The 1970s in Perspective*, Cambridge, MA, 2010.

*Figes, Orlando, *The Whisperers: Private Life in Stalin's Russia*, London, 2008.

Fink, Carole K., *Cold War: An International History*, 2nd edn, Boulder, CO, 2017.

Fischer-Galati, Stephen, *Twentieth-Century Rumania*, New York, 1970.

Fitzmaurice, John, *The Politics of Belgium: Crisis and Compromise in a Plural Society*, London, 1988.

*Flanner, Janet (Genêt), *Paris Journal 1944–1965*, New York, 1965.

Flora, Peter (ed.), *State, Society and Economy in Western Europe, 1815–1975*, 2 vols, Frankfurt, 1983.

Foster, R. F., *Modern Ireland 1600–1972*, London, 1989.

*Fox, Robert (ed.), *We Were There: An Eyewitness History of the Twentieth Century*, London, 2010.

Frei, Norbert, *Adenauer's Germany and the Nazi Past: The Politics of Amnesty and Integration*, New York, 2002.

Frei, Norbert, *1945 und wir. Das Dritte Reich im Bewußtsein der Deutschen*, Munich, 2005.

Frei, Norbert, *1968. Jugendrevolte und globaler Protest*, Munich, 2008.

Frei, Norbert et al., *Karrieren im Zwielicht. Hitlers Eliten nach 1945*, Frankfurt and New York, 2001.

Frei, Norbert and Süß, Dietmar (eds), *Privatisierung. Idee und Praxis seit den 1970er Jahren*, Göttingen, 2012.

Frevert, Ute, *Eurovisionen. Ansichten guter Europäer im 19. und 20. Jahrhundert*, Frankfurt am Main, 2003.

Friedrich, Jörg, *Die kalte Amnestie. NS-Täter in der Bundesrepublik*, Frankfurt am Main, 1984.

Friedrich, Jörg, *Yalu. An den Ufern des dritten Weltkriegs*, Berlin, 2007.

*Fritzsche, Peter (ed.), *The Turbulent World of Franz Göll: An Ordinary Berliner Writes the Twentieth Century*, Cambridge MA, 2011.

*Fukuyama, Francis, *The End of History and the Last Man*, London, 1992.

Fukuyama, Francis, 'The End of History?', *The National Interest* (Summer 1989), 3–18.

Fukuyama, Francis, *Political Order and Political Decay: From the Industrial Revolution to the Globalisation of Democracy*, London, 2015.

Fulbrook Mary, *Anatomy of a Dictatorship: Inside the GDR 1949–1989*, Oxford, 1995.

Fulbrook, Mary, *Interpretations of the Two Germanies, 1945–1990*, London, 2000.

Fulbrook, Mary, *History of Germany 1918–2000: The Divided Nation*, Oxford (1991), 2002.

Fulbrook Mary, *The People's State: East German Society from Hitler to Honecker*, Oxford, 2005.

Fulbrook, Mary, *Dissonant Lives: Generations and Violence through the German Dictatorships*, Oxford, 2011.

Fulbrook, Mary (ed.), *Europe since 1945*, Oxford, 2001.

Funder, Anna, *Stasiland*, London, 2003.

Furet, François, *The Passing of an Illusion: The Idea of Communism in the Twentieth Century*, Chicago, IL, and London, 1999.

Gaddis, John Lewis, *We Now Know: Rethinking Cold War History*, Oxford, 1997.

Gaddis, John Lewis, *The Cold War*, London, 2005.

Gallant, Thomas W., *Modern Greece: From the War of Independence to the Present*, London (2001), 2016.

Garton Ash, Timothy, *The Polish Revolution: Solidarity*, London (1983), 1999.

*Garton Ash, Timothy, *The Uses of Adversity: Essays on the Fate of Central Europe*, London (1989), 1999.

*Garton Ash, Timothy, *We the People: The Revolution of '89 Witnessed in Warsaw, Budapest, Berlin and Prague*, London (1990), 1999.

*Garton Ash, Timothy, *History of the Present: Essays, Sketches and Despatches from Europe in the 1990s*, London, 1999.

*Garton Ash, Timothy, *Facts are Subversive: Political Writing from a Decade without a Name*, London, 2009.

Garton Ash, Timothy, *The File: A Personal History*, London (1997), 2009.

Gassert, Philipp and Steinweis, Alan E. (eds), *Coping with the Nazi Past: West German Debates on Nazism and Generational Conflict, 1955–1975*, New York, 2007.

Gehler, Michael, *Europa. Ideen, Institutionen, Vereinigung*, Munich, 2010.

Geiselberger, Heinrich (ed.), *Die große Regression. Eine internationale Debatte über die gestige Situation der Zeit*, Berlin, 2017.

Genscher Hans-Dietrich and Winkler, Heinrich August, *Europas Zukunft – in bester Verfassung?*, Freiburg im Breisgau, 2013.

Giddens, Anthony, *Europe in the Global Age*, Cambridge, 2007.

Gilbert, Felix, *The End of the European Era, 1890 to the Present*, New York (1970), 1984.

Gilbert, Martin, *Challenge to Civilization: A History of the Twentieth Century, Vol. 3: 1952–1999*, London, 1999.

Gildea, Robert, *The Past in French History*, New Haven, CT, and London, 1994.

Gildea, Robert, *France since 1945*, Oxford, 2002.

*Gildea, Robert, Mark, James, Warring, Anette (eds), *Europe's 1968: Voices of Revolt*, Oxford, 2013.

Gillingham, John, *European Integration, 1950–2003: Superstate or New Market Economy?*, Cambridge, 2003.

Gillingham, John, *The EU: An Obituary*, London, 2016.

Gilmour, David, *The Pursuit of Italy: A History of a Land, its Regions and their Peoples*, London, 2011.

Ginsborg, Paul, *A History of Contemporary Italy 1943–1980*, London, 1990.

*Ginsborg, Paul, *Italy and its Discontents, 1980–2001*, London, 2003.

*Glenny, Misha, *The Fall of Yugoslavia*, London (1992), 1996.

Glenny, Misha, *The Balkans, 1804–1999: Nationalism, War and the Great Powers*, London, 1999.

Golan, Galia, *Reform Rule in Czechoslovakia: The Dubček Era, 1968–1969*, Cambridge, 1973.

*Goltz, Anna von der (ed.), *'Talkin' 'bout my generation': Conflicts of Generation Building and Europe's '1968'*, Göttingen, 2011.

Goltz, Anna von der, 'Generations of 68ers: Age-Related Constructions of Identity and Germany's "1968"', *Cultural and Social History*, 8/4 (2011), 473–90.

*Gorbachev, Mikhail, *Memoirs*, London, 1997.

Graham, Helen (ed.), *Interrogating Francoism: History and Dictatorship in Twentieth-Century Spain*, London, 2016.

Grant, Matthew and Ziemann, Benjamin (eds), *Understanding the Imaginary War: Culture, Thought and Nuclear Conflict, 1945–90*, Manchester, 2016.

Grenville, J. A. S., *A History of the World from the 20th to the 21st Century*, Abingdon (1994), 2005.

Grimm, Dieter, *Europa ja – aber welches? Zur Verfassung der europäischen Demokratie*, Munich, 2016.

Grob-Fitzgibbon, Benjamin, *Continental Drift: Britain and Europe from the End of Empire to the Rise of Euroscepticism*, Cambridge, 2016.

Guirao, Fernando, Lynch France M. B., and Pérez, Sigfrido M. Ramínez (eds), *Alan S. Milward and a Century of European Change*, New York and Abingdon, 2012.

Hall, Simon, *1956: The World in Revolt*, London, 2016.

*Hanhimäki, Jussi M. and Westad, Odd Arne (eds), *The Cold War: A History in Documents and Eyewitness Accounts*, Oxford, 2004.

Hanrieder, Wolfram, *Germany, America, Europe: Forty Years of German Foreign Policy*, New Haven, CT, and London, 1989.

Harper, John Lamberton, *The Cold War*, Oxford, 2011.

Harrison, Joseph, *An Economic History of Spain*, Manchester, 1978.

Harrison, Joseph, *The Spanish Economy in the Twentieth Century*, London, 1985.

Harrison, Joseph, *The Spanish Economy: From the Civil War to the European Community*, Cambridge, 1995.

Haslam, Jonathan, *Russia's Cold War*, New Haven, CT, and London, 2011.

Havel, Václav et al., *The Power of the Powerless: Citizens against the State in Central-Eastern Europe*, London, 1985.

Hayek, F. A. *The Road to Serfdom*, Abingdon (1944), 2001.

Hayman, Ronald, *Brecht: A Biography*, London, 1983.

*Heffer, Simon, *Like the Roman: The Life of Enoch Powell*, London, 1998.

*Heimann, Mary, *Czechoslovakia: The State that Failed*, New Haven, CT, and London, 2009.

*Hennessy, Peter, *Never Again: Britain 1945–1951*, New York, 1993.

*Hennessy, Peter, *Muddling Through: Power, Politics and the Quality of Government in Postwar Britain*, London, 1996.

*Hennessy, Peter, *Having it so Good: Britain in the Fifties*, London, 2006.

Herbert, Ulrich, *Geschichte Deutschlands im 20. Jahrhundert*, Munich, 2014.

Herbert, Ulrich, 'Europe in High Modernity: Reflections on a Theory of the 20th Century', *Journal of Modern European History*, 5/1 (2007), 5–20.

Herbert, Ulrich and Groehler, Olaf, *Zweierlei Bewältigung. Vier Beiträge über den Umgang mit der NS-Vergangenheit in den beiden deutschen Staaten*, Hamburg, 1992.

Hewison, Robert, *In Anger: British Culture in the Cold War, 1945–60*, London, 1981.

Hewitt, Gavin, *The Lost Continent*, London, 2013.

Hildermeier, Manfred, *Geschichte der Sowjetunion 1917–1991*, Munich, 1998.

Hillebrand, Ernst and Kellner, Anna Maria (eds), *Für ein anderes Europa. Beiträge zu einer notwendigen Debatte*, Bonn, 2014.

Hobsbawm, Eric, *Age of Extremes: The Short Twentieth Century 1914–1991*, London, 1994.

*Hobsbawm, Eric, *Interesting Times: A Twentieth-Century Life*, London, 2002.

Hobsbawm, Eric, *Fractured Times: Culture and Society in the Twentieth Century*, London, 2013.

Hobsbawm, Eric with Polito, Antonio, *The New Century*, London, 2000.

*Hoggart, Richard, *The Uses of Literacy: Aspects of Working-Class Life*, London (1957), 2009.

Hoggart, Richard and Johnson, Douglas, *An Idea of Europe*, London, 1987.

Hopkins, A. G., 'Rethinking Decolonization', *Past and Present*, 200 (2008), 211–47.

*Hosking, Geoffrey, *A History of the Soviet Union*, London, 1985.

Hosking, Geoffrey, 'Why has Nationalism Revived in Europe? The Symbolic Attractions and Fiscal Capabilities of the Nation-State', *Nations and Nationalism*, 22/2 (2016), 210–21.

Howard, Michael and Louis, Wm. Roger (eds), *The Oxford History of the Twentieth Century*, Oxford, 1998.

Hughes, H. Stuart, *Sophisticated Rebels: The Political Culture of European Dissent 1968–1987*, Cambridge MA, 1988.

Huntington, Samuel P., *The Clash of Civilizations and the Remaking of World Order*, London (1996), 2002.

Huskey, Eugene, 'Authoritarian Leadership in the Post-Communist World', *Daedalus*, 145/3 (2016), 69–82.

Ilic, Melanie and Smith, Jeremy (eds), *Soviet State and Society under Nikita Khrushchev*, London, 2009.

Isaacs, Jeremy and Downing, Taylor, *Cold War*, London (1998), 2008.

Jäckel, Eberhard, *Das deutsche Jahrhundert. Eine historische Bilanz*, Stuttgart, 1996.

Jackson, Julian, *Charles de Gaulle*, London, 1990.

James, Harold, *Rambouillet, 15. November 1975. Die Globalisierung der Wirtschaft*, Munich, 1997.

James, Harold, *Europe Reborn: A History, 1914–2000*, London, 2003.

James, Harold, *Finanzmarkt macht Geschichte. Lehren aus den Wirtschaftskrisen*, Göttingen, 2014.

*James, Harold and Stone, Marla (eds), *When the Wall Came Down: Reactions to German Unification*, London, 1992.

James, Lawrence, *The Rise and Fall of the British Empire*, London, 1994.

James, Lawrence, *Raj: The Making and Unmaking of British India*, New York, 1997.

Jarausch, Konrad H., *After Hitler: Recivilizing Germans, 1945–1995*, New York, 2006.

Jarausch, Konrad H., *Out of Ashes: A New History of Europe in the Twentieth Century*, Princeton, NJ, 2015.

Jarausch, Konrad H. (ed.), *Das Ende der Zuversicht? Die siebziger Jahre als Geschichte*, Göttingen, 2008.

Jelavich, Barbara, *History of the Balkans: Twentieth Century*, Cambridge, 1983.

Jelavich, Barbara, *Modern Austria, 1815–1986*, Cambridge, 1987.

Jerram, Leif, *Streetlife: The Untold History of Europe's Twentieth Century*, Oxford, 2013.

Jones, Polly (ed.), *The Dilemmas of De-Stalinization: Negotiating Cultural and Social Change in the Khrushchev Era*, London, 2006.

Judt, Tony, *Past Imperfect: French Intellectuals, 1944–1956*, Berkeley, CA, 1992.

Judt, Tony, *A Grand Illusion? An Essay on Europe*, London, 1997.

Judt, Tony, *The Burden of Responsibility: Blum, Camus, Aron and the French Twentieth Century*, Chicago, IL, and London, 1998.

*Judt, Tony, *Postwar: A History of Europe since 1945*, London, 2005.

Judt, Tony, *Reappraisals: Reflections on the Forgotten Twentieth Century*, London, 2009.

Judt, Tony, *Ill Fares the Land*, London, 2010.

Judt, Tony, *When the Facts Change: Essays 1995–2010*, London, 2015.

Judt, Tony, with Snyder, Timothy, *Thinking the Twentieth Century: Intellectuals and Politics in the Twentieth Century*, London, 2012.

Kaelble, Hartmut, *A Social History of Western Europe 1880–1980*, Dublin, 1989.

Kaelble, Hartmut, *Sozialgeschichte Europas 1945 bis zur Gegenwart*, Munich, 2007.

Kaelble, Hartmut, *The 1970s in Europe: A Period of Disillusionment or Promise?*, German Historical Institute, London, Annual Lecture, 2009, London, 2010.

Kaelble, Hartmut, *Kalter Krieg und Wohlfahrtsstaat. Europa 1945–1989*, Munich, 2011.

*Kagan, Robert, *Paradise and Power: America and Europe in the New World Order*, London, 2003.

Karlauf, Thomas, *Helmut Schmidt. Die späten Jahre*, Munich, 2016.

Keane, John, *Václav Havel: A Political Tragedy in Six Acts*, London, 1999.

Kedward, Rod, *La Vie en Bleu: France and the French since 1900*, London, 2006.

Kendall, Bridget, *The Cold War: A New Oral History of Life Between East and West*, London, 2017.

*Khrushchev, Nikita, *Khrushchev Remembers*, London, 1971.

King, Stephen D., *Grave New World: The End of Globalization, the Return of History*, New Haven, CT, and London, 2017.

Király, Béla K. and Jónas, Paul (eds), *The Hungarian Revolution of 1956 in Retrospect*, Boulder, CO, 1978.

Kleine-Ahlbrandt, W. Laird, *Europe Since 1945: From Conflict to Community*, Minneapolis-Saint Paul, MN, 1993.

Kocka, Jürgen, *Capitalism: A Short History*, Princeton, NJ, 2016.

Köhler, Henning, *Helmut Kohl. Ein Leben für die Politik*, Cologne, 2014.

König, Helmut, Schmidt, Julia and Sicking, Manfred (eds), *Europas Gedächtnis. Das neue Europa zwischen nationalen Erinnerungen und gemeinsamer Identität*, Bielefeld, 2008.

*Koning, Hans, *Nineteen Sixty-Eight: A Personal Report*, New York, 1987.

Kotkin, Stephen, *Armageddon Averted: The Soviet Collapse, 1970–2000*, Oxford, 2001.

*Kovály, Heda Margolius, *Under a Cruel Star: A Life in Prague 1941–1968*, London (1986), 2012.

Kozlov, Vladimir A., *Mass Uprisings in the USSR: Protest and Rebellion in the Post-Stalin Years*, New York, 2002.

Kramer, Alan, *The West Germany Economy 1945–1955*, New York and Oxford, 1991.

*Kramer, Mark, 'The Soviet Union and the 1956 Crises in Hungary and Poland: Reassessments and New Findings', *Journal of Contemporary History*, 33/2 (1998), 163–214.

*Krastev, Ivan, *After Europe*, Philadelphia, PA, 2017.

Krusche, Dieter (ed.), *Reclams Filmführer*, Stuttgart, 2000.

Kühnhardt, Ludger (ed.), *Crises in European Integration: Challenge and Response, 1945–2005*, New York and Oxford, 2008.

Kuper, Leo, *Genocide: Its Political Use in the Twentieth Century*, Harmondsworth, 1981.

Kuzio, Taras, *Putin's War Against Ukraine: Revolution, Nationalism and Crime*, Toronto, 2017.

Kyle, Keith, *Suez: Britain's End of Empire in the Middle East*, London (1991), 2003.

*Kynaston, David, *Family Britain 1951–57*, London, 2010.

Lacouture, Jean, *De Gaulle. Vol. 2, Le Politique*, Paris, 1985.

*Lange, Peter and Roß, Sabine (eds), *17. Juni 1953 – Zeitzeugen berichten. Protokoll eines Aufstands*, Münster, 2004.

Langguth, Gerd, *The Green Factor in German Politics: From Protest Movement to Political Party*, Boulder, CO, and London, 1984.

Lanzmann, Claude, *Shoah*, Paris, 1985; German edn, Munich, 1988.

*Laqueur, Walter, *Europe Since Hitler*, Harmondsworth, 1970.

Larkin, Maurice, *France since the Popular Front: Government and People, 1936–1986*, Oxford, 1988.

*Lasky, Melvin J. (ed.), *The Hungarian Revolution*, London, 1957.

Ledeen, Michael A., 'Renzo de Felice and the Controversy over Italian Fascism', *Journal of Contemporary History*, 11 (1976), 269–83.

Leffler, Melvyn P. and Westad, Odd Arne (eds), *The Cambridge History of the Cold War*, 3 vols, Cambridge, 2010.

Leggewie, Claus, *Der Kampf um die europäische Erinnerung. Ein Schlachtfeld wird besichtigt*, Munich, 2011.

Lever, Paul, *Berlin Rules: Europe and the German Way*, London, 2017.

Lewin, Moshe, *The Soviet Century*, London, 2005.

Lewis, Michael, *The Big Short: Inside the Doomsday Machine*, New York, 2010.

Lewis Michael, *Flash Boys*, New York, 2014.

Linz, Juan J. and Stephan, Alfred, *Problems of Democratic Transition and Consolidation: Southern Europe, South America and Post-Communist Europe*, Baltimore, MD, 1996.

*Lomax, Bill, *Hungary 1956*, London, 1976.

Loth, Wilfried, 'Helmut Kohl und die Währungsunion', *Vierteljahrshefte für Zeitgeschichte*, 61/4 (2013), 455–79.

Lüders, Michael, *Wer den Wind sät. Was westliche Politik im Orient anrichtet*, Munich, 2015.

Lüders, Michael, *Die den Sturm ernten. Wie der Westen Syrien ins Chaos stürzte*, Munich, 2017.

Luther, Kurt Richard and Pulzer, Peter (eds), *Austria 1945–95*, Aldershot, 1998.

Lynch, Frances M. B., *France and the International Economy: From Vichy to the Treaty of Rome*, London, 1997.

*MacCulloch, Diarmaid, *A History of Christianity*, London, 2009.

Madden, Thomas, *Istanbul: City of Majesty at the Crossroads of the World*, New York, 2016.

Maddison, Angus, *Monitoring the World Economy 1820–1992*, Paris, 1995.

Maddison, Angus, *The World Economy: A Millennial Perspective*, Paris, 2001

Maier, Charles S., *The Unmasterable Past: History, Holocaust and German National Identity*, Cambridge, MA, 1988.

*Maier, Charles S. (ed.), *The Cold War in Europe: Era of a Divided Continent*, New York, 1991.

Mak, Geert, *In Europe: Travels through the Twentieth Century*, London, 2008.

Mak, Geert, *Was, wenn Europa scheitert*, Munich, 2012.

*Malcolmson, Patricia and Robert (eds), *Nella Last in the 1950s*, London, 2010.

Mann, Michael, *The Dark Side of Democracy: Explaining Ethnic Cleansing*, Cambridge, 2005.

Mann, Michael, *Power in the 21st Century: Conversations with John A. Hall*, Cambridge, 2011.

Mann, Michael, *The Sources of Social Power, Vol. 4: Globalizations, 1945–2011*, Cambridge, 2013.

*Marsh, David, *The Euro: The Battle for the New Global Currency*, New Haven, CT, and London, 2011.

*Märthesheimer, Peter and Frenzel, Ivo (eds), *Im Kreuzfeuer: Der Fernsehfilm 'Holocaust'. Eine Nation ist betroffen*, Frankfurt am Main, 1979.

*Marwick, Arthur, *The Sixties: Cultural Revolution in Britain, France, Italy and the United States, c.1958–c.1974*, Oxford, 1998.

Mazower, Mark, *Dark Continent: Europe's Twentieth Century*, London, 1998.

Mazower, Mark, *The Balkans: From the End of Byzantium to the Present Day*, London, 2000.

McFaul, Michael and Stoner-Weiss, Kathryn, *After the Collapse of Communism: Comparative Lessons of Transition*, Cambridge, 2004.

McMillan, James, *Twentieth-Century France: Politics and Society 1898–1991*, London, 1992.

Menon, Rajan and Rumer, Eugene, *Conflict in Ukraine: The Unwinding of the Post-Cold War Order*, Cambridge, MA, 2015.

Meray, Tibor, *Thirteen Days that Shook the Kremlin*, New York, 1959.

*Merridale, Catherine, *Night of Stone: Death and Memory in Russia*, London, 2000.

Merridale, Catherine and Ward, Chris (eds), *Perestroika: The Historical Perspective*, London, 1991.

Merriman, John, *A History of Modern Europe: From the Renaissance to the Present*, New York, 1996.

Merseburger, Peter, *Willy Brandt 1913–1992. Visionär und Realist*, Stuttgart-Munich, 2002.

*Michnik, Adam, *Letters from Prison and Other Essays*, Berkeley, CA, 1985.

*Middelaar, Luuk van, *The Passage to Europe: How a Continent became a Union*, New Haven, CT, and London, 2014.

Millington, Barry (ed.), *The Wagner Compendium: A Guide to Wagner's Life and Music*, New York, 1992.

Milward, Alan S., *The Reconstruction of Western Europe 1945–1951*, London, 1984.

Milward, Alan S., *The European Rescue of the Nation-State*, London, 1992.

Mitscherlich, Alexander and Margarete, *Die Unfähigkeit zu Trauern*, Munich (1967), 1988.

Mommsen, Margareta, *Wer herrscht in Rußland? Der Kreml und die Schatten der Macht*, Munich, 2004.

Mommsen, Margareta, *Das Putin-Syndikat. Russland im Griff der Geheimdienstler*, Munich, 2017.

Mommsen, Margareta and Nußberger, Angelika, *Das System Putin*, Munich, 2007.

Monaco, James, *Film verstehen*, Reinbek bei Hamburg, 1980

Montefiore, Simon Sebag, *Stalin: The Court of the Red Tsar*, London, 2003.

*Moore, Charles, *Margaret Thatcher: The Authorized Biography. Vol. 2: Everything She Wants*, London, 2015.

Morgan, Kenneth O., *Labour in Power 1945–1951*, Oxford, 1985.

Münkler, Herfried, *The New Wars*, Cambridge, 2005.

Naimark, Norman M., *Fires of Hatred: Ethnic Cleansing in Twentieth-Century Europe*, Cambridge, MA, 2001.

Natoli, Claudio, 'Widerstand gegen Nationalsozialismus und Faschismus: Deutsche und italienische Forschungstendenzen im Vergleich', in Klaus-Dietmar Henke and Claudio Natoli (eds), *Mit dem Pathos der Nüchternheit*, Frankfurt and New York, 1991.

Nehring, Holger, *Politics of Security: British and West German Protest Movements and the Early Cold War, 1945–1970*, Oxford, 2013.

Nehring, Holger, 'National Internationalists: British and West German Protests against Nuclear Weapons, the Politics of Transnational Communications and the Social History of the Cold War, 1957–1964', *Contemporary European History*, 14/4 (2005), 559–82.

*Nicholson, Virginia, *Perfect Wives in Ideal Homes: The Story of Women in the 1950s*, London, 2015.

Noelle, Elisabeth and Neumann, Erich (eds), *The Germans: Public Opinion Polls 1947–1966*, Allensbach and Bonn, 1967.

Nora, Pierre, *Realms of Memory: Rethinking the French Past*, ed. Lawrence D. Kritzmann, New York, 1996.

*Novick, Peter, *The Holocaust and Collective Memory*, London, 2001.

Outhwaite, William, *Europe since 1989*, London, 2016.

Pakier, Małgorzata and Stråth, Bo (eds), *A European Memory? Contested Histories and Politics of Remembrance*, New York and Oxford, 2010.

*Parker, David (ed.), *Letters of Solidarity and Friendship: Czechoslovakia 1968–71*, Holmfirth, 2017.

Parker, Stephen, *Bertolt Brecht: A Literary Life*, London, 2014.

Paxton, Robert, *Vichy France: Old Guard and New Order 1940–1944*, New York, 1972.

Petersdorff, Dirk von, *Literaturgeschichte der Bundesrepublik Deutschland. Von 1945 bis zur Gegenwart*, Munich, 2011.

*Pevsner, Nikolaus, *An Outline of European Architecture*, Harmondsworth (1943), 1963.

Piketty, Thomas, *Capital in the Twenty-First Century*, Cambridge, MA, 2014.

Piketty, Thomas, *Chronicles: On our Troubled Times*, London, 2016.

Pleshakov, Constantine, *The Crimean Nexus: Putin's War and the Clash of Civilizations*, New Haven, CT, and London, 2017.

Plokhy, Serhii, *The Gates of Europe: A History of Ukraine*, London, 2015.

Preston, Paul, *The Triumph of Democracy in Spain*, London, 1987.

*Preston, Paul, *Franco*, London, 1993.

Priestland, David, *Merchant, Soldier, Sage: A New History of Power*, London, 2012.

Radisch, Iris, *Camus. Das Ideal der Einfachheit. Eine Biographie*, Reinbek bei Hamburg, 2013.

Rawnsley, Andrew, *The End of the Party: The Rise and Fall of New Labour*, London, 2010.

Reisman, Michael, 'Why Regime Change is (almost always) a Bad Idea', *The American Journal of International Law*, 98 (2004), 516–25.

Reitmayer, Morten and Schlemmer, Thomas (eds), *Die Anfänge der Gegenwart. Umbrüche in Westeuropa nach dem Boom*, Munich, 2014.

*Reynolds, David, *One World Divisible: A Global History Since 1945*, New York, 1999.

Reynolds, David, *In Command of History: Churchill Fighting and Writing the Second World War*, London, 2004.

Reynolds, David, *The Long Shadow: The Great War and the Twentieth Century*, London, 2013.

Richards, Steve, *The Rise of the Outsiders: How Mainstream Politics Lost its Way*, London, 2017.

Roberts, J. M., *Twentieth Century: A History of the World 1901 to the Present*, London, 1999.

*Rödder, Andreas, *21.0. Eine kurze Geschichte der Gegenwart*, Munich, 2015.

*Rogel, Carole, *The Breakup of Yugoslavia and the War in Bosnia*, Westport, CT, 1998.

Rose, Richard, *What is Europe?*, New York, 1996.

Rose, Richard, *Representing Europeans: A Pragmatic Approach*, Oxford, 2013.

Rosh, Lea and Jäckel, Eberhard, *'Der Tod ist ein Meister aus Deutschland.' Deportation und Ermordung der Juden. Kollaboration und Verweigerung in Europa*, Hamburg, 1990.

Rousso, Henry, *Le syndrome de Vichy de 1944 à nos jours*, Paris, 1990.

Rousso, Henry, *Vichy. L'événement, la mémoire, l'histoire*, Paris, 2001.

Rousso, Henry, *Frankreich und die 'dunklen Jahre'. Das Regime von Vichy in Geschichte und Gegenwart*, Göttingen, 2010.

Ruane, Kevin, *The Rise and Fall of the European Defence Community*, Basingstoke, 2000.

*Ruhl, Klaus-Jörg (ed.), *'Mein Gott, was soll aus Deutschland werden?' Die Adenauer-Ära 1949–1963*, Munich, 1985.

Runciman, David, *The Confidence Trap: A History of Democracy in Crisis from World War I to the Present*, Princeton, NY, 2015.

Ruzza, Carolo and Fella, Stefano, *Re-inventing the Italian Right: Territorial Politics, Populism and 'Post-Fascism'*, London, 2009.

Sabrow, Martin, 'A Myth of Unity? German Unification as a Challenge in Contemporary History', *Bulletin of the German Historical Institute London*, 38/2 (2016), 46–62.

Sabrow, Martin, '1990: An Epochal Break in German History?', *Bulletin of the German Historical Institute Washington DC*, 60 (2017), 31–42.

Sachs, Jeffrey, *Poland's Jump to the Market Economy*, Cambridge, MA, 1993.

Sakwa, Richard, *Frontline Ukraine: Crisis in the Borderlands*, London, 2016.

*Sandbrook, Dominic, *Never Had It So Good: A History of Britain from Suez to the Beatles*, London, 2005.

Sandbrook, Dominic, *White Heat: A History of Britain in the Swinging Sixties*, London, 2006.

Sandbrook, Dominic, *State of Emergency: The Way We Were: Britain, 1970–1974*, London, 2010.

Sandbrook, Dominic, *Seasons in the Sun: The Battle for Britain, 1974–1979*, London, 2012.

*Sassoon, Donald, *The Culture of the Europeans: From 1800 to the Present*, London, 2006.

Schabowski, Günter, *Das Politbüro. Ende eines Mythos*, Reinbek bei Hamburg, 1990.

Scharsach, Hans-Henning and Kuch, Kurt, *Haider. Schatten über Europa*, Cologne, 2000.

Schick, Jack M., *The Berlin Crisis, 1958–1962*, Philadelphia, PA, 1971.

Schildt, Axel and Siegfried, Detlef, *Deutsche Kulturgeschichte. Die Bundesrepublik 1945 bis zur Gegenwart*, Munich, 2009.

Schlögel, Karl, *Grenzland Europa. Unterwegs auf einem neuen Kontinent*, Munich, 2013.

Schmidt, Helmut, *Globalisierung. Politische, ökonomische und kulturelle Herausforderungen*, Stuttgart, 1998.

Schmidt, Helmut and Stern, Fritz, *Unser Jahrhundert. Ein Gespräch*, Munich, 2010.

*Schöllgen, Gregor, *Gerhard Schröder. Die Biographie*, Munich, 2016.

Schwarz, Hans-Peter, *Adenauer*, 2 vols, Munich, 1994.

Schwarz, Hans-Peter, *Das Gesicht des Jahrhunderts*, Berlin, 1998.

Schwarz, Hans-Peter, *Helmut Kohl. Eine politische Biographie*, Munich, 2012.

*Schwarz, Hans-Peter, 'Fragen an das 20. Jahrhundert', *Vierteljahrshefte für Zeitgeschichte*, 48 (2000), 1–36.

Seldon, Anthony with Baston, Lewis, *Major: A Political Life*, London, 1998.

Seldon, Anthony with Snowdon, Peter and Collings, Daniel, *Blair Unbound*, London, 2007.

*Service, Robert, *A History of Twentieth-Century Russia*, London, 1998.

*Service, Robert, *Stalin: A Biography*, London, 2004.

Sheehan, James, *The Monopoly of Violence: Why Europeans Hate Going to War*, London, 2007.

Shipman, Tim, *All Out War: The Full Story of How Brexit Sank Britain's Political Class*, London, 2016.

Shipway, Martin, *Decolonization and its Impact: A Comparative Approach to the End of the Colonial Empires*, Oxford, 2008.

Shore, Marci, *Caviar and Ashes: A Warsaw Generation's Life and Death in Marxism, 1918–1969*, New Haven, CT, and London, 2006.

Shore, Marci, *The Taste of Ashes: The Afterlife of Totalitarianism in Eastern Europe*, London, 2013.

Siegfried, André, *De la IVe à la Ve République au jour de jour*, Paris, 1958.

*Silber, Laura and Little, Allan, *The Death of Yugoslavia*, London, 1996.

Simms, Brendan, *Europe: The Struggle for Supremacy, 1453 to the Present*, London, 2013.

Simms, Brendan, *Britain's Europe: A Thousand Years of Conflict and Cooperation*, London, 2016.

Simpson, John, *Unreliable Sources: How the 20th Century was Reported*, London, 2010.

*Sittner, Gernot, *Helmut Kohl und der Mantel der Geschichte*, Munich, 2016.

*Skidelsky, Robert, *Britain since 1900: A Success Story?*, London, 2014.

Sontheimer, Kurt, *Antidemokratisches Denken in der Weimarer Republik*, Munich (1962), 1992.

Spohr, Kristina, *The Global Chancellor: Helmut Schmidt and the Reshaping of the International Order*, Oxford, 2016.

Spohr, Kristina and Reynolds, David (eds), *Transcending the Cold War: Summits, Statecraft, and the Dissolution of Bipolarity in Europe, 1970–1990*, Oxford, 2016.

Stahl, Walter (ed.), *The Politics of Postwar Germany*, New York, 1963.

Staritz, Dietrich, *Geschichte der DDR*, Frankfurt am Main, 1996.

Steinberg, Jonathan, *Why Switzerland?*, Cambridge, 1976.

Steininger, Rolf, *Eine Chance zur Wiedervereinigung? Die Stalin-Note vom 10. März 1952*, Bonn, 1985.

Stern, Fritz, *Dreams and Delusions: National Socialism in the Drama of the German Past*, New York, 1989.

Stern, Fritz, *Fünf Deutschland und ein Leben. Erinnerungen*, Munich, 2007.

Stern, Fritz, *Der Westen im 20. Jahrhundert. Selbstzerstörung, Wiederaufbau, Gefährdungen der Gegenwart*, Göttingen, 2009.

Stiglitz, Joseph E., *The Euro and its Threat to the Future of Europe*, London, 2016.

Stokes, Gale, *The Walls Came Tumbling Down: The Collapse of Communism in Eastern Europe*, New York, 1993.

Stone, Dan, *Goodbye to all that? The Story of Europe since 1945*, Oxford, 2014.

Stone, Dan (ed.), *The Oxford Handbook of Postwar European History*, Oxford, 2014.

Stöver, Bernd, *Der Kalte Krieg*, Munich, 2003.

Streeck, Wolfgang, *Buying Time: The Delayed Crisis of Democratic Capitalism*, London, 2014.

Streeck, Wolfgang, *How Will Capitalism End?*, London, 2016.

Suny, Ronald Grigor, *The Soviet Experiment*, New York, 1998.

Suny, Ronald Grigor (ed.), *The Cambridge History of Russia. Vol. 3, The Twentieth Century*, Cambridge, 2006.

*Swain, Geoffrey and Swain, Nigel, *Eastern Europe since 1945*, Basingstoke (1993), 2009.

Tanner, Jakob, *Geschichte der Schweiz im 20. Jahrhundert*, Munich, 2015.

*Taubman, William, *Khrushchev: The Man and his Era*, New York, 2003.

*Taubman, William, *Gorbachev: His Life and Times*, New York, 2017.

Taubman, William, Khrushchev, Sergei and Gleason, Abbott (eds), *Nikita Khrushchev*, New Haven, CT, and London, 2000.

*Taylor, A. J. P., *The Origins of the Second World War*, London (1961), 1964.

Taylor, Richard and Pritchard, Colin, *The Protest Makers: The British Nuclear Disarmament Movement of 1958–1965 Twenty Years On*, Oxford, 1980.

Thatcher, Margaret, *The Downing Street Years*, London, 1995.

Ther, Philipp, *Europe since 1989: A History*, Princeton, NJ, 2016.

Therborn, Göran, *European Modernity and Beyond: The Trajectory of European Societies 1945–2000*, London, 1995.

Thränhardt, Dietrich, *Geschichte der Bundesrepublik Deutschland*, Frankfurt am Main, 1986.

Timmermann, Brigitte, *The Third Man's Vienna: Celebrating a Film Classic*, Vienna, 2005.

Tismaneanu, Vladimir, *Fantasies of Salvation*, Princeton, NJ, 1998.

Tismaneanu, Vladimir (ed.), *The Revolutions of 1989*, London, 1999.

Todorov, Tzvetan, *Hope and Memory: Reflections on the Twentieth Century*, London, 2003.

*Tombs, Robert, *The English and their History*, London, 2014.

Tombs, Robert and Tombs, Isabelle, *That Sweet Enemy: The French and the British from the Sun King to the Present*, London, 2006.

Tomka, Béla, *A Social History of Twentieth-Century Europe*, Abingdon, 2013.

*Toynbee, Polly and Walker, David, *Cameron's Coup: How the Tories took Britain to the Brink*, London, 2015.

Trentmann, Frank, *Empire of Things: How We Became a World of Consumers, from the Fifteenth Century to the Twenty-First*, New York, 2016.

Urwin, Derek W., *Western Europe Since 1945: A Political History*, London, 1989.

Vachudova, Milada Anna, *Europe Undivided: Democracy, Leverage, and Integration after Communism*, Oxford, 2005.

Vadney, T. E., *The World Since 1945*, Harmondsworth, 1987.

Varoufakis, Yanis, *And the Weak Suffer What They Must? Europe, Austerity and the Threat to Global Stability*, London, 2016.

Vincent, Mary, *Spain 1833–2002: People and State*, Oxford, 2007.

Vinen, Richard, *A History in Fragments: Europe in the Twentieth Century*, London, 2000.

Wakeman, Rosemary (ed.), *Themes in Modern European History since 1945*, London, 2003.

Waller, Philip and Rowell, John (eds), *Chronology of the 20th Century*, Oxford, 1995.

Wapshott, Nicholas, *Keynes–Hayek: The Clash that Defined Modern Economics*, New York, 2011.

Wasserstein, Bernard, *Barbarism and Civilization: A History of Europe in Our Time*, Oxford, 2009.

Watson, Derek, *Molotov: A Biography*, Basingstoke, 2005.

Weber, Hermann, *Geschichte der DDR*, Munich, 1985.

*Weber, Hermann (ed.), *DDR. Dokumente zur Geschichte der Deutschen Demokratischen Republik 1945–1985*, Munich, 1986.

Wee, Hermann van der, *Prosperity and Upheaval: The World Economy 1945–1980*, Harmondsworth, 1987.

Wehler, Hans-Ulrich, *Deutsche Gesellschaftsgeschichte. Vol. 5: Bundesrepublik und DDR 1949–1990*, Munich, 2008.

Wehler, Hans-Ulrich, *Land ohne Unterschichten. Neue Essays zur deutschen Geschichte*, Munich, 2010.

Wehler, Hans-Ulrich, *Die neue Umverteilung. Soziale Ungleicheit in Deutschland*, Munich, 2013.

Wehler, Hans-Ulrich, *Die Deutschen und der Kapitalismus. Essays zur Geschichte*, Munich, 2014.

*Werth, Alexander, *France 1940–1955*, London, 1956.

*Weyrauch, Wolfgang (ed.), *Ich lebe in der Bundesrepublik. Fünfzehn Deutsche über Deutschland*, Munich, 1960.

*White, Charles, *The Adventures of the Sons of Neptune*, Scarborough, 2011.

Wiegrefe, Klaus, *Das Zerwürfnis. Helmut Schmidt, Jimmy Carter und die Krise der deutsch-amerikanischen Beziehungen*, Berlin, 2005.

Wilford, Hugh, *The CIA, the British Left and the Cold War: Calling the Tune?*, London, 2003.

Williams, Allan (ed.), *Southern Europe Transformed: Political and Economic Change in Greece, Italy, Portugal and Spain*, London, 1984.

Winkler, Heinrich August, *Auf ewig in Hitlers Schatten? Anmerkungen zur deutschen Geschichte*, Munich, 2007.

Winkler, Heinrich August, *Germany: The Long Road West. Vol. 2: 1933–1990*, Oxford, 2007.

*Winkler, Heinrich August, *Geschichte des Westens. Vol. 3: Vom Kalten Krieg zum Mauerfall*, Munich, 2014.

*Winkler, Heinrich August, *Geschichte des Westens. Vol. 4: Die Zeit der Gegenwart*, Munich, 2015.

Winkler, Heinrich August, *Zerreißproben. Deutschland, Europa und der Westen. Interventionen 1990–2015*, Munich, 2015.

Winkler, Heinrich August, *Zerbricht der Westen? Über die gegenwärtige Krise in Europa und Amerika*, Munich, 2017.

Winter, Martin, *Das Ende einer Illusion. Europa zwischen Anspruch, Wunsch und Wirklichkeit*, Munich, 2015.

Wirsching, Andreas, *Der Preis der Freiheit. Geschichte Europas in unserer Zeit*, Munich, 2012.

Wirsching, Andreas, *Demokratie und Globalisierung. Europa seit 1989*, Munich, 2015.

Wirsching Andreas (ed.), 'European Responses to the Crisis of the 1970s and 1980s', *Journal of Modern European History*, 9/2 (2011).

*Wise, Audrey, *Eyewitness in Revolutionary Portugal*, Nottingham, 1975.

Wittner, Lawrence S., *The Struggle against the Bomb, Vol. 1: One World or None: A History of the World Nuclear Disarmament Movement Through 1963*, Stanford, CA, 1993.

Wittner, Lawrence S., *The Struggle against the Bomb. Vol. 2: Resisting the Bomb: A History of the World Nuclear Disarmament Movement 1954–1970*, Stanford, CA, 1997.

*Wolff, Jochen (ed.), *Der Aufstand. Juni '53 – Augenzeugen berichten*, Berlin, 2003.

Wolfrum, Edgar, *Die Bundesrepublik Deutschland 1949–1990*, Stuttgart, 2005.

Woller, Hans, *Geschichte Italiens im 20. Jahrhundert*, Munich, 2010.

Wright, Vincent (ed.), *Privatization in Western Europe: Pressures, Problems and Paradoxes*, London, 1994.

Yekelchyk, Serhy, *The Conflict in Ukraine: What Everyone Needs to Know*, Oxford, 2015.

*Young, Hugo, *One of Us: A Biography of Margaret Thatcher*, London, 1990.

Young, John W. and Kent, John, *International Relations since 1945: A Global History*, Oxford, 2004.

*Ziemann, Benjamin, *Encounters with Modernity: The Catholic Church in West Germany, 1956–1975*, New York and Oxford, 2014.

Ziemann, Benjamin (ed.), *Peace Movements in Western Europe, Japan and the USA during the Cold War*, Essen, 2007.

Ziemann, Benjamin, 'The Code of Protest: Images of Peace in the West German Peace Movements, 1945–1990', *Contemporary European History*, 17/2 (2008), 237–61.

Ziemann, Benjamin, 'A Quantum of Solace? European Peace Movements during the Cold War and their Elective Affinities, *Archiv für Sozialgeschichte*, 49 (2009), 351–89.

Zöchling, Christa, *Haider. Licht und Schatten einer Karriere*, Vienna, 1999.

Zürcher, Erik J., *Turkey: A Modern History*, London (1993), 2004.

Index

Europe in 2018